PHILIP'S

ROAD ATLAS

2025 BIG EASY TO READ BRITAIN

T0301048

www.philips-maps.co.uk

First published in 2020 by Philip's
a division of Octopus Publishing Group Ltd
www.octopusbooks.co.uk
Carmelite House, 50 Victoria Embankment
London EC4Y 0DZ
An Hachette UK Company
www.hachette.co.uk

Fifth edition 2024
First impression 2024

ISBN 978-1-84907-662-3 spiral-bound
ISBN 978-1-84907-661-6 perfect-bound

Cartography by Philip's
Copyright © 2024 Philip's

This product includes
mapping data licensed from
Ordnance Survey®, with the
permission of the Controller of
His Majesty's Stationery Office.
© Crown copyright 2024. All rights reserved.
Licence number AC0000851689

Information for National Parks, Areas of Outstanding Natural
Beauty, National Trails and Country Parks in Wales supplied by
the Countryside Council for Wales.

Information for National Parks, Areas of Outstanding Natural
Beauty, National Trails and Country Parks in England supplied
by Natural England. Data for Regional Parks, Long Distance
Footpaths and Country Parks in Scotland provided by Scottish
Natural Heritage.

Gaelic name forms used in the Western Isles provided by
Comhairle nan Eilean.

Data for the National Nature Reserves in England provided by
Natural England. Data for the National Nature Reserves in Wales
provided by Countryside Council for Wales. Darparwyd data'n
ymwneud â Gwarchodfeydd Natur Cenedlaethol Cymru gan
Gyngor Cefn Gwlad Cymru.

Information on the location of National Nature Reserves in
Scotland was provided by Scottish Natural Heritage.

Data for National Scenic Areas in Scotland provided by
the Scottish Executive Office. Crown copyright material is
reproduced with the permission of the Controller of HMSO
and the Queen's Printer for Scotland. Licence number
C02W0003960.

Printed in Italy

*Data from Nielsen Total Consumer Market 2023 weeks 1–39

MIX
Paper | Supporting
responsible forestry
FSC® C015829

CONTENTS

II **Key to map symbols**

III **Restricted motorway junctions**

IV **Route planning maps**

XIV **Distances and journey times**

1 **Key to road map pages**

2 **Road maps of Britain**

161 **Urban approach maps**

161 Bristol *approaches*

162 Birmingham *approaches*

164 Cardiff *approaches*

165 Edinburgh *approaches*

166 Glasgow *approaches*

167 Leeds *approaches*

168 London *approaches*

172 Liverpool *approaches*

173 Manchester *approaches*

174 Newcastle *approaches*

175 **Town plans**

175 Aberdeen, Ayr, Bath

176 Birmingham, Blackpool, Bournemouth

177 Bradford, Brighton, Bristol

178 Bury St Edmunds, Cambridge, Canterbury, Cardiff

179 Carlisle, Chelmsford, Cheltenham, Chester

180 Chichester, Colchester, Coventry, Derby

181 Dorchester, Dumfries, Dundee, Durham

182 Edinburgh, Exeter, Gloucester

183 Glasgow, Grimsby, Harrogate

184 Hull, Inverness, Ipswich, Kendal

185 King's Lynn, Leeds, Lancaster

186 London

188 Leicester, Lincoln, Liverpool

189 Llandudno, Llanelli, Luton, Macclesfield

190 Manchester, Maidstone, Merthyr Tydfil

191 Middlesbrough, Milton Keynes, Newcastle upon Tyne, Newport

192 Newquay, Northampton, Norwich, Nottingham

193 Oxford, Perth, Peterborough, Plymouth

194 Poole, Portsmouth, Preston, Reading

195 St Andrews, Salisbury, Scarborough, Shrewsbury

196 Sheffield, Stoke-on-Trent (Hanley), Southampton

197 Southend-on-Sea, Stirling, Stratford-upon-Avon, Sunderland

198 Swansea, Swindon, Taunton, Telford

199 Torquay, Truro, Winchester, Windsor

200 Wolverhampton, Worcester, Wrexham, York

201 **Index to road maps of Britain**

Inside back cover: **County and unitary authority boundaries**

Road map symbols

M3	**Motorway, toll motorway**
5 8	**Motorway junction** – full, restricted access
S S	**Motorway service area** – full, restricted access
	Motorway under construction
A303	**Primary route** – dual, single carriageway
S S	**Service area, roundabout, multi-level junction**
4 5	**Numbered junction** – full, restricted access
	Primary route under construction
	Narrow primary route
Newbury	**Primary destination**
A303	**A road** – dual, single carriageway
	A road under construction, narrow A road
B3089	**B road** – dual, single carriageway
	B road under construction, narrow B road
	Minor road – over 4 metres, under 4 metres wide
	Minor road with restricted access
2	**Distance in miles**
	Tunnel
TOLL	**Toll, steep gradient** – arrow points downhill
	National trail – England and Wales
	Long distance footpath – Scotland
	Railway with station
	Level crossing, tunnel
	Preserved railway with station
	National boundary
	County / unitary authority boundary
	Car ferry, catamaran
	Passenger ferry, catamaran
	Hovercraft
CALAIS	**Ferry destination**
Ferry	**Car ferry** – river crossing
	Principal airport, other airport
MENDIP HILLS	**National Park, National Landscape** – England and Wales **National Scenic Area** – Scotland **forest park / regional park / national forest**
	Beach
	Linear antiquity
	Roman road
1643	**Hillfort, battlefield** – with date
261	**Viewpoint, nature reserve, spot height** – in metres
	Golf course, youth hostel, sporting venue
	Camp site, caravan site, camping and caravan site
P&R	**Shopping village, park and ride**
29	**Adjoining page number** – road maps

Road map scale
1: 150 000 • 1 cm = 1.5 km • 1 inch = 2·37 miles

0 1 2 3 4 5 6 7 8 km
0 1 2 3 4 5 miles

Parts of Scotland
1: 200 000 • 1 cm = 2.0 km • 1 inch = 3.16 miles

0 1 2 3 4 5 6 7 8 9 10 km
0 1 2 3 4 5 6 miles

Scottish Highlands and Islands
1: 250 000 • 1 cm = 2.5 km • 1 inch = 3.95 miles

0 1 2 3 4 5 6 7 8 9 10 11 12 km
0 1 2 3 4 5 6 7 8 miles

(Orkney and Shetland Islands at 1:300 000, approximately 4.75 miles to 1 inch)

Approach map symbols

M6	**Motorway**
	Toll motorway
6 5	**Motorway junction** – full, restricted access
S	**Service area**
	Under construction
A6	**Primary route** – dual, single carriageway
S	**Service area**
	Multi-level junction
	Roundabout
	Under construction
A195	**A road** – dual, single carriageway
B1288	**B road** – dual, single carriageway
	Minor road – dual, single carriageway
	Ring road
3	**Distance in miles**
COSELEY	**Railway with station**
LOXDALE	**Tramway with station**
M	**Underground or metro station**
	Congestion charge area

Town plan symbols

	Motorway
	Primary route – dual, single carriageway
	A road – dual, single carriageway
	B road – dual, single carriageway
	Minor through road
	One-way street
	Pedestrian roads
	Shopping streets
	Railway with station
City Hall	**Tramway with station**
	Bus or railway station building
	Shopping precinct or retail park
	Park
	Congestion charge zone
	Low Emission Zone (LEZ) or Clean Air Zone (CAZ) – See local authority websites for details
	Building of public interest, theatre, cinema
Bank	**Parking, shopmobility**
West St	**Underground station, metro station**
H	**Hospital, Police station**
PO	**Post office**

Tourist information

Abbey, cathedral or priory	**Church**	**House and garden**	**Safari park**
Ancient monument	**Country park** England and Wales Scotland	**Motor racing circuit**	**Theme park**
Aquarium	**Farm park**	**Museum**	**Tourist information**
Art gallery	**Picnic area**		**Zoo**
Bird collection or aviary	**Garden**	**Preserved railway**	**Other place of interest**
Castle	**Historic ship**	**Race course**	
	House	**Roman antiquity**	

Restricted motorway junctions

M1	Northbound	Southbound
2	No exit	No access
4	No exit	No access
6A	No exit. Access from M25 only	No access. Exit to M25 only
7	No exit. Access from A414 only	No access. Exit to A414 only
17	No access. Exit to M45 only	No access. Access from M45 only
19	No exit to A14	No access from A14
21A	No access	
23A		Exit to A42 only
24A	No exit	No access
35A	No access	No exit
43	No access. Exit to M621 only	No exit. Access from M621 only
48	No exit to A1(M) southbound	

M3	Eastbound	Westbound
8	No exit	No access
10	No access	No exit
13	No access to M27 eastbound	
14	No exit	No access

M4	Eastbound	Westbound
1	Exit to A4 eastbound only	Access from A4 westbound only
2	Access from A4 eastbound only	Access to A4 westbound only
21	No exit	No access
23	No access	No exit
25	No exit	No access
25A	No exit	No access
29	No exit	No access
38		No access
39	No exit or access	No exit
42	Access from A483 only	Exit to A483 only

M5	Northbound	Southbound
10	No exit	No access
11A	No access from A417 eastbound	No exit to A417 westbound

M6	Northbound	Southbound
3A	No access.	No exit. Access from M6 eastbound only
4A	No exit. Access from M42 southbound only	No access. Exit to M42 only
5	No access	No exit
10A	No access. Exit to M54 only	No exit. Access from M54 only
11A	No exit. Access from M6 Toll only	No access. Exit to M6 Toll only
20	No exit to M56 eastbound	No access from M56 westbound
20A	No exit	No access
24	No exit	No access
25	No access	No exit
30	No exit. Access from M61 northbound only	No access. Exit to M61 southbound only
31A	No access	No exit
45	No access	No exit

M6 Toll		
	Northbound	Southbound
T1		No exit
T2	No exit, no access	No access
T5	No exit	No access
T7	No access	No exit
T8	No access	No exit

M8	Eastbound	Westbound
6	No exit	No access
6A	No access	No exit
7	No Access	No exit
7A	No exit. Access from A725 northbound only	No access. Exit to A725 southbound only
8	No exit to M73 northbound	No access from M73 southbound
9	No access	No exit
13	No exit southbound	Access from M73 southbound only
14	No access	No exit

M9	Eastbound	Westbound
2	No access	No exit
3	No exit	No access
6	No access	No exit
8	No exit	No access

M11	Northbound	Southbound
4	No exit	No access
5	No access	No exit
8A	No access	No exit
9	No access	No exit
13	No access	No exit
14	No exit to A428 westbound	No exit. Access from A14 westbound only

M20	Eastbound	Westbound
2	No access	No exit
3	No exit Access from M26 eastbound only	No access Exit to M26 westbound only
10	No access	No exit
11A	No access	No exit

M23	Northbound	Southbound
7	No exit to A23 southbound	No access from A23 northbound
10A	No exit	No access

M25	Clockwise	Anticlockwise
5	No exit to M26 eastbound	No access from M26 westbound
19	No access	No exit
21	No exit to M1 southbound. Access from M1 southbound only	No exit to M1 southbound. Access from M1 southbound only
31	No exit	No access

M27	Eastbound	Westbound
10	No exit	No access
12	No access	No exit

M40	Eastbound	Westbound
3	No exit	No access
7	No exit	No access
8	No exit	No access
13	No exit	No access
14	No access	No exit
16	No access	No exit

M42	Northbound	Southbound
1	No exit	No access
7	No access Exit to M6 northbound only	No exit. Access from M6 northbound only
7A	No access. Exit to M6 southbound only	No exit
8	No exit. Access from M6 southbound only	Exit to M6 northbound only. Access from M6 southbound only

M45	Eastbound	Westbound
M1 J17	Access to M1 southbound only	No access from M1 southbound
With A45	No access	No exit

M48	Eastbound	Westbound
M4 J21	No exit to M4 westbound	No access from M4 eastbound
M4 J23	No access from M4 westbound	No exit to M4 eastbound

M49	Southbound	Northbound
18A	No exit to M5 northbound	No access from M5 southbound

M53	Northbound	Southbound
11	Exit to M56 eastbound only. Access from M56 westbound only	Exit to M56 eastbnd only. Access from M56 westbound only

M56	Eastbound	Westbound
2	No exit	No access
3	No access	No exit
4	No exit	No access
7		No access
8	No exit or access	No exit
9	No access from M6 northbound	No access to M6 southbound
15	No exit to M53	No access from M53 northbound

M57	Northbound	Southbound
3	No exit	No access
5	No exit	No access

M60	Clockwise	Anticlockwise
2	No exit	No access
3	No exit to A34 northbound	No exit to A34 northbound
4	No access from M56	No exit to M56
5	No exit to A5103 southbound	No exit to A5103 northbound
14	No exit	No access
16	No exit	No access
20	No access	No exit
22		No access
25	No access	
26		No exit or access
27	No exit	No access

M61	Northbound	Southbound
2	No access from A580 eastbound	No exit to A580 westbound
3	No access from A580 eastbound. No access from A666 southbound	No exit to A580 westbound
M6 J30	No exit to M6 southbound	No access from M6 northbound

M62	Eastbound	Westbound
23	No access	No exit

M65	Eastbound	Westbound
9	No access	No exit
11	No exit	No access

M66	Northbound	Southbound
1	No access	No exit

M67	Eastbound	Westbound
1A	No access	No exit
2	No exit	No access

M69	Northbound	Southbound
2	No exit	No access

M73	Northbound	Southbound
2	No access from M8 eastbound	No exit to M8 westbound

M74	Northbound	Southbound
3	No access	No exit
3A	No access	No access
7	No exit	No access
9	No exit or access	No access
10		No exit
11	No exit	No access
12	No access	No exit

M77	Northbound	Southbound
4	No exit	No access
6	No exit	No access
7	No exit	
8	No access	No access

M80	Northbound	Southbound
4A	No access	No exit
6A	No exit	No access
8	Exit to M876 northbound only. No access	Access from M876 southbound only. No exit

M90	Northbound	Southbound
1	Access from A90 northbound only	No access. Exit to A90 southbound only
2A	No access	No exit
7	No exit	No access
8	No exit	No access
10	No access from A912	No exit to A912

M180	Eastbound	Westbound
1	No access	No exit

M621	Eastbound	Westbound
2A	No exit	No access
4	No exit	
5	No exit	No access
6	No access	No exit

M876	Northbound	Southbound
2	No access	No exit

A1(M)	Northbound	Southbound
2	No access	No exit
3		No access
5	No exit	No exit, no access
14	No exit	No access
40	No access	No exit
43	No exit. Access from M1 only	No access. Exit to M1 only
57	No access	No exit
65	No access	No exit

A3(M)	Northbound	Southbound
1	No exit	No access
4	No access	No exit

A38(M) with Victoria Rd, (Park Circus) Birmingham

Northbound	No exit
Southbound	No access

A48(M)	Northbound	Southbound
M4 Junc 29	Exit to M4 eastbound only	Access from M4 westbound only
29A	Access from A48 eastbound only	Exit to A48 westbound only

A57(M)	Eastbound	Westbound
With A5103	No access	No exit
With A34	No access	No exit

A58(M)		Southbound
With Park Lane and Westgate, Leeds		No access

A64(M)		Eastbound	Westbound
With A58 Clay Pit Lane, Leeds		No access from A58	No exit to A58

A74(M)	Northbound	Southbound
18	No access	No exit
22		No exit to A75

A194(M)	Northbound	Southbound
A1(M) J65 Gateshead Western Bypass	Access from A1(M) northbound only	Exit to A1(M) southbound only

M1 (cont.)	Northbound	Southbound
16	No exit	No access
17	No exit	
18		No exit
19	No exit to A814 eastbound	No access from A814 westbound
20	No exit	No access
21	No access from M74	No exit
22	No exit. Access from M77 only	No access. Exit to M77 only
23	No access	No access
25	Exit to A739 northbound only. Access from A739 southbound only	
25A	No exit	No access
28	No exit	No access
28A	No exit	No access
29A	No exit	No access

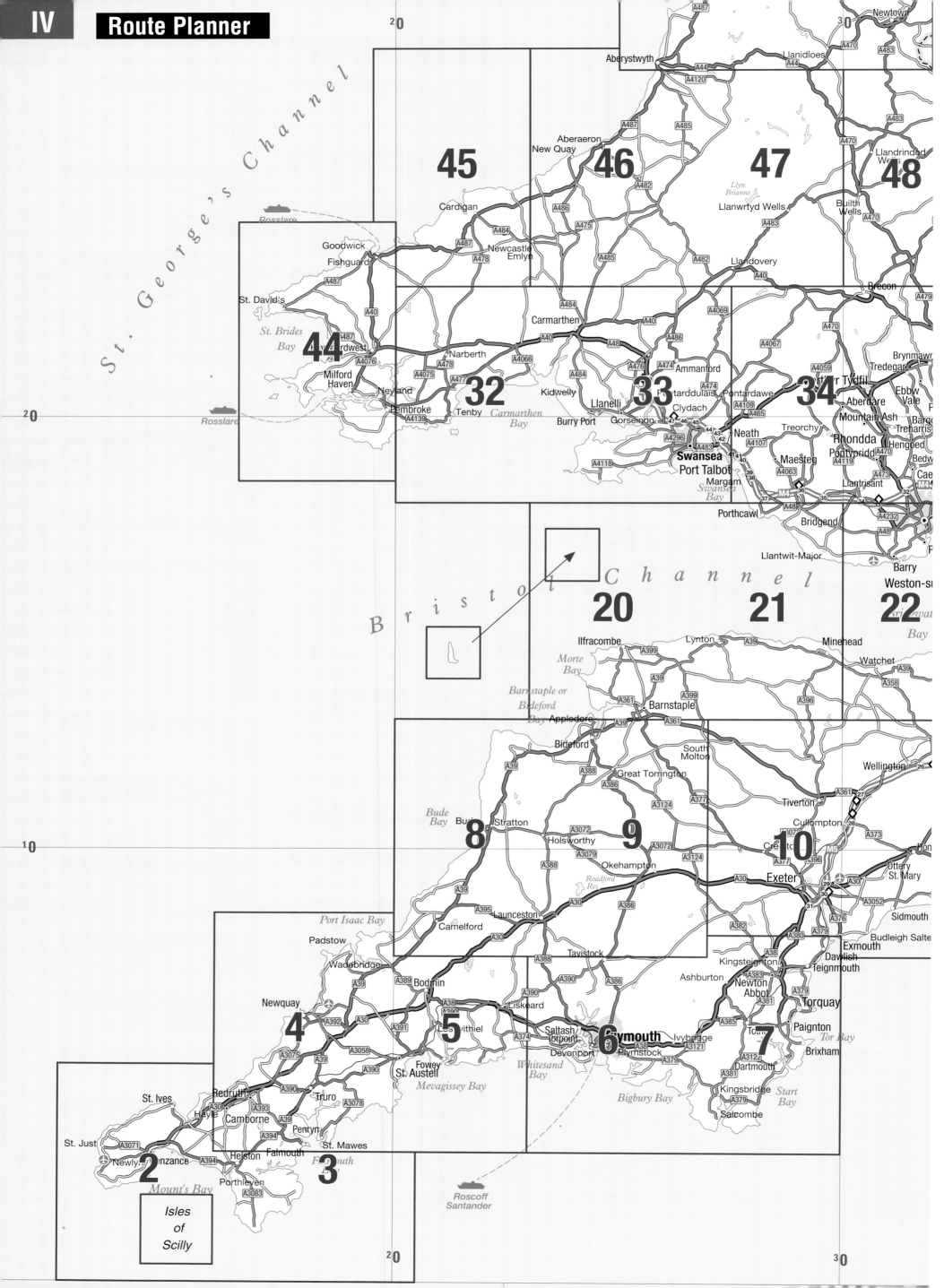

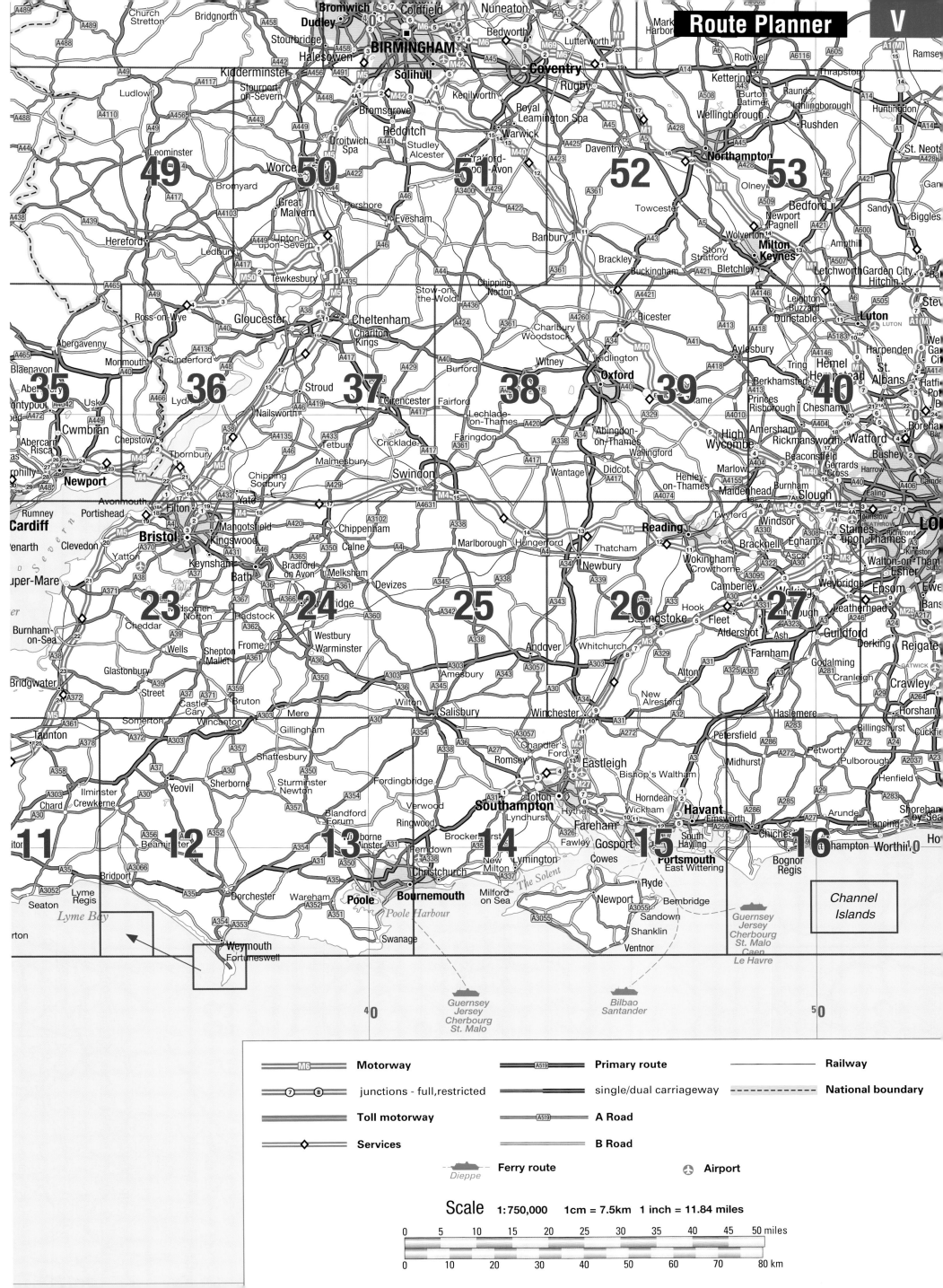

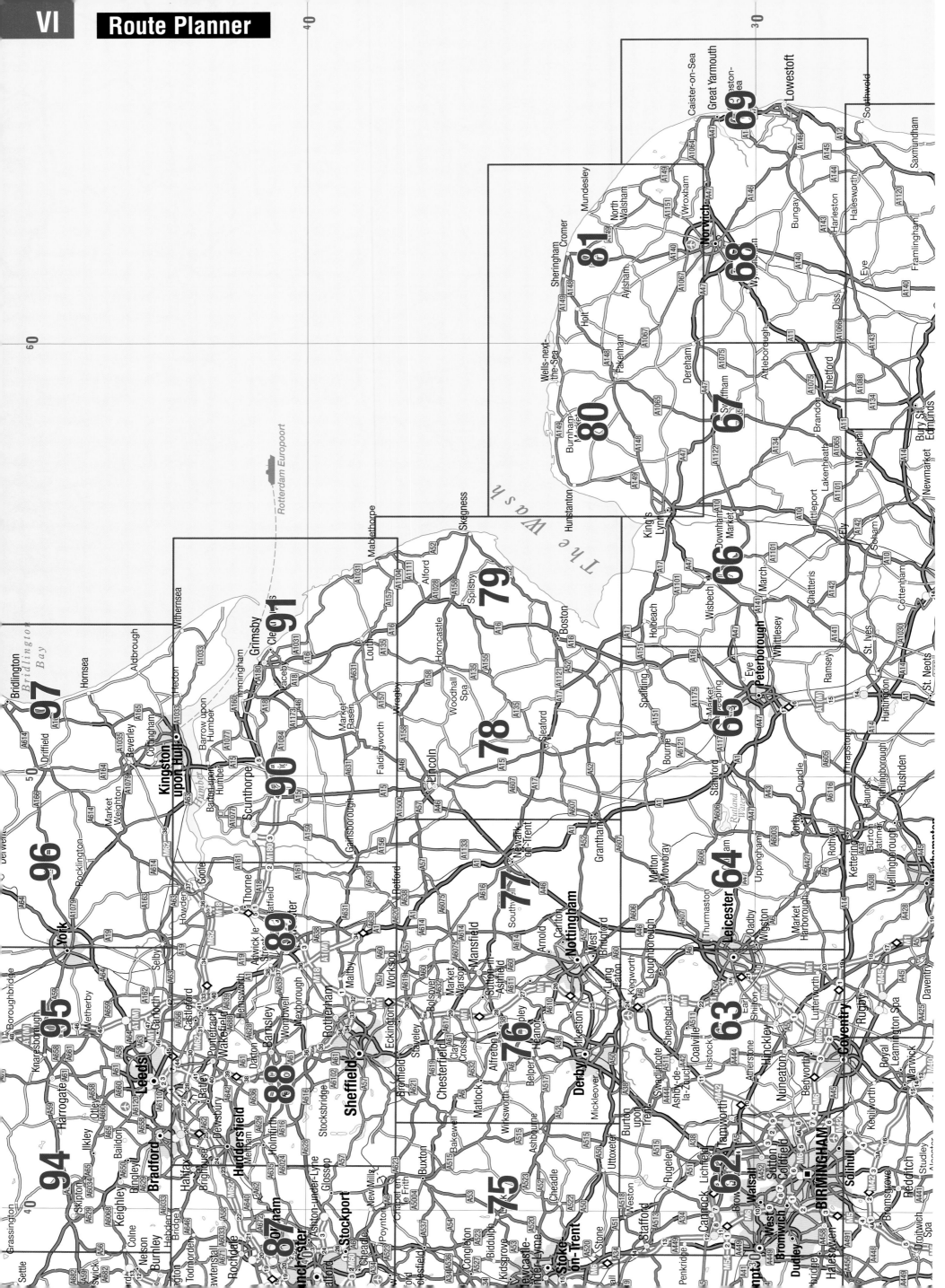

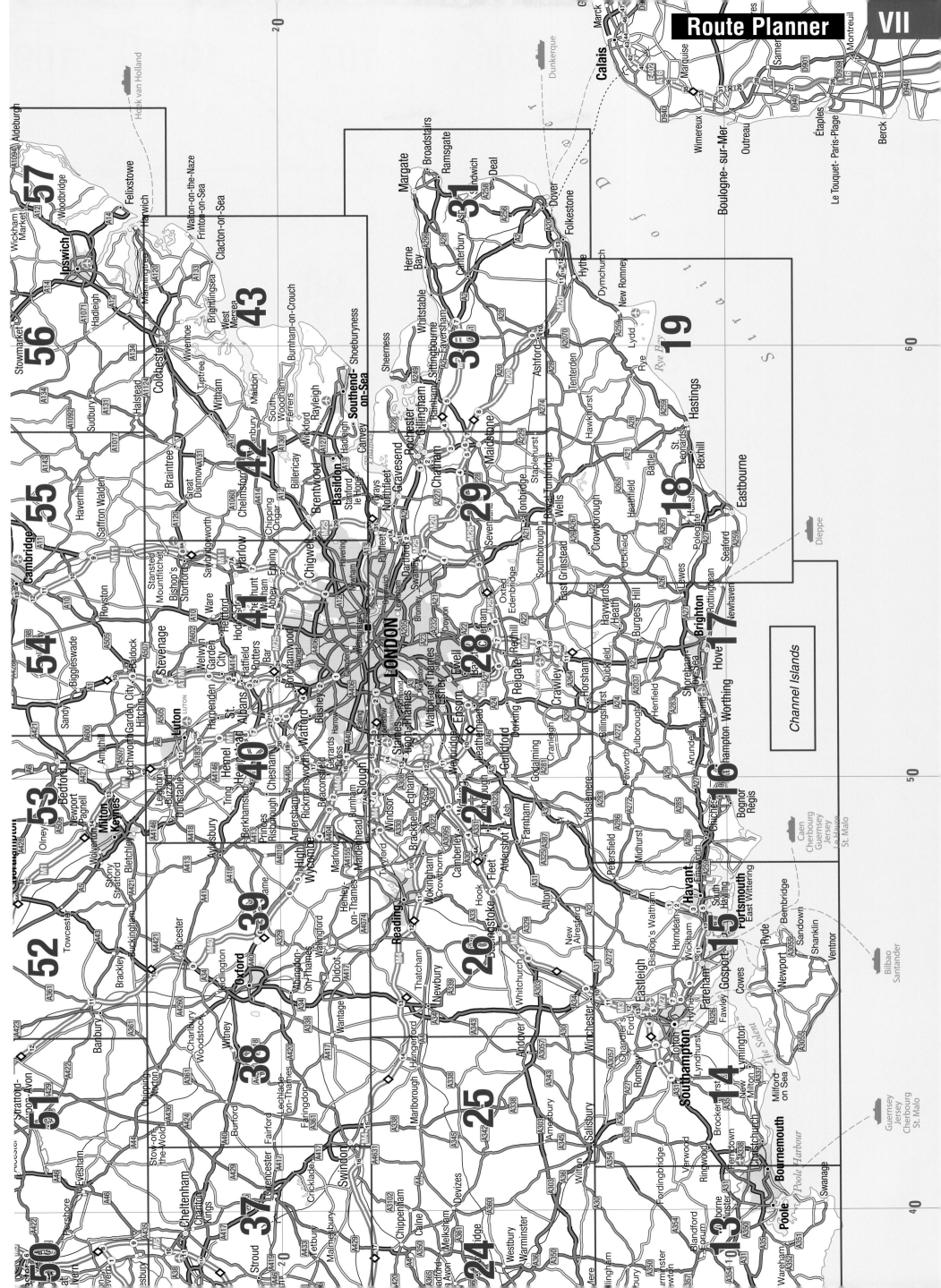

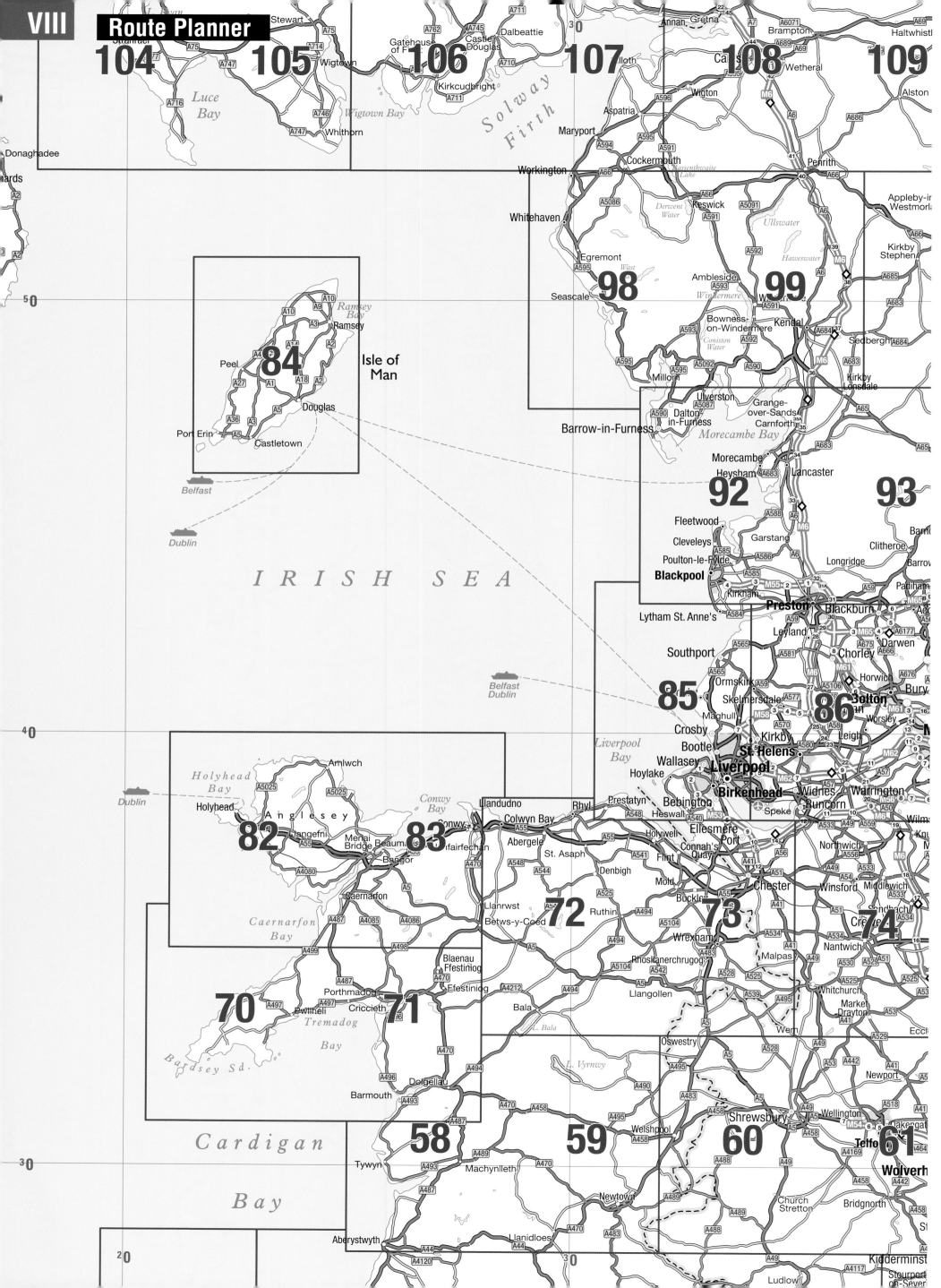

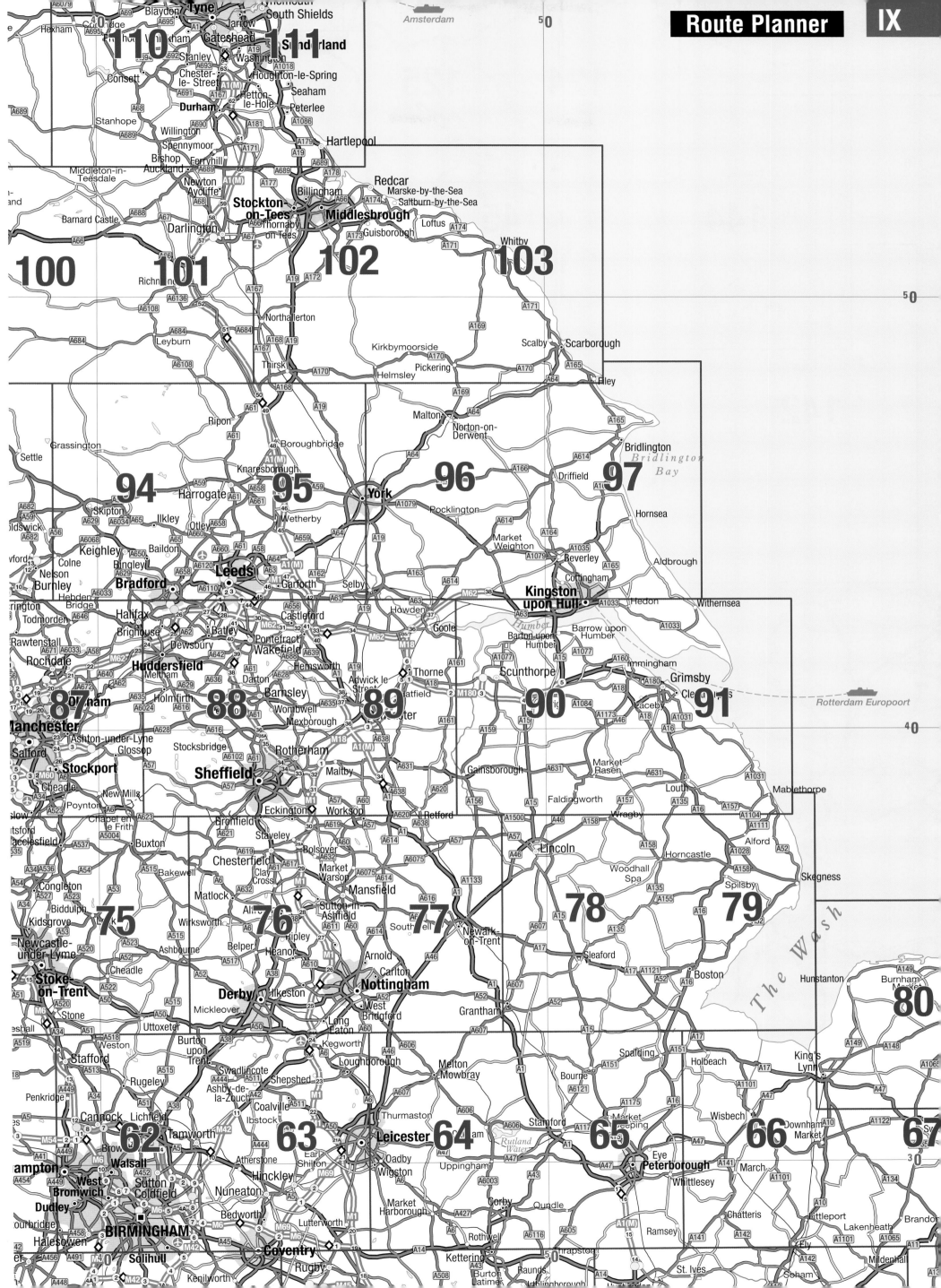

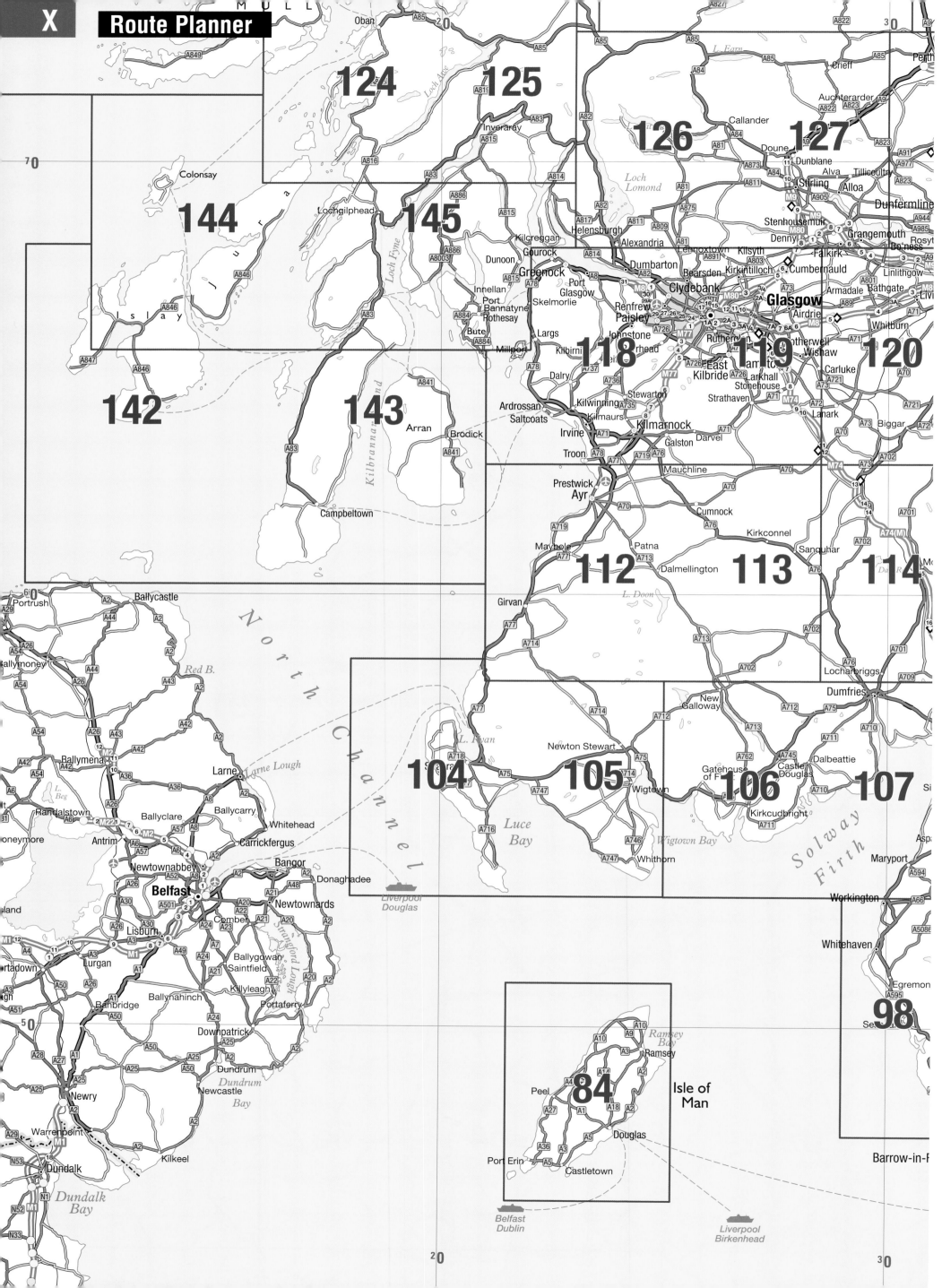

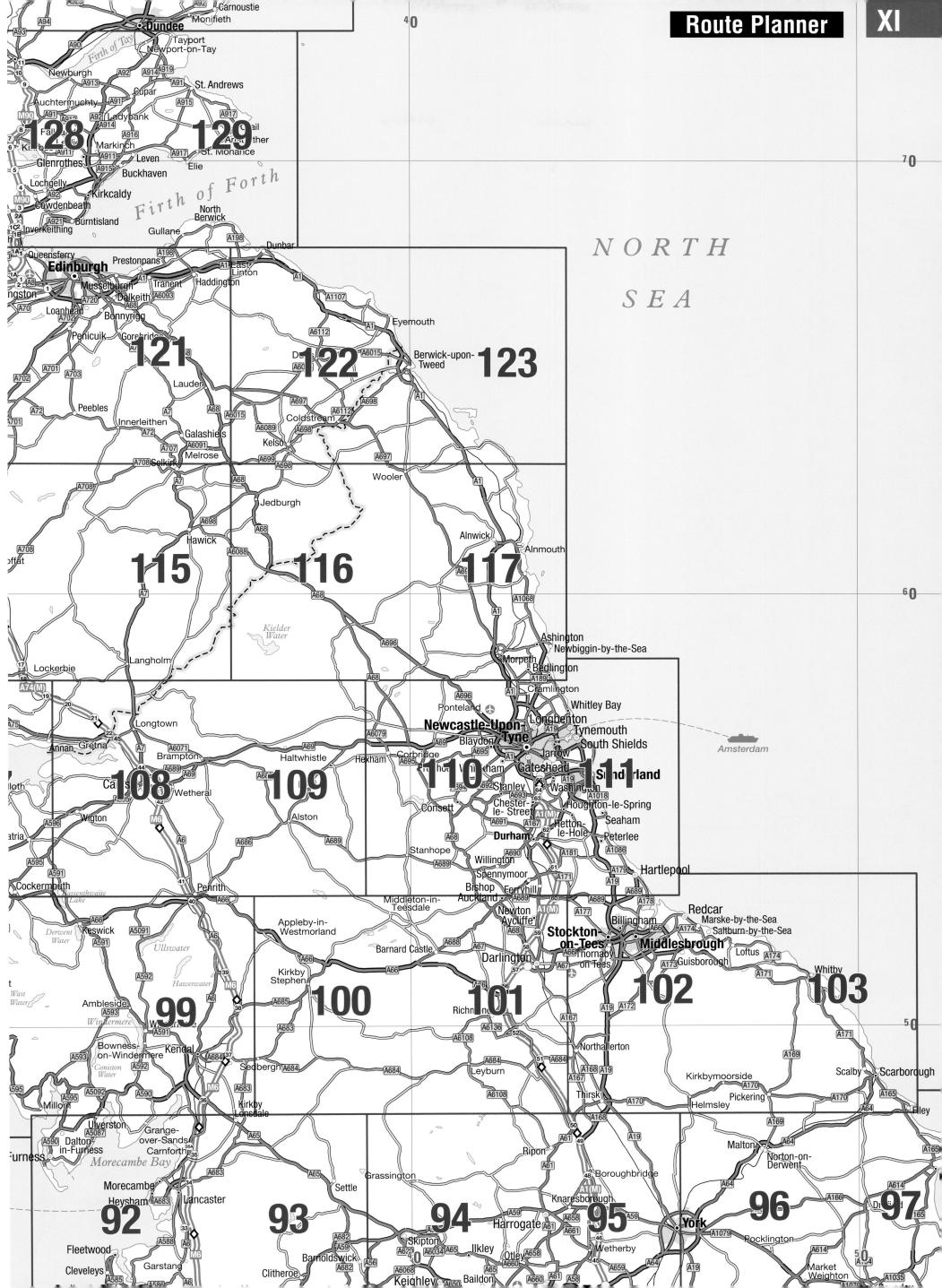

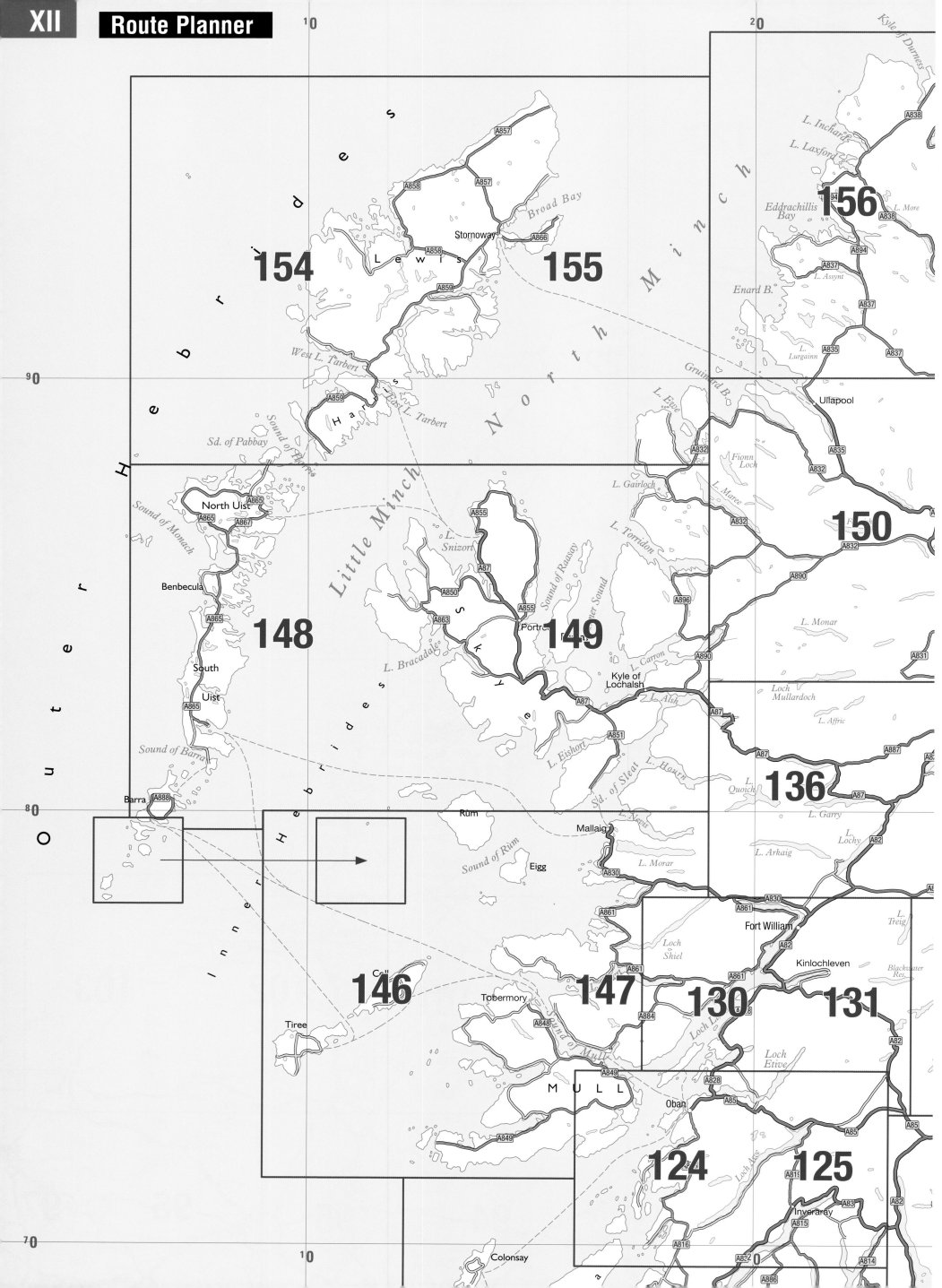

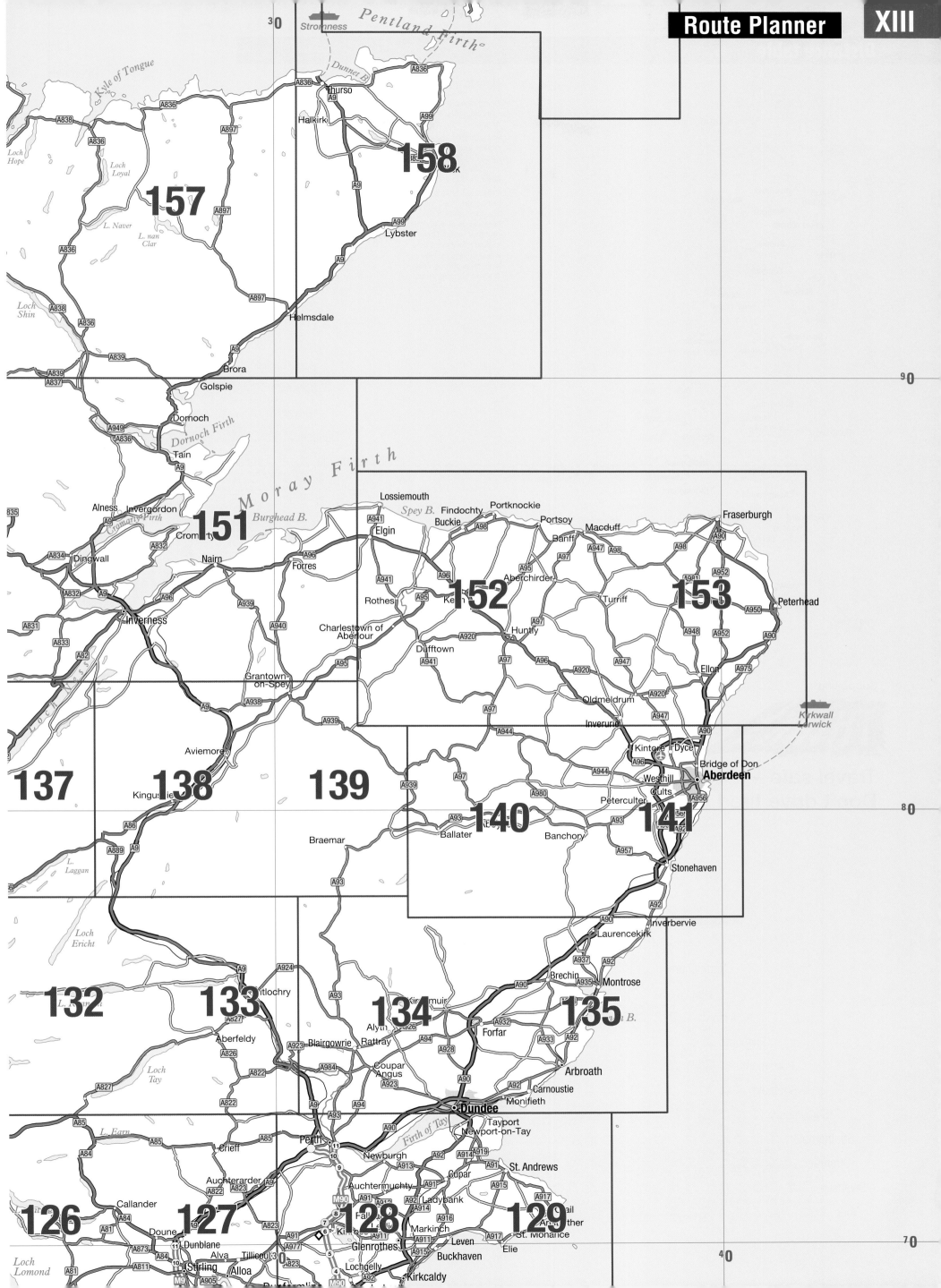

Distance table

How to use this table

Distances are shown in miles and kilometres with estimated journey times in hours and minutes.

For example: the distance between Dover and Fishguard is 331 miles or 533 kilometres with an estimated journey time of 6 hours, 20 minutes.

Estimated driving times are based on an average speed of 60mph on Motorways and 40mph on other roads. Drivers should allow extra time when driving at peak periods or through areas likely to be congested.

Supporting

THINK!

Travel safe – Don't drive tired

Map locations

John o' Groats · Kyle of Lochalsh · Inverness · Braemar · Aberdeen · Fort William · Dundee · Oban · Edinburgh · Glasgow · Berwick-upon-Tweed · Ayr · Stranraer · Carlisle · Newcastle upon Tyne · York · Kingston upon Hull · Leeds · Blackpool · Manchester · Doncaster · Liverpool · Sheffield · Lincoln · Holyhead · Nottingham · Norwich · Great Yarmouth · Shrewsbury · Leicester · Birmingham · Aberystwyth · Cambridge · Fishguard · Gloucester · Oxford · Harwich · Swansea · Cardiff · Bristol · London · Southampton · Brighton · Dover · Exeter · Bournemouth · Portsmouth · Plymouth · Land's End

Distance table

Each cell reads miles / kilometres / hours:minutes. The rightmost value in each row is the distance to London; the leftmost value is to the nearest preceding city in the list.

City	Miles	Kilometres	Time
London	—	—	—
Aberdeen	517	832	11:20
Aberystwyth	445 211	716 340	8:40 4:20
Ayr	317 183 394	510 295 634	6:10 4:20 7:20
Berwick-upon-Tweed	134 311 182 352	216 501 293 567	3:00 6:20 4:40 7:30
Birmingham	274 289 114 420 117	441 465 183 676 188	5:30 5:30 2:50 8:30 2:50
Blackpool	123 181 180 153 308 226	198 291 290 246 496 364	2:40 3:50 3:30 2:40 6:20 3:20
Bournemouth	270 147 412 436 207 564 107	435 237 663 702 333 908 172	5:00 3:10 7:50 8:30 5:00 10:30 2:40
Braemar	524 281 385 148 143 405 59 482	843 452 620 238 230 652 84 776	9:40 5:20 7:10 3:20 3:50 7:50 1:50 10:30
Brighton	534 92 286 163 409 446 253 573 84	859 148 460 262 658 718 407 922	9:40 2:10 5:20 3:50 7:40 8:00 5:10 10:30 1:50
Bristol	147 477 82 204 81 362 370 125 493 122	237 768 132 328 130 583 595 201 793 196	4:10 8:40 2:10 3:30 2:10 5:40 6:00 2:40 9:20 2:50
Cambridge	169 116 438 154 208 100 306 357 214 471 107	272 187 705 248 335 161 493 575 344 758 87	3:10 2:20 7:50 3:00 3:50 2:10 5:40 5:40 2:50 9:20 1:30
Cardiff	190 45 182 483 117 209 103 368 382 105 505 157	306 72 293 778 188 336 166 592 615 169 813 253	3:30 1:20 2:40 8:40 3:00 4:00 2:40 7:00 7:00 2:40 9:20 3:20
Carlisle	289 264 277 196 343 87 196 87 93 221 301	465 425 446 316 552 140 315 140 150 360 554	5:20 4:40 4:30 3:40 5:40 2:40 4:00 2:40 2:40 4:30 5:40
Doncaster	142 209 116 175 236 310 235 94 94 184 235 176 344 171	229 336 187 282 380 499 378 151 151 296 378 283 554 275	3:00 4:00 2:10 3:20 4:30 5:40 4:20 1:50 2:00 3:50 4:20 3:40 6:10 3:30
Dover	242 389 238 125 202 82 553 174 312 424 478 201 569 181 71	390 626 383 201 325 132 890 280 502 683 769 312 916 478 947 114	4:30 5:00 4:30 3:50 3:50 2:10 10:00 4:30 5:50 5:40 5:50 5:40 10:30 5:30
Dundee	523 275 152 441 406 430 517 52 495 239 349 113 117 376 67 448	842 443 245 710 654 692 832 84 797 385 562 182 188 605 108 721	9:10 5:00 3:10 8:00 7:40 7:40 9:10 1:20 8:30 4:30 6:20 2:40 2:30 7:10 1:50 8:40
Edinburgh	56 462 219 96 385 374 413 500 97 439 183 292 57 73 316 93 222 109	90 744 352 154 620 555 600 734 146 707 295 470 92 117 515 201 628	1:30 8:10 4:00 2:00 6:20 5:30 6:00 7:20 2:40 7:10 4:00 6:20 1:40 2:00 5:30 3:30 5:20
Exeter	450 518 248 251 353 121 284 76 184 550 82 282 157 428 446 201 569 181	724 834 399 404 568 195 401 122 296 885 132 454 253 689 718 323 916	8:00 9:10 4:40 4:30 6:20 2:30 4:30 1:40 2:40 9:40 2:20 3:10 3:10 7:50 7:50 4:10 3:40
Fishguard	230 399 460 331 398 478 180 435 248 468 794 357 336 274 597 600 90 811 418	370 642 740 533 640 770 290 700 399 753 1278 575 541 441 961 966 145 1305 673	4:30 7:30 8:30 6:20 7:40 8:50 3:50 8:20 4:50 9:00 15:10 7:00 6:20 6:50 11:00 11:30 3:40 14:50 7:20
Fort William	486 560 144 127 596 357 206 485 479 486 575 125 539 296 392 190 133 430 149 510	782 901 232 204 959 575 332 781 771 782 926 201 867 476 631 306 214 692 240 821	9:30 10:20 3:30 3:10 11:00 7:00 4:30 9:10 9:00 9:10 10:40 3:10 10:10 7:40 8:40 4:40 3:50 8:40 3:50 9:50
Glasgow	101 376 468 44 439 249 96 488 439 401 154 620 599 600 753 177 707 295 470 92 117 515 233 639	163 605 723 71 134 786 154 786 707 646 248 998 964 966 1212 285 1138 475 757 148 188 829 375 1028	2:50 8:30 8:00 1:20 2:00 8:40 2:00 8:40 7:10 6:40 2:40 11:30 10:30 10:50 14:00 4:40 11:40 8:00 7:40 2:20 2:40 9:40 5:10 11:40
Gloucester	346 454 153 111 349 410 191 150 247 56 123 35 159 443 99 174 56 318 330 102 468 109	557 731 246 179 562 660 307 241 398 90 198 56 256 713 159 280 90 512 531 164 753 175	6:10 8:30 3:10 2:10 6:10 7:10 3:30 2:50 4:20 1:20 2:20 1:00 3:00 8:00 2:40 3:10 1:50 6:50 5:50 2:30 8:30 2:30
Great Yarmouth	225 419 527 366 335 386 484 185 167 320 284 252 185 360 444 252 275 167 372 45 281 535 76	362 674 848 589 539 621 779 298 269 515 457 405 298 579 715 405 443 269 599 72 452 861 122	4:40 8:00 10:20 7:20 6:30 7:30 9:00 4:00 3:30 5:30 5:40 4:40 4:00 6:10 8:10 4:50 5:40 4:40 7:40 1:20 5:50 11:10 2:20
Harwich	82 196 432 543 337 279 413 469 125 194 336 246 67 217 504 187 275 167 372 65 281 535 76	132 316 695 874 542 449 665 755 201 312 541 396 108 349 811 301 443 269 599 105 452 861 122	2:10 4:00 8:10 10:30 6:40 5:20 7:40 8:40 2:50 4:00 5:40 4:40 1:40 3:40 8:10 4:30 5:40 4:40 7:40 1:20 5:50 11:10 2:20
Holyhead	349 334 191 130 438 167 282 333 394 360 181 231 216 270 206 288 141 148 311 305 111 439 269	562 538 307 531 705 269 454 536 634 580 291 372 348 435 332 538 686 463 227 238 501 491 179 707 433	7:10 7:00 4:00 6:40 8:40 4:50 5:40 6:40 7:30 7:00 3:50 4:50 5:00 5:40 5:30 6:50 7:00 3:50 4:30 6:30 3:30 8:10 5:20
Inverness	474 569 553 504 166 66 542 618 158 132 622 383 262 549 505 539 217 75 597 348 410 215 199 486 105 550	763 916 890 811 267 106 872 995 254 212 1001 617 422 884 813 867 350 121 961 560 737 346 320 782 169 885	9:40 11:00 11:00 9:30 4:00 1:40 10:30 11:30 3:20 3:20 11:30 7:30 5:20 10:20 11:00 11:30 7:20 1:40 11:50 8:10 9:40 4:40 4:20 9:40 2:50 10:40
John o' Groats	129 603 693 677 628 295 195 674 743 285 259 746 507 391 680 630 539 341 325 769 471 263 341 803 304 943	208 970 1116 1090 1011 475 314 1080 1197 459 417 1201 816 629 1094 1014 1075 1193 523 1165 769 924 550 528 967 373 1067	3:20 12:40 14:00 14:00 12:30 7:10 14:00 14:40 5:30 4:50 14:40 9:40 8:40 13:50 14:00 14:40 10:00 10:00 11:50 8:10 7:40 12:40 15:00 4:20 13:00 15:40
Kingston upon Hull	518 394 231 196 207 169 254 369 280 309 234 295 56 47 139 244 233 375 394 526 425 204 216 298 404 586 296	834 634 372 316 333 272 409 594 451 497 377 475 412 76 223 393 375 394 526 425 204 298 404 586 296	10:50 7:50 4:50 4:10 3:20 3:10 4:50 7:20 5:40 5:40 5:30 4:50 1:10 3:10 4:40 3:40 4:20 4:20 4:40 4:40 4:20 3:50 3:50 2:20 4:40 7:20 3:50
Kyle of Lochalsh	445 189 84 514 611 612 528 179 76 516 838 216 186 691 422 599 555 602 555 652 615 159 618 872 511 341 803 304 943	716 304 135 827 983 969 850 288 122 913 1011 348 299 1080 695 443 888 1048 695 995 789 712 471 263 212 499	9:00 4:00 2:10 11:20 13:20 12:10 12:10 10:20 4:40 12:10 12:10 5:20 4:40 12:50 6:50 12:20 7:50 9:40 12:10 7:50 6:30 4:50 10:10 14:30
Land's End	763 421 868 741 405 390 446 235 573 686 353 123 574 642 381 374 477 245 308 665 405 424 552 570 313 692 297	1228 678 1397 1193 652 628 718 378 922 1104 568 198 924 1033 613 602 768 394 602 1070 330 652 452 888 917 504 1114 478	15:10 8:20 17:20 14:20 8:30 8:00 9:10 4:50 10:50 13:20 7:20 2:00 10:50 12:00 7:40 7:20 9:20 4:20 7:50 10:40 6:50 10:40 10:40 8:30 9:40 6:30
Leeds	405 394 55 487 360 176 213 329 237 270 202 258 89 119 232 145 194 290 312 419 472 410 116 182 151 341 272 327 189	652 634 89 784 579 283 359 315 280 346 530 346 201 143 310 194 312 419 472 410 116 182 151 341 272 327 189	8:00 8:20 1:30 10:20 7:10 4:00 4:20 6:30 5:00 5:00 4:00 5:00 2:00 2:10 4:00 3:20 4:10 4:50 4:50 5:50 5:50 5:50 1:50 3:20 3:20 5:10 4:30 6:50 3:50
Leicester	95 320 500 102 588 461 190 147 140 85 314 422 209 196 296 349 185 74 206 150 68 120 166 288 158 140 39 252 299 153 414 97	153 515 805 164 947 742 306 237 225 137 505 679 336 315 476 562 298 119 332 240 193 267 626 254 225 63 406 481 246 666 156	2:00 6:30 9:50 2:10 11:50 8:50 4:00 3:10 3:20 1:40 5:40 7:00 4:10 3:40 5:30 5:30 3:50 1:40 3:50 2:40 1:10 2:10 3:50 4:50 2:40 2:40 1:10 5:10 6:00 3:10 7:00 2:00
Lincoln	51 68 371 476 44 554 427 216 155 128 159 391 299 247 247 258 314 9 191 208 85 183 197 325 336 206 145 360 441 320 616 211	82 109 597 766 71 892 687 348 249 206 256 468 642 438 398 415 505 325 410 335 137 295 317 523 541 331 233 580 710 515 991 340	1:20 1:30 6:50 7:40 1:00 10:10 7:40 4:00 3:40 4:10 4:30 3:30 3:20 3:40 4:10 3:40 4:10 0:20 3:10 4:10 1:50 4:10 4:10 6:30 5:50 4:40 3:40 6:30 7:40 6:00 11:40 4:10
Liverpool	129 130 75 361 407 130 511 382 102 265 240 140 164 329 216 286 299 86 120 169 194 161 272 318 234 49 93 219 213 104 341 202	208 209 121 581 655 209 822 615 164 427 386 225 348 530 257 381 480 138 193 272 312 259 438 512 377 79 150 352 343 167 549 325	2:50 2:40 1:50 6:30 7:30 2:40 9:40 7:40 2:40 5:20 5:20 2:40 4:10 6:40 4:30 4:50 5:20 2:10 2:40 3:20 4:00 3:20 5:20 6:40 6:10 1:20 2:10 4:50 4:50 2:20 6:40 4:10
Manchester	35 84 92 40 361 406 95 500 373 124 228 212 126 155 128 159 208 85 119 183 165 161 272 318 234 48 80 196 212 129 340 185	56 135 148 64 581 654 153 805 600 200 367 341 203 259 256 256 335 325 305 266 262 512 365 79 150 352 343 167 549 298	1:10 2:00 2:40 1:20 6:50 7:30 2:10 10:00 7:10 2:10 4:20 4:10 2:10 3:10 3:20 3:10 3:40 2:10 2:40 3:30 3:40 3:20 5:20 6:40 6:10 1:20 2:10 4:50 4:50 2:20 6:40 3:50
Newcastle upon Tyne	132 168 159 187 92 498 318 132 395 268 272 308 281 266 148 253 262 110 166 358 114 97 325 241 299 352 201 347 129 207 64 149 257 235 286	212 270 256 301 148 802 512 212 636 431 438 496 452 428 237 407 529 586 177 267 576 183 92 523 388 481 567 323 558 208 333 103 240 414 378 460	2:50 3:20 3:20 3:40 2:10 9:40 7:00 2:50 8:40 5:40 5:40 6:40 5:40 4:50 3:10 5:40 5:40 1:40 2:40 6:40 2:20 1:40 6:20 4:40 5:50 7:50 3:40 6:10 2:10 4:10 1:20 2:30 4:10 4:40 5:40
Norwich	264 185 220 105 119 176 421 582 149 571 73 20 328 620 811 552 496 589 679 237 84 373 267 528 615 444 798 183	425 298 354 169 192 283 678 937 240 1053 852 501 117 20 328 620 811 552 496 589 679 237 465 422 100 406 282 735 344 373 267 528 615 444 798 183	5:20 4:30 4:30 2:50 3:30 3:50 8:40 9:40 10:30 4:00 4:00 1:30 2:00 7:20 9:50 7:10 6:30 7:30 9:50 3:40 4:50 5:50 4:50 9:40 5:50 8:40 9:40 3:50
Nottingham	130 157 73 98 35 25 70 345 479 185 150 153 110 293 401 221 221 328 205 43 194 172 145 193 353 183 111 50 221 164 393 122	209 253 118 158 56 40 113 555 771 145 896 692 298 241 246 177 472 646 356 422 528 330 69 312 277 142 233 311 568 295 179 80 356 441 264 633 196	3:40 3:10 1:40 2:10 1:40 0:50 1:40 7:00 11:20 5:00 4:00 4:30 2:30 4:30 5:40 4:30 4:00 5:40 4:40 1:10 3:50 4:10 1:40 4:10 4:30 4:30 1:40 2:00 4:40 4:20 6:10 3:10
Oban	390 492 233 307 308 387 419 307 665 126 346 244 417 521 549 123 117 585 141 530 285 384 180 94 412 178 499	628 792 375 494 496 623 674 494 1070 206 557 393 188 687 843 829 710 148 79 481 549 123 117 188 942 557 303 768 227 853 459 618 289 151 663 286 803	7:30 9:40 4:50 6:00 6:10 7:30 7:50 6:40 12:40 2:30 5:30 3:50 2:50 8:00 12:40 9:10 7:40 1:40 1:30 9:50 5:30 5:30 5:50 4:30 9:40 5:40 4:20 8:10 4:20 9:30
Oxford	462 109 145 260 144 172 137 73 168 274 550 192 656 532 238 145 200 52 356 472 205 156 156 433 141 141 108 83 74 108 460 214 587 128 328 203 474 492 237 615 218	744 175 233 418 232 277 221 117 270 441 885 309 1056 856 383 233 322 84 573 760 330 251 696 227 233 418 174 134 119 174 740 345 945 206 528 326 763 792 382 990 351	8:30 2:10 4:50 5:10 3:20 3:20 2:50 1:30 3:10 5:40 10:40 3:20 9:50 8:40 4:40 3:20 4:30 1:20 6:50 7:40 4:10 2:40 2:40 7:40 2:20 2:40 1:40 1:40 1:10 1:40 9:40 4:20 8:10 4:20 9:30
Plymouth	199 587 267 343 410 283 293 242 316 49 674 550 571 1271 528 309 309 365 417 495 595 264 497 796 474 242 196 361 945 528 203 474 492 237 615 218	320 945 430 552 660 455 455 472 389 509 143 1085 577 1271 1069 528 309 309 528 672 797 588 253 797 958 888 797 549 490 842 528 527 763 792 382 990 351	4:00 10:30 5:10 7:00 7:40 5:10 5:50 5:50 6:50 1:40 11:20 6:40 6:10 20:30 9:40 6:40 6:40 8:40 11:20 5:40 4:20 6:40 10:40 9:00 8:10 4:20 9:30
Portsmouth	176 77 545 191 207 337 236 254 201 162 257 259 633 269 737 613 311 166 311 256 461 413 514 130 258 264 227 645 692 357 901 113	283 124 877 307 333 542 380 409 323 261 414 417 1019 433 1186 987 501 267 356 192 721 893 404 217 729 827 209 377 560 230 414 425 881 84 264 141 857 813 574 1450 182	4:50 1:40 10:40 4:50 4:20 6:10 4:30 4:40 4:10 4:10 4:50 4:50 10:10 4:50 11:40 9:50 6:40 3:20 4:40 3:40 7:10 9:00 4:30 3:10 2:40 5:00 2:40 5:20 5:50 3:20 10:10 2:00
Sheffield	303 283 135 339 37 146 83 72 46 62 113 62 427 189 387 303 168 146 126 248 348 378 468 142 176 160 245 355 256 360 159	370 455 217 546 60 235 133 116 74 100 53 681 687 742 400 306 203 399 560 399 273 255 245 393 458 515 229 283 257 360 256 593	3:20 5:20 2:40 5:10 2:40 1:40 1:10 1:40 1:00 1:40 7:10 4:30 7:20 6:00 5:10 4:30 2:40 2:30 2:30 2:20 4:20 5:40 5:40 1:50 2:40 2:40 3:20 4:30 3:20 6:00 3:20
Shrewsbury	82 207 263 461 500 382 172 378 362 124 438 615 288 441 330 109 176 103 103 166 364 191 118 165 76 426 433 124 642 258	132 333 423 742 805 610 277 608 582 200 705 989 463 710 531 176 283 166 364 124 438 615 288 441 330 283 209 58 75 91 642 258	2:10 3:50 4:40 8:40 9:00 7:00 4:00 7:20 6:50 2:40 8:10 11:40 5:40 8:40 6:10 2:10 3:20 2:40 3:20 2:00 7:10 4:30 2:20 3:10 1:40 8:10 6:50 2:00 11:40 4:20
Southampton	185 199 21 151 64 530 176 206 324 221 239 204 137 122 307 393 164 150 433 541 218 438 142 209 140 61 31 251 128 388 417 201 547 77	298 320 34 243 103 853 283 332 521 356 385 328 220 196 494 632 264 241 697 871 351 705 229 336 225 98 50 404 206 624 671 323 880 124	4:10 3:40 0:50 3:40 1:40 9:50 4:20 4:40 5:20 4:10 4:30 4:00 2:40 2:40 6:50 8:50 4:00 3:40 11:10 13:20 4:40 8:50 3:10 4:20 3:40 1:20 0:50 4:50 2:40 5:50 5:50 4:10 11:00 2:00
Stranraer	445 277 263 461 343 158 263 317 382 461 500 289 200 378 469 649 254 354 480 531 263 417 422 544 660 686 552 315 314 631 731 266 269 496 414 163 628 610 765 312 303 697 647	716 446 423 742 805 610 422 510 616 742 805 465 322 608 755 1044 409 570 772 854 423 671 679 876 1062 1104 888 507 505 1015 1176 428 433 798 667 263 1011 982 1231 502 488 1121	8:40 5:30 4:40 8:40 9:00 3:40 4:40 6:30 7:00 8:40 8:40 4:40 3:10 6:10 7:20 12:10 4:40 6:20 8:40 9:50 4:50 7:20 7:20 9:50 11:40 11:40 9:40 5:50 5:50 11:40 13:00 5:00 4:40 8:40 7:20 2:40 11:20 10:40 13:20
Swansea	417 161 118 217 182 206 141 506 192 301 187 195 233 177 248 285 594 696 572 184 267 329 89 409 496 67 161 412 274 232 309 41 227 85 222 505 167 216 119 383 379 73 507 194	671 259 190 349 293 332 227 815 309 485 559 301 314 285 399 459 956 1120 921 296 430 530 143 658 798 108 259 663 441 373 497 66 365 137 357 813 269 348 191 616 610 117 816 312	7:50 4:20 3:10 4:00 3:30 4:20 3:20 9:20 4:10 6:00 6:20 4:10 4:30 4:30 4:50 5:00 10:00 11:20 9:20 4:30 4:50 6:20 2:50 7:10 8:40 2:10 4:20 7:10 5:10 5:40 6:50 1:10 4:30 2:00 4:40 8:40 4:10 5:20 2:00 6:50 6:50 1:50 8:10 4:50
York	272 222 183 191 309 77 181 84 64 191 135 103 159 121 174 49 411 407 60 171 282 34 55 195 266 357 443 459 433 154 209 238 344 314 513 203	438 357 415 214 84 448 536 291 307 124 62 135 102 161 173 196 411 407 771 566 328 367 323 304 349 531 420 462 312 402 266 357 443 459 433 154 209 238 344 314 513 203	5:10 4:40 5:10 2:40 1:20 5:10 6:20 3:20 6:00 1:40 1:40 1:40 2:10 1:40 2:10 0:50 10:10 7:00 1:40 2:20 4:40 0:40 1:10 4:20 5:50 5:50 5:40 5:10 5:40 2:00 4:10 4:10 4:10 5:10 6:20 4:10

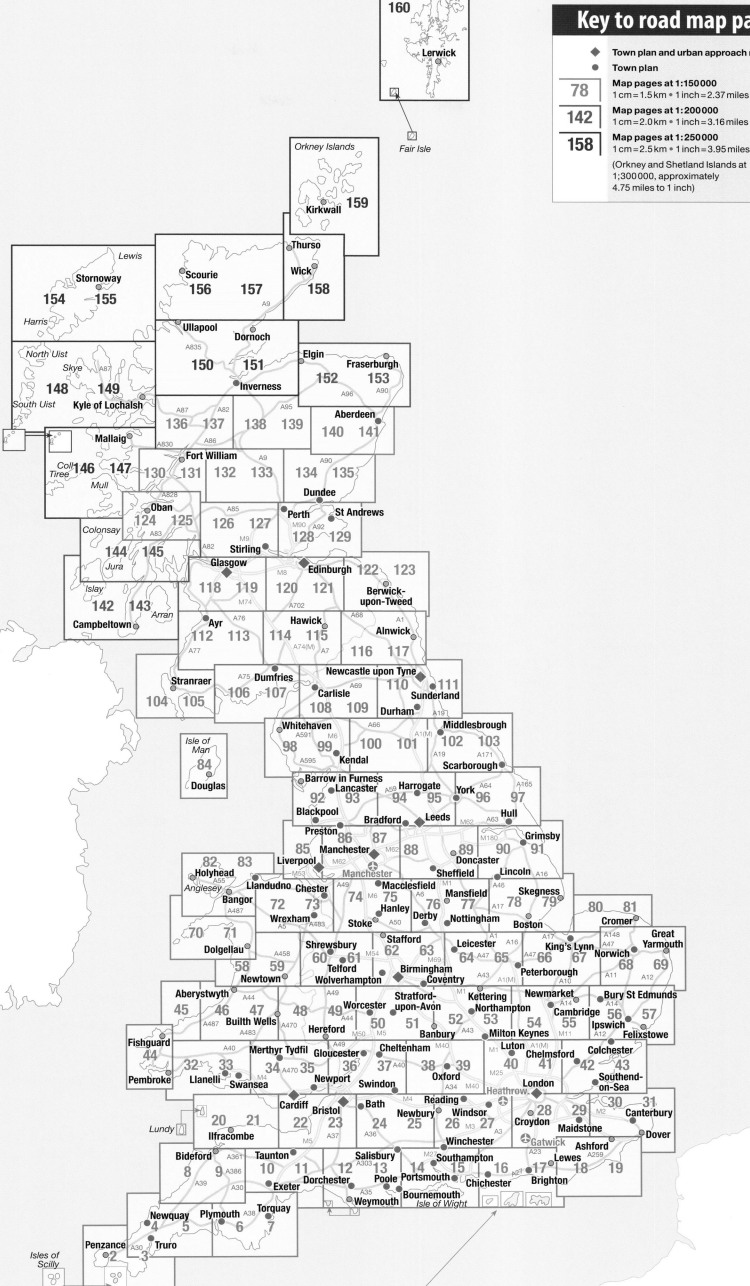

Key to road map pages

◆ Town plan and urban approach map
● Town plan

78	**Map pages at 1:150000** 1 cm = 1.5 km • 1 inch = 2.37 miles
142	**Map pages at 1:200000** 1 cm = 2.0 km • 1 inch = 3.16 miles
158	**Map pages at 1:250000** 1 cm = 2.5 km • 1 inch = 3.95 miles

(Orkney and Shetland Islands at 1;300000, approximately 4.75 miles to 1 inch)

Shetland Islands **160** Lerwick

Orkney Islands Kirkwall **159**

Fair Isle

Thurso

Wick

Lewis
Stornoway
154 **155**
Harris

Scourie
156 **157** **158**

A9

Ullapool
A835
Dornoch
150 **151**
Inverness

Elgin
Fraserburgh
152 **153**
A96 A90

North Uist
Skye A87
South Uist
148 **149**
Kyle of Lochalsh

Mallaig
A830
A87 A82 A95
136 **137** **138** **139**

Aberdeen
140 **141**

A86

Coll
Tiree **146** **147**
Mull

Fort William
130 **131** **132** **133**
A9

A90
134 **135**

A828
Oban
124 **125**
Colonsay
A83
A85
126 **127**

Dundee

Perth
St Andrews
M90 A92
128 **129**

144 **145**
Jura
A82
Stirling
M9

Islay
142 **143**
Arran
Campbeltown

Glasgow
118 **119**
M74
Edinburgh
120 **121**
A702
122 **123**
Berwick-upon-Tweed

M8

Ayr
112 **113**
A76
A77
Hawick
114 **115**
A74(M) A7
A68
A1
Alnwick
116 **117**

Stranraer
104 **105**
A75
Dumfries
106 **107**
Carlisle
108 **109**
A69
Durham
Newcastle upon Tyne
110 **111**
Sunderland
A1(M)
A19

Whitehaven
98 **99**
A591 M6
Kendal
A595
100 **101**
A66
102 **103**
A19 A171
Middlesbrough
Scarborough

Isle of Man
84
Douglas

Barrow in Furness
92 **93**
Lancaster
A59
Harrogate
94 **95**
York
96
A64 A165
97

Blackpool
Preston
86 **87**
Bradford
Leeds
88
M62 A63
Hull
A63

85
Liverpool
M62
Manchester
Doncaster
89
Sheffield
90 **91**
M180
Grimsby
Lincoln
A16

Anglesey
Holyhead
A55
82 **83**
Bangor
A487
Llandudno
Chester
72 **73**
A49
Macclesfield
74
M6
Hanley
75
A6
Mansfield
76 **77**
A17
Skegness
78 **79**
A46
80 **81**
Cromer
A148

Wrexham
A5
A483
70 **71**
Dolgellau
Stoke
A50
Derby
Nottingham
Boston
A47
Norwich
A17
68
Great Yarmouth
69
A12

Shrewsbury
60 **61**
Telford
A458
A54
Stafford
62
M54
63
M69
Leicester
64
A47
65
A1(M)
Peterborough
66 **67**
King's Lynn
A148
A11

Aberystwyth
45
A44
46 **47**
Newtown
A470
48
A49
Worcester
49
A44
Stratford-upon-Avon
Coventry
A43
Birmingham
Wolverhampton

Fishguard
44
Pembroke
A40
Merthyr Tydfil
32 **33** **34** **35**
A470
Llanelli
Swansea
M4
Hereford
A49
50
M5
51
Banbury
52 **53**
A43
Milton Keynes
54 **55**
Cambridge
A14
Newmarket
Bury St Edmunds
56 **57**
Ipswich
Felixstowe
A12

A487
Builth Wells
A483
A44

Gloucester
36
Cheltenham
37
A40
Oxford
38 **39**
M40
M1
Luton
40
A1(M)
Chelmsford
41
Colchester
42 **43**
Southend-on-Sea

Newport
Cardiff
Bristol
22 **23** **24**
Bath
Swindon
A34
Newbury
25
Reading
M4
Windsor
26 **27**
M25
Heathrow
London
28 **29**
Croydon
Gatwick
A23
Maidstone
30 **31**
Canterbury
Dover

Lundy
20 **21**
Ilfracombe
M5
A36
Winchester
Southampton
14 **15**
Portsmouth
Chichester
16 **17**
Lewes
A27
Brighton
18 **19**
A259
Ashford

Bideford
A361
Taunton
10 **11**
Dorchester
12
Salisbury
A303
13
Poole
Bournemouth
Isle of Wight

8
A39
9
A386
A30
Exeter
Weymouth
A35

Newquay
4 **5**
Plymouth
6
A38
Torquay
7

Penzance
2
A30
Truro
3

Isles of Scilly

Alderney

Channel Islands
Guernsey

Jersey

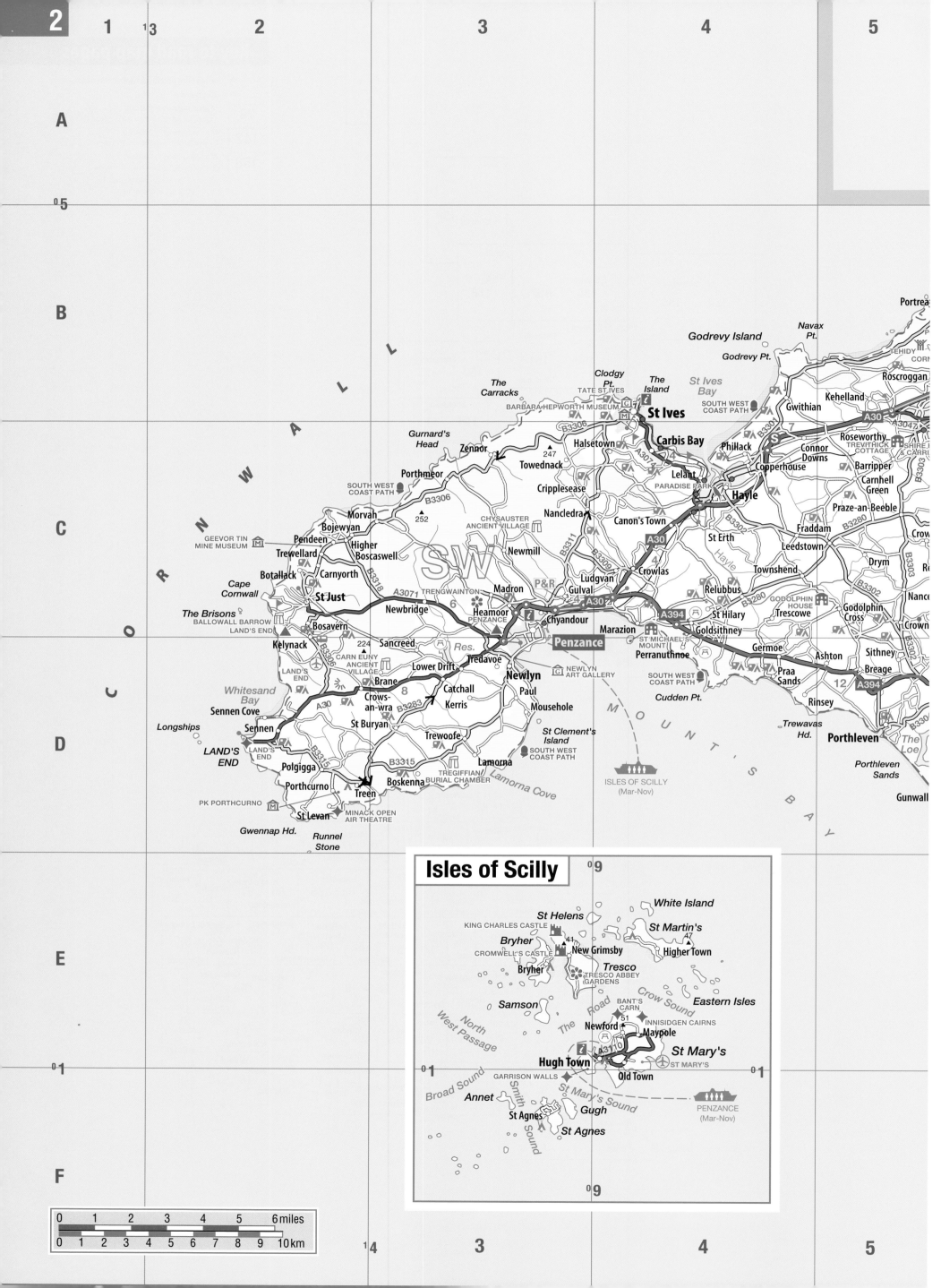

1 3 2 3 4 5

A

B

St Ives
Godrevy Island   Navax Pt.
Godrevy Pt.
Portrea
Roscroggan
TEHIDY CORN
The Carracks
Clodgy Pt.
TATE ST IVES   The Island   St Ives Bay   Gwithian
BARBARA HEPWORTH MUSEUM   SOUTH WEST COAST PATH
Kehelland
Gurnard's Head   B3306   Carbis Bay   A30
Zennor   Halsetown   Phillack   Roseworthy
Porthmeor   252   Towednack   Lelant   Connor Downs   TREVITHICK COTTAGE   SHIRE & CARRI
Cripplesease   PARADISE PARK   **Hayle**   Copperhouse   Barripper
SOUTH WEST COAST PATH   Nancledra   Canon's Town   Carnhell Green
B3306   Morvah   Praze-an-Beeble
Bojewyan   CHYSAUSTER ANCIENT VILLAGE   St Erth   Fraddam   Drym
Pendeen   Higher Boscaswell   Newmill   Crowlas   Leedstown   Crow
GEEVOR TIN MINE MUSEUM   252   Townshend   B3303
Trewellard   A30   Relubbus   B3280
Carnyorth   TRENGWAINTON   Ludgvan   Godolphin   Godolphin House   Nance
Botallack   B3318   Madron   Gulval   St Hilary   Trescowe   Cross
Cape Cornwall   A3071   P&R   A394
St Just   Heamoor   Germoe   Ashton   Sithney
The Brisons   Newbridge   PENZANCE   Chyandour   St Michael's Mount   Praa Sands   Breage
BALLOWALL BARROW   LAND'S END   Marazion   Goldsithney   Rinsey   B3302
Bosavern   224   Perranuthnoe   SOUTH WEST COAST PATH   12   A394
Kelynack   Sancreed   Res.   **Penzance**
CARN EUNY ANCIENT VILLAGE   Tredavoe   NEWLYN ART GALLERY   Cudden Pt.   Trewavas Hd.   **Porthleven**
LAND'S END   Lower Drift   **Newlyn**   Porthleven Sands
Brane   Paul   The Loe
Whitesand Bay   Crows-an-wra   Catchall   Mousehole
Sennen Cove   A30   Kerris   St Clement's Island   Gunwall
Longships   B3283   St Buryan   Trewoofe   Lamorna
Sennen   Lamorna   SOUTH WEST COAST PATH
LAND'S END   Polgigga   B3315   Boskenna   TREGIFFIAN BURIAL CHAMBER   Lamorna Cove
Porthcurno   B3315   Treen   ISLES OF SCILLY (Mar-Nov)
PK PORTHCURNO   St Levan   MINACK OPEN AIR THEATRE
Gwennap Hd.   Runnel Stone

C

D

E

F

CORNWALL
SW
MOUNT'S BAY

0 1 2 3 4 5 6 miles
0 1 2 3 4 5 6 7 8 9 10km

Isles of Scilly

9

White Island
St Helens
KING CHARLES CASTLE   St Martin's
Bryher   41   47
CROMWELL'S CASTLE   New Grimsby   Higher Town
Bryher   Tresco
TRESCO ABBEY GARDENS
Samson   Eastern Isles
North West Passage   BANT'S CARN   51   INNISIDGEN CAIRNS
Newford   Maypole
A3110   **St Mary's**
1   **Hugh Town**   1
Broad Sound   GARRISON WALLS   Old Town   ST MARY'S
Annet   The Road   Crow Sound
Smith Sound   St Mary's Sound   Gugh   PENZANCE (Mar-Nov)
St Agnes   St Agnes

9

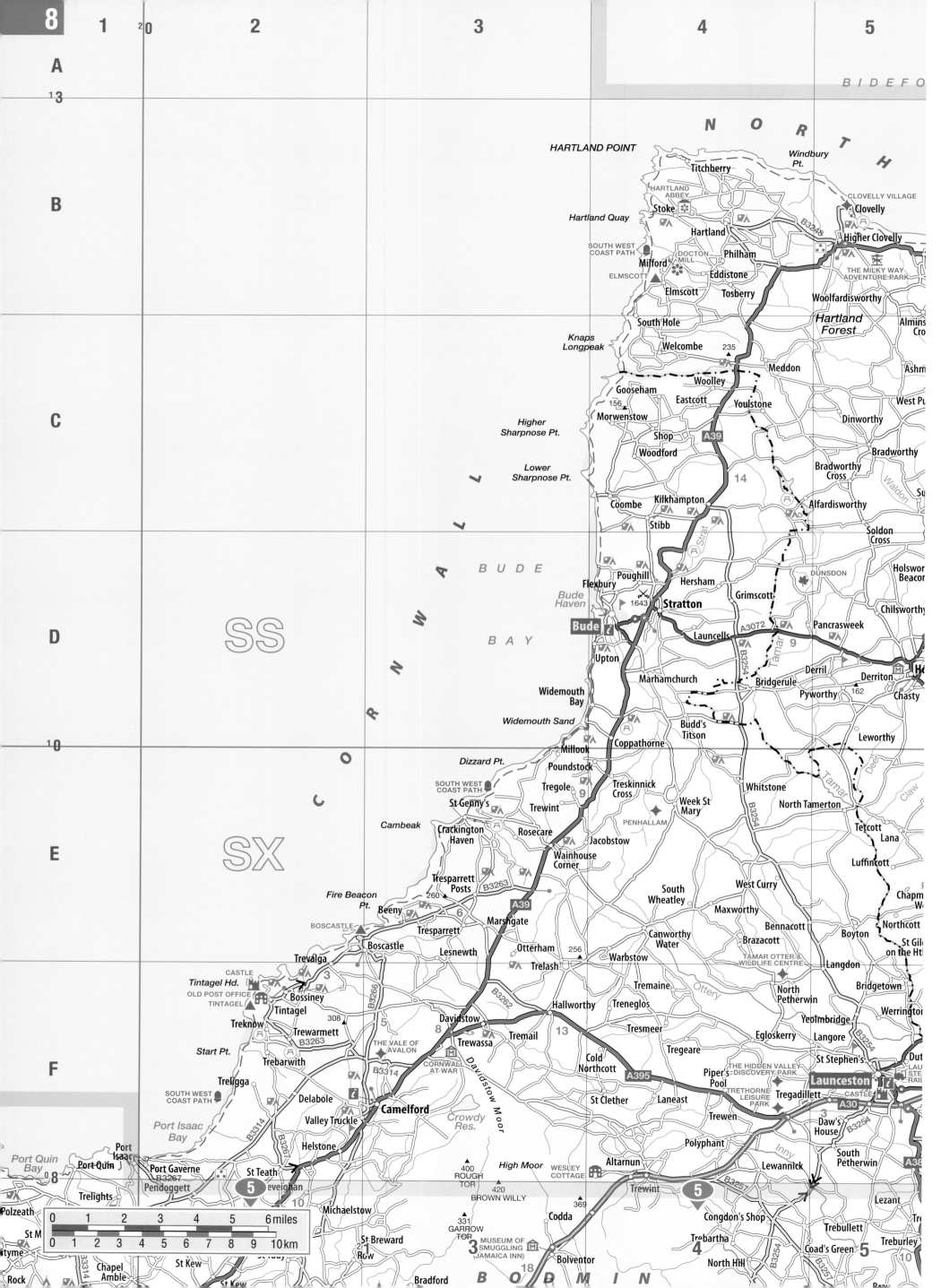

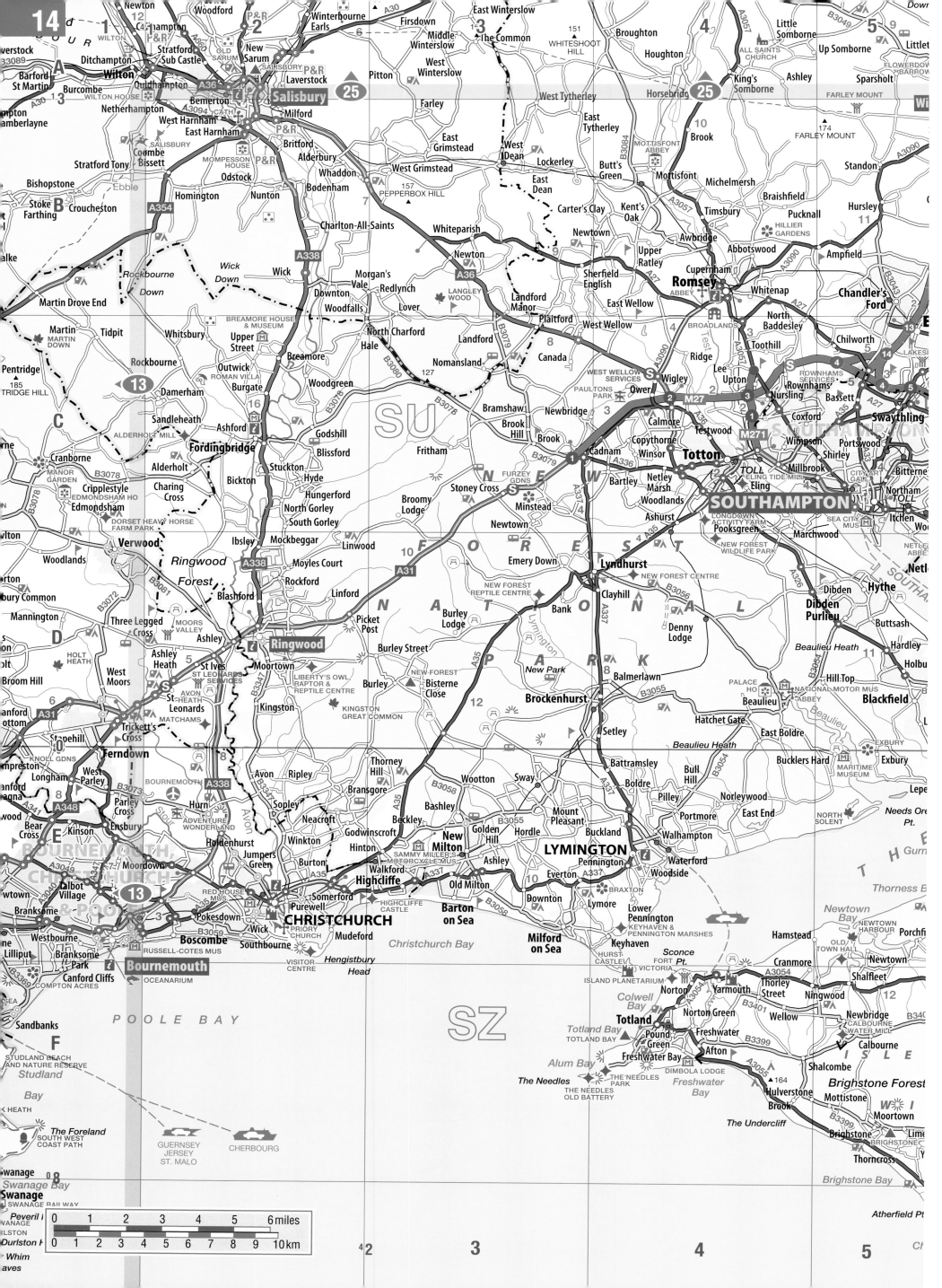

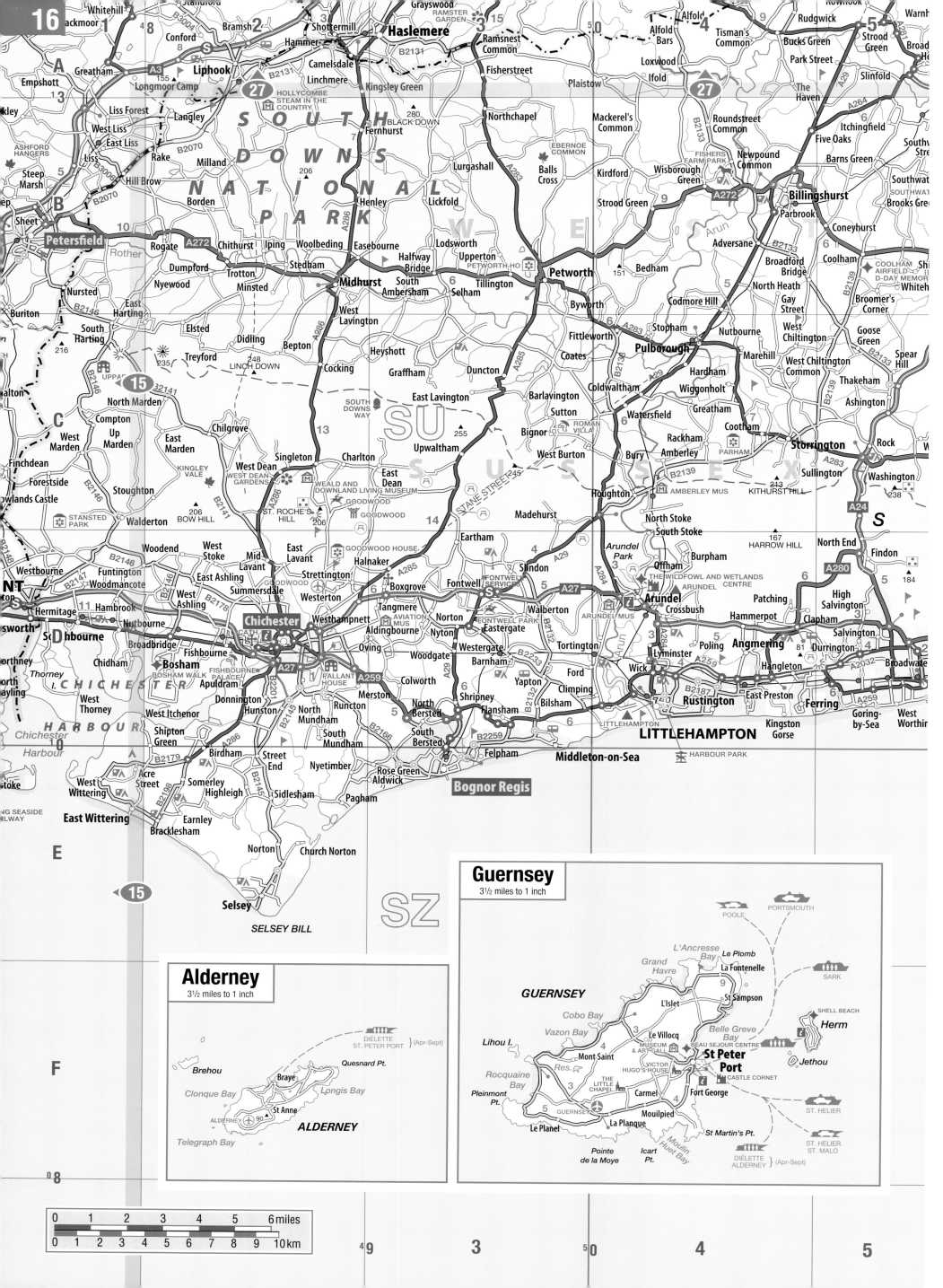

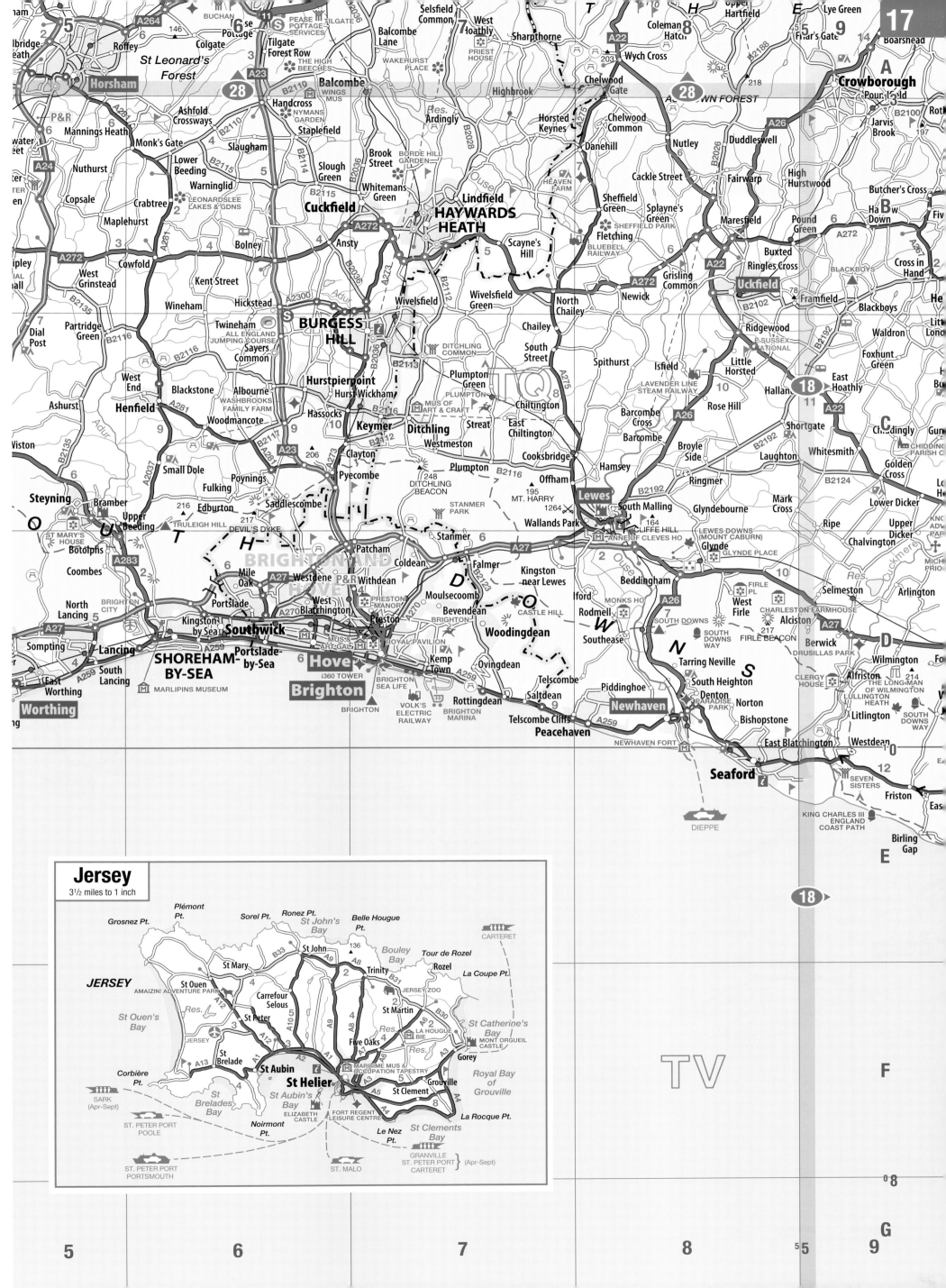

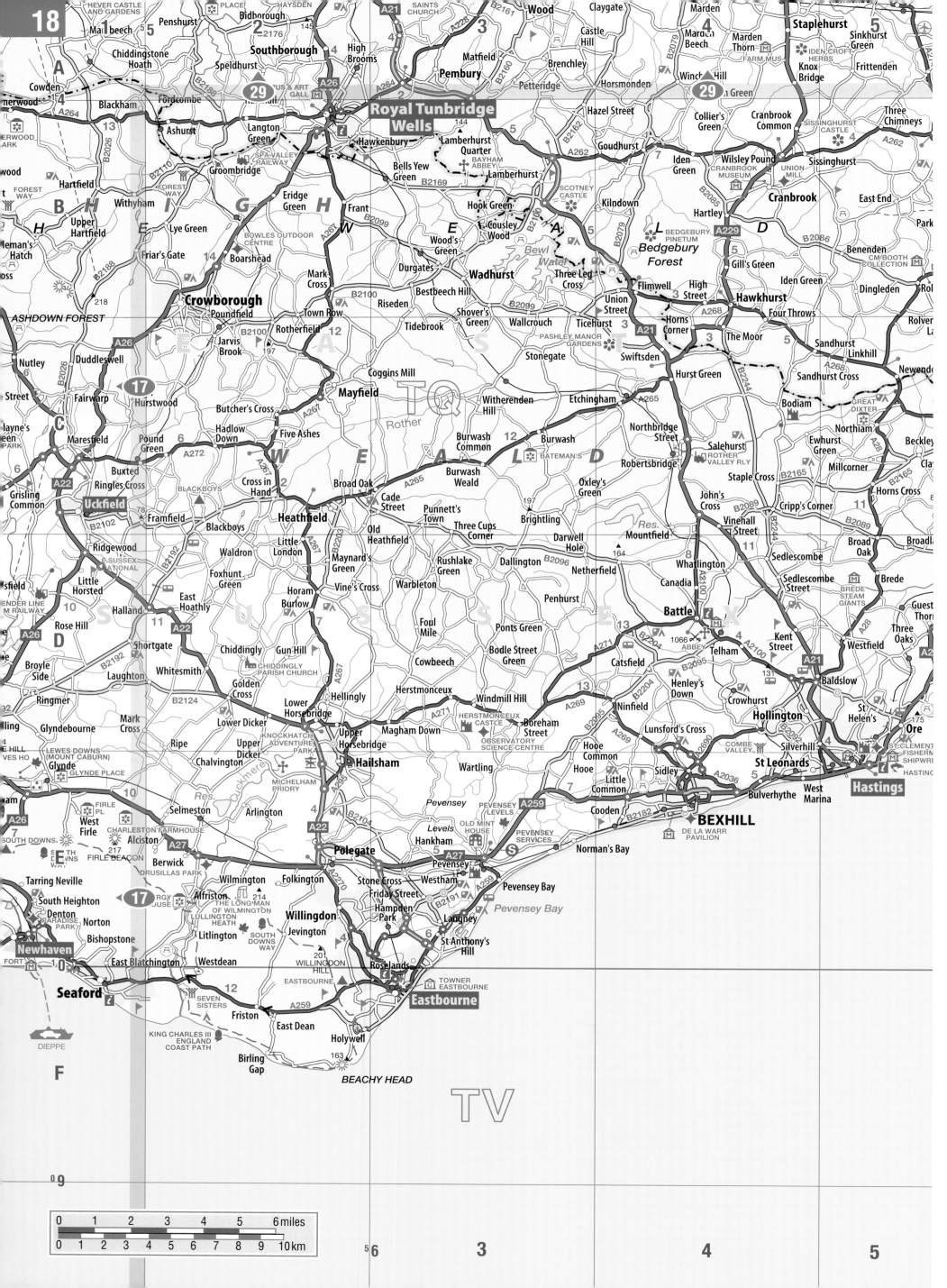

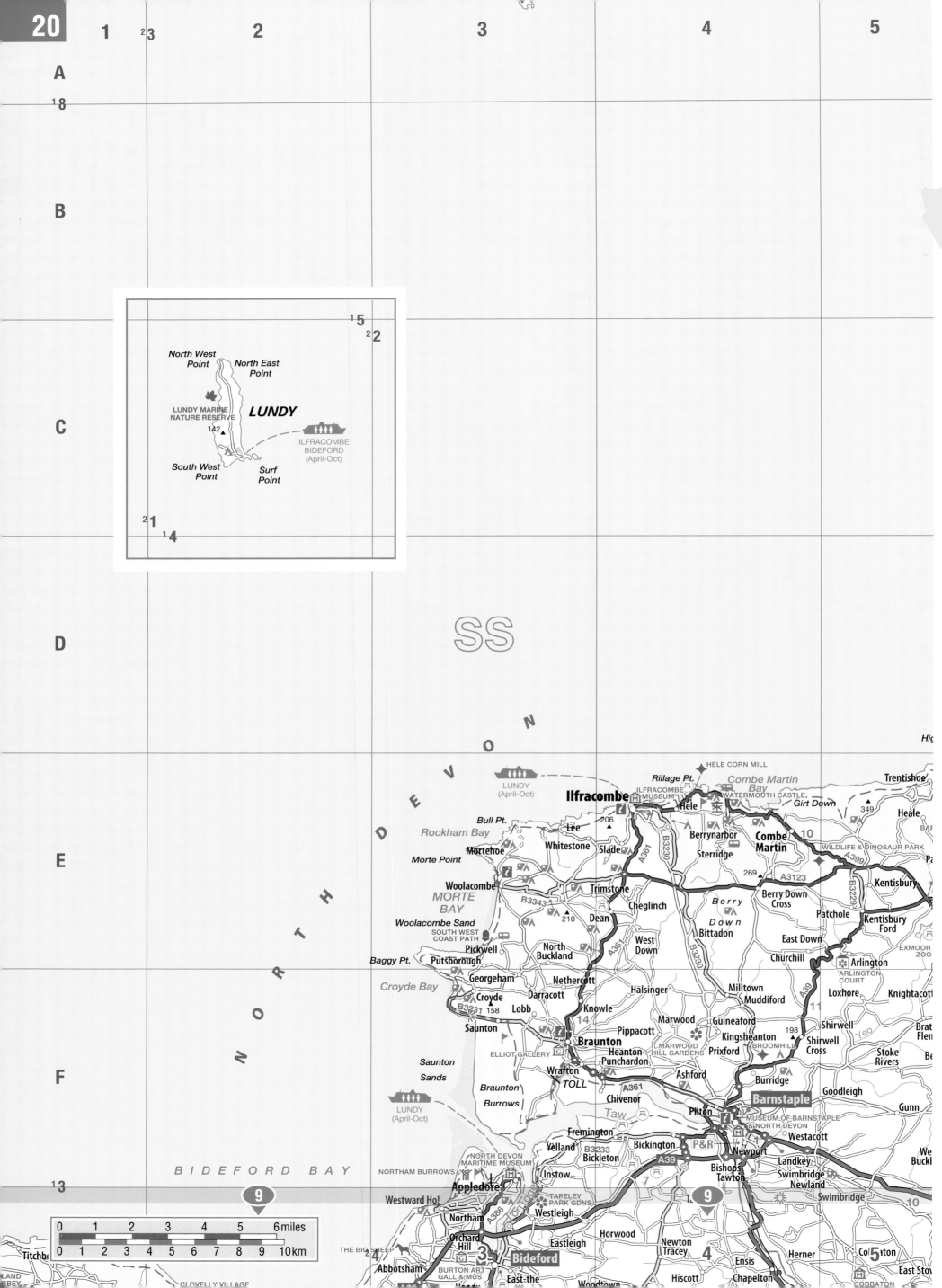

1   3   2   3   2   4   5

A

8

B

¹5
²2

North West
Point   North East
Point

LUNDY

LUNDY MARINE
NATURE RESERVE
C   142 ▲   ILFRACOMBE
BIDEFORD
(April-Oct)

South West
Point   Surf
Point

²1
¹4

D   SS

HELE CORN MILL
Rillage Pt.   Combe Martin   Trentishoe
Bay
LUNDY   ILFRACOMBE   WATERMOUTH CASTLE   Girt Down   349 ▲   Heale
(April-Oct)   MUSEUM   BAF
Ilfracombe   Hele   Combe   10
Bull Pt.   Berrynarbor   Martin   WILDLIFE & DINOSAUR PARK
Rockham Bay   Lee   206   Sterridge
Mortehoe   Whitestone   Slade   Berry Down   Kentisbury
Morte Point   Trimstone   269 ▲   A3123   Cross   Patchole
E   Woolacombe   Cheglinch   Berry   Kentisbury
MORTE   B3343   210   Dean   West   Down   East Down   Ford
BAY   SOUTH WEST   Down   Bittadon   Churchill   EXMOOR
Woolacombe Sand   North   Arlington   ZOO
COAST PATH   Pickwell   Buckland   Milltown   ARLINGTON
Baggy Pt.   Putsborough   Nethercott   Halsinger   Muddiford   COURT   Loxhore   Knightacott
Croyde Bay   Georgeham   Darracott   Marwood   Guineaford   198   Shirwell   Brat
B3231   Croyde   Knowle   MARWOOD   Kingsheanton   Shirwell   Flem
158   Lobb   Pippacott   HILL GARDENS   Prixford   BROOMHILL   Cross   Stoke
Saunton   Marwood   Rivers
ELLIOT GALLERY   Braunton   Heanton   Goodleigh   Gunn
F   Saunton   Puncharden   Ashford   Burridge   Barnstaple   We
Sands   Wrafton   Chivenor   Buckl
Braunton   TOLL   A361   Pilton   MUSEUM OF BARNSTAPLE
Burrows   Taw   & NORTH DEVON   Westacott
LUNDY   Fremington   Newport   Landkey
(April-Oct)   Yelland   Bickington   P&R   Bishops   Swimbridge
B3233   Bickleton   A39   Tawton   Newland   Swimbridge   10
BIDEFORD   BAY   NORTH DEVON   Instow   7   Woodtown   Col   ton
13   MARITIME MUSEUM   Appledore   TAPELEY   Horwood
NORTHAM BURROWS   PARK GDNS   Newton   Ensis
Westward Ho!   Northam   Westleigh   Tracey   Herner
9   A386   Eastleigh   THE BIG SHEEP   Orchard   Bideford   4   Hiscott   Chapelton   5   ton   East Stou
0   1   2   3   4   5   6 miles   Hill   BURTON ART   Woodtown
0 1 2 3 4 5 6 7 8 9 10km   GALL & MUS   Abbotsham   East-the
Titchbe   CLOVELLY VILLAGE   LAND
BBEY

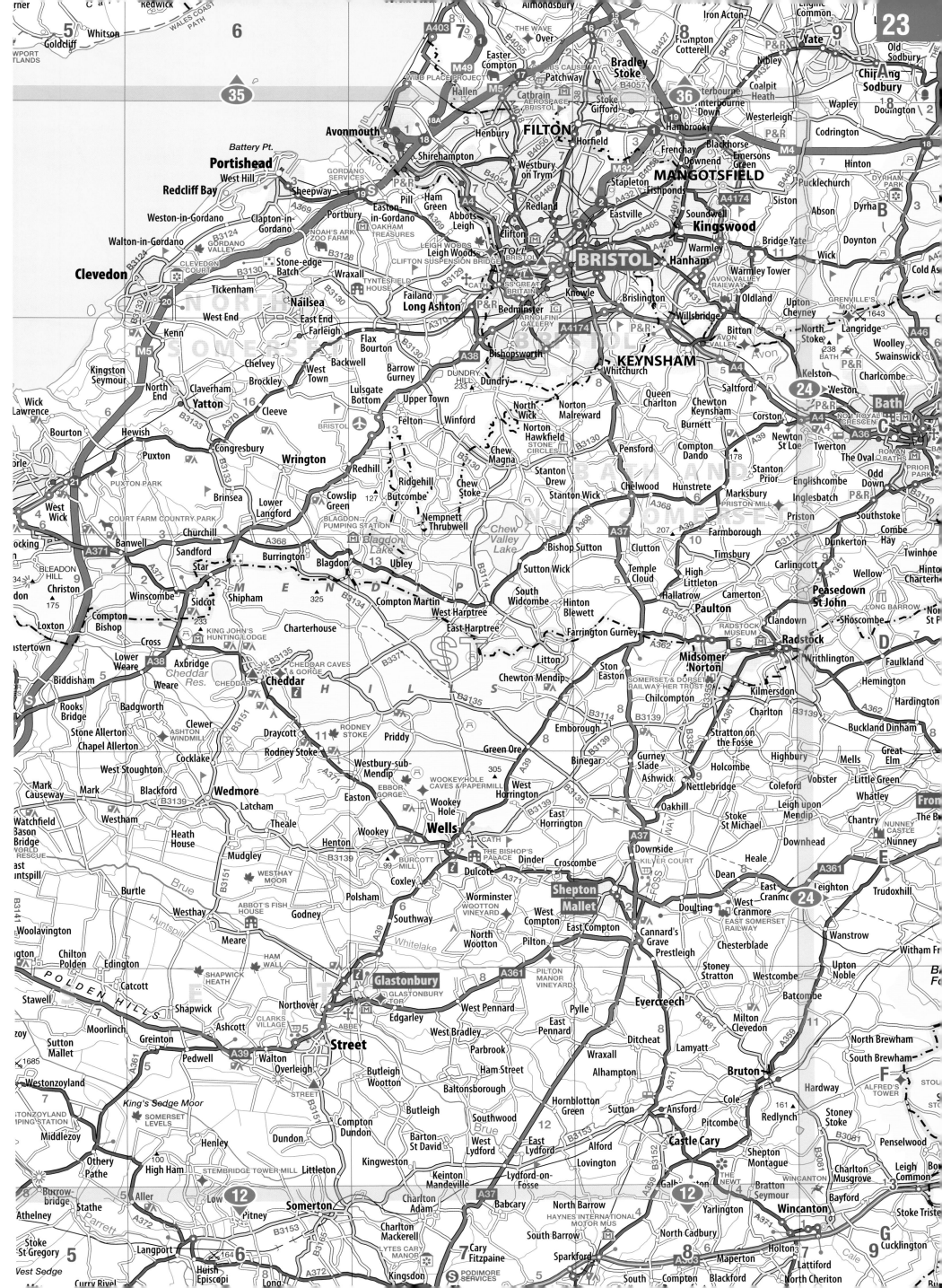

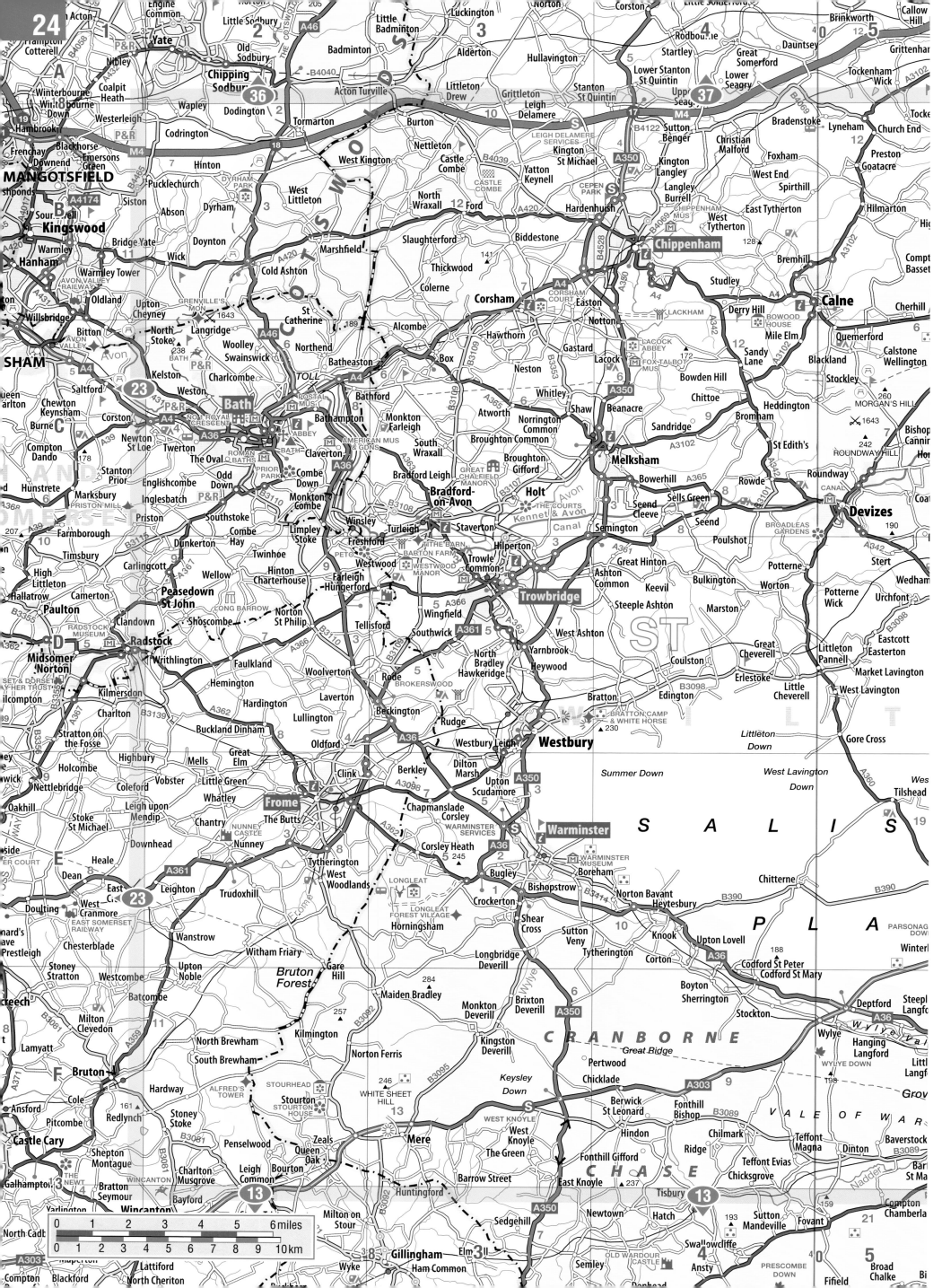

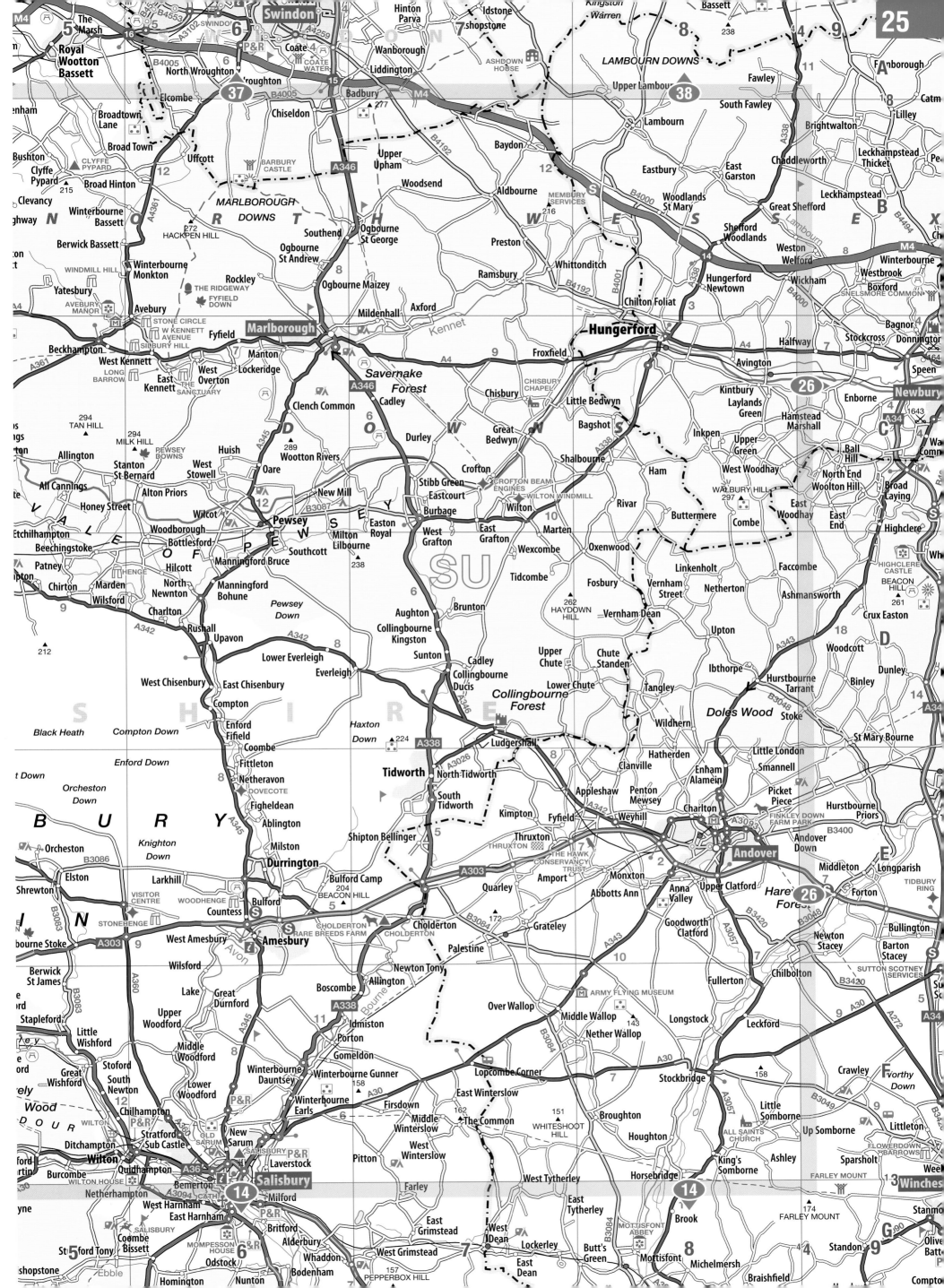

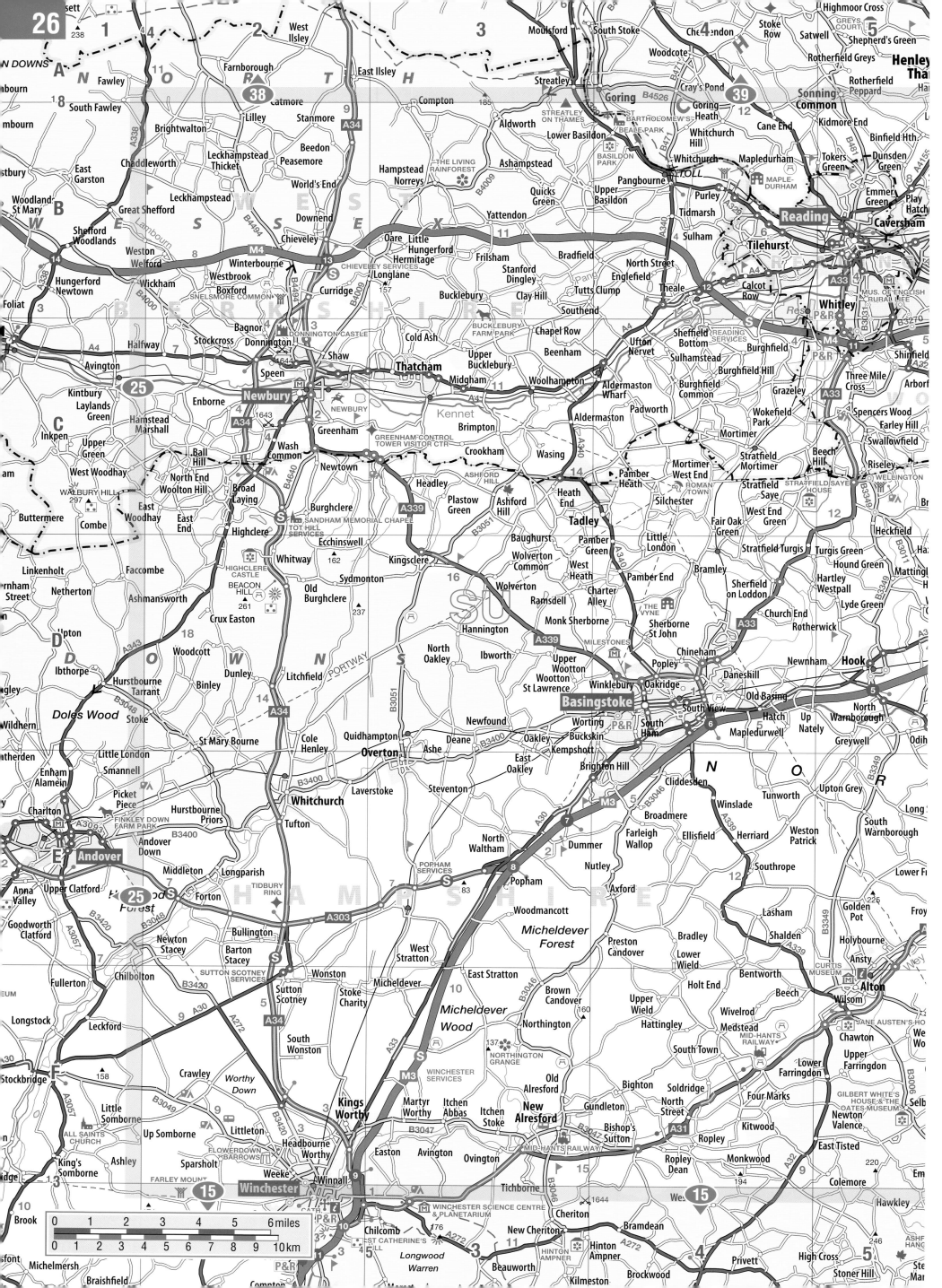

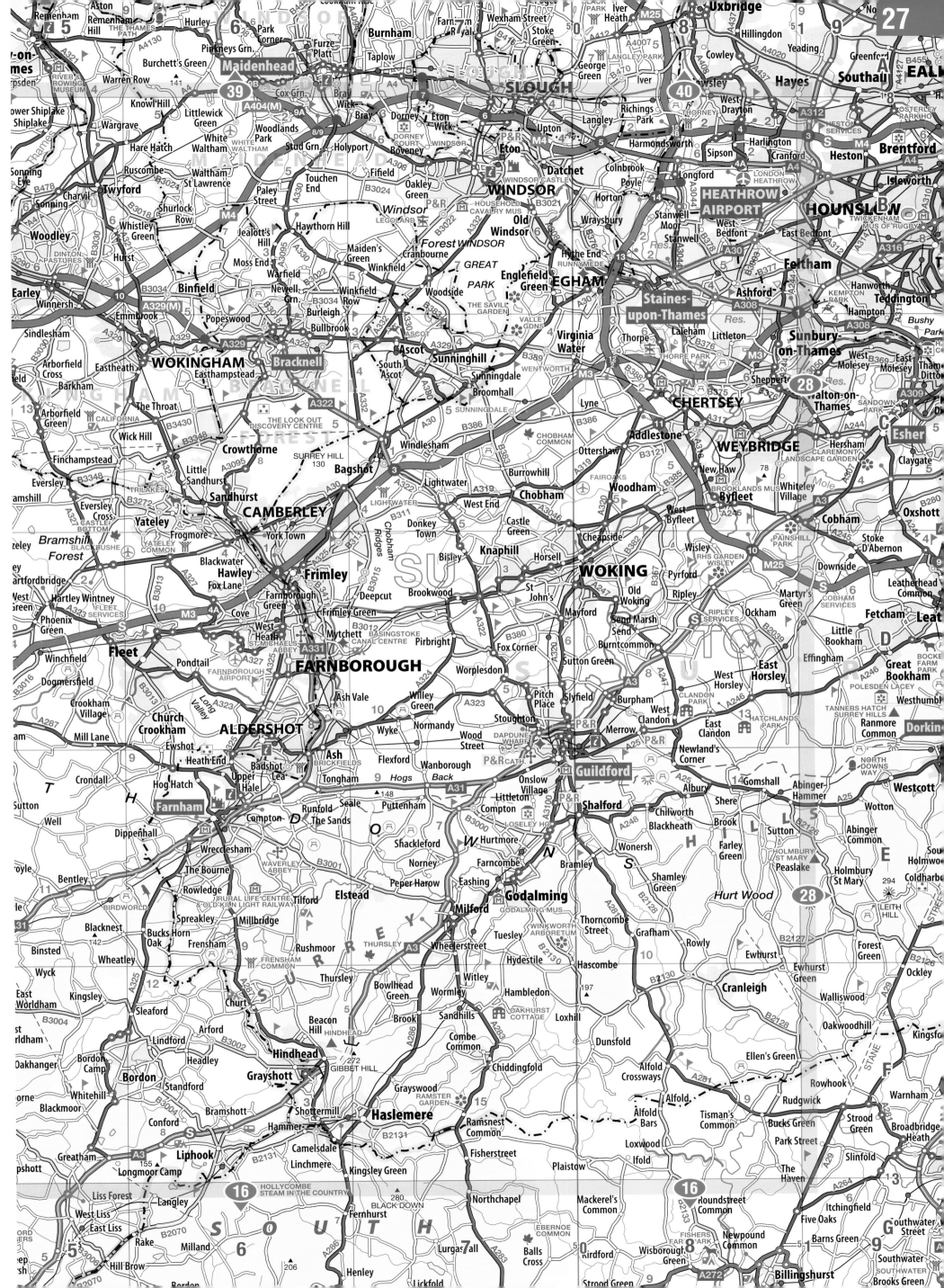

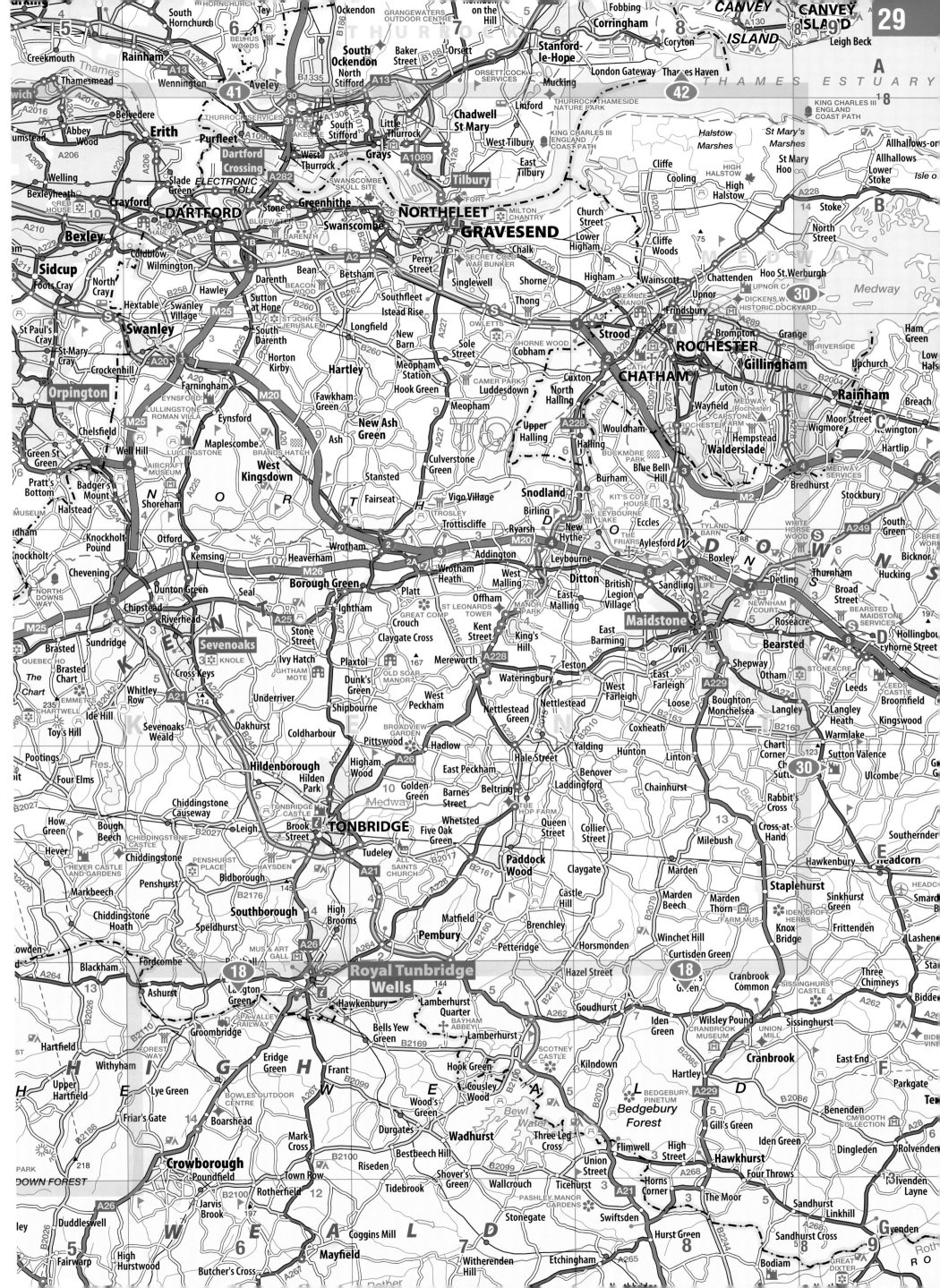

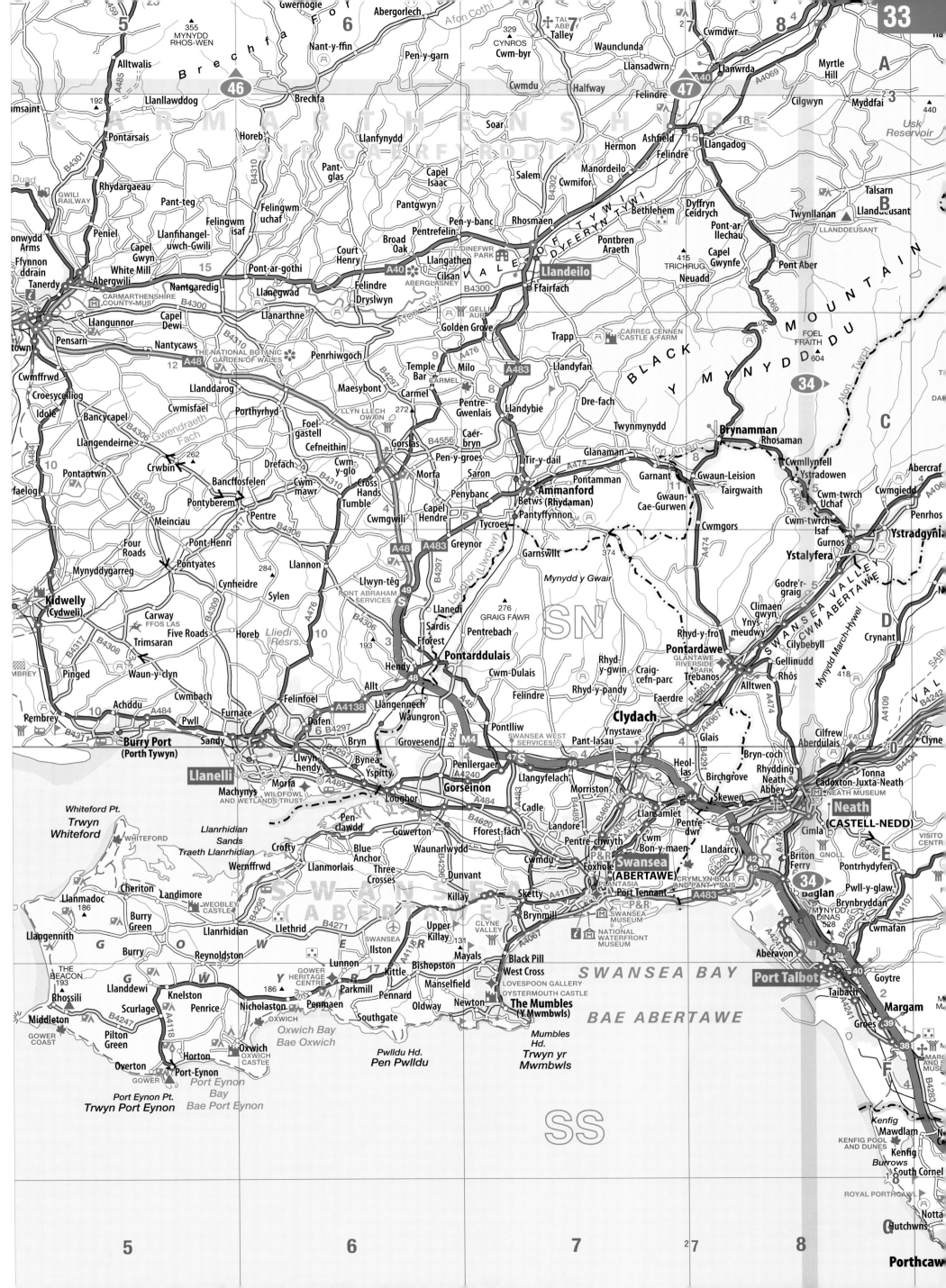

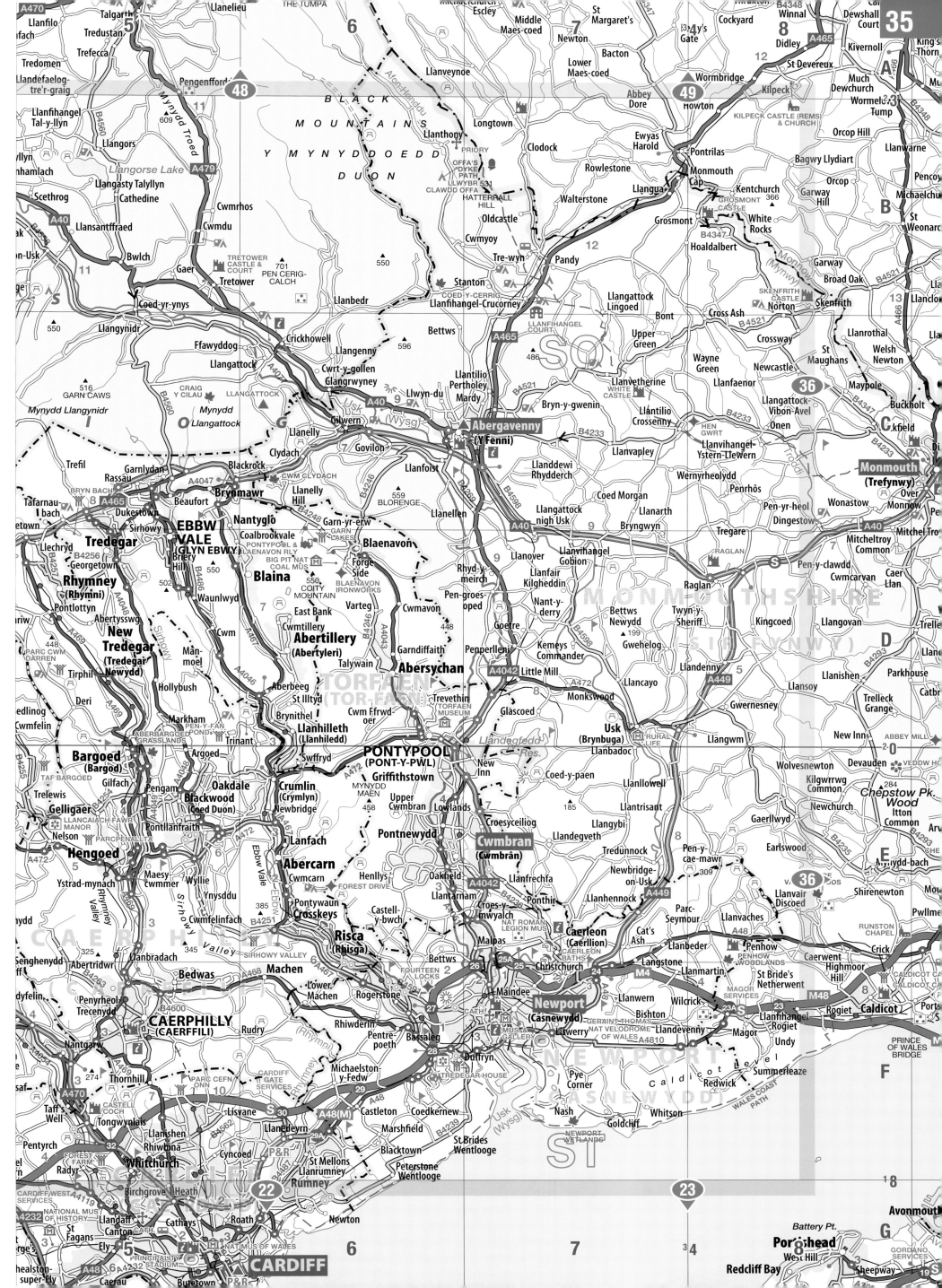

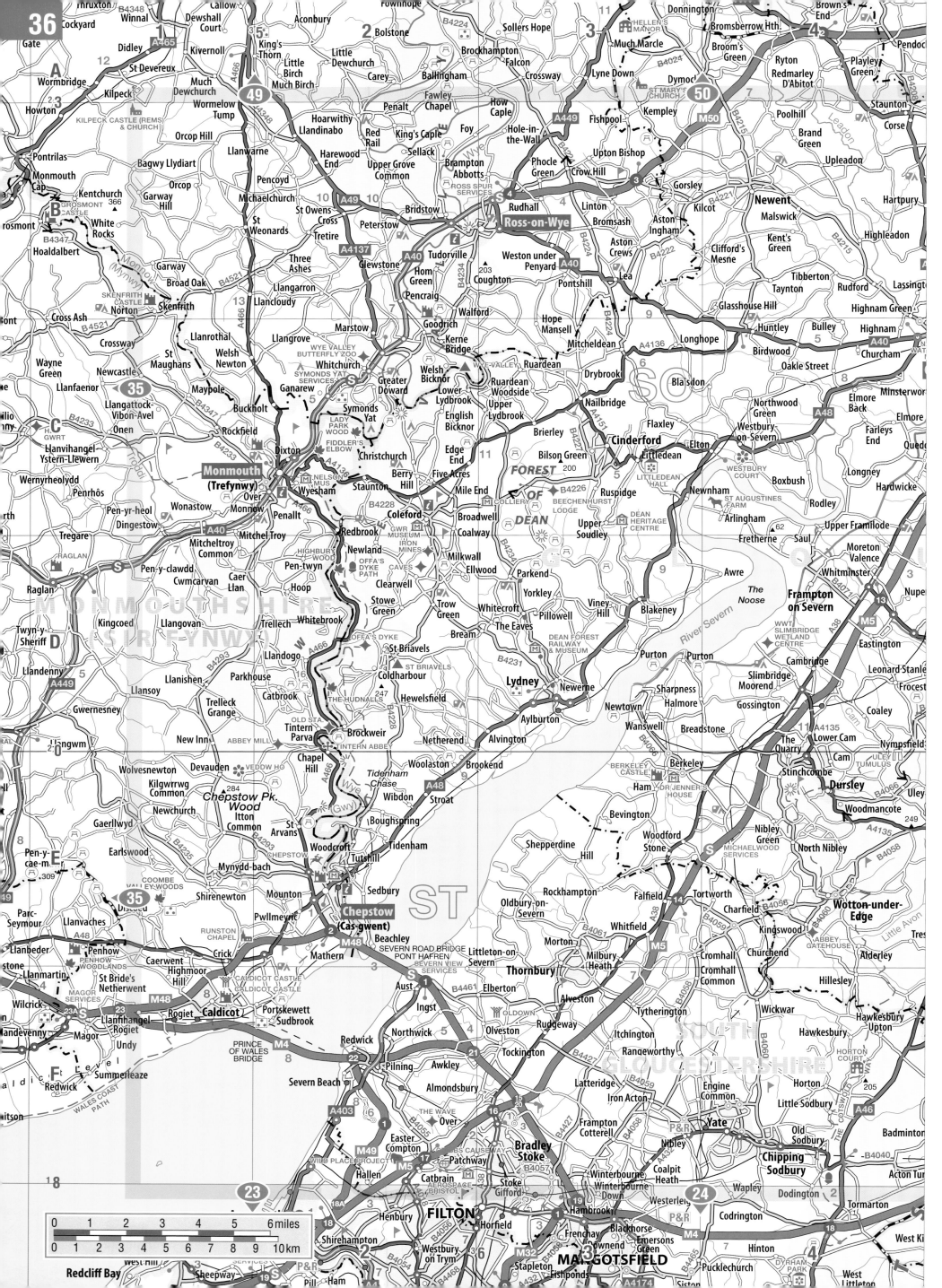

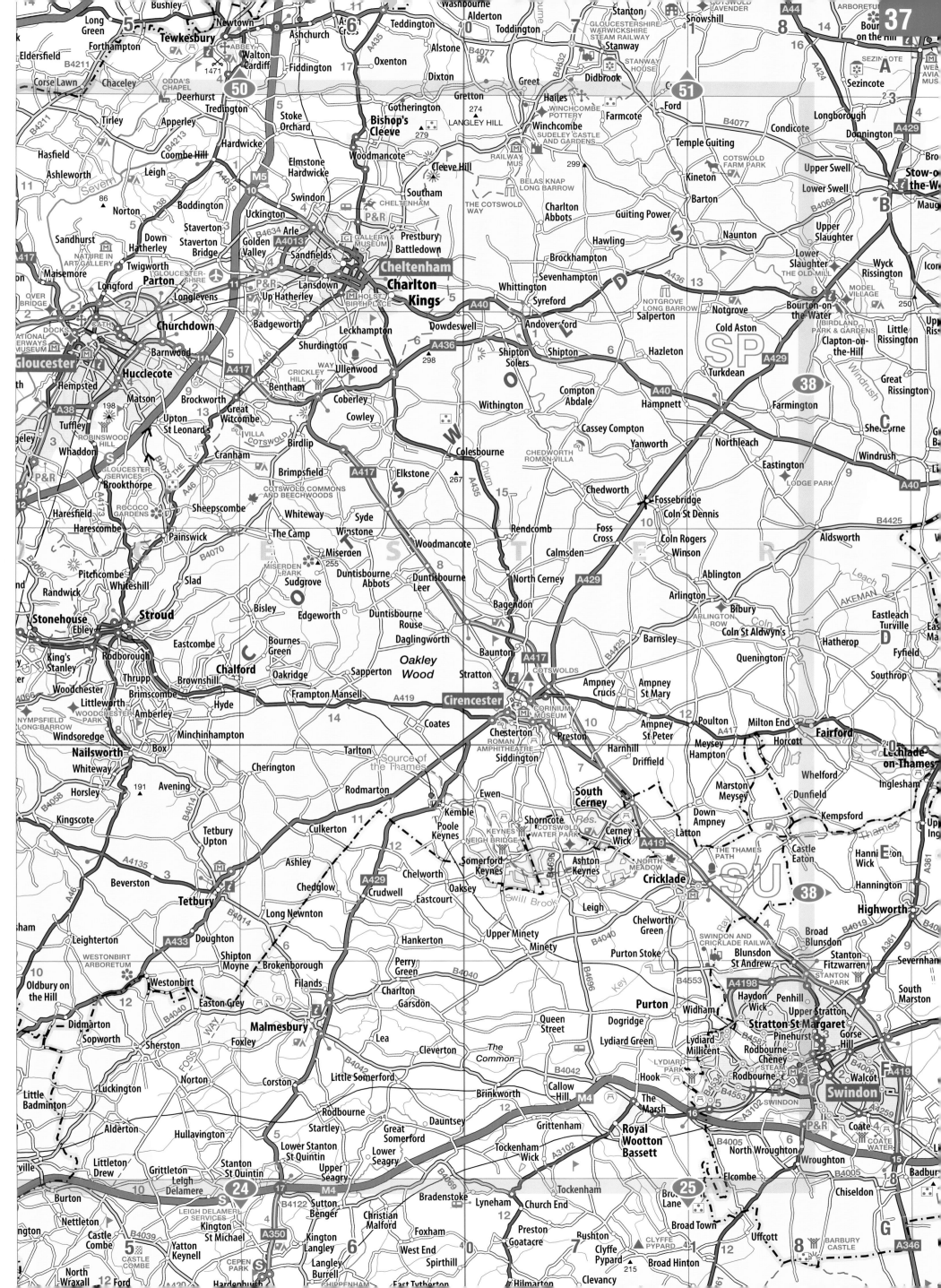

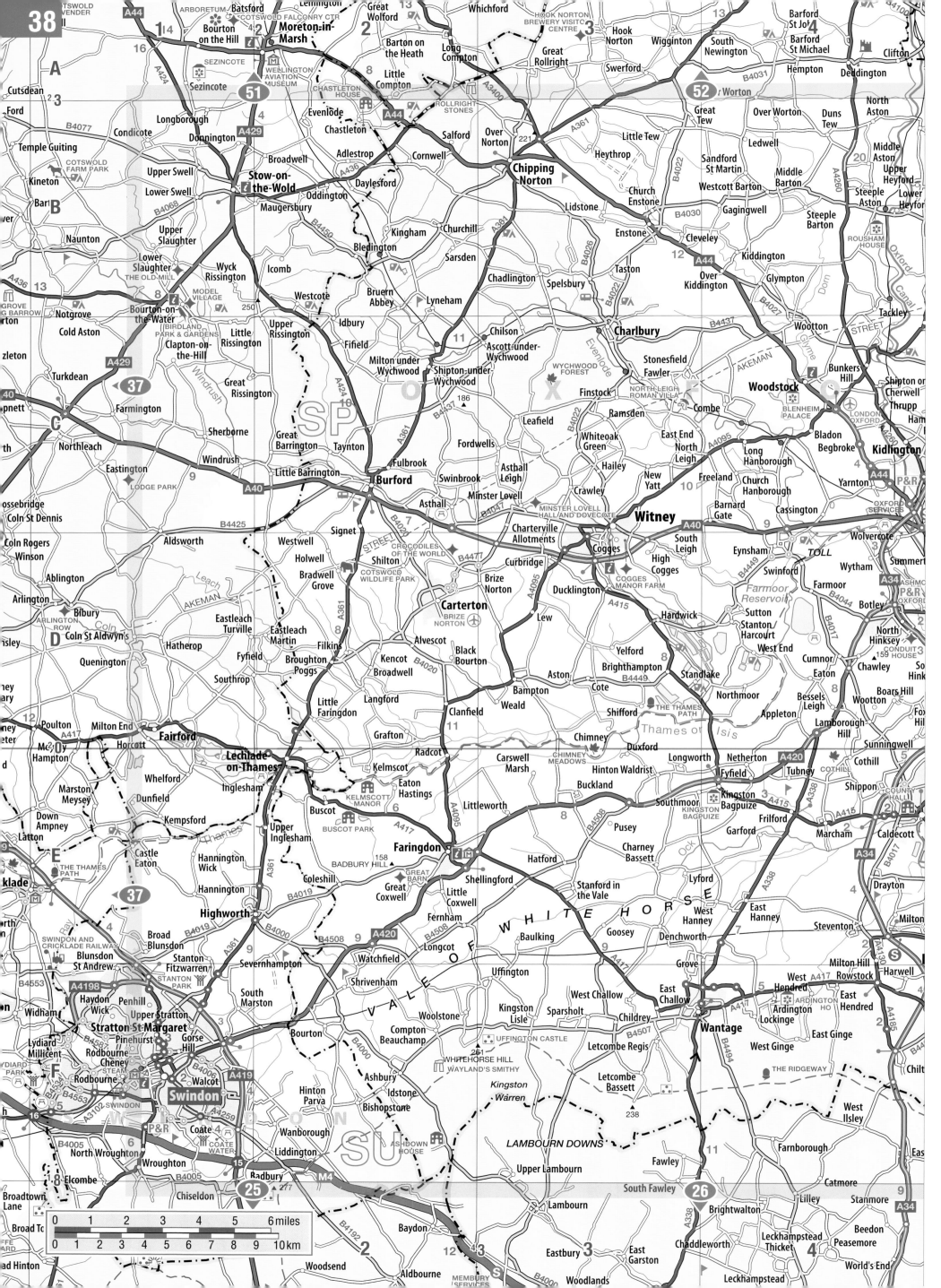

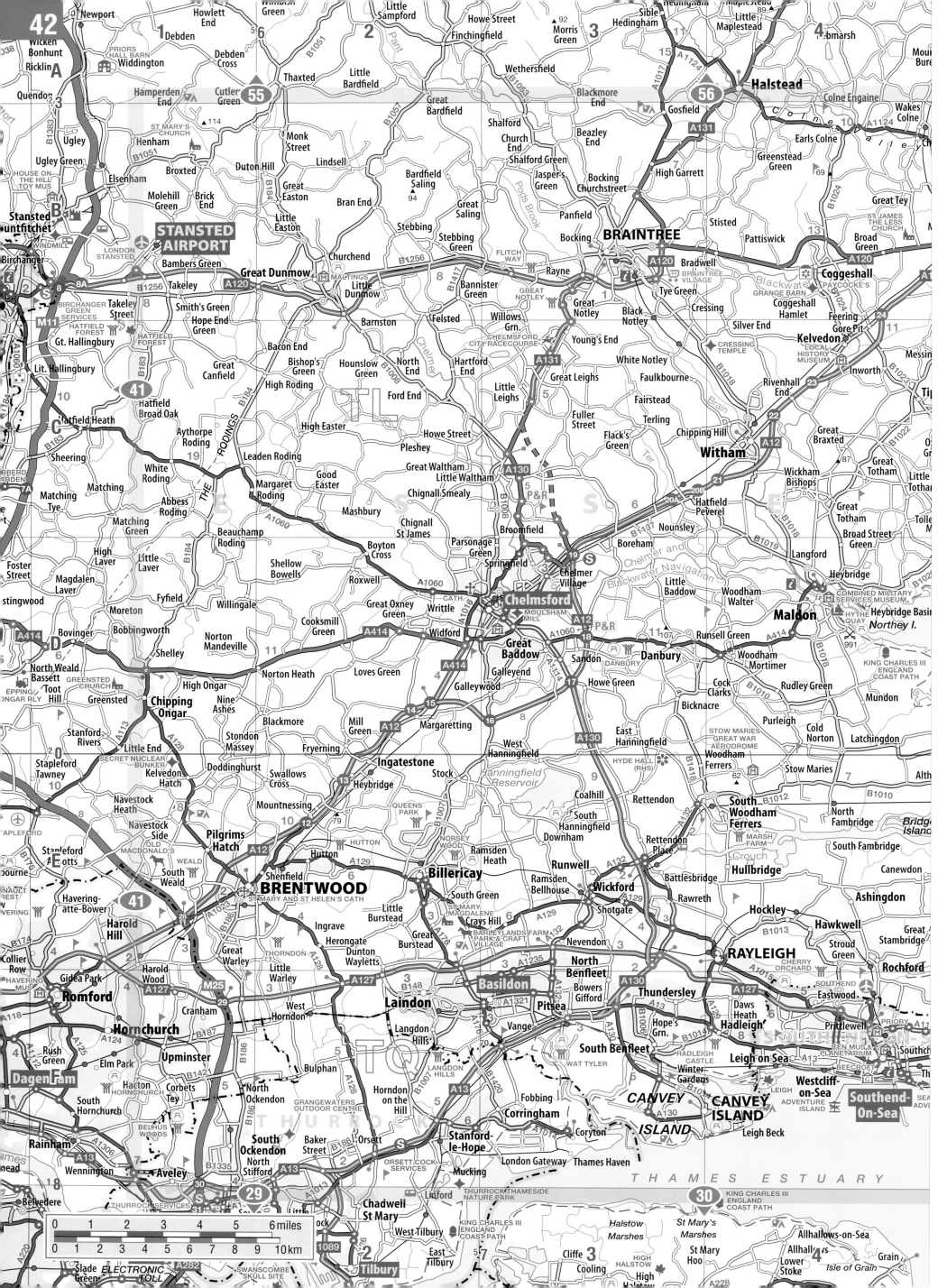

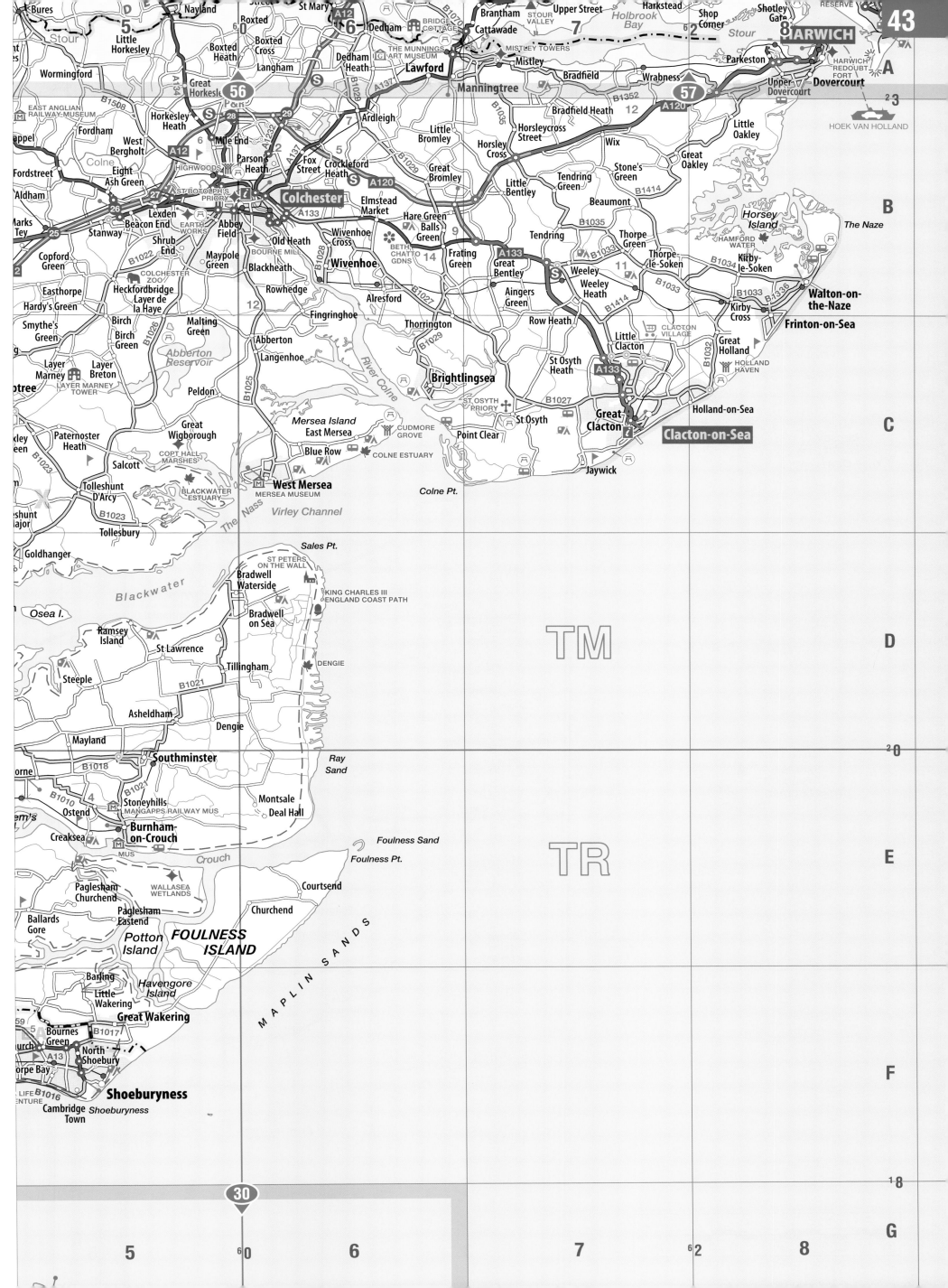

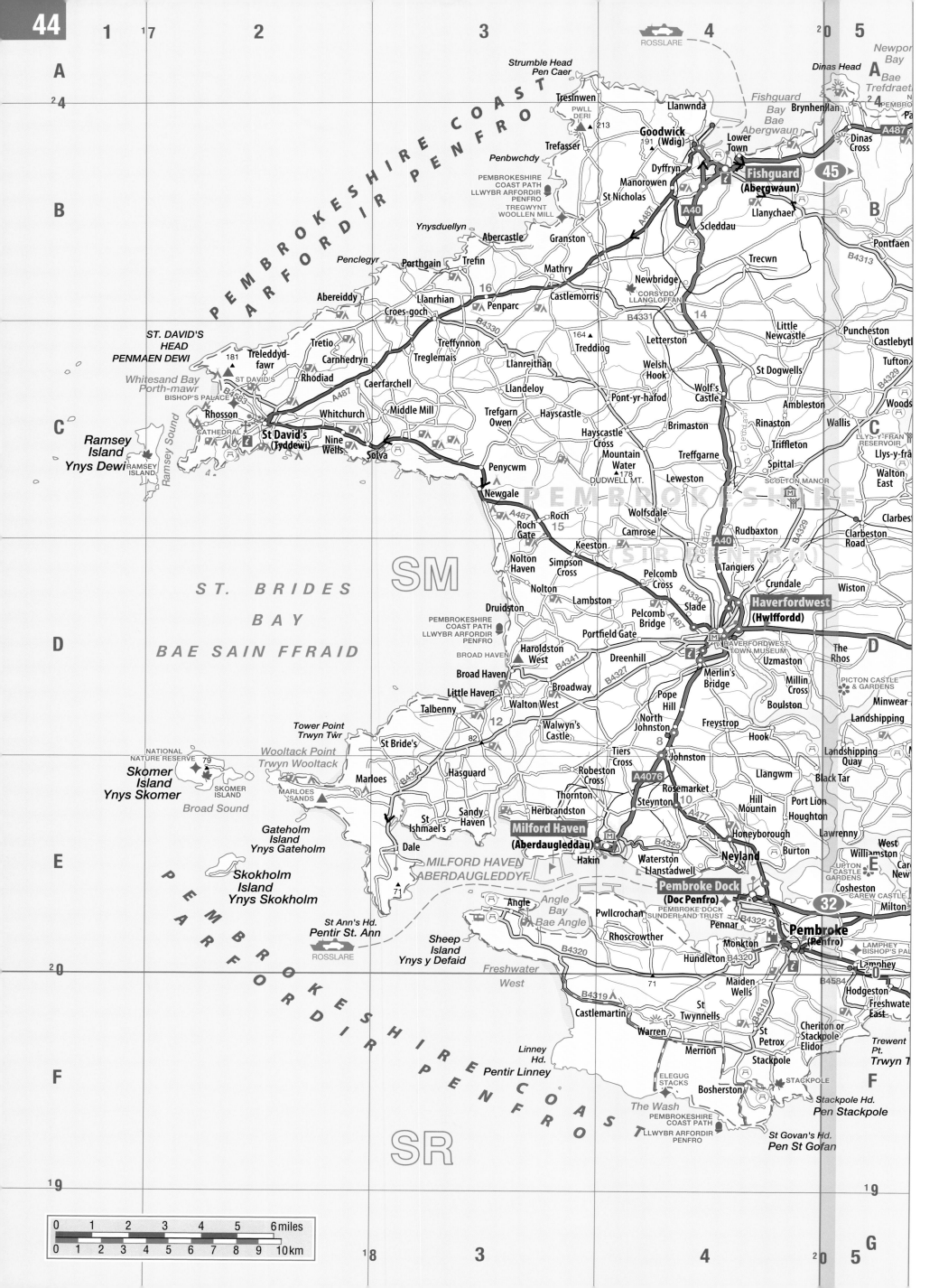

CARDIGAN

BAY

BAE

CEREDIGION

SN

Cwmtudu
Cwmtydu

Ynys-Lochtyn

Llangrannog D Blaencelyn

Pontgarreg

Plw

Penbryn B4334

Parcllyn Tresaith Penmorfa B4321
Felinwynt Pen
Cardigan I. MWNT Aberporth Brynhoffnant
Ynys 151 Blaenannerch Pent
Aberteifi Y Ferwig ABERPORTH Sarnau
Cemaes Head Gwbert WEST WALES Tan-y-groes
Pen Cemaes AIRPORT 16 Glynarthen B4334
Tremain Rhydlewis
B4548 Penparc Blaenporth B4333 Bettws
POPPIT SANDS Ifan Hawen
Cippyn Pantgwyn Beulah Penrhi
B4546 Cardigan Ponthirwaun Brongest Coed
St Dogmaels (Aberteifi) CASTLE Troed-uur E
ABBEY Bridgend Llangoedmor B4570 Bryngwyn Maesllyn
Moylgrove Llechryd Capel
COEDMOR Llandygwydd Tygwydd 46 B487
Monington CILGERRAN Carreg-wen 11 Cwm-cou Aber-banc
Croft Peñ-y- CASTLE NATIONAL CORACLE Llandyfriog
bryn Cilgerran CENTRE Cenarth Pentrecagal TEIFI
Glanrhyd 197 Bridell Abercych Newcastle 6 He
Pontgareg Llantood Rhos-hill Emlyn NATIONAL
Berry A487 Newchapel (Castell Newydd WOOL
Dinas Head Hill A478 CLYNFYW Penrherber Emlyn) MUSEUM Llang
Nevern B4582 Felindre Boncath CHEESE Aber Dref
Fishguard Brynhenllan Farchog PENGELLI Cilwendeg FARM Arad Felindre
Bay NEWPORT FOREST Bwlchygroes Cwmhiraeth Dre
Bae PEMBROKESHIRE Eglwyswrw Blaenffos Cwmcych Capel Iwan Cwmpe
Abergwaun Parrog 19 CASTELL DYFED SHIRE Star
Dinas HENLLYS FORT HORSE FARM Clydey 335
ower Cross Newport Crosswell Llanfair- Crymych MOELFRE F
wn A487 (Trefdraeth) Nant-Gwyn Cwmorgan
Fishguard 347 Afon Nevern Penygroes Tegryn Tanglwst
(Abergwaun) CARNINGLI TY CANOL Pontyglasier Eglwyswen 395
Ll Fychaer Cilgwyn Brynberian Hermon Llanfyrnach Bryn-Iwan
44 468 Pentre-galar Hen-feddau Trelech Hermon
Pontfaen 536 fawr
Trecwn B4313 FOEL- Mynachlog-ddu 247 Dinas
B4329 CWMCERWYN MYNYDD PRESELI 20 32
Little New Inn Rosebush Glandwr 20
Newcastle Puncheston 32
Castlebythe nclochog 289 Glandy Blaen- Bl
Glandy Glandwr waun G
Cross 3 Pant-y- 4 Pen 5 bont
Ambleston Woodstock New Moat Caws Llanglydwen Llanwinio Talog
Cwmbach
Hebron Cefn-y-pant

MYNYDD PRESELI

0 1 2 3 4 5 6 miles
0 1 2 3 4 5 6 7 8 9 10km

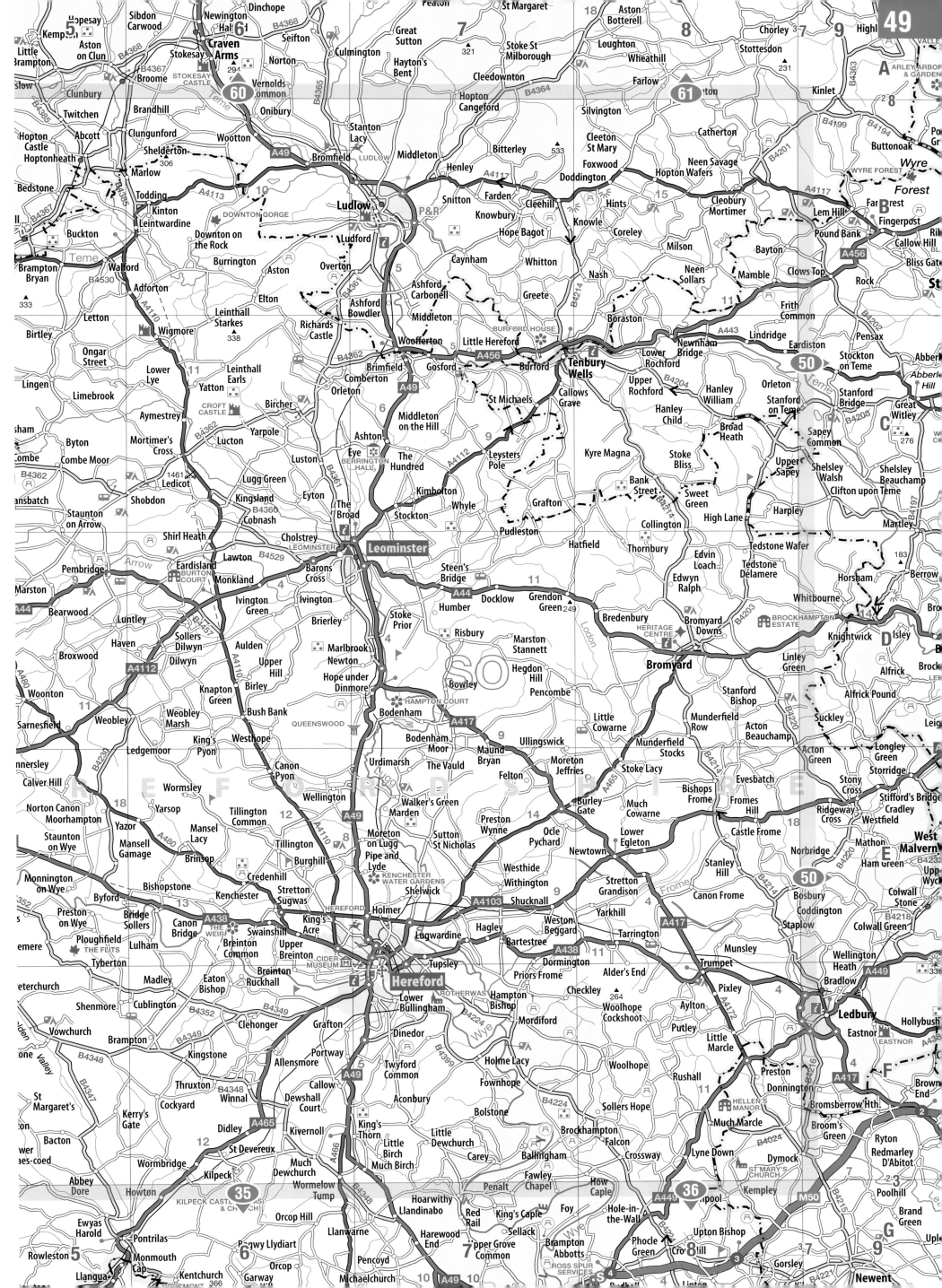

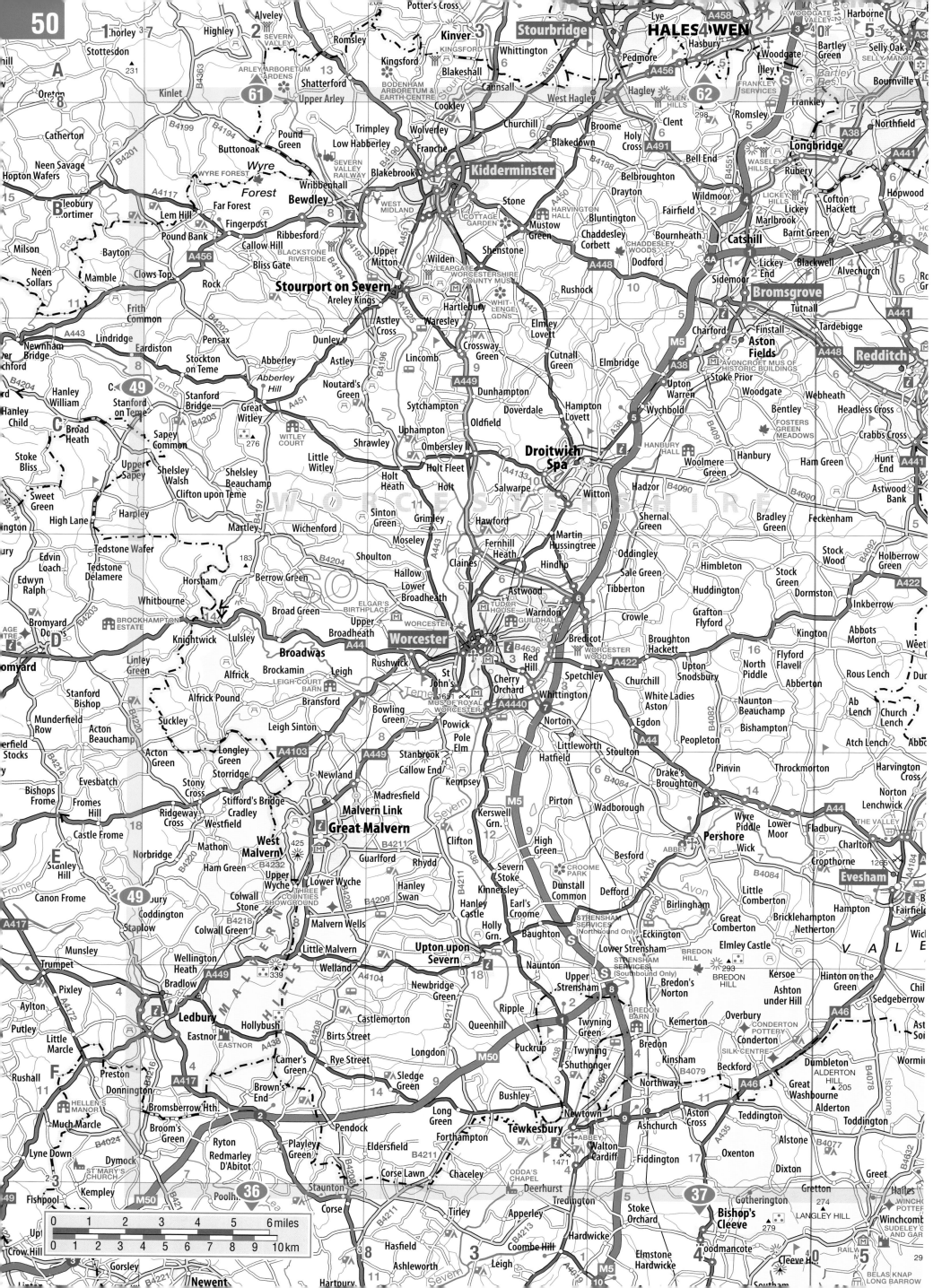

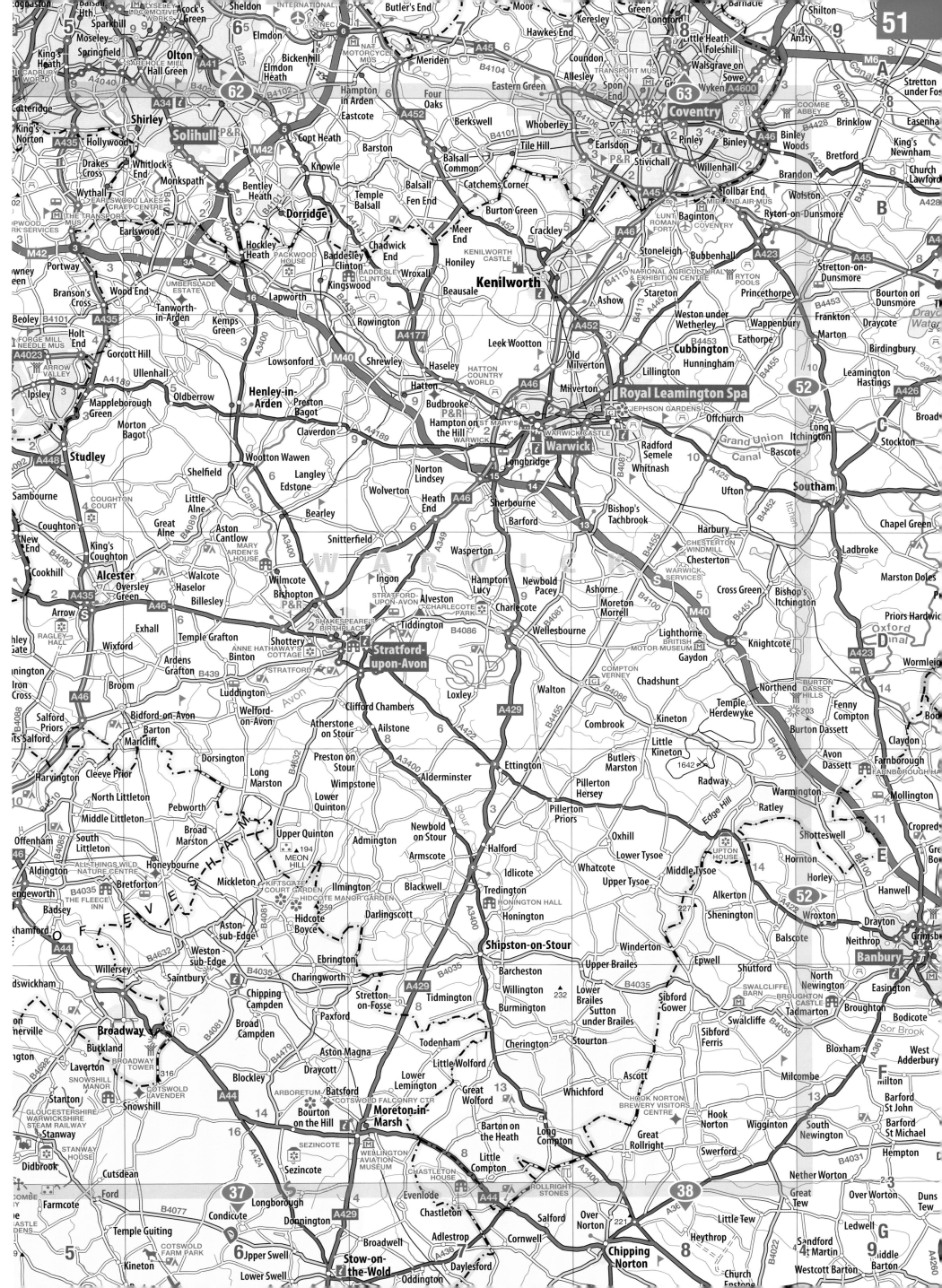

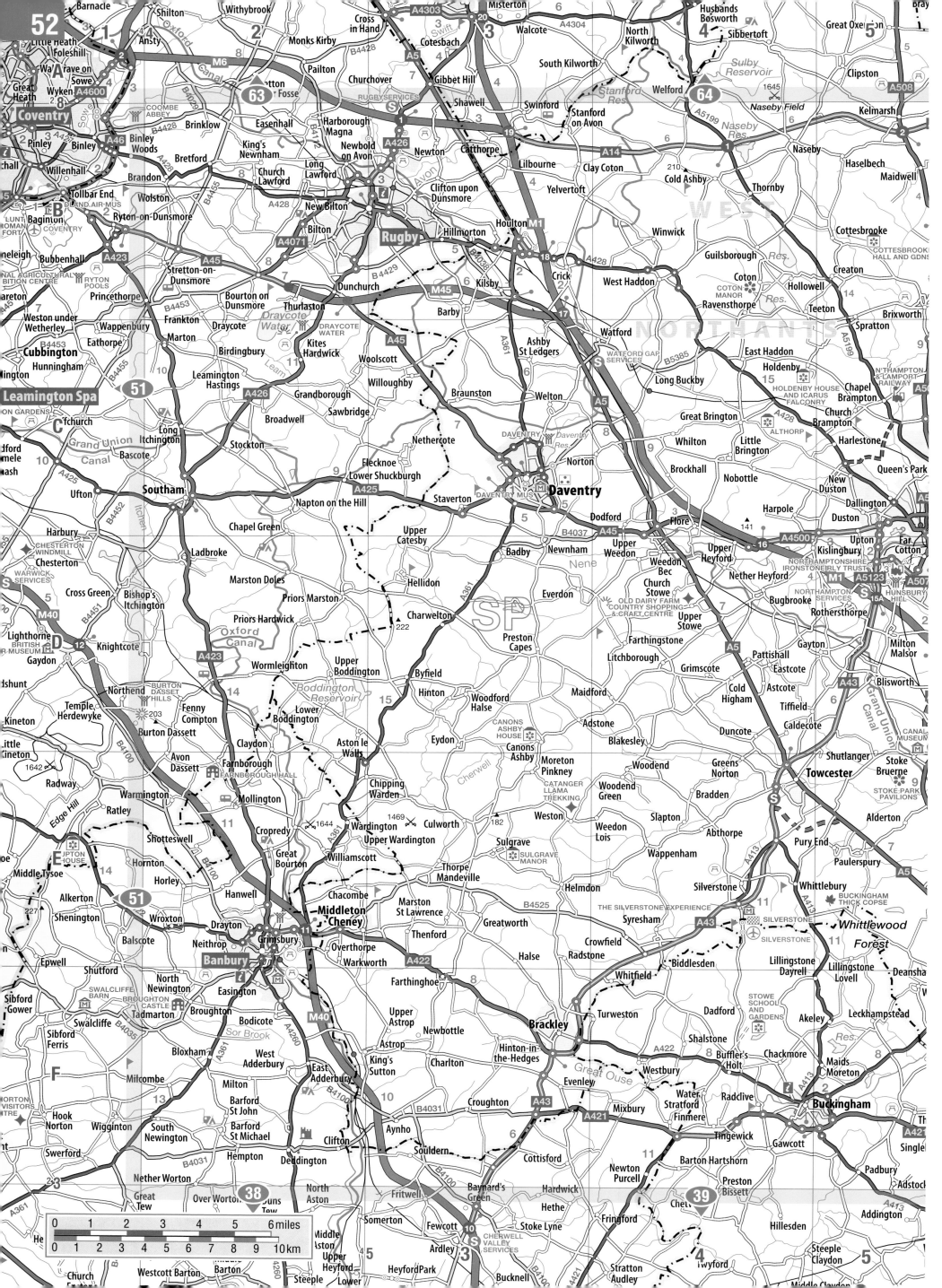

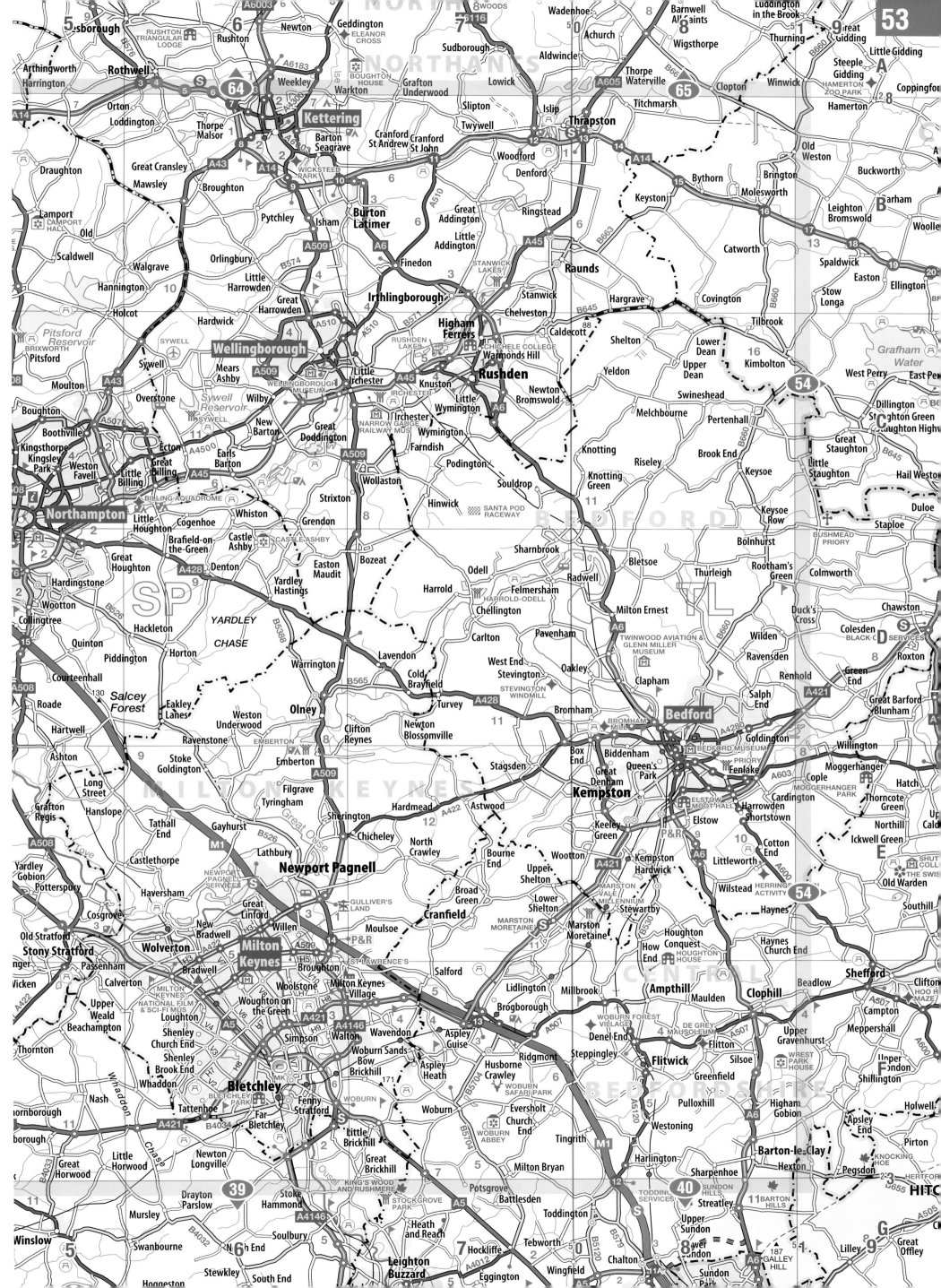

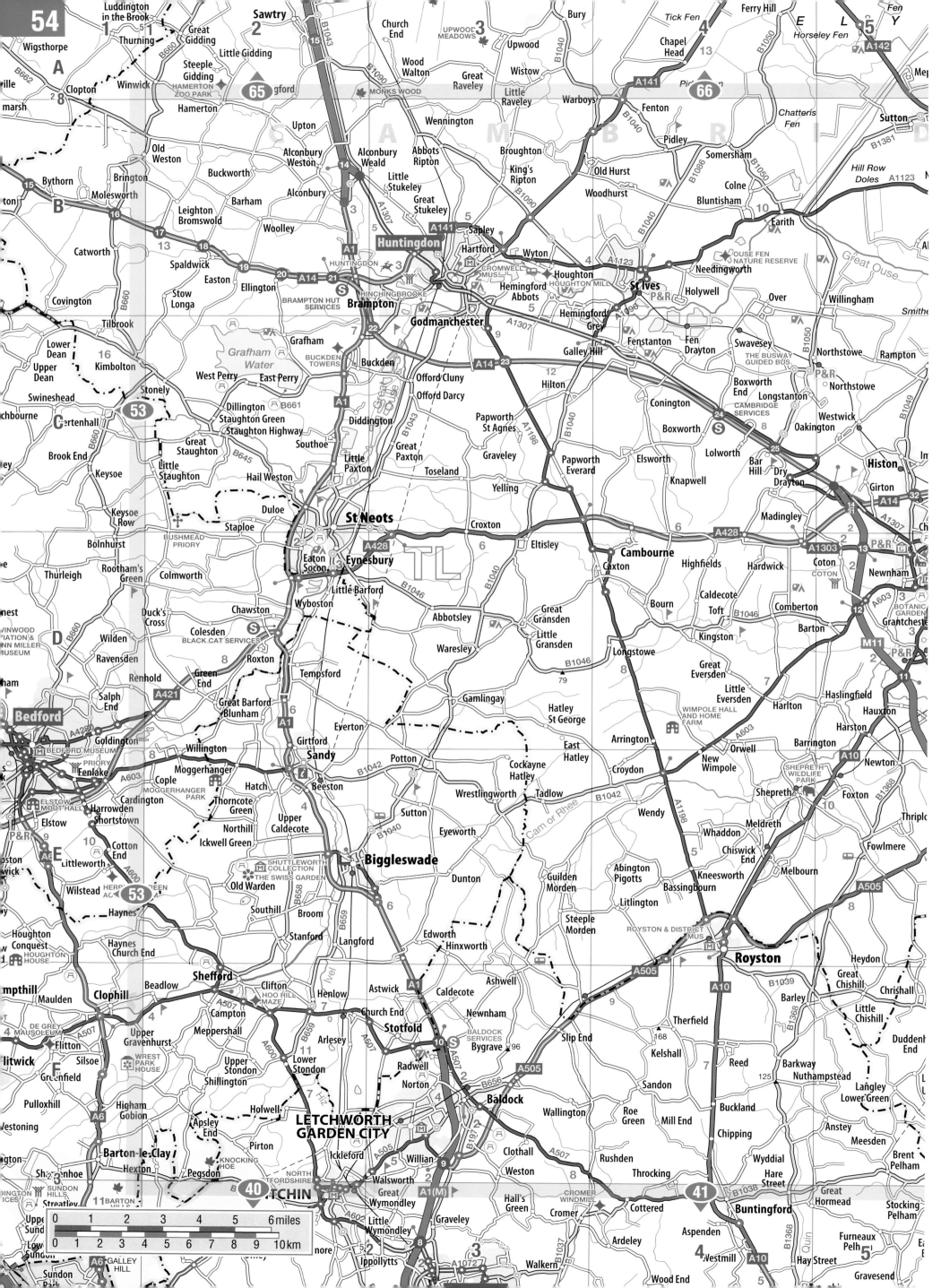

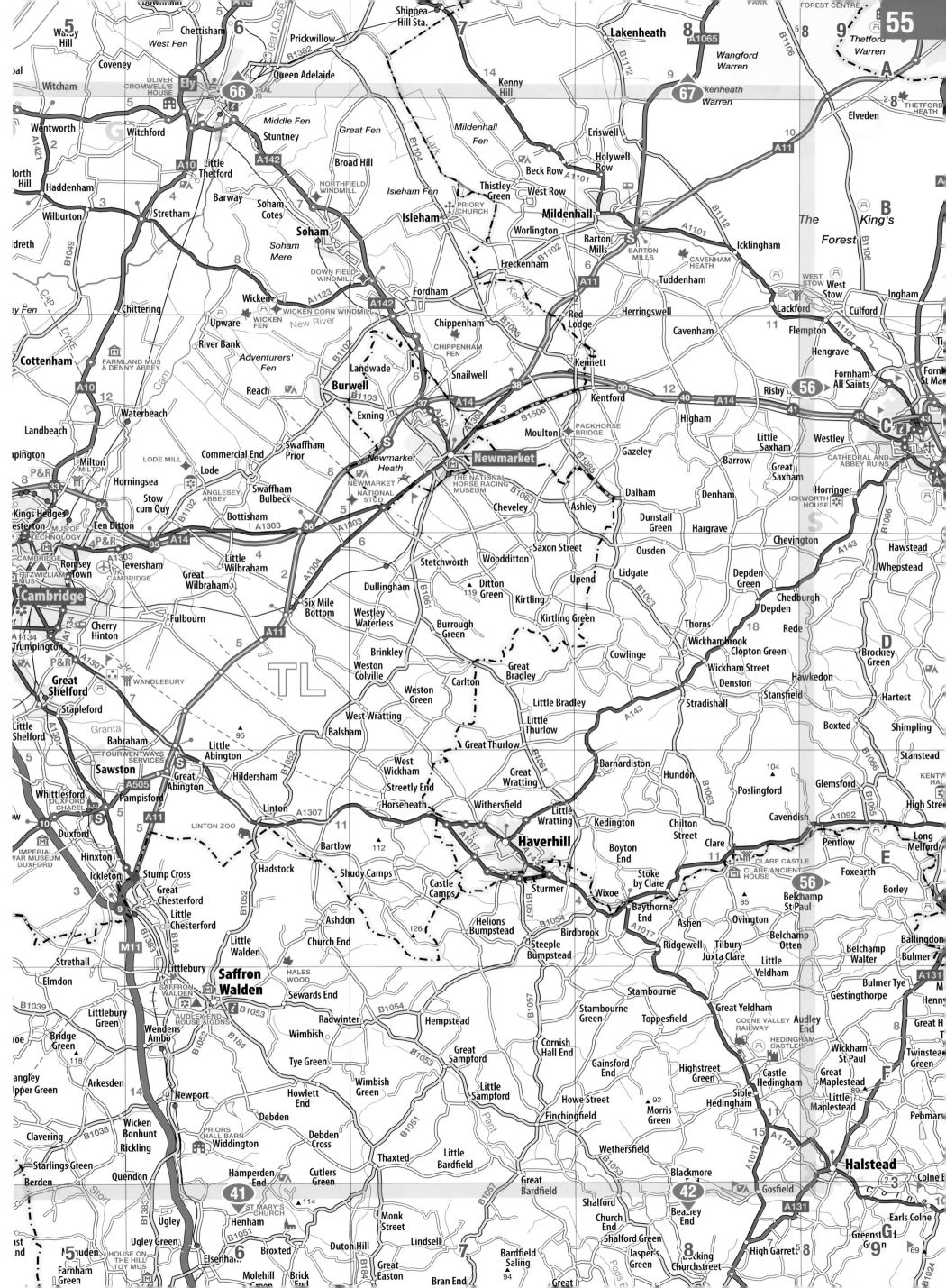

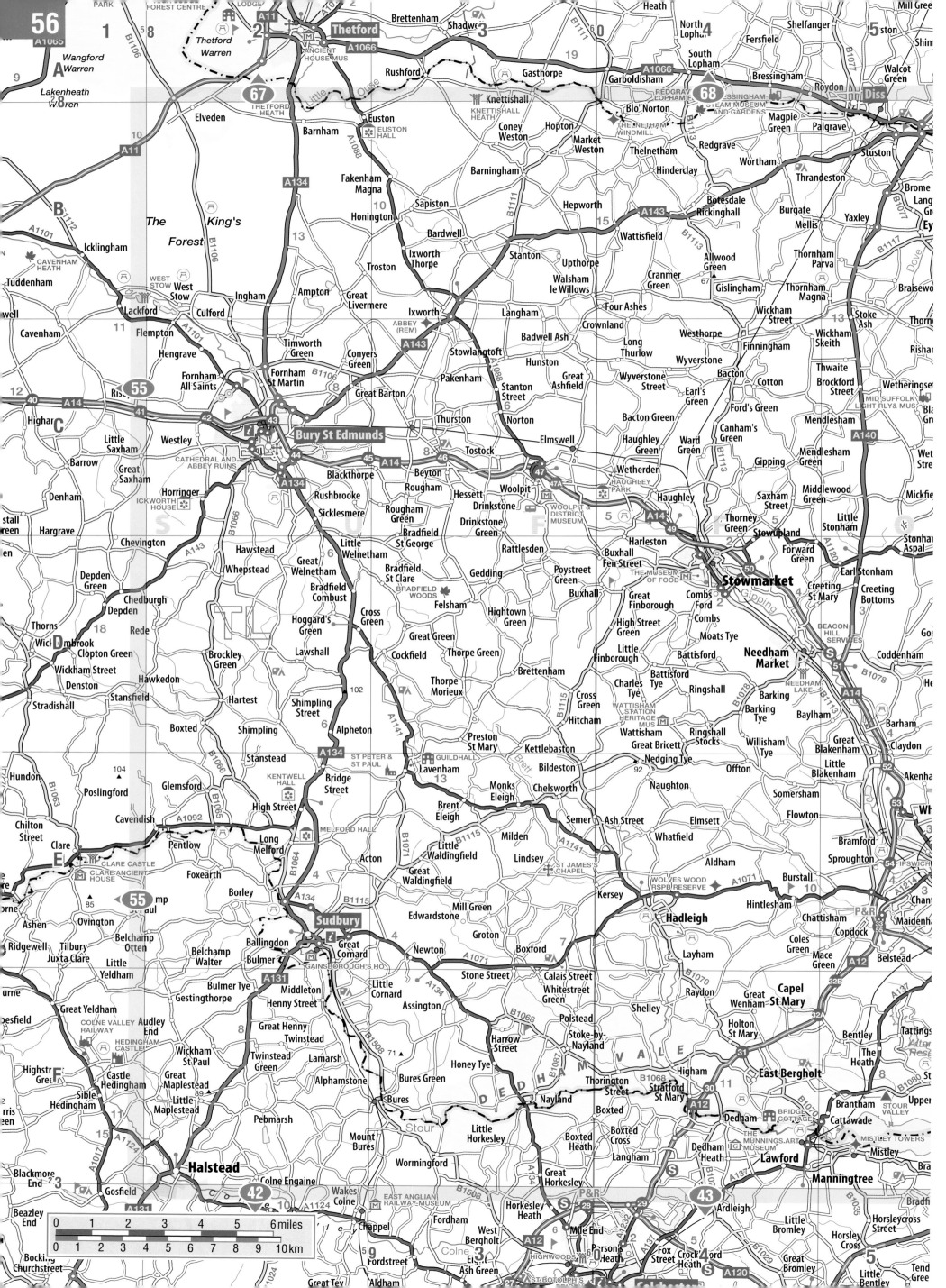

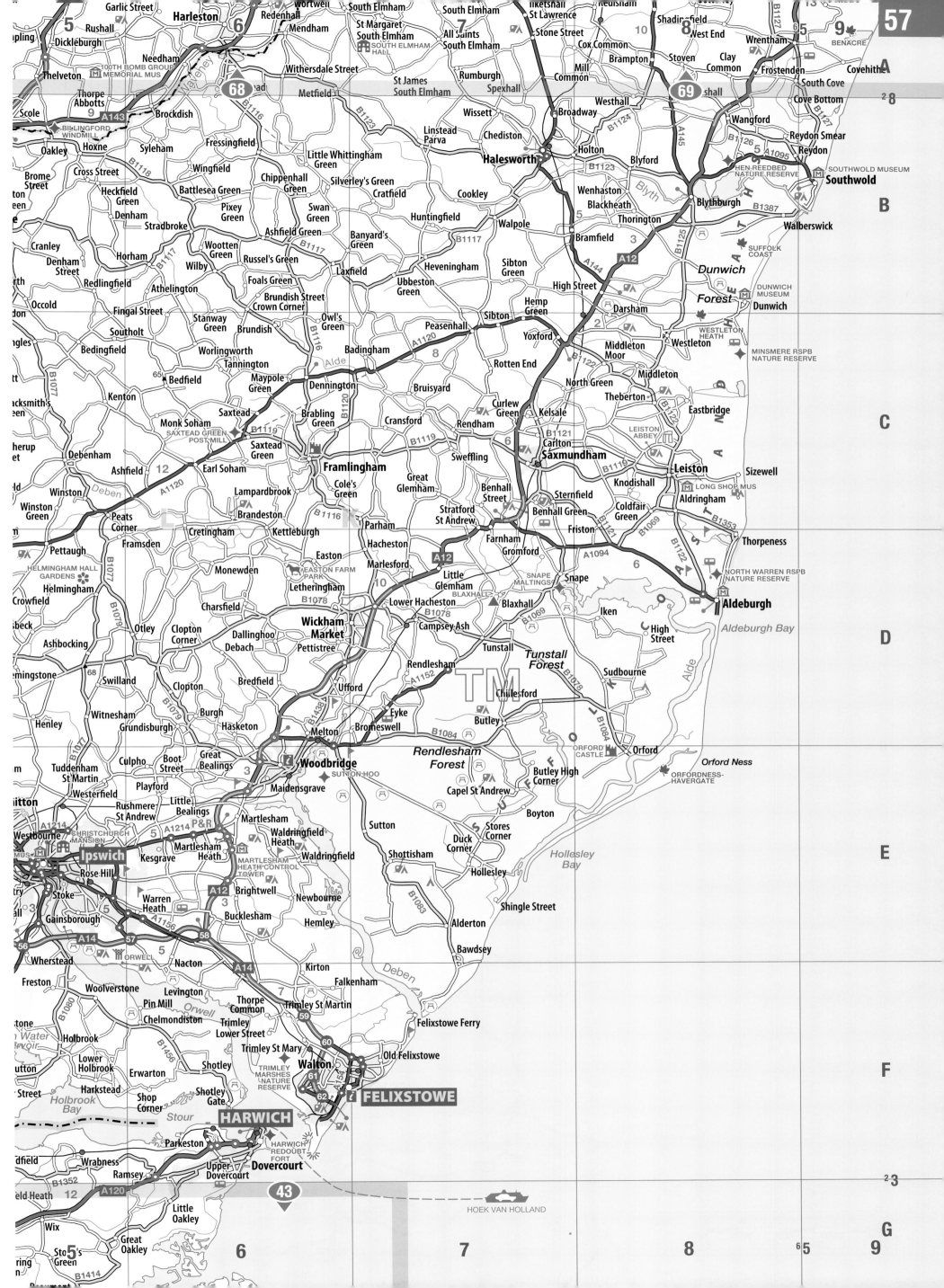

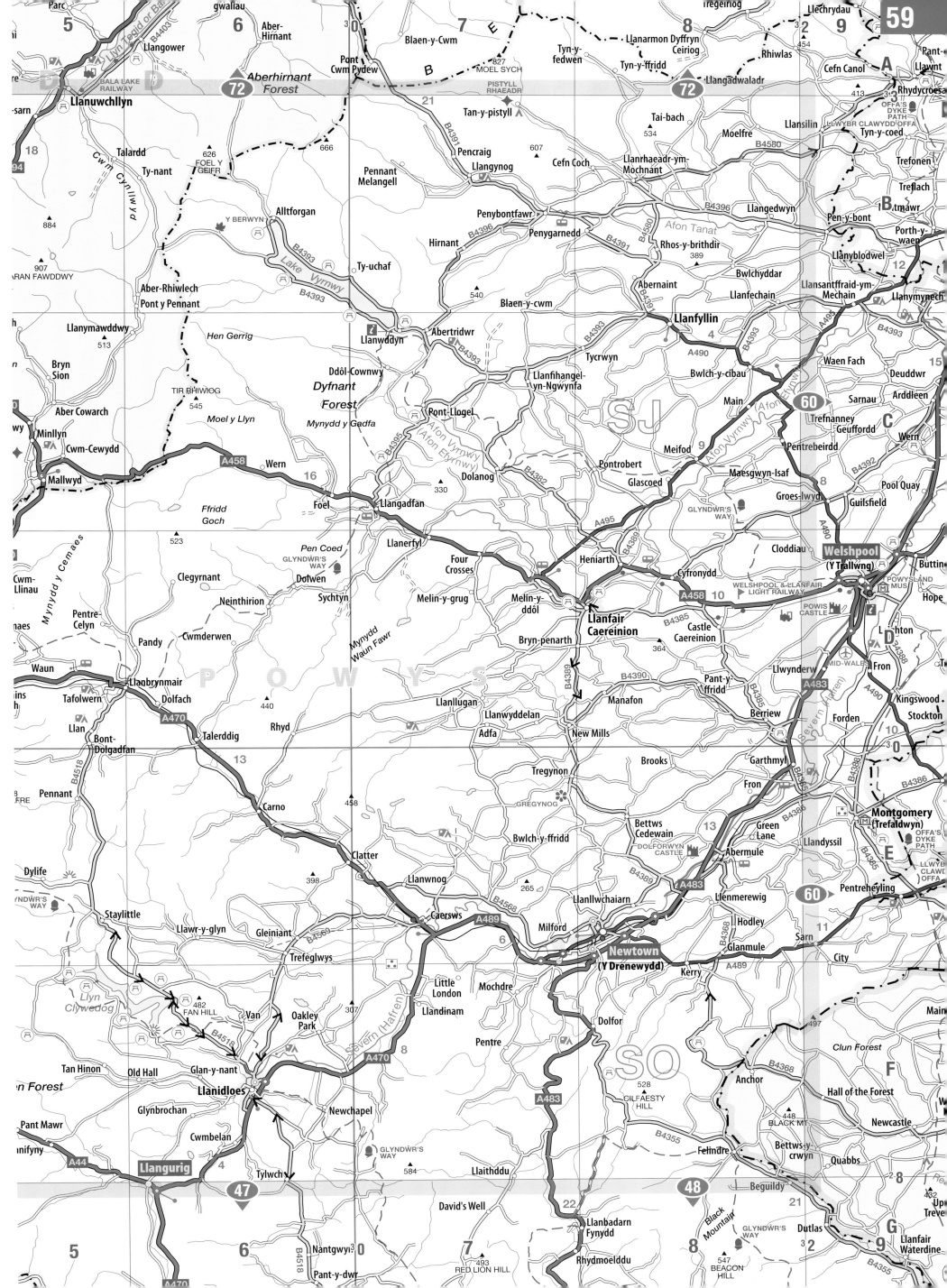

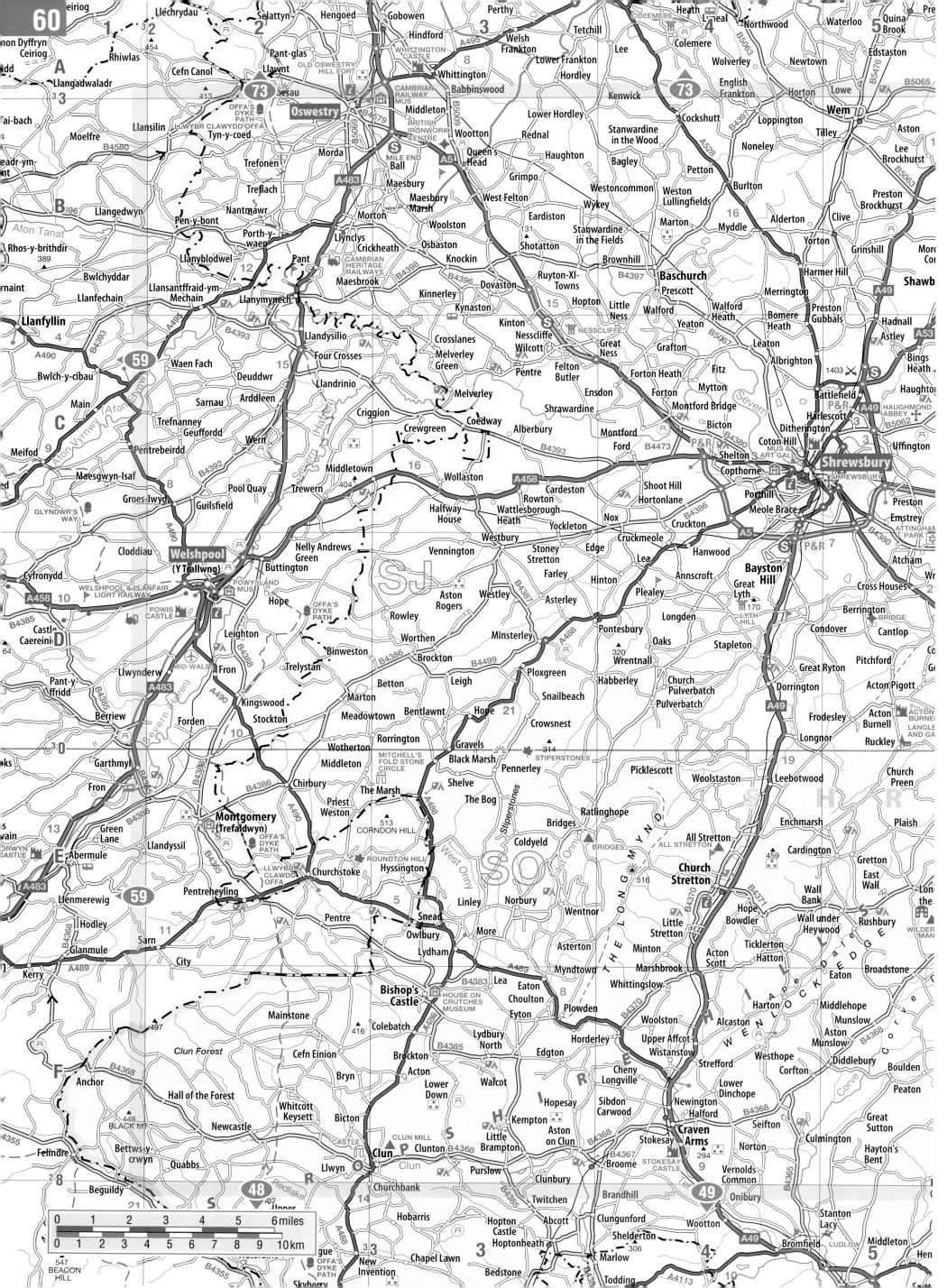

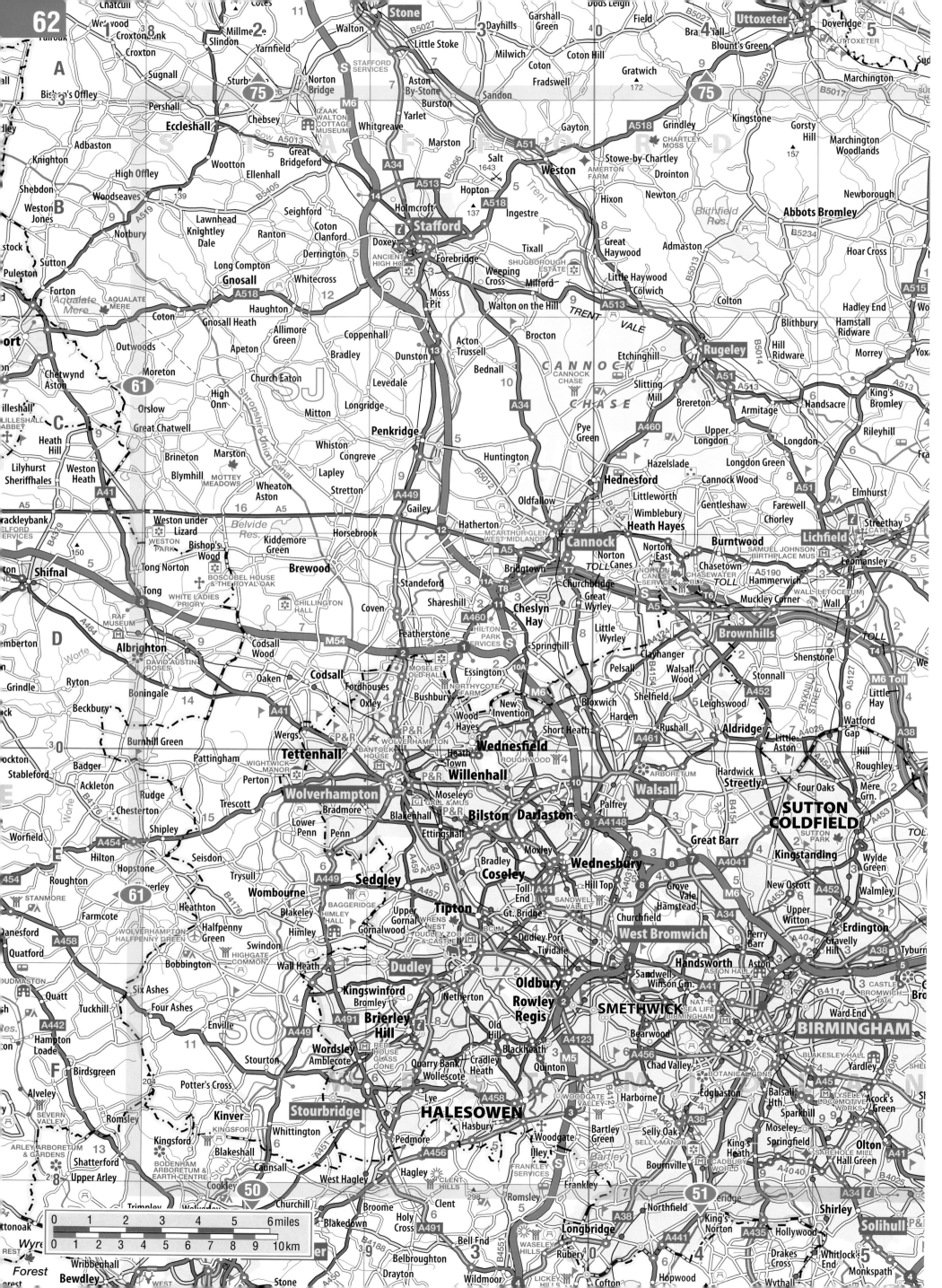

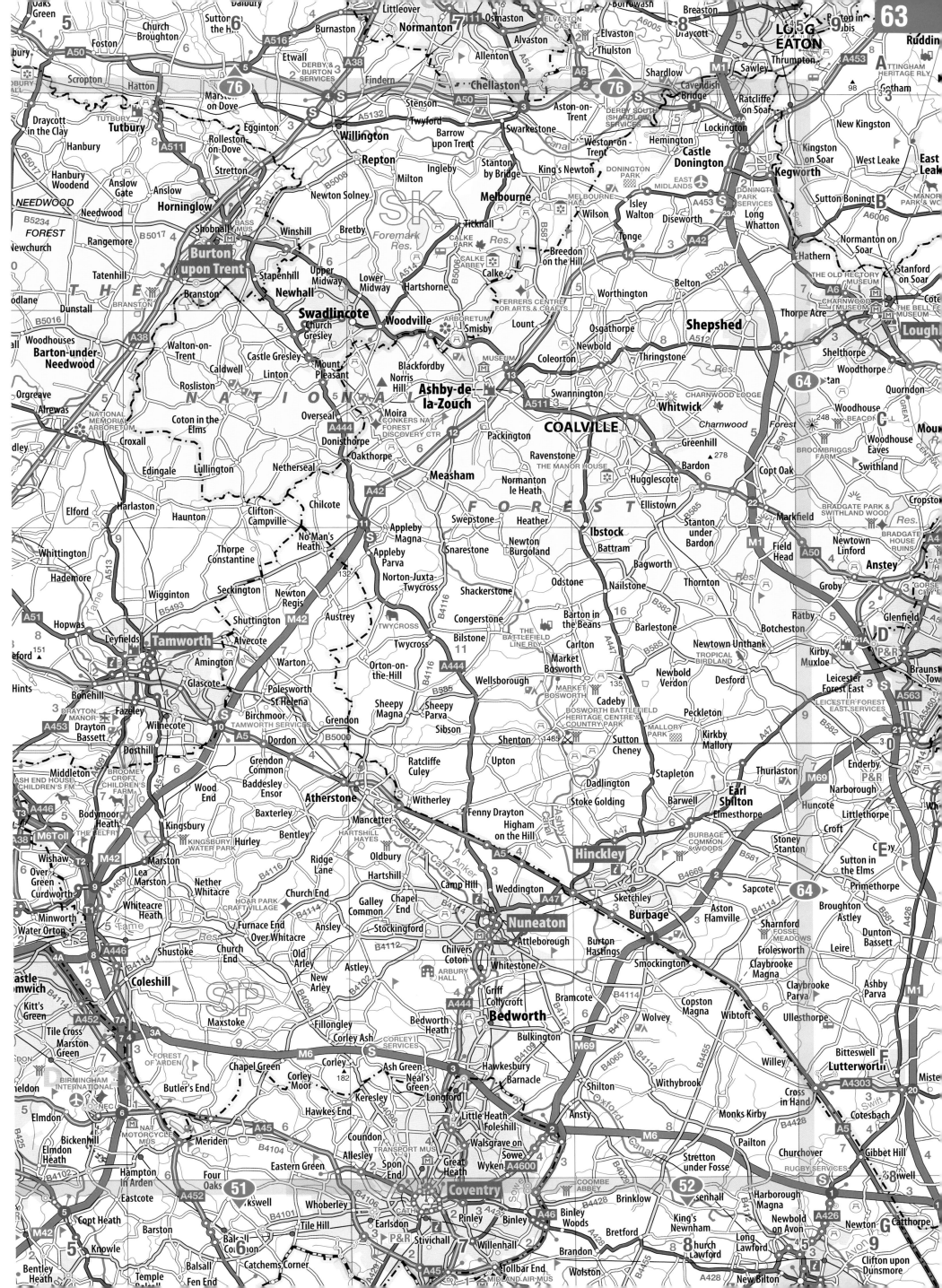

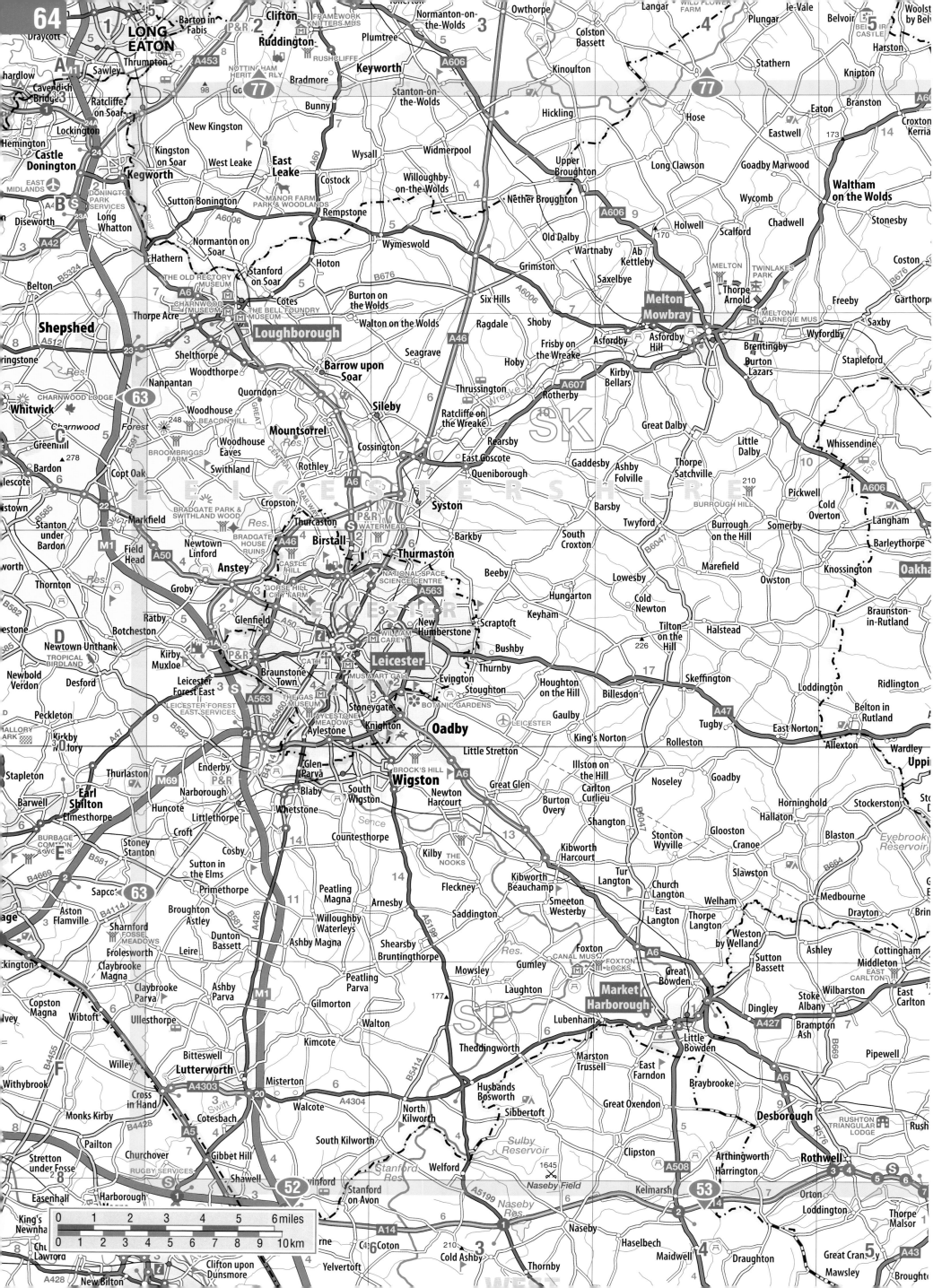

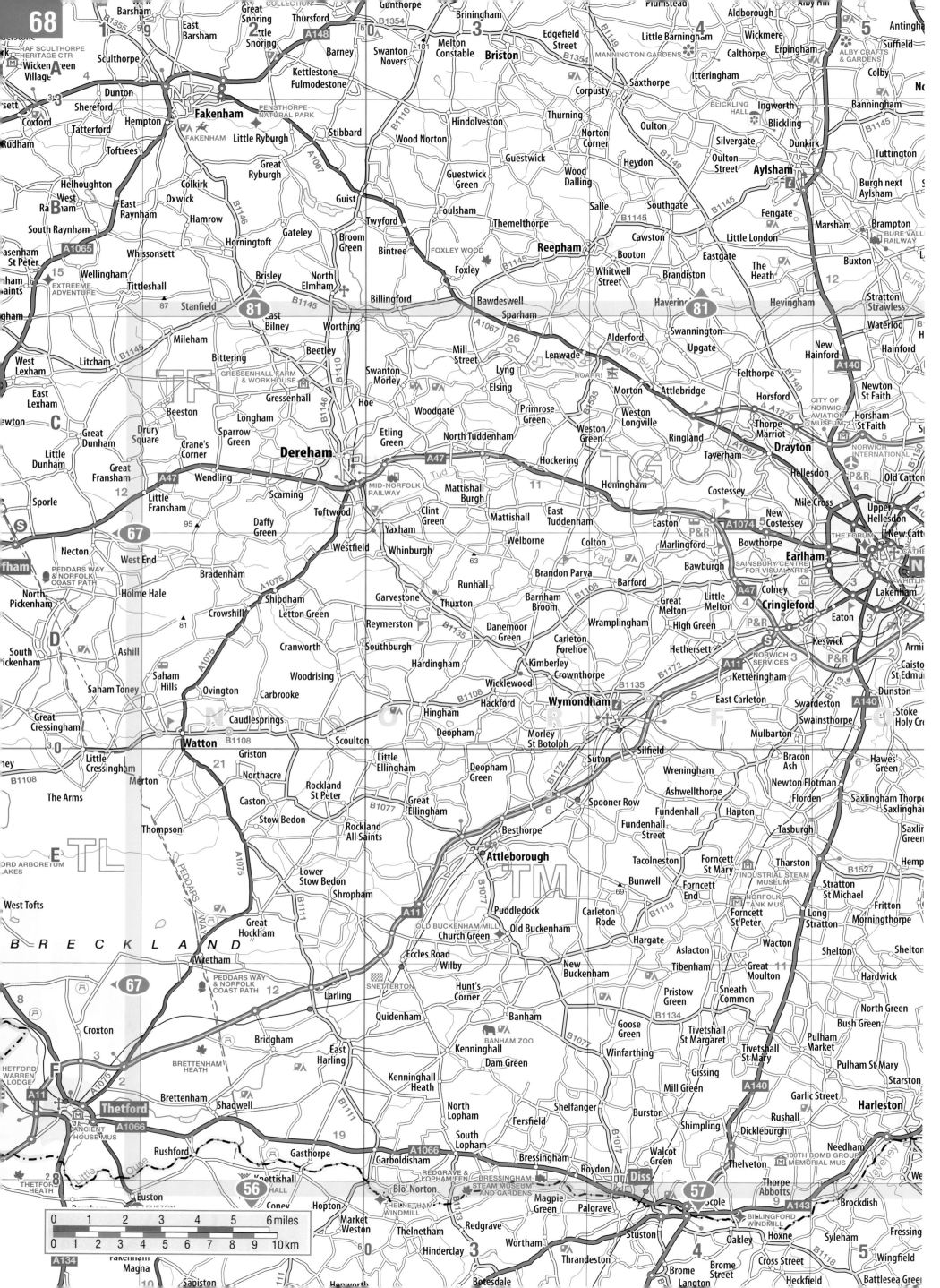

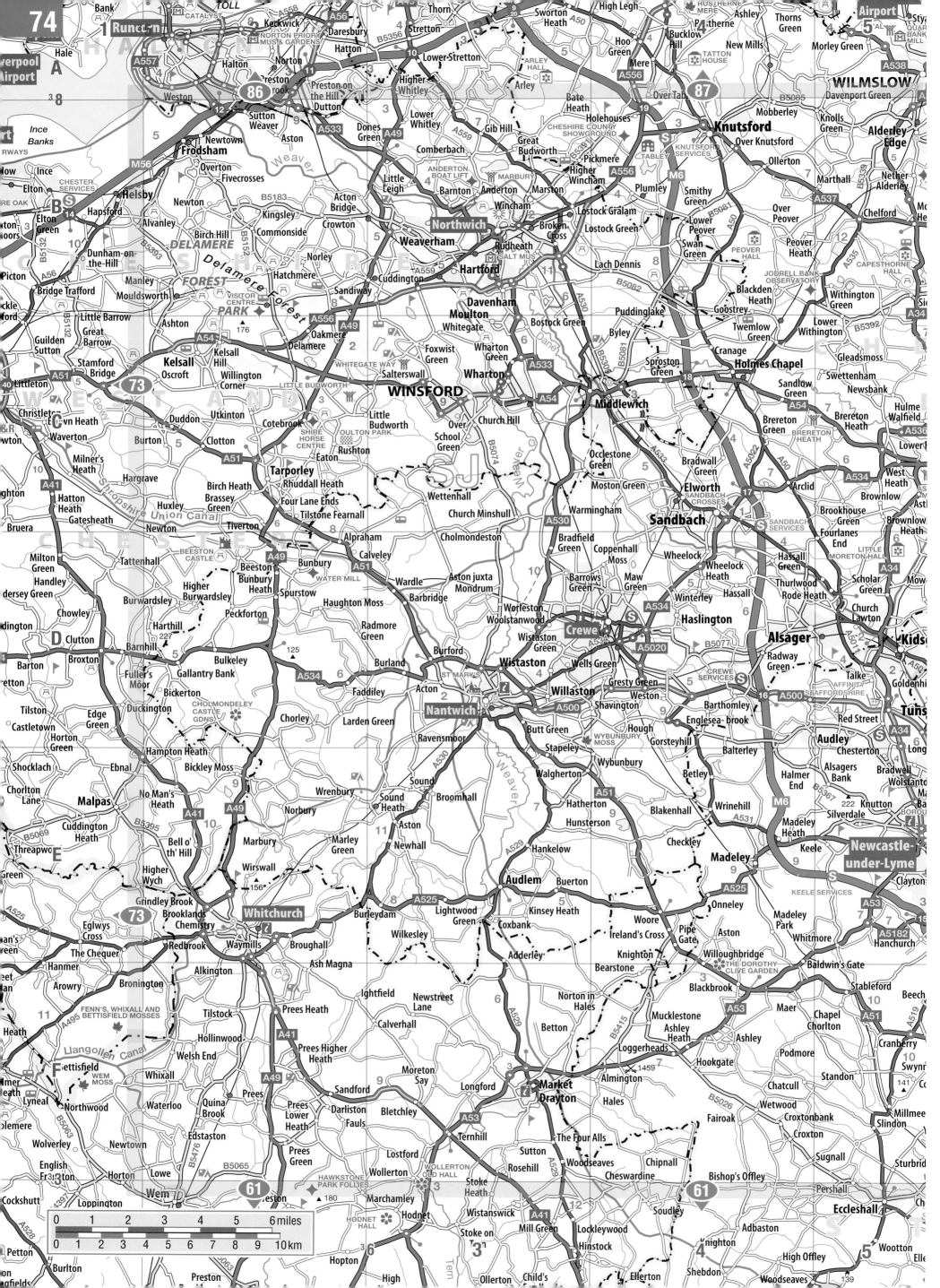

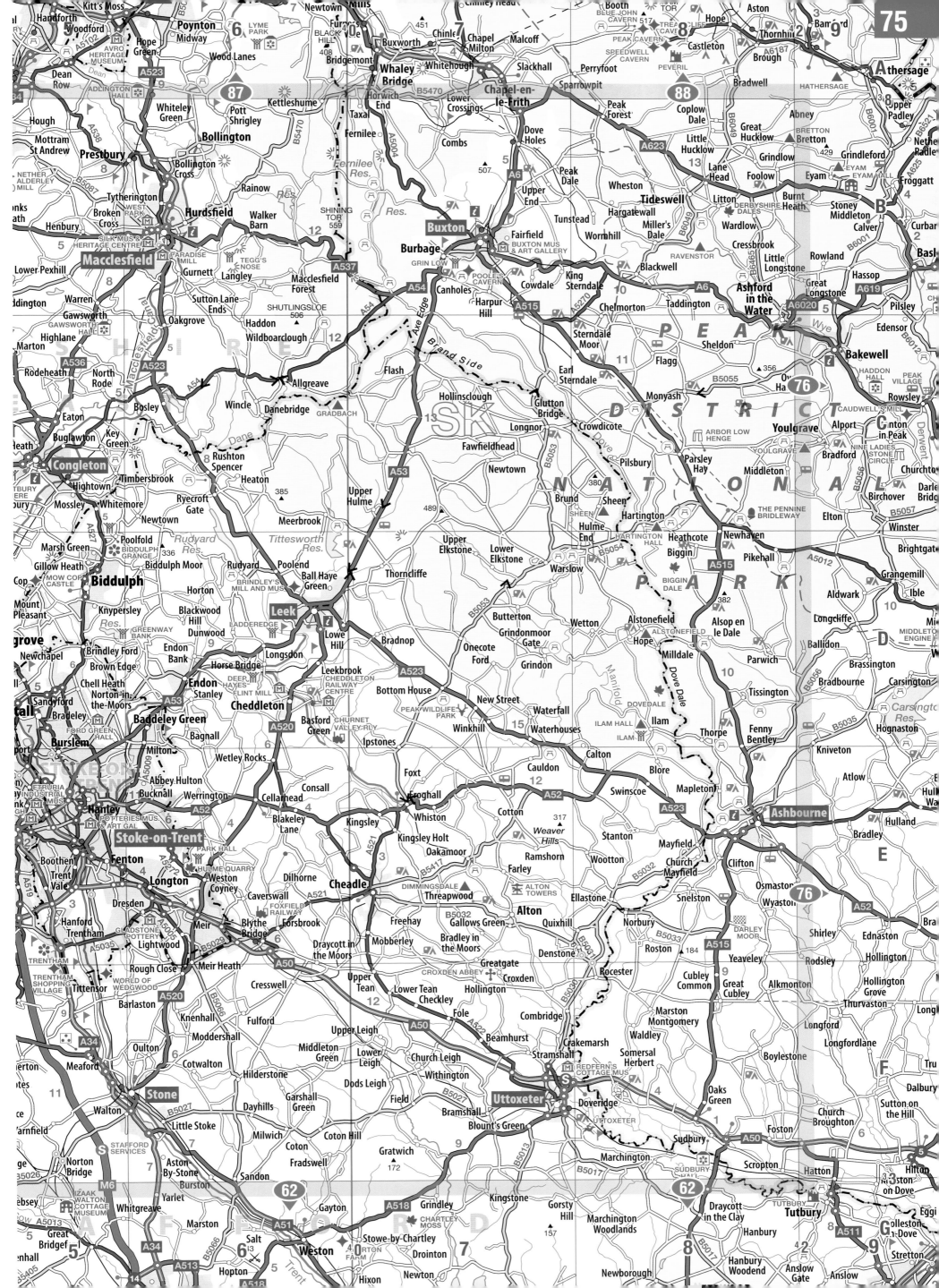

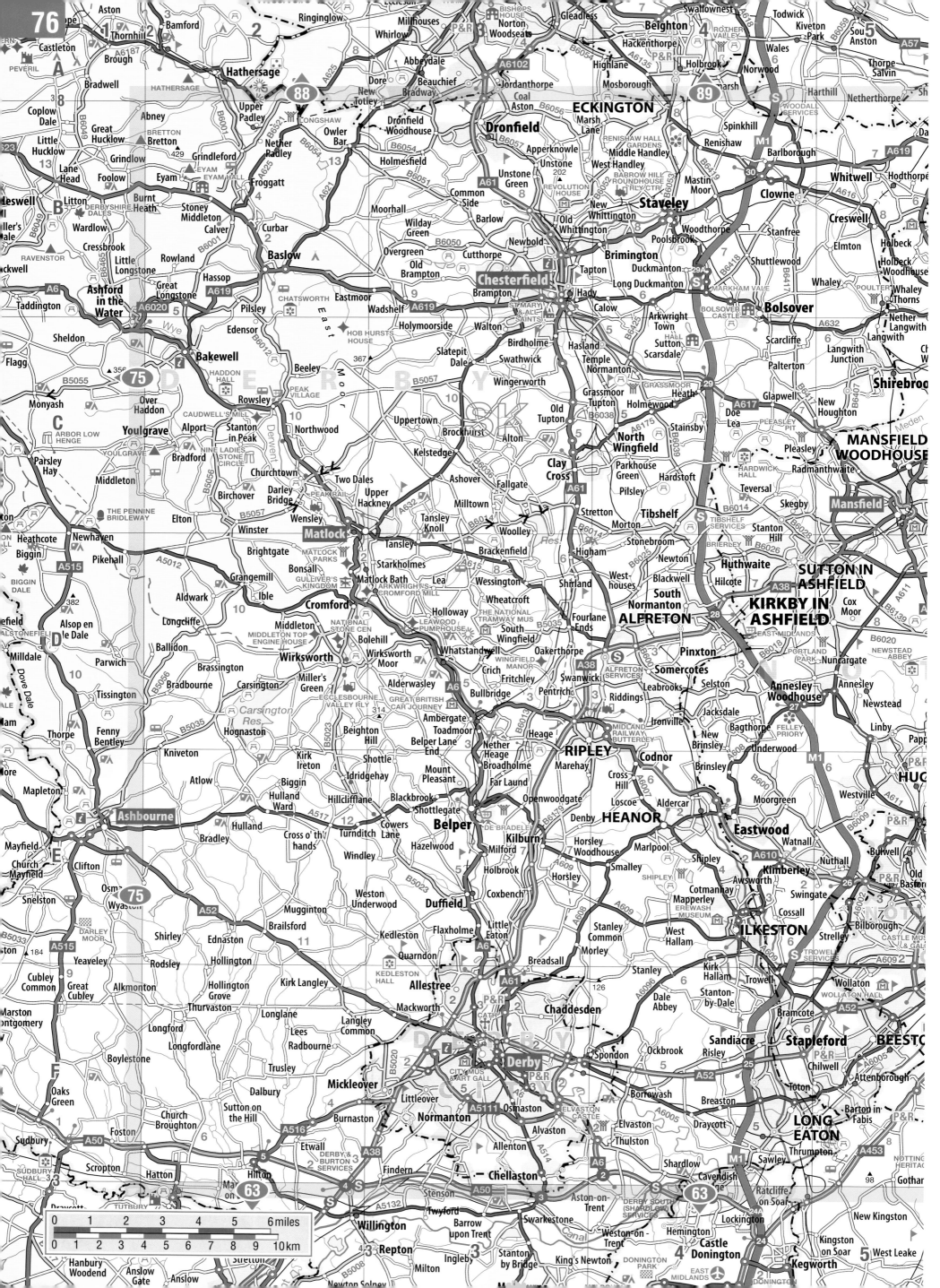

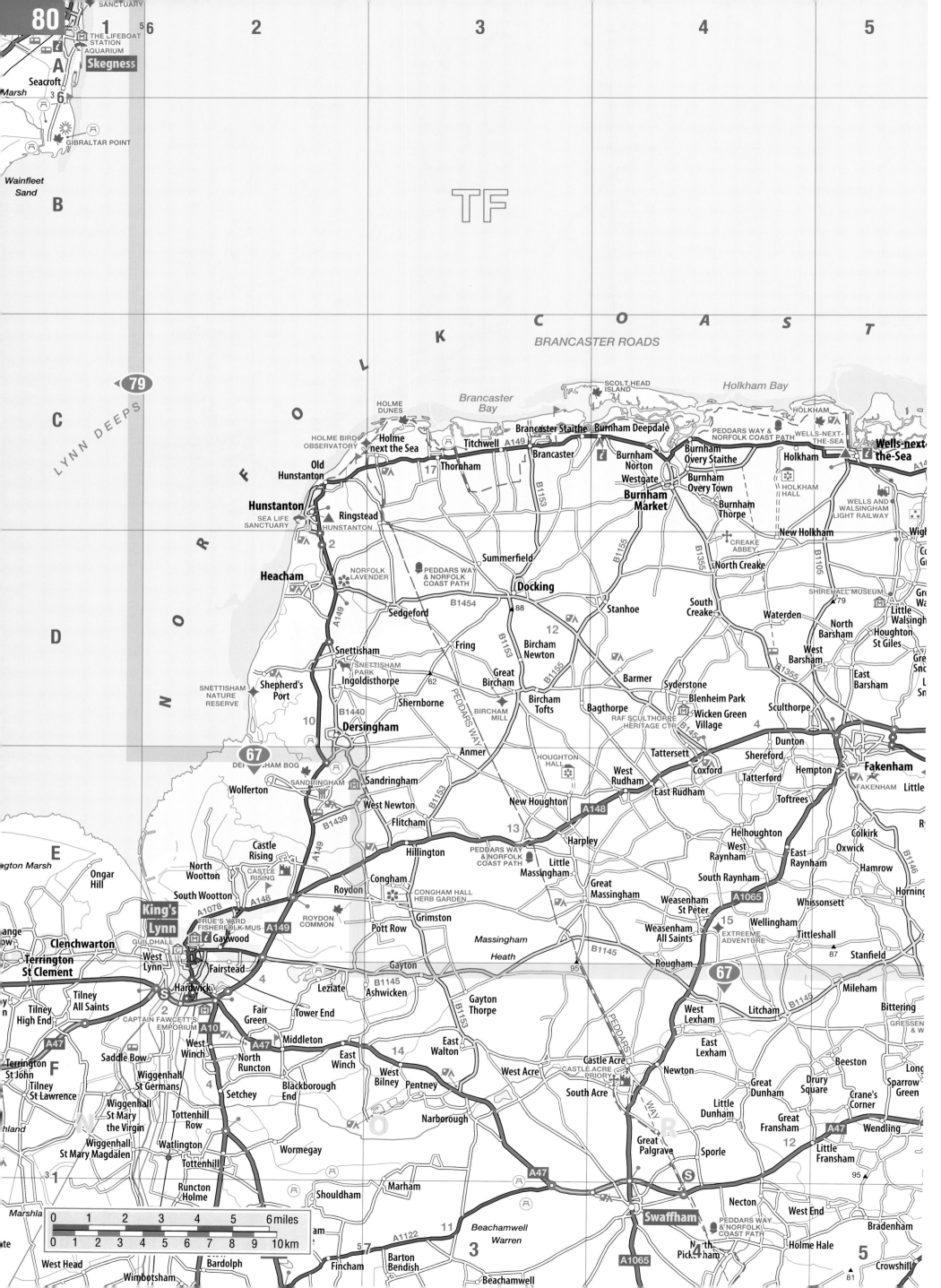

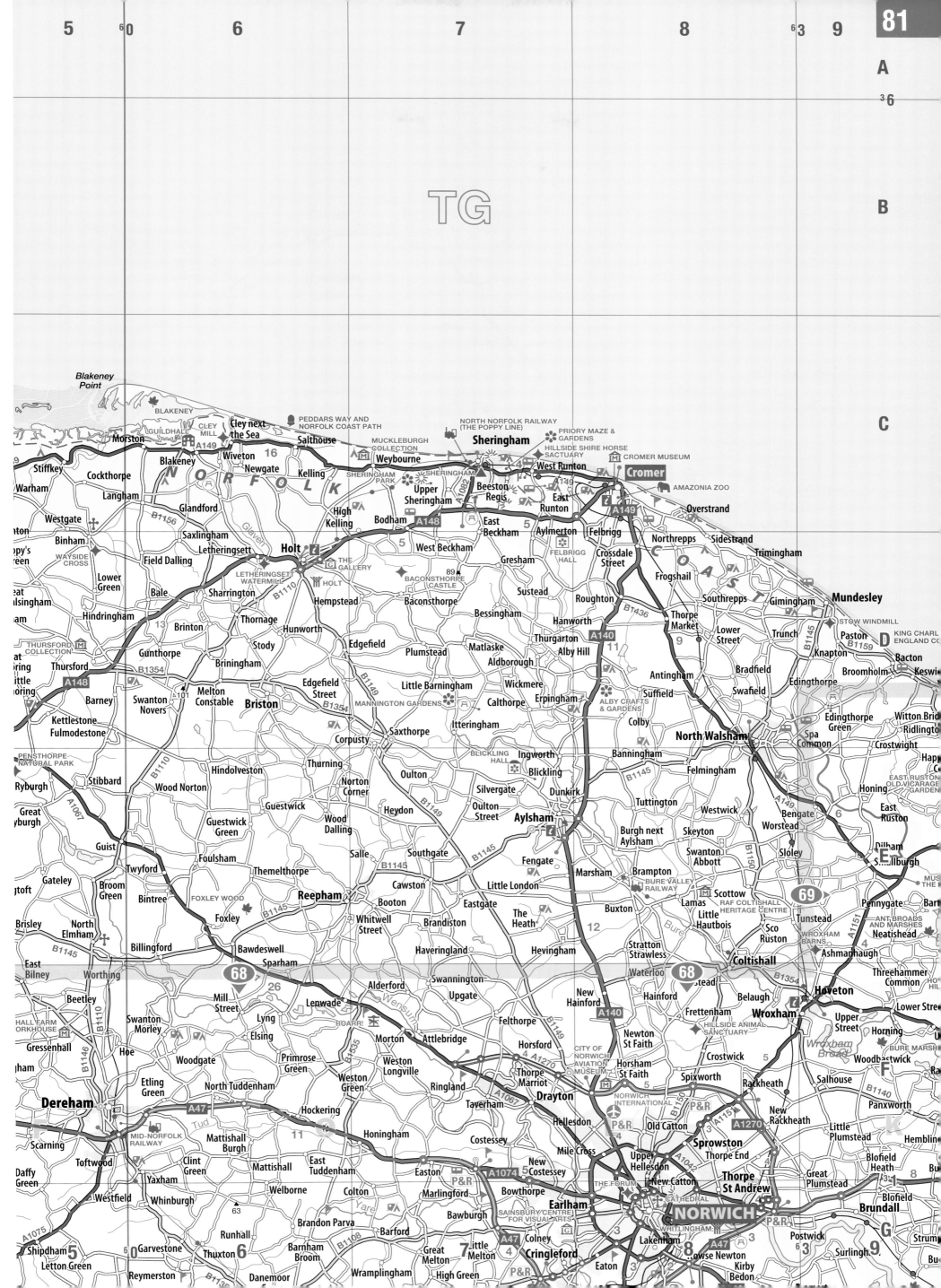

5 6 7 8 9

A
B
TG
C
D
E
F
G

Blakeney
Point

BLAKENEY
GUILDHALL
CLEY MILL
Cley next the Sea
PEDDARS WAY AND NORFOLK COAST PATH
NORTH NORFOLK RAILWAY (THE POPPY LINE)
PRIORY MAZE & GARDENS
HILLSIDE SHIRE HORSE SACTUARY
CROMER MUSEUM
Morston
Salthouse
MUCKLEBURGH COLLECTION
Weybourne
Sheringham
West Runton
Cromer
Stiffkey
Blakeney
Wiveton
16
Newgate
Kelling
SHERINGHAM PARK
Upper Sheringham
Beeston Regis
East Runton
A149
AMAZONIA ZOO
Warham
Cockthorpe
Langham
Glandford
High Kelling
Bodham
East Beckham
Aylmerton
Felbrigg
Overstrand
Westgate
B1156
Saxlingham
A148
5
West Beckham
5
Gresham
FELBRIGG HALL
Crossdale Street
Northrepps
Sidestrand
Trimingham
Binham
WAYSIDE CROSS
Field Dalling
Letheringsett
Holt
THE GALLERY
89
Sustead
Roughton
Frogshail
Southrepps
Gimingham
Mundesley
Lower Green
Bale
Sharrington
LETHERINGSETT WATERMILL
HOLT
BACONSTHORPE CASTLE
Bessingham
Hanworth
B1436
Thorpe Market
Lower Street
STOW WINDMILL
Trunch
B1145
Paston
B1159
Bacton
KING CHAR ENGLAND C
Hindringham
Brinton
13
Hempstead
Thornage
Hunworth
Edgefield
Plumstead
Matlaske
Thurgarton
Alby Hill
A140
11
Antingham
Bradfield
Swafield
Edingthorpe
Broomholm
Keswi
THURSFORD COLLECTION
Barney
Gunthorpe
Briningham
Edgefield Street
Little Barningham
Wickmere
Erpingham
Suffield
ALBY CRAFTS & GARDENS
Colby
Swafield
Knapton
Edingthorpe Green
Witton Brid
Ridlingto
Crostwight
Thursford
B1354
Melton Constable
Briston
B1354
MANNINGTON GARDENS
Calthorpe
North Walsham
Spa Common
Kettlestone
Fulmodestone
Swanton Novers
101
Corpusty
Saxthorpe
Itteringham
BLICKLING HALL
Ingworth
Banningham
Felmingham
Honing
Hap
Ce
EAST RUSTON OLD VICARAGE GARDEN
PENSTHORPE NATURAL PARK
Stibbard
Hindolveston
Thurning
Oulton
Blickling
B1145
East Ruston
Ryburgh
Wood Norton
Norton Corner
Silvergate
Dunkirk
Tuttington
Westwick
A149
Bengate
Worstead
Great yburgh
A1067
Guestwick
Heydon
Oulton Street
Aylsham
Sco Ruston
Sloley
Dilham
S...lburgh
Guist
Guestwick Green
Wood Dalling
Aylsham
B1145
Burgh next Aylsham
Skeyton
Swanton Abbott
B1150
Pennygate
Bart...
Gateley
Twyford
Foulsham
Salle
Southgate
Fengate
Marsham
Brampton
BURE VALLEY RAILWAY
Lamas
SCOTTOW RAF COLTISHALL HERITAGE CENTRE
Tunstead
A1151
ANT BROADS AND MARSHES
Neatishead
Broom Green
Bintree
FOXLEY WOOD
B1145
Reepham
Cawston
Booton
Brandiston
Eastgate
Little London
The Heath
Buxton
Little Hautbois
WROXHAM BARNS
Ashmanhaugh
Threehammer Common
Brisley
North Elmham
Billingford
Foxley
Whitwell Street
Haveringland
Hevingham
Stratton Strawless
Scottow
69
Coltishall
B1354
Hoveton
East Bilney
Worthing
68
Sparham
Bawdeswell
7
26
Alderford
Swannington
Upgate
New Hainford
Hainford
Waterloo
68
...stead
Hoveton
Wroxham
Upper Street
Lower St...
Beetley
Mill Street
Lenwade
ROARR!
Morton
Attlebridge
Felthorpe
A140
Frettenham
Belaugh
Wroxham
Horning
Swanton Morley
Lyng
Elsing
Weston Longville
Horsford
Newton St Faith
Crostwick
HILLSIDE ANIMAL SANCTUARY
5
Wroxbam Broad
BURE MARSH
Woodbastwick
HALL FARM WORKHOUSE
Hoe
Woodgate
Primrose Green
Weston Green
Ringland
Thorpe Marriot
Horsham St Faith
Spixworth
Rackheath
Salhouse
B1140
K
Gressenhall
B1146
North Tuddenham
Taverham
Drayton
CITY OF NORWICH AVIATION MUSEUM
A1067
NORWICH INTERNATIONAL
P&R
New Rackheath
Panxworth
Dereham
A47
Etling Green
Hockering
Honingham
Thorpe Marriot
Mile Cross
Old Catton
A1270
Sprowston
Thorpe End
Little Plumstead
Hembling
MID-NORFOLK RAILWAY
Scarning
Clint Green
Mattishall Burgh
11
Costessey
P&R
Hellesdon
New Catton
Upper Hellesdon
A1042
Thorpe St Andrew
Blofield Heath
B1...
Bu
Toftwood
Yaxham
Mattishall
East Tuddenham
New Costessey
Easton
SAINSBURY CENTRE FOR VISUAL ARTS
THE FORUM
A1270
Great Plumstead
Blofield
Daffy Green
Westfield
Whinburgh
Welborne
Colton
P&R
A1074
Marlingford
Bowthorpe
Earlham
NORWICH
CATHEDRAL
P&R
Brundall
A1075
Shipdham
5
Letton Green
Garveston
Thuxton
6
Runhall
Barnham Broom
Brandon Parva
B1108
Barford
Bawburgh
Great Melton
7
A47
4
Colney
Cringleford
Eaton
A47
8
Lakenham
Postwick
Surlingh
9
Reymerston
Danemoor
Wramplingham
High Green
little Melton
owse Newton
Kirby Bedon
Strum

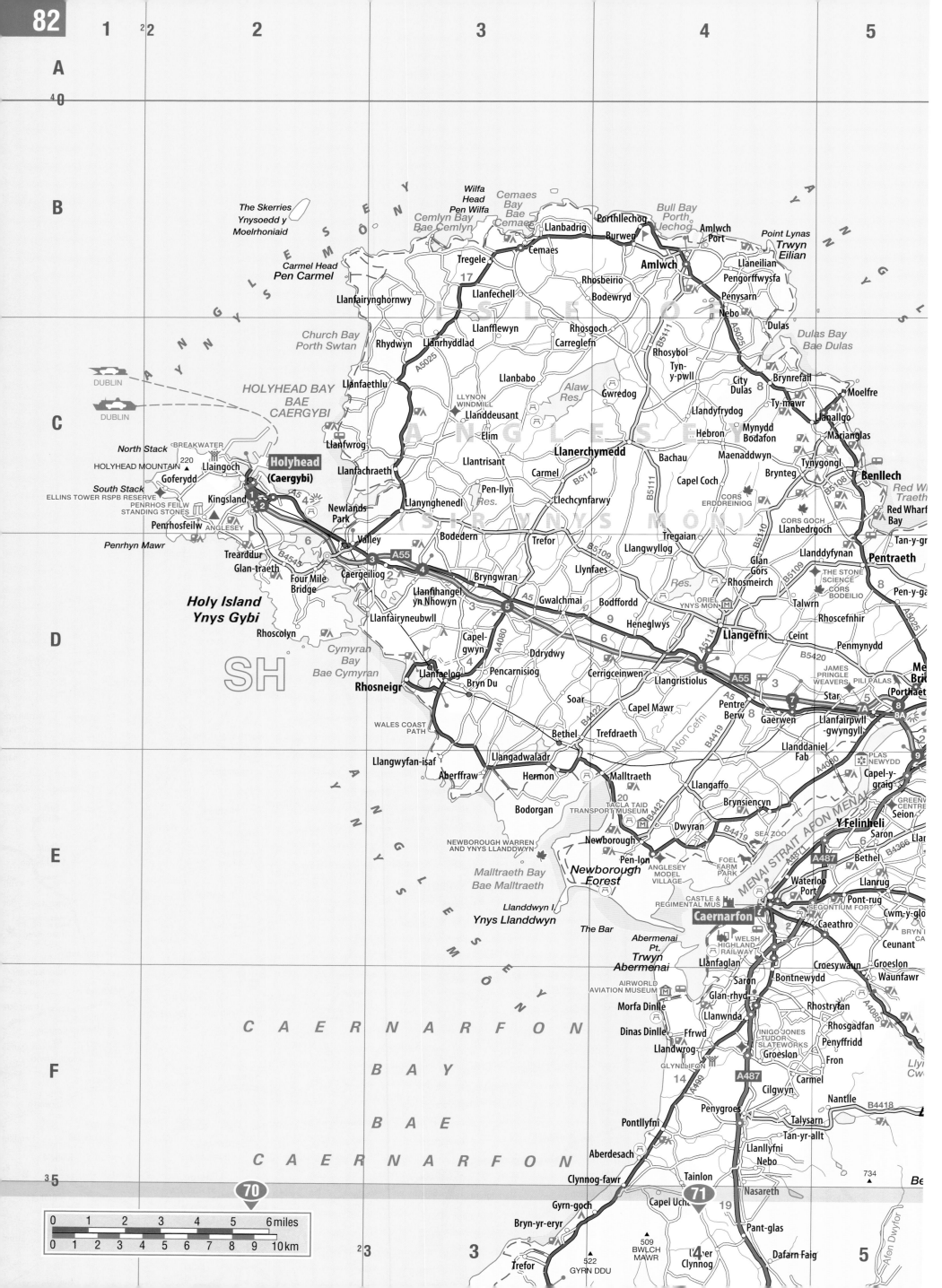

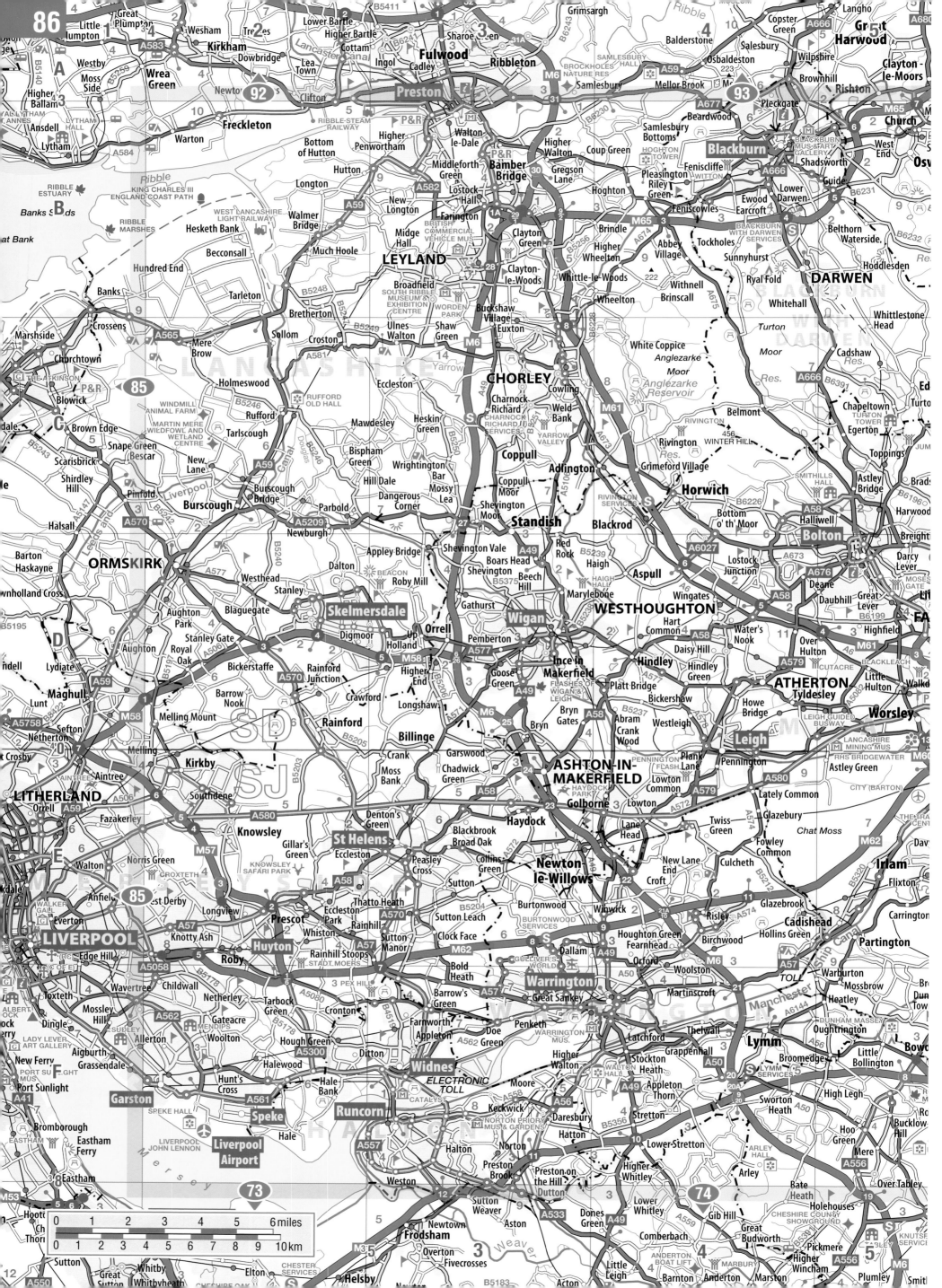

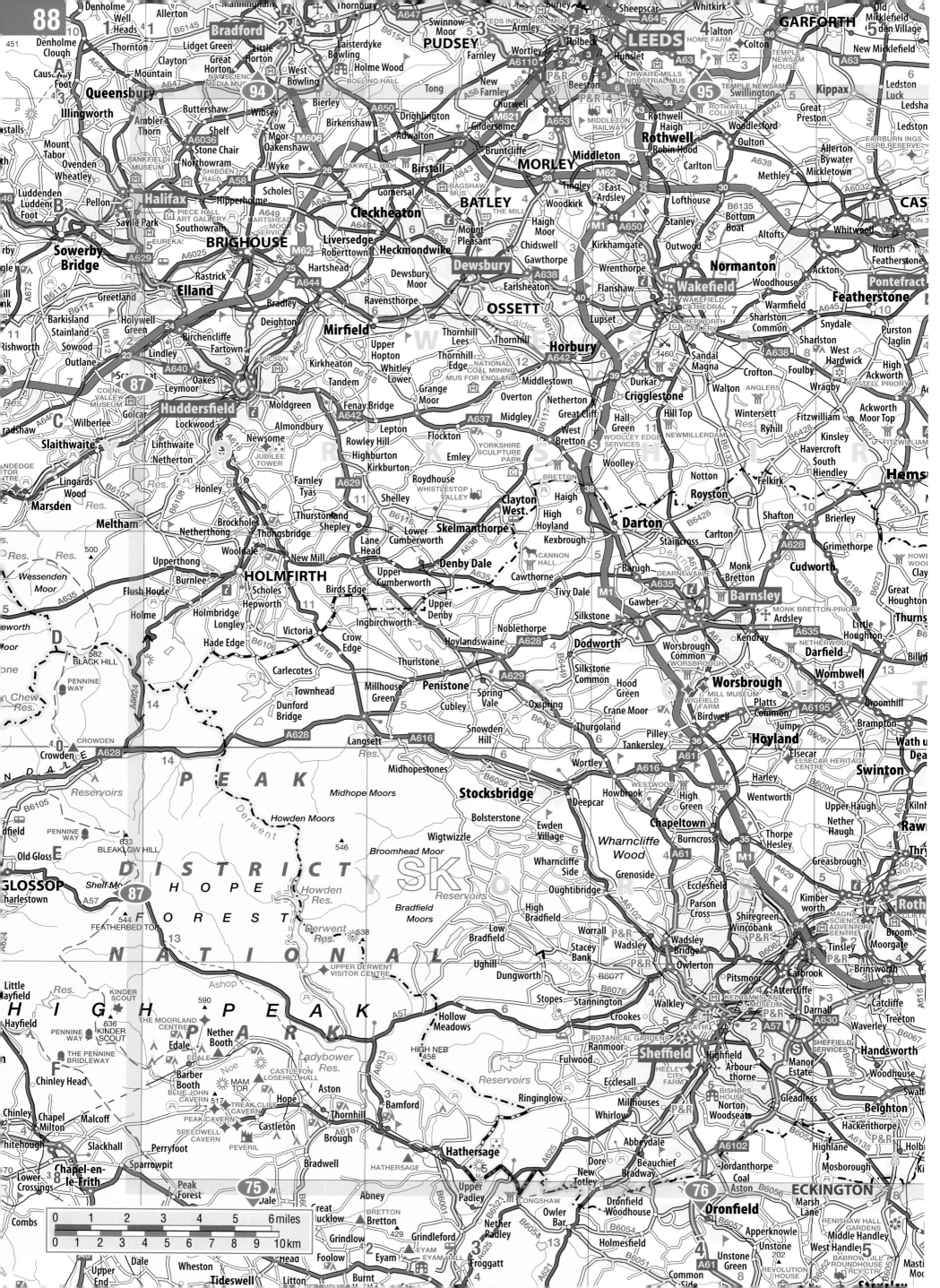

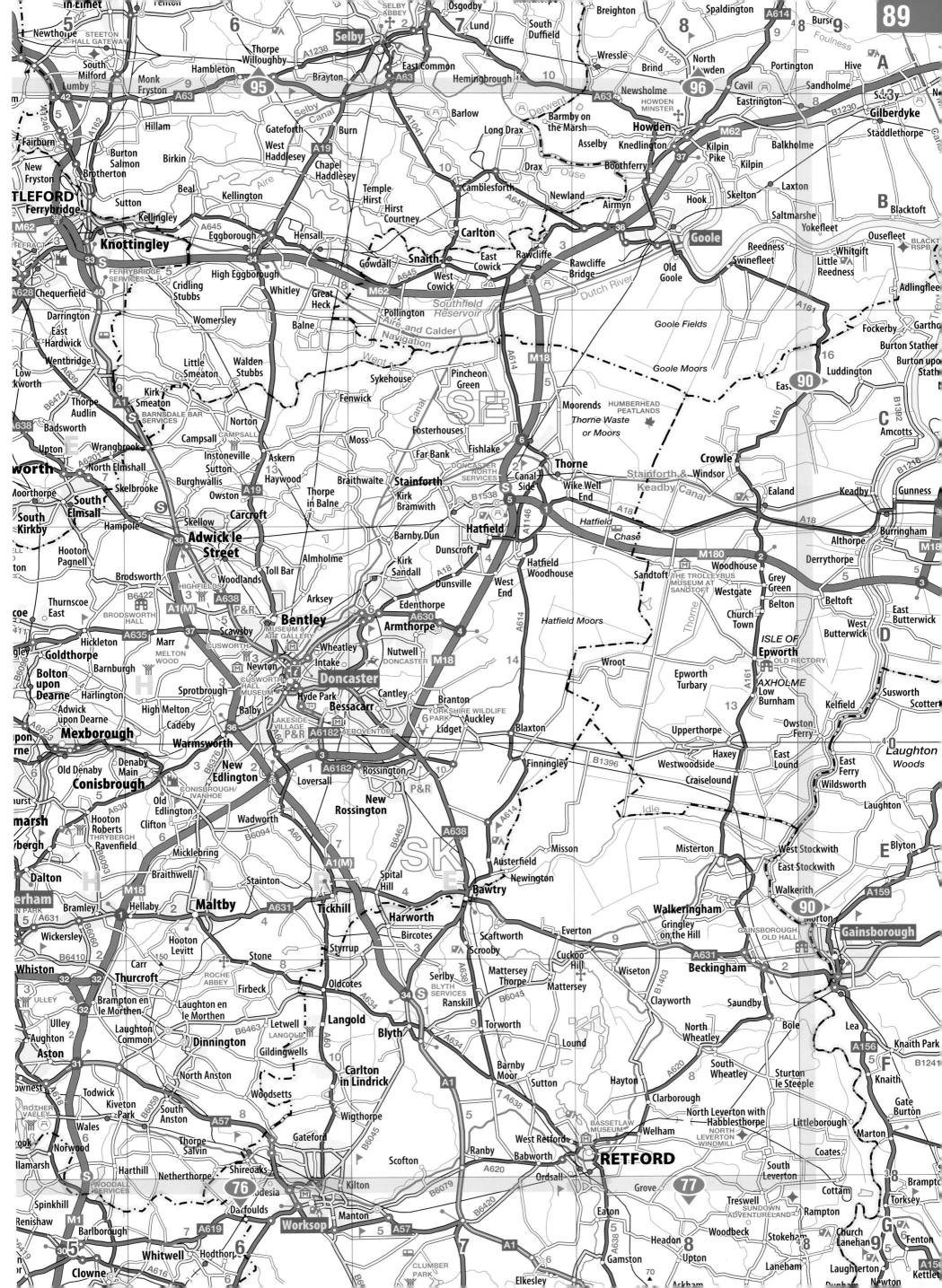

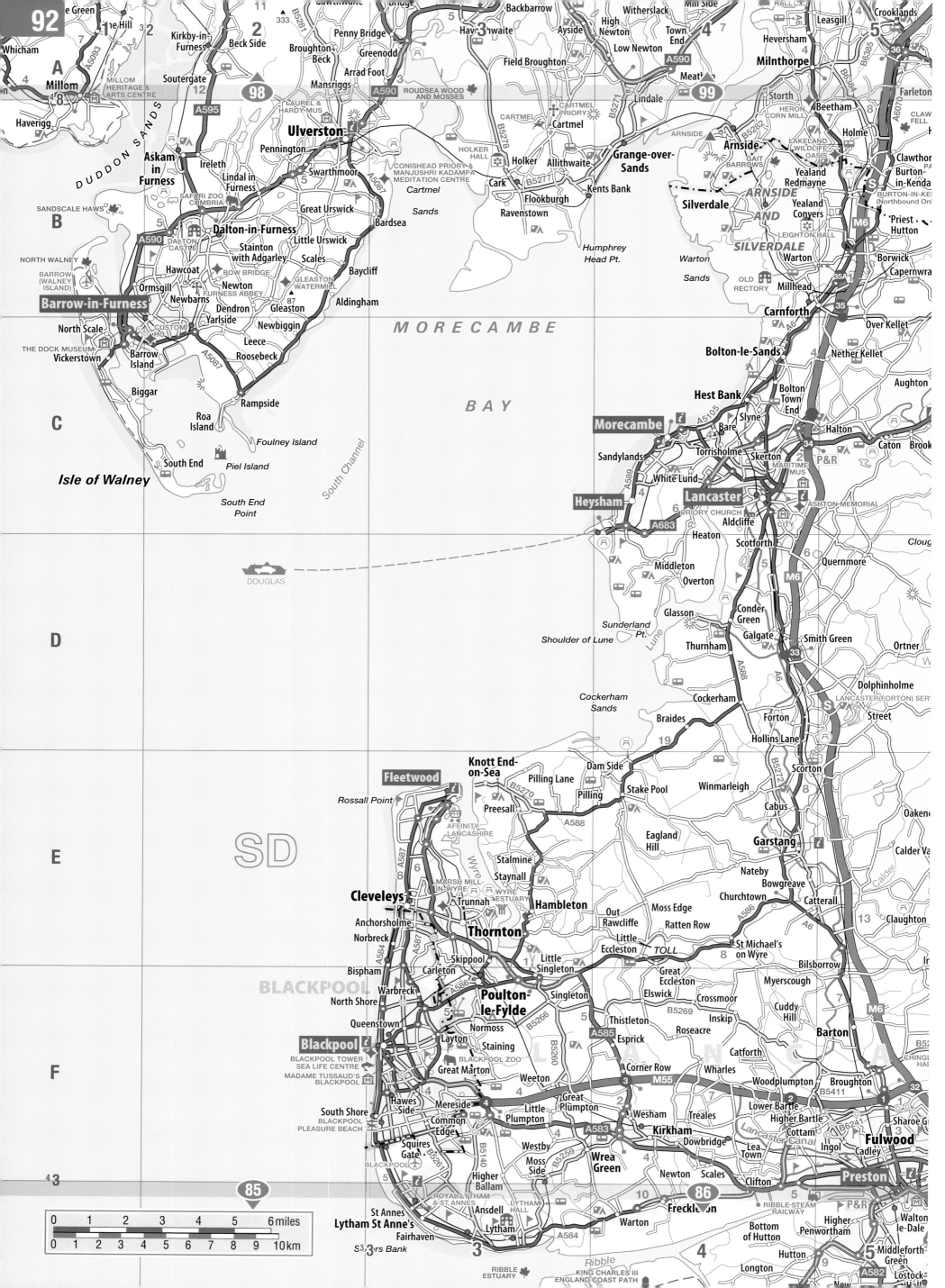

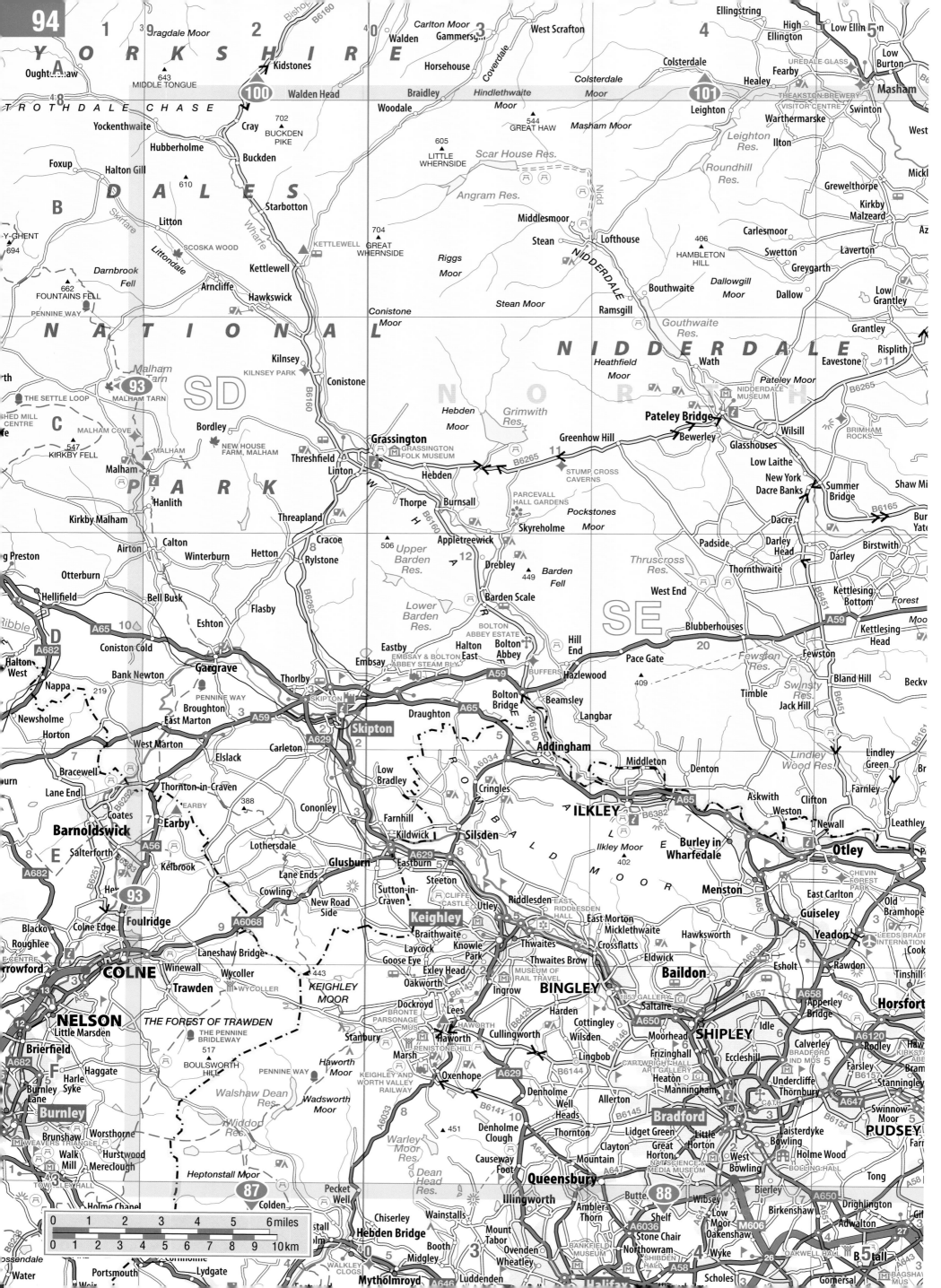

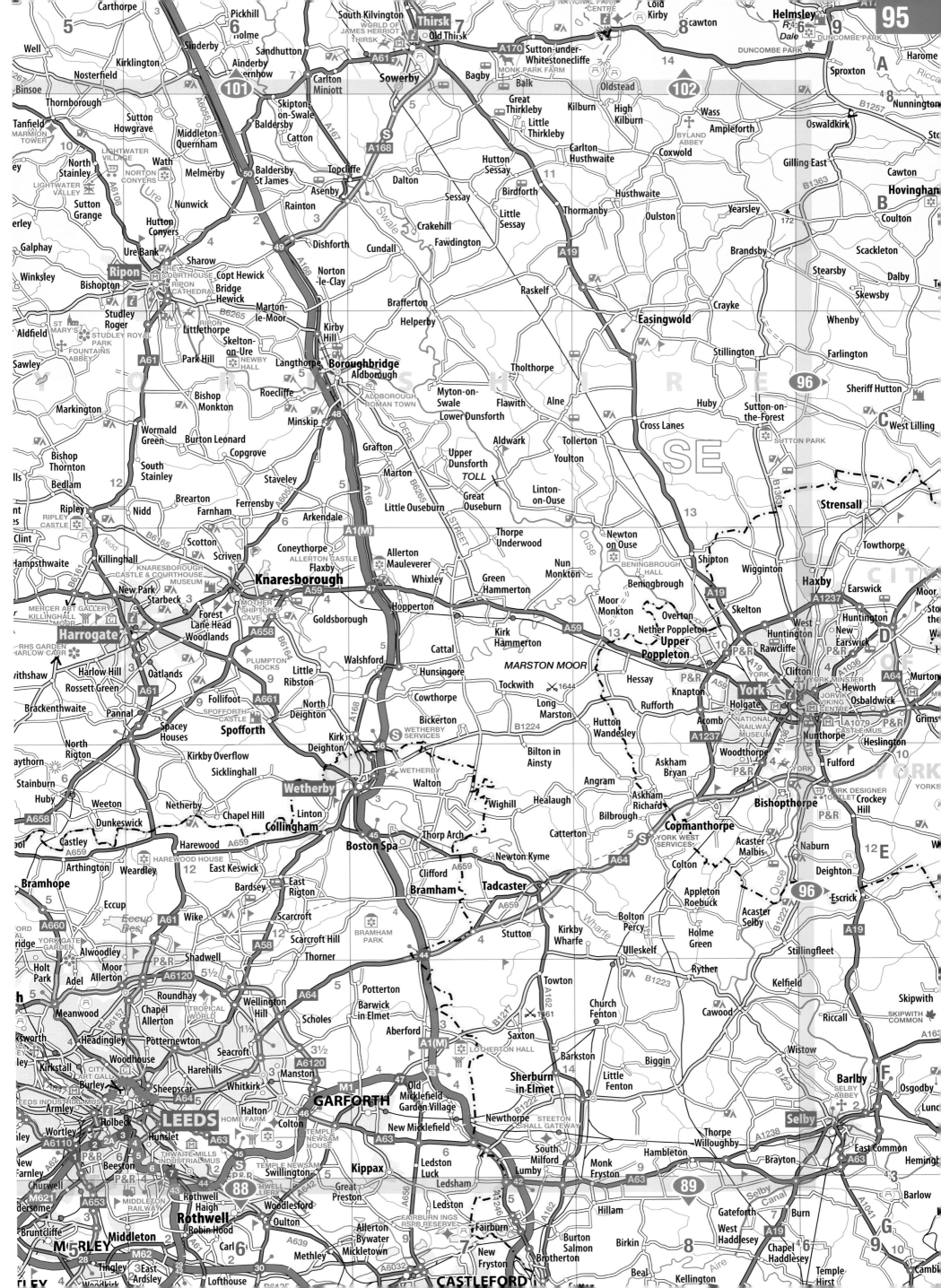

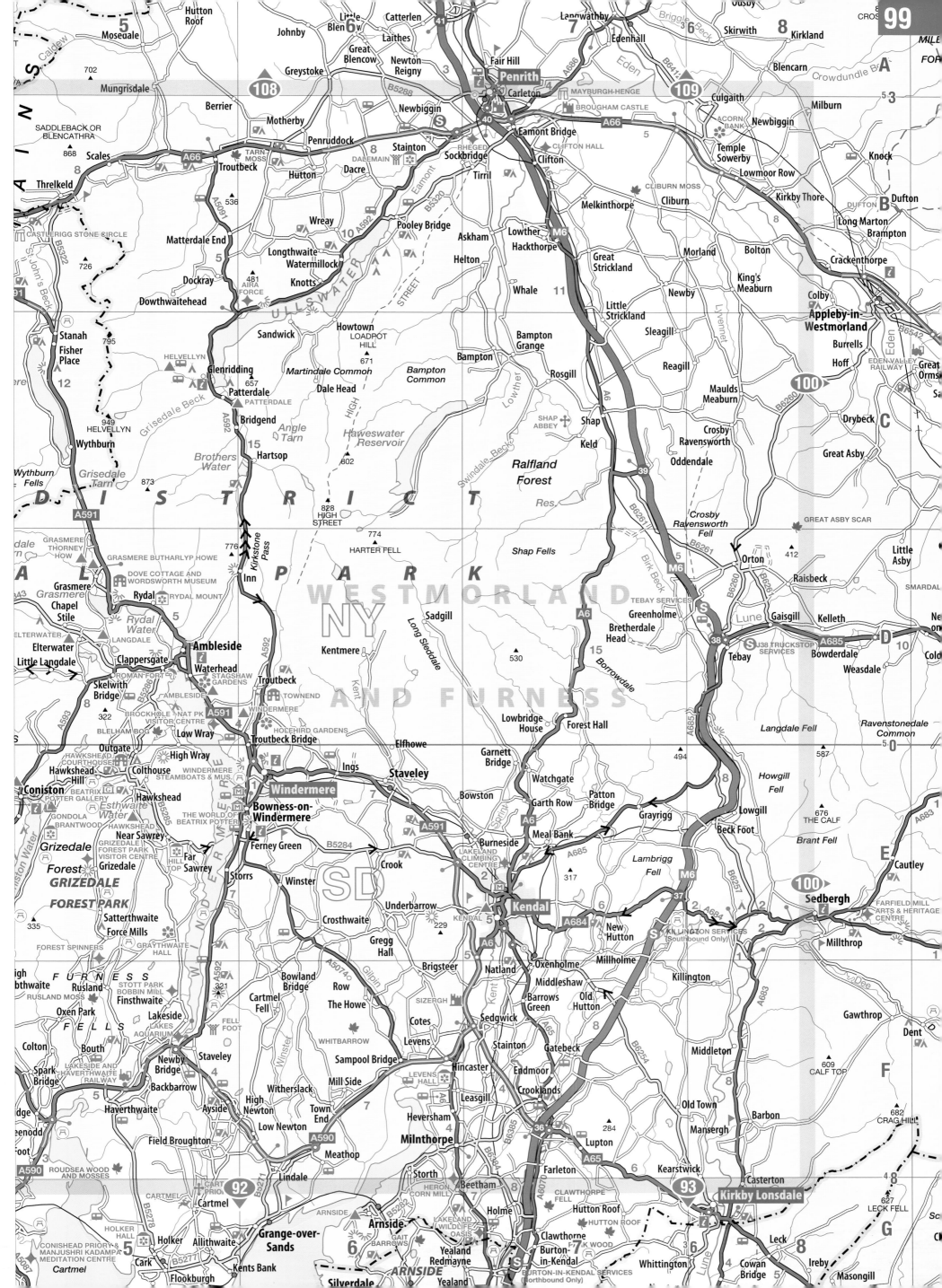

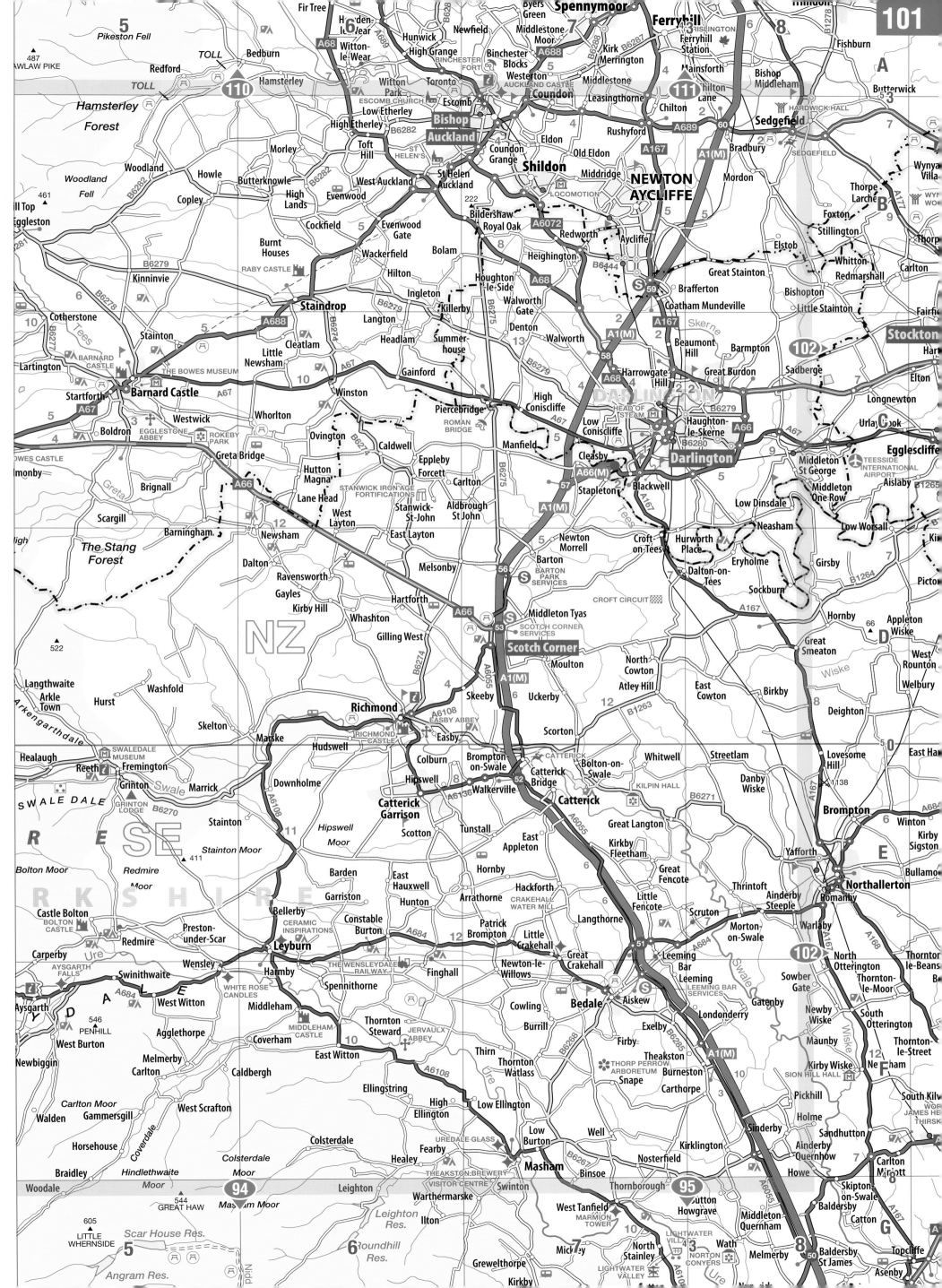

NZ OV

YORKSHIRE MOORS

SE

TA

NW

Map labels

1 18 2 3 20 4 5

A

B

C

D

E

F

CARLETON CASTLE
Bennane Hd.
112
Colmonell
B734 265 Knockdolian
Heronsford
Ballantrae Bay Glen Tig
Ballantrae Balkiss
Downan Pt.
Auchencrosh
439 BENERAIRD
A77
BELFAST
LARNE
Mark
Milleur Pt. Glen App 257
17
Corsewall Pt. Penwhirn Res.
Barnhills Portencalzie
North Cairn Cairnryan Main Water of L
South Cairn Corsewall B738
Loch Connell Kirkcolm Braid Fell
Dounan Bay The Wig
Mains of Airies Ervie
Low Salchrie LOCH RYAN
B796
Knocknain 6 A77
Slouchnawen Bay Leswalt Innermessan Auchmant
Craigencross A751
B738 Black Loch
B7043 CASTLE KENNEDY GARDENS
Glenstockadale A718 White Loch
Broadsea Bay Stranraer Aird Castle Kennedy
T H E CASTLE OF R H
St John Visitor Centre
Knockglass 3 Soulseat Loch GA
Stranraer Museum A75
Black Hd. Mark
182 Lochans
Dunskey Ho. B7077
5 A77 7 B7084 Torrs War
Portpatrick Awhirk 5 6
8 Stoneykirk A716
Port of Spittal Bay
B7042
Luce S

Cairngarroch Sandhead
Cairngarroch Bay KIRKMADRINE STONES Sandhead Bay
Money Hd.
Clachanmore
Hole Stone Bay Ardwell
Chapel Rossan
Ardwell Mains
Ardwell Pt. 10
Logan Mains
LOGAN BOTANIC GARDEN Balgowan Pt.
Mull of Logan
Port Nessock or Port Logan Bay
Port Logan B7065
Cairnywellan Hd. A716
Clanyard Bay
Low Clanyard
Laggantalluch Hd. Kirkmaiden Drumm
164
Damnaglaur B7041
Crammag Hd.
Cairngaan Ma
Port Kemin

Scale

0 1 2 3 4 5 6 miles
0 1 2 3 4 5 6 7 8 9 10 km

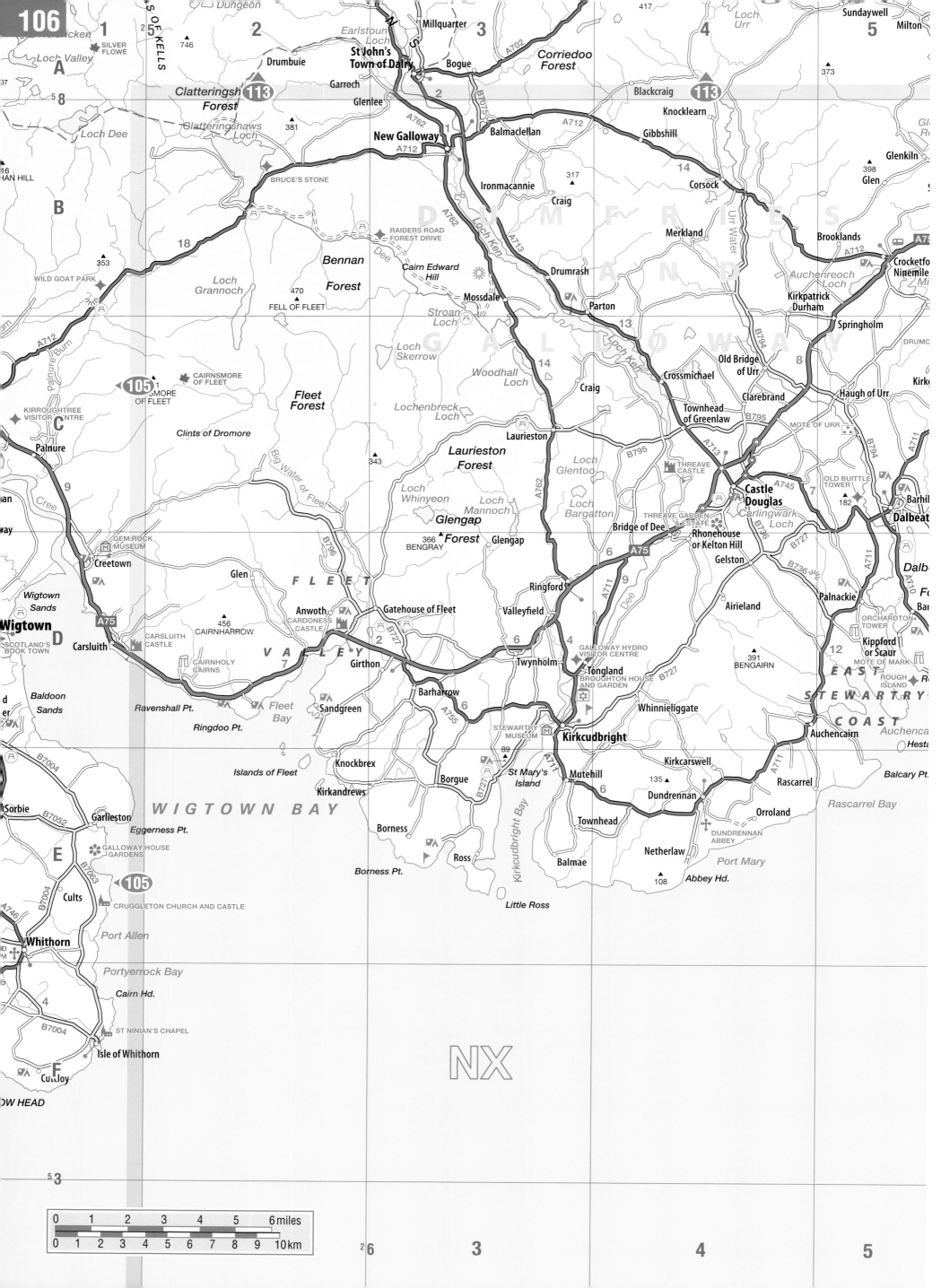

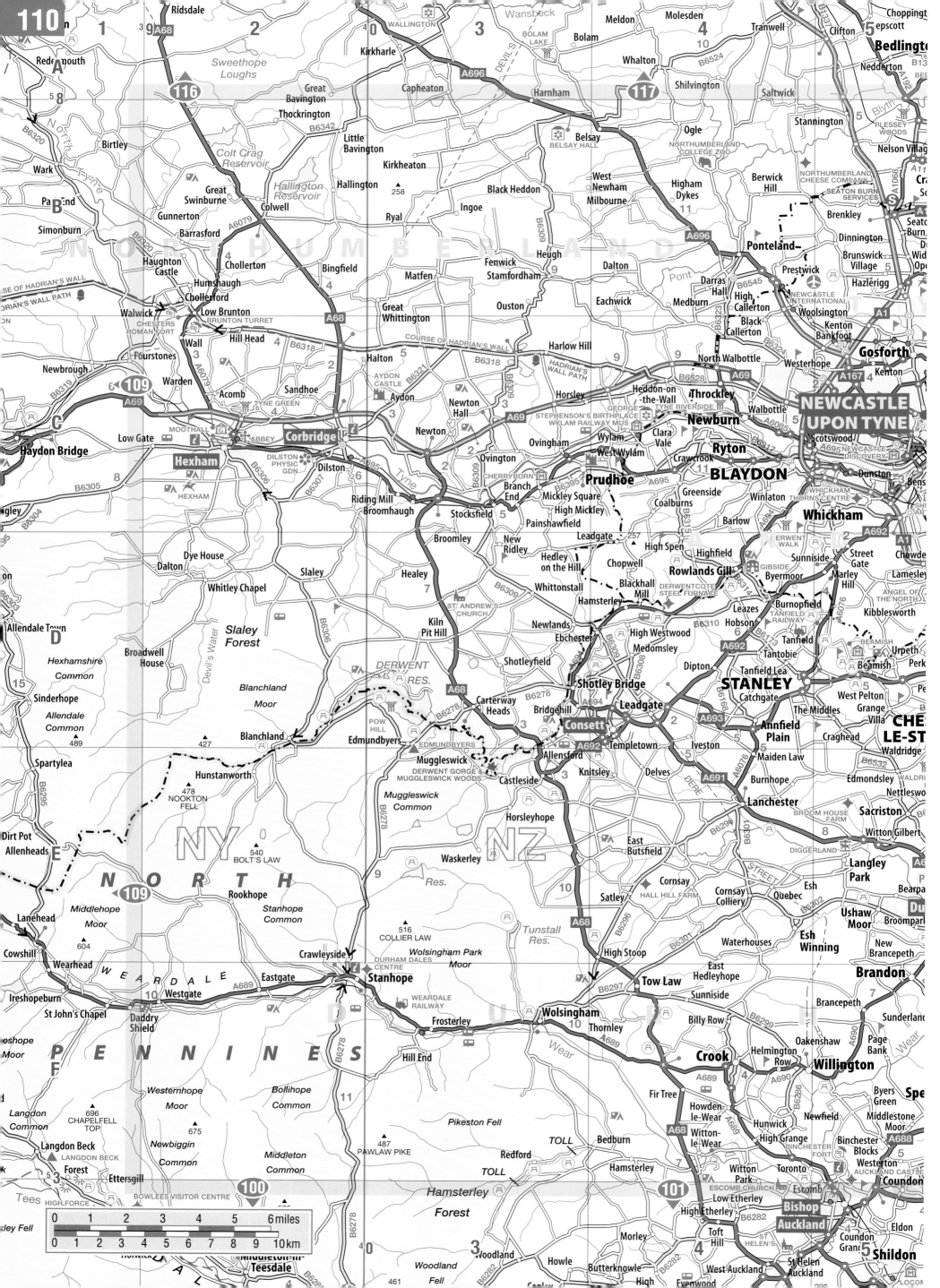

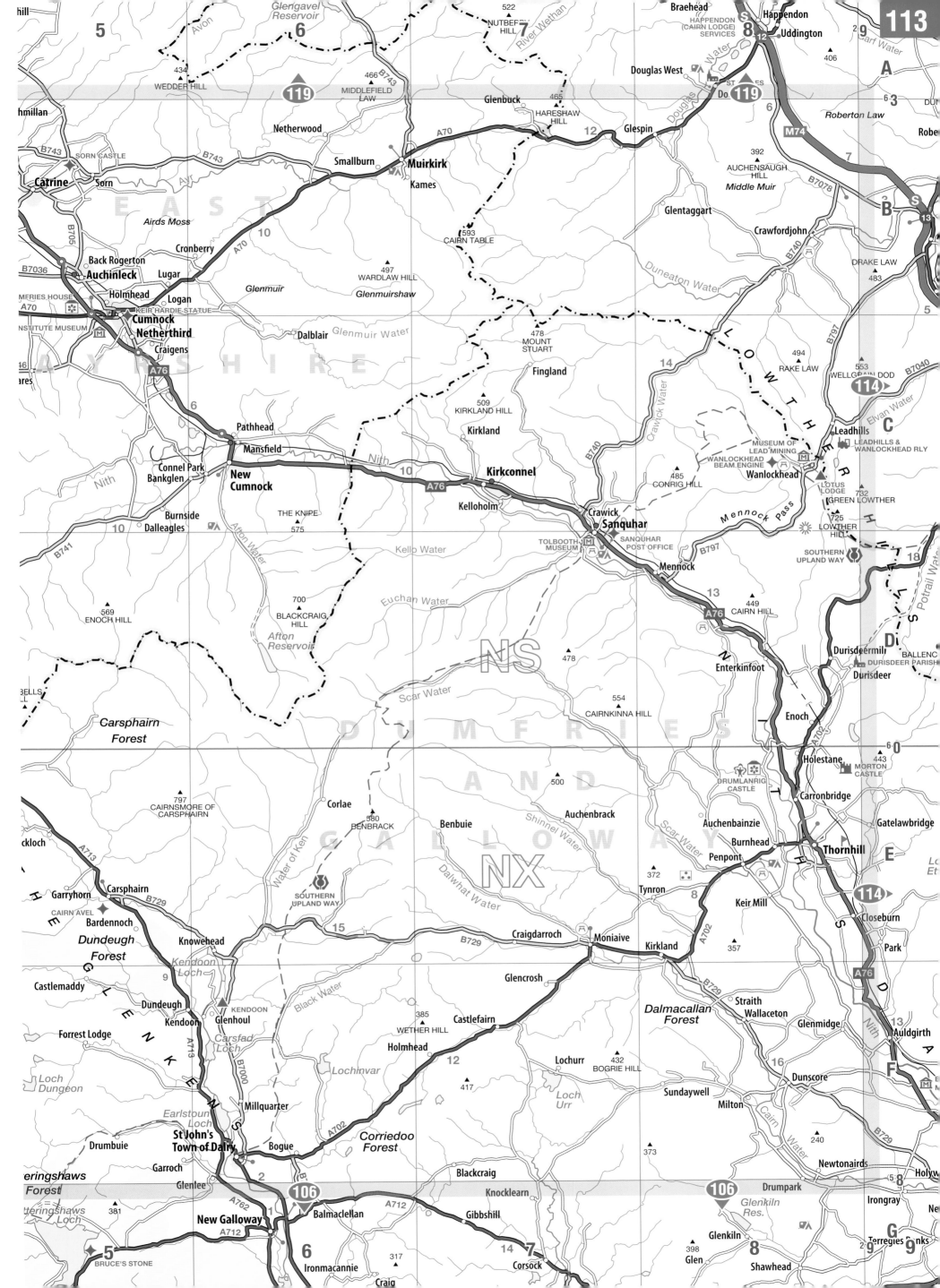

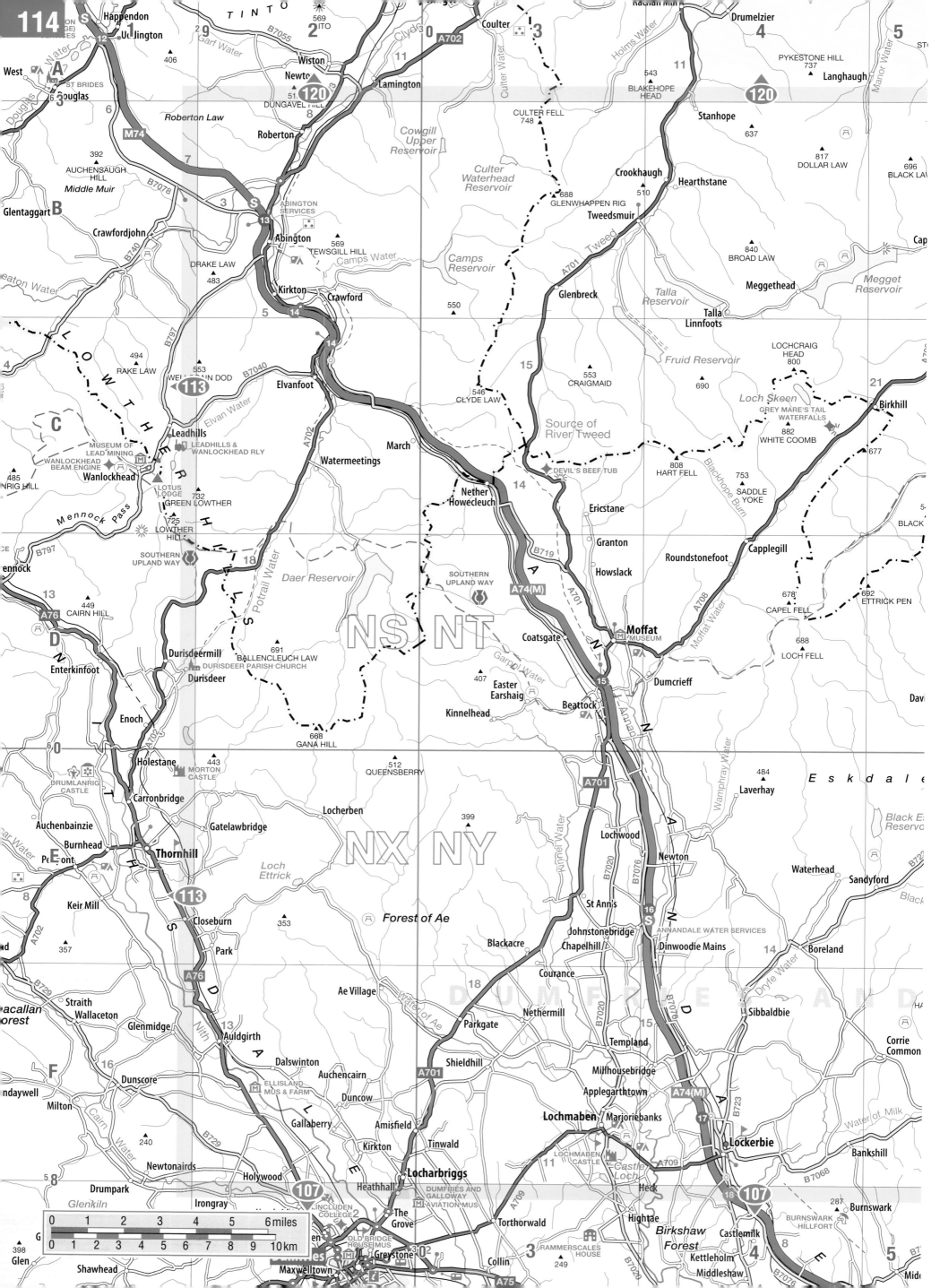

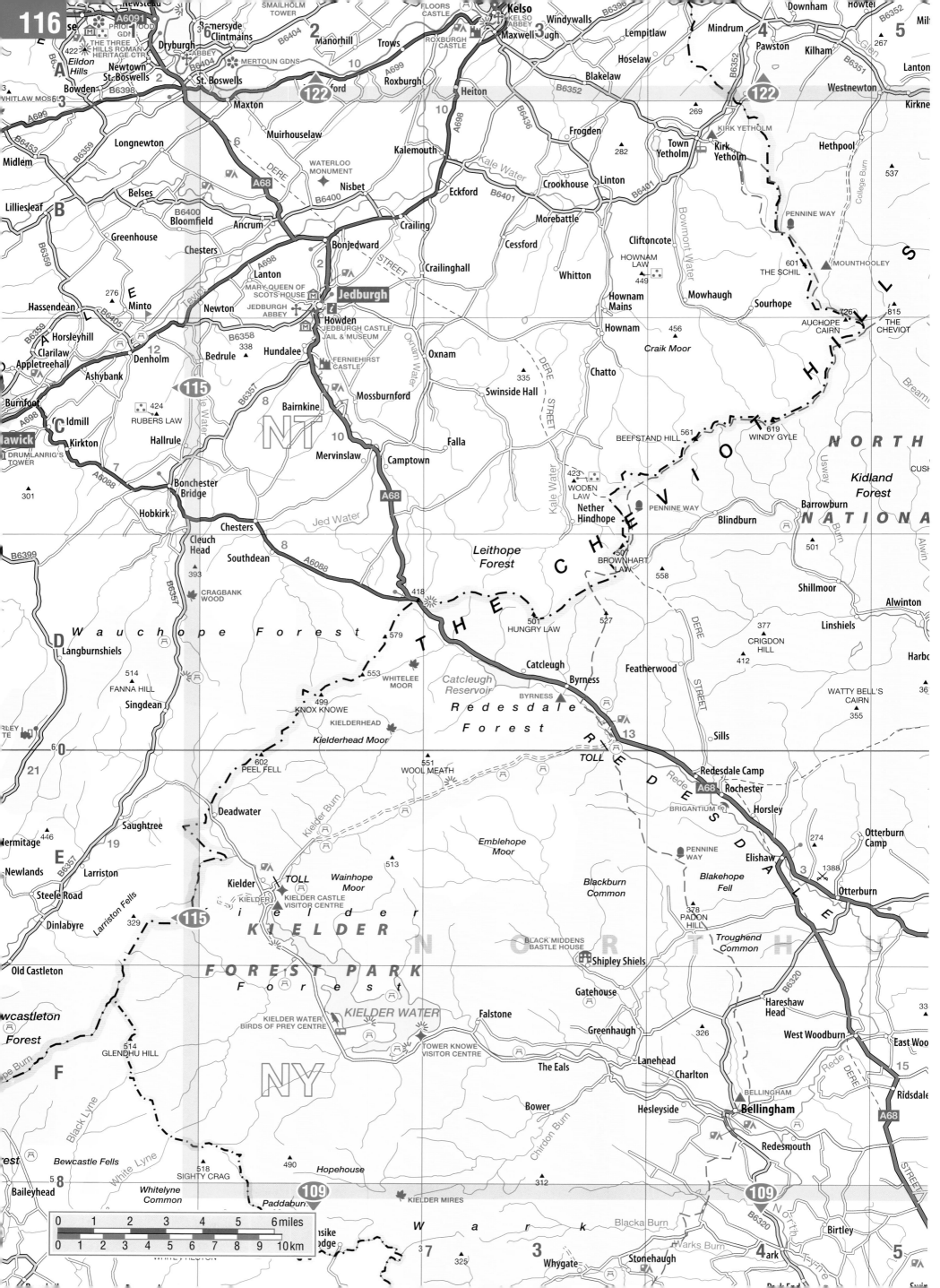

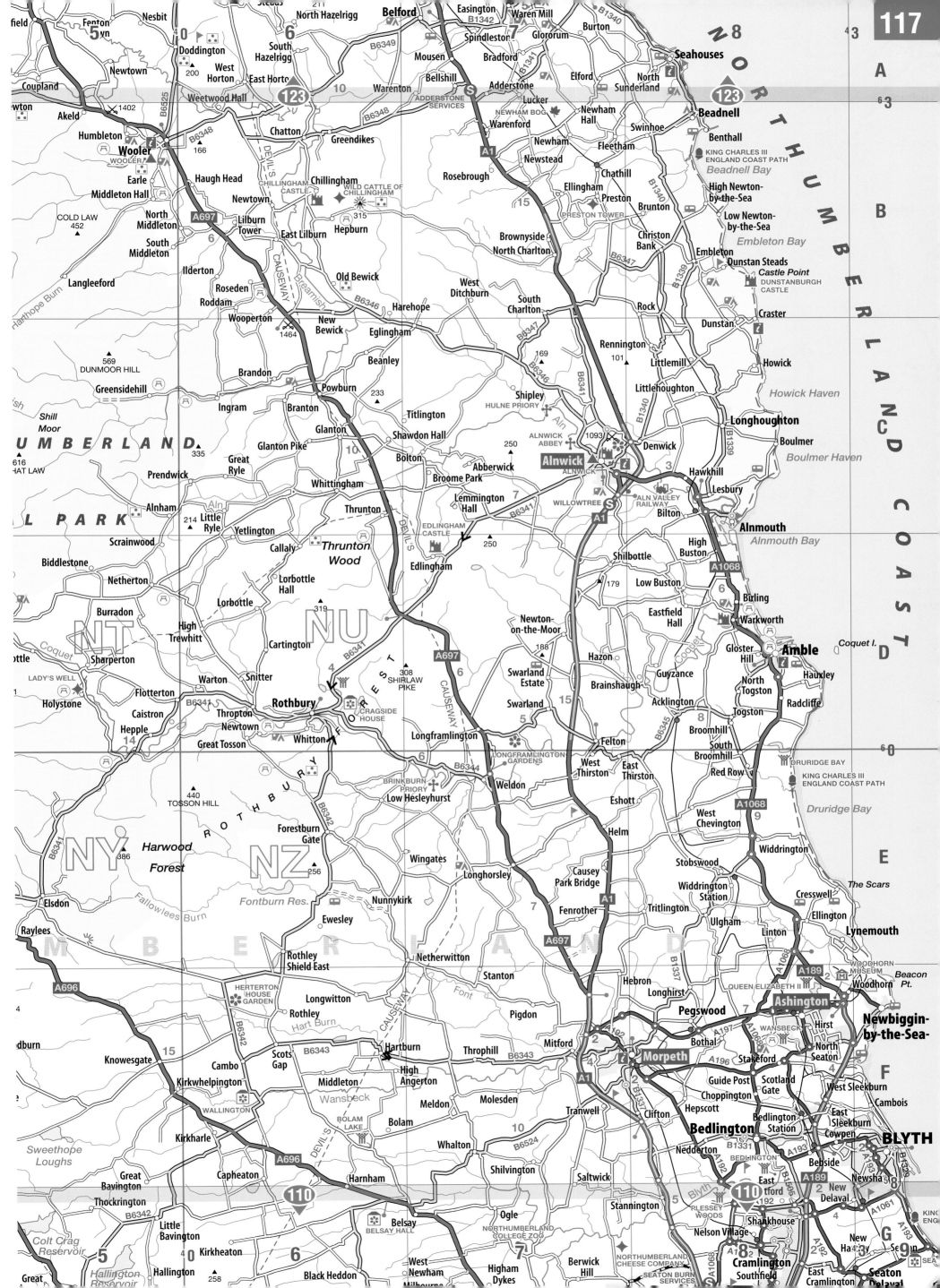

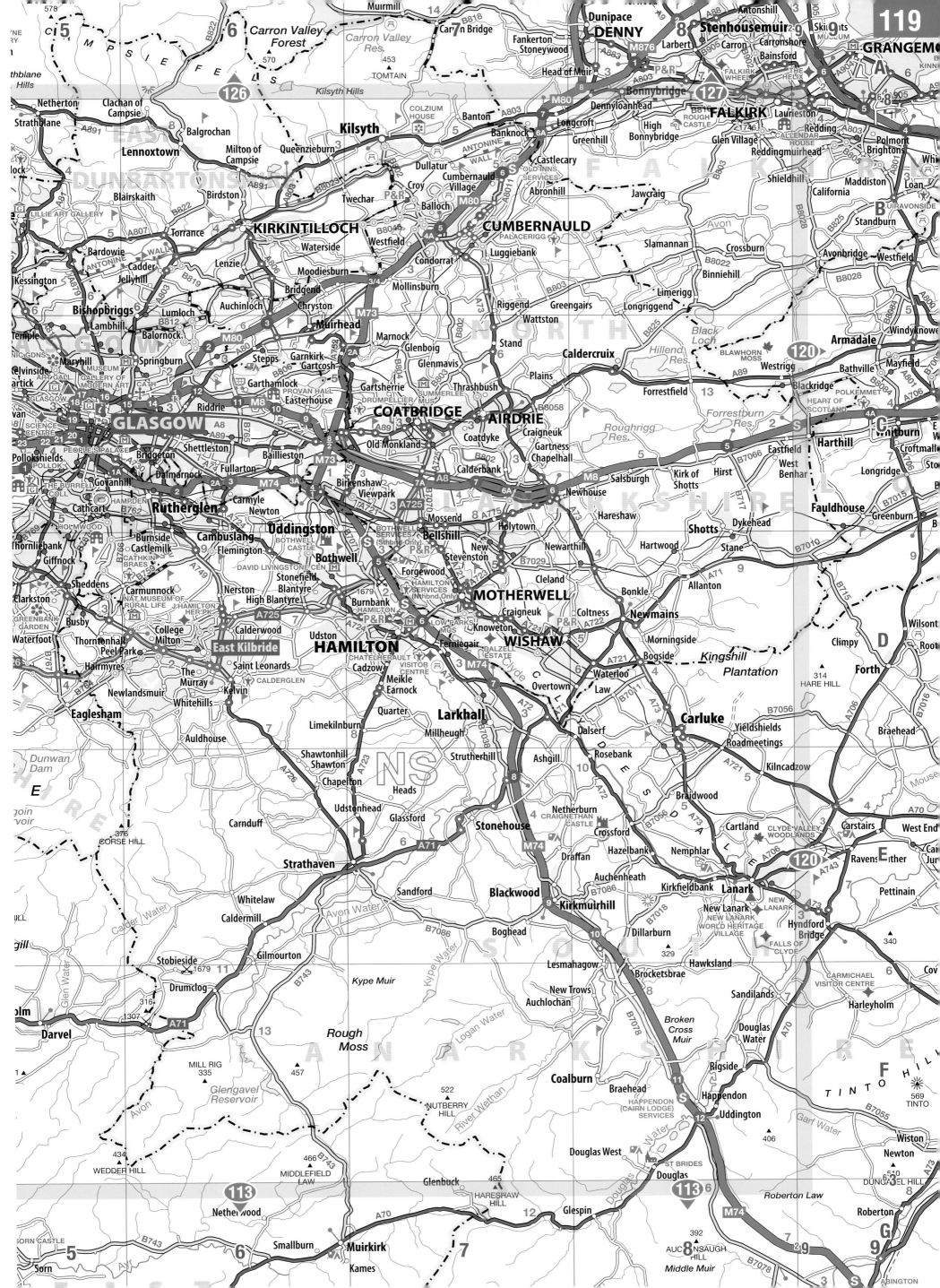

5   40   6   7   8   43   9

A

⁶8

B

Bay

M EYEMOUTH MUSEUM
emouth   C

NU

th

5   D

Lamberton
Beach
mberton

lappers
1333   Highfields   NORTHUMBERLAND

East   **Berwick-upon-Tweed**
B6461   Ord   M BERWICK-UPON-TWEED
5   Tweedmouth   BARRACKS & MAIN GUARD
end   Spittal   BERWICK
Tweed   Priory
A698   Park   Redshin Cove
108   A167
Murton   Scremerston   NORTH COAST
Thornton

West Allerdean   Cheswick
Shoresdean
Ancroft   Goswick   E
B6354   North Low
B6525
Berrington   Haggerston
Bowsden   South Low
A1   Beal   LINDISFARNE
82   12   Emmanuel Hd.
B6353   Causeway   Holy   *Holy Island*
Barmoor   West   Holy   Island   *(Lindisfarne)*
Barmoor   Lane End   Kyloe   Island   LINDISFARNE CASTLE
Castle   Fenwick   Sands   Castle Pt.
HERSLAW   West   Fenham   HERITAGE   LINDISFARNE
MILL   Kyloe   East   CENTRE   PRIORY
ADY WATERFORD HALL   Kyloe   Guile
157   Kyloe   Buckton   Pt.
Hills
Farne
Islands
B6353   Elwick   Ross
Kimmerston   Holburn   Budle
Nesbit   Detchant   Bay   Staple Sound
Fenton   Middleton   BAMBURGH   FARNE ISLANDS
Town   Hetton   CASTLE   Inner Sound
Steads   211   Budle
Doddington   North Hazelrigg   Easington   **Bamburgh**   F
200   Belford   5   Waren Mill
West   South   B1342   B1340
Newtown   Horton   Hazelrigg   Spindlestone   Glororum   Burton
East Horton   Mousen   Bradford   Elford   Seahouses
1402   10   Warenton   Bellshill   Adderstone   North
B6525   Weetwood Hall   S   Lucker   Sunderland   63
117   ADDERSTONE   Newham   Bead   117
Humbleton   Chatton   Greendikes   SERVICES   Hall   Benthall
166   NEWHAM BOG   Warenford   Swinhoe   KING CHARLES III
WOOLER   B6348   Newham   ENGLAND COAST PATH
Wooler   A1   Fleetham   *Bead* ll Bay   G
5   Earle   6   Chillingham   7   Newstead   8   9
Middleton Hall   Haugh Head   Chillingham   WILD CATTLE OF   Rosebrough   Chathill   High Newton-
Newtown   CHILLINGHAM   Ellingham   Preston   by-the-Sea
15

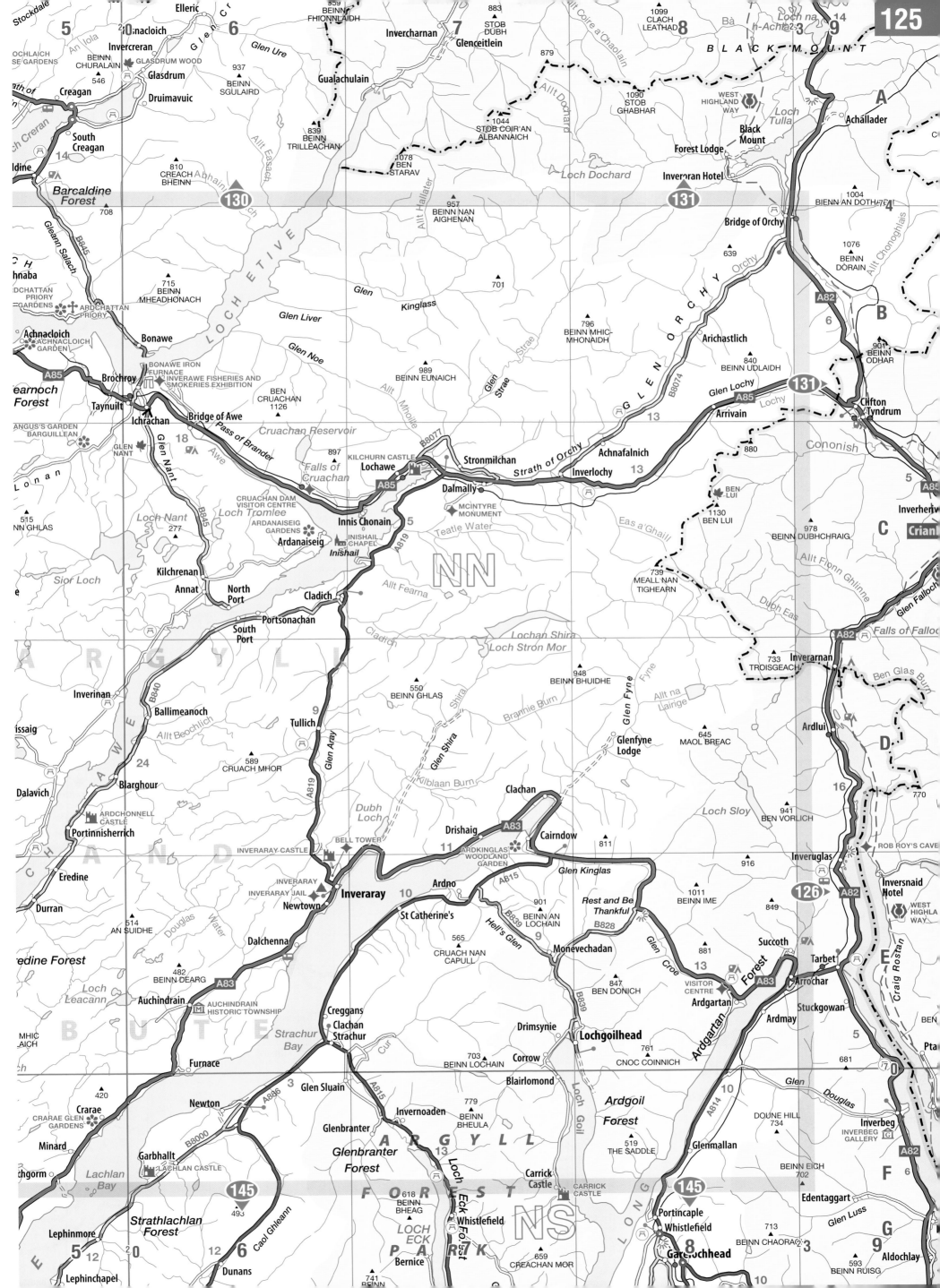

A

B

C

D

E

F

G

5 6 7 8 37 9

Dundee
Newport-on-Tay
Tayport
Tentsmuir Forest
Cupar
St Andrews
ST ANDREWS BAY
Eden Mouth
Leuchars
Guardbridge
Crail
Anstruther Easter
Pittenweem Anstruther Wester
St Monans
Elie
Earlsferry
Leven
Methil
Buckhaven
Isle of May
NO
NT
F O R T H
North Berwick
Bass Rock
Gullane
Dirleton
Aberlady
Dunbar
East Linton

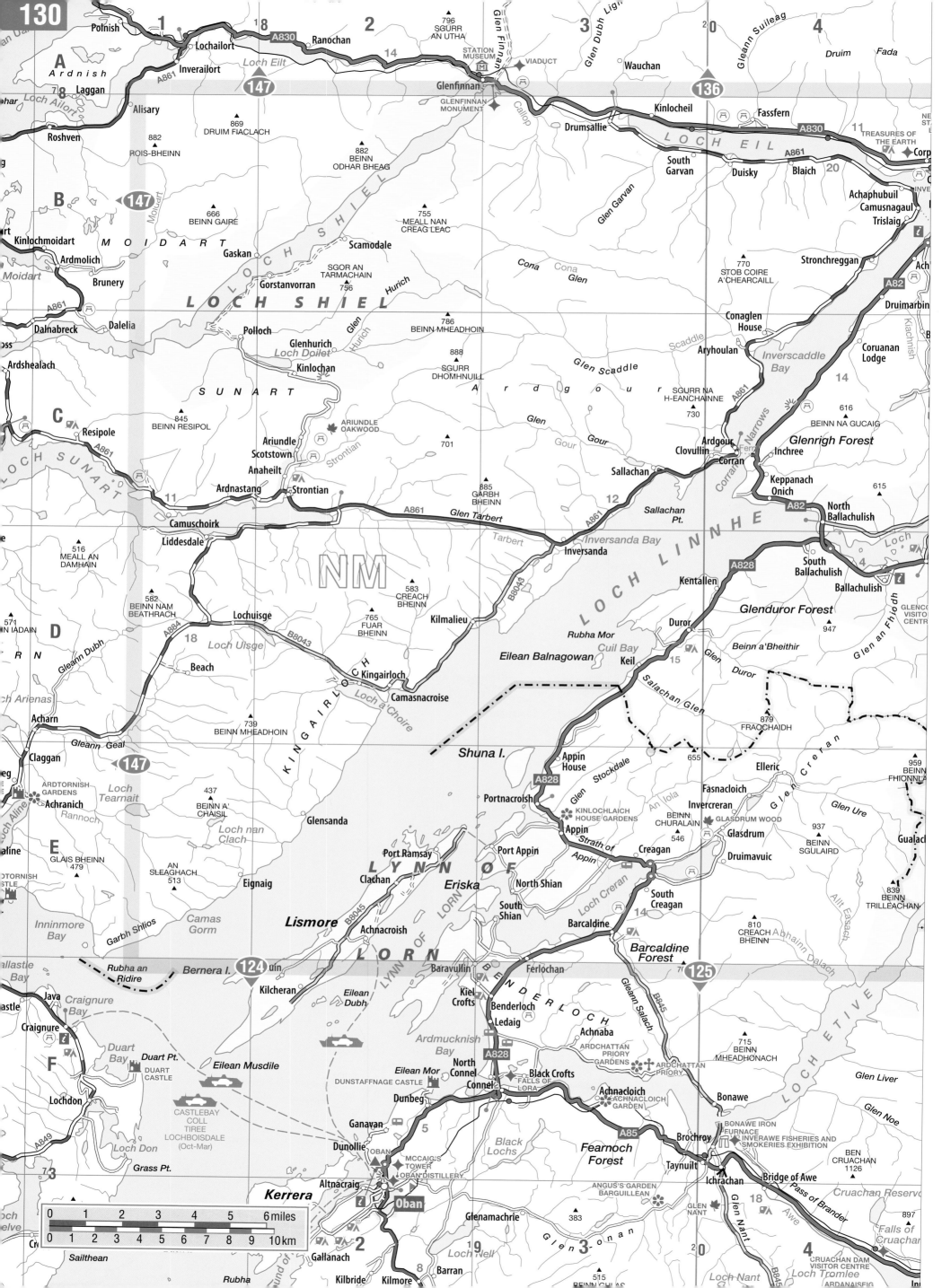

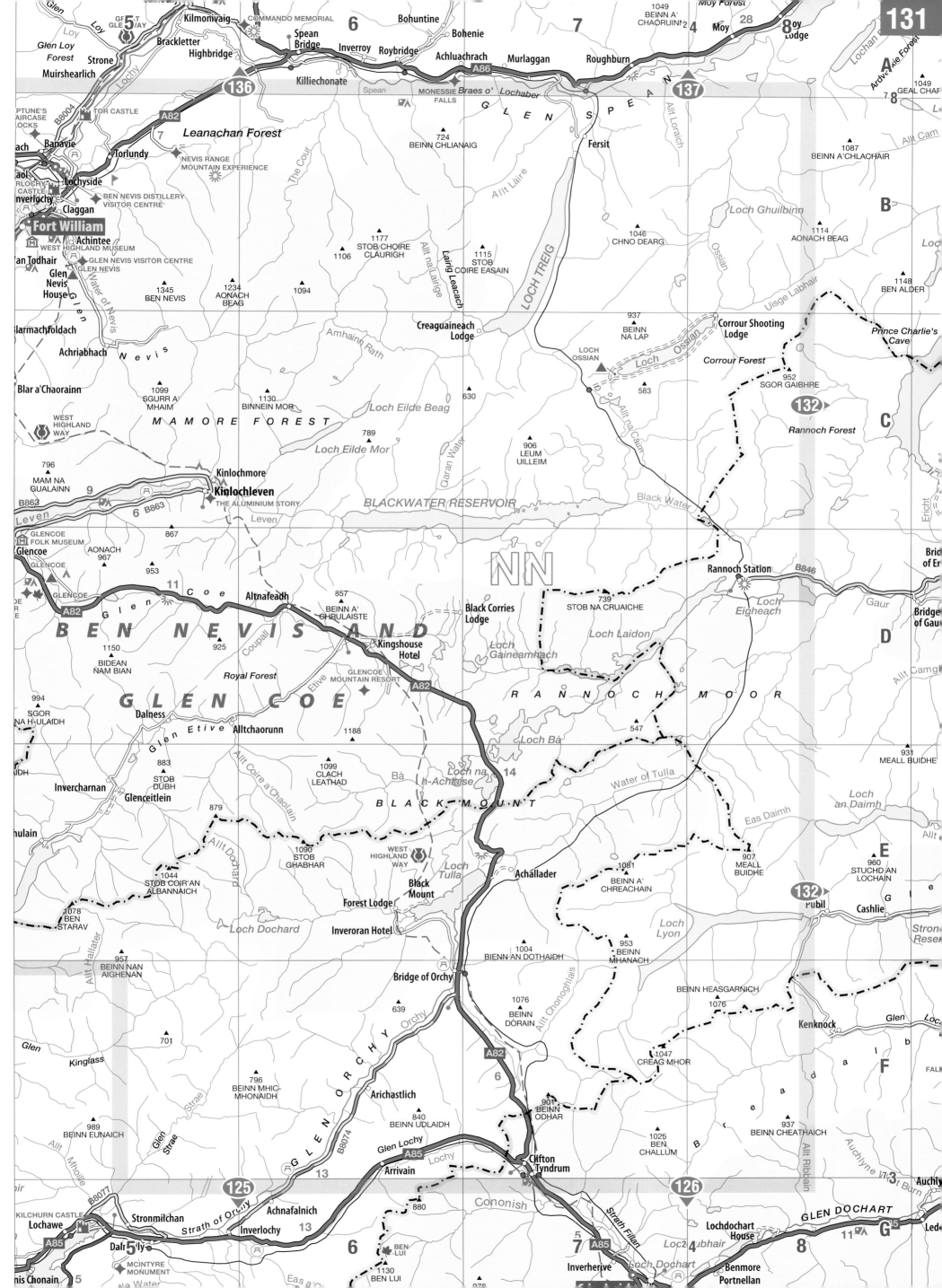

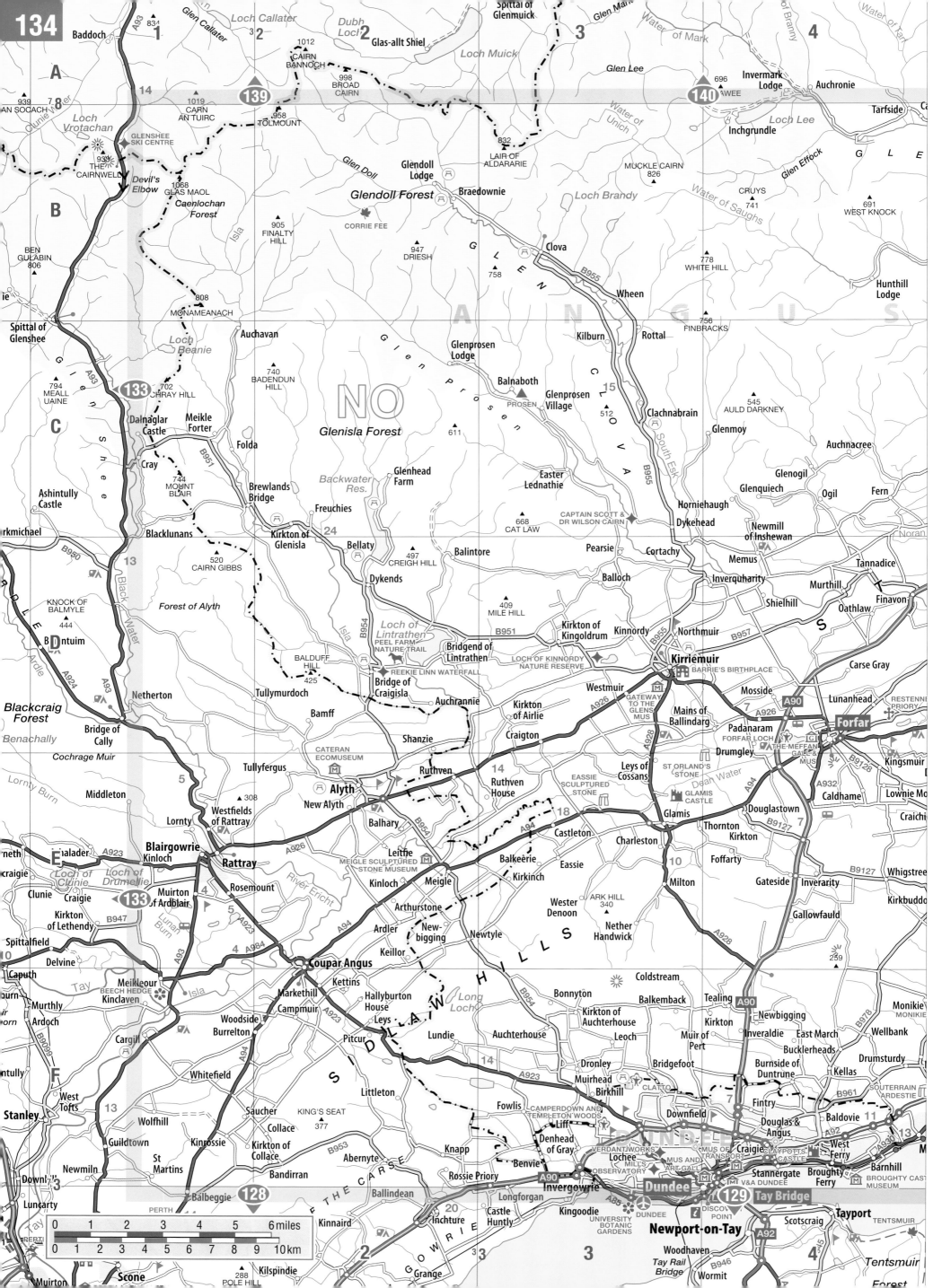

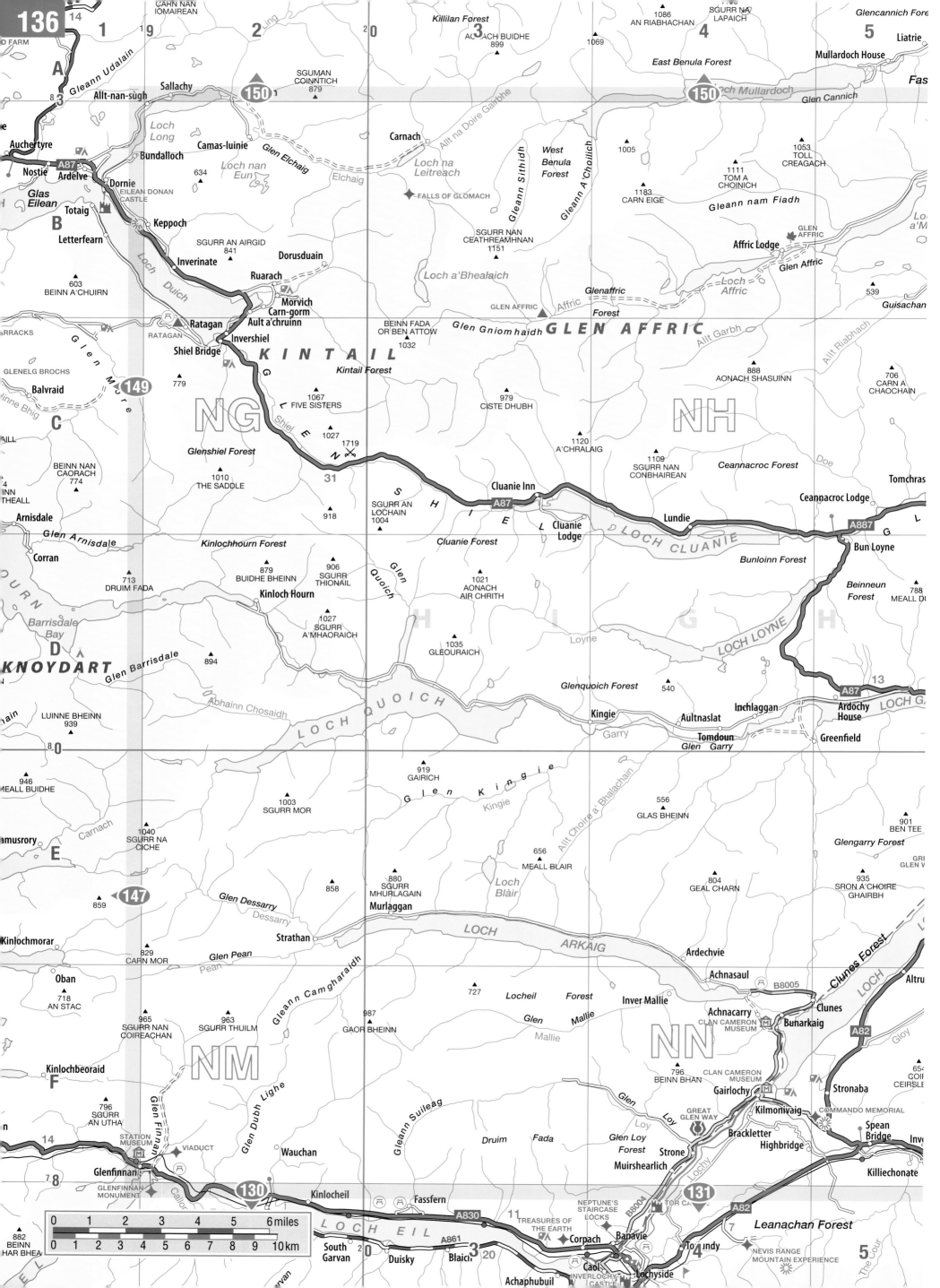

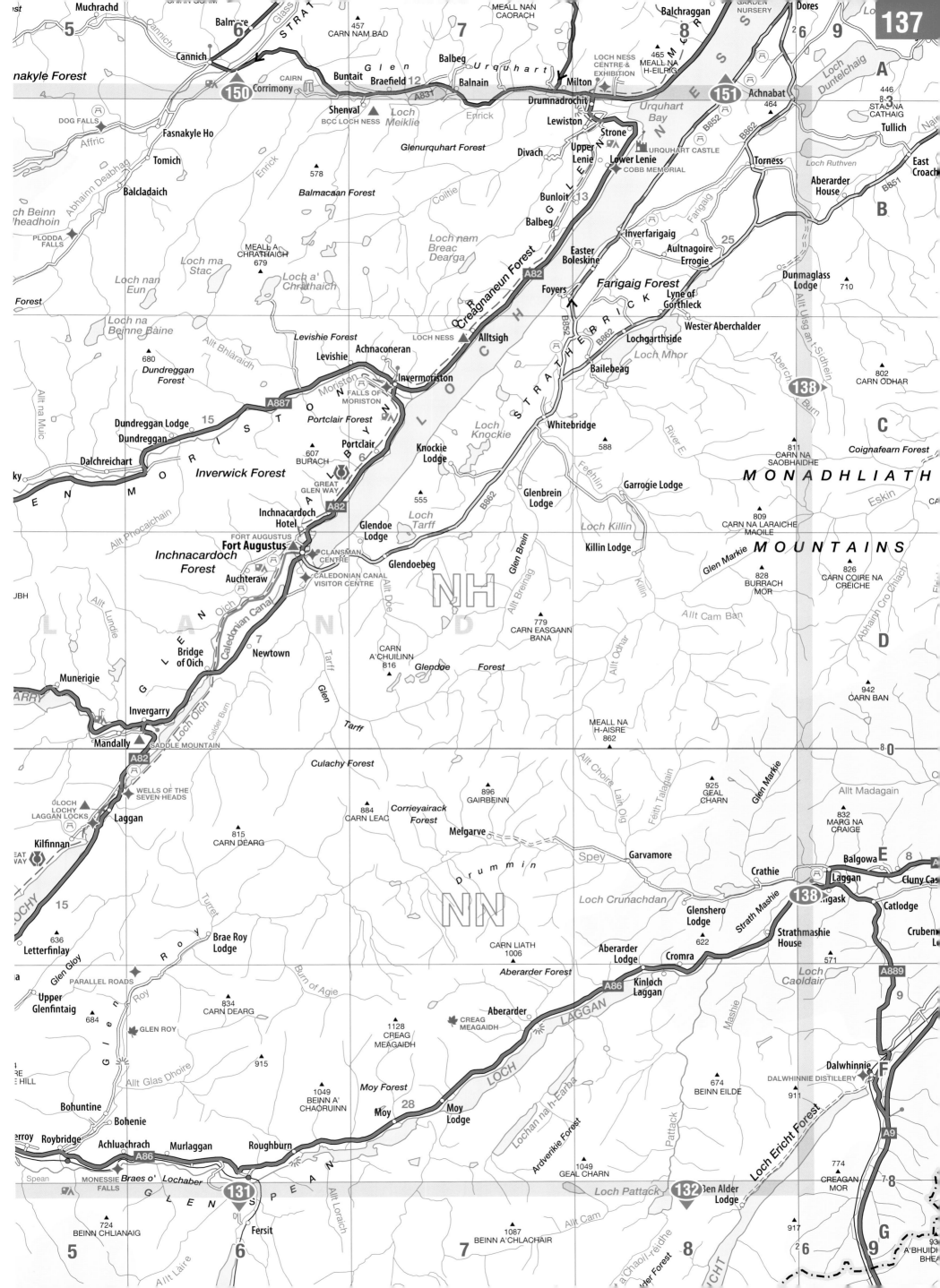

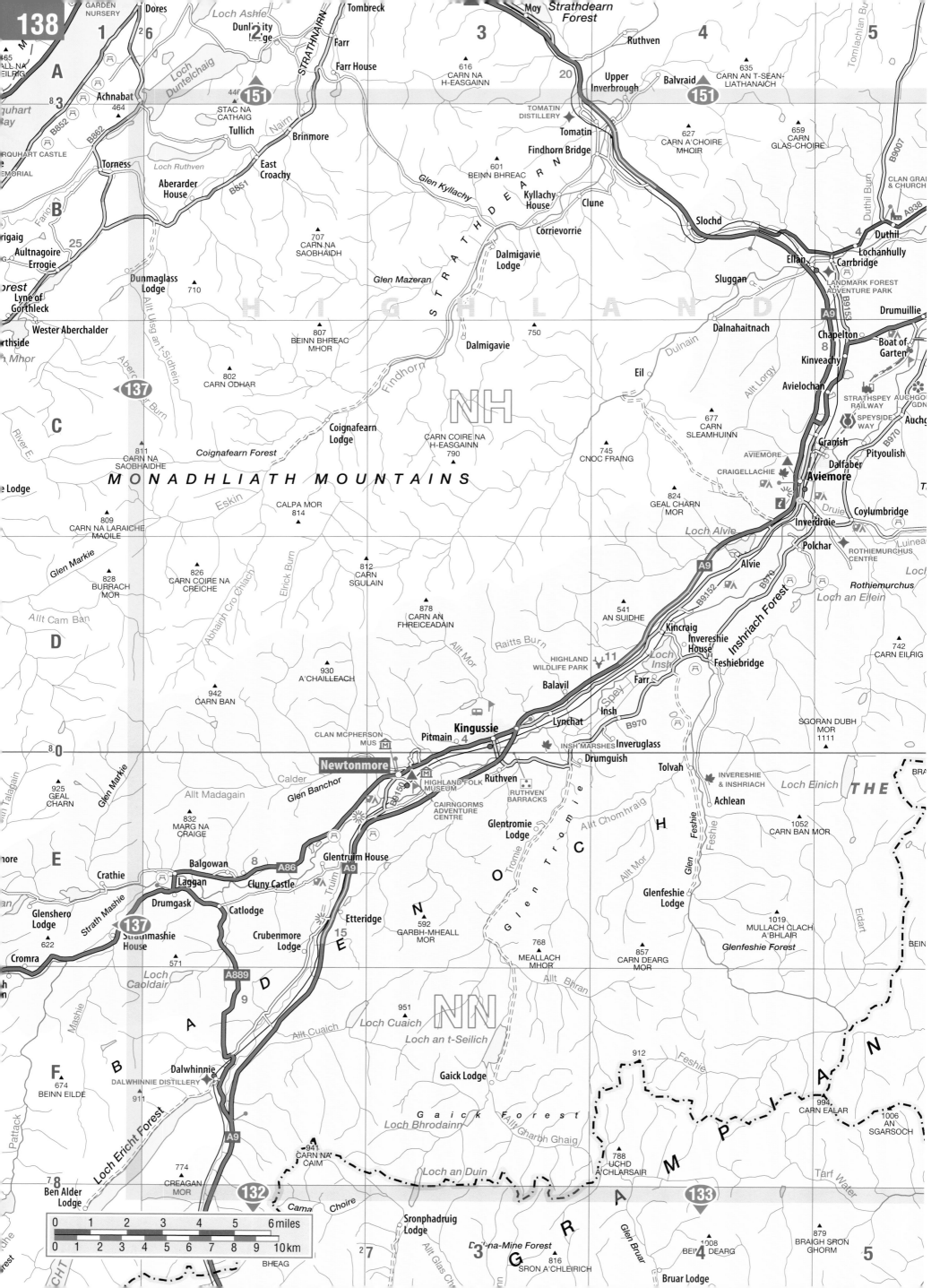

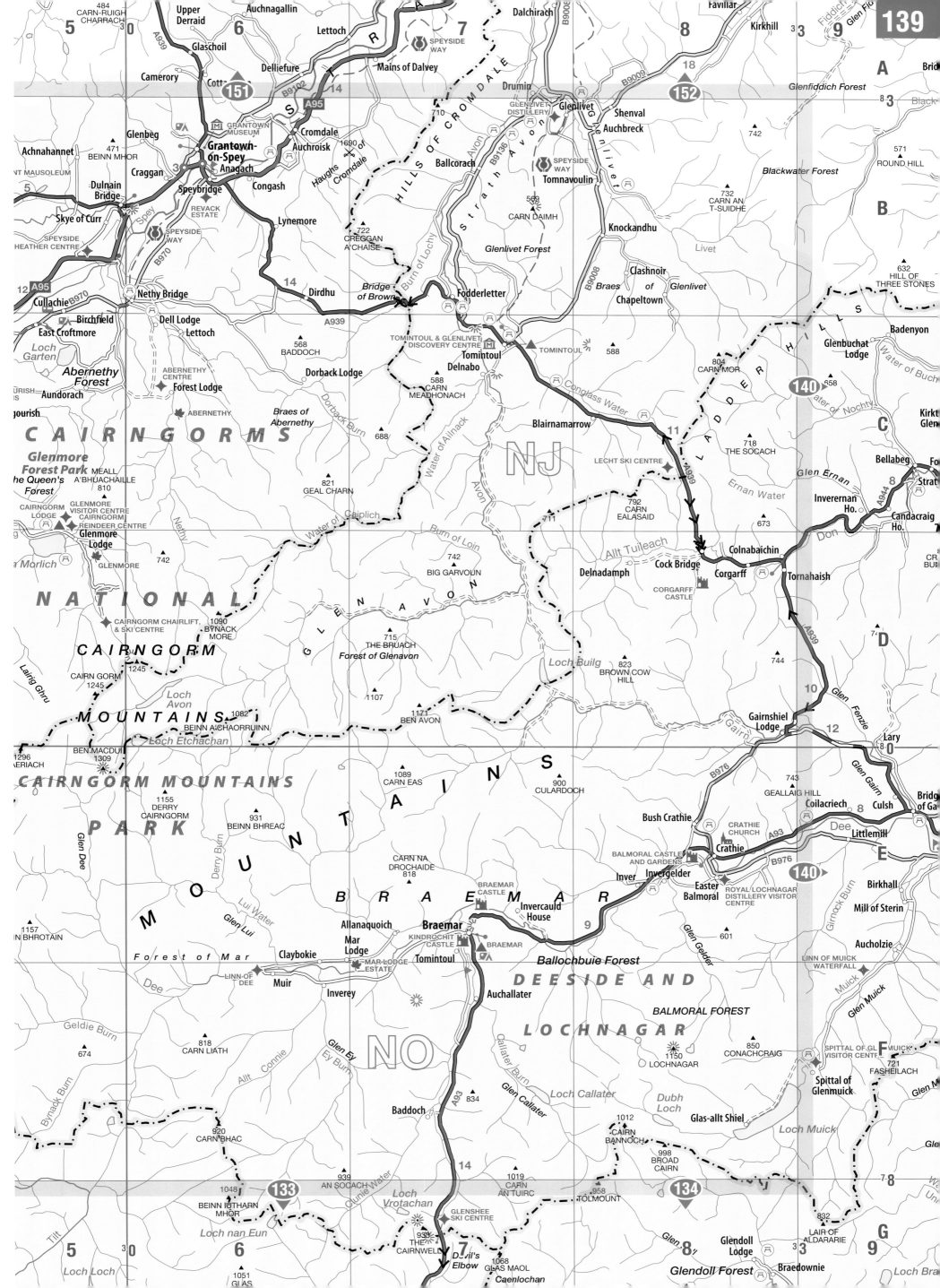

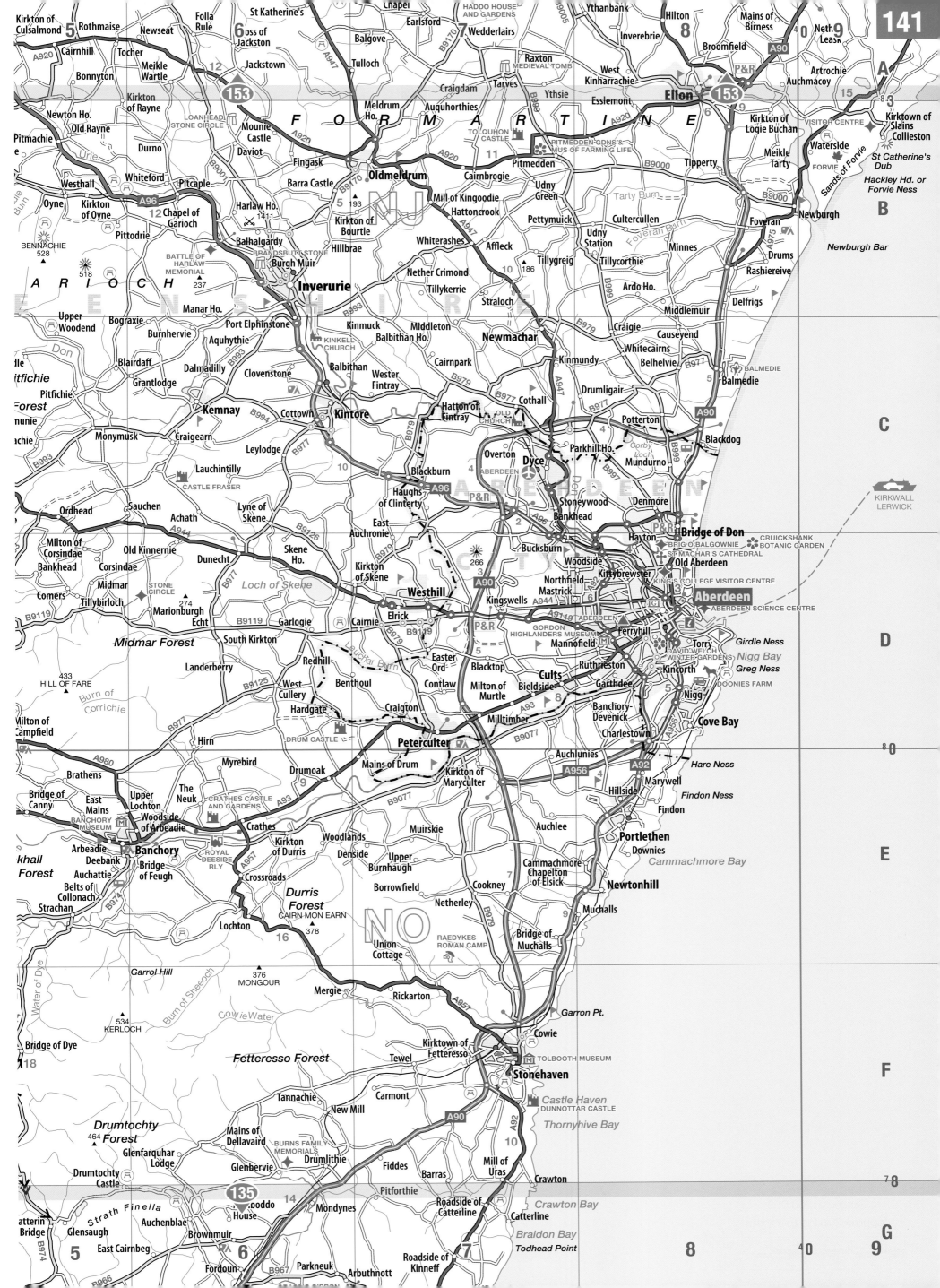

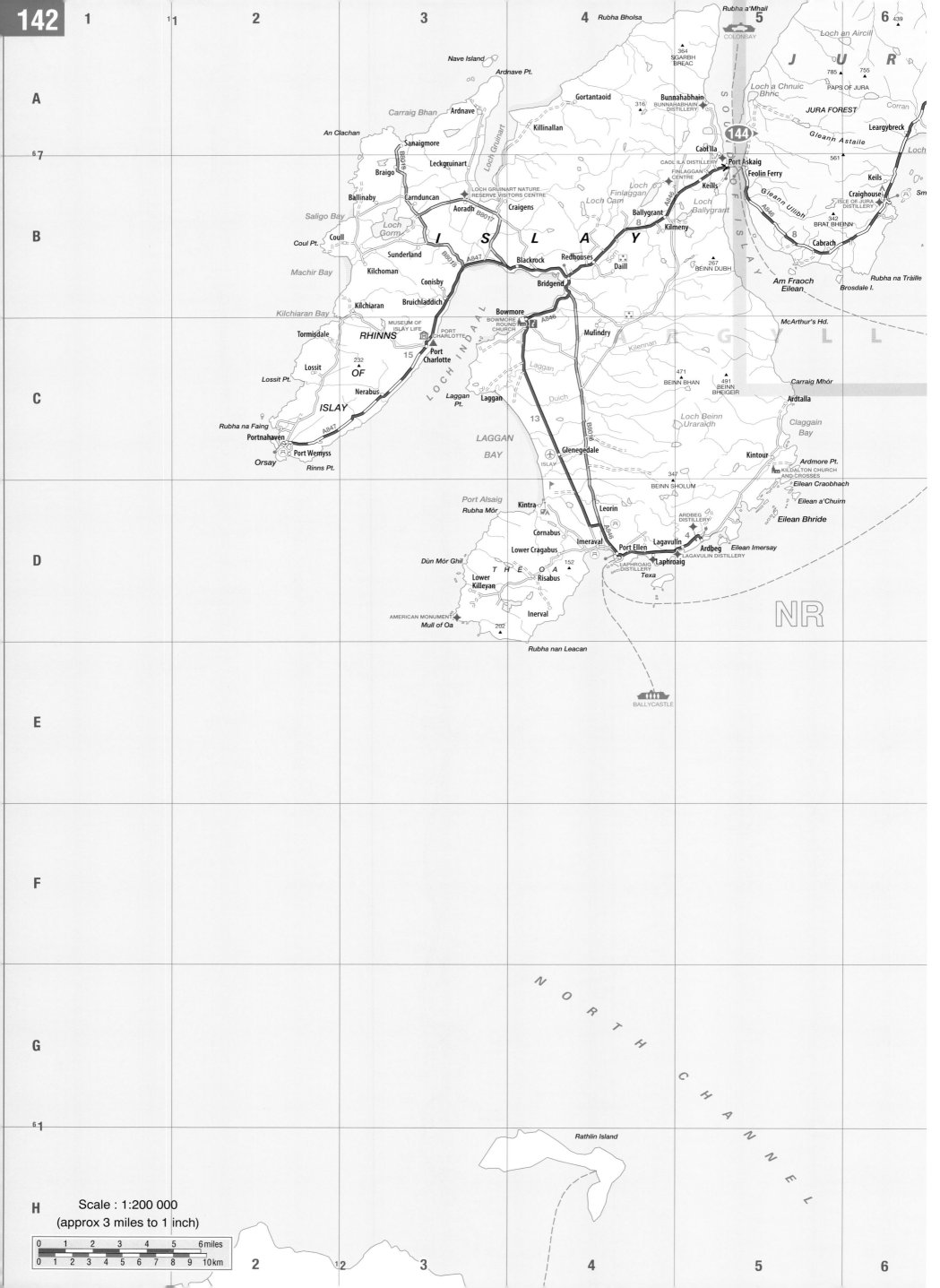

1   1   2   3   4   5   6 439

A

7

J U R A

Rubha Bholsa
Rubha a'Mhail
COLONSAY

Nave Island
Ardnave Pt.

364
SGARBH
BREAC

Loch an Aircill

785   755

Loch a Chnuic
Bhric

PAPS OF JURA

JURA FOREST

Corran

Leargybreck

Gleann Astaile

Loch

Gortantaoid

Bunnahabhain
BUNNAHABHAIN
DISTILLERY

An Clachan

Carraig Bhan   Ardnave

Sanaigmore

Killinallan

316

Keils

561

Leckgruinart

144

Caol Ila
CAOL ILA DISTILLERY

Port Askaig
Feolin Ferry

Craighouse
ISLE OF JURA
DISTILLERY

Braigo

B8018

Gleann Uillibh

Keills

Sm

Ballinaby

Carnduncan

LOCH GRUINART NATURE
RESERVE VISITORS CENTRE

Aoradh   B8017

Craigens

I   S   L   A   Y

Loch
Gruinart

FINLAGGAN
CENTRE

A846

Loch
Finlaggan   Ballygrant

Loch
Cam

Kilmeny

342
BRAT BHEINN

Loch
Ballygrant

B

Cabrach

267
BEINN DUBH

Am Fraoch
Eilean

Rubha na Tràille

Brosdale I.

Coul Pt.   Coull

Saligo Bay

Loch
Gorm

Sunderland

Kilchoman

Conisby

A847

B8018

Blackrock

Redhouses

Daill

1245
BEINN DUBH

Machir Bay

Bruichladdich

Bridgend

Kilchiaran Bay   Kilchiaran

MUSEUM OF
ISLAY LIFE

Port
Charlotte

Bowmore
BOWMORE
ROUND CHURCH

A846

Mulindry

Kilennan

A   R   G   Y   L   L

McArthur's Hd.

Tormisdale   RHINNS   15   Port Charlotte

Lossit   232

OF

Laggan
Pt.   Laggan

Laggan

Duich

471
BEINN BHAN

491
BEINN
BHEIGEIR

Carraig Mhór

Ardtalla

C

Lossit Pt.   Nerabus

ISLAY   13

Loch Beinn
Uraraidh

Claggain
Bay

Rubha na Faing

LAGGAN

Kintour

Ardmore Pt.

Portnahaven

A847

B8016

Glenegedale

KILDALTON CHURCH
AND CROSSES

Orsay   Port Wemyss

Rinns Pt.

BAY   ISLAY

347
BEINN SHOLUM

Eilean Craobhach

Eilean a'Chuirn

Eilean Bhride

Port Alsaig

Rubha Mór

Kintra

Leorin

ARDBEG
DISTILLERY

Dùn Mór Ghil

Cornabus

Imeraval

A846

Port Ellen

Lagavulin
4   Ardbeg

Eilean Imersay

D

THE OA

Lower Cragabus

Risabus

152

LAPHROAIG
DISTILLERY

Laphroaig
Texa

LAGAVULIN DISTILLERY

Lower
Killeyan

Inerval

NR

AMERICAN MONUMENT
Mull of Oa   202

Rubha nan Leacan

BALLYCASTLE

E

F

G

N   O   R   T   H   C   H   A   N   N   E   L

Rathlin Island

H

Scale : 1:200 000
(approx 3 miles to 1 inch)

0 1 2 3 4 5 6miles
0 1 2 3 4 5 6 7 8 9 10km

1   2   3   4   5   6

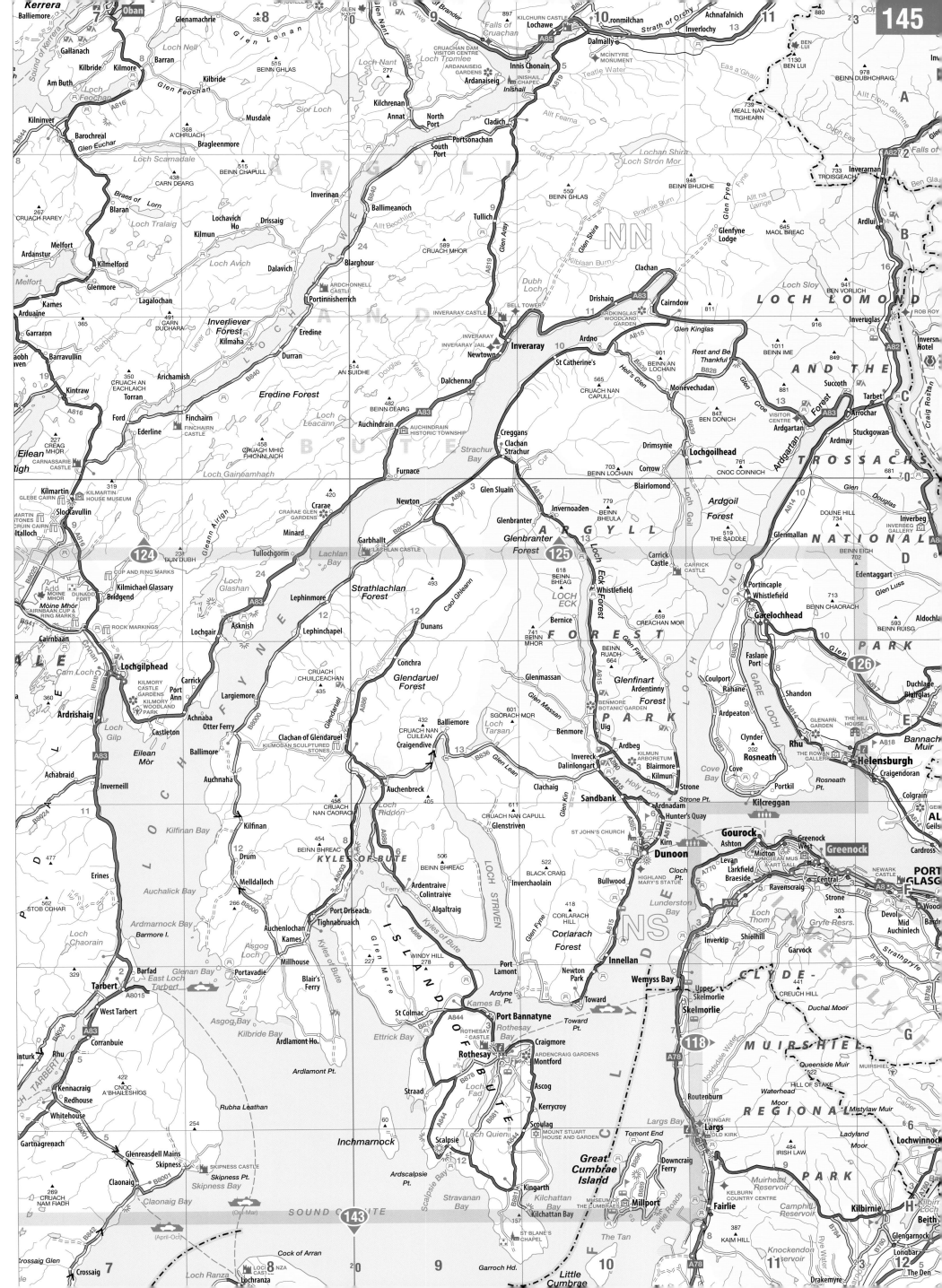

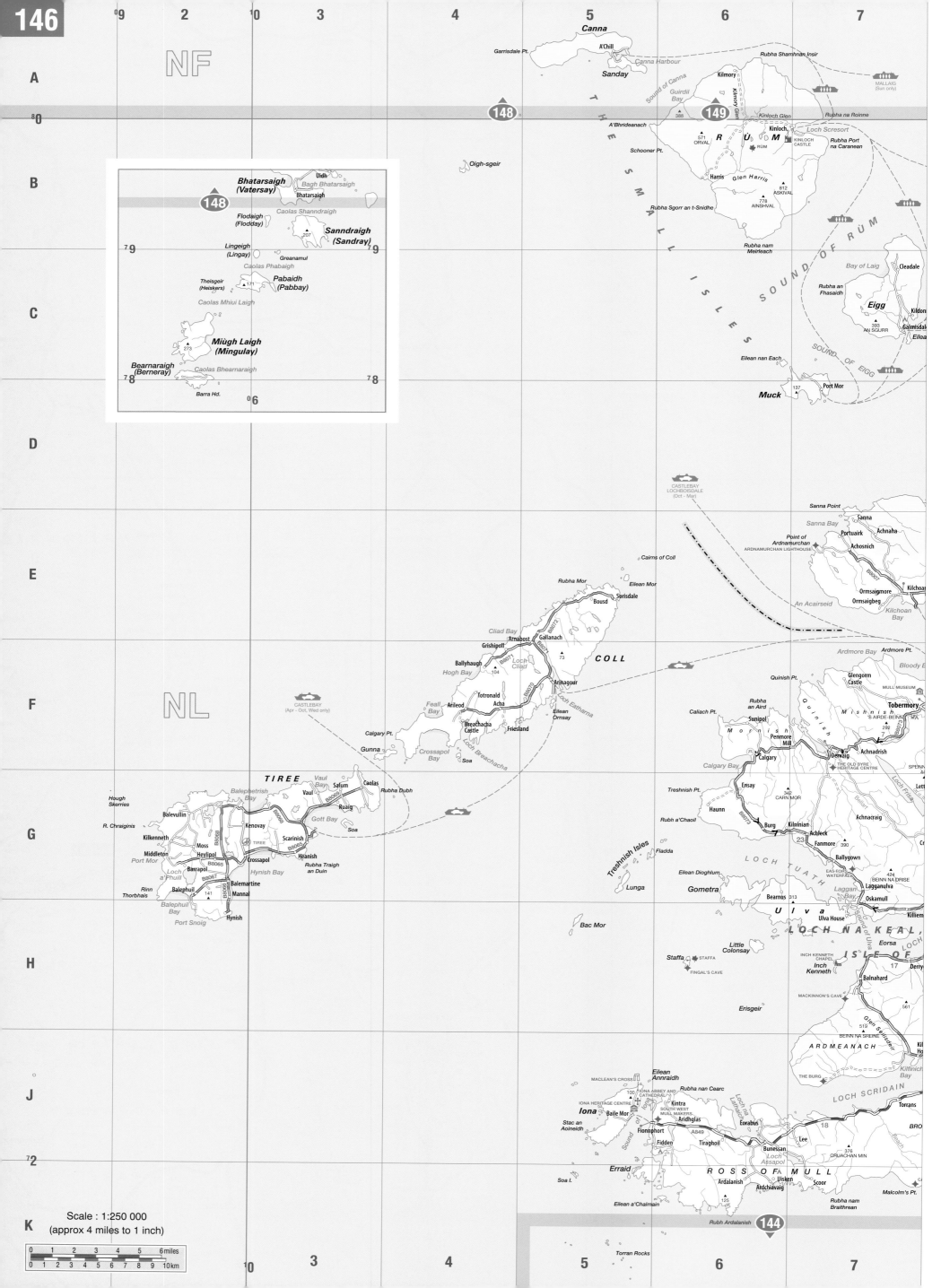

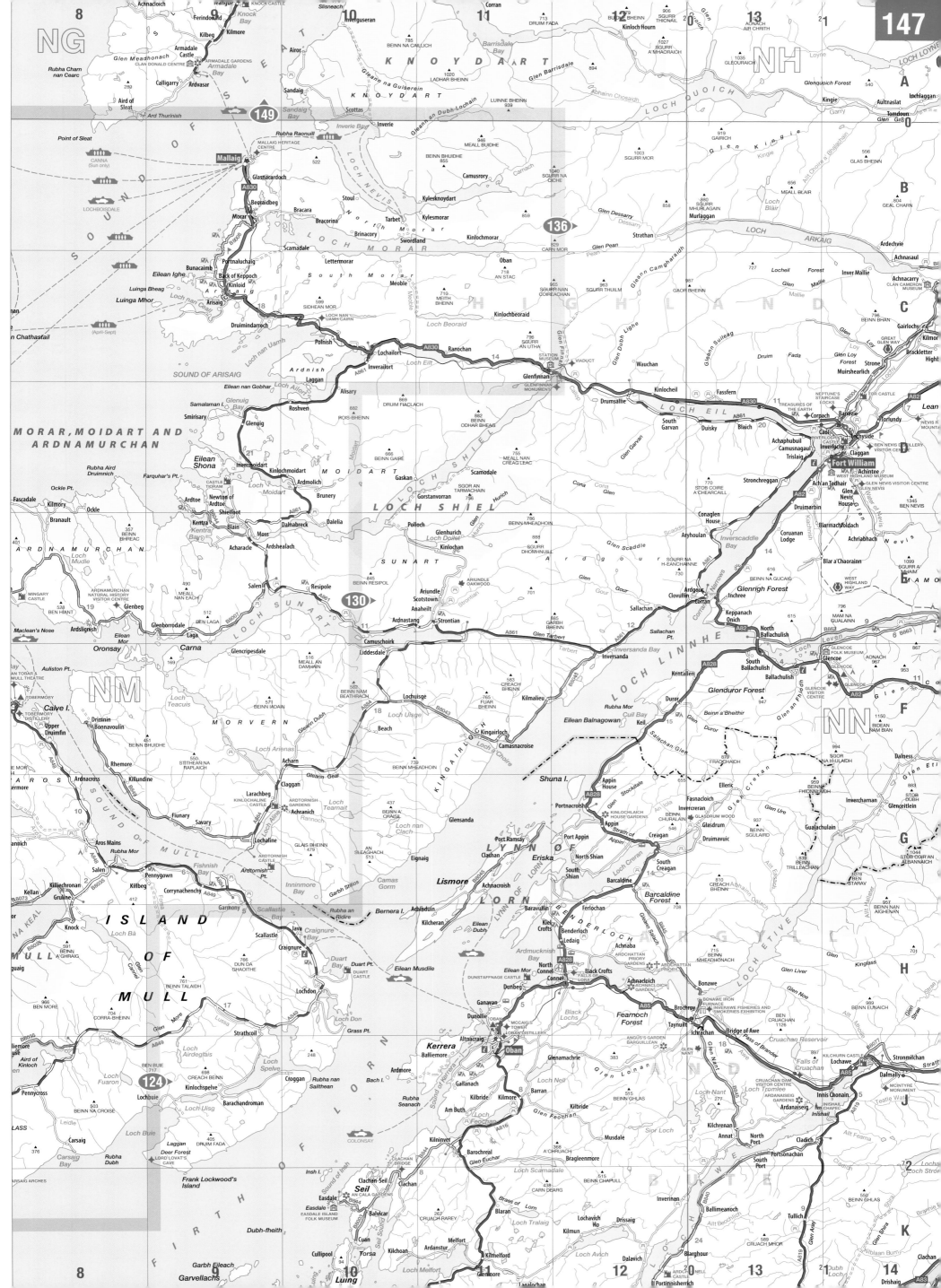

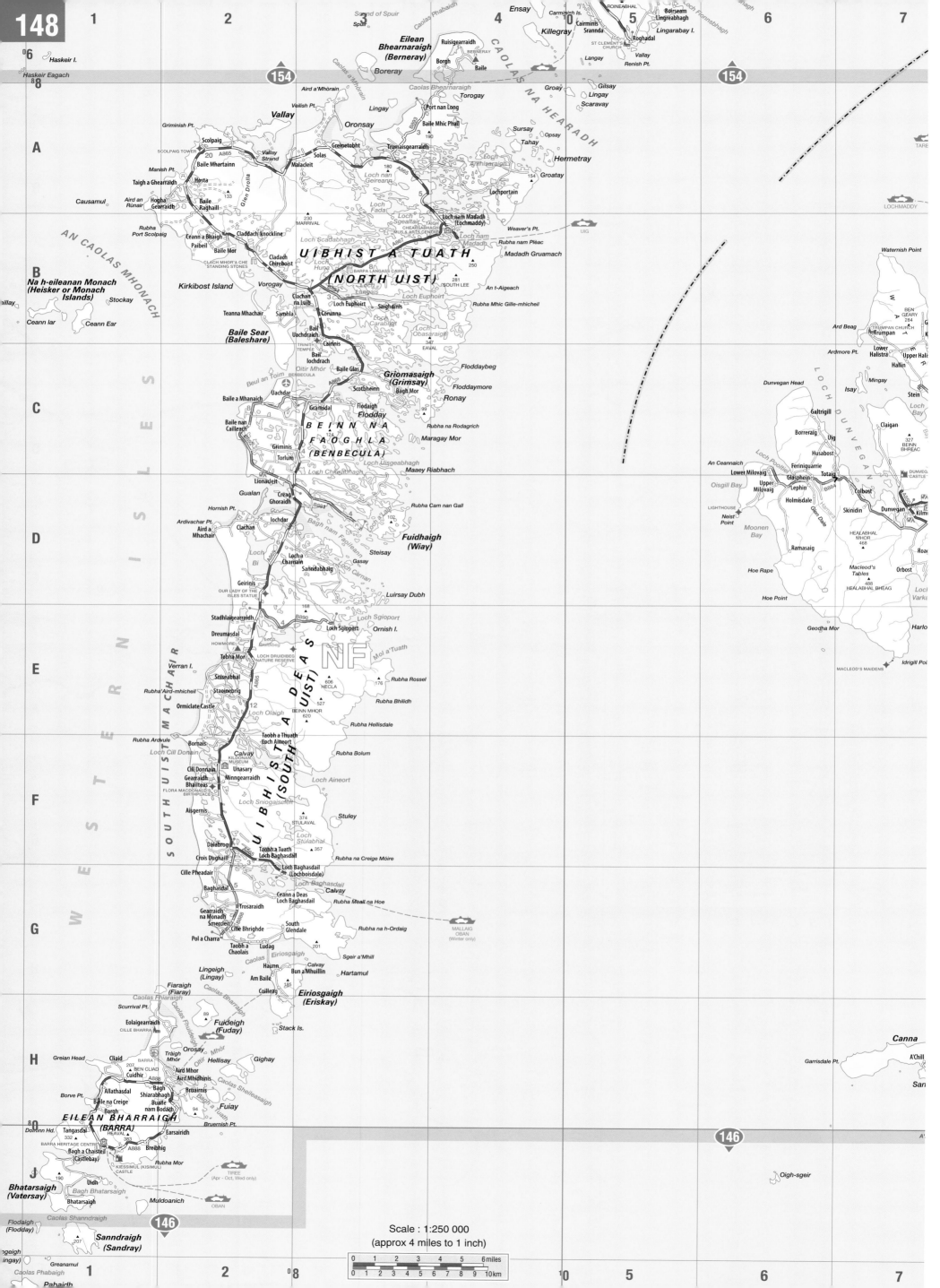

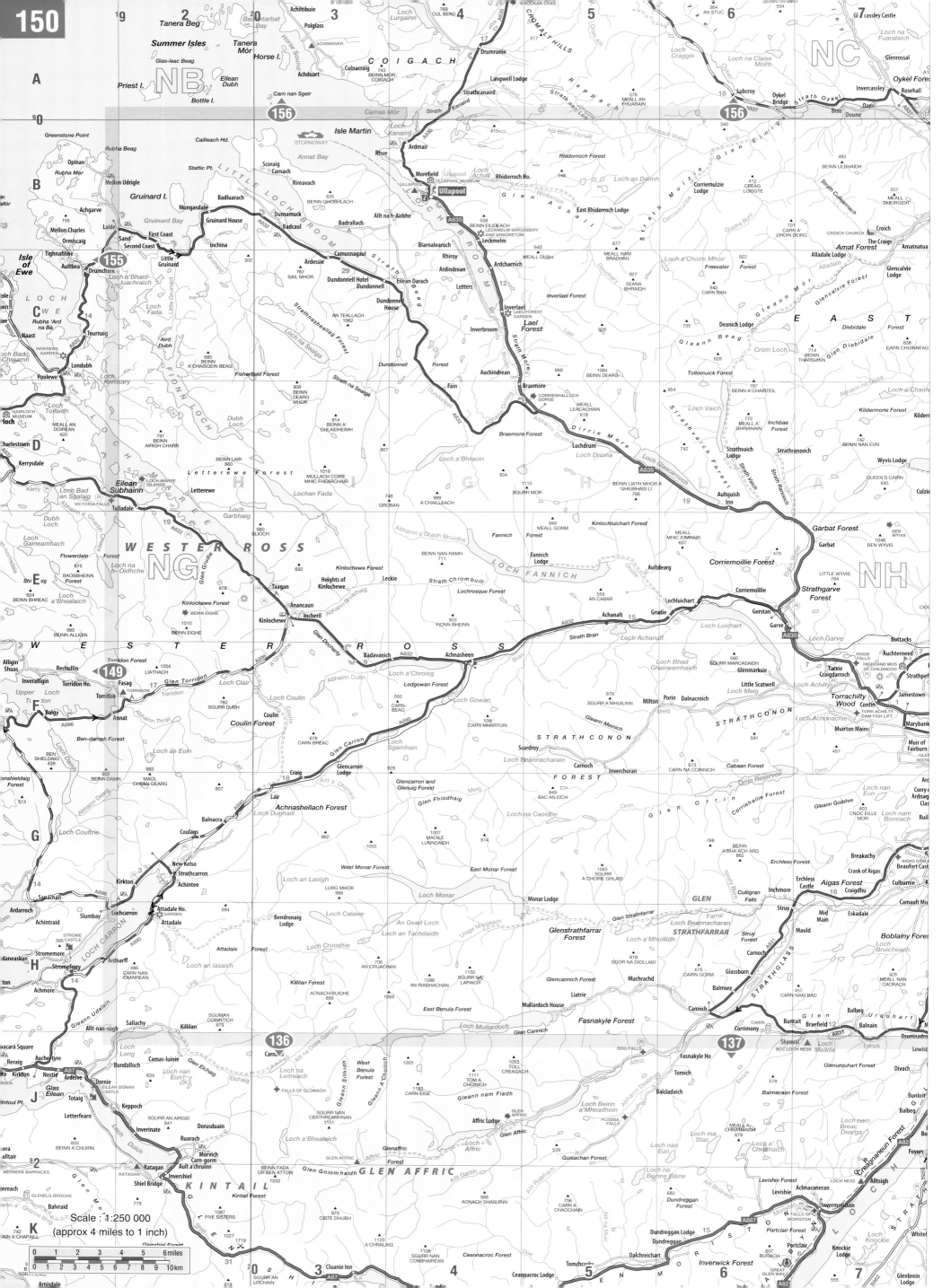

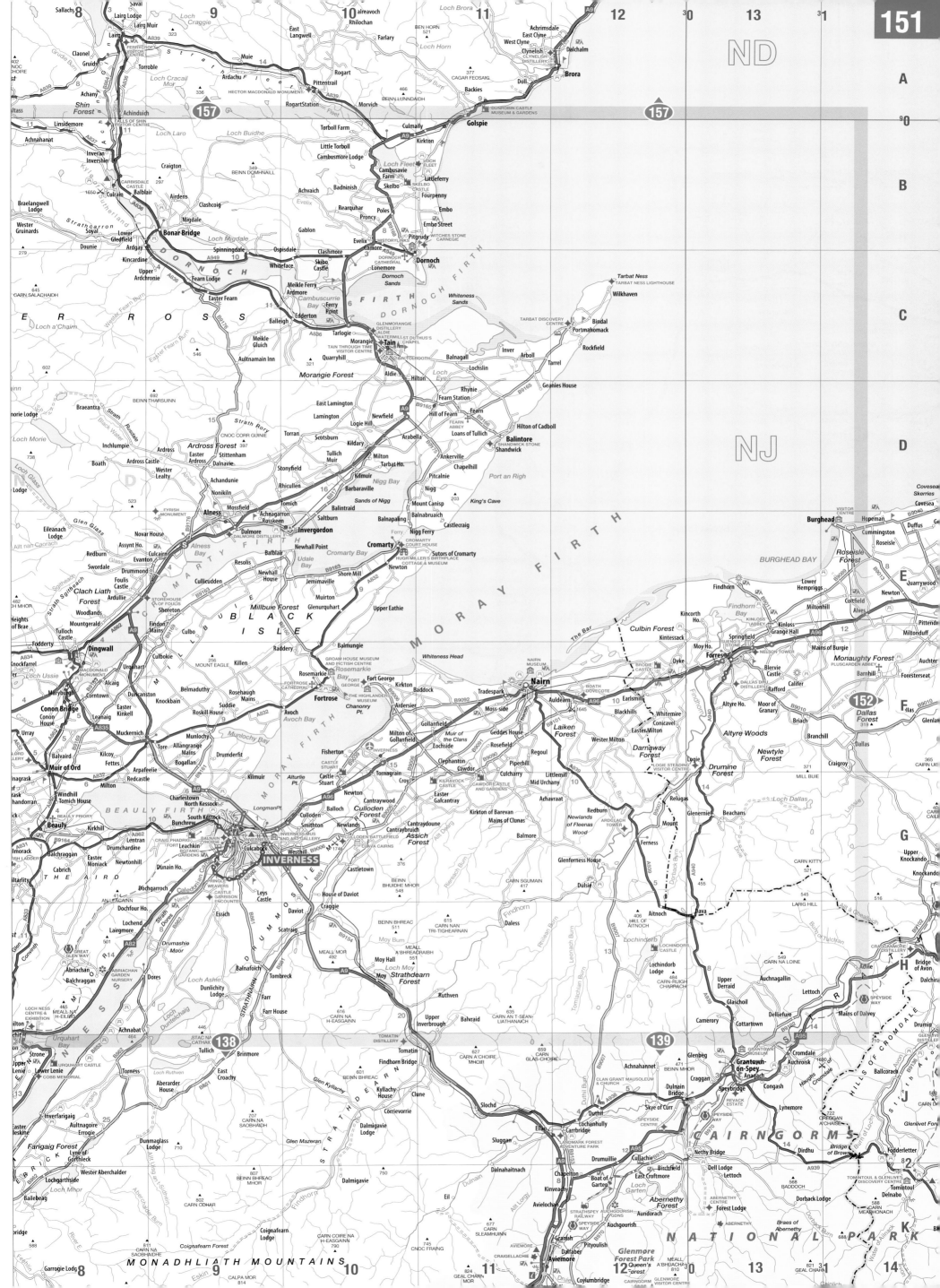

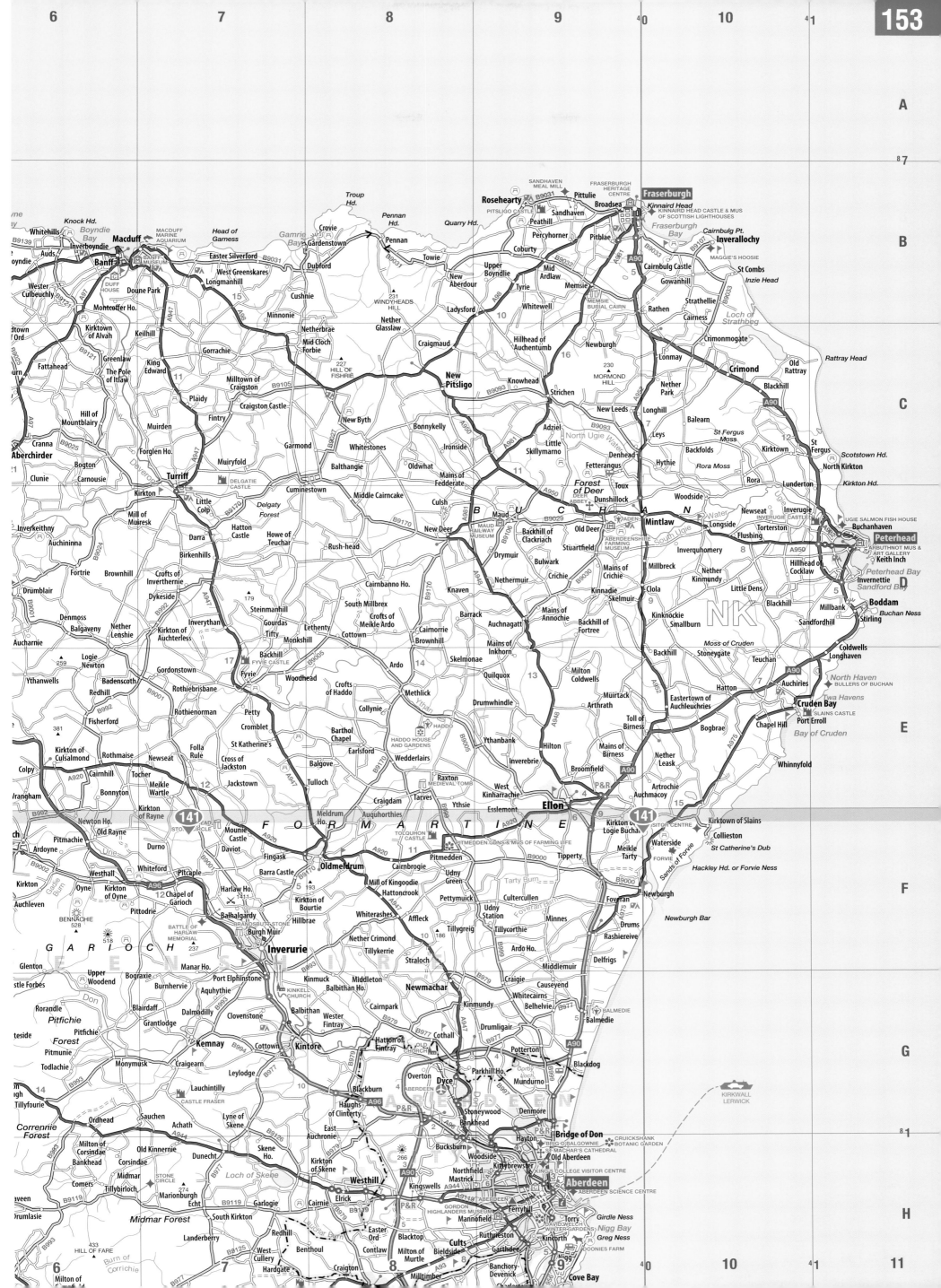

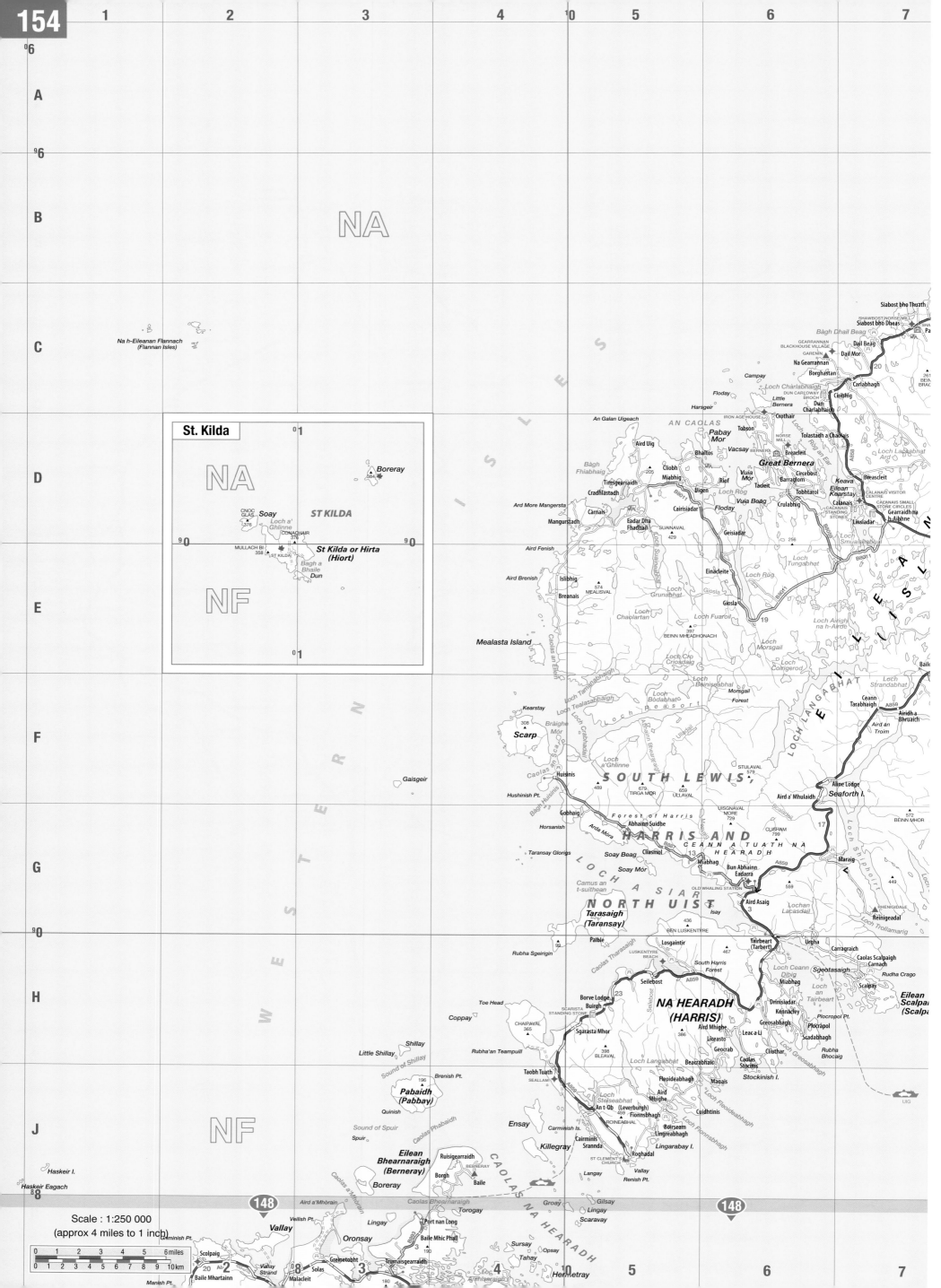

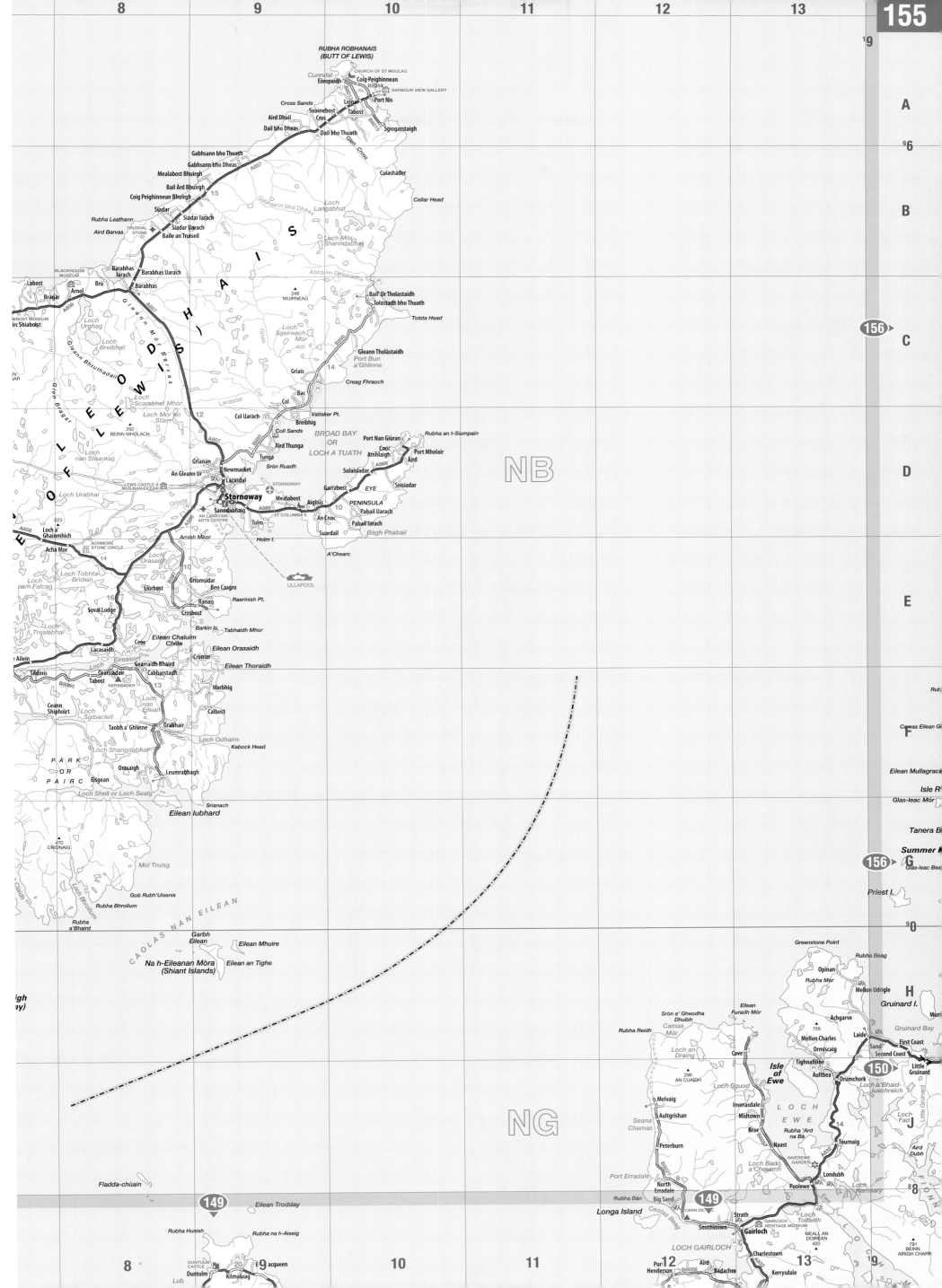

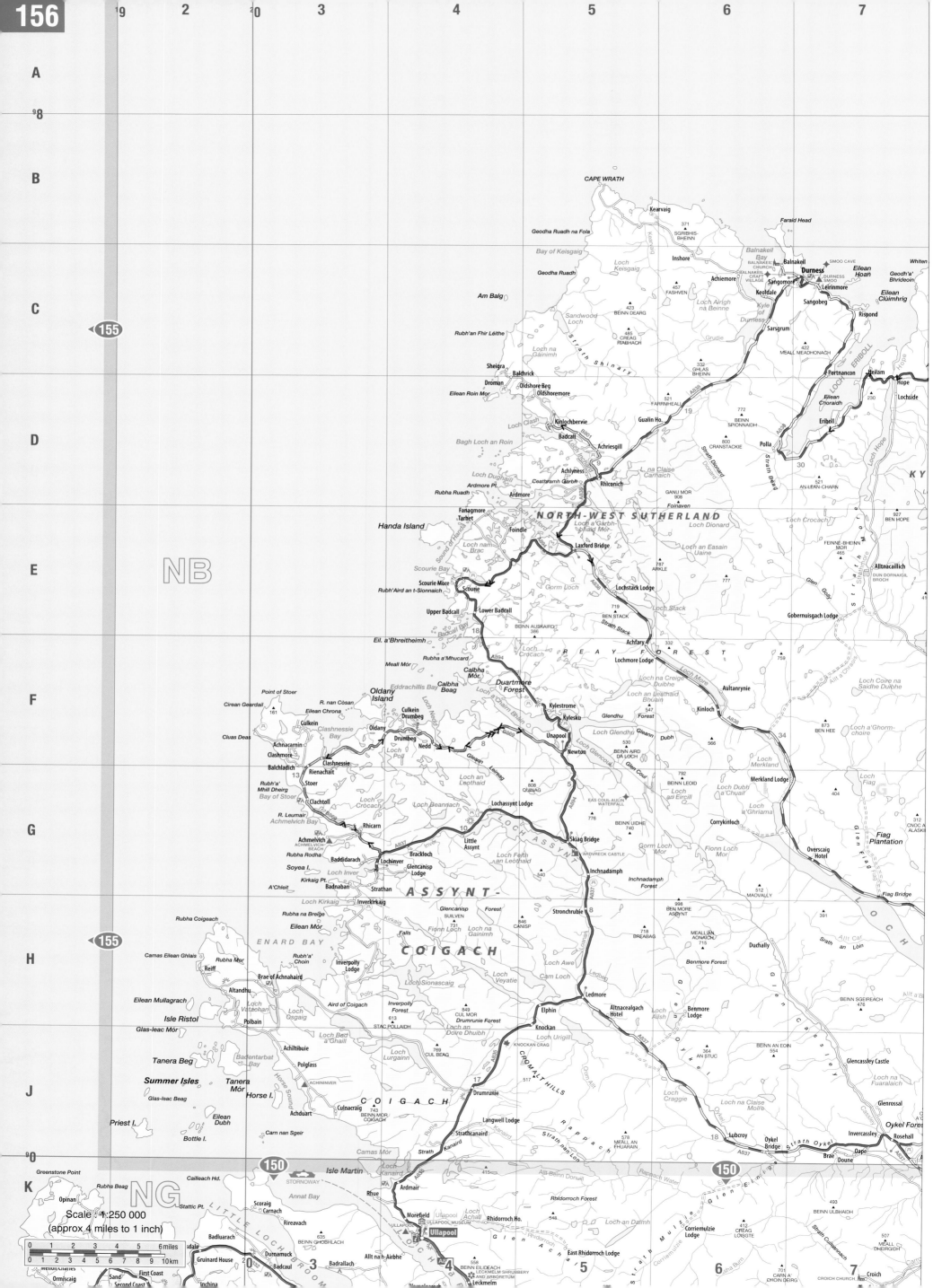

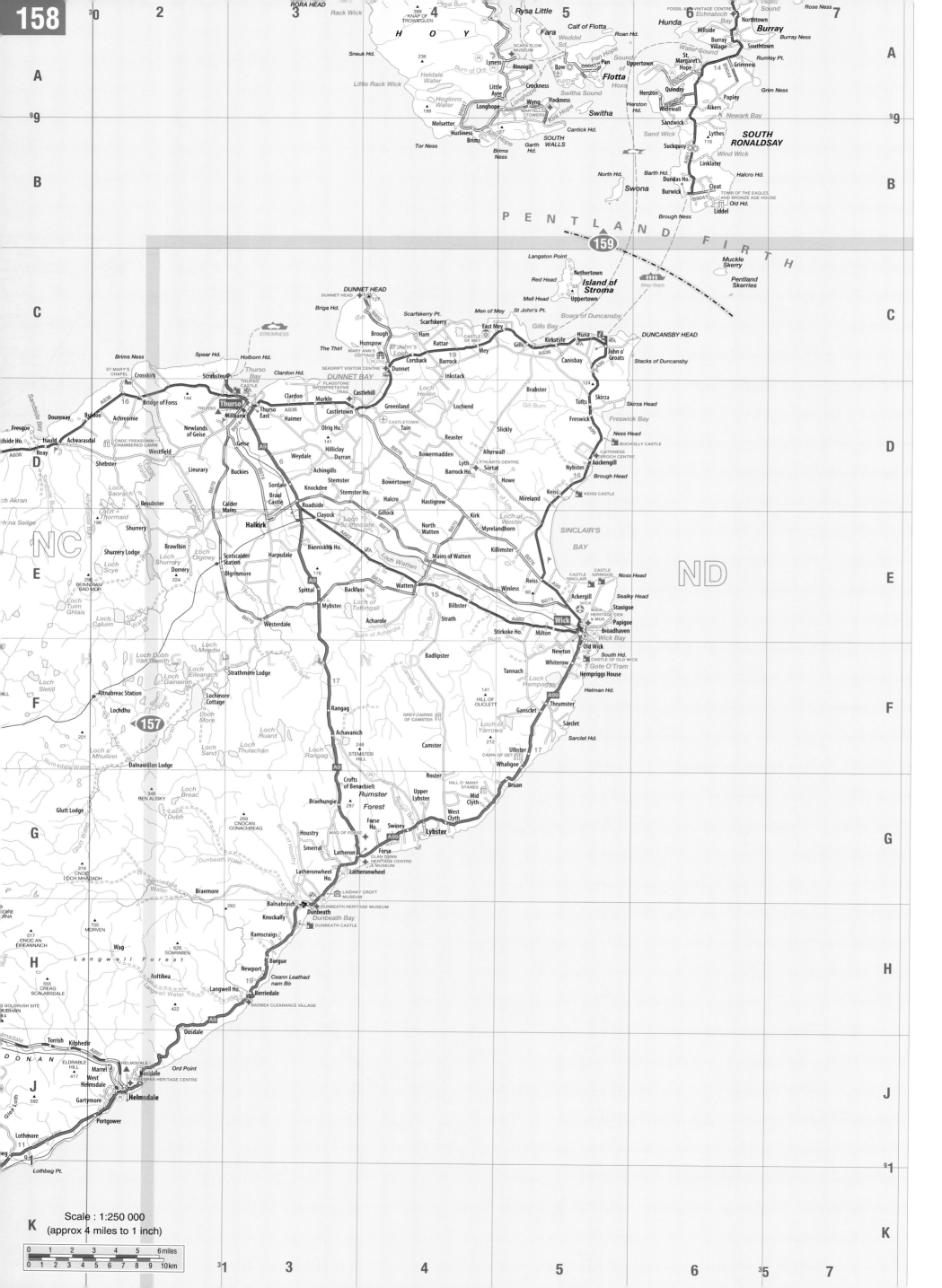

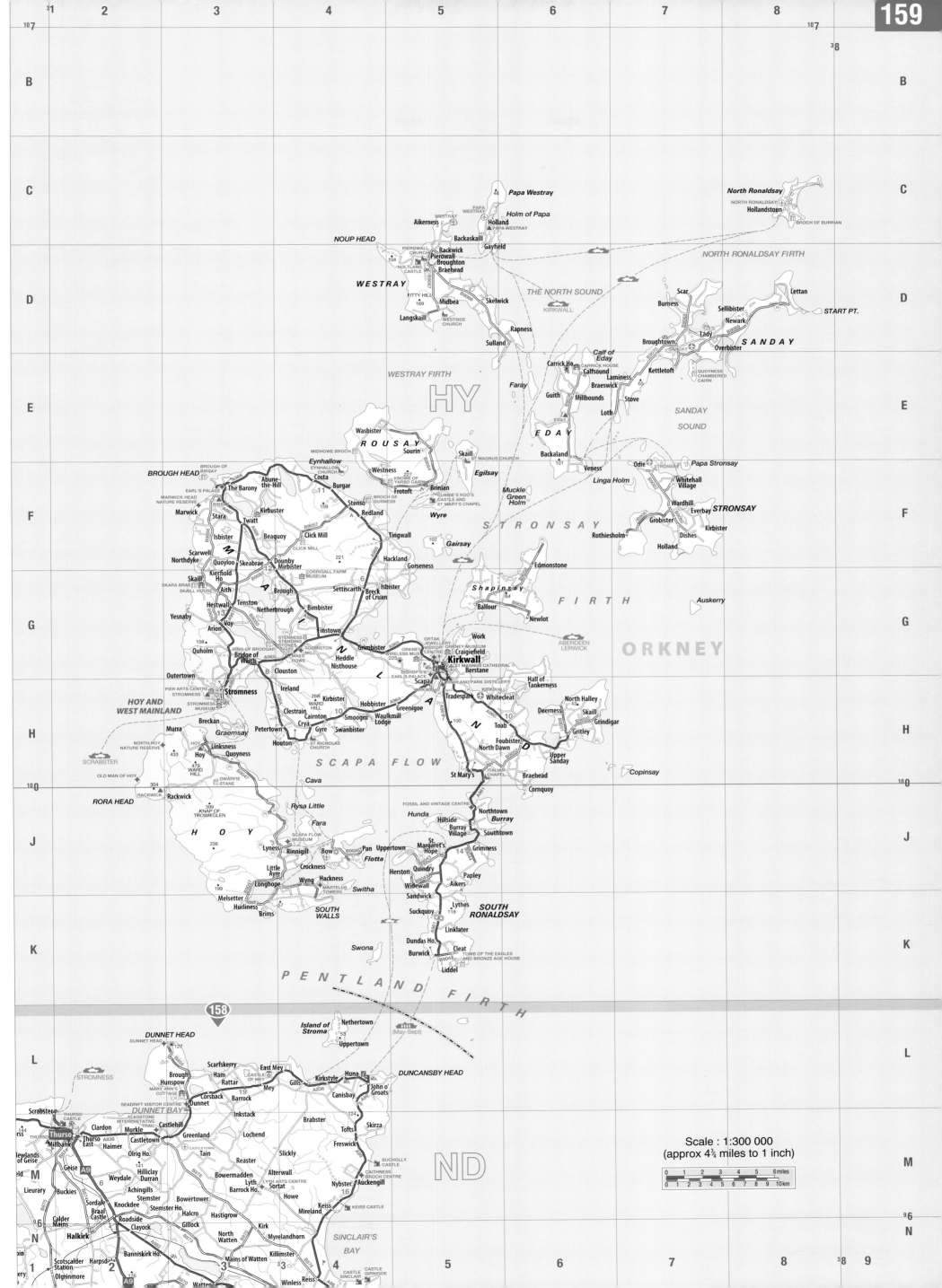

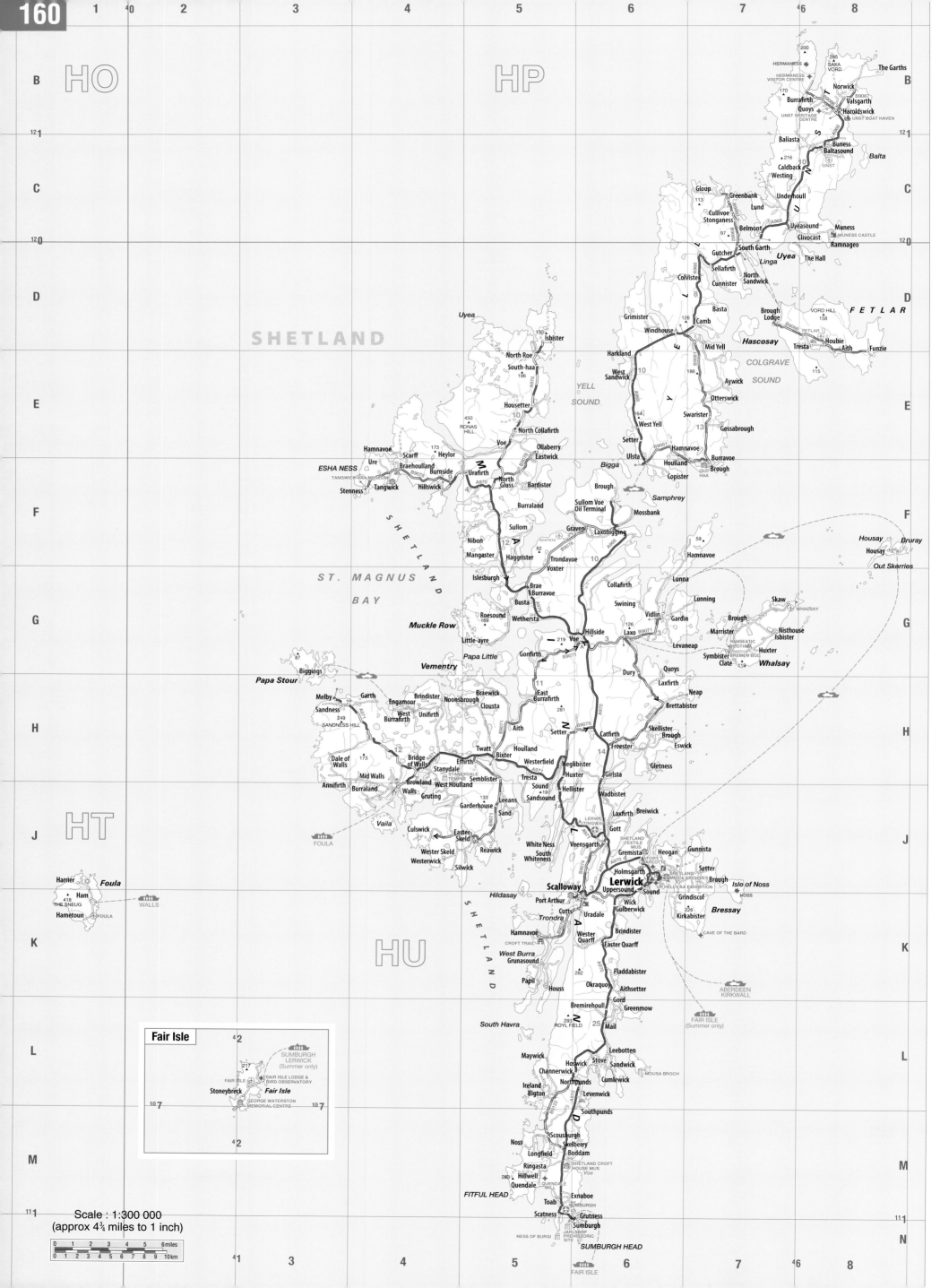

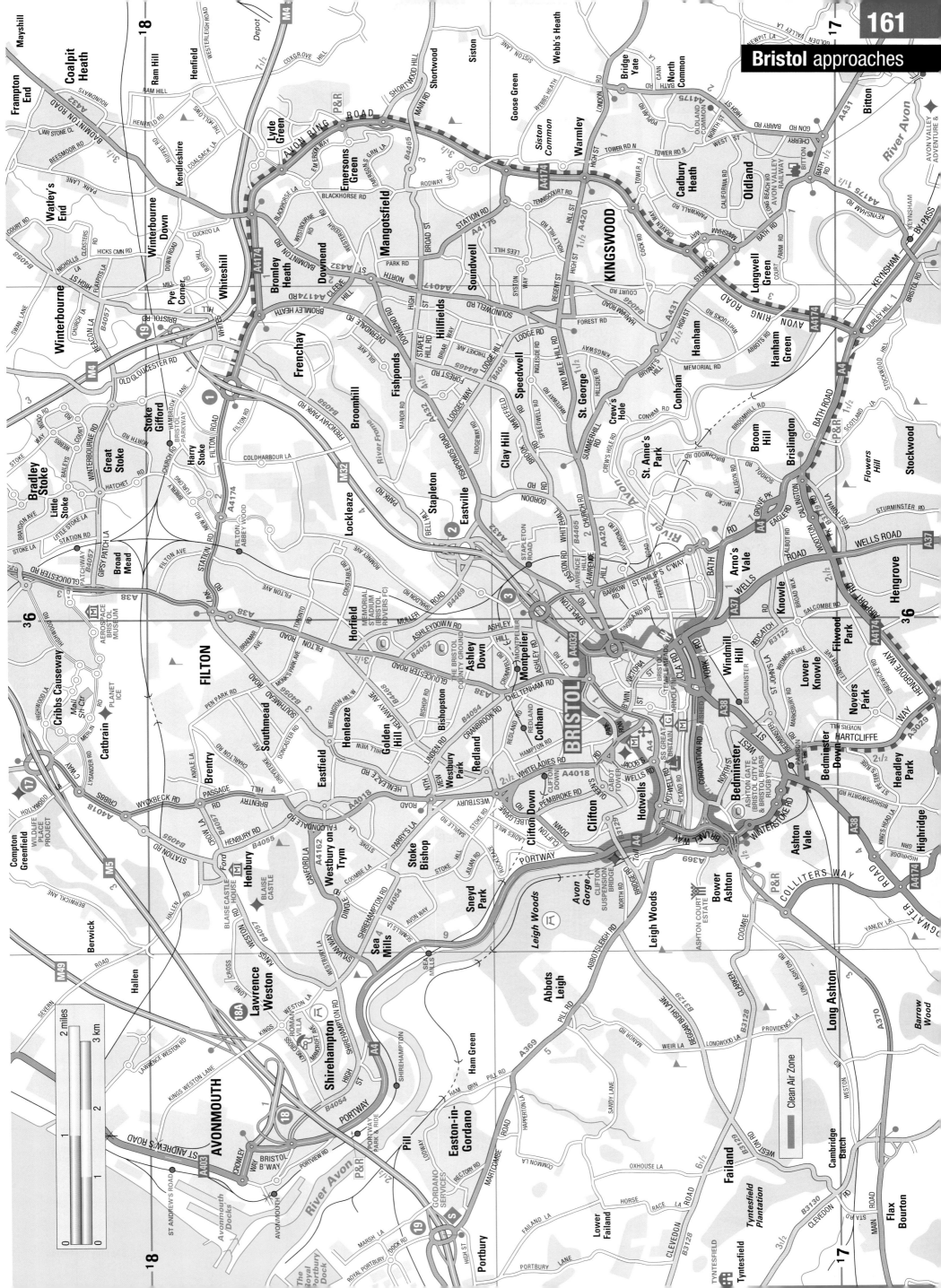

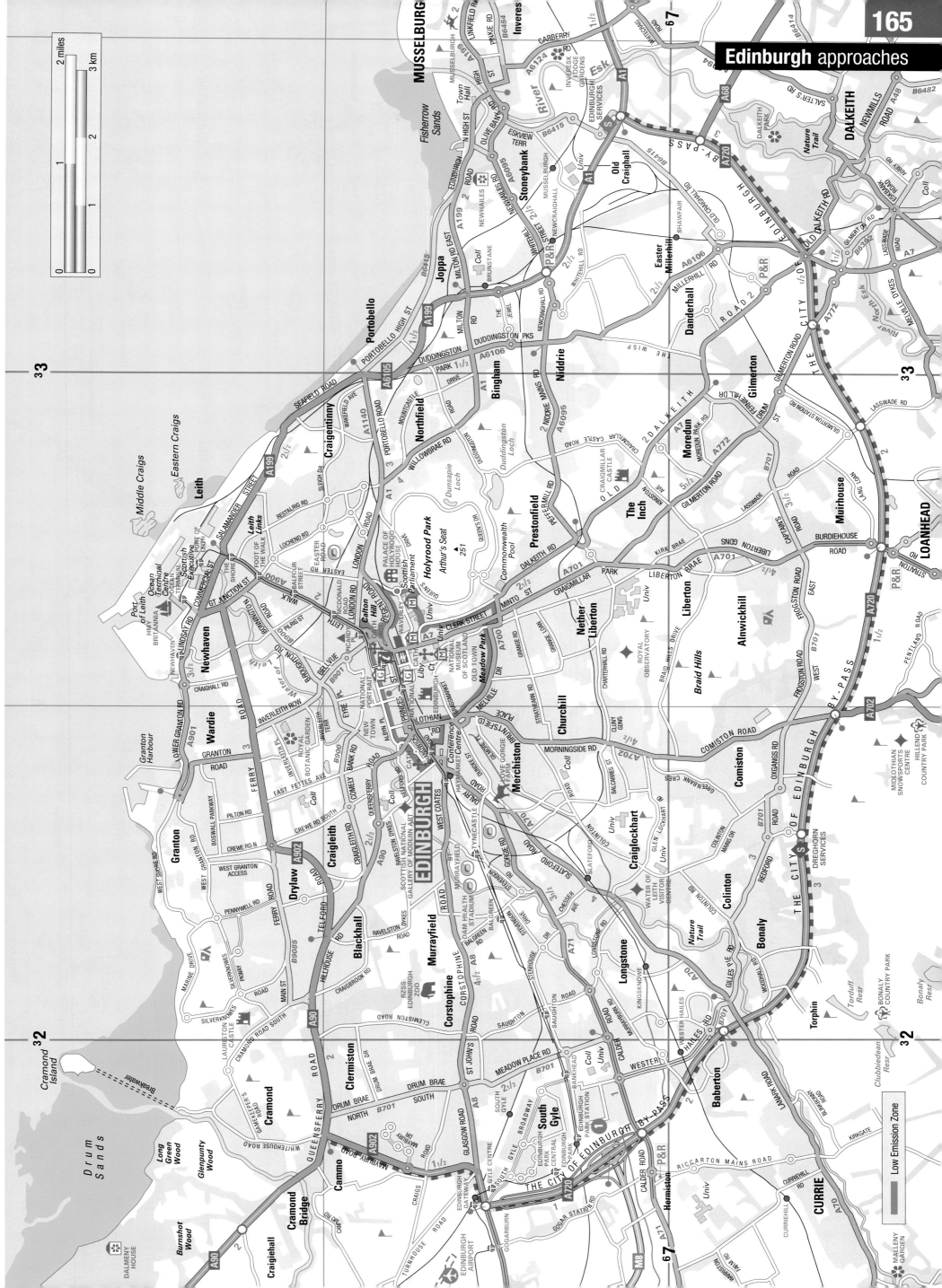

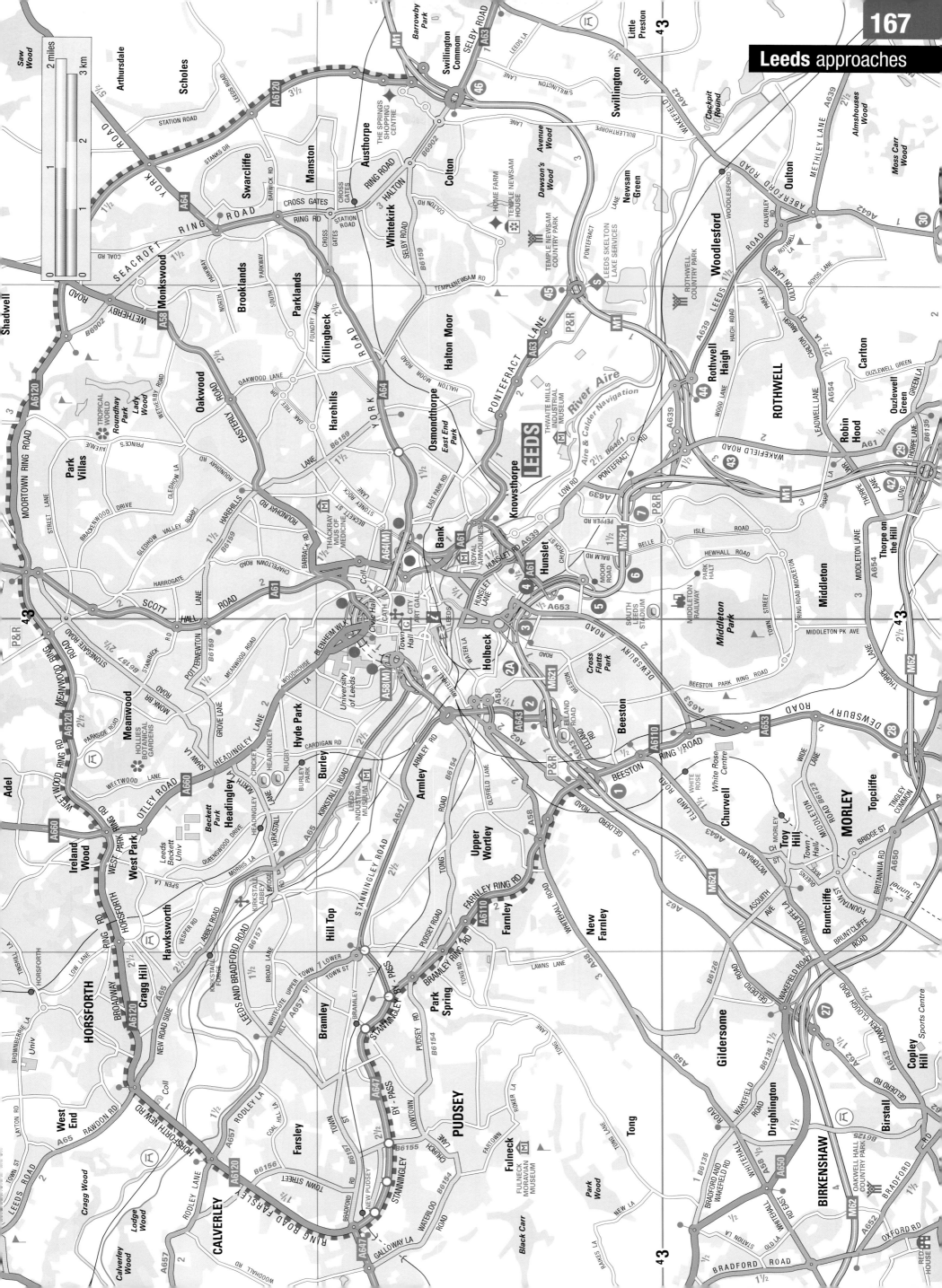

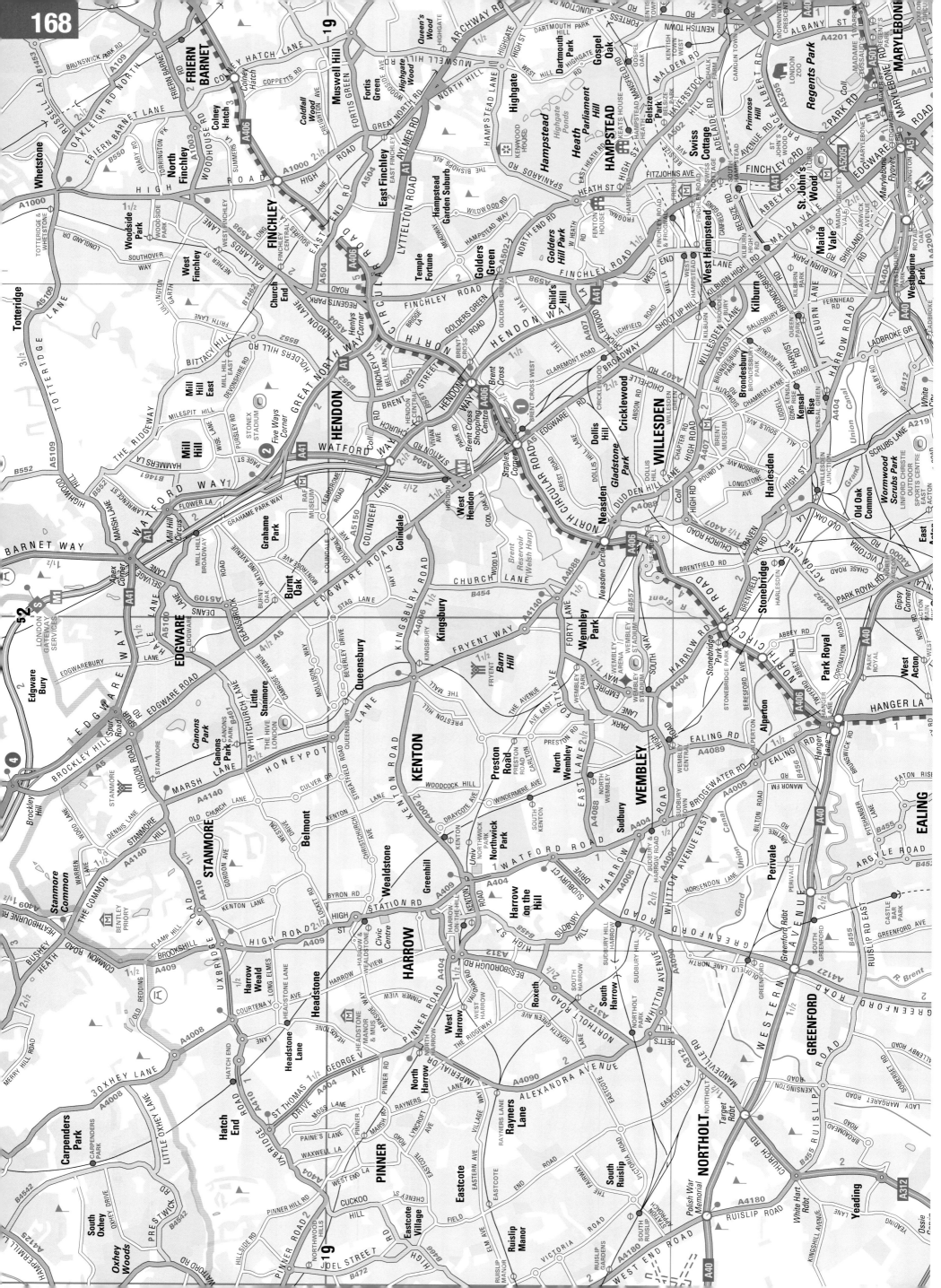

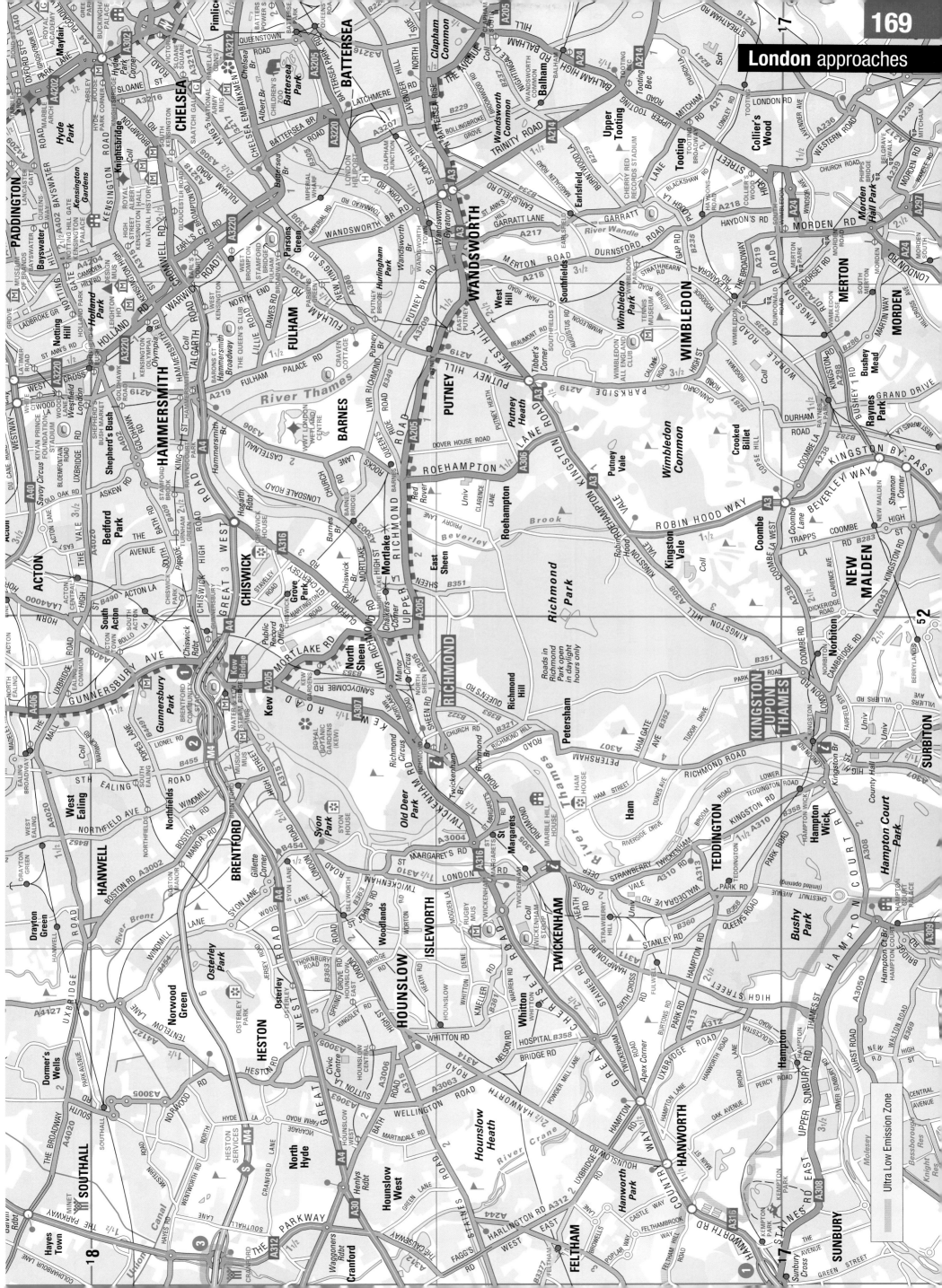

Ultra Low Emission Zone

52

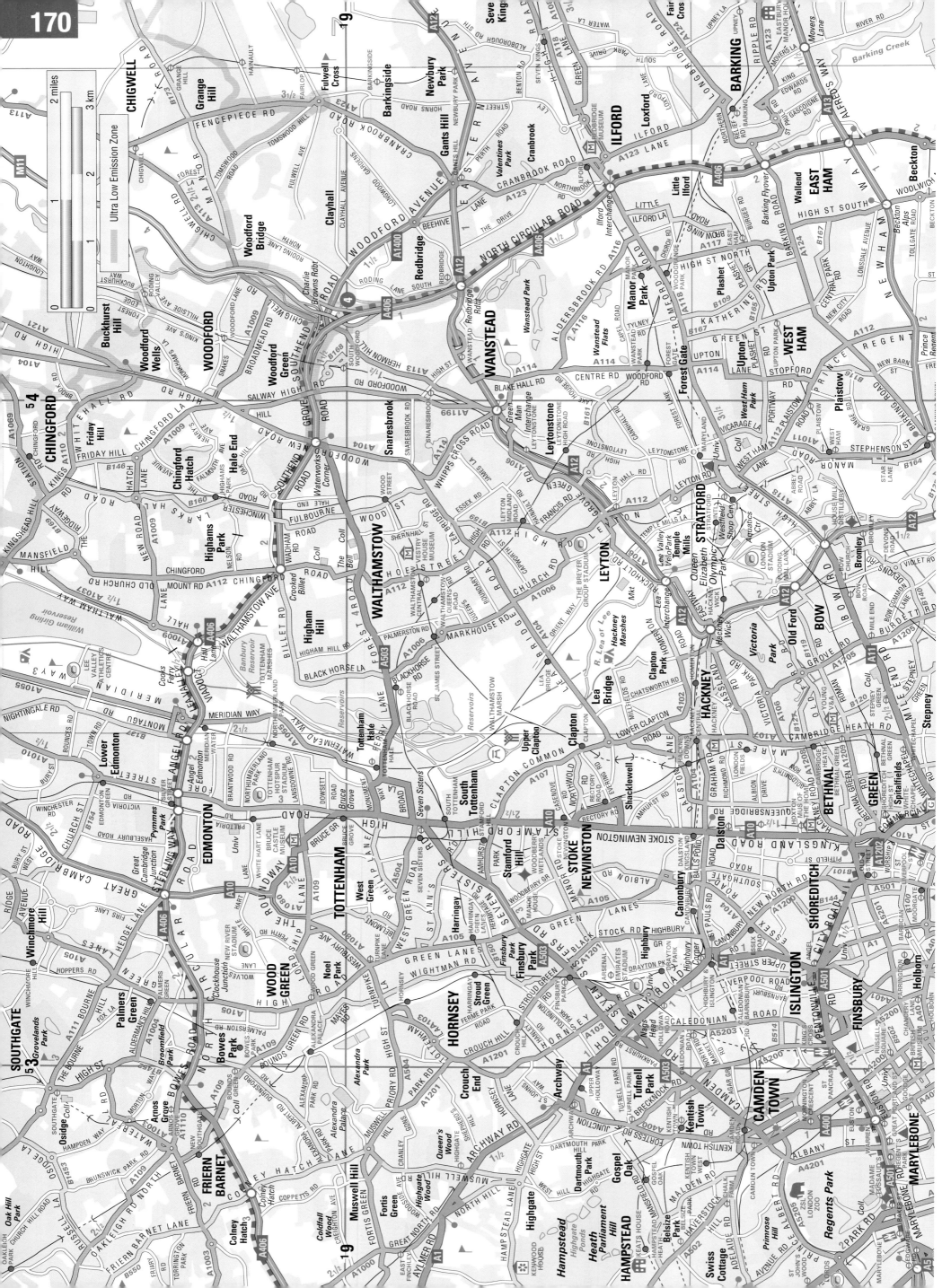

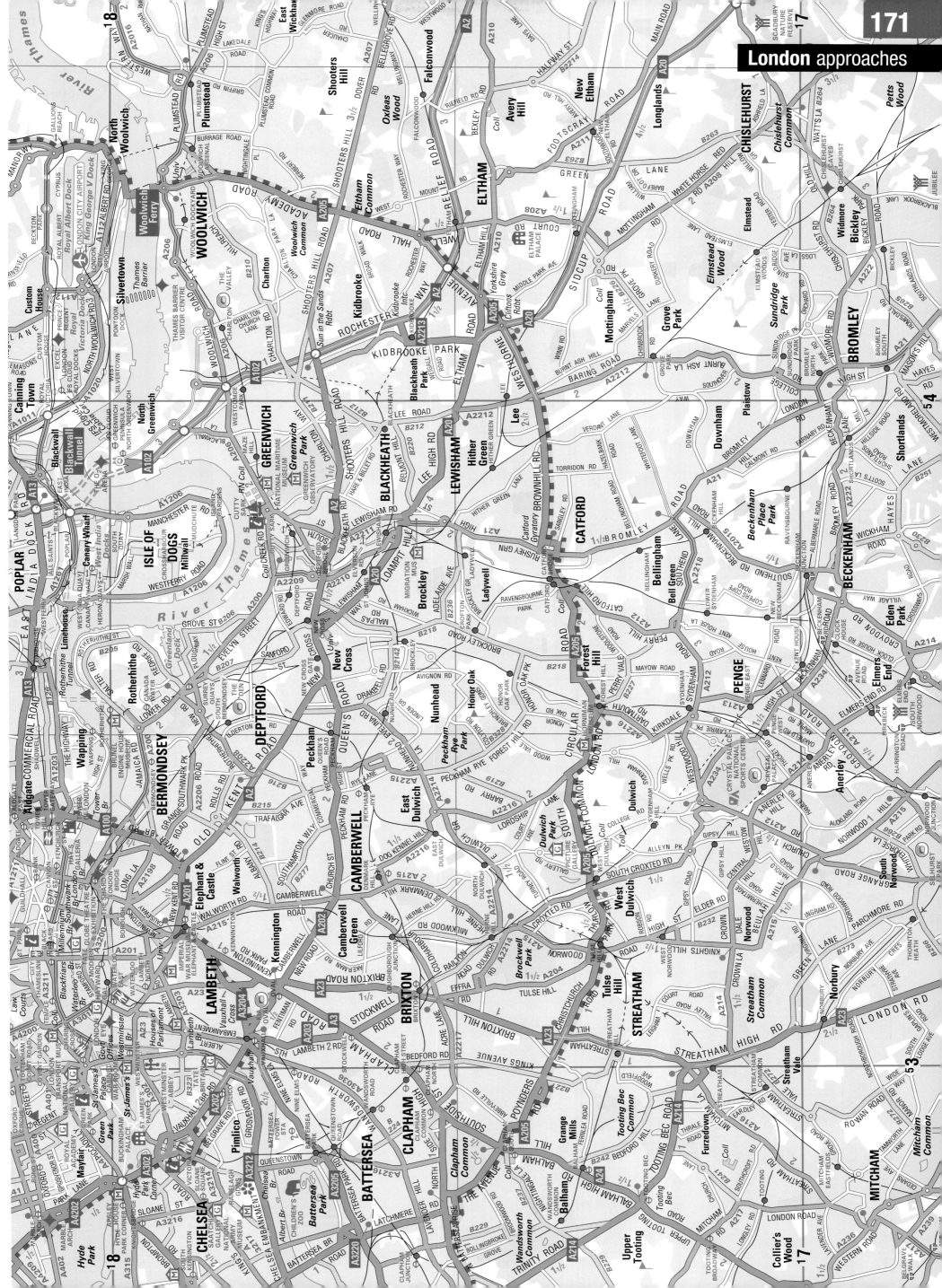

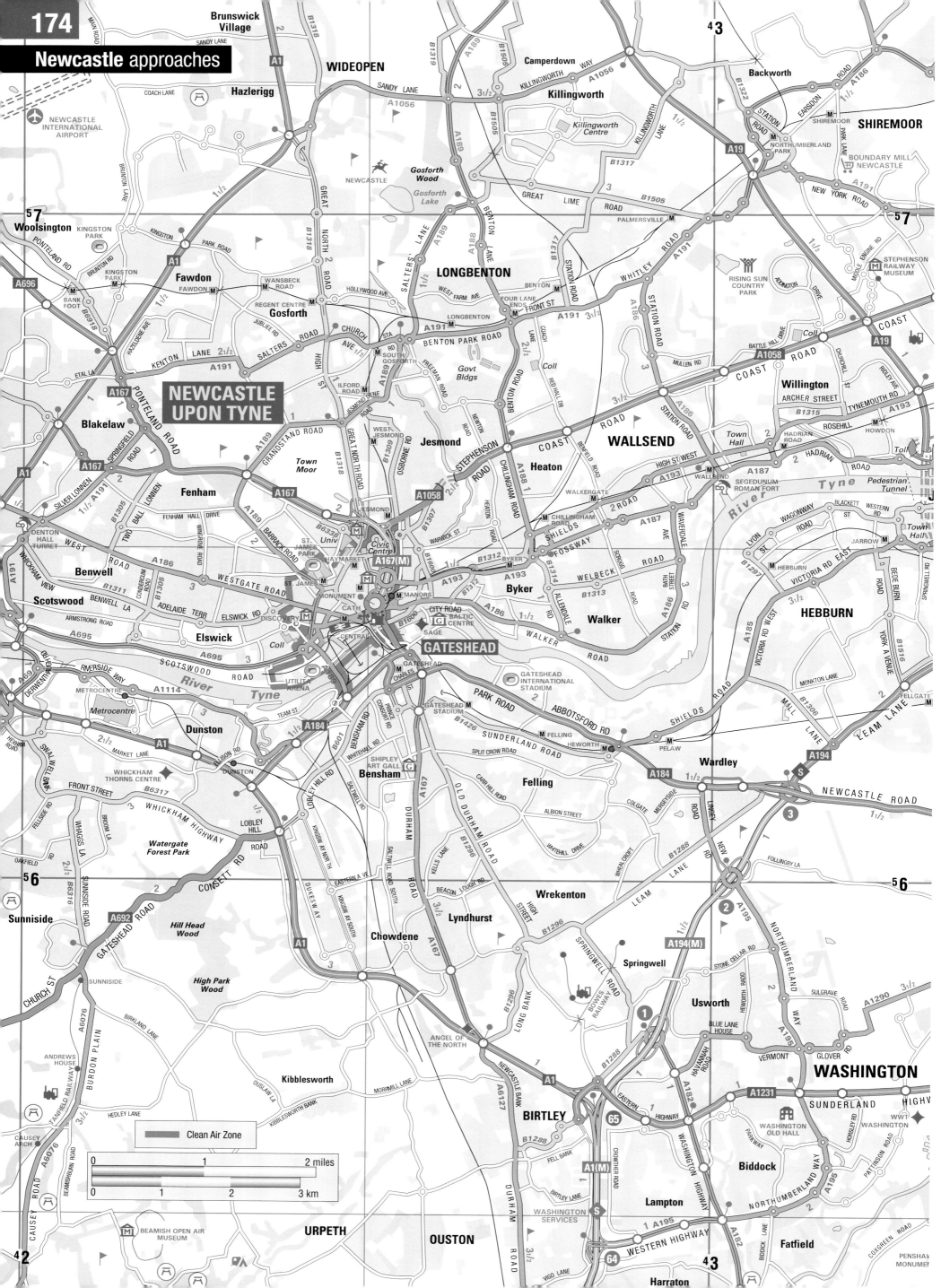

Town plan symbols

	Motorway
	Primary route – dual, single carriageway
	A road – dual, single carriageway
	B road – dual, single carriageway

	Minor through road	✛	Abbey or cathedral
	One-way street		Ancient monument
	Pedestrian roads		Aquarium
	Shopping streets		Art gallery
			Bird collection or aviary
	Railway with station		Building of interest
	Tramway with station		Castle
	Underground or Metro station		Church of interest
H	Hospital		Cinema
P	Parking		Garden
	Police		Historic ship
PO	Post Office		House
	Shopmobility		House and garden
▲	Youth hostel		Museum
			Preserved railway
	Bus or railway station building		Roman antiquity
	Shopping precinct or retail park		Safari park
			Theatre
	Park	i	Tourist information
	Congestion charge zone		Zoo
	Low Emission Zone (LEZ)/ Clean Air Zone (CAZ)	✦	Other place of interest

See local authority websites for details

Aberdeen

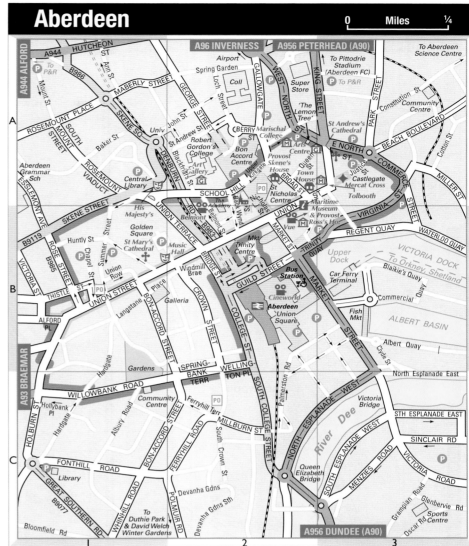

Ayr

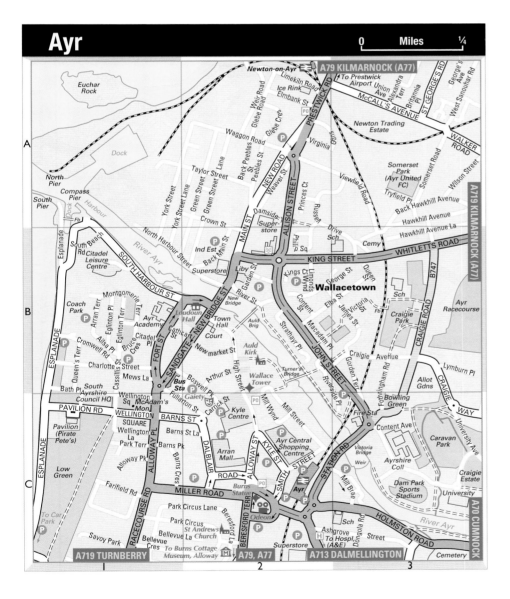

Bath

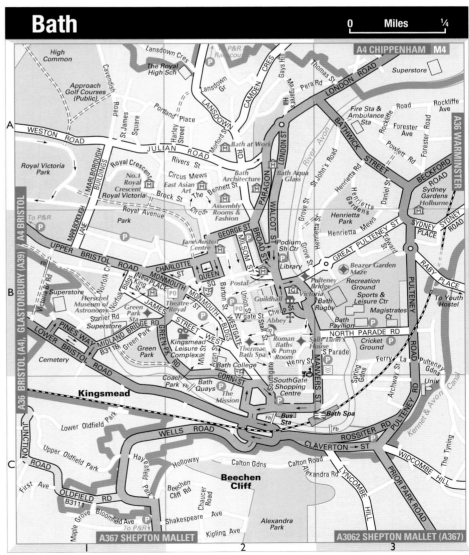

Birmingham

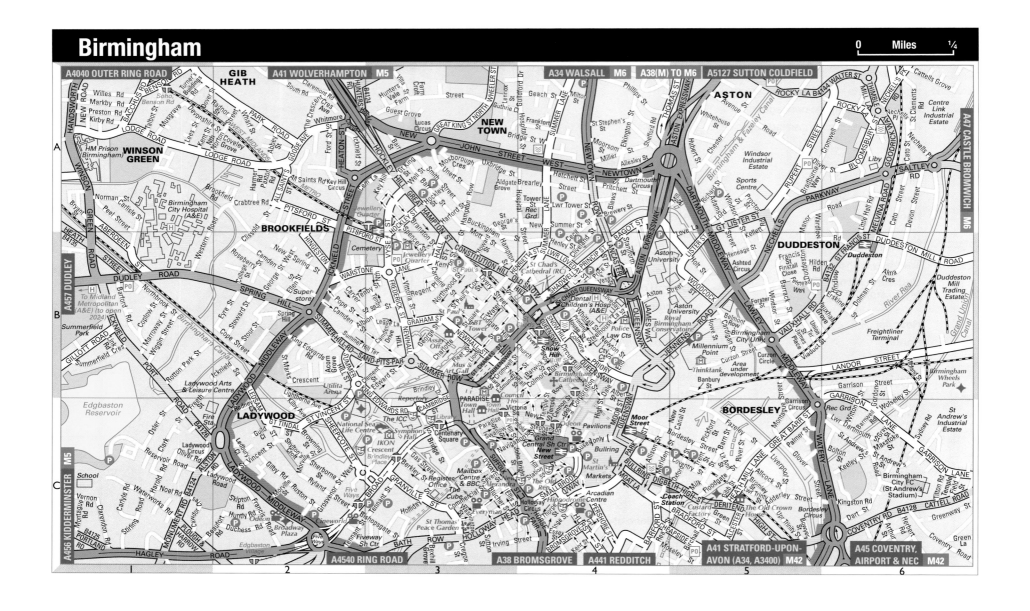

Blackpool

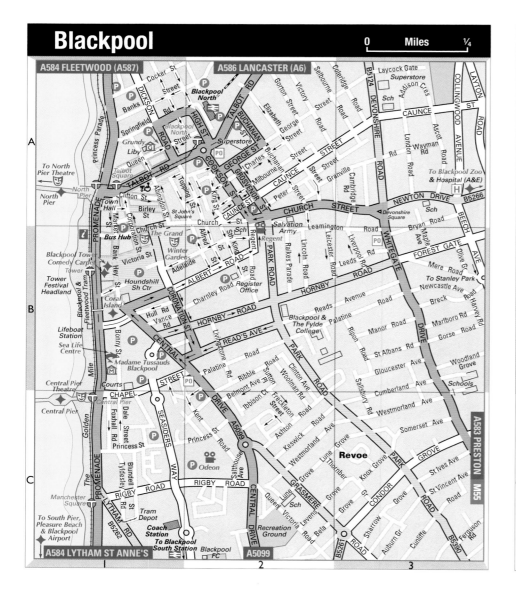

Bournemouth

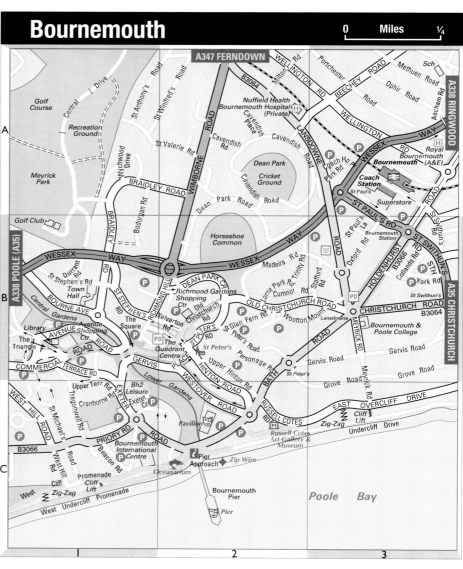

Bradford

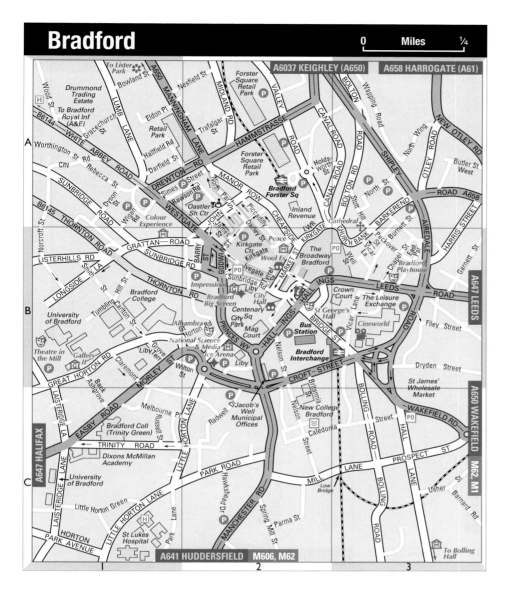

Brighton

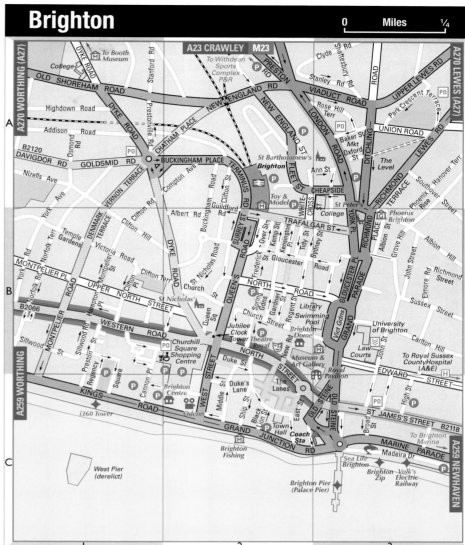

Bristol

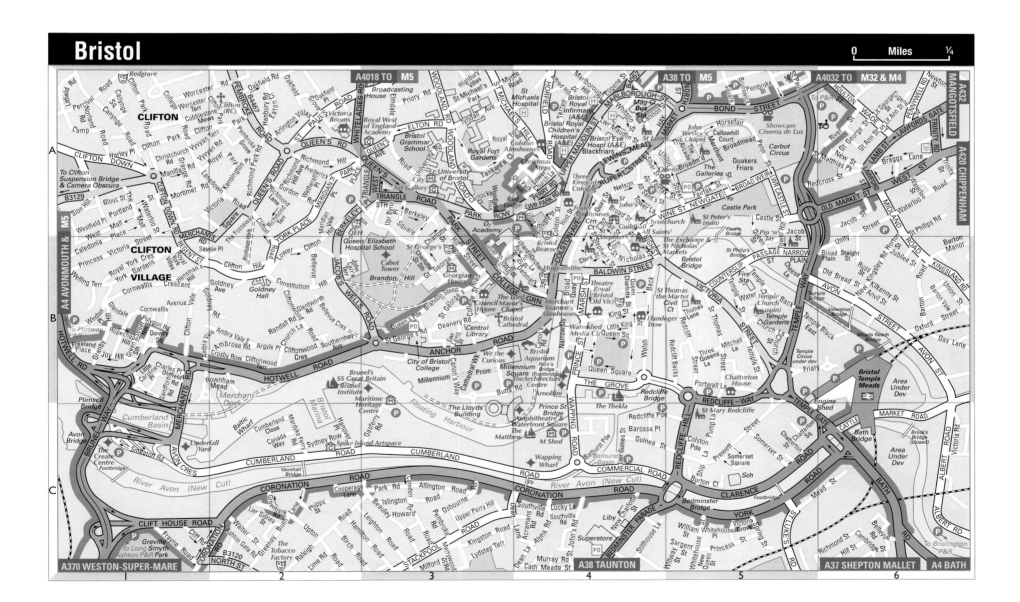

Bury St Edmunds

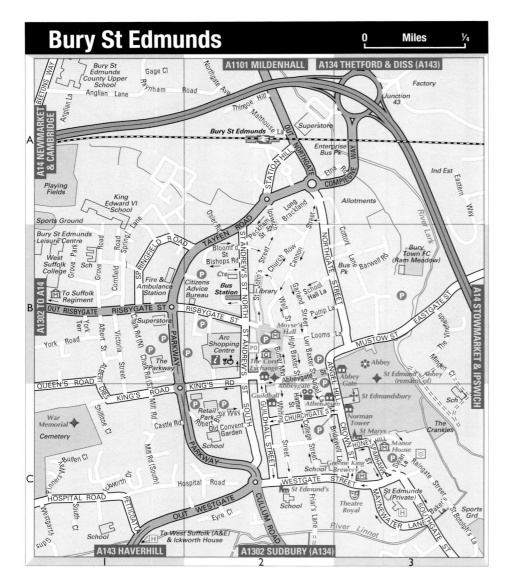

Cambridge

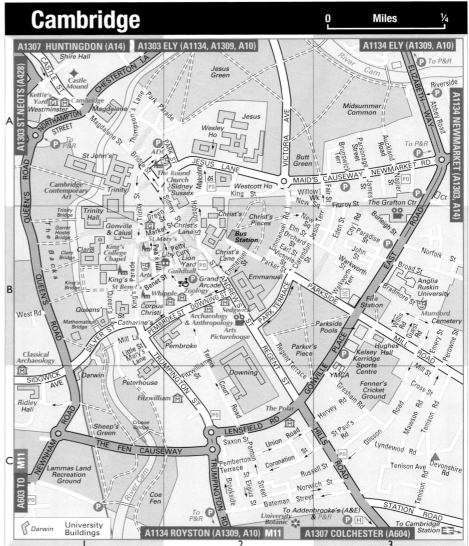

Canterbury

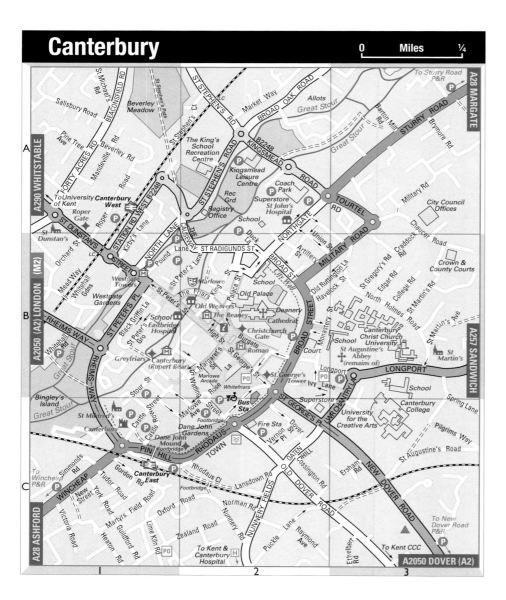

Cardiff / Caerdydd

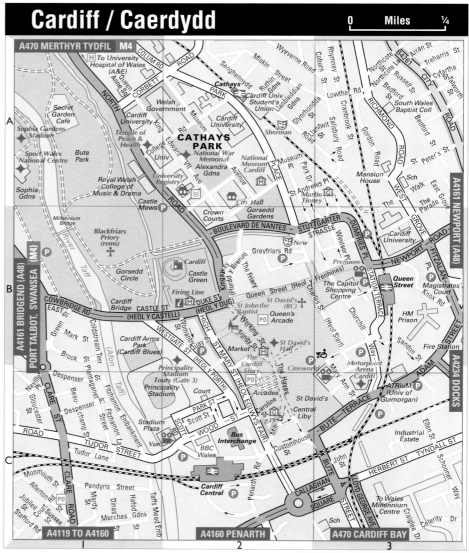

Carlisle

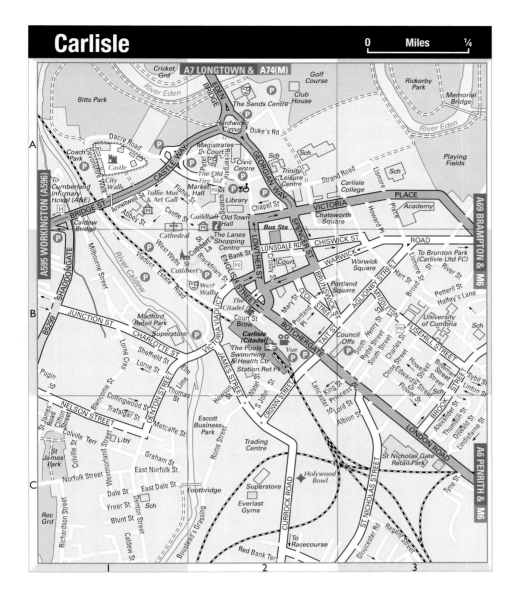

Chelmsford

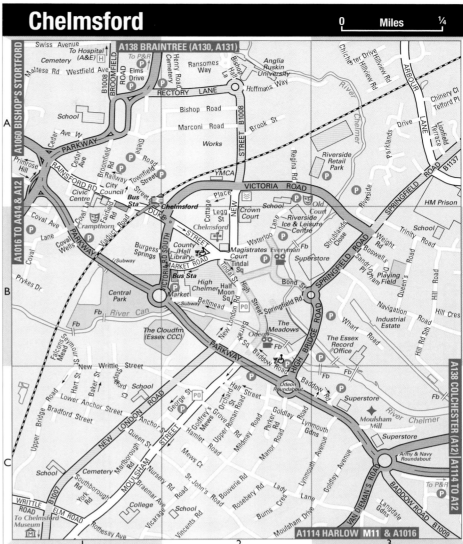

Cheltenham

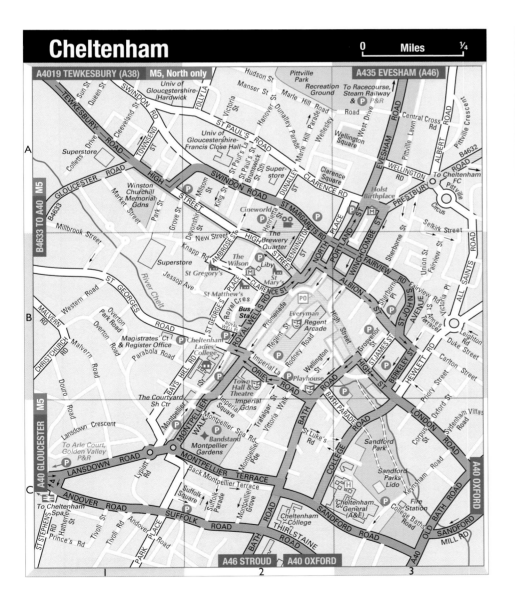

Chester

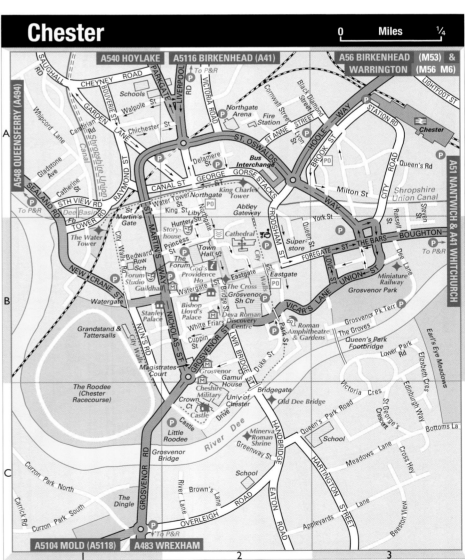

Chichester

0 Miles ¼

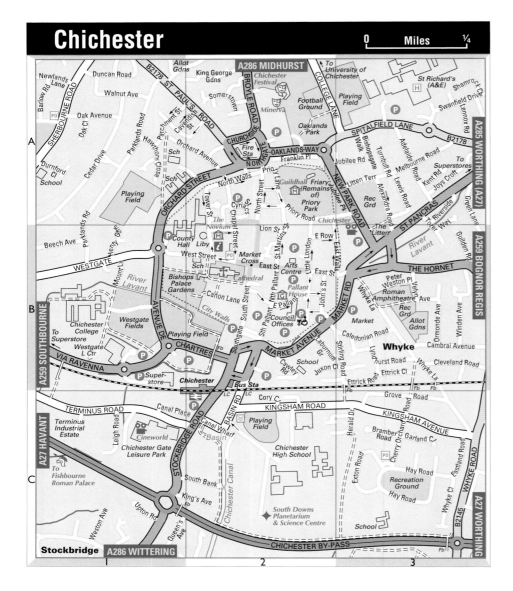

Colchester

0 Miles ¼

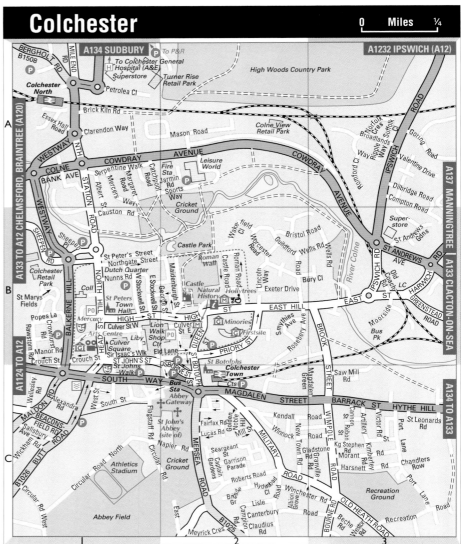

Coventry

0 Miles ¼

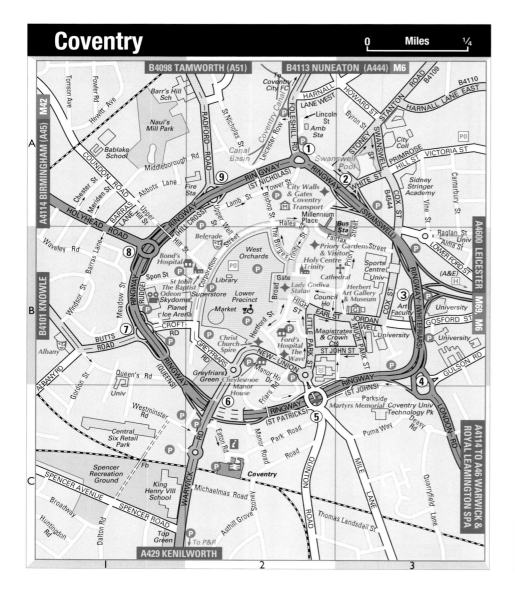

Derby

0 Miles ¼

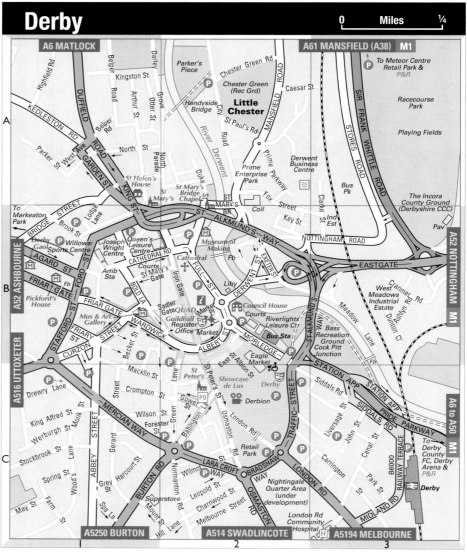

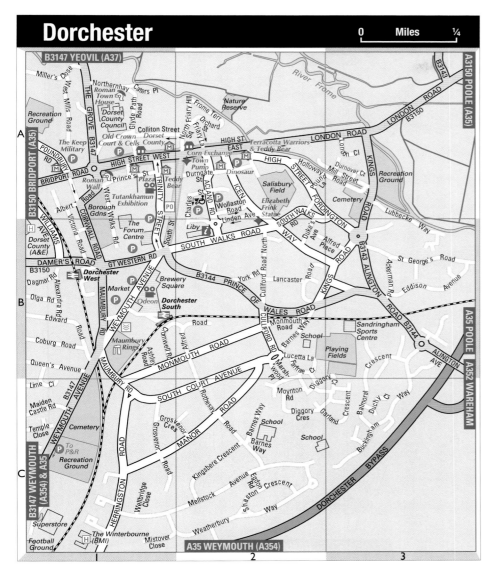

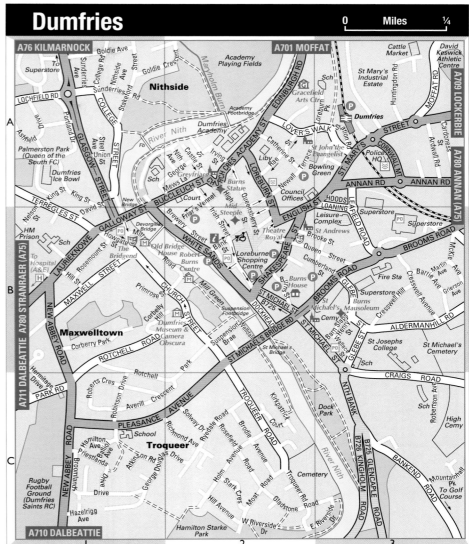

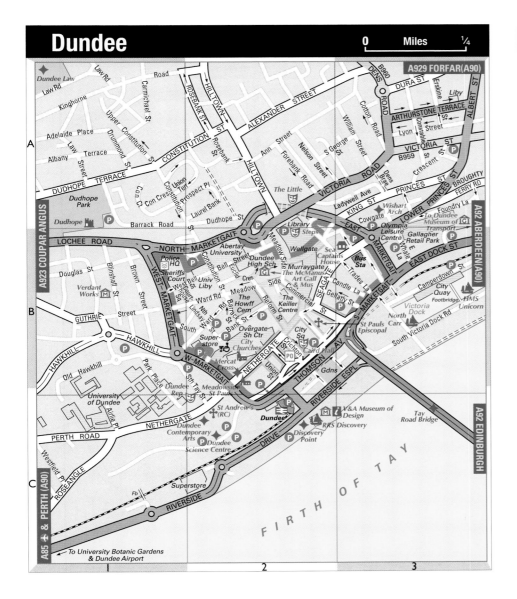

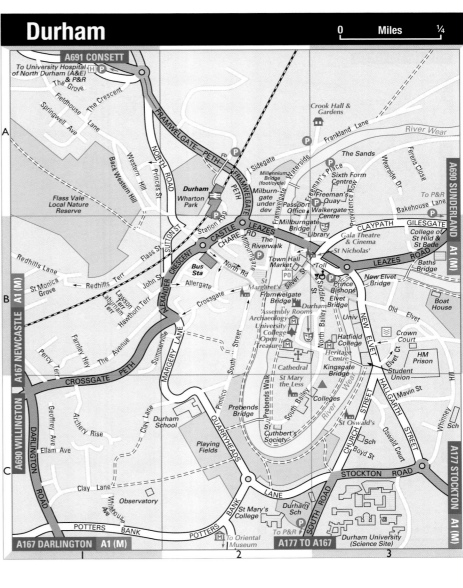

Edinburgh

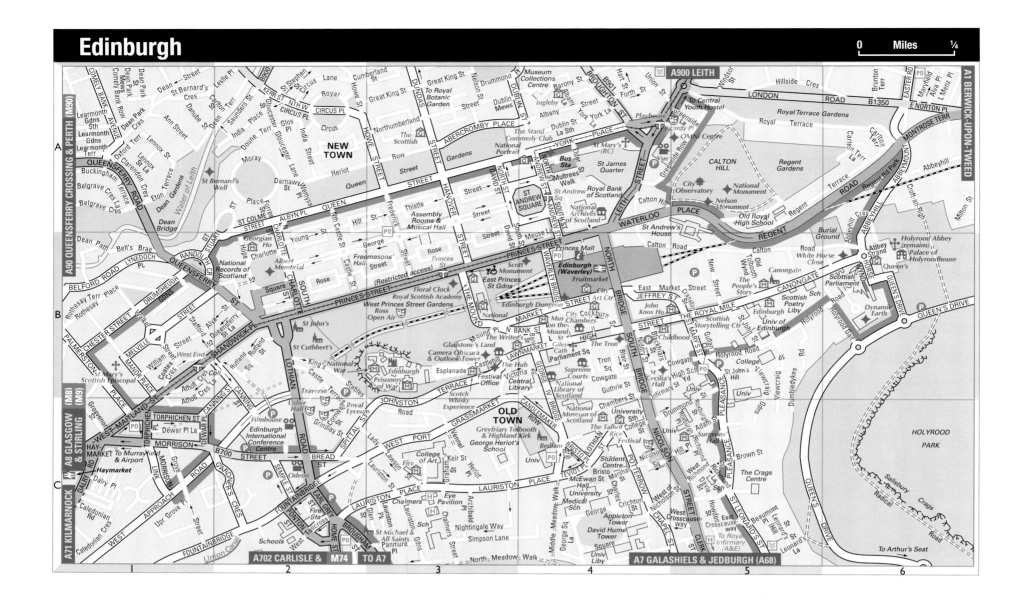

Exeter

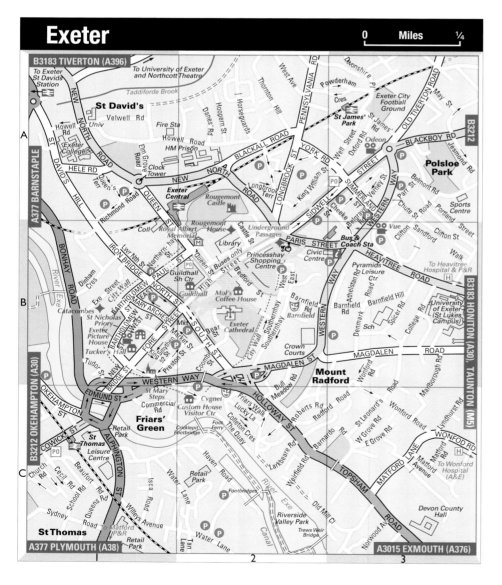

Gloucester

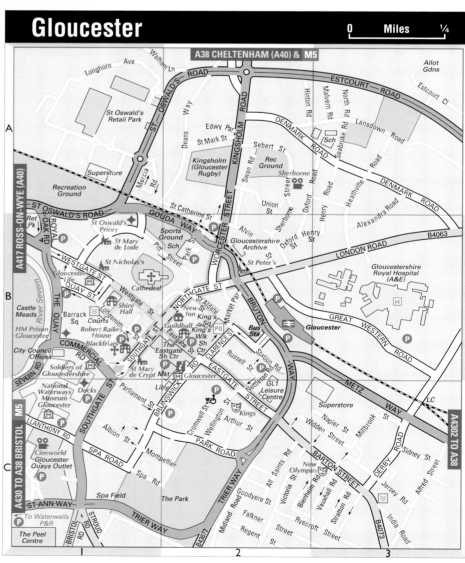

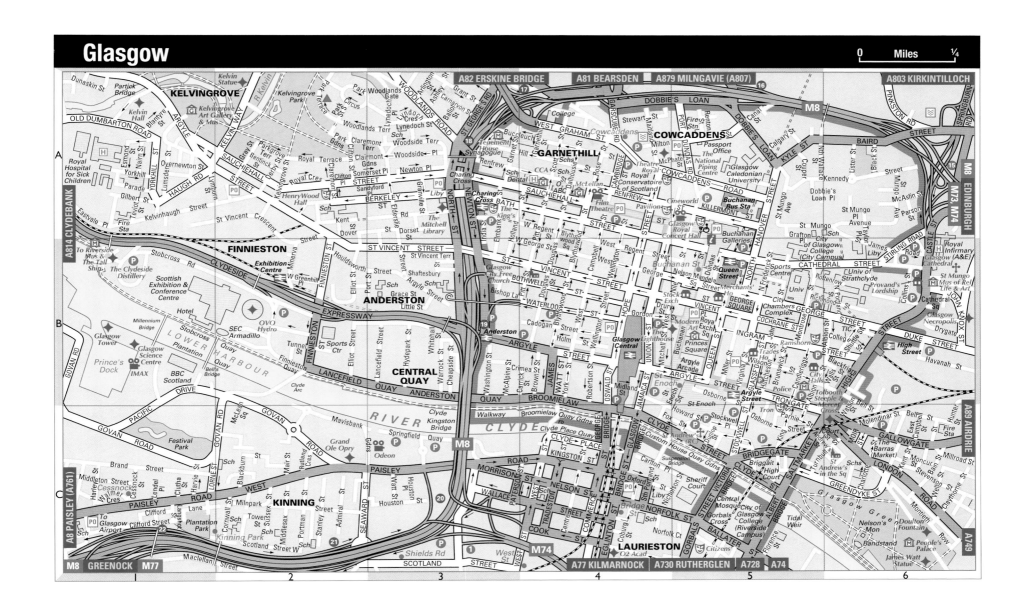

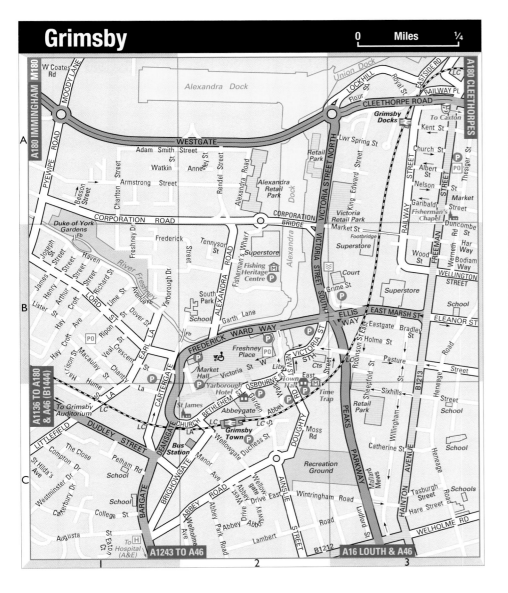

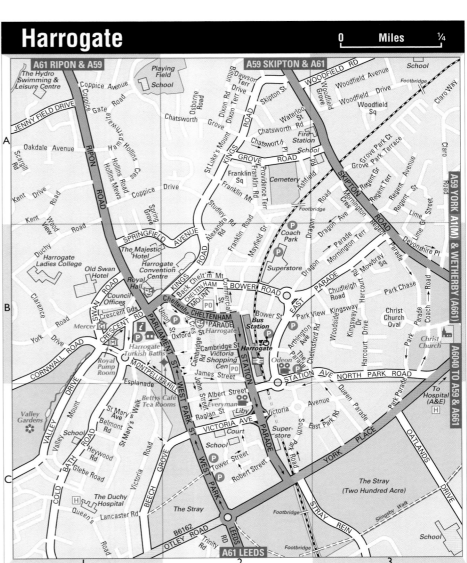

Hull

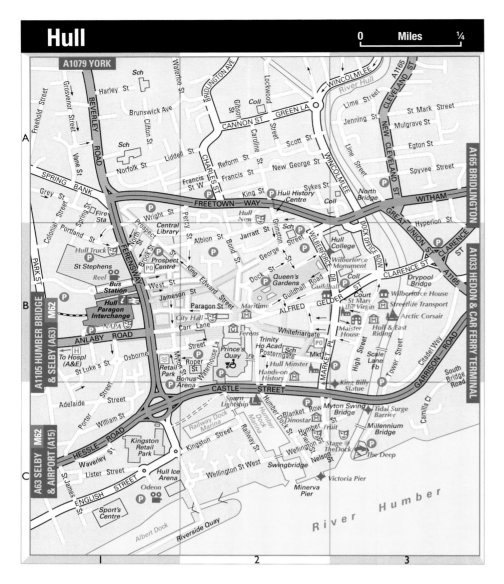

Inverness

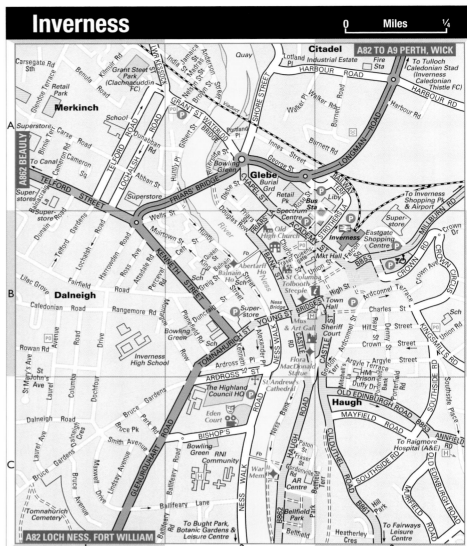

Ipswich

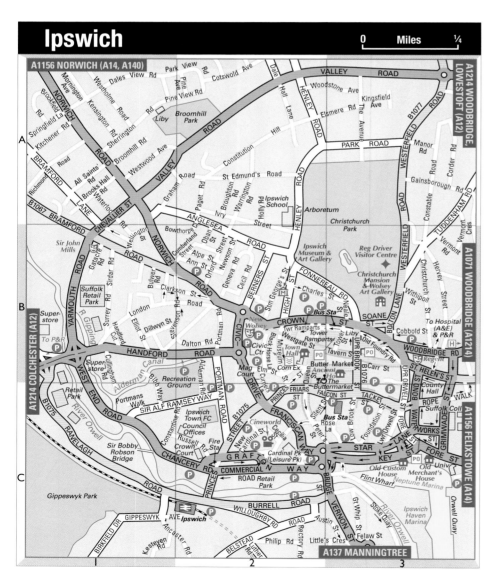

Kendal

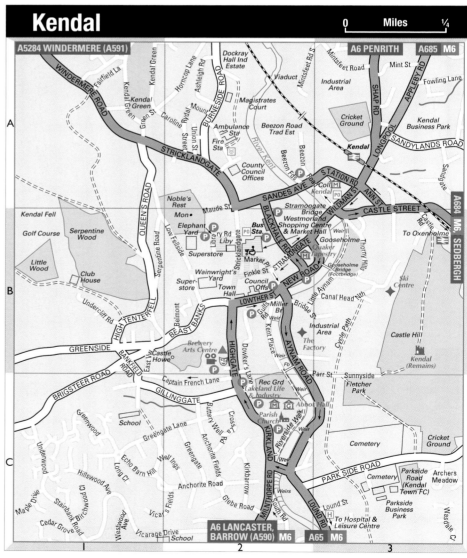

King's Lynn

0   Miles   ¼

Lancaster

0   Miles   ¼

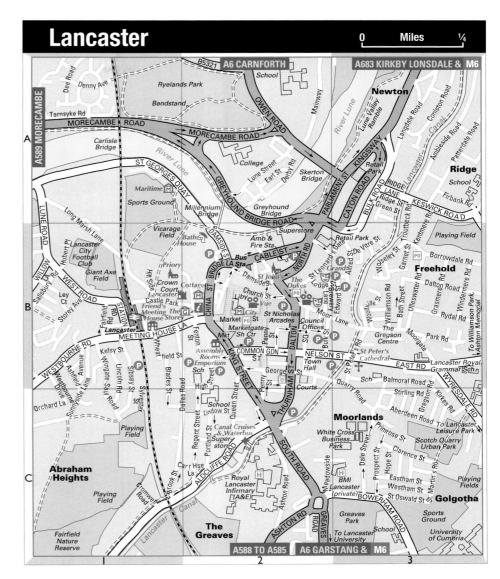

Leeds

0   Miles   ¼

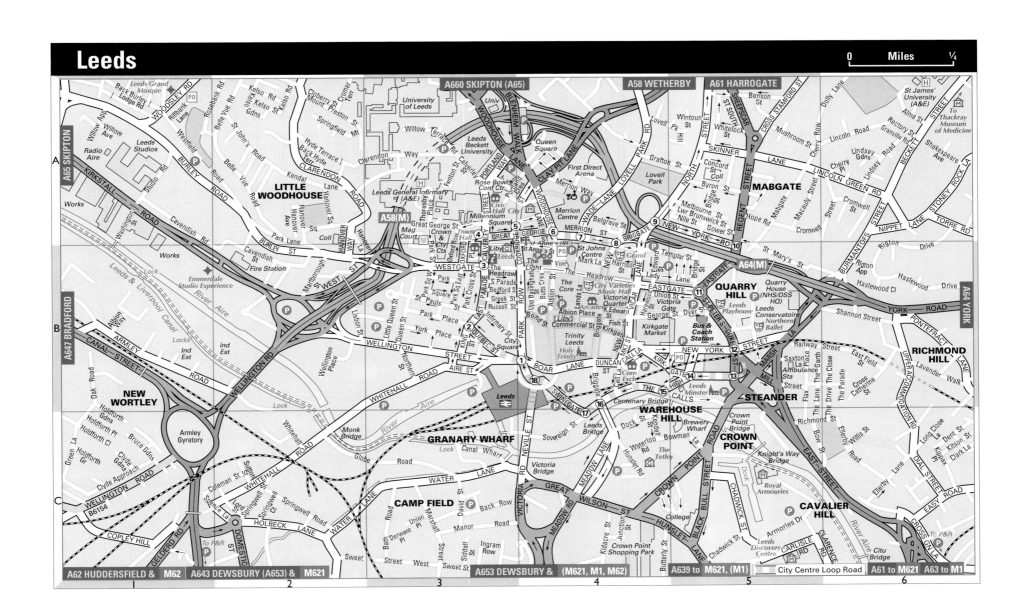

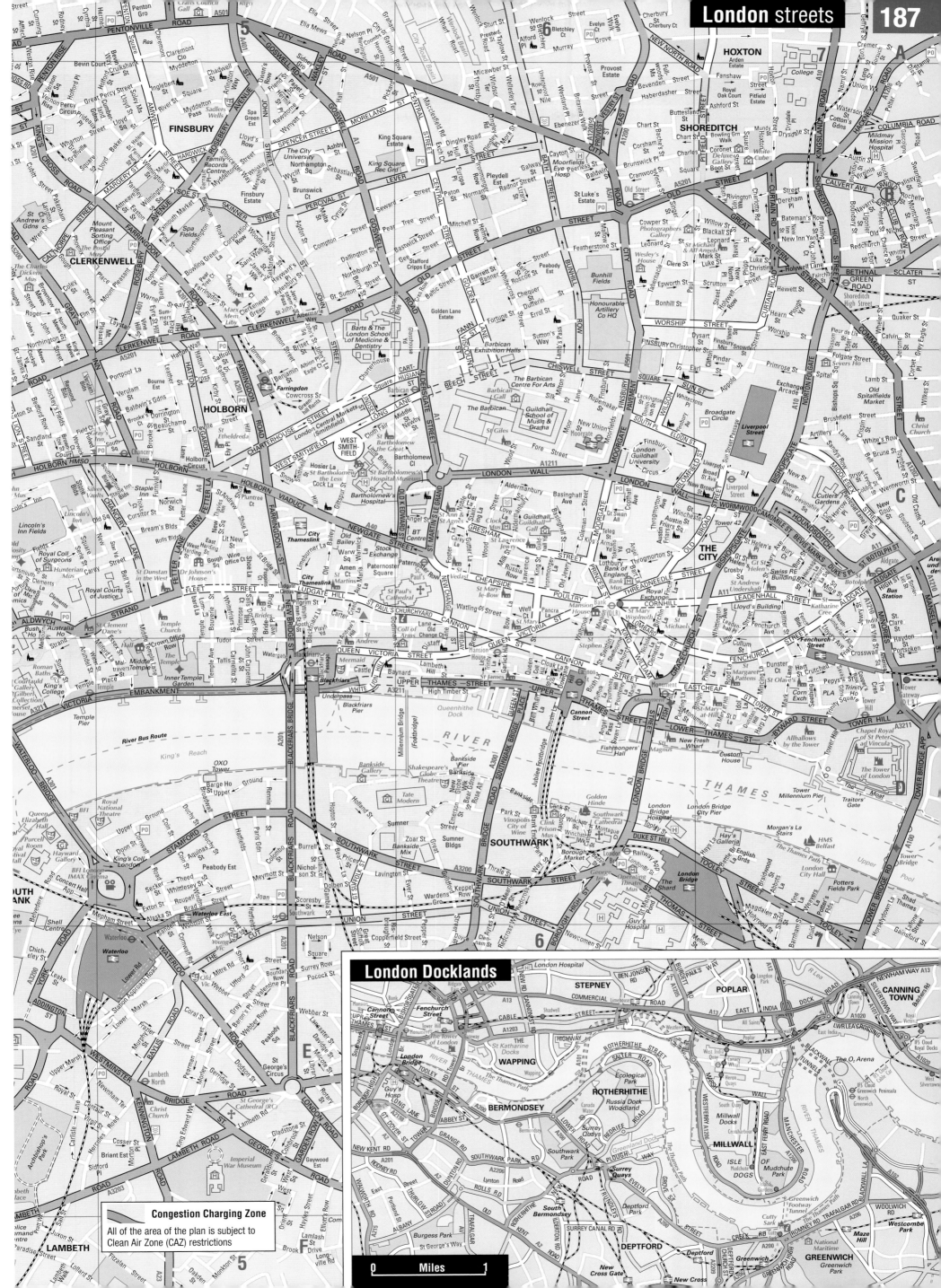

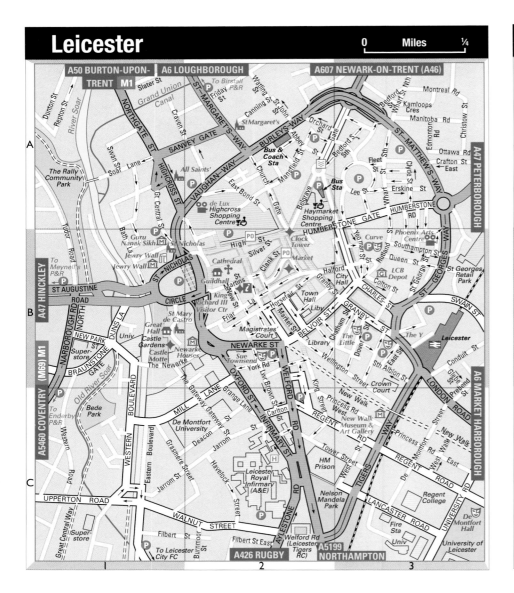

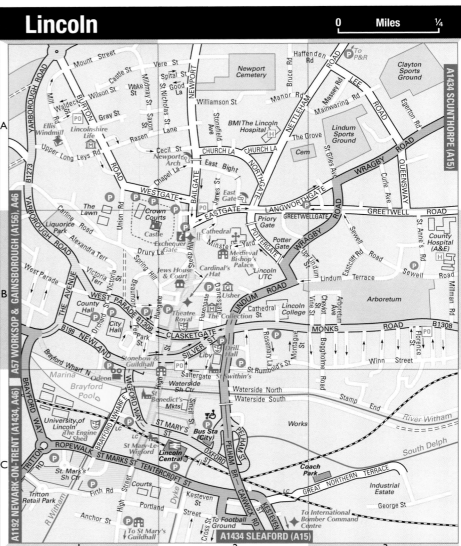

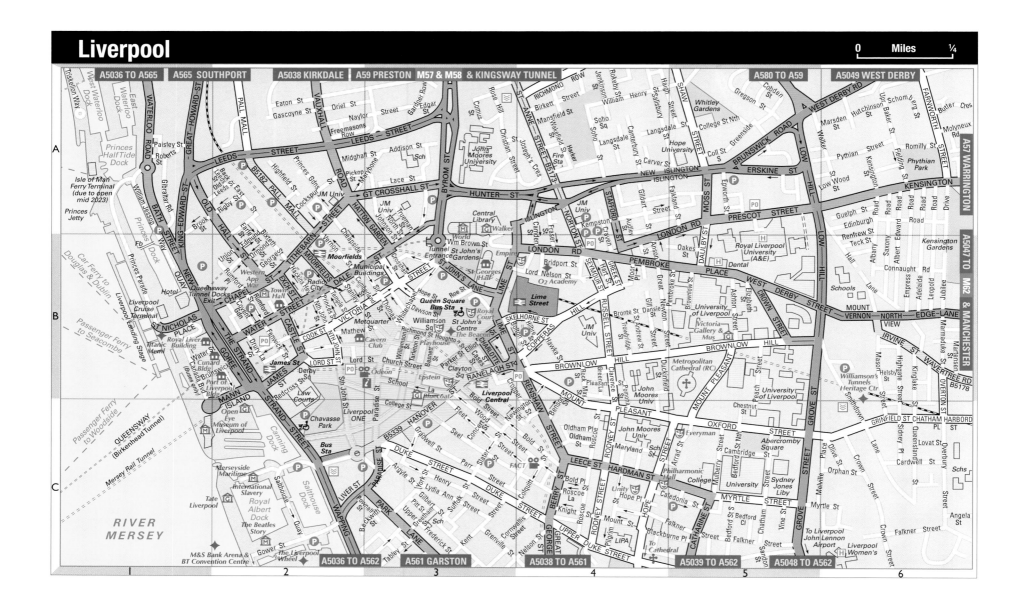

Llandudno

0   Miles   ¼

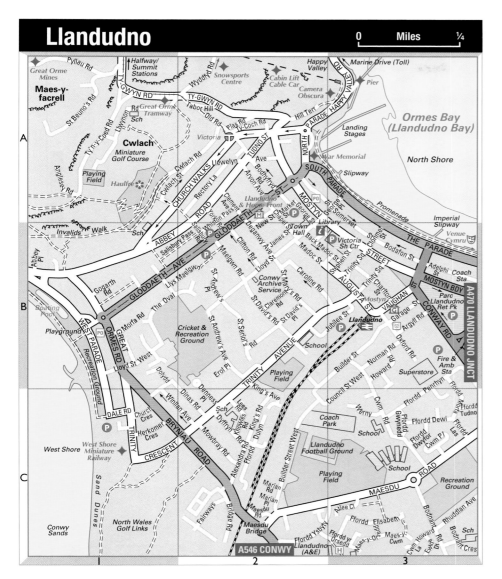

Llanelli

0   Miles   ¼

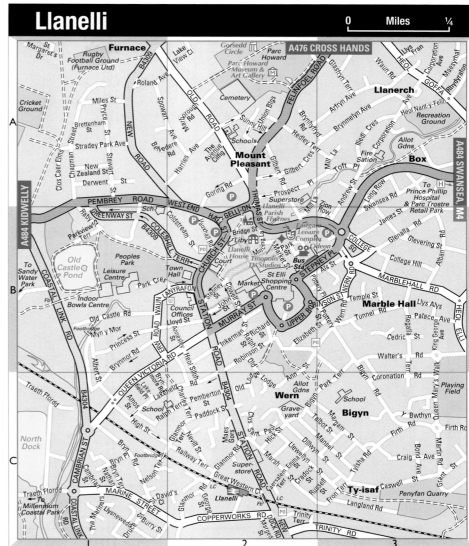

Luton

0   Miles   ¼

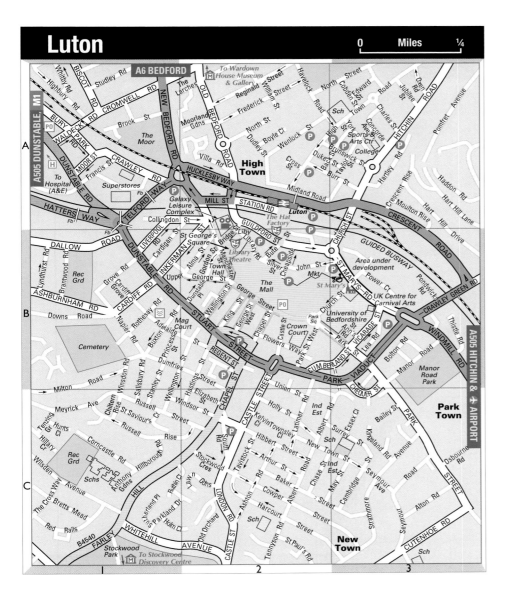

Macclesfield

0   Miles   ¼

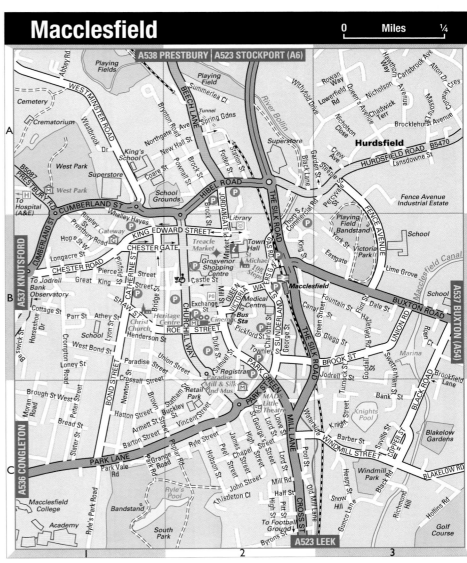

Manchester

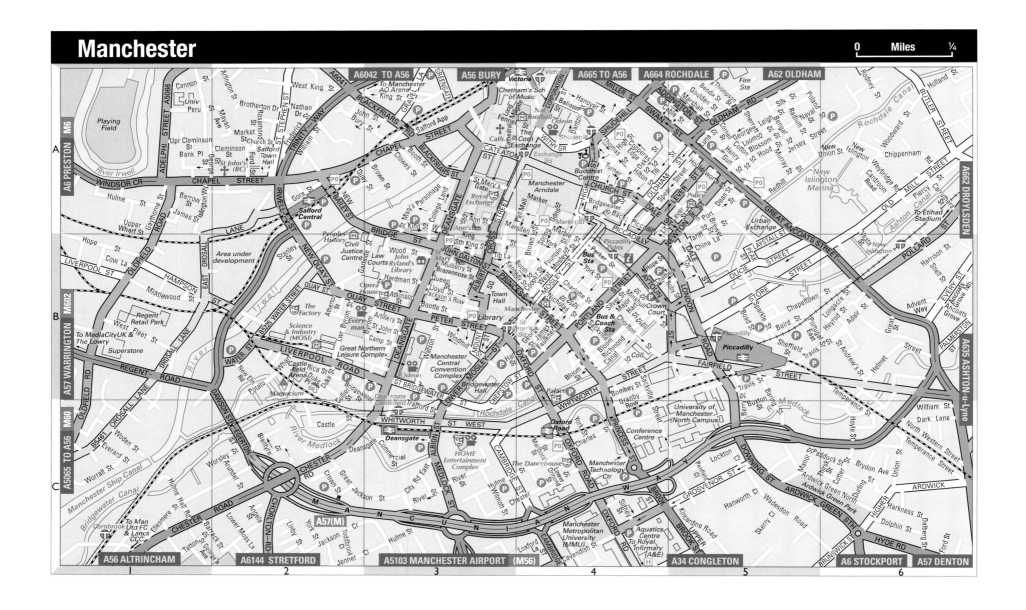

Maidstone

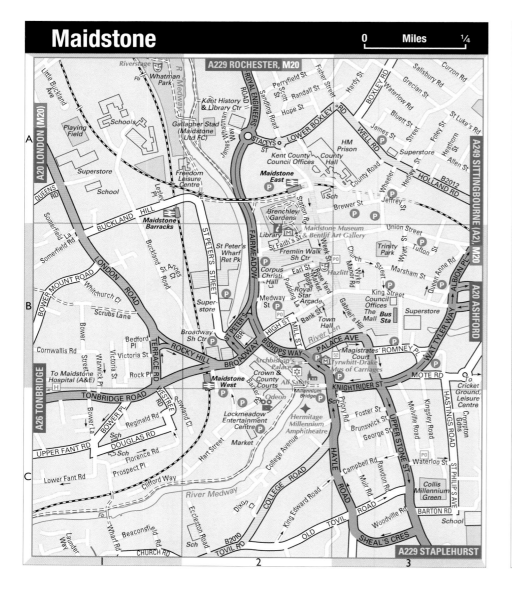

Merthyr Tydfil / Merthyr Tudful

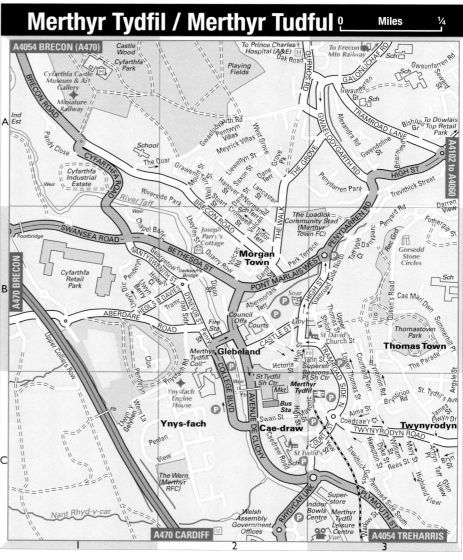

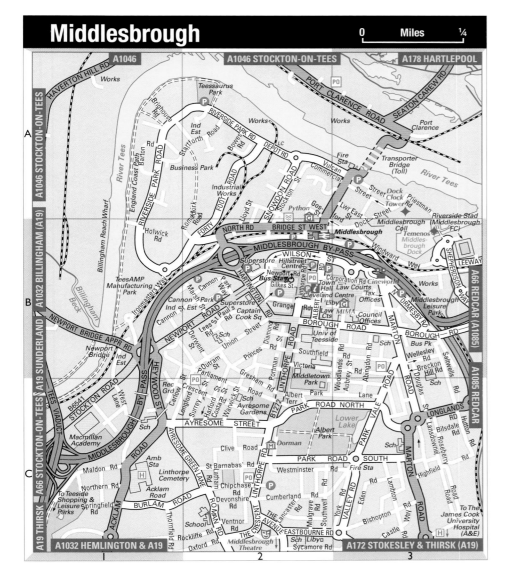

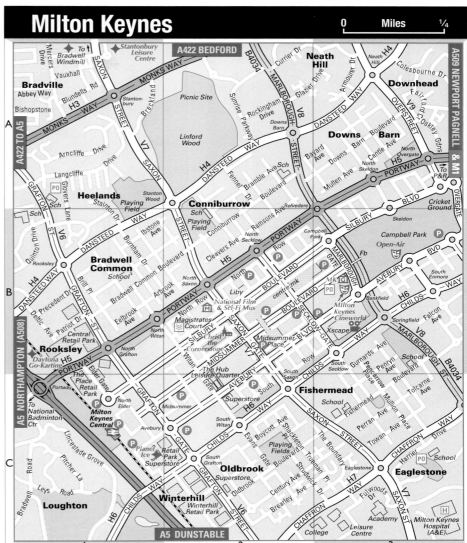

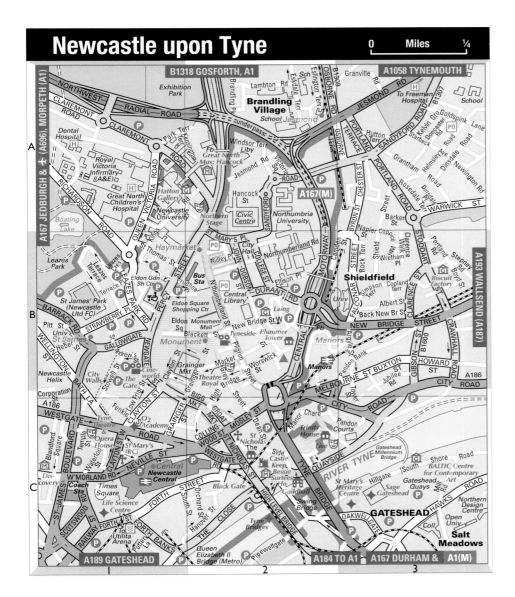

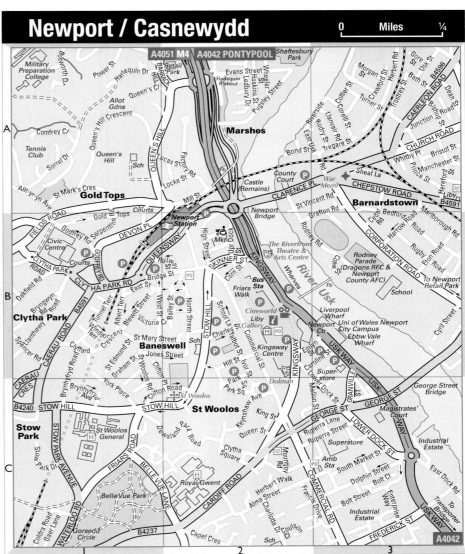

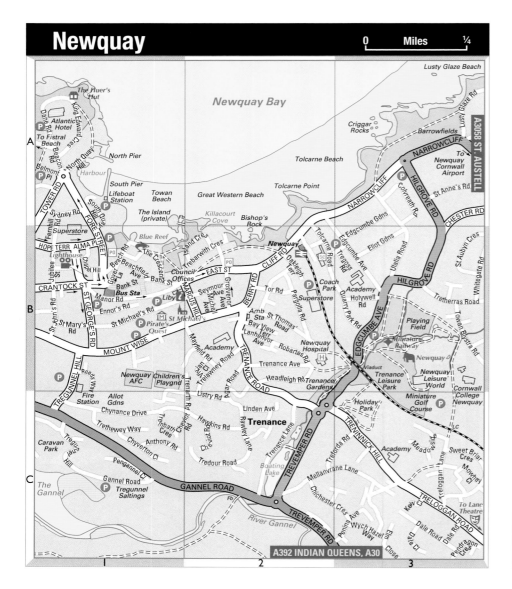

Newquay

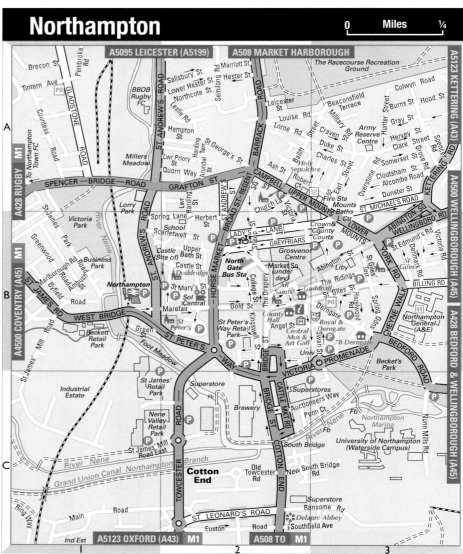

Northampton

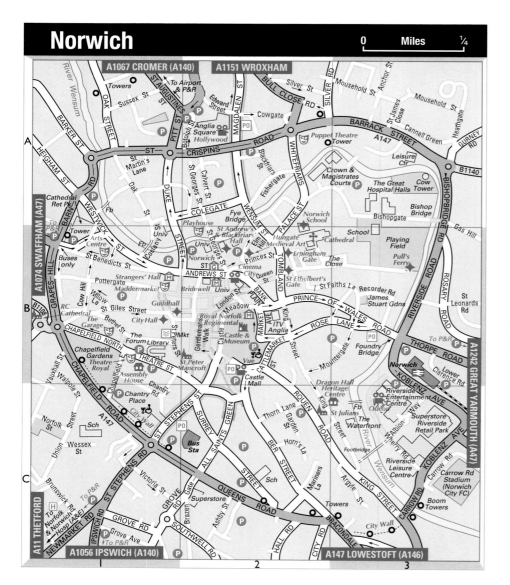

Norwich

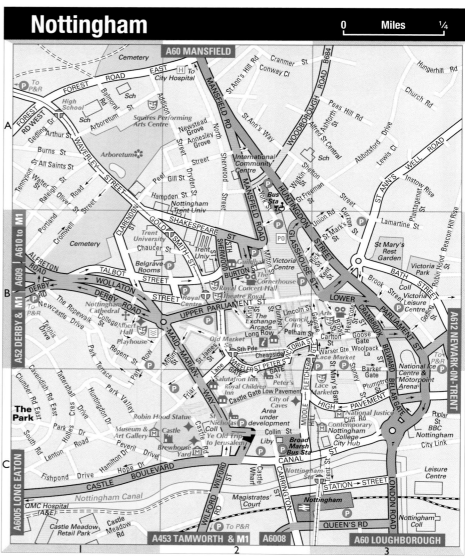

Nottingham

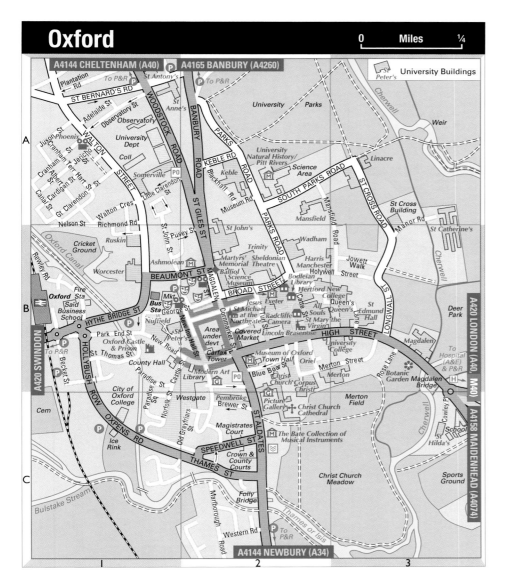

Oxford

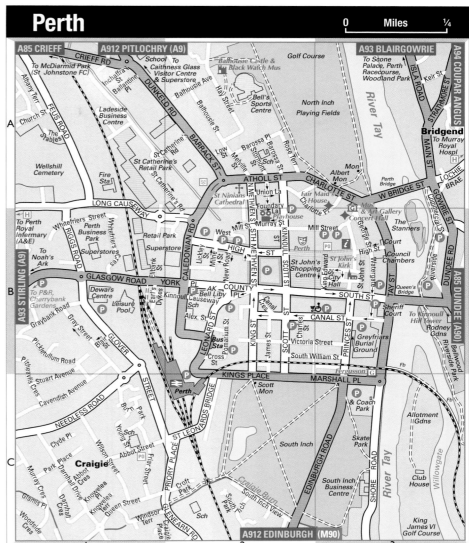

Perth

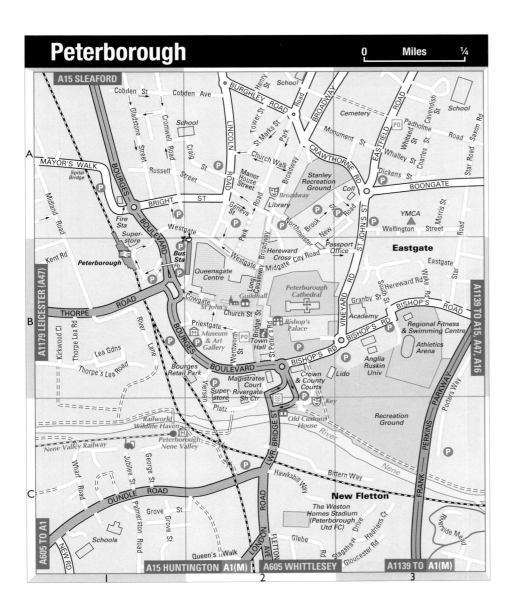

Peterborough

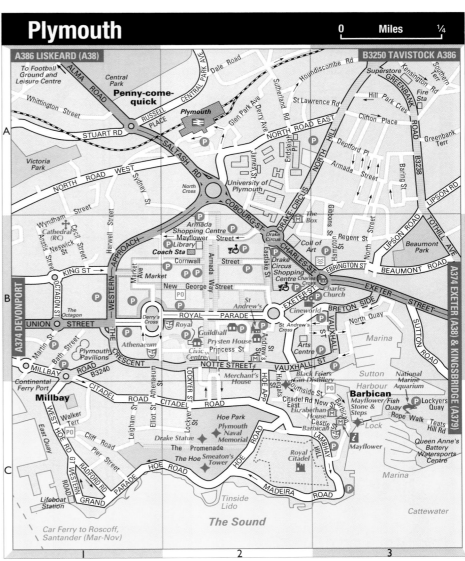

Plymouth

Poole

0 Miles ¼

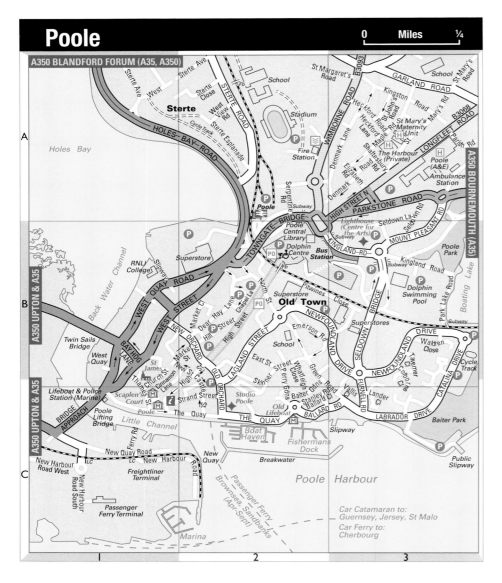

Portsmouth

0 Miles ¼

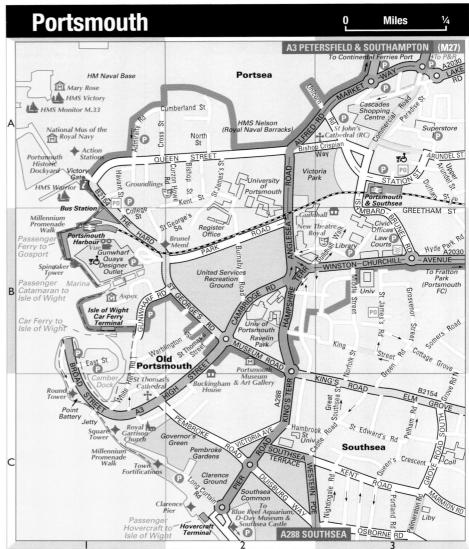

Preston

0 Miles ¼

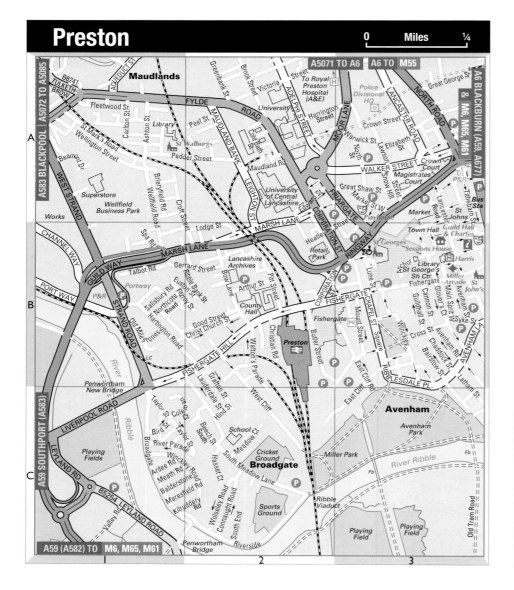

Reading

0 Miles ¼

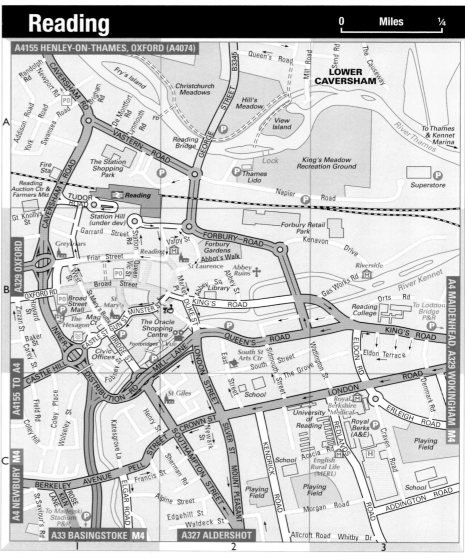

St Andrews

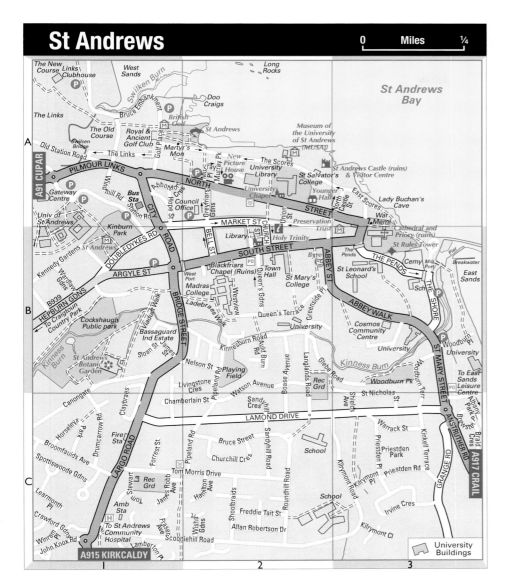

Salisbury

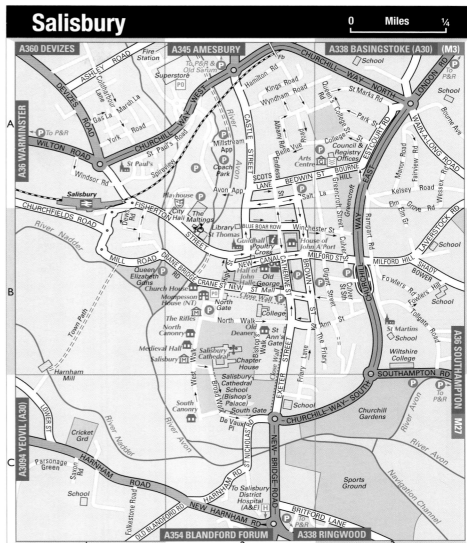

Scarborough

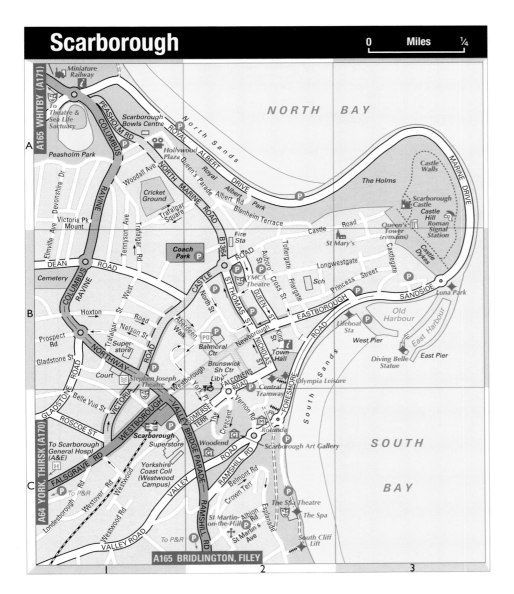

Shrewsbury

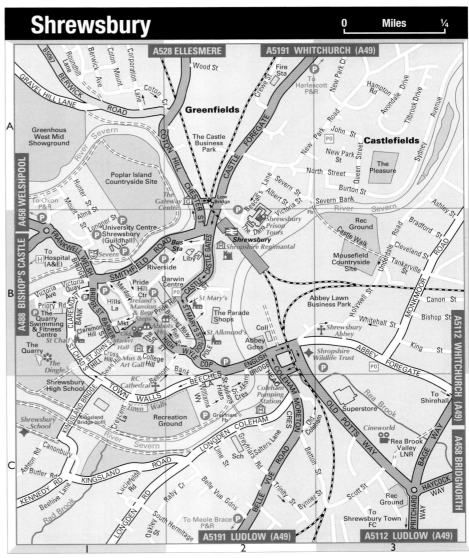

Sheffield

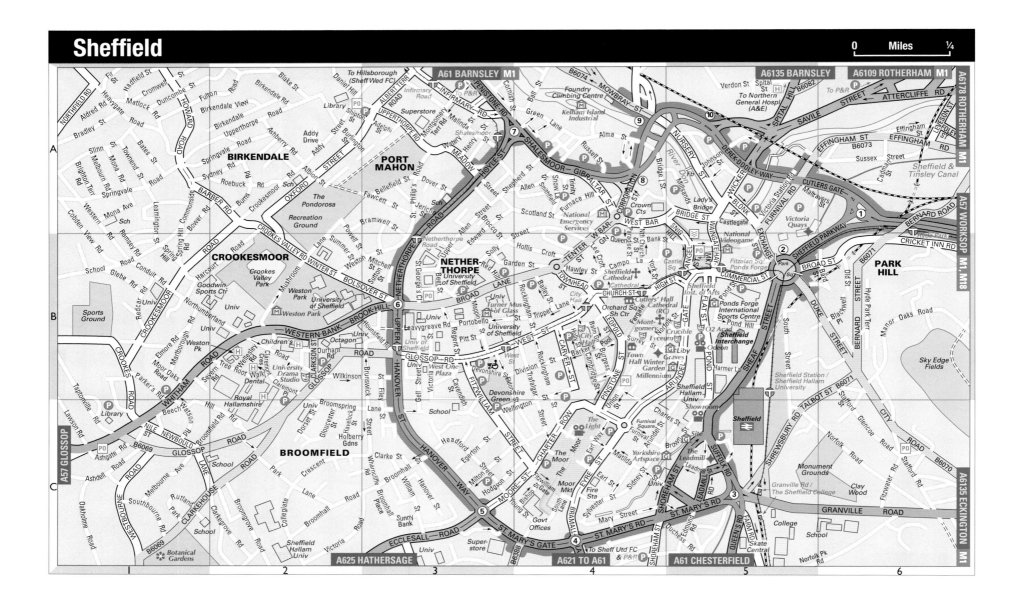

Stoke-on-Trent (Hanley)

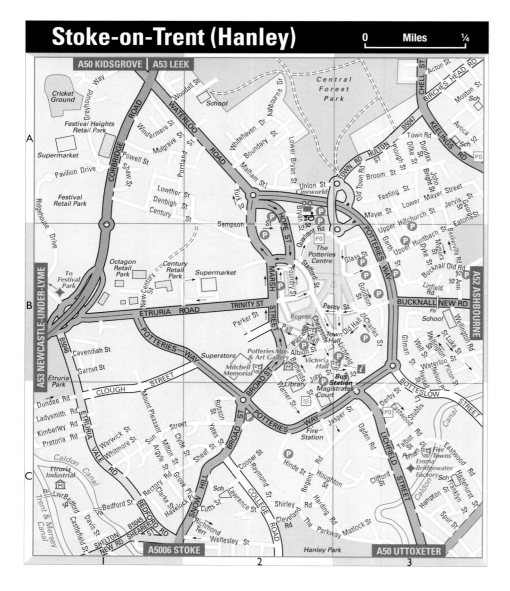

Southampton

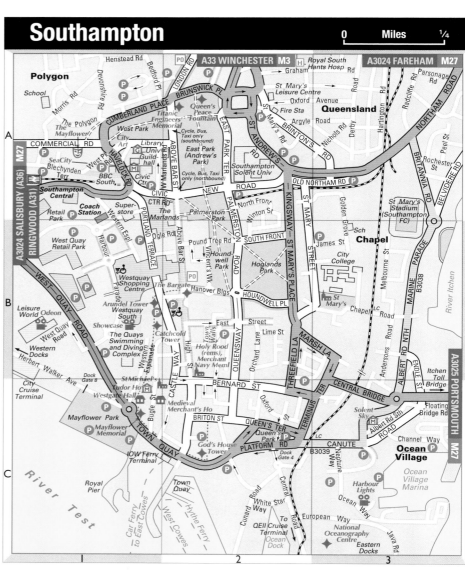

Southend-on-Sea

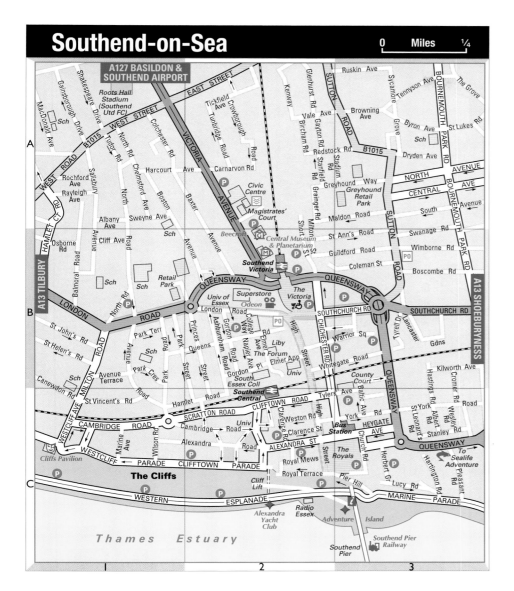

Stirling

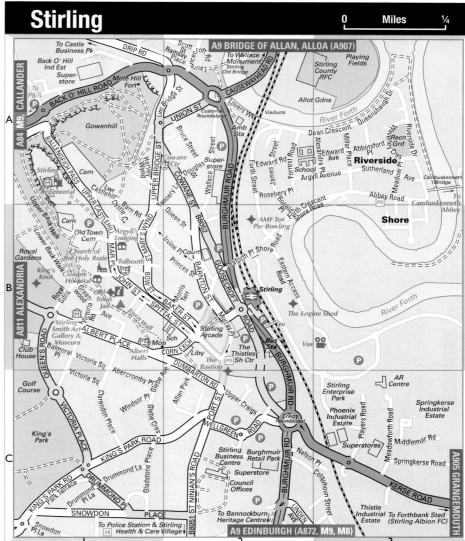

Stratford-upon-Avon

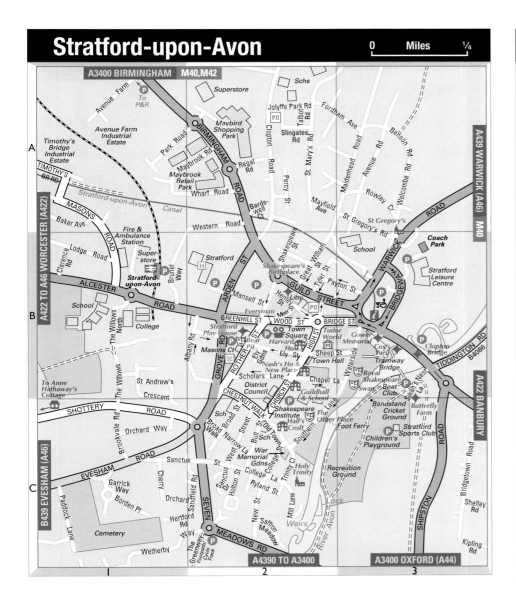

Sunderland

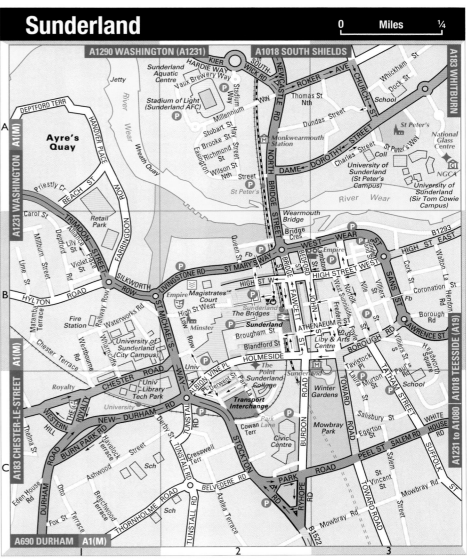

Swansea / Abertawe

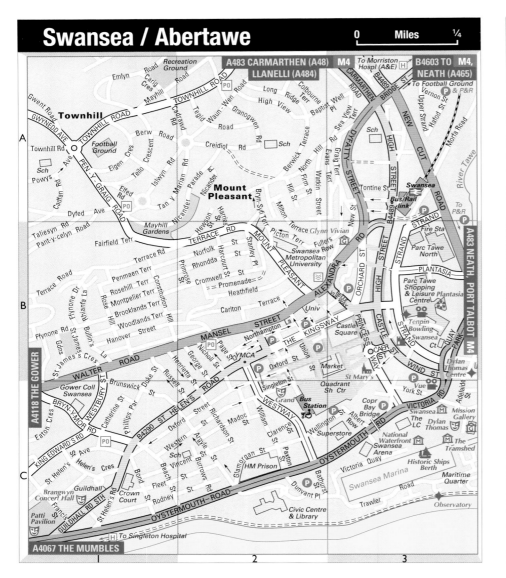

Swindon

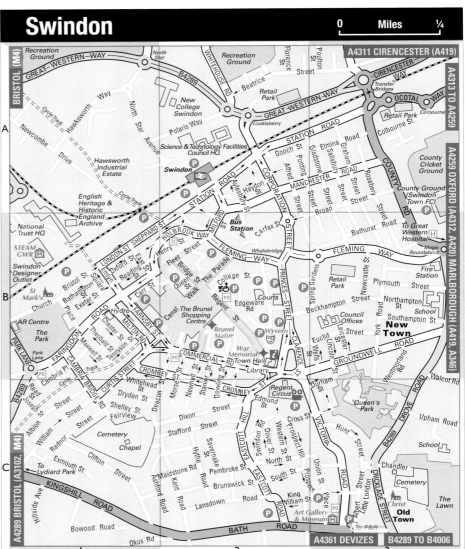

Taunton

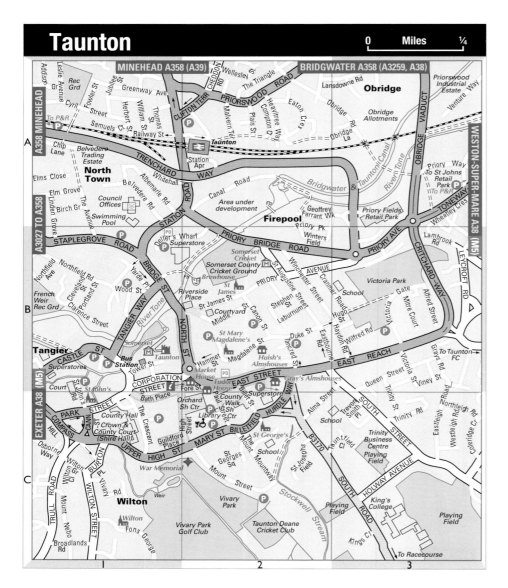

Telford

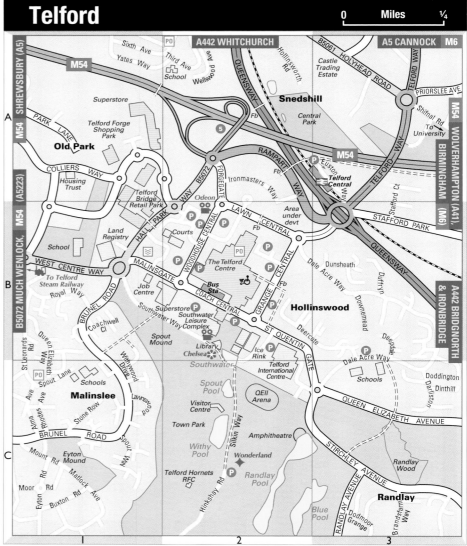

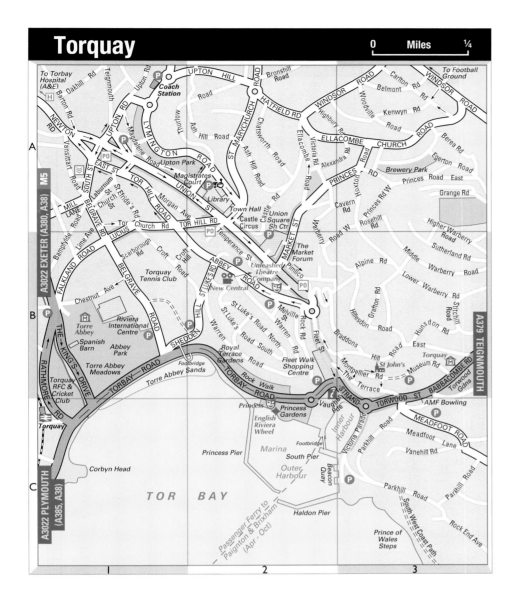

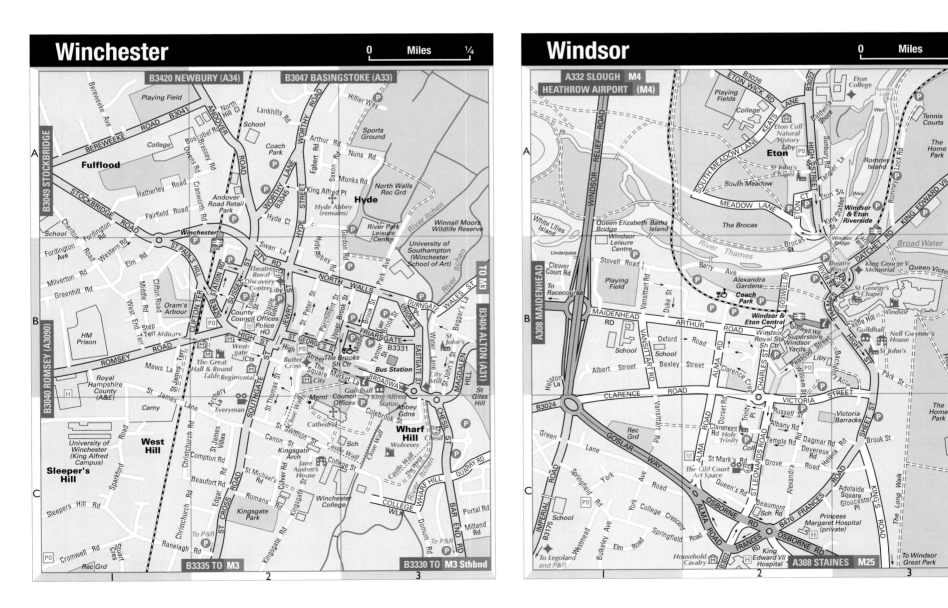

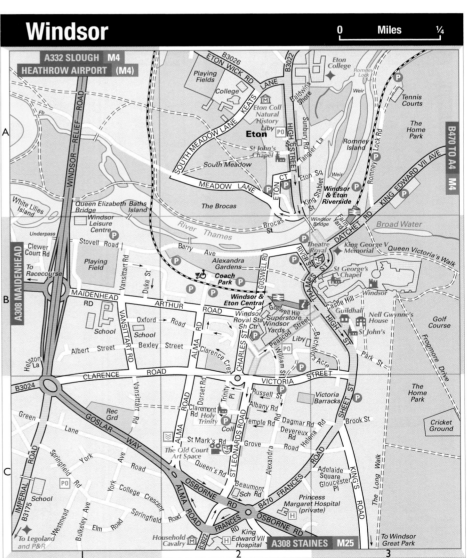

Wolverhampton

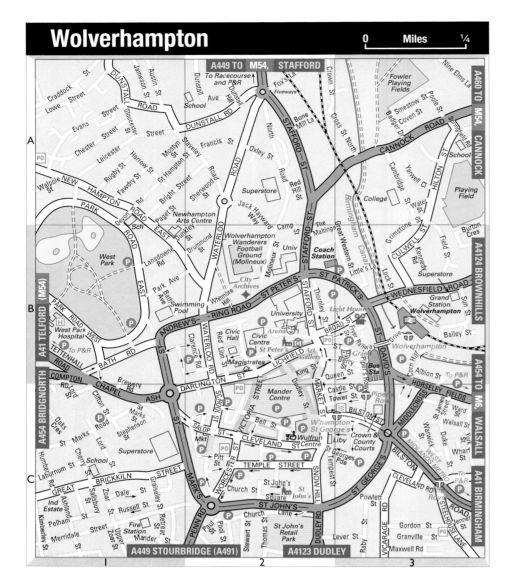

Worcester

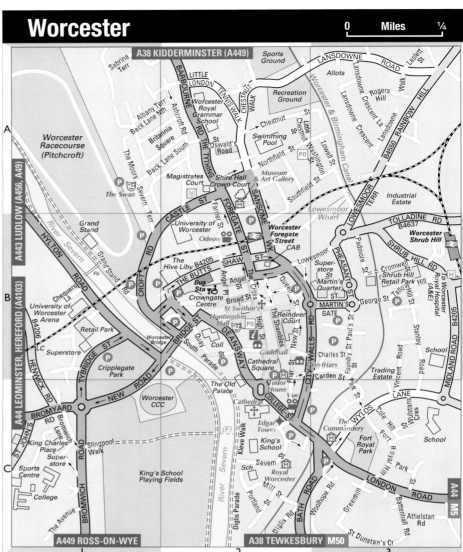

Wrexham / Wrecsam

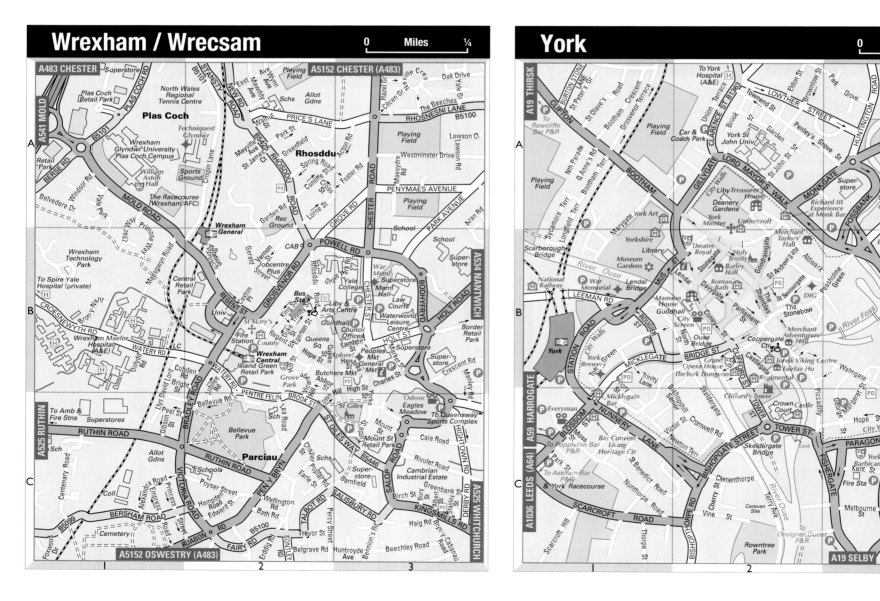

York

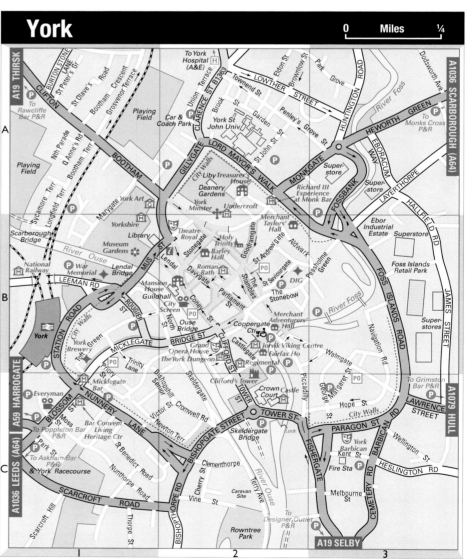

Abbreviations used in the index

Aberdeen	**Aberdeen City**	Guern	**Guernsey**
Aberds	**Aberdeenshire**	Gwyn	**Gwynedd**
Ald	**Alderney**	Halton	**Halton**
Anglesey	**Isle of Anglesey**	Hants	**Hampshire**
Angus	**Angus**	Hereford	**Herefordshire**
Argyll	**Argyll and Bute**	Herts	**Hertfordshire**
Bath	**Bath and North East Somerset**	Highld	**Highland**
BCP	**Bournemouth, Christchurch and Poole**	Hrtlpl	**Hartlepool**
		Hull	**Hull**
Bedford	**Bedford**	Invclyd	**Inverclyde**
Blackburn	**Blackburn with Darwen**	IoM	**Isle of Man**
Blackpool	**Blackpool**	IoW	**Isle of Wight**
Bl Gwent	**Blaenau Gwent**	Jersey	**Jersey**
Borders	**Scottish Borders**	Kent	**Kent**
Brack	**Bracknell**	Lancs	**Lancashire**
Bridgend	**Bridgend**	Leicester	**City of Leicester**
Brighton	**City of Brighton and Hove**	Leics	**Leicestershire**
Bristol	**City and County of Bristol**	Lincs	**Lincolnshire**
Bucks	**Buckinghamshire**	London	**Greater London**
Caerph	**Caerphilly**	Luton	**Luton**
Cambs	**Cambridgeshire**	Mbro	**Middlesbrough**
Cardiff	**Cardiff**	Medway	**Medway**
Carms	**Carmarthenshire**	Mers	**Merseyside**
C Beds	**Central Bedfordshire**	Midloth	**Midlothian**
Ceredig	**Ceredigion**	M Keynes	**Milton Keynes**
Ches E	**Cheshire East**	Mon	**Monmouthshire**
Ches W	**Cheshire West and Chester**	Moray	**Moray**
Clack	**Clackmannanshire**	M Tydf	**Merthyr Tydfil**
Conwy	**Conwy**	N Ayrs	**North Ayrshire**
Corn	**Cornwall**	Neath	**Neath Port Talbot**
Cumb	**Cumberland**	NE Lincs	**North East Lincolnshire**
Darl	**Darlington**	Newport	**City and County of Newport**
Denb	**Denbighshire**	N Lanark	**North Lanarkshire**
Derby	**City of Derby**	N Lincs	**North Lincolnshire**
Derbys	**Derbyshire**	N Nhants	**North Northamptonshire**
Devon	**Devon**	Norf	**Norfolk**
Dorset	**Dorset**	Northumb	**Northumberland**
Dumfries	**Dumfries and Galloway**	Nottingham	**City of Nottingham**
Dundee	**Dundee City**	Notts	**Nottinghamshire**
Durham	**Durham**	N Som	**North Somerset**
E Ayrs	**East Ayrshire**	N Yorks	**North Yorkshire**
Edin	**City of Edinburgh**	Orkney	**Orkney**
E Dunb	**East Dunbartonshire**	Oxon	**Oxfordshire**
E Loth	**East Lothian**	Pboro	**Peterborough**
E Renf	**East Renfrewshire**	Pembs	**Pembrokeshire**
Essex	**Essex**	Perth	**Perth and Kinross**
E Sus	**East Sussex**	Plym	**Plymouth**
E Yorks	**East Riding of Yorkshire**	Powys	**Powys**
Falk	**Falkirk**	Ptsmth	**Portsmouth**
Fife	**Fife**	Reading	**Reading**
Flint	**Flintshire**	Redcar	**Redcar and Cleveland**
Glasgow	**City of Glasgow**	Renfs	**Renfrewshire**
Glos	**Gloucestershire**	Rhondda	**Rhondda Cynon Taff**
Gtr Man	**Greater Manchester**	Rutland	**Rutland**

S Ayrs	**South Ayrshire**
Scilly	**Scilly**
S Glos	**South Gloucestershire**
Shetland	**Shetland**
Shrops	**Shropshire**
S Lanark	**South Lanarkshire**
Slough	**Slough**
Som	**Somerset**
Soton	**Southampton**
Southend	**Southend-on-Sea**
Staffs	**Staffordshire**
Stirling	**Stirling**
Stockton	**Stockton-on-Tees**
Stoke	**Stoke-on-Trent**
Suff	**Suffolk**
Sur	**Surrey**
Swansea	**Swansea**
Swindon	**Swindon**
S Yorks	**South Yorkshire**
T&W	**Tyne and Wear**
Telford	**Telford and Wrekin**
Thurrock	**Thurrock**
Torbay	**Torbay**
Torf	**Torfaen**
V Glam	**The Vale of Glamorgan**
W&F	**Westmorland and Furness**
Warks	**Warwickshire**
Warr	**Warrington**
W Berks	**West Berkshire**
W Dunb	**West Dunbartonshire**
Wilts	**Wiltshire**
Windsor	**Windsor and Maidenhead**
W Isles	**Western Isles**
W Loth	**West Lothian**
W Mid	**West Midlands**
W Nhants	**West Northamptonshire**
Wokingham	**Wokingham**
Worcs	**Worcestershire**
Wrex	**Wrexham**
W Sus	**West Sussex**
W Yorks	**West Yorkshire**
York	**City of York**

How to use the index

Example

Charlton Mackerell Som **12** B3

- grid square
- page number
- county or unitary authority

A

Abbas Combe 12 B5
Abberley 50 C2
Abberton
  Essex 43 C6
  Worcs 50 D4
Abberwick 117 C7
Abbess Roding . .42 C1
Abbey 11 C6
Abbey-cwm-hir .48 B2
Abbeydale 88 F4
Abbey Dore 49 F5
Abbey Field 43 B5
Abbey Hulton . . .75 E6
Abbey
  St Bathans 122 C3
Abbeystead 93 D5
Abbey Town 107 D8
Abbey Village . .86 B4
Abbey Wood 29 B5
Abbots Bickington .9 C5
Abbots Bromley . .62 B4
Abbotsbury 12 F3
Abbotsham 9 B6
Abbotskerswell . . .7 C6
Abbots Langley . .40 D3
Abbots Leigh 23 B7
Abbotsley 54 D3
Abbots Morton . .50 D5
Abbots Ripton . .54 B3
Abbots Salford . .51 D5
Abbotswood 14 B4
Abbotts Ann 25 E8
Abcott 49 B5
Abdon 61 F5
Aber 46 E3
Aberaeron 46 C3
Aberaman 34 D4
Aberangell 58 C5
Aber-Arad 46 F2
Aberarder 137 F7
Aberarder
  House 138 B2
Aberarder
  Lodge 137 F8
Aberargie 128 C3
Aberarth 46 C3
Aberavon 33 E8
Aber-banc 46 E2
Aberbeeg 35 D6
Abercanaid 34 D4
Abercarn 35 E6
Abercastle 44 B3
Abercegir 58 D5
Aberchirder 152 C6
Aber Cowarth . . .59 C5
Abercraf 34 C2
Abercrombie 129 D7
Abercych 45 E4
Abercynafon 34 C4
Abercynon 34 D4
Aberdalgie 128 B2
Aberdâr
  = Aberdare 34 D3
Aberdare
  = Aberdâr 34 D3
Aberdaron 70 E2
Aberdaugleddau
  = Milford Haven . .44 E4

Aberdeen 141 D8
Aberdesach 82 F4
Aberdour 128 F3
Aberdovey
  = Aberdyfi 58 E3
Aberdulais 34 D1
Aberdyfi
  = Aberdovey 58 E3
Aberedw 48 E2
Abereiddy 44 B2
Abererch 70 D4
Aberfan 34 D4
Aberfeldy 133 E5
Aberffraw 82 E3
Aberffrwd 47 B5
Aberford 95 F7
Aberfoyle 126 D4
Abergavenny =
  Y Fenni 35 C6
Abergele 72 B3
Aber-Giâr 46 E4
Abergorlech 46 F4
Abergwaun
  = Fishguard 44 B4
Abergwesyn 47 D7
Abergwili 33 B5
Abergwynant 58 C3
Abergwyngregyn .83 D6
Abergynolwyn . . .58 D3
Aber-Hirnant 72 F3
Aberhonddu
  = Brecon 34 B4
Aberhosan 58 E5
Aberkenfig 34 F2
Aberlady 129 F6
Aberlemno 135 D5
Aberllefenni 58 D4
Abermagwr 47 B5
Abermaw
  = Barmouth 58 C3
Abermeurig 46 D4
Abermule 59 E8
Abernaint 59 B8
Abernant 32 B4
Aber-nant 34 D4
Abernethy 128 C3
Abernyte 134 F2
Aberpennar
  = Mountain Ash . .34 E4
Aberporth 45 D4
Abersoch 70 E4
Abersychan 35 D6
Abertawe
  = Swansea 33 E7
Aberteifi
  = Cardigan 45 E3
Aberthin 22 B2
Abertillery
  = Abertyleri 35 D6
Abertridwr
  Caerph 35 F5
  Powys 59 C7
Abertyleri
  = Abertillery 35 D6
Abertysswg 35 D5
Aberuthven 127 C8
Aber-Village 35 B5
Aberyscir 34 B3
Aberystwyth 58 F2

Abhainn Suidhe 154 G5
Abingdon-on-
  Thames 38 E4
Abinger Common . .28 E2
Abinger Hammer .27 E8
Abington 114 B2
Abington Pigotts .54 E4
Ab Kettleby 64 B4
Ab Lench 50 D5
Ablington
  Glos 37 D8
  Wilts 25 E6
Abney 75 B8
Aboyne 140 E4
Abram 86 D4
Abriachan 151 H8
Abridge 41 E7
Abronhill 119 B7
Abson 24 B2
Abthorpe 52 E4
Abune-the-Hill . . 159 F3
Aby 79 B7
Acaster Malbis . .95 E8
Acaster Selby . . .95 E8
Accrington 87 B5
Acha 146 F4
Achabraid 145 E7
Achachork 149 D9
Achafolla 124 D3
Achagary 157 D10
Achahoish 144 F6
Achalader 133 E8
Achallader 131 E7
Acha Mor 155 E8
Achanalt 150 E5
Achanamara 144 E6
Achandunie 151 D9
Ach'an Todhair . .130 B4
Achany 157 J8
Achaphubuil 130 B4
Acharacle 147 E9
Acharn
  Highld 147 F10
  Perth 132 E4
Acharole 158 E4
Achath 141 C6
Achavanich 158 F3
Achavraat 151 G12
Achddu 33 D5
Achduart 156 J3
Achentoul 157 F11
Achfary 156 F5
Achgarve 155 H13
Achiemore
  Highld 156 C6
  Highld 157 D11
A'Chill 148 H7
Achiltibuie 156 J3
Achina 157 C10
Achinduich 157 J8
Achinduin 124 B4
Achingills 158 D3
Achintee
  Highld 131 B5
  Highld 150 G2
Achintraid 149 E13
Achlean 138 E4
Achleck 146 G7
Achluachrach . . .137 F5
Achlyness 156 D5
Achmelvich 156 G3

Achmore
  Highld 149 E13
  Stirling 132 F2
Achnaba
  Argyll 124 B5
  Argyll 145 E8
Achnabat 151 H8
Achnacarnin 156 F3
Achnacarry 136 F4
Achnacloich
  Argyll 125 B5
  Highld 149 H10
Achnaconeran . .137 C7
Achnacraig 146 G7
Achnacroish 130 E2
Achnadrish 146 F7
Achnafalnich . . .125 C8
Achnagarron 151 E9
Achnaha 146 E7
Achnahanat 151 B8
Achnahannet . . .139 B5
Achnairn 157 H8
Achnaluachrach .157 J9
Achnasaul 136 F4
Achnasheen 150 F4
Achosnich 146 E7
Achranich 147 G10
Achreamie 157 C13
Achriabhach 131 C5
Achriesgill 156 D5
Achrimsdale 157 J12
Achtoty 157 C9
Achurch 65 F7
Achuvoldrach . . .157 D8
Achvaich 151 B10
Achvarasdal 157 C12
Ackergill 158 E5
Acklam
  Mbro 102 C2
  N Yorks 96 C3
Ackleton 61 E7
Acklington 117 D8
Ackton 88 B5
Ackworth Moor
  Top 88 C5
Acle 69 C7
Acock's Green . . .62 F5
Acol 31 C7
Acomb
  Northumb 110 C2
  York 95 D8
Aconbury 49 F7
Acre 87 B5
Acrefair 73 E6
Acre Street 15 E8
Acton
  Ches E 74 D3
  Dorset 13 G7
  London 41 F5
  Shrops 60 F3
  Suff 56 E2
  Wrex 73 D7
Acton
  Beauchamp . . .49 D8
Acton Bridge 74 B2
Acton Burnell . . .60 D5
Acton Green 49 D8
Acton Pigott 60 D5
Acton Round 61 E6
Acton Scott 60 F4
Acton Trussell . . .62 C3

Acton Turville 37 F5
Adbaston 61 B7
Adber 12 B3
Adderley 74 E3
Adderstone 123 F7
Addiewell 120 C2
Addingham 94 E3
Addington
  Bucks 39 B7
  Kent 29 D7
  London 28 C4
Addinston 121 D8
Addiscombe 28 C4
Addlestone 27 C8
Addlethorpe 79 C8
Adel 95 F5
Adeney 61 C7
Adfa 59 D7
Adforton 49 B6
Adisham 31 D6
Adlestrop 38 B2
Adlingfleet 90 B2
Adlington 86 C4
Admaston
  Staffs 62 B4
  Telford 61 C6
Admington 51 E7
Adstock 52 F5
Adstone 52 D3
Adversane 16 B4
Advie 152 E1
Adwalton 88 B3
Adwell 39 E6
Adwick le Street . .89 D6
Adwick upon
  Dearne 89 D5
Adziel 153 C9
Ae Village 114 F2
Affleck 141 B7
Affpuddle 13 E6
Affric Lodge 136 B4
Afon-wen 72 B5
Afton 14 F4
Agglethorpe 101 F5
Agneash 84 D4
Aigburth 85 F4
Aiginis 155 D9
Aike 97 E6
Aikerness 159 C5
Aikers 159 J5
Aiketgate 108 E4
Aikton 108 D2
Ailey 48 E5
Ailstone 51 D7
Ailsworth 65 E8
Ainderby
  Quernhow 102 F1
Ainderby
  Steeple 101 E8
Aingers Green . . .43 B7
Ainsdale 85 C4
Ainsdale-on-Sea 85 C4
Ainstable 108 E5
Ainsworth 87 C5
Ainthorpe 103 D5
Aintree 85 E4
Aird
  Argyll 124 E3
  Dumfries 104 D4
  Highld 149 A12
  W Isles 155 D10

Aird a Mhachair 148 D2
Aird a' Mhulaidh 154 F6
Aird Asaig 154 G6
Aird Dhail 155 A9
Airdens 151 B9
Aird Mhidhinis . 148 H2
Aird Mhighe
  W Isles 154 H6
  W Isles 154 J5
Aird Mhor 148 H2
Aird of Sleat . . .149 H10
Airdrie 119 C7
Airdtorrisdale . . .157 C9
Aird Uig 154 D5
Airidh a
  Bhruaich 154 F7
Airieland 106 D4
Airmyn 89 B8
Airntully 133 F7
Airor 149 H12
Airth 127 F7
Airton 94 D2
Airyhassen 105 E7
Aisby
  Lincs 78 F3
  Lincs 90 E2
Aisgernis 148 F2
Aiskew 101 F7
Aislaby
  N Yorks 103 D6
  N Yorks 103 F5
  Stockton 102 C2
Aisthorpe 78 A2
Aith
  Orkney 159 G3
  Shetland 160 D8
  Shetland 160 H5
Aithsetter 160 K6
Aitkenhead 112 D3
Aitnoch 151 H12
Akeld 117 B5
Akeley 52 F5
Akenham 56 E5
Albaston 6 B2
Alberbury 60 C3
Albourne 17 C6
Albrighton
  Shrops 60 C4
  Shrops 62 D2
Alburgh 69 F5
Albury
  Herts 41 B7
  N Yorks 95 C7
  Sur 27 E8
Albury End 41 B7
Alby Hill 81 D7
Alcaig 151 F8
Alcaston 60 F4
Alcester 51 D5
Alciston 18 E2
Alcombe
  Som 21 E8
  Wilts 24 C3
Alconbury 54 B2
Alconbury Weald
  Cambs 54 B3
Alconbury
  Weston 54 B2
Aldbar Castle . . .135 D5
Aldborough
  Norf 81 D7

Aldborough continued
  N Yorks 95 C7
Aldbourne 25 B7
Aldbrough 97 F8
Aldbrough
  St John 101 C7
Aldbury 40 C2
Aldcliffe 92 C4
Aldclune 133 C6
Aldeburgh 57 D8
Aldeby 69 E7
Aldenham 40 E4
Alderbury 14 B2
Aldercar 76 E4
Alderford 68 C4
Alderholt 14 C2
Alderley 36 E4
Alderley Edge . . .74 B5
Aldermaston 26 C3
Aldermaston
  Wharf 26 C4
Alderminster 51 E7
Alder's End 49 E8
Aldersey Green . .73 D8
Aldershot 27 D6
Alderton
  Glos 50 F5
  Shrops 60 B4
  Suff 57 E7
  Wilts 37 F5
  W Nhants 52 E5
Alderwasley 76 D3
Aldfield 95 C5
Aldford 73 D8
Aldham
  Essex 43 B5
  Suff 56 E4
Aldie 151 C10
Aldingbourne 16 D3
Aldingham 92 B2
Aldington
  Kent 19 B7
  Worcs 51 E5
Aldington Frith . . .19 B7
Aldochlay 126 E2
Aldreth 54 B5
Aldridge 62 D4
Aldringham 57 C8
Aldsworth 38 C1
Aldunie 140 B2
Aldwark
  Derbys 76 D2
  N Yorks 95 C7
Aldwick 16 E3
Aldwincle 65 F7
Aldworth 26 B3
Alexandria 118 B3
Alfardisworthy . . .8 C4
Alfington 11 E6
Alfold 27 F8
Alfold Bars 27 F8
Alfold Crossways .27 F8
Alford
  Aberds 140 C4
  Lincs 79 B7
  Som 23 F8
Alfreton 76 D4
Alfrick 50 D2
Alfrick Pound 50 D2
Alfriston 18 E2
Algaltraig 145 F9

Algarkirk 79 F5
Alhampton 23 F8
Aline Lodge 154 F6
Alisary 147 D10
Alkborough 90 B2
Alkerton 51 E8
Alkham 31 E6
Alkington 74 F2
Alkmonton 75 F8
Alladale Lodge . 150 C7
Allaleigh 7 D6
Allanaquoich . . .139 E7
Allangrange
  Mains 151 F9
Allanton
  Borders 122 D4
  N Lanark 119 D8
Allathasdal 148 H1
All Cannings 25 C5
Allendale Town . .109 D8
Allenheads 109 E8
Allensford 110 D3
Allens Green 41 C7
Allensmore 49 F6
Allenton 76 F3
Aller 12 B2
Allerby 107 F7
Allerford 21 E8
Allerston 103 F6
Allerthorpe 96 E3
Allerton
  Mers 86 F2
  W Yorks 94 F4
Allerton Bywater .88 B5
Allerton
  Mauleverer 95 D7
Allesley 63 F7
Allestree 76 F3
Allet 3 B6
Allexton 64 D5
Allgreave 75 C6
Allhallows 30 B2
Allhallows-on-
  Sea 30 B2
Alligin Shuas . . .149 C13
Allimore Green . .62 C2
Allington
  Lincs 77 E8
  Wilts 25 C5
  Wilts 25 F7
Allithwaite 92 B3
Alloa 127 E7
Allonby 107 E7
Alloway 112 C3
All Saints South
  Elmham 69 F6
All Stretton 60 E4
Allt 33 D6
Alltbeithe 136 C3
Alltchaorunn 131 D5
Alltforgan 59 B6
Alltmawr 48 E2
Alltnacaillich 156 E7
Allt na h-Airbhe 150 B4
Allt-nan-sùgh . . .136 B2
Alltsigh 137 C7
Alltwalis 46 F3
Alltwen 33 D8
Alltyblaca 46 E4
Allwood Green . . .56 B4
Almeley 48 D5
Almer 13 E7

Almholme 89 D6
Almington 74 F4
Alminstone Cross . .8 B5
Almondbank 128 B2
Almondbury 88 C2
Almondsbury 36 F3
Alne 95 C7
Alness 151 E9
Alnham 117 C5
Alnmouth 117 C8
Alnwick 117 C7
Alperton 40 F4
Alphamstone 56 F2
Alpheton 56 D2
Alphington 10 E4
Alport 76 C2
Alpraham 74 D2
Alresford 43 B6
Alrewas 63 C5
Alsager 74 D4
Alsagers Bank . . .74 E5
Alsop en le Dale .75 D8
Alston
  Devon 11 D8
  W&F 109 E7
Alstone 50 F4
Alstonefield 75 D8
Alswear 10 B2
Altandhu 156 H2
Altanduin 157 G11
Altarnun 8 F4
Altass 156 J7
Alterwall 158 D4
Altham 93 F7
Althorne 43 E5
Althorpe 90 D2
Alticry 105 D6
Altnabreac
  Station 157 E13
Altnacealgach
  Hotel 156 H5
Altnacraig 124 C4
Altnafeadh 131 D6
Altnaharra 157 F8
Altofts 88 B4
Alton
  Derbys 76 C3
  Hants 26 F5
  Staffs 75 E7
Alton Pancras . . .12 D5
Alton Priors 25 C6
Altrincham 87 F5
Altrua 136 F5
Altskeith 126 D3
Altyre House 151 F13
Alva 127 E7
Alvanley 73 B8
Alvaston 76 F3
Alvechurch 50 B5
Alvecote 63 D6
Alvediston 13 B7
Alveley 61 F7
Alverdiscott 9 B7
Alverstoke 15 E7
Alverstone 15 F6
Alverton 77 E7
Alves 152 B1
Alvescot 38 D2

Abb – Alv

Alveston
S Glos 36 F3
Warks 51 D7
Alvie 138 D4
Alvingham 91 E7
Alvington 36 D3
Alwalton 65 E8
Alweston 12 C4
Alwinton 116 D5
Alwoodley 95 E5
Alyth 134 E2
Amatnatua 150 B7
Am Baile 148 G2
Ambergate 76 D3
Amber Hill 78 E5
Amberley
Glos 37 D5
W Sus 16 C4
Amble 117 D8
Amblecote 62 F2
Ambler Thorn 87 B8
Ambleside 99 E5
Ambleston 44 C5
Ambrosden 39 C6
Am Buth 124 C4
Amcotts 90 C2
Amersham 40 E2
Amesbury 25 E6
Amington 63 D6
Amisfield 114 F2
Amlwch 82 B4
Amlwch Port 82 B4
Ammanford
= Rhydaman 33 C7
Amod 143 E8
Amotherby 96 B3
Ampfield 14 B5
Ampleforth 95 B8
Ampney Crucis 37 D7
Ampney St Mary . . . 37 D7
Ampney St Peter . . . 37 D7
Amport 25 E7
Ampthill 53 F8
Ampton 56 B2
Amroth 32 D2
Amulree 133 F5
Anagach 139 B6
Anaheilt 130 C2
Anancaun 150 E3
An Caol 149 C11
Ancaster 78 E2
Anchor 59 F8
Anchorsholme 92 E3
An Cnoc 155 D9
Ancroft 123 E5
Ancrum 116 B2
Anderby 79 B8
Anderson 13 E6
Anderton 74 B3
Andover 25 E8
Andover Down 25 E8
Andoversford 37 C7
Andreas 84 C4
Anfield 85 E4
Angersleigh 11 C6
Angle 44 E3
An Gleann Ur 155 D9
Angmering 16 D4
Angram
N Yorks 95 E8
N Yorks 100 E3
Anie 126 C4
Ankerville 151 D11
Anlaby 90 B4
Anmer 80 E3
Annan 107 C8
Annat
Argyll 125 C6
Highld 149 C13
Anna Valley 25 E8
Annbank 112 B4
Annesley
Woodhouse 76 D5
Annfield Plain . . . 110 D4
Annifirth 160 J3
Annitsford 111 B5
Annscroft 60 D4
Ansdell 85 E4
Ansford 23 F8
Ansley 63 E6
Anslow 63 B6
Anslow Gate 63 B6
Anstey
Herts 54 F5
Leics 64 D2
Anstruther
Easter 129 D7
Anstruther
Wester 129 D7
Ansty
Hants 26 E5
Warks 63 F7
Wilts 13 B7
W Sus 17 B6
Anthill
Common 15 C7
Anthorn 107 D8
Antingham 81 D8
An t-Ob
= Leverburgh . . . 154 J5
Anton's Gowt 79 E5
Antonshill 127 F7
Antony 5 D8
Anwick 78 D4
Anwoth 106 D2
Aoradh 142 B3
Apes Hall 67 E5
Apethorpe 65 E7
Apeton 62 C2
Apley 78 B4
Apperknowle 76 B3
Apperley 37 B5
Apperley Bridge . . . 94 F4
Appersett 100 E3
Appin 130 E3
Appin House 130 E3
Appleby 90 C4
Appleby-in-
Westmorland . . . 100 B1
Appleby Magna . . . 63 D7
Appleby Parva 63 D7
Applecross 149 D12
Applecross
House 149 D12

Appledore
Devon 11 C5
Devon 20 F3
Kent 19 C6
Appledore Heath . 19 B6
Appleford 39 E5
Applegarthtown . . 114 F4
Appleshaw 25 E8
Applethwaite 98 B4
Appleton
Halton 86 F3
Oxon 38 D4
Appleton-le-
Moors 103 F5
Appleton-le-
Street 96 B3
Appleton
Roebuck 95 E8
Appleton Thorn . . 86 F4
Appleton Wiske . 102 D1
Appletreehall . . . 115 C8
Appletreewick . . . 94 C3
Appley 11 B5
Appley Bridge 86 D3
Apse Heath 15 F6
Apsley End 54 F2
Apuldram 16 D2
Aquhythie 141 C6
Arabella 151 D11
Arbeadie 141 E5
Arberth
= Narberth 32 C2
Arbirlot 135 E6
Arboll 151 C11
Arborfield 27 C5
Arborfield Cross . 27 C5
Arborfield
Garrison 27 C5
Arbourthorne 88 F4
Arbroath 135 E6
Arbuthnott 135 B7
Archiestown 152 D2
Arclid 74 C4
Ardachu 157 J9
Ardalanish 146 K6
Ardanaiseig 125 C6
Ardaneaskan 149 E13
Ardanstur 124 D4
Ardargie House
Hotel 128 C2
Ardarroch 149 E13
Ardbeg
Argyll 142 D5
Argyll 145 E10
Ardcharnich 150 C4
Ardchiavaig 146 K6
Ardchullarie
More 126 C4
Ardchyle 126 B4
Ard-dhubh 149 D12
Arddleen 60 C2
Ardechvie 136 E4
Ardeley 41 B6
Ardelve 149 F13
Arden 126 F2
Ardens Grafton . . 51 D6
Ardentinny 145 E10
Ardentraive 145 F9
Ardeonaig 132 F3
Ardersier 151 F10
Ardessie 150 C3
Ardfern 124 E4
Ardgartan 125 E8
Ardgay 151 B8
Ardgour 130 C4
Ardheslaig 149 C12
Ardiecow 152 B5
Ardindrean 150 C4
Ardingly 17 B7
Ardington 38 F4
Ardlair 140 B4
Ardlamont
House 145 G8
Ardleigh 43 B6
Ardler 134 E2
Ardley 39 B5
Ardlui 126 C2
Ardlussa 144 E5
Ardmair 150 B4
Ardmay 125 E8
Ardminish 143 D7
Ardmolich 147 D10
Ardmore
Argyll 124 C3
Highld 151 C10
Highld 156 D5
Ardnacross 147 G8
Ardnadam 145 F10
Ardnagrask 151 G8
Ardnarff 149 E13
Ardnastang 130 C2
Ardnave 142 A3
Ardno 125 E7
Ardo 153 E8
Ardoch 133 F7
Ardochy House . . 136 D5
Ardo House 141 B8
Ardoyne 141 B5
Ardpatrick 144 G6
Ardpatrick
House 144 H6
Ardpeaton 145 E11
Ardrishaig 145 E7
Ardross
Fife 129 D7
Highld 151 D9
Ardrossan 118 E2
Ardross Castle . . 151 D9
Ardshealach 147 E9
Ardsley 88 D4
Ardslignish 147 E8
Ardtalla 142 C5
Ardtoe 147 D9
Ardtrostan 127 B5
Arduaine 124 D3
Ardullie 151 E8
Ardvasar 149 H11
Ardvorlich 126 B5
Ardwell 104 E5
Ardwell Mains . . . 104 E5
Ardwick 87 E6
Areley Kings 50 B3
Arford 27 F6

Arichastlich . . . 125 B8
Aridhglas 146 J6
Arileod 146 F4
Arinacrinachd . 149 C12
Arinagour 146 F5
Arion 159 G3
Arisaig 147 C9
Ariundle 130 C2
Arkendale 95 C6
Arkesden 55 F5
Arkholme 93 B5
Arkleton 115 E6
Arkle Town 101 D5
Arkley 41 E5
Arksey 89 D6
Arle 37 B6
Arlecdon 98 C2
Arlesey 54 F2
Arleston 61 C6
Arley 86 F4
Arlingham 36 C4
Arlington
Devon 20 E5
E Sus 18 E2
Glos 37 D8
Armadale
Highld 157 C10
W Loth 120 C2
Armadale
Castle 149 H11
Armathwaite 108 E5
Arminghall 69 D5
Armitage 62 C4
Armley 95 F5
Armscote 51 E7
Armthorpe 89 D7
Arnabost 146 F5
Arncliffe 94 B2
Arncroach 129 D7
Arne 13 F7
Arnesby 64 E3
Arngask 128 C3
Arnisdale 149 G13
Arnish 149 D10
Arniston Engine . 121 C6
Arnol 155 C8
Arnold
E Yorks 97 E7
Notts 77 E5
Arnprior 126 E5
Arnside 92 B4
Aros Mains 147 G8
Arowry 73 F8
Arpafeelie 151 F9
Arrad Foot 99 F5
Arram 97 E6
Arrathorne 101 E7
Arreton 15 F6
Arrington 54 D4
Arrivain 125 B8
Arrochar 125 E8
Arrow 51 D5
Arthington 95 E5
Arthingworth 64 F4
Arthog 58 C3
Arthrath 153 E9
Arthurstone 134 E2
Artrochie 153 E10
Arundel 16 D4
Aryhoulan 130 C4
Asby 98 B2
Ascog 145 G10
Ascot 27 C7
Ascott 51 F8
Ascott-under-
Wychwood 38 C3
Asenby 95 B6
Asfordby 64 C4
Asfordby Hill 64 C4
Asgarby
Lincs 78 E4
Lincs 79 C6
Ash
Kent 29 C6
Kent 31 D6
Som 12 B2
Sur 27 D6
Ashampstead 26 B3
Ashbocking 57 D5
Ashbourne 75 E8
Ashbrittle 11 B5
Ash Bullayne 10 D2
Ashburton 7 C5
Ashbury
Devon 9 E7
Oxon 38 F2
Ashby 90 D3
Ashby by Partney . 79 C7
Ashby cum Fenby . 91 D6
Ashby de la
Launde 78 D3
Ashby-de-la-
Zouch 63 C7
Ashby Folville 64 C4
Ashby Magna 64 E2
Ashby Parva 64 F2
Ashby Puerorum . 79 B6
Ashby St Ledgers . 52 C3
Ashby St Mary . . . 69 D6
Ashchurch 50 F4
Ashcombe 7 B7
Ashcott 23 F6
Ashdon 55 E6
Ashe 26 E3
Asheldham 43 D5
Ashen 55 E8
Ashendon 39 C7
Ashfield
Carms 33 B7
Stirling 127 D6
Suff 57 C6
Ashfield Green . . 57 B6
Ashford
Crossways 17 B6
Ashford
Devon 20 F4
Hants 14 C2
Kent 30 E4
Sur 27 B8
Ashford Bowdler . 49 B7
Ashford
Carbonell 49 B7
Ashford Hill 26 C3
Ashford in the
Water 75 C8
Ashgill 119 E7
Ash Green 63 F7

Ashill
Devon 11 C5
Norf 67 D8
Som 11 C8
Ashingdon 42 E4
Ashington
Northumb 117 F8
Som 12 B3
W Sus 16 C5
Ashintully
Castle 133 C8
Ashkirk 115 B7
Ashlett 15 D5
Ashleworth 37 B5
Ashley
Cambs 55 C7
Ches E 87 F5
Devon 9 C8
Dorset 14 C2
Glos 37 E6
Hants 14 E3
Hants 25 F8
N Nhants 64 E4
Staffs 74 F4
Ashley Green 40 D2
Ashley Heath
Dorset 14 D2
Staffs 74 F4
Ash Magna 74 F2
Ashmanhaugh . . . 69 B6
Ashmansworth . . 26 D2
Ashmansworthy . . 8 C5
Ash Mill 10 B2
Ashmore 13 C7
Ashover 76 C3
Ashow 51 B8
Ash Priors 11 B6
Ashreigney 9 C8
Ash Street 56 E4
Ashtead 28 D2
Ash Thomas 10 C5
Ashton
Ches W 74 C2
Corn 2 D5
Hants 15 C6
Hereford 49 C7
Invclyd 118 B2
N Nhants 65 F7
W Nhants 53 E5
Ashton Common . 24 D3
Ashton-in-
Makerfield 86 E3
Ashton Keynes . . 37 E7
Ashton under Hill . 50 F4
Ashton-under-
Lyne 87 E7
Ashton upon
Mersey 87 E5
Ashurst
Hants 14 C4
Kent 18 B2
W Sus 17 C5
Ashurstwood 28 F5
Ash Vale 27 D6
Ashwater 9 E5
Ashwell
Herts 54 F3
Rutland 65 C5
Som 11 C8
Ashwellthorpe . . . 68 E4
Ashwick 23 E8
Ashwicken 67 C7
Ashybank 115 C8
Askam in Furness 92 B2
Askern 89 C6
Askerswell 12 E3
Askett 39 D8
Askham
Notts 77 B7
W&F 99 B7
Askham Bryan . . . 95 E8
Askham Richard . . 95 E8
Asknish 145 D8
Askrigg 100 E4
Askwith 94 E4
Aslackby 78 F3
Aslacton 68 E4
Aslockton 77 F7
Asloun 140 C4
Aspatria 107 E8
Aspenden 41 B6
Asperton 79 F5
Aspley Guise 53 F7
Aspley Heath 53 F7
Aspull 86 D4
Asselby 89 B8
Asserby 79 B7
Assington 56 F3
Assynt House . . 151 E8
Astbury 74 C5
Astcote 52 D4
Asterley 60 D3
Asterton 60 E3
Asthall 38 C2
Asthall Leigh 38 C3
Astley
Shrops 60 C5
Warks 63 F7
Worcs 50 C2
Astley Abbotts . . 61 E7
Astley Bridge 86 C5
Astley Cross 50 C3
Astley Green 86 E5
Aston
Ches E 74 E3
Ches W 74 B2
Derbys 88 F2
Hereford 49 B6
Herts 41 B5
Oxon 38 D3
Shrops 60 B5
Staffs 74 E4
S Yorks 89 F5
Telford 61 D6
W Mid 62 F4
Wokingham 39 F7
Aston Abbotts . . 39 B8
Aston Botterell . . 61 F6
Aston-by-Stone . . 75 F6
Aston Cantlow . . . 51 D6
Aston Clinton . . . 40 C1
Aston Crews 36 B3
Aston Cross 50 F4
Aston End 41 B5
Aston Eyre 61 E6
Aston Fields 50 C4

Aston Flamville . . 63 E8
Aston Ingham . . . 36 B3
Aston juxta
Mondrum 74 D3
Aston le Walls . . . 52 D2
Aston Magna 51 F6
Aston Munslow . . 60 F5
Aston on Clun . . . 60 F3
Aston-on-Trent . . 63 B8
Aston Rogers 60 D3
Aston Rowant . . . 39 E7
Aston Sandford . . 39 D7
Aston Somerville . 50 F5
Aston Subedge . . 51 E6
Aston Tirrold 39 F5
Aston Upthorpe . . 39 F5
Astrop 52 F3
Astwick 54 F3
Astwood
M Keynes 53 E7
Worcs 50 D3
Astwood Bank . . . 50 C5
Aswarby 78 F3
Aswardby 79 B6
Atcham 60 D5
Atch Lench 50 D5
Athelhampton . . . 13 E5
Athelington 57 B6
Athelney 11 B8
Athelstaneford . . 121 B8
Atherington 9 B7
Atherstone 63 E7
Atherstone on
Stour 51 D7
Atherton 86 D4
Atley Hill 101 D7
Atlow 76 E2
Attadale 150 H2
Attadale House . 150 H2
Attenborough . . . 76 F5
Atterby 90 E3
Attercliffe 88 F4
Attleborough
Norf 68 E3
Warks 63 E7
Attlebridge 68 C4
Atwick 97 D7
Atworth 24 C3
Aubourn 78 C2
Auchagallon 143 E9
Auchallater 139 F7
Auchandoir 140 C3
Auchavan 134 C1
Auchbreck 139 B8
Auchenback 118 D5
Auchenblae 135 B7
Auchenbrack . . . 113 E7
Auchenbreck . . . 145 E9
Auchencairn
Dumfries 106 D4
Dumfries 114 F2
Auchencrow 122 C4
Auchendinny . . . 121 C5
Auchengray 120 D2
Auchenhalrig . . . 152 B3
Auchenheath . . . 119 E8
Auchenlochan . . 145 F8
Auchenmalg 105 D6
Auchensoul 112 E2
Auchentiber 118 E3
Auchgourish . . . 138 C5
Auchincarroch . . 126 F3
Auchindrain 125 E6
Auchindrean . . . 150 C4
Auchininna 153 D6
Auchinleck 113 B5
Auchinloch 119 B6
Auchinroath 152 C2
Auchintoul 140 C4
Auchiries 153 E10
Auchlee 141 E7
Auchleven 140 B5
Auchlochan 119 F8
Auchlossan 140 D4
Auchlunies 141 E7
Auchlyne 126 B4
Auchmacoy 153 E9
Auchmair 140 B2
Auchmantle 105 C5
Auchmillan 112 B5
Auchmithie 135 E6
Auchmuirbridge . 128 D4
Auchmull 135 B5
Auchnacree 134 C4
Auchnagallin 151 H13
Auchnagatt 153 D9
Auchnaha 145 E8
Auchnashelloch . 127 C6
Aucholzie 140 E2
Auchrannie 134 D2
Auchroisk 139 B6
Auchronie 140 F3
Auchterarder . . . 127 C8
Auchteraw 137 D6
Auchterderran . . 128 E4
Auchterhouse . . . 134 F3
Auchtermuchty . . 128 C4
Auchterneed 150 F7
Auchtertool 128 E4
Auchtertyre 152 C1
Auchtubh 126 B4
Auckengill 158 D5
Auckley 89 D7
Audenshaw 87 E7
Audlem 74 E3
Audley 74 D4
Audley End 56 F2
Auds 153 B6
Aughton
E Yorks 96 F3
Lancs 85 D4
Lancs 93 C5
S Yorks 89 F5
Wilts 25 D7
Aughton Park . . . 86 D2
Auldearn 151 F12
Aulden 49 D6
Auldgirth 114 F2
Auldhame 129 F7
Auldhouse 119 D6
Ault a'chruinn . . 136 B2
Aultanrynie 156 F6
Aultbea 155 J13

Aultdearg 150 E5
Aultgrishan 155 J12
Aultguish Inn . . . 150 D6
Aultibea 157 G13
Aultiphurst 157 C11
Aultmore 152 C4
Aultnagoire 137 B8
Aultnamain Inn . 151 C9
Aulton 140 B5
Aundorach 139 C5
Aunsby 78 F3
Auquhorthies . . . 141 B7
Aust 36 F2
Austendike 66 B2
Austerfield 89 E7
Austrey 63 D6
Austwick 93 C7
Authorpe 91 F8
Authorpe Row . . . 79 B8
Avebury 25 C6
Aveley 42 F1
Avening 37 E5
Averham 77 D7
Aveton Gifford . . . 6 E4
Avielochan 138 C5
Aviemore 138 C4
Avington
Hants 26 F3
W Berks 25 C8
Avoch 151 F10
Avon 14 E2
Avonbridge 120 B2
Avon Dassett 52 E2
Avonmouth 23 B7
Avonwick 6 D5
Awbridge 14 B4
Awhirk 104 D4
Awkley 36 F2
Awliscombe 11 D6
Awre 36 D4
Awsworth 76 E4
Axbridge 23 D6
Axford
Hants 26 E4
Wilts 25 B7
Axminster 11 E7
Axmouth 11 E7
Axton 85 F2
Aycliff 31 E7
Aycliffe 101 B7
Aydon 110 C3
Aylburton 36 D3
Ayle 109 E7
Aylesbeare 10 E5
Aylesbury 39 C8
Aylesby 91 D6
Aylesford 29 D8
Aylesham 31 D6
Aylestone 64 D2
Aylmerton 81 D7
Aylsham 81 E7
Aylton 49 F8
Aylworth 37 B8
Aymestrey 49 C6
Aynho 52 F3
Ayot St Lawrence 40 C4
Ayot St Peter . . . 41 C5
Ayr 112 B3
Aysgarth 101 F5
Ayside 99 F5
Ayston
E Yorks 97 D5
Pboro 65 D7
Ayton 122 C5
Aywick 160 E7
Azerley 95 B5

B

Babbacombe 7 C7
Babbinswood 73 F7
Babcary 12 B3
Babel 47 F7
Babell 73 B5
Babraham 55 D6
Babworth 89 F7
Bac 155 C9
Bachau 82 C4
Backaland 159 E6
Backaskaill 159 C5
Backbarrow 99 F5
Backe 32 C3
Backfolds 153 C10
Backford 73 B8
Backford Cross . . 73 B7
Backhill
Aberds 153 E7
Aberds 153 E10
Backhill of
Clackriach 153 D9
Backhill of
Fortree 153 D9
Backhill of
Trustach 140 E5
Backies 157 J11
Backlass 158 E4
Back of
Keppoch 147 C9
Back Rogerton . . 113 B5
Backwell 23 C6
Backworth 111 B6
Bacon End 42 C2
Baconsthorpe . . . 81 D7
Bacton
Hereford 49 F5
Norf 81 D9
Suff 56 C4
Bacton Green . . . 56 C4
Bacup 87 B6
Badachro 149 A12
Badanloch
Lodge 157 F10
Badavanich 150 F4
Badbury 38 F1
Badby 52 D3
Badcall 156 D5
Badcaul 150 B3
Baddeley Green . 75 D6
Baddesley
Clinton 51 B7
Baddesley Ensor . 63 E6
Baddidarach 156 G3
Baddoch 139 F7
Baddock 151 F10
Badenscoth 153 E7
Badenyon 140 C2
Badger 61 E7
Badger's Mount . 29 C5

Badgeworth 37 C6
Badgworth 23 D5
Badicaul 149 F12
Badingham 57 C7
Badlesmere 30 D4
Badlipster 158 F4
Badluarach 150 B2
Badminton 37 F5
Badnaban 156 G3
Badninish 151 B10
Badrallach 150 B3
Badsey 51 E5
Badshot Lea 27 E6
Badsworth 89 C5
Badwell Ash 56 C3
Bae Colwyn
= Colwyn Bay . . 83 D8
Bagby 102 F2
Bag Enderby 79 B6
Bagendon 37 D7
Bagh a Chaisteil
= Castlebay . . . 148 J1
Baghasdal 148 G2
Bagh Mor 148 C3
Bagh
Shiarabhagh . . . 148 H2
Bagillt 73 B6
Baginton 51 B8
Baglan 33 E8
Bagley 60 B4
Bagnall 75 D6
Bagnor 26 C2
Bagshot
Sur 27 C7
Wilts 25 C8
Bagthorpe
Norf 80 D3
Notts 76 D4
Bagworth 63 D8
Bagwy Llydiart . . 35 B8
Baildon 94 F4
Baile Ailein 155 E7
Baile
Mhanaich 148 C2
Baile a
Mhanaich 148 C2
Baile an Truiseil 155 B8
Baile glas 148 C3
Baile Mhartainn 148 A2
Baile Mhic Phail 148 A3
Baile Mor 146 J5
Baile nan
Cailleach 148 C2
Baile Raghaill . 148 A2
Baileyhead 108 B5
Bailiesward 152 E4
Bailieston 119 C6
Bail'lochdrach . . 148 C3
Bail Uachdraich 148 B3
Bail'Ur
Tholastaidh . . . 155 C10
Bainbridge 100 E4
Bainsford 127 F7
Bainshole 152 E6
Bainton
E Yorks 97 D5
Pboro 65 D7
Bairnkine 116 C2
Baker's End 41 C6
Baker Street 42 F2
Bakewell 76 C2
Bala = Y Bala . . . 72 F3
Balachuirn 149 D10
Balavil 138 D3
Balbeg
Highld 137 B7
Highld 150 H7
Balbeggie 128 B3
Balbithan 141 C6
Balbithan House 141 C7
Balblair
Highld 151 B8
Highld 151 E10
Perth 133 D6
Balby 89 D6
Balchladich 156 F3
Balchraggan
Highld 151 G8
Highld 151 H8
Balchrick 156 D4
Balchristie 129 D6
Balcladaich 137 B5
Balcombe 28 F4
Balcombe Lane . . 28 F4
Balcomie 129 C8
Balcurvie 128 D5
Baldersby 95 B6
Baldersby
St James 95 B6
Balderstone 93 F6
Balderton
Ches W 73 C7
Notts 77 D8
Baldhu 3 B6
Baldinnie 129 C6
Baldock 54 F3
Baldovie 134 F4
Baldrine 84 D4
Baldslow 18 D4
Baldwin 84 D3
Baldwinholme . . 108 D3
Baldwin's Gate . . 74 E4
Bale 81 D6
Balearn 153 C10
Balemartine 146 G2
Balephuil 146 G2
Balerno 120 C4
Balevullin 146 G2
Balfield 135 C5
Balfour 159 G5
Balfron 126 F4
Balfron Station . . 126 F4
Balgaveny 153 D6
Balgavies 135 D5
Balgonar 128 E2
Balgove 153 E8
Balgowan 138 E2
Balgown 149 B8
Balgrochan 119 B6
Balgy 149 C13
Balhaldie 127 D7
Balhalgardy 141 B6
Balham 28 B3
Balhary 134 E2

Baliasta 160 C8
Baligill 157 C11
Balintore
Angus 134 D3
Highld 151 D11
Balintraid 151 D10
Balk 102 F2
Balkeerie 134 E3
Balkemback 134 F3
Balkholme 89 B8
Ball 60 B3
Ballabeg 84 E2
Ballacannell . . . 84 D4
Ballachulish 130 D4
Ballajora 84 C4
Ballaleigh 84 D3
Ballamodha 84 E2
Ballantrae 104 A4
Ballaquine 84 D4
Ballards Gore . . . 43 E5
Ballasalla
IoM 84 C3
IoM 84 E2
Ballater 140 E2
Ballaugh 84 C3
Ballchraggan . . . 151 D10
Ballechin 133 D6
Balleigh 151 C10
Ballencrieff 121 B7
Ballentoul 133 C5
Ball Haye Green . 75 D6
Ball Hill 26 C2
Ballidon 76 D2
Balliemore
Argyll 124 C4
Argyll 145 E9
Ballikinrain 126 F4
Ballimeanoch . . . 125 D6
Ballimore
Argyll 145 E8
Stirling 126 C4
Ballinaby 142 B3
Ballindean 128 B4
Ballingdon 56 E2
Ballinger
Common 40 D2
Ballingham 49 F7
Ballingry 128 E3
Ballinlick 133 E6
Ballinluig 133 D6
Ballintuim 133 D8
Balloch
Angus 134 D3
Highld 151 G10
N Lanark 119 B7
W Dunb 126 F2
Ballochan 140 E4
Ballochford 152 E3
Ballochmorrie . . 112 F2
Balls Cross 16 B3
Balls Green 43 B6
Ballygown 146 G7
Ballygrant 142 B4
Ballyhaugh 146 F4
Balmacara 149 F13
Balmacara
Square 149 F13
Balmaclellan . . . 106 B3
Balmacneil 133 D6
Balmacqueen . . . 149 A9
Balmae 106 E3
Balmaha 126 E3
Balmalcolm 128 D5
Balmeanach 149 D10
Balmedie 141 C8
Balmer Heath . . . 73 F8
Balmerino 129 B5
Balmerlawn 14 D4
Balmichael 143 E10
Balmirmer 135 F5
Balmore
Highld 149 D7
Highld 150 H6
Highld 151 G11
Perth 133 D6
Balmule 128 F4
Balmullo 129 B6
Balmungie 151 F10
Balnaboth 134 C3
Balnabruaich . . . 151 E10
Balnabruich 158 H3
Balnacoil 157 H11
Balnacra 150 G2
Balnafoich 151 H9
Balnagall 151 C11
Balnaguard 133 D6
Balnahard
Argyll 144 D3
Argyll 146 H7
Balnain 150 H7
Balnakeil 156 C6
Balnaknock 149 B9
Balnapaling 151 E10
Balne 89 C6
Balochroy 143 C8
Balone 129 C6
Balornock 119 C6
Balquharn 133 F7
Balquhidder 126 B4
Balsall 51 B7
Balsall Common . 51 B7
Balsall Heath . . . 62 F4
Balscott 51 E8
Balsham 55 D6
Baltasound 160 C8
Balterley 74 D4
Baltersan 105 C8
Balthangie 153 C8
Baltonsborough . 23 F7
Balvaird 151 F8
Balvicar 124 D3
Balvraid
Highld 149 G13
Highld 151 H11
Bamber Bridge . . 86 B3
Bambers Green . . 42 B1
Bamburgh 123 F7
Bamff 134 D2
Bamford
Derbys 88 F3
Gtr Man 87 C6
Bampton
Devon 10 B4
Oxon 38 D3
W&F 99 C7
Bampton Grange 99 C7

Banavie 131 B5
Banbury 52 E2
Bancffosfelen . . . 33 C5
Banchory 141 E5
Banchory-
Devenick 141 D8
Bancycapel 33 C5
Bancyfelin 32 C4
Bancyffordd 46 F3
Bandirran 134 F2
Banff 153 B6
Bangor 83 D5
Bangor-is-y-coed
= Bangor-on-Dee 73 E7
Bangor-on-Dee
= Bangor-is-y-
coed 73 E7
Banham 68 F3
Bank 14 D3
Bankend 107 C7
Bankfoot 133 F7
Bankglen 113 C6
Bankhead
Aberdeen 141 C7
Aberds 141 D5
Bank Newton . . . 94 D2
Banknock 119 B7
Banks
Cumb 109 C5
Lancs 85 B4
Bankshill 114 F4
Bank Street 49 C8
Banningham 81 E8
Banniskirk
House 158 E3
Bannister Green . 42 B2
Bannockburn . . . 127 E7
Banstead 28 D3
Bantham 6 E4
Banton 119 B7
Banwell 23 D5
Banyard's Green . 57 B6
Bapchild 30 C3
Barabhas 155 C8
Barabhas Iarach 155 C8
Barabhas
Uarach 155 B8
Barachandroman
. . . . 124 C2
Barassie 118 F3
Baravullin 124 E4
Barbaraville 151 D10
Barber Booth . . . 88 F2
Barbieston 112 C4
Barbon 99 F8
Barbridge 74 D3
Barbrook 21 E6
Barby 52 B3
Barcaldine 130 E3
Barcheston 51 F7
Barcombe 17 C8
Barcombe Cross . 17 C8
Barden 101 E6
Barden Scale . . 94 D3
Bardfield Saling . 42 B2
Bardister 160 F5
Bardney 78 C4
Bardon 63 C8
Bardon Mill 109 C7
Bardowie 119 B5
Bardrainney 118 B3
Bardsea 92 B3
Bardsey 95 E6
Bardwell 56 B3
Bare 92 C4
Barfad 145 G7
Barford
Norf 68 D4
Warks 51 C7
Barford St John . . 52 F2
Barford
St Martin 25 F5
Barford
St Michael 52 F2
Barfrestone 31 D6
Bargod
= Bargoed 35 E5
Bargoed
= Bargod 35 E5
Bargrennan 105 B7
Barham
Cambs 54 B2
Kent 31 D6
Suff 56 D5
Barharrow 106 D3
Barhill 106 C5
Bar Hill 54 C4
Barholm 65 C7
Barkby 64 D3
Barkestone-le-
Vale 77 F7
Barkham 27 C5
Barking
London 41 F7
Suff 56 D4
Barkingside 41 F7
Barking Tye 56 D4
Barkisland 87 C8
Barkston
Lincs 78 E2
N Yorks 95 F7
Barkway 54 F4
Barlaston 75 F5
Barlavington 16 C3
Barlborough 76 B4
Barley
Herts 54 F4
Lancs 93 E8
Barley Mow 111 D5
Barleythorpe . . . 64 D5
Barling 43 F5
Barlow
Derbys 76 B3
N Yorks 89 B7
T&W 110 C4
Barmby Moor . . . 96 E3
Barmby on the
Marsh 89 B7
Barmer 80 D4
Barmoor Castle . 123 F5
Barmoor Lane
End 123 F6
Barmouth
= Abermaw 58 C3
Barmpton 101 C8

Barmston 97 D7
Barnack 65 D7
Barnacle 63 F7
Barnard Castle . 101 C5
Barnard Gate . . 38 C4
Barnardiston 55 E8
Barnburgh 89 D5
Barnby 69 F7
Barnby Dun 89 D7
Barnby in the
  Willows 77 D8
Barnby Moor . . .89 F7
Barnes Street . . .29 E7
Barnet 41 E5
Barnetby le Wold 90 D4
Barney 81 D5
Barnham
  Suff 56 B2
  W Sus 16 D3
Barnham Broom . 68 D3
Barnhead 135 D6
Barnhill
  Ches W 73 D8
  Dundee 134 F4
  Moray 152 C1
Barnhills 104 B3
Barningham
  Durham 101 C5
  Suff 56 B3
Barnoldby le
  Beck 91 D6
Barnoldswick . . .93 E8
Barns Green 16 B5
Barnsley
  Glos 37 D7
  S Yorks 88 D4
Barnstaple 20 C4
Barnston
  Essex 42 C2
  Mers 85 F3
Barnstone 77 F7
Barnt Green 50 B5
Barnton
  Ches W 74 B3
  Edin 120 B4
Barnwell All
  Saints 65 F7
Barnwell
  St Andrew 65 F7
Barnwood 37 C5
Barochreal 124 C4
Barons Cross . . . 49 D6
Barr 112 E2
Barra Castle . . . 141 B6
Barrachan 105 E7
Barrack 153 D8
Barraglom 154 D6
Barrahormid . . . 144 E6
Barran 124 C4
Barrapol 146 G2
Barras
  Aberds 141 F7
  W&F 100 C3
Barrasford 110 B2
Barravullin 124 E4
Barregarrow 84 D3
Barrhead 118 D4
Barrhill 112 F2
Barrington
  Cambs 54 E4
  Som 11 C8
Barripper 2 C5
Barrmill 118 D3
Barrock 158 C4
Barrock House . 158 D4
Barrow
  Lancs 93 F7
  Rutland 65 C5
  Suff 55 C8
Barroway Drove . 67 D5
Barrowburn 116 C4
Barrowby 77 F8
Barrowcliff 103 F8
Barrowden 65 D6
Barrowford 93 F8
Barrow Green . . 30 C3
Barrow Gurney . . 23 C7
Barrow Haven . . .90 B4
Barrow-in-
  Furness 92 C2
Barrow Island . . 92 C1
Barrow Nook . . .86 D2
Barrows Green
  Ches E 74 D3
  W&F 99 F7
Barrow's Green . .86 F3
Barrow Street . . .24 F3
Barrow upon
  Humber 90 B4
Barrow upon
  Soar 64 C2
Barrow upon
  Trent 63 B7
Barry 135 F5
Barry = Y Barri . . 22 C3
Barry Island 22 C3
Barsby 64 C3
Barsham 69 F6
Barston 51 B7
Bartestree 49 E7
Barthol Chapel . 153 E8
Barthomley 74 D4
Bartley 14 C4
Bartley Green . . .62 F4
Bartlow 55 E6
Barton
  Cambs 54 D5
  Ches W 73 D8
  Glos 37 B8
  Lancs 85 D4
  Lancs 92 F5
  N Yorks 101 D7
  Oxon 39 D5
  Torbay 7 C7
  Warks 51 D6
Barton Bendish .67 D7
Barton
  Hartshorn 52 F4
Barton in Fabis .76 F5
Barton in the
  Beans 63 D7
Barton-le-Clay . .54 F2
Barton-le-Street .96 B3
Barton-le-
  Willows 96 C3
Barton Mills 55 B8
Barton on Sea . . .14 E3

Barton on the
  Heath 51 F7
Barton St David . .23 F7
Barton Seagrave .53 B6
Barton Stacey . . .26 E2
Barton Turf 69 B6
Barton-under-
  Needwood . . . 63 C5
Barton-upon-
  Humber 90 B4
Barton Waterside 90 B4
Barugh 88 D4
Barway 55 B6
Barwell 63 E8
Barwick
  Herts 41 C6
  Som 12 C3
Barwick in Elmet .95 F6
Baschurch 60 B4
Bascote 52 C2
Basford Green . .75 D6
Bashall Eaves . . .93 E6
Bashley 14 E3
Basildon 42 F3
Basingstoke 26 D4
Baslow 76 B2
Bason Bridge . . .22 E5
Bassaleg 35 F6
Bassett 14 C5
Bassingbourn . . .54 E4
Bassingfield 77 F6
Bassingham 78 C2
Bassingthorpe . .65 B6
Basta 160 D7
Baston 65 C8
Bastwick 69 C7
Baswick Steer . . .97 E6
Batchworth
  Heath 40 E3
Batcombe
  Dorset 12 D4
  Som 23 F8
Bate Heath 74 B3
Batford 40 C4
Bath 24 C2
Bathampton 24 C2
Bathealton 11 B5
Batheaston 24 C2
Bathford 24 C2
Bathgate 120 C2
Bathley 77 D7
Bathpool
  Corn 5 B7
  Som 11 B7
Bathville 120 C2
Batley 88 B3
Batsford 51 F6
Battersby 102 D3
Battersea 28 B3
Battisborough
  Cross 6 E3
Battisford 56 D4
Battisford Tye . . .56 D4
Battle
  E Sus 18 D4
  Powys 48 F2
Battledown 37 B6
Battlefield 60 C5
Battlesbridge . . .42 E3
Battlesden 40 B2
Battlesea Green . .57 B6
Battleton 10 B4
Battram 63 D8
Battramsley 14 E4
Baughton 50 E3
Baughurst 26 D3
Baulking 38 E3
Baumber 78 B5
Baunton 37 D7
Baverstock 24 F5
Bawburgh 68 D4
Bawdeswell 81 E6
Bawdrip 22 F5
Bawdsey 57 E7
Bawtry 89 E7
Baxenden 87 B5
Baxterley 63 E6
Baybridge 15 B6
Baycliff 92 B2
Baydon 25 B7
Bayford
  Herts 41 D6
  Som 12 B5
Bayles 109 E7
Baylham 56 D5
Baynard's Green . .39 B5
Bayston Hill 60 D4
Baythorn End . . .55 E8
Bayton 49 B8
Beach 130 D1
Beachampton . . .53 F5
Beachamwell 67 D7
Beachans 151 G13
Beacharr 143 D7
Beachborough . . 19 B8
Beachley 36 E2
Beacon 11 D6
Beacon End 43 B5
Beacon Hill 27 F6
Beacon's Bottom 39 E7
Beaconsfield 40 F2
Beacrabhaic . . . 154 H6
Beadlam 102 F4
Beadlow 54 F2
Beadnell 117 B8
Beaford 9 C7
Beal
  Northumb 123 E6
  N Yorks 89 B6
Beamhurst 75 F7
Beaminster 12 D2
Beamish 110 D5
Beamsley 94 D3
Bean 29 B6
Beanacre 24 C4
Beanley 117 C6
Beaquoy 159 F4
Bear Cross 13 E8
Beardwood 86 B4
Beare Green 28 E2
Bearley 51 C6
Bearnus 146 G6
Bearpark 110 E5
Bearsbridge . . . 109 D7
Bearsden 118 B5
Bearsted 29 D8
Bearstone 74 F4

Bearwood
  BCP 13 E8
  Hereford 49 D5
  W Mid 62 F4
Beattock 114 D3
Beauchamp
  Roding 42 C1
Beauchief 88 F4
Beaufort 35 C5
Beaufort Castle .151 G8
Beaulieu 14 D4
Beauly 151 G8
Beaumaris
  = Biwmares . . . 83 D6
Beaumont
  Cumb 108 D3
  Essex 43 B7
Beaumont Hill . . 101 C7
Beausale 51 B7
Beauworth 15 B6
Beaworthy 9 E6
Beazley End 42 B3
Bebington 85 F4
Bebside 117 F8
Beccles 69 E7
Becconsall 86 B2
Beckbury 61 D7
Beckenham 28 C4
Beckermet 98 D2
Beckfoot
  Cumb 98 D3
  Cumb 107 E7
Beck Foot 99 E8
Beckford 50 F4
Beckhampton . . .25 C5
Beck Hole 103 D6
Beckingham
  Lincs 77 D8
  Notts 89 F8
Beckington 24 D3
Beckley
  E Sus 19 C5
  Hants 14 E3
  Oxon 39 C5
Beck Row 55 B7
Beck Side 98 F4
Beckton 41 F7
Beckwithshaw . . .95 D5
Becontree 41 F7
Bedale 101 F7
Bedburn 110 F4
Bedchester 13 C6
Beddau 34 F4
Beddgelert 71 C6
Beddingham 17 D8
Beddington 28 C4
Bedfield 57 C6
Bedford 53 D8
Bedham 16 B4
Bedhampton 15 D8
Bedingfield 57 C5
Bedlam 95 C5
Bedlington 117 F8
Bedlington
  Station 117 F8
Bedlinog 34 D4
Bedminster 23 B7
Bedmond 40 D3
Bednall 62 C3
Bedrule 116 C2
Bedstone 49 B5
Bedwas 35 F5
Bedworth 63 F7
Bedworth Heath .63 F7
Bed-y-coedwr . . .71 E8
Beeby 64 D3
Beech
  Hants 26 F4
  Staffs 75 F5
Beech Hill
  Gtr Man 86 D3
  W Berks 26 C4
Beechingstoke . . 25 D5
Beedon 26 B2
Beeford 97 D7
Beeley 76 C2
Beelsby 91 D6
Beenham 26 C3
Beeny 8 E3
Beer 11 F7
Beercrocombe . . 11 B8
Beer Hackett 12 C3
Beesands 7 E6
Beesby 91 F8
Beeson 7 E6
Beeston
  C Beds 54 E2
  Ches W 74 D2
  Norf 68 C2
  Notts 76 F5
  W Yorks 95 F5
Beeston Regis . . .81 C7
Beeswing 107 C5
Beetham 92 B4
Beetley 68 C2
Begbroke 38 C4
Begelly 32 D2
Beggar's Bush . . .48 C4
Beguildy 48 B3
Beighton
  Norf 69 D6
  S Yorks 88 F5
Beighton Hill 76 D2
Beith 118 D3
Bekesbourne 31 D5
Belaugh 69 C5
Belbroughton 50 B4
Belchamp Otten .56 E2
Belchamp St Paul .55 E8
Belchamp Walter .56 E2
Belchford 79 B5
Belford 123 F7
Belhaven 122 B2
Belhelvie 141 C8
Belhinnie 140 B3
Bellabeg 140 C2
Bellamore 112 F2
Bellanoch 144 D6
Bellaty 134 D2
Bell Bar 41 D5
Bell Busk 94 D2
Belleau 79 B7
Bellehiglash . . . 152 E1
Bell End 50 B4
Bellerby 101 E6
Bellever 6 B4
Belliehill 135 C5
Bellingdon 40 D2

Bellingham 116 F4
Belloch 143 E7
Bellochantuy . . 143 E7
Bell o'th'Hill 74 E2
Bellsbank 112 D4
Bellshill
  N Lanark 119 C7
  Northumb 123 F7
Bellspool 120 F5
Bellsquarry 120 C3
Bells Yew Green . .18 B3
Belmaduthy 151 F9
Belmesthorpe . . .65 C7
Belmont
  Blackburn 86 C5
  London 28 C3
  S Ayrs 112 B3
  Shetland 160 C7
Belnacraig 140 C2
Belowda 4 C4
Belper 76 E3
Belper Lane End .76 E3
Belsay 110 B4
Belses 115 B8
Belsford 7 D5
Belstead 56 E5
Belston 112 B3
Belstone 9 E8
Belthorn 86 B5
Beltinge 31 C5
Beltoft 90 D2
Belton
  Leics 63 B8
  Lincs 78 F2
  N Lincs 89 D8
  Norf 69 D7
Belton in Rutland 64 D5
Beltring 29 E7
Belts of
  Collonach 141 E5
Belvedere 29 B5
Belvoir 77 F8
Bembridge 15 F7
Bemersyde 121 F8
Bemerton 25 F6
Bempton 97 B7
Benacre 69 F8
Ben Alder
  Lodge 132 B2
Ben Armine
  Lodge 157 H10
Benbuie 113 E7
Ben Casgro 155 E9
Benderloch 124 B5
Bendronaig
  Lodge 150 H3
Benenden 18 B5
Benfield 105 C7
Bengate 69 B6
Bengeworth 50 E5
Benhall Green . . .57 C7
Benhall Street . . .57 C7
Benholm 135 C8
Beningbrough . . .95 D8
Benington
  Herts 41 B5
  Lincs 79 E6
Benllech 82 C5
Benmore
  Argyll 145 E10
  Stirling 126 B3
Benmore Lodge 156 H6
Bennacott 8 E4
Bennan 143 F10
Benniworth 91 F6
Benover 29 E8
Bensham 110 C5
Benslie 118 E3
Benson 39 E6
Bent 135 B6
Bent Gate 87 B5
Benthall
  Northumb 117 B8
  Shrops 61 D6
Bentham 37 C6
Benthoul 141 D7
Bentlawnt 60 D3
Bentley
  E Yorks 97 F6
  Hants 27 E5
  Suff 56 F5
  S Yorks 89 D6
  Warks 63 E6
  Worcs 50 C4
Bentley Heath . . .51 B6
Benton 21 F5
Bentpath 115 E6
Bents 120 C2
Bentworth 26 E4
Benvie 134 F3
Benwick 66 E3
Beoley 51 C5
Beoraidbeg . . . 147 B9
Bepton 16 C2
Berden 41 B7
Bere Alston 6 C2
Bere Ferrers 6 C2
Bergh Apton . . . 69 D6
Berinsfield 39 E5
Berkeley 36 E3
Berkhamsted . . .40 D2
Berkley 24 E3
Berkswell 51 B7
Bermondsey 28 B4
Bernera 149 F13
Bernice 145 D10
Bernisdale 149 C9
Berrick Salome . .39 E6
Berriedale 158 H3
Berrier 99 B5
Berriew 59 D8
Berrington
  Northumb 123 E6
  Shrops 60 D5
Berrow 22 D5
Berrow Green . . .50 D2
Berry Down
  Cross 20 E4
Berryfield 39 C7
Berry Hill
  Glos 36 C2
  Pembs 45 E2
Berryhillock 152 B5
Berrynarbor 20 E4
Berry Pomeroy . .7 C6
Bersham 73 E7

Berstane 159 G5
Berwick 18 E2
Berwick Bassett . .25 B6
Berwick Hill 110 B4
Berwick St James 25 F5
Berwick St John . .13 B7
Berwick
  St Leonard 24 F4
Berwick-upon-
  Tweed 123 D5
Bescar 85 C4
Besford 50 E4
Bessacarr 89 D7
Bessels Leigh . . .38 D4
Bessingby 97 C7
Bessingham 81 D7
Bestbeech Hill . . .18 B3
Besthorpe
  Norf 68 E3
  Notts 77 C8
Bestwood 77 E5
Bestwood Village .77 E5
Beswick 97 E6
Betchworth 28 E3
Bethania
  Ceredig 46 C4
  Gwyn 71 C8
  Gwyn 83 F6
Bethel
  Anglesey 82 D3
  Gwyn 72 F3
  Gwyn 82 E5
Bethersden 30 E3
Bethesda
  Gwyn 83 E6
  Pembs 32 C1
Bethlehem 33 B7
Bethnal Green . . .41 F6
Betley 74 E4
Betsham 29 B7
Betteshanger . . .31 D7
Bettiscombe 11 E8
Bettisfield 73 F8
Betton
  Shrops 60 D3
  Shrops 74 F3
Bettws
  Bridgend 34 F3
  Mon 35 C6
  Newport 35 E6
Bettws Cedewain .59 E8
Bettws Gwerfil
  Goch 72 E4
Bettws Ifan 46 E2
Bettws Newydd. . .35 D7
Bettws-y-crwyn . .60 F2
Bettyhill 157 C10
Betws 33 C7
Betws Bledrws . . 46 D4
Betws-Garmon . .82 F5
Betws-y-Coed . . .83 F7
Betws-yn-Rhos . .72 B3
Beulah
  Ceredig 45 E4
  Powys 47 D8
Bevendean 17 D7
Bevercotes 77 B6
Beverley 97 F6
Beverston 37 E5
Bevington 36 E3
Bewaldeth 108 F2
Bewcastle 109 B5
Bewdley 50 B2
Bewerley 94 C4
Bewholme 97 D7
Bexhill 18 E4
Bexley 29 B5
Bexleyheath 29 B5
Bexwell 67 D6
Beyton 56 C3
Bhaltos 154 D5
Bhatarsaigh . . . 148 J1
Bibury 37 D8
Bicester 39 B5
Bickenhall 11 C7
Bickenhill 63 F5
Bicker 78 F5
Bickershaw 86 D4
Bickerstaffe 86 D2
Bickerton
  Ches E 74 D2
  N Yorks 95 D7
Bickington
  Devon 7 B5
  Devon 20 F4
Bickleigh
  Devon 6 C3
  Devon 10 D4
Bickleton 20 F4
Bickley 28 C5
Bickley Moss 74 E2
Bicknacre 42 D3
Bicknoller 22 F3
Bicknor 30 D2
Bickton 14 C2
Bicton
  Shrops 60 C4
  Shrops 60 F2
Bidborough 29 E6
Biddenden 19 B5
Biddenham 53 E8
Biddestone 24 B3
Biddisham 23 D5
Biddlesden 52 E4
Biddlestone 117 D5
Biddulph 75 D5
Biddulph Moor . .75 D6
Bideford 9 B6
Bidford-on-Avon 51 D6
Bidston 85 E3
Bielby 96 E3
Bierley
  IoW 15 G6
  W Yorks 94 F4
Bierton 39 C8
Bigbury 6 E4
Bigbury on Sea . .6 E4
Bigby 90 D4
Biggar
  S Lanark 120 F3
  W&F 92 C1
Biggin
  Derbys 75 D8
  Derbys 76 E2
  N Yorks 95 F8
Biggings 160 G3
Biggin Hill 28 D5

Biggleswade 54 E2
Bighouse 157 C11
Bighton 26 F4
Bignor 16 C3
Big Sand 149 A12
Bilberry 4 C5
Bilborough 76 E5
Bilbrook 22 E2
Bilbrough 95 E8
Bilbster 158 E4
Bildershaw 101 B7
Bildeston 56 E3
Billericay 42 E2
Billesdon 64 D4
Billesley 51 D6
Billingborough . . .78 F4
Billinge 86 D3
Billingford 81 E6
Billingham 102 B2
Billinghay 78 D4
Billingley 88 D5
Billingshurst 16 B4
Billingsley 61 F7
Billington
  C Beds 40 B2
  Lancs 93 F7
Billockby 69 C7
Billy Row 110 F4
Bilsborrow 92 F5
Bilsby 79 B7
Bilsham 16 D3
Bilsington 19 B7
Bilson Green 36 C3
Bilsthorpe 77 C6
Bilsthorpe Moor .77 D6
Bilston
  Midloth 121 C5
  W Mid 62 E3
Bilstone 63 D7
Bilting 30 E4
Bilton
  E Yorks 97 F7
  Northumb 117 C8
  Warks 52 B2
Bilton in Ainsty . .95 E7
Bimbister 159 G4
Binbrook 91 E6
Binchester
  Blocks 110 F5
Bincombe 12 F4
Binegar 23 E8
Bines Green 17 C5
Binfield 27 B6
Binfield Heath . . .26 B5
Bingfield 110 B2
Bingham 77 F7
Bingley 94 F4
Bings Heath 60 C5
Binham 81 D5
Binley
  Hants 26 D2
  W Mid 51 B8
Binley Woods . . .51 B8
Binniehill 119 B8
Binsoe 94 B5
Binstead 15 E6
Binsted 27 E5
Bintree 81 E6
Binweston 60 D3
Birch
  Essex 43 C5
  Gtr Man 87 D6
Bircham Newton . 80 D3
Bircham Tofts . . .80 D3
Birchanger 41 B8
Birchencliffe 88 C2
Bircher 49 C6
Birch Green 43 C5
Birchgrove
  Cardiff 22 B3
  Swansea 33 E8
Birch Heath 74 C2
Birch Hill 74 B2
Birchington 31 C6
Birchmoor 63 D6
Birchover 76 C2
Birch Vale 87 F8
Birchwood
  Lincs 78 C2
  Warr 86 E4
Bircotes 89 E7
Birdbrook 55 E8
Birdforth 95 B7
Birdham 16 E2
Birdholme 76 C3
Birdingbury 52 C2
Birdlip 37 C6
Birds Edge 88 D3
Birdsall 96 C4
Birdsgreen 61 F7
Birdsmoor Gate . 11 D8
Birdston 119 B6
Birdwell 88 D4
Birdwood 36 C4
Birgham 122 F3
Birkby 101 D8
Birkdale 85 C4
Birkenhead 85 F4
Birkenhills 153 D7
Birkenshaw
  N Lanark 119 C6
  W Yorks 88 B3
Birkhall 140 E2
Birkhill
  Angus 134 F3
  Borders 114 C5
Birkholme 65 B6
Birley 49 D6
Birling
  Kent 29 C7
  Northumb 117 D8
Birling Gap 18 F2
Birmingham 62 F4
Birnam 133 E7
Birse 140 E4
Birsemore 140 E4
Birstall
  Leics 64 D2
  W Yorks 88 B3
Birstwith 94 D5
Birthorpe 78 F4
Birtley
  Hereford 49 C5
  Northumb 109 B8

Birtley continued
  T&W 111 D5
Birts Street 50 F2
Bisbrooke 65 E5
Biscathorpe 91 F6
Biscot 40 B3
Bisham 39 F8
Bishampton 50 D4
Bish Mill 10 B2
Bishop
  Auckland 101 B7
Bishopbridge . . .90 E4
Bishopbriggs . . . 119 C6
Bishop Burton . . .97 F5
Bishop
  Middleham 111 F6
Bishopmill 152 B2
Bishop Monkton . 95 C6
Bishop Norton . . .90 E3
Bishopsbourne . .31 D5
Bishops Cannings 25 C5
Bishop's Castle . .60 F3
Bishop's Caundle 12 C4
Bishop's Cleeve . .37 B6
Bishops Frome . .49 E8
Bishop's Green . .42 C2
Bishop's Hull 11 B7
Bishop's Itchington 51 D8
Bishops Lydeard . .11 B6
Bishops Nympton 10 B2
Bishop's Offley . .61 B7
Bishop's
  Stortford 41 B7
Bishop's Sutton . 26 F4
Bishop's
  Tachbrook 51 C8
Bishops Tawton . .20 F4
Bishopsteignton . .7 B7
Bishopstoke 15 C5
Bishopston 33 F6
Bishopstone
  Bucks 39 C8
  E Sus 17 D8
  Hereford 49 E6
  Swindon 38 F2
  Wilts 13 B8
Bishopstrow 24 E3
Bishop Sutton . . .23 D7
Bishop's
  Waltham 15 C6
Bishop's Wood . . 62 D2
Bishopsworth . . .23 C7
Bishop Thornton . 95 C5
Bishopthorpe . . .95 E8
Bishopton
  Darl 102 B1
  Dumfries 105 F8
  N Yorks 95 B6
  Renfs 118 B4
Bishop Wilton . . .96 D3
Bishton 35 F7
Bisley
  Glos 37 D6
  Sur 27 D7
Bispham 92 E3
Bispham Green . .86 C2
Bissoe 3 B6
Bisterne Close . . .14 D3
Bitchfield 65 B6
Bittadon 20 E4
Bittaford 6 D4
Bittering 68 C2
Bitterley 49 B7
Bitterne 15 C5
Bitteswell 64 F2
Bitton 23 C8
Bix 39 F7
Bixter 160 H5
Blaby 64 E2
Blackacre 114 E3
Blackadder
  West 122 D4
Blackawton 7 D6
Blackborough . . .11 D5
Blackborough
  End 67 C6
Black Bourton . . .38 D2
Blackboys 18 C2
Blackbrook
  Derbys 76 E3
  Mers 86 E3
  Staffs 74 F4
Blackburn
  Aberds 141 C7
  Aberds 152 E5
  Blackburn 86 B4
  W Loth 120 C2
Black Callerton . 110 C4
Black Clauchrie . 112 F2
Black Corries
  Lodge 131 D6
Blackcraig 113 F7
Black Crofts 124 B5
Blackden Heath . .74 B4
Blackdog 141 C8
Black Dog 10 D3
Blackfell 111 D5
Blackfield 14 D5
Blackford
  Cumb 108 C3
  Perth 127 D7
  Som 12 B4
  Som 23 E6
Blackfordby 63 C7
Blackgang 15 G5
Blackhall
  Colliery 111 F7
Blackhall Mill . . . 110 D4
Blackhall Rocks .111 F7
Blackham 29 F5
Blackhaugh 121 F7
Blackheath
  Essex 43 B6
  Suff 57 B8
  Sur 27 E8
  W Mid 62 F3
Black Heddon . . 110 B3
Blackhill
  Aberds 153 C10
  Aberds 153 D10
  Highld 149 C8
Blackhills
  Highld 151 F12
  Northumb 109 B8

Blackhills continued
  Moray 152 D2
Blackhorse 23 B8
Blackland 24 C5
Black Lane 87 D5
Blacklaw 153 C6
Blackley 87 D6
Blacklunans 134 C1
Black Marsh 60 E3
Blackmill 34 F3
Blackmoor 27 F5
Blackmoor Gate . .21 E5
Blackmore 42 D2
Blackmore End
  Essex 55 F8
  Herts 40 C4
Black Mount . . . 131 E6
Blackness 120 B3
Blacknest 27 E5
Black Notley 42 B3
Blacko 93 E8
Black Pill 33 E7
Blackpool
  Blackpool 92 F3
  Devon 7 E6
  Pembs 32 C1
Blackpool Gate . 108 B5
Blackridge 119 C8
Blackrock
  Argyll 142 B4
  Mon 35 C6
Blackrod 86 C4
Blackshaw 107 C7
Blackshaw Head . .87 B7
Blacksmith's
  Green 56 C5
Blackstone 17 C6
Black Tar 44 E4
Blackthorn 39 C6
Blackthorpe 56 C3
Blacktoft 90 B2
Blacktop 141 D7
Black Torrington . .9 D6
Blacktown 35 F6
Blackwall Tunnel .41 F6
Blackwater
  Corn 3 B6
  Hants 27 D6
  IoW 15 F6
Blackwaterfoot . 143 F9
Blackwell
  Darl 101 C7
  Derbys 75 B8
  Derbys 76 D4
  Warks 51 E7
  Worcs 50 B4
  W Sus 28 F4
Blackwood 119 F7
Blackwood
  = Coed Duon . . .35 E5
Blackwood Hill . .75 D6
Blacon 73 C7
Bladnoch 105 D8
Bladon 38 C4
Blaenannerch . . .45 E4
Blaenau
  Ffestiniog 71 C8
Blaenavon 35 D6
Blaencelyn 46 D2
Blaendyryn 47 F8
Blaenffos 45 F3
Blaengarw 34 E3
Blaengwrach 34 D2
Blaen-gwynfi 34 E2
Blaenpennal 46 C5
Blaenplwyf 46 B4
Blaenporth 45 E4
Blaenrhondda . . .34 D3
Blaen-waun 32 B3
Blaen-y-coed 32 B4
Blaencwm 47 B7
Blaen-y-Cwm
  Denb 72 F4
  Gwyn 71 E8
  Powys 59 B7
Blagdon
  N Som 23 D7
  Torbay 7 C6
Blagdon Hill 11 C7
Blagill 109 E7
Blaguegate 86 D2
Blaich 130 B4
Blain 147 E9
Blaina 35 D6
Blair Atholl 133 C5
Blairbeg 143 E11
Blairdaff 141 C5
Blair Drummond 127 E6
Blairgowrie 134 E1
Blairhall 128 F2
Blairingone 128 E2
Blairland 118 E3
Blairlogie 127 E7
Blairlomond 125 F7
Blairmore 145 E10
Blairnamarrow . . 139 C8
Blairquhosh 126 F4
Blair's Ferry 145 G8
Blairskaith 119 B5
Blaisdon 36 C4
Blakebrook 50 B3
Blakedown 50 B3
Blakelaw 122 F3
Blakeley 62 E2
Blakeley Lane . . .75 E6
Blakemere 49 E5
Blakeney
  Glos 36 D3
  Norf 81 C6
Blakenhall
  Ches E 74 E4
  W Mid 62 E3
Blakeshall 62 F2
Blakesley 52 D4
Blanchland 110 D2
Blandford
  Forum 13 D6
Blandford
  St Mary 13 D6
Bland Hill 94 D5
Blanefield 119 B5
Blankney 78 C3
Blantyre 119 D6
Blar
  a'Chaorainn . . 131 C5
Blaran 124 D4
Blarghour 125 D5

Blarmachfoldach
  . . . . 130 C4
Blarnalearoch . . 150 B4
Blashford 14 D2
Blaston 64 E5
Blatherwycke . . .65 E6
Blawith 98 F4
Blaxhall 57 D7
Blaxton 89 D7
Blaydon 110 C4
Bleadon 22 D5
Bleak Hey Nook . .87 D8
Blean 30 C5
Bleasby
  Lincs 90 F5
  Notts 77 E7
Bleasdale 93 E5
Bleatarn 100 C2
Blebocraigs 129 C6
Bleddfa 48 C4
Bledington 38 B2
Bledlow 39 D7
Bledlow Ridge . . .39 E7
Blegbie 121 C7
Blencarn 109 F6
Blencogo 107 E8
Blendworth 15 C8
Blenheim Park . . .80 D4
Blennerhasset . . 107 E8
Blervie Castle . . 151 F13
Bletchingdon . . .39 C5
Bletchingley 28 D4
Bletchley
  M Keynes 53 F6
  Shrops 74 F3
Bletherston 32 B1
Bletsoe 53 D8
Blewbury 39 F5
Blickling 81 E7
Blidworth 77 D5
Blindburn 116 C4
Blindcrake 107 F8
Blindley Heath . .28 E4
Blisland 5 B6
Blissford 14 C2
Bliss Gate 50 B2
Blisworth 52 D5
Blithbury 62 B4
Blitterlees 107 D8
Blockley 51 F6
Blofield 69 D6
Blofield Heath . . .69 C6
Blo' Norton 56 B4
Bloomfield 115 B8
Blore 75 E8
Blount's Green . .75 F7
Blowick 85 C4
Bloxham 52 F2
Bloxholm 78 D3
Bloxwich 62 D3
Bloxworth 13 E6
Blubberhouses . .94 D4
Blue Anchor
  Som 22 E2
  Swansea 33 E6
Blue Row 43 C6
Blundeston 69 E8
Blunham 54 D2
Blunsdon
  St Andrew 37 F8
Bluntington 50 B3
Bluntisham 54 B4
Blunts 5 C8
Blyborough 90 E3
Blyford 57 B8
Blymhill 62 C2
Blyth
  Northumb 117 F9
  Notts 89 F7
Blyth Bridge . . . 120 E4
Blythburgh 57 B8
Blythe 121 E8
Blythe Bridge . . .75 E6
Blyton 90 E2
Boarhills 129 C7
Boarhunt 15 D7
Boars Head 86 D3
Boars Hill 38 D4
Boarstall 39 C6
Boasley Cross . . .9 E6
Boath 151 D8
Boat of Garten . . 138 C5
Bobbing 30 C2
Bobbington 62 E2
Bobbingworth . . .41 D8
Bocaddon 5 D6
Bochastle 126 D5
Bocking 42 B3
Bocking
  Churchstreet . .42 B3
Boddam
  Aberds 153 D11
  Shetland 160 M5
Boddington 37 B5
Bodedern 82 C3
Bodelwyddan . . .72 B4
Bodenham
  Hereford 49 D7
  Wilts 14 B2
Bodenham Moor .49 D7
Bodermid 70 E2
Bodewryd 82 B3
Bodfari 72 B4
Bodffordd 82 D4
Bodham 81 C7
Bodiam 18 C4
Bodicote 52 F2
Bodieve 4 B4
Bodinnick 5 D6
Bodle Street
  Green 18 D3
Bodmin 5 C5
Bodney 67 E8
Bodorgan 82 E3
Bodsham 30 E5
Boduan 70 D4
Bodymoor Heath .63 E5
Bogallan 151 F9
Bogbrae 153 E10
Bogend
  Borders 122 E3
  S Ayrs 118 F3
Boghall 120 C2
Boghead 119 E7

Bogmoor......152 B3
Bogniebrae....152 D5
Bognor Regis...16 E3
Bograxie......141 C6
Bogside......119 D8
Bogton......153 C6
Bogue......113 F6
Bohenie......137 F5
Bohortha......3 C7
Bohuntine......137 F5
Boirseam......154 J5
Bojewyan......2 C2
Bolam
  Durham......101 B6
  Northumb......117 F6
Bolberry......6 F4
Bold Heath......86 F3
Boldon......111 C6
Boldon Colliery. 111 C6
Boldre......14 E4
Boldron......101 C5
Bole......89 F8
Bolehill......76 D2
Boleside......121 F7
Bolham......10 C4
Bolham Water...11 C6
Bolingey......4 D2
Bollington......75 B6
Bollington Cross. 75 B6
Bolney......17 B6
Bolnhurst......53 D8
Bolshan......135 D6
Bolsover......76 B4
Bolsterstone......88 E3
Bolstone......49 F7
Boltby......102 F2
Bolter End......39 E7
Bolton
  E Loth......121 B8
  E Yorks......96 D3
  Gtr Man......86 D5
  Northumb......117 C7
  W&F......99 B8
Bolton Abbey....94 D3
Bolton Bridge...94 D3
Bolton-by-
  Bowland......93 E7
Boltonfellend. 108 C4
Boltongate......108 E2
Bolton-le-Sands 92 C4
Bolton Low
  Houses......108 E2
Bolton-on-
  Swale......101 E7
Bolton Percy...95 E8
Bolton Town End 92 C4
Bolton upon
  Dearne......89 D5
Bolventor......5 B6
Bomere Heath....60 C4
Bonar Bridge...151 B9
Bonawe......125 B6
Bonby......90 C4
Boncath......45 F4
Bonchester
  Bridge......115 C8
Bonchurch......15 G6
Bondleigh......9 D8
Bonehill
  Devon......6 B5
  Staffs......63 D5
Bo'ness......127 F8
Bonhill......118 B3
Boningale......62 D2
Bonjedward......116 B2
Bonkle......119 D8
Bonnavoulin....147 F8
Bonnington
  Edin......120 C4
  Kent......19 B7
Bonnybank......129 D5
Bonnybridge...127 F7
Bonnykelly......153 C8
Bonnyrigg and
  Lasswade......121 C6
Bonnyton
  Aberds......153 E6
  Angus......134 F3
  Angus......135 D6
Bonsall......76 D2
Bonskeid House 133 C5
Bont......35 C7
Bontddu......58 C3
Bont-Dolgadfan. 59 D5
Bont-goch......58 F3
Bonthorpe......79 B7
Bontnewydd
  Ceredig......46 C5
  Gwyn......82 F4
Bont-newydd...72 B4
Bont Newydd
  Gwyn......71 C8
  Gwyn......71 E8
Bontuchel......72 D4
Bonvilston......22 B2
Bon-y-maen....33 E7
Booker......39 E8
Boon......121 E8
Boosbeck......102 C4
Boot......98 D3
Booth......87 B8
Boothby Graffoe. 78 D2
Boothby Pagnell. 78 F2
Boothen......75 E5
Boothferry......89 B8
Boothville......53 C5
Booth Wood....87 C8
Bootle
  Cumb......98 F3
  Mers......85 E4
Booton......81 E7
Boot Street......57 E6
Boquhan......126 F4
Boraston......49 B8
Borden
  Kent......30 C2
  W Sus......16 B2
Bordley......94 C2
Bordon......27 F6
Bordon Camp...27 F5
Boreham
  Essex......42 D3
  Wilts......24 E3
Boreham Street. 18 D3
Borehamwood....40 E4

Boreland
  Dumfries......114 E4
  Stirling......132 F2
Borgh
  W Isles......148 H1
  W Isles......154 J4
Borghastan......154 C7
Borgie......157 D9
Borgue
  Dumfries......106 E3
  Highld......158 H3
Borley......56 E2
Bornais......148 F2
Bornesketaig....149 A8
Borness......106 E3
Boroughbridge....95 C6
Borough Green......29 D7
Borras Head......73 D7
Borreraig......148 C6
Borrobol
  Lodge......157 G11
Borrohol......114 E4
Borrowash......76 F4
Borrowby......102 F2
Borrowdale......98 C4
Borrowfield......141 E7
Borth......58 E3
Borthwickbrae. 115 C7
Borthwickshiels 115 C7
Borth-y-Gest....71 D6
Borve......149 D9
Borve Lodge....154 H5
Borwick......92 B5
Bosavern......2 C2
Bosbury......49 E8
Boscastle......8 E3
Boscombe
  BCP......14 E2
  Wilts......25 F7
Boscoppa......4 D5
Bosham......16 D2
Bosherston......44 F4
Bosley......75 C6
Bossall......96 C3
Bossiney......8 F2
Bossingham......31 E5
Bossington......21 E7
Bostock Green....74 C3
Boston......79 E6
Boston Long
  Hedges......79 E6
Boston Spa......95 E7
Boston West......79 E5
Boswinger......3 B8
Botallack......2 C2
Botany Bay......41 E5
Botcherby......108 D4
Botcheston......63 D8
Botesdale......56 B4
Bothal......117 F8
Bothamsall......77 B6
Bothel......107 F8
Bothenhampton...12 E2
Bothwell......119 D7
Botley
  Bucks......40 D2
  Hants......15 C6
  Oxon......38 D4
Botolph Claydon. 39 B7
Botolphs......17 D5
Bottacks......150 E7
Bottesford
  Leics......77 F8
  N Lincs......90 D2
Bottisham......55 C6
Bottlesford......25 D6
Bottom Boat......88 B4
Bottomcraig....129 B5
Bottom House....75 D7
Bottom of Hutton 86 B2
Bottom
  o'th'Moor......86 C4
Botusfleming......6 C2
Botwnnog......70 D3
Bough Beech......29 E5
Boughrood......48 F3
Boughspring......36 E2
Boughton
  Norf......67 D6
  Notts......77 C6
  W Nhants......53 C5
Boughton Aluph. 30 E4
Boughton Lees...30 E4
Boughton
  Malherbe......30 E2
Boughton
  Monchelsea...29 D8
Boughton Street. 30 D4
Boulby......103 C5
Boulden......60 F5
Boulmer......117 C8
Boulston......44 D4
Boultenstone....140 C3
Boultham......78 C2
Bourn......54 D4
Bourne......65 B7
Bourne End
  Bucks......40 F1
  C Beds......53 E7
  Herts......40 D3
Bournemouth...13 E8
Bournes Green
  Glos......37 D6
  Southend......43 F5
Bournheath......50 B4
Bournmoor......111 D6
Bournville......62 F4
Bourton
  Dorset......24 F2
  N Som......23 C5
  Oxon......38 F2
  Shrops......61 E5
Bourton on
  Dunsmore......52 B2
Bourton on the
  Hill......51 F6
Bourton-on-the-
  Water......38 B1
Bousd......146 E5
Boustead Hill. 108 D2
Bouth......99 F5
Bouthwaite......94 B4
Boveney......40 F2
Boverton......21 C8
Bovey Tracey......7 B6
Bovingdon......40 D3
Bovingdon Green
  Bucks......40 F1

Bovingdon Green
  continued
  Herts......40 D3
Bovinger......41 D8
Bovington Camp. 13 F6
Bow
  Borders......121 E7
  Devon......10 D2
  Orkney......159 J4
Bowbank......100 B4
Bow Brickhill....53 F7
Bowburn......111 F6
Bowcombe......15 F5
Bowd......11 E6
Bowden
  Borders......121 F8
  Devon......7 E6
Bowden Hill......24 C4
Bowderdale......100 D1
Bowdon......87 F5
Bower......116 F3
Bowerchalke......13 B8
Bowerhill......24 C4
Bower Hinton....12 C2
Bowermadden...158 D4
Bowers Gifford...42 F3
Bowershall......128 E2
Bowertower......158 D4
Bowes......100 C4
Bowgreave......92 E4
Bowgreen......87 F5
Bowhill......115 B7
Bowhouse......107 C7
Bowland Bridge. 99 F6
Bowley......49 D7
Bowlhead Green. 27 F7
Bowling
  W Dunb......118 B4
  W Yorks......94 F4
Bowling Bank....73 E7
Bowling Green....50 D3
Bowmanstead....99 E5
Bowmore......142 C4
Bowness-on-
  Solway......108 C2
Bowness-on-
  Windermere...99 E6
Bow of Fife....128 C5
Bowsden......123 E5
Bowside Lodge 157 C11
Bowston......99 E6
Bow Street......58 F3
Bowthorpe......68 D4
Box
  Glos......37 D5
  Wilts......24 C3
Boxbush......36 C4
Box End......53 E8
Boxford
  Suff......56 E3
  W Berks......26 B2
Boxgrove......16 D3
Boxley......29 D8
Boxmoor......40 D3
Boxted
  Essex......56 F4
  Suff......56 D2
Boxted Cross....56 F4
Boxted Heath....56 F4
Boxworth......54 C4
Boxworth End....54 C4
Boyden Gate....31 C6
Boylestone......75 F8
Boyndie......153 B6
Boynton......97 C7
Boysack......135 E6
Boyton
  Corn......8 E5
  Suff......57 E7
  Wilts......24 F4
Boyton Cross....42 D2
Boyton End......55 E8
Bozeat......53 D7
Braaid......84 E3
Braal Castle....158 D3
Brabling Green...57 C6
Brabourne......30 E4
Brabourne Lees. .30 E4
Brabster......158 D5
Bracadale......149 E8
Bracara......147 B10
Braceborough....65 C7
Bracebridge......78 C2
Bracebridge
  Heath......78 C2
Bracebridge Low
  Fields......78 C2
Braceby......78 F3
Bracewell......93 E8
Brackenfield....76 D3
Brackenthwaite
  Cumb......108 E2
  N Yorks......95 D5
Bracklesham....16 E2
Brackletter......136 F4
Brackley
  Argyll......143 D8
  W Nhants......52 F3
Brackloch......156 G4
Bracknell......27 C6
Braco......127 D7
Bracobrae......152 C5
Bracon Ash......68 E4
Bracorina......147 B10
Bradbourne......76 D2
Bradbury......101 B8
Bradda......84 F1
Bradden......52 E4
Braddock......5 C6
Bradeley......75 D5
Bradenham
  Bucks......39 E8
  Norf......68 D2
Bradenstoke....24 B5
Bradfield
  Essex......56 F5
  Norf......81 D8
  W Berks......26 B4
Bradfield
  Combust......56 D2
Bradfield Green. 74 D3
Bradfield Heath. 43 B7
Bradfield
  St Clare......56 D3
Bradfield
  St George......56 C3
Bradford
  Corn......5 B6

Bradford continued
  Derbys......76 C2
  Devon......9 D6
  Northumb......123 F7
  W Yorks......94 F4
Bradford Abbas . 12 C3
Bradford Leigh...24 C3
Bradford-on-
  Avon......24 C3
Bradford-on-
  Tone......11 B6
Bradford Peverell 12 E4
Brading......15 F7
Bradley
  Derbys......76 E2
  Hants......26 E4
  NE Lincs......91 D6
  Staffs......62 C2
  W Mid......62 E3
  W Yorks......88 B2
Bradley Green....50 C4
Bradley in the
  Moors......75 E7
Bradley Stoke....36 F3
Bradlow......50 F2
Bradmore
  Notts......77 F5
  W Mid......62 E2
Bradninch......10 D5
Bradnop......75 D7
Bradpole......12 E2
Bradshaw
  Gtr Man......86 C5
  W Yorks......87 C8
Bradstone......9 F5
Bradwall Green.. 74 C4
Bradway......88 F4
Bradwell
  Derbys......88 F2
  Essex......42 B4
  M Keynes......53 F6
  Norf......69 D8
  Staffs......74 E5
Bradwell Grove. .38 D2
Bradwell on Sea. 43 D6
Bradwell
  Waterside......43 D5
Bradworthy......8 C5
Bradworthy Cross .8 C5
Brae
  Dumfries......107 B5
  Highld......155 J13
  Highld......156 J7
  Shetland......160 G5
Braeantra......151 D8
Braedownie......134 B2
Braefield......150 H7
Braegrum......128 B2
Braehead
  Dumfries......105 D8
  Orkney......159 D5
  Orkney......159 H6
  S Lanark......119 F8
  S Lanark......120 D2
Braehead of
  Lunan......135 D6
Braehoulland....160 F4
Braehungie....158 G3
Braelangwell
  Lodge......151 B8
Braemar......139 E7
Braemore
  Highld......150 D4
  Highld......158 G2
Brae of
  Achnahaird...156 H3
Brae Roy Lodge. 137 E6
Braeside......118 B2
Braes of Enzie. 152 C3
Braeswick......159 E7
Braewick......160 H5
Brafferton
  Darl......101 B7
  N Yorks......95 B7
Brafield-on-the-
  Green......53 D6
Bragar......155 C7
Bragbury End....41 B5
Bragleenmore...124 C5
Braichmelyn....83 E6
Braid......120 C5
Braides......92 D4
Braidley......101 F5
Braidwood......119 E8
Braigo......142 B3
Brailsford......76 E2
Brainshaugh....117 D8
Braintree......42 B3
Braiseworth....56 B5
Braishfield......14 B4
Braithwaite
  Cumb......98 B4
  S Yorks......89 C7
  W Yorks......94 E3
Braithwell......89 E6
Bramber......17 C5
Bramcote
  Notts......76 F5
  Warks......63 F8
Bramdean......15 B7
Bramerton......69 D5
Bramfield
  Herts......41 C5
  Suff......57 B7
Bramford......56 E5
Bramhall......87 F6
Bramham......95 E7
Bramhope......95 E5
Bramley
  Hants......26 D4
  Sur......27 E8
  S Yorks......89 E5
  W Yorks......94 F5
Brampford Speke.10 E4
Brampton
  Cambs......54 B3
  Cumb......108 C5
  Derbys......76 B3
  Hereford......49 F6
  Lincs......77 B8
  Norf......81 E8
  Suff......69 F7
  S Yorks......88 D5
  W&F......100 B1
Brampton
  Abbotts......36 B3
  Brampton Ash...64 F4

Brampton Bryan. .49 B5
Brampton en le
  Morthen......89 F5
Bramshall......75 F7
Bramshaw......14 C3
Bramshill......26 C5
Bramshott......27 F6
Branault......147 E8
Brancaster......80 C3
Brancaster
  Staithe......80 C3
Brancepeth....110 F5
Branch End....110 C3
Branchill......151 F13
Branderburgh...152 A2
Brandesburton...97 E7
Brandeston......57 C6
Brand Green......36 B4
Brandhill......49 B6
Brandis Corner....9 D6
Brandon
  Durham......110 F5
  Lincs......78 E2
  Northumb......117 C6
  Suff......67 F7
  Warks......52 B2
Brandon Bank....67 F6
Brandon Creek....67 E6
Brandon Parva....68 D3
Brandsby......95 B8
Brandy Wharf....90 E4
Brane......2 D3
Branksome......13 E8
Branksome Park. 13 E8
Bransby......77 B8
Branscombe......11 F6
Bransford......50 D2
Bransgore......14 E2
Branshill......127 E7
Bransholme......97 F7
Branson's Cross. 51 B5
Branston
  Leics......64 B5
  Lincs......78 C3
  Staffs......63 B6
Branston Booths 78 C3
Branstone......15 F6
Bransty......98 C1
Brant Broughton 78 D2
Branthwaite
  Cumb......98 B2
  Cumb......108 F2
Brantingham....90 B3
Branton
  Northumb......117 C6
  S Yorks......89 D7
Branxholme....115 C7
Branxholm Park 115 C7
Branxton......122 F4
Brassey Green....74 C2
Brassington......76 D2
Brasted......29 D5
Brasted Chart....29 D5
Brathens......141 E5
Bratoft......79 C7
Brattleby......90 F3
Bratton
  Telford......61 C6
  Wilts......24 D4
Bratton Clovelly....9 E6
Bratton Fleming. .20 F5
Bratton Seymour. 12 B4
Braughing......41 B6
Braunston......52 C3
Braunston Town 64 D2
Braunston-in-
  Rutland......64 D5
Braunton......20 F3
Brawby......96 B3
Brawl......157 C11
Brawlbin......158 E2
Bray......27 B7
Braybrooke......64 F4
Braye......16 I1
Brayford......21 F5
Bray Shop......5 B8
Braystones......98 D2
Braythorn......94 E5
Brayton......95 F9
Bray Wick......27 B6
Brazacott......8 E4
Breach......30 C2
Breachacha
  Castle......146 F4
Breachwood
  Green......40 B4
Breacleit......154 D6
Breaden Heath. .73 F8
Breadsall......76 F3
Breadstone......36 D4
Breage......2 D5
Breakachy......150 G7
Bream......36 D3
Breamore......14 C2
Brean......22 D4
Breanais......154 E4
Brearton......95 C6
Breascleit......154 D7
Breaston......76 F4
Brechfa......46 F4
Brechin......135 C5
Breck of Cruan. 159 H3
Breckrey......149 B10
Brecon
  =Aberhonddu...34 B4
Bredbury......87 E7
Brede......18 D5
Bredenbury......49 D8
Bredfield......57 D6
Bredgar......30 C2
Bredhurst......29 C8
Bredicot......50 D4
Bredon......50 F4
Bredon's Norton. 50 F4
Bredwardine......48 E5
Breedon on the
  Hill......63 B8
Breibhig
  W Isles......148 J1
  W Isles......155 D9
Breich......120 C2
Breightmet......86 D5
Breighton......96 F3
Breinton......49 F6

Breinton
  Common......49 E6
Breiwick......160 J6
Bremhill......24 B4
Bremirehoull....160 L6
Brenchley......29 E7
Brendon......21 E6
Brenkley......110 B5
Brent Eleigh......56 E3
Brentford......28 B2
Brentingby......64 C4
Brent Knoll......22 D5
Brent Pelham....54 F5
Brentwood......42 E1
Brenzett......19 C7
Brereton......62 C4
Brereton Green. .74 C4
Brereton Heath. .74 C5
Bressingham....68 F3
Bretby......63 B6
Bretford......52 B2
Bretforton......51 E5
Bretherdale
  Head......99 D7
Bretherton......86 B2
Brettabister....160 H6
Brettenham
  Norf......68 F2
  Suff......56 D3
Bretton
  Derbys......76 B2
  Flint......73 C7
Brewer Street......28 D4
Brewlands
  Bridge......134 C1
Brewood......62 D2
Briach......151 F13
Briants Puddle...13 E6
Brick End......42 B1
Brickendon......41 D6
Bricket Wood....40 D4
Brickhampton....50 E4
Bride......84 B4
Bridekirk......107 F8
Bridell......45 E3
Bridestowe......9 F7
Brideswell......152 E5
Bridford......10 F3
Bridfordmills....10 F3
Bridge......31 D5
Bridge End......78 F4
Bridgefoot
  Angus......134 F3
  Cumb......98 B2
Bridge Green....55 F5
Bridgehampton. 12 B3
Bridge Hewick...95 B6
Bridgehill......110 D3
Bridgemary......15 D6
Bridgemont......87 F8
Bridgend
  Aberds......140 C4
  Aberds......152 E5
  Angus......135 C5
  Argyll......142 B4
  Argyll......143 G8
  Argyll......145 D7
  Fife......129 C5
  Moray......152 E3
  N Lanark......119 B6
  Pembs......45 E3
  W&F......99 C5
Bridgend = Pen-y-
  Bont Ar Ogwr...21 B8
Bridgend of
  Lintrathen......134 D2
Bridge of Alford 140 C4
Bridge of Allan. 127 E6
Bridge of Avon 152 E1
Bridge of Awe. 125 C6
Bridge of Balgie 132 E2
Bridge of Cally. 133 D8
Bridge of Canny .141 E5
Bridge of
  Craigisla......134 D2
Bridge of Dee. 106 D4
Bridge of Don. 141 C8
Bridge of Dun. 135 D6
Bridge of Dye...140 F5
Bridge of Earn. 128 C3
Bridge of Ericht 132 D2
Bridge of Feugh. 141 E6
Bridge of Forss 157 C13
Bridge of Gairn. 140 E2
Bridge of Gaur. 132 D2
Bridge of
  Muchalls......141 E7
Bridge of Oich. 137 D6
Bridge of Orchy 125 B8
Bridge of Waith. 159 G3
Bridge of Walls. 160 H4
Bridge of Weir. 118 C3
Bridgerule......8 D4
Bridges......60 E3
Bridge Sollers....49 E6
Bridge Street....56 E2
Bridgeton......119 C6
Bridgetown
  Corn......8 F5
  Som......21 F8
Bridge Trafford. 73 B8
Bridge Yate......23 B8
Bridgham......68 F2
Bridgnorth......61 E7
Bridgtown......62 D3
Bridgwater......22 F5
Bridlington......97 C7
Bridport......12 E2
Bridstow......36 B2
Brierfield......93 F8
Brierley
  Glos......36 C3
  Hereford......49 D6
  S Yorks......88 C5
Brierley Hill......62 F3
Briery Hill......35 D5
Brigg......90 D4
Briggswath......103 D6
Brigham
  Cumb......107 F7
  E Yorks......97 D6
Brighouse......88 B2
Brighstone......14 F5
Brightgate......76 D2
Brighthampton. .38 D3
Brightling......18 C3
Brightlingsea....43 C6

Brighton
  Brighton......17 D7
  Corn......4 D4
Brighton Hill......26 E4
Brightons......120 B2
Brightwalton....26 B2
Brightwell......57 E6
Brightwell
  Baldwin......39 E6
Brightwell cum
  Sotwell......39 E5
Brigsley......91 D6
Brig o'Turk......126 D4
Brigsteer......99 F6
Brigstock......65 F6
Brill......39 C6
Brilley......48 E4
Brimaston......44 C4
Brimfield......49 C7
Brimington......76 B4
Brimley......7 B5
Brimpsfield......37 C6
Brimpton......26 C3
Brims......159 K3
Brimscombe......37 D5
Brimstage......85 F4
Brinacory......147 B10
Brind......96 F3
Brindister
  Shetland......160 H4
  Shetland......160 K6
Brindle......86 B4
Brindley Ford....75 D5
Brineton......62 C2
Bringhurst......64 E5
Brington......53 B8
Brinian......159 F5
Briningham......81 D6
Brinkhill......79 B6
Brinkley......55 D7
Brinklow......52 B2
Brinkworth......37 F7
Brinmore......138 B2
Brinscall......86 B4
Brinsea......23 C6
Brinsley......76 E4
Brinsop......49 E6
Brinsworth......88 F5
Brinton......81 D6
Brisco......108 D4
Brisley......81 E5
Brislington......23 B8
Bristol......23 B7
Briston......81 D6
Britannia......87 B6
Britford......14 B2
Brithdir......58 C4
British Legion
  Village......29 D8
Briton Ferry....33 E8
Britwell Salome. 39 E6
Brixham......7 D7
Brixton
  Devon......6 D3
  London......28 B4
Brixton Deverill. 24 F3
Brixworth......52 B5
Brize Norton......38 D2
Broad Blunsdon. 38 E1
Broadbottom....87 E7
Broadbridge....16 D2
Broadbridge
  Heath......28 F2
Broad Campden. 51 F6
Broad Chalke....13 B8
Broadclyst......10 E4
Broadfield
  Gtr Man......87 C6
  Lancs......86 B3
  Pembs......32 D2
  W Sus......28 F3
Broadford......149 F11
Broadford Bridge.16 B4
Broad Green
  C Beds......53 E7
  Essex......42 B4
  Worcs......50 D2
Broadhaugh....115 D7
Broadhaven....158 E5
Broad Haven......44 D3
Broadheath......87 F5
Broad Heath......49 C8
Broadhembury....11 D6
Broadhempston....7 C6
Broad Hill......55 B6
Broad Hinton......25 B6
Broadholme
  Derbys......76 E3
  Lincs......77 B8
Broadland Row. 18 D5
Broadlay......32 D4
Broad Layings....26 C2
Broadley
  Lancs......87 C6
  Moray......152 B3
Broadley
  Common......41 D7
Broad Marston...51 E6
Broadmayne....12 F5
Broadmeadows 121 F7
Broadmere......26 E4
Broadmoor......32 D1
Broadoak......31 C5
Broad Oak
  Carms......33 B6
  Cumb......98 E3
  Dorset......12 E2
  E Sus......13 D5
  E Sus......18 C5
  Hereford......36 B1
  Mers......86 E3
Broadrashes......152 C4
Broadsea......153 B9
Broadstairs......31 C7
Broadstone
  BCP......13 E8
  Shrops......60 F5
Broad Street......30 D2
Broad Street
  Green......42 D4
Broad Town....25 B5
Broadtown Lane. 25 B5
Broadwas......50 D2
Broadwater
  Herts......41 B5
  W Sus......17 D5

Broadway
  Carms......32 D3
  Pembs......44 D3
  Som......11 C8
  Suff......57 B7
  Worcs......51 F5
Broadwell
  Glos......36 C2
  Glos......38 B2
  Oxon......38 D2
  Warks......52 C2
Broadwell
  House......110 D2
Broadwey......12 F4
Broadwindsor....12 D2
Broadwoodkelly....9 D8
Broadwoodwidger. 9 F6
Brobury......48 E5
Brochel......149 D10
Brochloch......113 C6
Brochroy......125 B6
Brockamin......50 D2
Brockbridge......15 C7
Brockdam......117 B7
Brockdish......57 B6
Brockenhurst......14 D4
Brocketsbrae....119 F8
Brockford Street 56 C5
Brockhall......52 C4
Brockham......28 E2
Brockhampton
  Glos......37 B7
  Hereford......49 F7
Brockholes......88 C2
Brockhurst
  Derbys......76 C3
  Hants......15 D7
Brocklebank....108 E3
Brocklesby......90 C5
Brockley......23 C6
Brockley Green....56 D2
Brockleymoor...108 F4
Brockton
  Shrops......60 D3
  Shrops......60 F3
  Shrops......61 D5
  Shrops......61 E5
  Shrops......61 D7
  Telford......61 C7
  W&F......100 C2
Brockweir......36 D2
Brockwood......15 B7
Brockworth......37 C5
Brocton......62 C3
Brodick......143 E11
Brodsworth......89 D6
Brogaig......149 B9
Brogborough....53 F7
Brokenborough. .37 F6
Broken Cross
  Ches E......75 B5
  Ches W......74 B3
Bromborough....85 F4
Brome......56 B5
Brome Street......57 B5
Bromeswell......57 D7
Bromfield
  Cumb......107 E8
  Shrops......49 B6
Bromham
  Bedford......53 D8
  Wilts......24 C4
Bromley
  London......28 C5
  W Mid......62 F3
Bromley
  Common......28 C5
Bromley Green....19 B6
Brompton
  Medway......29 C8
  N Yorks......102 E1
  N Yorks......103 F7
Brompton-on-
  Swale......101 E7
Brompton Ralph. 22 F7
Brompton Regis. 21 F8
Bromsash......36 B3
Bromsberrow
  Heath......50 F2
Bromsgrove......50 B4
Bromyard......49 D8
Bromyard
  Downs......49 D8
Bronaber......71 D8
Brongest......46 E2
Bronington......73 F8
Bronllys......48 F3
Bronnant......46 C5
Bronwydd Arms. 33 B5
Bronydd......48 E4
Brongarth......73 E7
Brook
  Carms......32 D3
  Hants......14 B4
  Hants......14 C3
  IoW......14 F4
  Kent......30 E4
  Sur......27 E8
  Sur......27 F7
Brooke
  Norf......69 E6
  Rutland......64 D5
Brookenby......91 E6
Brookend......36 E2
Brook End......53 C8
Brookfield......118 C4
Brook Hill......14 C3
Brookhouse......92 C5
Brookhouse
  Green......74 C5
Brookland......19 C6
Brooklands
  Dumfries......106 B5
  Gtr Man......87 E5
  Shrops......74 E2
Brookmans Park. 41 D5
Brooks......59 E8
Brooks Green....16 B5
Brook Street
  Kent......19 B6
  Kent......29 E6
  W Sus......17 B7
Brookthorpe....37 C5
Brookville......67 E6
Brookwood......27 D7
Broom
  C Beds......54 E2
  S Yorks......88 E5
  Warks......51 D5
  Worcs......50 B4

Broome
  Norf......69 E6
  Shrops......60 F4
Broomedge......86 F5
Broome Park....117 C6
Broomer's
  Corner......16 B5
Broomfield
  Aberds......153 E9
  Essex......42 C3
  Kent......30 D2
  Kent......31 C5
  Som......22 F4
Broomfleet......90 B2
Broom Green......81 E5
Broomhall
  Ches E......74 E3
  Windsor......27 C7
Broomhaugh....110 C3
Broomhill
  Norf......67 D6
  Northumb......117 D8
  S Yorks......88 D5
Broom Hill......13 D8
Broomholm......81 D9
Broomley......110 C3
Broom's Green....50 F2
Broomy Lodge....14 C3
Brora......157 J12
Broseley......61 D6
Brotherhouse Bar 66 C2
Brotherstone...122 F2
Brothertoft......79 E5
Brotherton......89 B5
Brotton......102 C4
Broubster......157 C13
Brough
  Derbys......88 F2
  E Yorks......90 B3
  Highld......158 C4
  Notts......77 D8
  Orkney......159 G4
  Shetland......160 F7
  Shetland......160 F7
  Shetland......160 H6
  Shetland......160 J7
  Shetland......160 J7
  W&F......100 C2
Broughall......74 E2
Brough Lodge. 160 D7
Brough
  Sowerby......100 C2
Broughton
  Borders......120 F4
  Cambs......54 B3
  Flint......73 C7
  Hants......25 F8
  Lancs......92 F5
  M Keynes......53 E6
  N Lincs......90 D3
  N Nhants......53 B6
  N Yorks......94 D2
  N Yorks......96 B3
  Orkney......159 D5
  Oxon......52 F2
  V Glam......21 B8
Broughton Astley.64 E2
Broughton Beck. 98 F4
Broughton
  Common......24 C3
Broughton
  Gifford......24 C3
Broughton
  Hackett......50 D4
Broughton in
  Furness......98 F4
Broughton Mills. .98 E4
Broughton Moor 107 F7
Broughton Park. 87 D6
Broughton Poggs 38 D2
Broughtown......159 D7
Broughty Ferry. 134 F4
Browhouses....108 C2
Browland......160 H4
Brown Candover. 26 F3
Brown Edge
  Lancs......85 C4
  Staffs......75 D6
Brown Heath....73 C8
Brownhill
  Aberds......153 D6
  Aberds......153 D8
  Blackburn......93 F6
  Shrops......60 B4
Brownhills
  Fife......129 C7
  W Mid......62 D4
Brownlow......74 C5
Brownlow Heath. .74 C5
Brownmuir......135 B7
Brown's End......50 F2
Brownshill......37 D5
Brownston......6 D4
Brownyside......117 B7
Broxa......103 E7
Broxbourne......41 D6
Broxburn
  E Loth......122 B2
  W Loth......120 B3
Broxholme......78 B2
Broxted......42 B1
Broxton......73 D8
Broxwood......49 D5
Broyle Side......17 C8
Brù......155 C8
Bruairnis......148 H2
Bruan......158 G5
Bruar Lodge....133 B5
Brucehill......118 B3
Bruera......73 C8
Bruern Abbey....38 B2
Bruichladdich....142 B3
Bruisyard......57 C7
Brumby......90 D2
Brund......75 C8
Brundall......69 D6
Brundish......57 C6
Brundish Street. .57 B6
Brunery......147 D10
Brunshaw......93 F8
Brunswick
  Village......110 B5
Bruntcliffe......88 B3
Bruntingthorpe. .64 E3
Brunton
  Fife......128 B5
  Northumb......117 B8

Brunton *continued*
Wilts 25 D7
Brushford
Devon 9 D8
Som. 10 B4
Bruton 23 F8
Bryanston 13 D6
Brydekirk 107 B8
Bryher 2 E3
Brymbo 73 D6
Brympton 12 C3
Bryn
Carms 33 D6
Gtr Man. 86 D3
Neath 34 E2
Shrops 60 F2
Brynamman 33 C8
Brynberian 45 F3
Brynbryddan 34 E1
Brynbuga = *Usk* 35 D7
Bryncae 34 F3
Bryncethin 34 F3
Bryncir 71 C5
Bryn-coch 33 E8
Bryncroes 70 D3
Bryncrug 58 D3
Bryn Du 82 D3
Bryneglwys 72 E5
Brynford 73 B5
Bryn Gates 86 D3
Bryn-glas 83 E8
Bryn Golau 34 F3
Bryngwran 82 D3
Bryngwyn
Ceredig 45 E4
Mon. 35 D7
Powys 48 E3
Brynhenllan 45 F2
Brynhoffnant 46 D2
Brynithel 35 D6
Bryn-Iwan 46 F2
Brynmawr 35 C5
Bryn-mawr 70 D3
Brynmenyn 34 F3
Brynmill 33 E7
Brynna 34 F3
Bryn-nantllech 72 C3
Bryn-penarth 59 D8
Brynrefail
Anglesey 82 C4
Gwyn. 83 E5
Bryn Rhyd-yr-Arian 72 C3
Brynsadler 34 F4
Bryn Saith Marchog 72 D4
Brynsiencyn 82 E4
Bryn Sion 59 C5
Brynteg
Anglesey 82 C4
Ceredig 46 E3
Bryn-y-gwenin 35 C7
Bryn-y-maen 83 D8
Bryn-yr-eryr 70 C4
Buaile nam Bodach 148 H2
Bualintur 149 F9
Buarthmeini 72 F2
Bubbenhall 51 B8
Bubwith 96 F3
Buccleuch 115 C6
Buchanhaven 153 D11
Buchanty 127 B8
Buchlyvie 126 E4
Buckabank 108 E3
Buckden
Cambs 54 C2
N Yorks 94 B2
Buckenham 69 D6
Buckerell 11 D6
Buckfast 6 C5
Buckfastleigh 6 C5
Buckhaven 129 E5
Buckholm 121 F7
Buckholt 36 C2
Buckhorn Weston 13 B5
Buckhurst Hill 41 E7
Buckie 152 B4
Buckies 158 D3
Buckingham 52 F4
Buckland
Bucks 40 C1
Devon 6 E4
Glos 51 F5
Hants 14 E4
Herts 54 F4
Kent 31 E7
Oxon 38 E3
Sur 28 D3
Buckland Brewer 9 B6
Buckland Common 40 D2
Buckland Dinham 24 D2
Buckland Filleigh 9 D6
Buckland in the Moor 6 B5
Buckland Monachorum 6 C2
Buckland Newton 12 D4
Buckland St Mary 11 C7
Bucklebury 26 B3
Bucklegate 79 F6
Bucklerheads 134 F4
Bucklers Hard 14 E5
Bucklesham 57 E6
Buckley = *Bwcle* 73 C6
Bucklow Hill 86 F5
Buckminster 65 B5
Bucknall
Lincs 78 C4
Stoke 75 E6
Bucknell
Oxon 39 B5
Shrops 49 B5
Buckpool 152 B4
Bucksburn 141 D7
Buck's Cross 8 B5
Bucks Green 27 F8
Buckshaw Village 86 B3
Bucks Horn Oak 27 E6
Buckskin 26 D4
Buck's Mills 9 B5
Buckton
E Yorks 97 B7
Hereford 49 B5
Northumb 123 F6
Buckworth 54 B2
Budbrooke 51 C7
Budby 77 C6
Budd's Titson 8 D4
Bude 8 D4
Budlake 10 E4
Budle 123 F7
Budleigh Salterton 11 F5
Budock Water 3 C6
Buerton 74 E3
Buffler's Holt 52 F4
Bugbrooke 52 D4
Buglawton 75 C5
Bugle 4 D5
Bugley 24 E3
Bugthorpe 96 D3
Buildwas 61 D6
Builth Road 48 D2
Builth Wells = *Llanfair-ym-Muallt* 48 D2
Buirgh 154 H5
Bulby 65 B7
Bulcote 77 E6
Buldoo 157 C12
Bulford 25 E6
Bulford Camp 25 E6
Bulkeley 74 D2
Bulkington
Warks 63 F7
Wilts 24 D4
Bulkworthy 9 C5
Bullamoor 102 E1
Bullbridge 76 D3
Bullbrook 27 C6
Bulley 36 C4
Bullgill 107 F7
Bull Hill 14 E4
Bullington
Hants 26 E2
Lincs 78 B3
Bull's Green 41 C5
Bullwood 145 F10
Bulmer
Essex 56 E2
N Yorks 96 C2
Bulmer Tye 56 F2
Bulphan 42 F2
Bulverhythe 18 E4
Bulwark 153 D9
Bulwell 76 E5
Bulwick 65 E6
Bumble's Green 41 D7
Bun Abhainn Eadarra 154 G6
Bunacaimb 147 C9
Bun a'Mhuillin 148 G2
Bunarkaig 136 F4
Bunbury 74 D2
Bunbury Heath 74 D2
Bunchrew 151 G9
Bundalloch 149 F13
Buness 160 C8
Bunessan 146 J6
Bungay 69 F6
Bunkers Hill 38 C4
Bunker's Hill
Lincs 78 B2
Lincs 79 D5
Bunloit 137 B8
Bun Loyne 136 D5
Bunnahabhain 142 A5
Bunny 64 B2
Buntait 150 H6
Buntingford 41 B6
Bunwell 68 E4
Burbage
Derbys 75 B7
Leics 63 E8
Wilts 25 C7
Burchett's Green 39 F8
Burcombe 25 F5
Burcot 39 E5
Burcott 40 B1
Burdon 111 D6
Bures 56 F3
Bures Green 56 F3
Burford
Ches E 74 D3
Oxon 38 C2
Shrops 49 C7
Burg 146 G6
Burgar 159 F4
Burgate
Hants 14 C2
Suff 56 B4
Burgess Hill 17 C7
Burgh 57 D6
Burgh by Sands 108 D3
Burgh Castle 69 D7
Burghclere 26 C2
Burghead 151 E14
Burghfield 26 C4
Burghfield Common 26 C4
Burghfield Hill 26 C4
Burgh Heath 28 D3
Burghill 49 E6
Burgh le Marsh 79 C8
Burgh Muir 141 B6
Burgh next Aylsham 81 E8
Burgh on Bain 91 F6
Burgh St Margaret 69 C7
Burgh St Peter 69 E7
Burghwallis 89 C6
Burham 29 C8
Buriton 15 B8
Burland 74 D3
Burlawn 4 B4
Burleigh 27 C6
Burlescombe 11 C5
Burleston 13 E5
Burley
Hants 14 D3
Rutland 65 C5
W Yorks 95 F5
Burleydam 74 E3
Burley Gate 49 E7
Burley in Wharfedale 94 E4
Burley Lodge 14 D3
Burley Street 14 D3
Burlingjobb 48 D4
Burlow 18 D2
Burlton 60 B4
Burmarsh 19 B7
Burmington 51 F7
Burn 89 B6
Burnaston 76 F2
Burnbank 119 D7
Burnby 96 E4
Burncross 88 E4
Burneside 99 E7
Burness 159 D7
Burneston 101 F8
Burnett 23 C8
Burnfoot
Borders 115 C7
Borders 115 C8
E Ayrs 112 D4
Perth 127 D8
Burnham
Bucks 40 F2
N Lincs 90 C4
Burnham Deepdale 80 C4
Burnham Green 41 C5
Burnham Market 80 C4
Burnham Norton 80 C4
Burnham-on-Crouch 43 E5
Burnham-on-Sea 22 E5
Burnham Overy Staithe 80 C4
Burnham Overy Town 80 C4
Burnham Thorpe 80 C4
Burnhead
Dumfries 113 E8
S Ayrs 112 D2
Burnhervie 141 C6
Burnhill Green 61 D7
Burnhope 110 E4
Burnhouse 118 D3
Burniston 103 E8
Burnlee 88 D2
Burnley 93 F8
Burnley Lane 93 F8
Burnmouth 123 C5
Burn of Cambus 127 D6
Burnopfield 110 D4
Burnsall 94 C3
Burnside
Angus 135 D5
E Ayrs 113 C5
Fife 128 D3
Shetland 160 F4
S Lanark 119 C6
W Loth 120 B3
Burnside of Duntrune 134 F4
Burnswark 107 B8
Burntcommon 27 D8
Burnt Heath 76 B2
Burnthouse 3 C6
Burnt Houses 101 B6
Burntisland 128 F4
Burnton 112 D4
Burntwood 62 D4
Burnt Yates 95 C5
Burnwynd 120 C4
Burpham
Sur 27 D8
W Sus 16 D4
Burradon
Northumb 117 D5
T&W 111 B5
Burrafirth 160 B8
Burraland
Shetland 160 F5
Shetland 160 J4
Burras 3 C5
Burravoe
Shetland 160 F7
Shetland 160 G5
Burray Village 159 J5
Burrells 100 C1
Burrelton 134 F2
Burridge
Devon 20 F4
Hants 15 C6
Burrill 101 F7
Burringham 90 D2
Burrington
Devon 9 C8
Hereford 49 B6
N Som 23 D6
Burrough Green 55 D7
Burrough on the Hill 64 C4
Burrow-bridge 11 B8
Burrowhill 27 C7
Burry 33 E5
Burry Green 33 E5
Burry Port = *Porth Tywyn* 33 D5
Burscough 86 C2
Burscough Bridge 86 C2
Bursea 96 F4
Burshill 97 E6
Bursledon 15 D5
Burslem 75 E5
Burstall 56 E4
Burstock 12 D2
Burston
Norf 68 F4
Staffs 75 F6
Burstow 28 E4
Burstwick 91 B6
Burtersett 100 F3
Burtle 23 E5
Burton
BCP 14 E2
Ches W 73 B7
Ches W 74 C2
Lincs 78 B2
Northumb 123 F7
Pembs 44 E4
Som 22 E3
Wilts 24 B3
Burton Agnes 97 C7
Burton Bradstock 12 F2
Burton Dassett 51 D8
Burton Fleming 97 B6
Burton Green
W Mid 51 B7
Wrex 73 D7
Burton Hastings 63 E8
Burton-in-Kendal 92 B5
Burton in Lonsdale 93 B6
Burton Joyce 77 E6
Burton Latimer 53 B7
Burton Lazars 64 C4
Burton-le-Coggles 65 B6
Burton Leonard 95 C6
Burton on the Wolds 64 B2
Burton Overy 64 E3
Burton Pedwardine 78 E4
Burton Pidsea 97 F8
Burton Salmon 89 B5
Burton Stather 90 C2
Burton upon Stather 90 C2
Burton upon Trent 63 B6
Burtonwood 86 E3
Burwardsley 74 D2
Burwarton 61 F6
Burwash 18 C3
Burwash Common 18 C3
Burwash Weald 18 C3
Burwell
Cambs 55 C6
Lincs 79 B6
Burwen 82 B4
Burwick 159 K5
Bury
Cambs 66 F2
Gtr Man 87 C6
Som 10 B4
W Sus 16 C4
Bury Green 41 B7
Bury St Edmunds 56 C2
Burythorpe 96 C3
Busby 119 D5
Buscot 38 E2
Bush Bank 49 D6
Bushbury 62 D3
Bushby 64 D3
Bush Crathie 139 E8
Bushey 40 E4
Bushey Heath 40 E4
Bush Green 68 F5
Bushley 50 F3
Bushton 25 B5
Buslingthorpe 90 F4
Busta 160 G5
Butcher's Cross 18 C2
Butcombe 23 C7
Butetown 22 B3
Butleigh 23 F7
Butleigh Wootton 23 F7
Butler's Cross 39 D8
Butler's End 63 F6
Butlers Marston 51 E8
Butley 57 D7
Butley High Corner 57 E7
Butterburn 109 B6
Buttercrambe 96 D3
Butterknowle 101 B6
Butterleigh 10 D4
Buttermere
Cumb 98 C3
Wilts 25 C8
Buttershaw 88 B2
Butterstone 133 E7
Butterton 75 D7
Butterwick
Durham 102 B1
Lincs 79 E6
N Yorks 96 B3
N Yorks 97 B5
Butt Green 74 D3
Buttington 60 D2
Buttonoak 50 B2
Buttsash 14 D5
Butt's Green 14 B4
Buxhall 56 D4
Buxhall Fen Street 56 D4
Buxley 122 D4
Buxted 17 B8
Buxton
Derbys 75 B7
Norf 81 E8
Buxworth 87 F8
Bwcle = *Buckley* 73 C6
Bwlch 35 B5
Bwlchgwyn 73 D6
Bwlch-Llan 46 D4
Bwlchnewydd 32 B4
Bwlchtocyn 70 E4
Bwlch-y-cibau 59 C8
Bwlchyddar 59 B8
Bwlch-y-fadfa 46 E3
Bwlch-y-ffridd 59 E7
Bwlchygroes 45 F4
Bwlch-y-sarnau 48 B2
Byermoor 110 D4
Byers Green 110 F5
Byfield 52 D3
Byfleet 27 C8
Byford 49 E5
Bygrave 54 F3
Byker 111 C5
Bylchau 72 C3
Byley 74 C4
Bynea 33 E6
Byrness 116 D3
Bythorn 53 B8
Byton 49 C5
Byworth 16 B3

C

Cabharstadh 155 E8
Cablea 133 F6
Cabourne 90 D5
Cabrach
Argyll 144 G3
Moray 140 B2
Cabrich 151 G8
Cabus 92 E4
Cackle Street 17 B8
Cadbury 10 D4
Cadbury Barton 9 C8
Cadder 119 B6
Caddington 40 C3
Caddonfoot 121 F7
Cadeby
Leics 63 D8
S Yorks 89 D6
Cadeleigh 10 D4
Cade Street 18 C3
Cadgwith 3 E6
Cadham 128 D4
Cadishead 86 E5
Cadle 33 E7
Cadley
Lancs 92 F5
Wilts 25 C7
Wilts 25 D7
Cadmore End 39 E7
Cadnam 14 C3
Cadney 90 D4
Cadole 73 C6
Cadoxton 22 C3
Cadoxton-Juxta-Neath 34 E1
Cadshaw 86 C5
Cadzow 119 D7
Caeathro 82 E4
Caehopkin 34 C2
Caenby 90 F4
Caenby Corner 90 F3
Caerau
Bridgend 34 E2
Cardiff 22 B3
Caér-bryn 33 C6
Caerdeon 58 C3
Caerdydd = *Cardiff* 22 B3
Caerfarchell 44 C2
Caerffili = *Caerphilly* 35 F5
Caerfyrddin = *Carmarthen* 33 B5
Caergeiliog 82 D3
Caergwrle 73 D7
Caergybi = *Holyhead* 82 C2
Caerleon = *Caerllion* 35 E7
Caer Llan 36 D1
Caerllion = *Caerleon* 35 E7
Caernarfon 82 E4
Caerphilly = *Caerffili* 35 F5
Caersws 59 E7
Caerwedros 46 D2
Caerwent 36 E1
Caerwych 71 D7
Caerwys 72 B5
Caethle 58 E3
Caim 83 C6
Caio 47 F5
Cairinis 148 B3
Cairisiadar 154 D5
Cairminis 154 J5
Cairnbaan 145 D7
Cairnbanno House 153 D8
Cairnborrow 152 D4
Cairnbrogie 141 B7
Cairnbulg Castle 153 B10
Cairncross
Angus 134 B4
Borders 122 C4
Cairndow 125 D7
Cairness 153 B10
Cairneyhill 128 F2
Cairnfield House 152 B4
Cairngaan 104 F5
Cairngarroch 104 E4
Cairnhill 153 E6
Cairnie
Aberds 141 D7
Aberds 152 D4
Cairnorrie 153 D8
Cairnpark 141 C7
Cairnryan 104 C4
Cairnton 159 H4
Caister-on-Sea 69 C8
Caistor 90 D5
Caistor St Edmund 68 D5
Caistron 117 D5
Caitha Bowland 121 E7
Calais Street 56 F3
Calanais 154 D7
Calbost 155 F9
Calbourne 14 F5
Calceby 79 B6
Calcot Row 26 B4
Calcott 31 C5
Caldback 160 C8
Caldbeck 108 F3
Caldbergh 101 F5
Caldecote
Cambs 54 D4
Cambs 65 F8
Herts 54 F3
W Nhants 52 D4
Caldecott
N Nhants 53 C7
Oxon 38 E4
Rutland 65 E5
Calderbank 119 C7
Calder Bridge 98 D2
Calderbrook 87 C7
Caldercruix 119 C8
Calder Hall 98 D2
Calder Mains 158 E2
Caldermill 119 E6
Calder Vale 92 E5
Calderwood 119 D6
Caldhame 134 E4
Caldicot 36 F1
Caldwell
Derbys 63 C6
N Yorks 101 C6
Caldy 85 F3
Caledrhydiau 46 D3
Calfsound 159 E6
Calgary 146 F6
Califer 151 F13
California
Falk 120 B2
Norf 69 C8
Calke 63 B7
Callakille 149 C11
Callaly 117 D6
Callander 126 D5
Callaughton 61 E6
Callestick 4 D2
Calligarry 149 H11
Callington 5 C8
Callow 49 F6
Callow End 50 E3
Callow Hill
Wilts 37 F7
Worcs 50 B2
Callows Grave 49 C7
Calmore 14 C4
Calmsden 37 D7
Calne 24 B5
Calow 76 B4
Calshot 15 D5
Calstock 6 C2
Calstone Wellington 24 C5
Calthorpe 81 D7
Calthwaite 108 E4
Calton
N Yorks 94 D2
Staffs 75 D8
Calveley 74 D2
Calver 76 B2
Calverhall 74 F3
Calver Hill 49 E5
Calverleigh 10 C4
Calverley 94 F5
Calvert 39 B6
Calverton
M Keynes 53 F5
Notts 77 E6
Calvine 133 C5
Calvo 107 D8
Cam 36 E4
Camas-luinie 136 B2
Camasnacroise 130 D2
Camastianavaig 149 E10
Camasunary 149 G10
Camault Muir 151 G8
Camb 160 D7
Camber 19 D6
Camberley 27 C6
Camberwell 28 B4
Camblesforth 89 B7
Cambo 117 F6
Cambois 117 F9
Camborne 3 B5
Cambourne 54 D4
Cambridge
Cambs 55 D5
Glos 36 D4
Cambridge Town 43 F5
Cambus 127 E7
Cambusavie Farm 151 B10
Cambusbarron 127 E6
Cambuskenneth 127 E7
Cambuslang 119 C6
Cambusmore Lodge 151 B10
Camden 41 F5
Camelford 8 F3
Camelsdale 27 F6
Camerory 151 H13
Camer's Green 50 F2
Camerton
Bath 23 D8
Cumb 107 F7
E Yorks 91 B6
Camghouran 132 D2
Cammachmore 141 E8
Cammeringham 90 F3
Camore 151 B10
Campbeltown 143 F8
Camperdown 111 B5
Camp Hill 63 E7
Campmuir 134 F2
Campsall 89 C6
Campsey Ash 57 D7
Campton 54 F2
Camptown 116 C2
Camrose 44 C4
Camserney 133 E5
Camster 158 F4
Camuschoirk 130 C1
Camuscross 149 G11
Camusnagaul
Highld 130 B4
Highld 150 C3
Camusrory 147 B11
Camusteel 149 D12
Camusterrach 149 D12
Camusvrachan 132 E3
Canada 14 C3
Canadia 18 D4
Canal Side 89 C7
Candacraig House 140 C2
Candlesby 79 C7
Candy Mill 120 E3
Cane End 26 B4
Canewdon 42 E4
Canford Bottom 13 D8
Canford Cliffs 13 F8
Canford Magna 13 E8
Canham's Green 56 C4
Canholes 75 B7
Canisbay 158 C5
Cann 13 B6
Cannard's Grave 23 E8
Cann Common 13 B6
Cannich 150 H6
Cannington 22 F4
Cannock 62 D3
Cannock Wood 62 C4
Canonbie 108 B3
Canon Bridge 49 E6
Canon Frome 49 E8
Canon Pyon 49 E6
Canons Ashby 52 D3
Canonstown 2 C4
Canterbury 30 D5
Cantley
Norf 69 D6
S Yorks 89 D7
Cantlop 60 D5
Canton 22 B3
Cantraybruich 151 G10
Cantraydoune 151 G10
Cantraywood 151 G10
Cantsfield 93 B6
Canvey Island 42 F3
Canwick 78 C2
Canworthy Water 8 E4
Caol 131 B5
Caolas 146 G3
Caolas Scalpaigh 154 H7
Caolas Stocinis 154 H6
Caol Ila 142 A5
Capel 28 E2
Capel Bangor 58 F3
Capel Betws Lleucu 46 D5
Capel Carmel 70 E2
Capel Coch 82 C4
Capel Curig 83 F7
Capel Cynon 46 E2
Capel Dewi
Carms 33 B5
Ceredig 46 E3
Ceredig 58 F3
Capel Garmon 83 F8
Capel-gwyn 82 D3
Capel Gwyn 33 B5
Capel Gwynfe 33 B8
Capel Hendre 33 C6
Capel Hermon 71 E8
Capel Isaac 33 B6
Capel Iwan 45 F4
Capel le Ferne 31 F6
Capel Llanilltern 34 F4
Capel Mawr 82 D4
Capel St Andrew 57 E7
Capel St Mary 56 F4
Capel Seion 46 B5
Capel Tygwydd 45 E4
Capel Uchaf 70 C5
Capelulo 83 D7
Capel-y-graig 82 E5
Capenhurst 73 B7
Capernwray 92 B5
Capheaton 117 F6
Cappercleuch 115 B5
Capplegill 114 D4
Capton 7 D6
Caputh 133 F7
Carbis Bay 2 C4
Carbost
Highld 149 D9
Highld 149 E8
Carbrook 88 F4
Carbrooke 68 D2
Carburton 77 B6
Carcant 121 D6
Carcary 135 D6
Carclaze 4 D5
Car Colston 77 E7
Carcroft 89 C6
Cardenden 128 E4
Cardeston 60 C3
Cardiff = *Caerdydd* 22 B3
Cardigan = *Aberteifi* 45 E3
Cardington
Bedford 53 E8
Shrops 60 E5
Cardinham 5 C6
Cardonald 118 C5
Cardow 152 D1
Cardrona 121 F6
Cardross 118 B3
Cardurnock 107 D8
Careby 65 C7
Careston Castle 135 D5
Carew 32 D1
Carew Cheriton 32 D1
Carew Newton 32 D1
Carey 49 F7
Carfrae 121 C8
Cargenbridge 107 B6
Cargill 134 F1
Cargo 108 D3
Cargreen 6 C2
Carham 122 F4
Carhampton 22 E2
Carharrack 3 B6
Carie
Perth 132 D3
Perth 132 F3
Carines 4 D2
Carisbrooke 15 F5
Cark 92 B3
Carlabhagh 154 C7
Carland Cross 4 D3
Carlby 65 C7
Carlecotes 88 D2
Carlesmoor 94 B4
Carleton
Cumb 108 D4
Lancs 92 F3
N Yorks 94 E2
W&F 99 B7
Carleton Forehoe 68 D3
Carleton Rode 68 E4
Carlingcott 23 D8
Carlin How 103 C5
Carlisle 108 D4
Carlops 120 D4
Carlton
Bedford 53 D7
Cambs 55 D7
Leics 63 D7
Notts 77 E6
N Yorks 89 B7
N Yorks 101 C6
N Yorks 101 F5
N Yorks 102 F4
Stockton 102 B1
Suff 57 C7
S Yorks 88 C4
W Yorks 88 B4
Carlton Colville 69 F8
Carlton Curlieu 64 E3
Carlton Husthwaite 95 B7
Carlton in Cleveland 102 D3
Carlton in Lindrick 89 F6
Carlton le Moorland 78 D2
Carlton Miniott 102 F1
Carlton on Trent 77 C7
Carlton Scroop 78 E2
Carluke 119 D8
Carmarthen = *Caerfyrddin* 33 B5
Carmel
Anglesey 82 C3
Carms 33 C6
Flint 73 B5
Guern 16 I2
Gwyn 82 F4
Carmont 141 F7
Carmunnock 119 D6
Carmyle 119 C6
Carmyllie 135 E5
Carnaby 97 C7
Carnach
Highld 136 B3
Highld 150 B3
W Isles 154 H7
Carnachy 157 D10
Càrnais 154 D5
Carnbee 129 D7
Carnbo 128 D2
Carnbrea 3 B5
Carnduff 119 E6
Carnduncan 142 B3
Carne 3 C8
Carnforth 92 B4
Carn-gorm 136 B2
Carnhedryn 44 C3
Carnhell Green 2 C5
Carnkie
Corn 3 C5
Corn 3 C6
Carno 59 E6
Carnoch
Highld 150 F5
Highld 150 H6
Carnock 128 F2
Carnon Downs 3 B6
Carnousie 153 C6
Carnoustie 135 F5
Carnwath 120 E2
Carnyorth 2 C2
Carperby 101 F5
Carpley Green 100 F4
Carr 89 E6
Carradale 143 E9
Carragraich 154 H6
Carrbridge 138 B5
Carrefour Selous 17 I3
Carreglefn 82 C3
Carreg-wen 45 E4
Carr Hill 111 C5
Carrick
Argyll 145 E8
Fife 129 B6
Carrick Castle 145 D10
Carrick House 159 E6
Carriden 128 F2
Carrington
Gtr Man 86 E5
Lincs 79 D6
Midloth 121 C6
Carrog
Conwy 71 C8
Denb 72 E5
Carron
Falk 127 F7
Moray 152 D2
Carronbridge 113 E8
Carron Bridge 127 F6
Carronshore 127 F7
Carrshield 109 E8
Carrutherstown 107 B8
Carrville 111 E6
Carsaig
Argyll 144 E6
Argyll 147 J8
Carscreugh 105 D6
Carsegowan 105 D8
Carse Gray 134 D4
Carse House 144 G6
Carseriggan 105 C7
Carsethorn 107 D6
Carshalton 28 C3
Carsington 76 D2
Carskiey 143 H7
Carsluith 105 D8
Carsphairn 113 E5
Carstairs 120 E2
Carstairs Junction 120 E2
Carswell Marsh 38 E3
Carter's Clay 14 B4
Carterton 38 D2
Carterway Heads 110 D3
Carthew 4 D5
Carthorpe 101 F8
Cartington 117 D6
Cartland 119 E8
Cartmel 92 B3
Cartmel Fell 99 F6
Carway 33 D5
Cary Fitzpaine 12 B3
Cascob 48 C4
Cas-gwent = *Chepstow* 36 E2
Cashlie 132 E1
Cashmoor 13 C7
Casnewydd = *Newport* 35 F7
Cassey Compton 37 C7
Cassington 38 C4
Cassop 111 F6
Castell 72 C5
Castellau 34 F4
Castell-Howell 46 E3
Castell-Nedd = *Neath* 33 E8
Castell Newydd Emlyn = *Newcastle Emlyn* 46 E2
Castell-y-bwch 35 E6
Casterton 93 B6
Castle Acre 67 C8
Castle Ashby 53 D6
Castlebay = *Bagh a Chaisteil* 148 J1
Castle Bolton 101 E5
Castle Bromwich 62 F5
Castle Bytham 65 C6
Castlebythe 32 B1
Castle Caereinion 59 D8
Castle Camps 55 E7
Castle Carrock 108 D5
Castlecary 119 B7
Castle Cary 23 F8
Castle Combe 24 B3
Castlecraig 151 E11
Castle Donington 63 B8
Castle Douglas 106 C4
Castle Eaton 37 E8
Castle Eden 111 F7
Castlefairn 113 F7
Castle Forbes 140 C5
Castleford 88 B5
Castle Frome 49 E8
Castle Green 27 C7
Castle Gresley 63 C6
Castle Heaton 122 E5
Castle Hedingham 55 F8
Castlehill
Borders 120 F5
Highld 158 D3
W Dunb 118 B3
Castle Hill 29 E7
Castle Huntly 128 B5
Castle Kennedy 104 D5
Castlemaddy 113 F5
Castlemartin 44 F4
Castlemilk
Dumfries 107 B8
Glasgow 119 D6
Castlemorris 44 B4
Castlemorton 50 F2
Castle O'er 115 E5
Castle Pulverbatch 60 D4
Castle Rising 67 B6
Castleside 110 E3
Castle Stuart 151 G10
Castlethorpe 53 E6
Castleton
Angus 134 E3
Argyll 145 E7
Derbys 88 F2
Gtr Man 87 C6
Newport 35 F6
N Yorks 102 D4
Castletown
Ches W 73 D8
Highld 151 G10
Highld 158 D3
IoM 84 F2
T&W 111 D6
Castleweary 115 D7
Castley 95 E5
Caston 68 E2
Castor 65 E8
Catacol 143 D10
Catbrain 36 F2
Catbrook 36 D2
Catchall 2 D3
Catchems Corner 51 B7
Catchgate 110 D4
Catcleugh 116 D3
Catcliffe 88 F5
Catcott 23 F5
Caterham 28 D4
Catfield 69 B6
Catfirth 160 H6
Catford 28 B4
Catforth 92 F4
Cathays 22 B3
Cathcart 119 C5
Cathedine 35 B5
Catherington 15 C7
Catherton 49 B8
Catlodge 138 E2
Catlowdy 108 B4
Catmore 38 F4
Caton 92 C5
Caton Green 92 C5
Catrine 113 B5
Cat's Ash 35 E7
Catsfield 18 D4
Catshill 50 B4
Cattal 95 D7
Cattawade 56 F5
Catterall 92 E4
Catterick 101 E7
Catterick Bridge 101 E7
Catterick Garrison 101 E6
Catterlen 108 F4
Catterline 135 B8
Catterton 95 E8
Catthorpe 52 B3
Cattistock 12 E3
Catton
Northumb 109 D8
N Yorks 95 B6
Catwick 97 E7
Catworth 53 B8
Caudlesprings 68 D2
Caulcott 39 B5
Cauldcots 135 E6
Cauldhame 126 E5
Cauldmill 115 C8
Cauldon 75 E7
Caulkerbush 107 D6
Caulside 115 F7
Caunsall 62 F2
Caunton 77 D7
Causewayend 120 F3
Causeway End 105 C8
Causeway Foot 94 F3
Causewayhead
Cumb 107 D8
Stirling 127 E6
Causeyend 141 C8
Causey Park Bridge 117 E7
Cautley 100 E1
Cavendish 56 E2
Cavendish Bridge 63 B8
Cavenham 55 C8
Caversfield 39 B5
Caversham 26 B5
Caverswall 75 E6
Cavil 96 F3
Cawdor 151 F11
Cawkwell 79 B5
Cawood 95 F8
Cawsand 6 D2
Cawston 81 E7
Cawthorne 88 D3
Cawthorpe 65 B7
Cawton 96 B2
Caxton 54 D4
Caynham 49 B7
Caythorpe
Lincs 78 E2
Notts 77 E6
Cayton 103 F8
Ceann a Bhaigh 148 B2
Ceannacroc Lodge 136 C5
Ceann a Deas Loch Baghasdail 148 G2
Ceann Shiphoirt 155 F7
Ceann Tarabhaigh 154 F7

Cearsiadair 155 E8
Cefn Berain 72 C3
Cefn-brith 72 D3
Cefn Canol 73 F6
Cefn-coch 83 E8
Cefn Coch 59 B8
Cefn-coed-y-
  cymmer 34 D4
Cefn Cribbwr 34 F2
Cefn Cross 34 F2
Cefn-ddwysarn 72 F3
Cefn Einion 60 F2
Cefneithin 33 C6
Cefn-gorwydd 47 E8
Cefn-mawr 73 E6
Cefn-y-bedd 73 D7
Cefn-y-pant 32 B2
Cei-bach 46 D3
Ceinewydd
  = New Quay 46 D2
Ceint 82 D4
Cellan 46 E5
Cellarhead 75 E6
Cemaes 82 B3
Cemmaes 58 D5
Cemmaes Road 58 D5
Cenarth 45 E4
Cenin 71 C5
Central 118 B2
Ceos 155 E8
Ceres 129 C6
Cerne Abbas 12 D4
Cerney Wick 37 E7
Cerrigceinwen 82 D4
Cerrigydrudion . . 72 E3
Cessford 116 B3
Ceunant 82 E5
Chaceley 50 F3
Chacewater 3 B6
Chackmore 52 F4
Chacombe 52 E2
Chadderton 87 D7
Chadderton Fold 87 D6
Chaddesden 76 F3
Chaddesley
  Corbett 50 B3
Chaddleworth 26 B2
Chadlington 38 B3
Chadshunt 51 D8
Chad Valley 62 F4
Chadwell 64 B4
Chadwell St Mary . 29 B7
Chadwick End 51 B7
Chadwick Green . 86 E3
Chaffcombe 11 C8
Chagford 10 F2
Chailey 17 C7
Chainbridge 66 D4
Chain Bridge 79 E6
Chainhurst 29 E8
Chalbury 13 D8
Chalbury
  Common 13 D8
Chaldon 28 D4
Chaldon Herring . 13 F5
Chale 15 G5
Chale Green 15 G5
Chalfont
  Common 40 E3
Chalfont St Giles . 40 E2
Chalfont St Peter . 40 E2
Chalford 37 D5
Chalgrove 39 E6
Chalk 29 B7
Challacombe 21 E5
Challoch 105 C7
Challock 30 D4
Chalton
  C Beds 40 B3
  Hants 15 C8
Chalvington 18 E2
Chancery 46 B4
Chandler's Ford . 14 B5
Channel Tunnel . . 19 B8
Channerwick 160 L6
Chantry
  Som 24 E2
  Suff 56 E5
Chapel 128 E4
Chapel Allerton
  Som 23 D6
  W Yorks 95 F6
Chapel Amble 4 B4
Chapel Brampton . 52 C5
Chapel Chorlton . . 74 F5
Chapel End 63 E7
Chapel-en-le-
  Frith 87 F8
Chapelgate 66 B4
Chapel Green
  Warks 52 C2
  Warks 63 F6
Chapel Haddlesey 89 B6
Chapelhall 119 C7
Chapel Head 66 F3
Chapelhill
  Dumfries 114 E3
  Highld 151 D11
  N Ayrs 118 E2
  Perth 128 B4
  Perth 133 F7
Chapel Hill
  Aberds 153 E10
  Lincs 78 D5
  Mon 36 E2
  N Yorks 95 E6
Chapelknowe . . 108 B3
Chapel Lawn 48 B5
Chapel-le-Dale . . 93 B7
Chapel Milton . . . 87 F8
Chapel of
  Garioch 141 B6
Chapel Row 26 C3
Chapel
  St Leonards . . 79 B8
Chapel Stile 99 D5
Chapelton
  Angus 135 E6
  Devon 9 B7
  Highld 138 C5
  S Lanark 119 E6
Chapeltown
  Blackburn 86 C5
  Moray 139 B8
  S Yorks 88 E4

Chapmanslade . . 24 E3
Chapmans Well 9 E5
Chapmore End 41 C6
Chappel 42 B4
Chard 11 C8
Chardstock 11 D8
Charfield 36 E4
Charford 50 C4
Charing 30 E3
Charing Cross 14 C2
Charing Heath 30 E3
Charingworth 51 F7
Charlbury 38 C3
Charlcombe 24 C2
Charlcote 51 D7
Charles 21 F5
Charlesfield 107 C8
Charleston
  Aberdeen 141 D8
  Renfs 118 C4
Charlestown
  Aberdeen 141 D8
  Corn 4 D5
  Derbys 87 E8
  Dorset 12 G4
  Fife 128 F2
  Gtr Man 87 D6
  Highld 149 A13
  Highld 151 G9
  W Yorks 87 B7
Charlestown of
  Aberlour 152 D2
Charles Tye 56 D4
Charlesworth 87 E8
Charleton 7 E5
Charlton
  Hants 25 E8
  Herts 40 B4
  London 28 B5
  Northumb 116 F4
  Som 23 D8
  Telford 61 C5
  Wilts 13 B7
  Wilts 25 D6
  Wilts 37 F6
  W Nhants 52 F3
  Worcs 50 E5
  W Sus 16 C2
Charlton Abbots . 37 B7
Charlton Adam . . 12 B3
Charlton-All-
  Saints 14 B2
Charlton Down . . 12 E4
Charlton
  Horethorne . . . 12 B4
Charlton Kings . . 37 B6
Charlton
  Mackerell 12 B3
Charlton
  Marshall 13 D6
Charlton
  Musgrove 12 B5
Charlton on
  Otmoor 39 C5
Charltons 102 C4
Charlwood 28 E3
Charlynch 22 F4
Charminster 12 E4
Charmouth 11 E8
Charndon 39 B6
Charney Bassett . 38 E3
Charnock
  Richard 86 C3
Charsfield 57 D6
Chart Corner 29 D8
Charter Alley 26 D3
Charterhouse 23 D6
Charterville
  Allotments 38 C3
Chartham 30 D5
Chartham Hatch . 30 D5
Chartridge 40 D2
Chart Sutton 30 E2
Charvil 27 B5
Charwelton 52 D3
Chasetown 62 D4
Chastleton 38 B2
Chasty 8 D5
Chatburn 93 E7
Chatcull 74 F4
Chatham 29 C8
Chathill 117 B7
Chattenden 29 B8
Chatteris 66 F3
Chattisham 56 E4
Chatto 116 C3
Chatton 117 B6
Chawleigh 10 C2
Chawley 38 D4
Chawston 54 D2
Chawton 26 F5
Cheadle
  Gtr Man 87 F6
  Staffs 75 E7
Cheadle Heath . . 87 F6
Cheadle Hulme . . 87 F6
Cheam 28 C3
Cheapside 27 D8
Chearsley 39 C7
Chebsey 62 B2
Checkendon 39 F6
Checkley
  Ches E 74 E4
  Hereford 49 F7
  Staffs 75 F7
Chedburgh 55 D8
Cheddar 23 D6
Cheddington 40 C2
Cheddleton 75 D6
Cheddon
  Fitzpaine 11 B7
Chedglow 37 E6
Chedgrave 69 E6
Chedington 12 D2
Chediston 57 B7
Chedworth 37 C7
Chedzoy 22 F5
Cheeklaw 122 D3
Cheeseman's
  Green 19 B7
Cheglinch 20 E4
Cheldon 10 C2
Chelford 74 B5
Chellaston 76 F3
Chell Heath 75 D5
Chellington 53 D7
Chelmarsh 61 F7
Chelmer Village . 42 D3

Chelmondiston . . 57 F6
Chelmorton 75 C8
Chelmsford 42 D3
Chelsea 28 B3
Chelsfield 29 C5
Chelsworth 56 E3
Cheltenham 37 B6
Chelveston 53 C7
Chelvey 23 C6
Chelwood 23 C8
Chelwood
  Common 17 B8
Chelwood Gate . . 17 B8
Chelworth 37 E6
Chelworth Green 37 E7
Chemistry 74 E2
Chenies 40 E3
Cheny Longville . . 60 F4
Chepstow
  = Cas-gwent 36 E2
Chequerfield 89 B5
Cherhill 24 B5
Cherington
  Glos 37 E6
  Warks 51 F7
Cheriton
  Devon 21 E6
  Hants 15 B6
  Kent 19 B8
  Swansea 33 E5
Cheriton Bishop . 10 E2
Cheriton
  Fitzpaine 10 D3
Cheriton or Stackpole
  Elidor 44 F4
Cherrington 61 B6
Cherrybank 128 B3
Cherry Burton . . . 97 E5
Cherry Hinton . . . 55 D5
Cherry Orchard . . 50 D3
Cherry
  Willingham 78 B3
Chertsey 27 C8
Cheselbourne 13 E5
Chesham 40 D2
Chesham Bois . . . 40 E2
Cheshunt 41 D6
Cheslyn Hay 62 D3
Chessington 28 C2
Chester 73 C8
Chesterblade 23 E8
Chesterfield 76 B3
Chester-le-
  Street 111 D5
Chester Moor . . . 111 E5
Chesters
  Borders 116 B2
  Borders 116 B2
Chesterton
  Cambs 55 C5
  Cambs 65 E8
  Glos 37 D7
  Oxon 39 B5
  Shrops 61 E7
  Staffs 74 E5
  Warks 51 D8
Chesterwood . . . 109 C8
Chestfield 30 C5
Cheston 6 D4
Cheswardine 61 B7
Cheswick 123 E6
Chetnole 12 D4
Chettiscombe 10 C4
Chettisham 66 F5
Chettle 13 C7
Chetton 61 E6
Chetwode 39 B6
Chetwynd Aston . 61 C7
Cheveley 55 C7
Chevening 29 D5
Chevington 55 D8
Chevithorne 10 C4
Chew Magna 23 C7
Chew Stoke 23 C7
Chewton
  Keynsham 23 C8
Chewton Mendip . 23 D7
Chicheley 53 E7
Chichester 16 D2
Chickerell 12 F4
Chicklade 24 F4
Chicksgrove 24 F4
Chidden 15 C7
Chiddingfold 27 F7
Chiddingly 18 D2
Chiddingstone . . 29 E5
Chiddingstone
  Causeway 29 E6
Chiddingstone
  Hoath 29 E5
Chideock 12 E2
Chidham 15 D8
Chidswell 88 B3
Chieveley 26 B2
Chignall
  St James 42 D2
Chignall Smealy . 42 C2
Chigwell 41 E7
Chigwell Row . . . 41 E7
Chilbolton 25 F8
Chilcomb 15 B6
Chilcombe 12 E3
Chilcompton 23 D8
Chilcote 63 C6
Childer Thornton 73 B7
Child Okeford . . . 13 C6
Childrey 38 F3
Child's Ercall 61 B6
Childswickham . . 51 F5
Childwall 86 F2
Childwick Green . 40 C4
Chilfrome 12 E3
Chilgrove 16 C2
Chilham 30 D4
Chilhampton 25 F5
Chilla 9 D6
Chillaton 9 F6
Chillenden 31 D6
Chillerton 15 F5
Chillesford 57 D7
Chillingham 117 B6
Chillington
  Devon 7 E5
  Som 11 C8
Chilmark 24 F4
Chilson 38 C3
Chilsworthy
  Corn 6 B2

Chilsworthy continued
  Devon 8 D5
Chilthorne
  Domer 12 C3
Chiltington 17 C7
Chilton
  Bucks 39 C6
  Durham 101 B7
  Oxon 38 F4
Chilton Cantelo . . 12 B3
Chilton Foliat 25 B8
Chilton Lane 111 F6
Chilton Polden . . 23 F5
Chilton Street . . . 55 E8
Chilton Trinity . . . 22 F4
Chilwell 76 F5
Chilworth
  Hants 14 C5
  Sur 27 E8
Chimney 38 D3
Chineham 26 D4
Chingford 41 E6
Chinley 87 F8
Chinley Head 87 F8
Chinnor 39 D7
Chipnall 74 F4
Chippenhall
  Green 57 B6
Chippenham
  Cambs 55 C7
  Wilts 24 B4
Chipperfield 40 D3
Chipping
  Herts 54 F4
  Lancs 93 E6
Chipping
  Campden 51 F6
Chipping Hill 42 C4
Chipping Norton . 38 B3
Chipping Ongar . 42 D1
Chipping Sodbury 36 F4
Chipping Warden 52 E2
Chipstable 10 B5
Chipstead
  Kent 29 D5
  Sur 28 D3
Chirbury 60 E2
Chirk = Y Waun . . 73 F6
Chirk Bank 73 F6
Chirmorrie 105 B6
Chirnside 122 D4
Chirnsidebridge 122 D4
Chirton 25 D5
Chisbury 25 C7
Chiselborough . . 12 C2
Chiseldon 25 B6
Chiserley 87 B8
Chislehampton . . 39 E5
Chislehurst 28 B5
Chislet 31 C6
Chiswell Green . . 40 D4
Chiswick 28 B3
Chiswick End . . . 54 E4
Chisworth 87 E7
Chithurst 16 B2
Chittering 55 B5
Chitterne 24 E4
Chittlehamholt . . 9 B8
Chittlehampton . . 9 B8
Chittoe 24 C4
Chivenor 20 F4
Chobham 27 C7
Choicelee 122 D3
Cholderton 25 E7
Cholesbury 40 D2
Chollerford 110 B2
Chollerton 110 B2
Cholmondeston . 74 C3
Cholsey 39 F5
Cholstrey 49 D6
Chop Gate 102 E3
Choppington . . . 117 F8
Chopwell 110 D4
Chorley
  Ches E 74 D2
  Lancs 86 C3
  Shrops 61 F6
  Staffs 62 C4
Chorleywood . . . 40 E3
Chorlton cum
  Hardy 87 E6
Chorlton Lane . . . 73 E8
Choulton 60 F3
Chowdene 111 D5
Chowley 73 D8
Chrishall 54 F5
Christchurch
  BCP 14 E2
  Cambs 66 E4
  Glos 36 C2
  Newport 35 F7
Christian Malford . 24 B4
Christleton 73 C8
Christmas
  Common 39 E7
Christon 23 D5
Christon Bank . . . 117 B8
Christow 10 F3
Chryston 119 B6
Chudleigh 7 B6
Chudleigh
  Knighton 7 B6
Chulmleigh 9 C8
Chunal 87 E8
Church 86 B5
Churcham 36 C4
Church Aston . . . 61 C7
Churchbank 48 B4
Church Brampton 52 C5
Churchbridge . . . 62 D3
Church
  Broughton 76 F2
Church
  Crookham 27 D6
Churchdown 37 C5
Church Eaton . . . 62 C2
Churchend
  Essex 42 B2
  Essex 43 E6
  S Glos 36 E4
Church End
  Cambs 66 D3
  Cambs 66 F2
  C Beds 40 B2
  C Beds 53 F7
  C Beds 54 F2
  Essex 42 B3

Church End continued
  Essex 55 E6
  E Yorks 97 D6
  Herts 41 B7
  Lincs 78 F5
  Warks 63 E6
  Wilts 24 B5
Church Enstone . 38 B3
Church Fenton . . 95 F8
Churchfield 62 E4
Churchgate
  Street 41 C7
Church Green
  Devon 11 E6
  Norf 68 E3
Church Gresley . . 63 C6
Church
  Hanborough . . 38 C4
Church Hill 74 C3
Church Houses . 102 E4
Churchill
  Devon 11 D8
  Devon 20 E4
  N Som 23 D6
  Oxon 38 B2
  Worcs 50 B3
  Worcs 50 D4
Churchinford 11 C7
Church Knowle . . 13 F7
Church Laneham 77 B8
Church Langton . 64 E4
Church Lawford . 52 B2
Church Lawton . . 74 D5
Church Leigh 75 F7
Church Lench . . . 50 D5
Church Mayfield . 75 E8
Church Minshull . 74 C3
Church Norton . . 16 E2
Churchover 64 F2
Church Preen . . . 60 E5
Church
  Pulverbatch . . 60 D4
Churchstanton . . 11 C6
Church Stoke . . . 60 E2
Churchstow 6 E5
Church Stowe . . . 52 D4
Church Street . . . 29 B8
Church Stretton . 60 E4
Churchtown
  Derbys 76 C2
  IoM 84 C4
  Lancs 92 E4
  Mers 85 C4
Church Town
  N Lincs 89 D8
  Sur 28 D4
Church Village . . . 34 F4
Church Warsop . . 77 C5
Churnsike
  Lodge 109 B6
Churston Ferrers . 7 D7
Churt 27 F6
Churton 73 D8
Churwell 88 B3
Chute Standen . . 25 D8
Chwilog 70 D5
Chyandour 2 C3
Cilan Uchaf 70 E3
Cilcain 73 C5
Cilcennin 46 C4
Cilfor 71 D7
Cilfrew 34 D1
Cilfynydd 34 E4
Cilgerran 45 E3
Cilgwyn
  Carms 33 B8
  Gwyn 82 F4
  Pembs 45 F2
Ciliau Aeron 46 D3
Cill Donnain 148 F2
Cille Bhrighde . . 148 G2
Cille Pheadair . . 148 G2
Cilmaengwyn . . . 34 D2
Cilmery = Cilmeri 48 D2
Cilsan 33 B6
Ciltalgarth 72 E2
Cilwendeg 45 F4
Cilybebyll 33 D8
Cilycwm 47 F6
Cimla 34 E1
Cinderford 36 C3
Cippyn 45 E3
Circebost 154 D6
Cirencester 37 D7
Ciribhig 154 C6
City
  London 41 F6
  Powys 60 F2
City Dulas 82 C4
Clachaig 145 E10
Clachan
  Argyll 124 D3
  Argyll 125 D7
  Argyll 130 E2
  Argyll 144 H6
  Highld 149 L10
  W Isles 148 D2
Clachan na Luib 148 B3
Clachan of
  Campsie 119 B6
Clachan of
  Glendaruel . . 145 E8
Clachan-Seil . . . 124 D3
Clachan
  Strachur 125 E6
Clachbreck 144 F6
Clachnabrain . . 134 C3
Clachtoll 156 G3
Clackmannan . . 127 E8
Clacton-on-Sea . 43 C7
Cladach
  Chireboist . . . 148 B2
Claddach-
  knockline . . . 148 B2
Cladich 125 C6
Claggan
  Highld 131 B5
  Highld 147 G9
  Highld 147 G9
Claigan 148 C7
Claines 50 D3
Clandown 23 D8
Clanfield
  Hants 15 C7
  Oxon 38 D2
Clanville 23 F6
Claonaig 145 H7

Claonel 157 J8
Clapgate
  Dorset 13 D8
  Herts 41 B7
Clapham
  Bedford 53 D8
  London 28 B3
  N Yorks 93 C7
  W Sus 16 D4
Clappers 122 D5
Clappersgate . . . 99 D5
Clapton 12 D2
Clapton-in-
  Gordano 23 B6
Clapton-on-the-
  Hill 38 C1
Clapworthy 9 B8
Clara Vale 110 C4
Clarbeston 32 B1
Clarbeston Road . 32 B1
Clarborough 89 F8
Clardon 158 D3
Clare 55 E8
Clarebrand 106 C4
Clarencefield . . . 107 C7
Clarilaw 115 C8
Clark's Green 28 F2
Clarkston 119 D5
Clashandorran . . 151 G8
Clashcoig 151 B9
Clashindarroch . 152 E4
Clashmore
  Highld 151 C10
  Highld 156 F3
Clashnessie 156 F3
Clashnoir 139 B8
Clate 160 G7
Clathy 127 C8
Clatt 140 B4
Clatter 59 E6
Clatterford 15 F5
Clatterin Bridge 135 B6
Clatworthy 22 F2
Claughton
  Lancs 92 E5
  Lancs 93 C5
  Mers 85 F4
Claverdon 51 C6
Claverham 23 C6
Clavering 55 F5
Claverley 61 E7
Claverton 24 C2
Clawdd-newydd 72 D4
Clawthorpe 92 B5
Clawton 9 E5
Claxby
  Lincs 79 B7
  Lincs 90 E5
Claxton
  Norf 69 D6
  N Yorks 96 C2
Claybokie 139 E6
Claybrooke
  Magna 63 F8
Claybrooke Parva 63 F8
Clay Common . . . 69 F7
Clay Coton 52 B3
Clay Cross 76 C3
Claydon
  Oxon 52 D2
  Suff 56 D5
Claygate
  Dumfries 108 B3
  Kent 29 E8
  Sur 28 C2
Claygate Cross . . 29 D7
Clayhanger
  Devon 10 B5
  W Mid 62 D4
Clayhidon 11 C6
Clayhill
  E Sus 18 C5
  Hants 14 D4
Clay Hill 26 B3
Clay Lake 66 B2
Clayock 158 E3
Claypole 77 E8
Clayton
  Staffs 75 E5
  S Yorks 89 D5
  W Sus 17 C6
  W Yorks 94 F4
Clayton-le-Moors 93 F7
Clayton-le-
  Woods 86 B3
Clayton West . . . 88 C3
Clayworth 89 F8
Cleadale 146 C7
Cleadon 111 C6
Clearbrook 6 C3
Clearwell 36 D2
Cleasby 101 C7
Cleat 159 K5
Cleatlam 101 C6
Cleator 98 C2
Cleator Moor . . . 98 C2
Clebrig 157 F8
Cleckheaton 88 B2
Cleedownton . . . 61 F5
Cleehill 49 B7
Clee St Margaret . 61 F5
Cleethorpes 91 D7
Cleeton St Mary . 49 B8
Cleeve
  Devon 23 C6
  Ches W 73 D8
Cleeve Hill 37 B6
Cleeve Prior 51 E5
Clegyrnant 59 D6
Clehonger 49 F6
Cleish 128 E2
Cleland 119 D8
Clench Common . 25 C6
Clenchwarton . . . 67 B5
Clent 50 B4
Cleobury
  Mortimer 49 B8
Cleobury North . . 61 F6
Cleongart 143 E7
Clephanton 151 F11
Clerklands 115 B8
Clestrain 159 H4
Cleuch Head . . . 115 C8
Clevancy 25 B5
Clevedon 23 B6
Cleveley 38 B3

Cleveleys 92 E3
Cleverton 37 F6
Clevis 21 B7
Clewer 23 D6
Cley next the Sea 81 C6
Cliaid 148 H1
Cliasmol 154 G5
Cliburn 99 B7
Click Mill 159 F4
Cliddesden 26 E4
Cliff
  Medway 29 B8
  N Yorks 96 F2
Cliff End 19 D5
Cliffe Woods 29 B8
Clifford
  Hereford 48 E4
  W Yorks 95 E7
Clifford
  Chambers 51 D6
Clifford's Mesne . 36 B4
Cliffsend 31 C7
Clifton
  Bristol 23 B7
  C Beds 54 F2
  Derbys 75 E8
  Lancs 92 F4
  Northumb 117 F8
  N Yorks 94 E4
  Oxon 52 F2
  Stirling 131 F7
  S Yorks 89 E6
  York 95 D8
Clifton Campville 63 C6
Cliftoncote 116 B4
Clifton Green . . . 87 D5
Clifton Hampden 39 E5
Clifton Reynes . . 53 D7
Clifton upon
  Dunsmore . . . 52 B3
Clifton upon
  Teme 50 C2
Cliftonville 31 B7
Climaen gwyn . . . 33 D8
Climping 16 D4
Climpy 120 D2
Clink 24 E2
Clint 95 D5
Clint Green 68 C3
Clintmains 122 F2
Cliobh 154 D5
Clippesby 69 C7
Clipsham 65 C6
Clipston 64 F4
Clipstone 77 C5
Clitheroe 93 E7
Cliuthar 154 H6
Clive 60 B5
Clivocast 160 C8
Clixby 90 D5
Clocaenog 72 D4
Clochan 152 B4
Clock Face 86 E3
Clockmill 122 D3
Cloddiau 60 D2
Clodock 35 B7
Clola 153 D10
Clophill 53 F8
Clopton
  N Nhants 65 F7
  Suff 57 D6
Clopton Corner . 57 D6
Clopton Green . . 55 D8
Closeburn 113 E8
Close Clark 84 E2
Closworth 12 C3
Clothall 54 F3
Clotton 74 C2
Clough Foot 87 B7
Cloughton 103 E8
Cloughton
  Newlands . . . 103 E8
Clousta 160 H5
Clouston 159 G3
Clova
  Aberds 140 B3
  Angus 134 B3
Clove Lodge 100 C4
Clovelly 8 B5
Clovenfords 121 F7
Clovenstone 141 C6
Clovullin 130 C4
Clow Bridge 87 B6
Clowne 76 B4
Clows Top 50 B2
Cloy 73 E7
Cluanie Inn 136 C3
Cluanie Lodge . . 136 C3
Clun 60 F3
Clunbury 60 F3
Clunderwen 32 C2
Clune 138 B3
Clunes 136 F5
Clungunford 49 B5
Clunie
  Aberds 153 C6
  Perth 133 E8
Clunton 60 F3
Cluny 128 E4
Cluny Castle 138 E2
Clutton
  Bath 23 D8
  Ches W 73 D8
Clwt-grugoer . . . 72 C3
Clwt-y-bont 83 E5
Clydach
  Swansea 33 D7
Clydach Vale 34 E3
Clydebank 118 B4
Clydey 45 F4
Clyffe Pypard . . . 25 B5
Clynder 145 E11
Clyne 34 D2
Clynelish 157 J11
Clynnog-fawr . . . 82 F4
Clyro 48 E4
Clyst Honiton . . . 10 E5
Clyst Hydon 10 D5
Clyst St George . . 10 F4
Clyst
  St Lawrence . . 10 D5
Clyst St Mary . . . 10 E4
Cnoc Amhlaigh 155 D10

Cnwch-coch 47 B5
Coachford 152 D4
Coad's Green 5 B7
Coal Aston 76 B3
Coalbrookdale . . 61 D6
Coalbrookvale . . 35 D5
Coalburn 119 F8
Coalburns 110 C4
Coalcleugh 109 E8
Coaley 36 D4
Coalhall 112 C4
Coalhill 42 E3
Coalpit Heath . . . 36 F3
Coalport 61 D6
Coalsnaughton . . 127 E8
Coaltown of
  Balgonie 128 E4
Coaltown of
  Wemyss 128 E5
Coalville 63 C8
Coalway 36 C2
Coat 12 B2
Coatbridge 119 C7
Coatdyke 119 C7
Coate
  Swindon 38 F1
  Wilts 24 C5
Coates
  Cambs 66 E3
  Glos 37 D6
  Lancs 93 E8
  Notts 90 F2
  W Sus 16 C3
Coatham 102 B3
Coatham
  Mundeville . . 101 B7
Coatsgate 114 D3
Cobbaton 9 B8
Cobbler's Green . 69 E5
Coberley 37 C6
Cobham
  Kent 29 C7
  Sur 28 C2
Cobholm Island . 69 D8
Cobleland 126 E4
Cobnash 49 C6
Cock Bank 73 E7
Cock Bridge 139 D8
Cockburnspath . 122 B3
Cock Clarks 42 D4
Cockenzie and Port
  Seton 121 B7
Cockerham 92 D4
Cockermouth . . . 107 F8
Cockernhoe
  Green 40 B4
Cockfield
  Durham 101 B6
  Suff 56 D3
Cockfosters 41 E5
Cocking 16 C2
Cockington 7 C6
Cocklake 23 E6
Cockley Beck . . . 98 D4
Cockley Cley 67 D7
Cockshutt 60 B4
Cockthorpe 81 C5
Cockwood 10 F4
Cockyard 49 F6
Codda 5 B6
Coddenham 56 D5
Coddington
  Ches W 73 D8
  Hereford 50 E2
  Notts 77 D8
Codford St Mary . 24 F4
Codford St Peter . 24 F4
Codicote 41 C5
Codmore Hill . . . 16 B4
Codnor 76 E4
Codrington 24 B2
Codsall 62 D2
Codsall Wood . . . 62 D2
Coed Duon
  = Blackwood . . 35 E5
Coedely 34 F4
Coedkernew 35 F6
Coed Mawr 83 D5
Coed Morgan . . . 35 C7
Coedpoeth 73 D6
Coed-Talon 73 D6
Coedway 60 C3
Coed-y-bryn 46 E2
Coed-y-paen 35 E7
Coed-yr-ynys . . . 35 B5
Coed
  Ystumgwern . 71 E6
Coelbren 34 C2
Coffinswell 7 C6
Cofton Hackett . . 50 B5
Cogan 22 B3
Cogenhoe 53 C6
Cogges 38 D3
Coggeshall 42 B4
Coggeshall
  Hamlet 42 B4
Coggins Mill 18 C2
Coignafearn
  Lodge 138 C2
Coig
  Peighinnean 155 A10
Coig Peighinnean
  Bhuirgh 155 B9
Coilacriech 140 E2
Coilantogle 126 D4
Coilleag 148 G2
Coillore 149 E8
Coity 34 F3
Col 155 C9
Colaboll 157 H8
Colan 4 C3
Colaton Raleigh . 11 F5
Colbost 148 D7
Colburn 101 E6
Colby
  IoM 84 E2
  Norf 81 D8
  W&F 100 B1
Colchester 43 B6
Colcot 22 C3
Cold Ash 26 C3
Cold Ashby 52 B4
Cold Ashton 24 B2
Cold Aston 37 C8

Coldbeck 100 D2
Coldblow 29 B6
Cold Blow 32 C2
Cold Brayfield . . . 53 D7
Coldeast 7 B6
Colden 87 B7
Colden Common . 15 B5
Coldfair Green . . 57 C8
Coldham 66 D4
Cold Hanworth . . 90 F4
Coldharbour
  Glos 36 D2
  Kent 29 D6
  Sur 28 E2
Cold Hatton 61 B6
Cold Hesledon . . 111 E7
Cold Higham . . . 52 D4
Cold Kirby 102 F3
Cold Newton . . . 64 D4
Cold Northcott . . 8 F4
Cold Norton 42 D4
Cold Overton . . . 64 C5
Coldrain 128 D2
Coldred 31 E6
Coldridge 9 D8
Cole 23 F8
Colebatch 60 F3
Colebrook 10 D5
Colebrooke 10 E2
Coleby
  Lincs 78 C2
  N Lincs 90 C2
Coleford
  Devon 10 D2
  Glos 36 C2
  Som 23 E8
Cole Green 41 C5
Cole Henley 26 D2
Colehill 13 D8
Coleman's Hatch . 29 F5
Colemere 73 F8
Colemore 26 F5
Coleorton 63 C8
Colerne 24 B3
Colesbourne 37 C6
Colesden 54 D2
Cole's Green 57 C6
Coleshill
  Bucks 40 E2
  Oxon 38 E2
  Warks 63 F6
Colestocks 11 D5
Colgate 28 F3
Colgrain 126 F2
Colinsburgh 129 D6
Colinton 120 C5
Colintraive 145 F9
Colkirk 80 E5
Collace 134 F2
Collafirth 160 G6
Collaton St Mary . 7 D6
College Milton . . 119 D6
Collessie 128 C4
Collier Row 41 E8
Collier's End 41 B6
Collier's Green . . 18 B4
Collier Street . . . 29 E8
Colliery Row 111 E6
Collieston 141 B9
Collin 107 B7
Collingbourne
  Ducis 25 D7
Collingbourne
  Kingston 25 D7
Collingham
  Notts 77 C8
  W Yorks 95 E6
Collington 49 C8
Collingtree 53 D5
Collins Green . . . 86 E3
Colliston 135 E6
Collycroft 63 F7
Collynie 153 E8
Collyweston 65 D6
Colmonell 104 A5
Colmworth 54 D2
Colnabaichin . . 139 D8
Colnbrook 27 B8
Colne
  Cambs 54 B4
  Lancs 93 E8
Colne Edge 93 E8
Colne Engaine . . 56 F2
Colney 68 D4
Colney Heath . . . 41 D5
Colney Street . . . 40 D4
Coln Rogers 37 D7
Coln St Aldwyn's . 37 D8
Coln St Dennis . . 37 C7
Colpy 153 E6
Colquhar 121 E6
Colsterdale 101 F6
Colsterworth . . . 65 B6
Colston Bassett . 77 F6
Coltfield 151 E13
Coltishall 69 C5
Coltness 119 D8
Colton
  Norf 68 D4
  N Yorks 95 E8
  Staffs 62 B4
  W&F 99 F5
  W Yorks 95 F6
Col Uarach 155 D9
Colva 48 D4
Colvend 107 D5
Colvister 160 D7
Colwall Green . . . 50 E2
Colwall Stone . . . 50 E2
Colwell 110 B2
Colwich 62 B4
Colwick 77 E6
Colwinston 21 B8
Colworth 16 D3
Colwyn Bay
  = Bae Colwyn . 83 D8

Colyford 11 E7
Colyton 11 E7
Combe
  Hereford.....48 C5
  Oxon.....38 C4
  W Berks.....25 C8
Combe Common.27 F7
Combe Down....24 C2
Combe Florey....22 F3
Combe Hay.....24 D2
Combeinteignhead 7 B7
Combe Martin...20 E4
Combe Moor.....49 C5
Combe Raleigh..11 D6
Comberbach....74 B3
Comberton
  Cambs.....54 D4
  Hereford.....49 C6
Combe
  St Nicholas.....11 C8
Combpyne.....11 E7
Combridge.....75 F7
Combrook.....51 D8
Combs
  Derbys.....75 B7
  Suff.....56 D4
Combs Ford.....56 D4
Combwich.....22 E4
Comers.....141 D5
Comins Coch....58 D3
Commercial End. 55 C6
Commins Capel
  Betws.....46 D5
Commins Coch.. 58 D5
Commondale... 102 C4
Common Edge...92 F3
Commonmoor.....5 C7
Commonside....74 B2
Common Side....76 B3
Compstall.....87 E7
Compton
  Devon.....7 C6
  Hants.....15 B5
  Sur.....27 E6
  Sur.....27 E7
  W Berks.....26 B3
  Wilts.....25 D6
  W Sus.....15 C8
Compton Abbas. 13 C6
Compton Abdale .37 C7
Compton Bassett .24 B5
Compton
  Beauchamp.....38 F2
Compton Bishop. 23 D5
Compton
  Chamberlayne...13 B8
Compton Dando. 23 C8
Compton Dundon.23 F6
Compton Martin. 23 D7
Compton
  Pauncefoot ...12 B4
Compton Valence 12 E3
Comrie
  Fife.....128 F2
  Perth.....127 B6
Conaglen House 130 C4
Conchra.....145 E9
Concraigie.....133 E8
Conder Green....92 D4
Conderton.....50 F4
Condicote.....38 B1
Condorrat.....119 B7
Condover.....60 D4
Coneyhurst.....16 B5
Coneysthorpe....96 B3
Coneythorpe.....95 D6
Coney Weston....56 B3
Conford.....27 F6
Congash.....139 B6
Congdon's Shop..5 B7
Congerstone....63 D7
Congham.....80 E3
Congleton.....75 C5
Congl-y-wal ...71 C8
Congresbury....23 C6
Congreve.....62 C3
Conicavel.....151 F12
Coningsby.....78 D5
Conington
  Cambs.....54 C4
  Cambs.....65 F8
Conisbrough....89 E6
Conisby.....142 B3
Conisholme.....91 E8
Coniston
  E Yorks.....97 F7
  W&F.....99 E5
Coniston Cold....94 D2
Conistone.....94 C2
Connah's Quay ..73 C6
Connel.....124 B5
Connel Park....113 C6
Connor Downs....2 C4
Conon Bridge ..151 F8
Conon House....151 F8
Cononley.....94 E2
Conordan.....149 E10
Consall.....75 E6
Consett.....110 D4
Constable
  Burton.....101 E6
Constantine.....3 D6
Constantine Bay. 4 B3
Contin.....150 F7
Contlaw.....141 D7
Conwy.....83 D7
Conyer.....30 C3
Conyers Green ..56 C2
Cooden.....18 E4
Cooil.....84 E3
Cookbury.....9 D6
Cookham.....40 F1
Cookham Dean...40 F1
Cookham Rise...40 F1
Cookhill.....51 D5
Cookley
  Suff.....57 B7
  Worcs.....62 F2
Cookley Green ..39 E6
Cookney.....141 E7
Cooksbridge....17 C8
Cooksmill Green 42 D2
Coolham.....16 B5
Cooling.....29 B8
Coombe
  Corn.....4 D4
  Corn.....8 C4

Coombe continued
  Hants.....15 B7
  Wilts.....25 D6
Coombe Bissett .14 B2
Coombe Hill.....37 B5
Coombe Keynes ..13 F6
Coombes.....17 D5
Coopersale
  Common.....41 D7
Cootham.....16 C4
Copdock.....56 E5
Copford Green ...43 B5
Copgrove.....95 C6
Copister.....160 F6
Cople.....54 E2
Copley.....101 B5
Coplow Dale....75 B8
Copmanthorpe...95 E8
Coppathorne.....8 D4
Coppenhall.....62 C3
Coppenhall Moss 74 D4
Coppenford.....65 F8
Copperhouse.....2 C4
Coppingford.....65 F8
Copplestone.....10 D2
Coppull.....86 C3
Coppull Moor....86 C3
Copsale.....17 B5
Copster Green...93 F6
Copston Magna ..63 F8
Copt Heath.....51 B6
Copt Hewick....95 B6
Copthorne
  Shrops.....60 C4
  Sur.....28 F4
Copy's Green....80 D5
Copythorne.....14 C4
Corbets Tey....42 F1
Corbridge.....110 C2
Corby.....65 F5
Corby Glen.....65 B6
Cordon.....143 E11
Coreley.....49 B8
Cores End.....40 F2
Corfe.....11 C7
Corfe Castle....13 F7
Corfe Mullen....13 E7
Corfton.....60 F4
Corgarff.....139 D8
Corhampton.....15 B7
Corlae.....113 E6
Corley.....63 F7
Corley Ash.....63 F6
Corley Moor....63 F6
Cornaa.....84 D4
Cornabus.....142 D4
Cornel.....83 E7
Corner Row.....92 F4
Corney.....98 E3
Cornforth.....111 F6
Cornhill.....152 C5
Cornhill-on-
  Tweed.....122 F4
Cornholme.....87 B7
Cornish Hall End..55 F7
Cornquoy.....159 J6
Cornsay.....110 E4
Cornsay Colliery 110 E4
Corntown
  Highld.....151 F8
  V Glam.....21 B8
Cornwell.....38 B2
Cornwood.....6 D4
Cornworthy.....7 D6
Corpach.....130 B4
Corpusty.....81 D7
Corran
  Highld.....130 C4
  Highld.....149 H13
Corranbuie.....145 G7
Corrany.....84 D4
Corrie.....143 D11
Corrie Common ..114 F5
Corriecravie....143 F10
Corriemoillie...150 E6
Corriemulzie
  Lodge.....156 B6
Corrievarkie
  Lodge.....132 B2
Corrievorrie...138 B3
Corrimony.....150 H6
Corringham
  Lincs.....90 E2
  Thurrock.....42 F3
Corris.....58 D4
Corris Uchaf....58 D4
Corrour Shooting
  Lodge.....131 C8
Corrow.....125 E7
Corry.....149 F11
Corrykinloch...156 G6
Corrymuckloch..133 F5
Corrynachenchy 147 G9
Corry of
  Ardnagrask...151 G8
Corsback.....158 C4
Corscombe ...12 D3
Corse
  Aberds.....152 D6
  Glos.....36 B4
Corse Lawn.....50 F3
Corse of Kinnoir 152 D5
Corsewall.....104 C4
Corsham.....24 B3
Corsindae.....141 D5
Corsley.....24 E3
Corsley Heath...24 E3
Corsock.....106 B4
Corston
  Bath.....23 C8
  Wilts.....37 F6
Cors-y-Gedol ...71 E6
Cortachy.....134 D3
Corton
  Suff.....69 E8
  Wilts.....24 E4
Corton Denham ..12 B4
Coruanan Lodge 130 C4
Corwen.....72 E4
Coryton
  Devon.....9 F6
  Thurrock.....42 F3
Cosby.....64 E2
Coseley.....62 E3
Cosgrove.....53 E5
Cosham.....15 D7

Cosheston.....32 D1
Cossall.....76 E4
Cossington
  Leics.....64 C3
  Som.....23 E5
Costa.....159 F4
Costessey.....68 C4
Costock.....64 B2
Coston.....64 B5
Cote.....38 D3
Cotebrook.....74 C2
Cotehill.....108 D4
Cotes
  Leics.....64 B2
  Staffs.....74 F5
  W&F.....99 F6
Cotesbach.....64 F2
Cotgrave.....77 F6
Cothall.....141 C7
Cotham.....77 E7
Cothelstone.....22 F3
Cotherstone....101 C5
Cothill.....38 E4
Cotleigh.....11 D7
Cotmanhay.....76 E4
Cotmaton.....11 F6
Coton
  Cambs.....54 D5
  Staffs.....62 B2
  Staffs.....75 F6
  W Nhants.....52 B4
Coton Clanford..62 B2
Coton Hill
  Shrops.....60 C4
  Staffs.....75 F6
Coton in the Elms 63 C6
Cott.....7 C5
Cottam
  E Yorks.....97 C5
  Lancs.....92 F5
  Notts.....77 B8
Cottartown....151 H13
Cottenham.....54 C5
Cotterdale....100 E3
Cottered.....41 B6
Cotteridge.....50 B5
Cotterstock....65 E7
Cottesbrooke...52 B5
Cottesmore.....65 C6
Cotteylands.....10 C4
Cottingham
  E Yorks.....97 F6
  N Nhants.....64 E5
Cottingley.....94 F4
Cottisford.....52 F3
Cotton
  Staffs.....75 E7
  Suff.....56 C4
Cotton End.....53 E8
Cottown
  Aberds.....140 B4
  Aberds.....141 C6
  Aberds.....153 D8
Cotwalton.....75 F6
Couch's Mill.....5 D6
Coughton
  Hereford.....36 B2
  Warks.....51 C5
Coulaghailtro... 144 G6
Coulags.....150 G2
Coulby Newham 102 C3
Coulderton.....98 D1
Coulin.....150 F3
Coull
  Aberds.....140 D4
  Argyll.....142 B3
Coulport.....145 E11
Coulsdon.....28 D3
Coulston.....24 D4
Coulter.....120 F3
Coulton.....96 B2
Cound.....61 D5
Coundon
  Durham.....101 B7
  W Mid.....63 F7
Coundon
  Grange.....101 B7
Countersett....100 F4
Countess.....25 E6
Countess Wear ..10 F4
Countesthorpe ..64 E2
Countisbury....21 E6
County Oak.....28 F3
Coupar Angus..134 E2
Coup Green.....86 B3
Coupland
  Cumb.....100 C2 –
Coupland
  Northumb.....122 F5
  E Ayrs.....113 C5
Cour.....143 D9
Courance.....114 E3
Court-at-Street.19 B7
Courteenhall....53 D5
Court Henry....33 B6
Courtsend.....43 E6
Courtway.....22 F4
Cousland.....121 C6
Cousley Wood...18 B3
Cove
  Argyll.....145 E11
  Borders.....122 B3
  Devon.....10 C4
  Hants.....27 D6
  Highld.....155 H13
Cove Bay.....141 D8
Cove Bottom....57 B8
Covehithe.....69 F8
Coven.....62 D3
Coveney.....66 F4
Covenham
  St Bartholomew .91 E7
Covenham
  St Mary.....91 E7
Coventry.....51 B8
Coverack.....3 E6
Coverham.....101 F6
Covesea.....152 A1
Covington
  Cambs.....53 B8
  S Lanark.....120 F2
Cowan Bridge...93 B6
Cow Ark.....93 E6
Cowbeech.....18 D3
Cowbit.....66 C2
Cowbridge
  Lincs.....79 E6
  Som.....21 E8
Cowbridge
  =Y Bont-Faen ..21 B8
Cowdale.....75 B7
Cowden.....29 E5

Cowdenbeath...128 E3
Cowdenburn....120 D5
Cowers Lane....76 E3
Cowes.....15 E5
Cowesby.....102 F2
Cowfold.....17 B6
Cowgill.....100 F2
Cowie
  Aberds.....141 F7
  Stirling.....127 F7
Cowley
  Devon.....10 E4
  Glos.....37 C6
  London.....40 F3
  Oxon.....39 D5
Cowleymoor.....10 C4
Cowling
  Lancs.....86 C3
  N Yorks.....94 E2
  N Yorks.....101 F7
Cowlinge.....55 D8
Cowpe.....87 B6
Cowpen.....117 F8
Cowpen Bewley 102 B2
Cowplain.....15 C7
Cowshill.....109 E8
Cowslip Green.. 23 C6
Cowstrandburn 128 E2
Cowthorpe.....95 D7
Coxbank.....74 E3
Coxbench.....76 E3
Cox Common....69 F6
Coxford
  Norf.....80 E4
  Soton.....14 C4
Cox Green.....27 B6
Coxheath.....29 D8
Coxhill.....31 E6
Coxhoe.....111 F6
Coxley.....23 E7
Cox Moor.....76 D5
Coxwold.....95 B8
Coychurch.....21 B8
Coylton.....112 B4
Coylumbridge ..138 C5
Coynach.....140 D3
Coynachie.....152 E4
Coytrahen.....34 F2
Crabadon.....7 D5
Crabbs Cross.....50 C5
Crabtree.....17 B6
Crackenthorpe 100 B1
Crackington Haven 8 E3
Crackley.....51 B7
Crackleybank...61 C7
Crackpot.....100 E4
Cracoe.....94 C2
Craddock.....11 C5
Cradhlastadh...154 D5
Cradley.....50 E2
Cradley Heath...62 F3
Crafthole.....5 D8
Craggan.....139 B6
Craggie
  Highld.....151 H10
  Highld.....157 H11
Cragg Vale.....87 B8
Craghead.....110 D5
Crai.....34 B2
Craibstone....152 C4
Craichie.....135 E5
Craig
  Dumfries.....106 B3
  Dumfries.....106 C3
  Highld.....150 G3
Craiganor
  Lodge.....132 D3
Craig Castle....140 B3
Craig-cefn-parc..33 D7
Craigdam.....153 E8
Craigdarroch
  Dumfries.....113 E7
  Highld.....150 F7
Craigdhu.....150 G7
Craigearn.....141 C6
Craigellachie...152 D2
Craigencross...104 C4
Craigend
  Perth.....128 B3
  Stirling.....127 F6
Craigendive....145 E9
Craigendoran...126 F2
Craigends.....118 C4
Craigens
  Argyll.....142 B3
  E Ayrs.....113 C5
Craighat.....126 F3
Craighead.....129 D8
Craighlaw
  Mains.....105 C7
Craighouse....144 G4
Craigie
  Aberds.....141 C8
  Dundee.....134 F4
  Perth.....128 B3
  Perth.....133 E8
  S Ayrs.....118 F4
Craigiefield...159 G5
Craigielaw.....121 B7
Craiglockhart..120 B5
Craigmalloch...112 E4
Craigmaud.....153 C8
Craigmillar....121 B5
Craigmore.....145 G10
Craignant.....73 F6
Craigneuk
  N Lanark.....119 C7
  N Lanark.....119 D7
Craignure.....124 B3
Craigo.....135 C6
Craigow.....128 D2
Craig Penllyn...21 B8
Craigrothie....129 C5
Craigroy.....151 F14
Craigruie.....126 B3
Craigston Castle 153 C7
Craigton
  Aberdeen....141 D7
  Angus.....134 D3
  Angus.....135 E5
  Highld.....151 G9
Craigtown....157 D11
Craig-y-don....83 C7
Craig-y-nos....34 C2
Craik.....115 D6
Crail.....129 D8
Crailing.....116 B2
Crailinghall...116 B2

Craiseloune.....89 E8
Crakehill.....95 B7
Crakemarsh.....75 F7
Crambe.....96 C3
Cramlington ...111 B5
Cramond.....120 B4
Cramond Bridge 120 B4
Cranage.....74 C4
Cranberry.....74 F5
Cranborne.....13 C8
Cranbourne.....27 B7
Cranbrook
  Devon.....10 E5
  Kent.....18 B4
Cranbrook
  Common.....18 B4
Crane Moor.....88 D4
Crane's Corner ..68 C2
Cranfield.....53 E7
Cranford.....28 B2
Cranford
  St Andrew.....53 B7
Cranford St John .53 B7
Cranham
  Glos.....37 C5
  London.....42 F1
Crank.....86 E3
Crank Wood.....86 D4
Cranleigh.....27 F8
Cranley.....57 B5
Cranmer Green...56 B4
Cranmore.....14 F4
Cranna.....153 C6
Crannich.....147 G8
Crannoch.....152 C4
Cranoe.....64 E4
Cransford.....57 C7
Cranshaws.....122 C4
Cranstal.....84 B4
Crantock.....4 C2
Cranwell.....78 E3
Cranwich.....67 E7
Cranworth.....68 D2
Craobh Haven ..124 E3
Crapstone.....6 C3
Crarae.....125 F5
Crask Inn.....157 G8
Craskins.....140 D4
Crask of Aigas .150 G7
Craster.....117 C8
Craswall.....48 F4
Cratfield.....57 B7
Crathes.....141 E6
Crathie
  Aberds.....139 E8
  Highld.....137 E8
Crathorne.....102 D2
Craven Arms....60 F4
Crawcrook.....110 C4
Crawford
  Lancs.....86 D2
  S Lanark.....114 B2
Crawfordjohn..113 B8
Crawick.....113 C7
Crawley
  Hants.....26 F2
  Oxon.....38 C3
  W Sus.....28 F3
Crawley Down...28 F4
Crawleyside....110 E2
Crawshawbooth..87 B6
Crawton.....135 B8
Cray
  N Yorks.....94 B2
  Perth.....133 C8
Crayford.....29 B6
Crayke.....95 B8
Crays Hill.....42 E3
Cray's Pond.....39 F6
Creacombe.....10 C3
Creagan.....130 E3
Creag Ghoraidh 148 D2
Creaguaineach
  Lodge.....131 C7
Creaksea.....43 E5
Creaton.....52 B5
Creca.....108 B2
Credenhill.....49 E6
Crediton.....10 D3
Creebridge....105 C8
Creech
  Heathfield.....11 B7
Creech
  St Michael.....11 B7
Creed.....3 B8
Creekmouth.....41 F7
Creeting Bottoms 56 D5
Creeting St Mary 56 D4
Creeton.....65 B7
Creetown.....105 D8
Creggans.....125 E6
Cregneash.....84 F1
Creg-ny-Baa....84 D3
Cregrina.....48 D3
Creich.....128 B5
Creigiau.....34 F4
Cremyll.....6 D2
Creslow.....39 B8
Cressage.....61 D5
Cressbrook.....75 B8
Cresselly.....32 D1
Cressing.....42 B3
Cresswell
  Northumb.....117 E8
  Staffs.....75 F6
Cresswell Quay .32 D1
Creswell.....76 B5
Cretingham.....57 C6
Cretshengan...144 G6
Crewe
  Ches E.....74 D4
  Ches W.....73 D8
Crewgreen.....60 C3
Crewkerne.....12 D2
Crianlarich....126 B2
Cribyn.....46 D4
Criccieth.....71 D5
Crich.....76 D3
Crichie.....153 D9
Crichton.....121 C6
Crick
  Mon.....36 E1
  W Nhants.....52 B3
Crickadarn.....48 E2
Cricket
  Malherbie.....11 C8
Cricket
  St Thomas.....11 D8

Crickheath.....60 B2
Crickhowell.....35 C6
Cricklade.....37 E8
Cricklewood....41 F5
Cridling Stubbs..89 B6
Crieff.....127 B7
Criggion.....60 C2
Crigglestone....88 C4
Crimond.....153 C10
Crimonmogate 153 C10
Crimplesham....67 D6
Crinan.....144 D6
Cringleford.....68 D4
Cringles.....94 E3
Crinow.....32 C2
Cripplesease.....2 C4
Cripplestyle.....13 C8
Cripp's Corner ..18 C4
Croasdale.....98 C2
Crockenhill.....29 C6
Crockernwell...10 E2
Crockerton.....24 E3
Crocketford or
  Ninemile Bar ..106 B5
Crockey Hill....96 E2
Crockham Hill ..28 D5
Crockleford
  Heath.....43 B6
Crockness.....159 J4
Crock Street....11 C8
Croeserw.....34 E2
Croes-goch.....44 B3
Croes-lan.....46 E2
Croesor.....71 C7
Croesyceiliog
  Carms.....33 C5
  Torf.....35 E7
Croes-y-mwyalch 35 E7
Croesywaun.....82 F5
Croft
  Hereford.....49 F8
  Lincs.....79 C8
  Warr.....86 E4
Croftamie.....126 F3
Croftmalloch...120 C2
Crofton
  Wilts.....25 C7
  W Yorks.....88 C4
Croft-on-Tees...101 D7
Crofts of
  Benachielt....158 G3
Crofts of Haddo 153 E8
Crofts of
  Inverthernie...153 D7
Crofts of Meikle
  Ardo.....153 D8
Crofty.....33 E6
Croggan.....124 C3
Croich.....150 B7
Crois Dughaill ..148 F2
Cromarty.....151 E10
Cromblet.....153 E7
Cromdale.....139 B6
Cromer
  Herts.....41 B5
  Norf.....81 C8
Cromford.....76 D2
Cromhall.....36 E3
Cromhall
  Common.....36 F3
Cromor.....155 E9
Cromra.....137 E8
Cromwell.....77 C7
Cronberry.....113 B6
Crondall.....27 E5
Cronk-y-Voddy. 84 D3
Cronton.....86 F2
Crook
  Durham.....110 F4
  W&F.....99 E6
Crookedholm ..118 F4
Crookes.....88 F4
Crookham
  Northumb.....122 F5
  W Berks.....26 C3
Crookham
  Village.....27 D5
Crookhaugh....114 B4
Crookhouse....116 B3
Crooklands.....99 F7
Crook of Devon 128 D2
Cropredy.....52 E2
Cropston.....64 C2
Cropthorne.....50 E4
Cropton.....103 F5
Cropwell Bishop .77 F6
Cropwell Butler .77 F6
Cros.....155 A10
Crosbost.....155 E8
Crosby
  Cumb.....107 F7
  IoM.....84 E3
  N Lincs.....90 C2
Crosby
  Ravensworth..99 C8
Crosby Villa....107 F7
Croscombe.....23 E7
Cross.....23 D6
Crossaig.....143 C9
Crossal.....149 E9
Crossapol.....146 G2
Cross Ash.....35 C8
Cross-at-Hand ..29 E8
Crossbush.....16 D4
Crosscanonby..107 F7
Crossdale
  Street.....81 D8
Crossens.....85 C4
Crossflatts.....94 E4
Crossford
  Fife.....128 F2
  S Lanark.....119 E8
Crossgate.....66 B2
Crossgatehall .121 C6
Crossgates
  Fife.....128 F3
  Powys.....48 C2
Crossgill.....93 C5
Cross Green
  Devon.....9 F5
  Suff.....56 D3
  Suff.....56 D3
  Warks.....51 D8
Cross-hands.....32 C2

Cross Hands
  Carms.....33 C6
  Pembs.....32 C1
Crosshill
  E Ayrs.....112 B4
  Fife.....128 E3
  S Ayrs.....112 D3
Cross Hill.....76 E4
Crosshouse.....118 F3
Cross Houses....60 D5
Crossings.....108 B5
Cross in Hand
  E Sus.....18 C2
  Leics.....64 F2
Cross Inn
  Ceredig.....46 C4
  Ceredig.....46 D2
  Rhondda.....34 F4
Crosskeys.....35 E6
Cross Keys.....29 D6
Crosskirk....157 B13
Cross Lane Head.61 E7
Crosslanes.....60 C3
Cross Lanes
  Corn.....3 D5
  N Yorks.....95 C8
  Wrex.....73 E7
Crosslee.....118 C4
Crosslee.....115 C6
Crossmichael..106 C4
Crossmoor.....92 F4
Cross Oak.....35 B5
Cross of
  Jackston.....153 E7
Cross o'th'hands .76 E2
Crossroads
  Aberds.....141 E6
  E Ayrs.....118 F4
Cross Street.....57 B5
Crossway
  Hereford.....49 F8
  Mon.....35 C8
  Powys.....48 D2
Crossway Green. 50 C3
Crosswell.....45 F3
Crosswood.....47 B5
Crosthwaite....99 E6
Croston.....86 C2
Crostwick.....69 C5
Crostwight.....69 B6
Crothair.....154 D6
Crouch.....29 D7
Crouchend.....13 B8
Crouch Hill.....12 C5
Crouch House
  Green.....28 E5
Croughton.....52 F3
Crovie.....153 B8
Crowan.....2 C5
Crowborough...18 B2
Crowcombe.....22 F3
Crowdecote.....75 C8
Crowden.....87 E8
Crowdhill.....14 C6
Crow Edge.....88 D2
Crowell.....39 E7
Crowfield
  Suff.....56 D5
  W Nhants.....52 E4
Crow Hill.....36 B3
Crowhurst
  E Sus.....18 D4
  Sur.....28 E4
Crowhurst Lane
  End.....28 E4
Crowland.....66 C2
Crowlas.....2 C4
Crowle
  N Lincs.....89 C8
  Worcs.....50 D4
Crowmarsh
  Gifford.....39 F6
Crown Corner....57 B6
Crownhill.....6 D2
Crownland.....56 C4
Crownthorpe....68 D3
Crowntown.....2 C5
Crows-an-wra....2 D2
Crowshill.....68 D2
Crowsnest.....60 D3
Crowthorne.....27 C6
Crowton.....74 B2
Croxall.....63 C5
Croxby.....91 E5
Croxdale.....111 F5
Croxden.....75 F7
Croxley Green...40 E3
Croxton
  Cambs.....54 C3
  N Lincs.....90 C4
  Norf.....67 F8
  Staffs.....74 F4
Croxtonbank....74 F4
Croxton Kerrial .64 B5
Croy
  Highld.....151 G10
  N Lanark.....119 B7
Croyde.....20 F3
Croydon
  Cambs.....54 E4
  London.....28 C4
Crubenmore
  Lodge.....138 E2
Cruckmeole.....60 D4
Cruckton.....60 C4
Cruden Bay....153 E10
Crudgington....61 C6
Crudwell.....37 E6
Crug.....48 B3
Crugmeer.....4 B4
Crugybar.....47 F5
Crulabhig.....154 D6
Crumlin
  =Crymlyn.....35 E6
Crumpsall.....87 D6
Crundale
  Kent.....30 E4
  Pembs.....44 D4
Cruwys Morchard 10 D3
Crux Easton....26 D2
Crwbin.....33 C5
Crya.....159 H4
Cryers Hill....40 E1
Crymlyn.....83 D6
Crymych.....45 F3
Crynant.....34 D1

Crynfryn.....46 C4
Cuaig.....149 C12
Cuan.....124 D3
Cubbington.....51 C8
Cubeck.....100 F4
Cubert.....4 D2
Cubley.....88 D3
Cubley Common..75 F8
Cublington
  Bucks.....39 B8
  Hereford.....49 F6
Cuckfield.....17 B7
Cucklington.....13 B5
Cuckney.....77 B5
Cuckoo Hill....89 E8
Cuddesdon.....39 D6
Cuddington
  Bucks.....39 C7
  Ches W.....74 B3
Cuddington
  Heath.....73 E8
Cuddy Hill.....92 F4
Cudham.....28 C5
Cudliptown.....6 B3
Cudworth
  Som.....11 C8
  S Yorks.....88 D4
Cuffley.....41 D6
Cuiashader....155 B10
Cuidhir.....148 H1
Cuidhtinis.....154 J5
Culbo.....151 E9
Culbokie.....151 F9
Culburnie.....150 G7
Culcabock.....151 G9
Culcairn.....151 E9
Culcharry.....151 F11
Culcheth.....86 E4
Culdrain.....152 E5
Culduie.....149 D12
Culford.....56 B2
Culgaith.....99 B8
Culham.....39 E5
Culkein.....156 F3
Culkein
  Drumbeg.....156 F4
Culkerton.....37 E6
Cullachie.....139 B5
Cullen.....152 B5
Cullercoats....111 B6
Cullicudden....151 E9
Cullingworth....94 F3
Cullipool.....124 D3
Cullivoe.....160 C7
Culloch.....127 C6
Culloden.....151 G10
Cullompton.....10 D5
Culmaily.....151 B11
Culmazie.....105 D7
Culmington.....60 F4
Culmstock.....11 C6
Culnacraig.....156 J3
Culnaknock....149 B10
Culpho.....57 E6
Culrain.....151 B8
Culross.....127 F8
Culroy.....112 C3
Culsh
  Aberds.....140 E2
  Aberds.....153 D8
Culshabbin.....105 D7
Culswick.....160 J4
Cultercullen...141 B8
Cults
  Aberdeen....141 D7
  Aberds.....152 E5
  Dumfries.....105 E8
Culverstone
  Green.....29 C7
Culverthorpe....78 E3
Culworth.....52 E3
Culzie Lodge...151 D8
Cumbernauld..119 B7
Cumbernauld
  Village.....119 B7
Cumberworth....79 B8
Cuminestown...153 C8
Cumlewick....160 L6
Cummersdale..108 D3
Cummertrees...107 C8
Cummingston...152 B1
Cumnock.....113 B5
Cumnor.....38 D4
Cumrew.....108 D5
Cumwhinton...108 D4
Cumwhitton...108 D5
Cundall.....95 B7
Cunninghamhead
  .....118 E3
Cunnister.....160 D7
Cupar.....129 C5
Cupar Muir....129 C5
Cupernham.....14 B4
Curbar.....76 B2
Curbridge
  Hants.....15 C6
  Oxon.....38 D3
Curdridge.....15 C6
Curdworth.....63 E5
Curland.....11 C7
Curlew Green....57 C7
Currarie.....112 E1
Curridge.....26 B2
Currie.....120 C4
Curry Mallet....11 B8
Curry Rivel....11 B8
Curtisden Green..29 E8
Curtisknowle....6 D5
Cury.....3 D5
Cushnie.....153 B7
Cushuish.....22 F3
Cusop.....48 E4
Cutcloy.....105 F8
Cutcombe.....21 F8
Cutgate.....87 C6
Cutiau.....58 C3
Cutlers Green...55 F6
Cutnall Green...50 C3
Cutsdean.....51 F5
Cutthorpe.....76 B3
Cutts.....160 K6
Cuxham.....39 E6
Cuxton.....29 C8
Cuxwold.....91 D5
Cwm
  Bl Gwent.....35 D5
  Denb.....72 B4
  Swansea.....33 E7

Cwmafan.....34 E1
Cwmaman.....34 E4
Cwmann.....46 E4
Cwmavon.....35 D6
Cwmbach
  Carms.....32 B3
  Carms.....33 D5
  Powys.....48 D2
  Powys.....48 F3
Cwmbâch.....34 D4
Cwmbelan.....59 F6
Cwmbran
  =Cwmbrân.....35 E6
Cwmbrwyno.....58 F4
Cwmcarn.....35 E6
Cwmcarvan.....36 D1
Cwm-Cewydd...59 C5
Cwm-cou.....45 E4
Cwmcych.....45 F4
Cwmdare.....34 D3
Cwmderwen.....59 D6
Cwmdu
  Carms.....46 F5
  Powys.....35 B5
  Swansea.....33 E7
Cwmduad.....46 F2
Cwm-Dulais.....33 D7
Cwmdwr.....47 F6
Cwmfelin
  Bridgend.....34 F2
  M Tydf.....34 D4
Cwmfelin Boeth. 32 C2
Cwm-felin-fach.. 35 E5
Cwmfelin Mynach 32 B3
Cwmffrwd.....33 C5
Cwm Ffrwd-oer. 35 D6
Cwmgiedd.....34 C1
Cwmgors.....33 C8
Cwmgwili.....33 C6
Cwmgwrach.....34 D2
Cwm-hesgen.....71 E8
Cwmhiraeth.....46 F2
Cwm-hwnt.....34 D3
Cwmifor.....33 B7
Cwm Irfon.....47 E7
Cwmisfael.....33 C5
Cwm-Llinau.....58 D5
Cwmllynfell....33 C8
Cwm-mawr.....33 C6
Cwmorgan.....45 F4
Cwm-parc.....34 E3
Cwmpengraig...46 F2
Cwm Penmachno 71 C8
Cwmrhos.....35 B5
Cwmsychpant..46 E3
Cwmtillery.....35 D6
Cwm-twrch Isaf. 34 C1
Cwm-twrch
  Uchaf.....34 C1
Cwmwysg.....34 B2
Cwm-y-glo
  Carms.....33 C6
  Gwyn.....82 E5
Cwmyoy.....35 B6
Cwmystwyth....47 B6
Cwrt.....58 D3
Cwrt-newydd...46 E3
Cwrt-y-cadno...47 E5
Cwrt-y-gollen.. 35 C6
Cydweli
  =Kidwelly.....33 D5
Cyffordd Llandudno
  Junction.....83 D7
Cyffylliog.....72 D4
Cyfronydd.....59 D8
Cymer.....34 E2
Cyncoed.....35 F5
Cynghordy.....47 E7
Cynheidre.....33 D5
Cynwyd.....72 E4
Cynwyl Elfed....32 B4
Cywarch.....59 C5

D

Dacre
  N Yorks.....94 C4
  W&F.....99 B6
Dacre Banks....94 C4
Daddry Shield..109 F8
Dadford.....52 F4
Dadlington.....63 E8
Dafarn Faig....71 C5
Dafen.....33 D6
Daffy Green.....68 D2
Dagenham.....41 F7
Daglingworth...37 D6
Dagnall.....40 C2
Dail Beag.....154 C7
Dail bho Dheas. 155 A9
Dail bho Thuath 155 A9
Daill.....142 B4
Dail Mor.....154 C7
Dairsie or
  Osnaburgh...129 C6
Daisy Hill.....86 D4
Dalabrog.....148 F2
Dalavich.....125 D5
Dalbeattie....106 C5
Dalblair.....113 C6
Dalbog.....135 B5
Dalby
  IoM.....84 E2
  N Yorks.....96 B2
Dalchalloch...132 C4
Dalchalm.....157 J12
Dalchenna.....125 E6
Dalchirach....152 E1
Dalchork.....157 H8
Dalchreichart..137 C5
Dalchruin.....127 C6
Dalderby.....78 C5
Dale
  Pembs.....44 E3
Dale Abbey.....76 F4
Dale Head.....99 C6
Dalelia.....147 E10
Dale of Walls...160 H3
Daless.....151 H11
Dalfaber.....138 C5
Dalgarven.....118 E3

Dalgety Bay 128 F3
Dalginross 127 B6
Dalguise 133 E6
Dalhalvaig 157 D11
Dalham 55 C8
Dalinlongart 145 E10
Dalkeith 121 C6
Dallam 86 E3
Dallas 151 F14
Dalleagles 113 C5
Dallinghoo 57 D6
Dallington
E Sus 18 D3
W Nhants 52 C5
Dallow 94 B4
Dalmadilly 141 C6
Dalmally 125 C7
Dalmarnock 119 C6
Dalmary 126 E4
Dalmellington 112 D4
Dalmeny 120 B4
Dalmigavie 138 C3
Dalmigavie Lodge 138 B3
Dalmore 151 E9
Dalmuir 118 B4
Dalnabreck 147 E9
Dalnacardoch Lodge 132 B4
Dalnacroich 150 F6
Dalnaglar Castle 133 C8
Dalnahaitnach 138 B4
Dalnaspidal Lodge 132 B3
Dalnavaid 133 C7
Dalnavie 151 D9
Dalnawillan Lodge 157 E13
Dalness 131 D5
Dalnessie 157 H9
Dalqueich 128 D2
Dalreavoch 157 J10
Dalry 118 E2
Dalrymple 112 C3
Dalserf 119 D8
Dalston 108 D3
Dalswinton 114 F2
Dalton
Dumfries 107 B8
Lancs 86 D2
Northumb 110 B4
Northumb 110 D2
N Yorks 95 B7
N Yorks 101 D6
S Yorks 89 E5
Dalton-in-Furness 92 B2
Dalton-le-Dale 111 E7
Dalton-on-Tees 101 D7
Dalton Piercy 111 F7
Dalveich 126 B5
Dalvina Lodge 157 E9
Dalwhinnie 138 F2
Dalwood 11 D7
Dalwyne 112 E3
Damerham 14 C2
Damgate 69 D7
Dam Green 68 F3
Damnaglaur 104 F5
Damside 120 E4
Dam Side 92 E4
Danbury 42 D3
Danby 103 D5
Danby Wiske 101 E8
Dandaleith 152 D2
Danderhall 121 C6
Danebridge 75 C6
Dane End 41 B6
Danehill 17 B8
Danemoor Green 68 D3
Danesford 61 E7
Daneshill 26 D4
Dangerous Corner 86 C3
Danskine 121 C8
Darcy Lever 86 D5
Darenth 29 B6
Daresbury 86 F3
Darfield 88 D5
Darfoulds 77 B5
Dargate 30 C4
Dargavel Renfs 118 B3
Darite 5 C7
Darlaston 62 E3
Darley 94 D5
Darley Bridge 76 C2
Darley Head 94 D4
Darlingscott 51 E7
Darlington 101 C7
Darliston 74 F2
Darlton 77 B7
Darnall 88 F4
Darnick 121 F8
Darowen 58 D5
Darra 153 D7
Darracott 20 F3
Darras Hall 110 B4
Darrington 89 B5
Darsham 57 C8
Dartford 29 B6
Dartford Crossing 29 B6
Dartington 7 C5
Dartmeet 6 B4
Dartmouth 7 D6
Darton 88 D4
Darvel 119 F5
Darwell Hole 18 D3
Darwen 86 B4
Datchet 27 B7
Datchworth 41 C5
Datchworth Green 41 C5
Daubhill 86 D5
Daugh of Kinermony 152 D2
Dauntsey 37 F6
Dava 151 H13
Davenham 74 B3
Davenport Green 74 B5
Daventry 52 C3
Davidson's Mains 120 B5
Davidstow 8 F3
David's Well 48 B2
Davington 115 D5
Daviot
Aberds 141 B6
Highld 151 H10
Davoch of Grange 152 C4
Davyhulme 87 E5
Dawley 61 D6
Dawlish 7 B7
Dawlish Warren 7 B7
Dawn 83 D8
Daws Heath 42 F4
Daw's House 8 F5
Dawsmere 79 F7
Dayhills 75 F6
Daylesford 38 B2
Ddôl-Cownwy 59 C7
Ddrydwy 82 D3
Deadwater 116 E2
Deaf Hill 111 F6
Deal 31 D7
Deal Hall 43 E6
Dean
Cumb 98 B2
Devon 6 C5
Devon 20 E4
Dorset 13 C7
Hants 15 C6
Som 23 E8
Deanburnhaugh 115 C6
Deane
Gtr Man 86 D4
Hants 26 D3
Deanich Lodge 150 C6
Deanland 13 C7
Dean Prior 6 C5
Dean Row 87 F6
Deans 120 C3
Deanscales 98 B2
Deanshanger 53 F5
Deanston 127 D6
Dearham 107 F7
Debach 57 D6
Debden
Essex 41 E7
Essex 55 F6
Debden Cross 55 F6
Debenham 57 C5
Dechmont 120 B3
Deddington 52 F2
Dedham 56 F4
Dedham Heath 56 F4
Deebank 141 E5
Deene 65 E6
Deenethorpe 65 E6
Deepcar 88 E3
Deepcut 27 D7
Deepdale 100 F2
Deeping Gate 65 D8
Deeping St James 65 D8
Deeping St Nicholas 66 C2
Deerhill 152 C4
Deerhurst 37 B5
Deerness 159 H6
Defford 50 E4
Defynnog 34 B3
Deganwy 83 D7
Deighton
N Yorks 102 D1
W Yorks 88 C2
York 96 E2
Deiniolen 83 E5
Delabole 8 F2
Delamere 74 C2
Delfrigs 141 B8
Delliefure 151 H13
Dell Lodge 139 C6
Delnabo 139 C7
Delnadamph 139 D8
Delph 87 D7
Delves 110 E4
Delvine 133 E8
Dembleby 78 F3
Denaby Main 89 E5
Denbigh = Dinbych 72 C4
Denbury 7 C6
Denby 76 E3
Denby Dale 88 D3
Denchworth 38 E3
Dendron 92 B2
Denel End 53 F8
Denend 152 E6
Denford 53 B7
Dengie 43 D5
Denham
Bucks 40 F3
Suff 55 C8
Suff 57 B5
Denham Street 57 B5
Denhead
Aberds 153 C9
Fife 129 C6
Denhead of Arbilot 135 E5
Denhead of Gray 134 F3
Denholm 115 C8
Denholme 94 F3
Denholme Clough 94 F3
Denio 70 D4
Denmead 15 C7
Denmore 141 C8
Denmoss 153 D6
Dennington 57 C6
Denny 127 F7
Dennyloanhead 127 F7
Denny Lodge 14 D4
Denshaw 87 C7
Denside 141 E7
Densole 31 E6
Denston 55 D8
Denstone 75 E8
Dent 100 F2
Denton
Cambs 65 F8
Darl 101 C7
E Sus 17 D8
Gtr Man 87 E7
Kent 31 E6
Lincs 77 F8
Norf 69 F5
N Yorks 94 E4
Oxon 39 D5
W Nhants 53 D6
Denton's Green 86 E2
Denver 67 D6
Denwick 117 C8
Deopham 68 D3
Deopham Green 68 E3
Depden 55 D8
Depden Green 55 D8
Deptford
London 28 B4
Wilts 24 F5
Derby 76 F3
Derbyhaven 84 F2
Dereham 68 C2
Deri 35 D5
Derril 8 D5
Derringstone 31 E6
Derrington 62 B2
Derriton 8 D5
Derryguaig 146 H7
Derry Hill 24 B4
Derrythorpe 90 D2
Dersingham 80 D2
Dervaig 146 F7
Derwen 72 D4
Derwenlas 58 E4
Desborough 64 F5
Desford 63 D8
Detchant 123 F6
Detling 29 D8
Deuddwr 60 C2
Devauden 36 E1
Devil's Bridge 47 B6
Devizes 24 C5
Devol 118 B3
Devonport 6 D2
Devonside 127 E8
Devoran 3 C6
Dewar 121 E6
Dewlish 13 E5
Dewsbury 88 B3
Dewsbury Moor 88 B3
Dewshall Court 49 F6
Dhoon 84 D4
Dhoor 84 C4
Dhowin 84 B4
Dial Post 17 C5
Dibden 14 D5
Dibden Purlieu 14 D5
Dickleburgh 68 F4
Didbrook 51 F5
Didcot 39 F5
Diddington 54 C2
Diddlebury 60 F5
Didley 49 F6
Didling 16 C2
Didmarton 37 F5
Didsbury 87 E6
Didworthy 6 C4
Digby 78 D3
Digg 149 B9
Diggle 87 D8
Digmoor 86 D2
Digswell Park 41 C5
Dihewyd 46 D3
Dilham 69 B6
Dilhorne 75 E6
Dillarburn 119 E8
Dillington 54 C2
Dilston 110 C2
Dilton Marsh 24 E3
Dilwyn 49 D6
Dinas
Carms 45 F4
Gwyn 70 D3
Dinas Cross 45 F2
Dinas Dinlle 82 F4
Dinas-Mawddwy 59 C5
Dinas Powys 22 B3
Dinbych = Denbigh 72 C4
Dinbych-y-Pysgod = Tenby 32 D2
Dinder 23 E7
Dinedor 49 F7
Dingestow 36 C1
Dingle 85 F4
Dingleden 18 B5
Dingley 64 F4
Dingwall 151 F8
Dinlabyre 115 E8
Dinmael 72 E4
Dinnet 140 E3
Dinnington
Som 12 C2
S Yorks 89 F6
T&W 110 B5
Dinorwic 83 E5
Dinton
Bucks 39 C7
Wilts 24 F5
Dinwoodie Mains 114 E4
Dinworthy 8 C5
Dippen 143 F11
Dippenhall 27 E6
Dipple
Moray 152 C3
S Ayrs 112 D2
Diptford 6 D5
Dipton 110 D4
Dirdhu 139 B6
Dirleton 129 F7
Dirt Pot 109 E8
Discoed 48 C4
Diseworth 63 B8
Dishes 159 F7
Dishforth 95 B6
Disley 87 F7
Diss 56 B5
Disserth 48 D2
Distington 98 B2
Ditchampton 25 F5
Ditcheat 23 F8
Ditchingham 69 E6
Ditchling 17 C7
Ditherington 60 C5
Dittisham 7 D6
Ditton
Halton 86 F2
Kent 29 D8
Ditton Green 55 D7
Ditton Priors 61 F6
Divach 137 B7
Divlyn 47 F6
Dixton
Glos 50 F4
Mon 36 C2
Dobcross 87 D7
Dobwalls 5 C7
Doccombe 10 F2
Dochfour House 151 H9
Dochgarroch 151 G9
Docking 80 D3
Docklow 49 D7
Dockray 99 B5
Dockroyd 94 F3
Doc Penfro = Pembroke Dock 44 E4
Dodburn 115 D7
Doddinghurst 42 E1
Doddington
Cambs 66 E3
Kent 30 D3
Lincs 78 B2
Northumb 123 F5
Shrops 49 B8
Doddiscombsleigh 10 F3
Dodford
W Nhants 52 C4
Worcs 50 B4
Dodington 24 A2
Dodleston 73 C7
Dods Leigh 75 F7
Dodworth 88 D4
Doe Green 86 F3
Doe Lea 76 C4
Dogdyke 78 D5
Dogmersfield 27 D5
Dogridge 37 F7
Dogsthorpe 65 D8
Dog Village 10 E4
Dolanog 59 C7
Dolau
Powys 48 C3
Rhondda 34 F3
Dolbenmaen 71 C6
Dolfach 59 D6
Dolfor 59 F8
Dol-fôr 58 D5
Dolgarrog 83 E7
Dolgellau 58 C4
Dolgran 46 F3
Dolhendre 72 F2
Doll 157 J11
Dollar 127 E8
Dolley Green 48 C4
Dollwen 58 F3
Dolphin 73 B5
Dolphinholme 92 D5
Dolphinton 120 E4
Dolton 9 C7
Dolwen
Conwy 83 D8
Powys 59 D6
Dolwyd 83 D8
Dolwyddelan 83 F7
Dôl-y-Bont 58 F3
Dol-y-cannau 48 E4
Dolyhir 48 D4
Doncaster 89 D6
Dones Green 74 B3
Donhead St Andrew 13 B7
Donhead St Mary 13 B7
Donibristle 128 F3
Donington 78 F5
Donington on Bain 91 F6
Donington South Ing 78 F5
Donisthorpe 63 C7
Donkey Town 27 C7
Donnington
Glos 38 B1
Hereford 50 F2
Shrops 61 D5
Telford 61 C7
W Berks 26 C2
W Sus 16 D2
Donnington Wood 61 C7
Donyatt 11 C8
Doonfoot 112 C3
Dorback Lodge 139 C6
Dorchester
Dorset 12 E4
Oxon 39 E5
Dordon 63 D6
Dore 88 F4
Dores 151 H8
Dorking 28 E2
Dormansland 28 E5
Dormanstown 102 B3
Dormington 49 E7
Dormston 50 D4
Dornal 105 B6
Dorney 27 B7
Dornie 149 F13
Dornoch 151 C10
Dornock 108 C2
Dorrery 158 E2
Dorridge 51 B6
Dorrington
Lincs 78 D3
Shrops 60 D4
Dorsington 51 E6
Dorstone 48 E5
Dorton 39 C6
Dorusduain 136 B2
Dosthill 63 E6
Dottery 12 E2
Doublebois 5 C6
Dougarie 143 E9
Doughton 37 E5
Douglas
IoM 84 E3
S Lanark 119 F8
Douglas & Angus 134 F4
Douglastown 134 E4
Douglas Water 119 F8
Douglas West 119 F8
Doulting 23 E8
Dounby 159 F3
Doune
Highld 156 J7
Stirling 127 D6
Doune Park 153 B7
Douneside 140 D3
Dounie 151 B8
Dounreay 157 C12
Dousland 6 C3
Dovaston 60 B3
Dove Holes 75 B7
Dovenby 107 F7
Dover 31 E7
Dovercourt 57 F6
Doverdale 50 C3
Doveridge 75 F8
Doversgreen 28 E3
Dowally 133 E7
Dowbridge 92 F4
Dowdeswell 37 C6
Dowlais 34 D4
Dowland 9 C7
Dowlish Wake 11 C8
Down Ampney 37 E8
Downcraig Ferry 145 H10
Downderry 5 D8
Downe 28 C5
Downend
IoW 15 F6
S Glos 23 B8
W Berks 26 B2
Downfield 134 F3
Downgate 5 B8
Downham
Essex 42 E3
Lancs 93 E7
Northumb 122 F4
Downham Market 67 D6
Down Hatherley 37 B5
Downhead 23 E8
Downhill
Perth 133 F7
T&W 111 D6
Downholland Cross 85 D4
Downholme 101 E6
Downies 141 E8
Downley 39 E8
Down St Mary 10 D2
Downside
Som 23 E8
Sur 28 D2
Down Thomas 6 D3
Downton
Hants 14 E3
Wilts 14 B2
Downton on the Rock 49 B6
Dowsby 65 B8
Dowsdale 66 C2
Dowthwaitehead 99 B5
Doxey 62 B3
Doxford 117 B7
Doxford Park 111 D6
Doynton 24 B2
Draffan 119 E7
Dragonby 90 C3
Drakeland Corner 6 D3
Drakemyre 118 D2
Drake's Broughton 50 E4
Drakes Cross 51 B5
Drakewalls 6 B2
Draughton
N Yorks 94 D3
W Nhants 53 B5
Drax 89 B7
Draycote 52 B2
Draycott
Derbys 76 F4
Glos 51 F6
Som 23 D6
Draycott in the Clay 63 B5
Draycott in the Moors 75 E6
Drayford 10 C2
Drayton
Leics 64 E5
Lincs 78 F5
Norf 68 C4
Oxon 38 E4
Oxon 52 E2
Ptsmth 15 D7
Som 12 B2
Worcs 50 B4
Drayton Bassett 63 D5
Drayton Beauchamp 40 C2
Drayton Parslow 39 B8
Drayton St Leonard 39 E5
Drebley 94 D3
Dreemskerry 84 C4
Dreenhill 44 D4
Drefach
Carms 33 C6
Carms 46 F2
Dre-fach
Carms 33 C7
Ceredig 46 E4
Drefelin 46 F2
Dreghorn 118 F3
Drellingore 31 E6
Drem 121 B8
Dresden 75 E6
Dreumasdal 148 E2
Drewsteignton 10 E2
Driby 79 B6
Driffield
E Yorks 97 D6
Glos 37 E7
Drigg 98 E2
Drighlington 88 B3
Drimnin 147 F8
Drimpton 12 D2
Drimsynie 125 E7
Drinisiadar 154 H6
Drinkstone 56 C3
Drinkstone Green 56 C3
Drishaig 125 D7
Drissaig 124 D5
Drochil 120 E4
Drointon 62 B4
Droitwich Spa 50 C3
Droman 156 D4
Dron 128 C3
Dronfield 76 B3
Dronfield Woodhouse 76 B3
Drongan 112 C4
Dronley 134 F3
Droxford 15 C7
Droylsden 87 E7
Druid 72 E4
Druidston 44 D3
Druimarbin 130 B4
Druimavuic 130 E4
Druimdrishaig 144 F6
Druimindarroch 147 C9
Druimyeon More 143 C7
Drum
Argyll 145 F8
Perth 128 D2
Drumbeg 156 F4
Drumblade 152 D5
Drumblair 153 D6
Drumbuie
Dumfries 113 F5
Highld 149 E12
Drumburgh 108 D2
Drumburn 107 C6
Drumchapel 118 B5
Drumchardine 151 G8
Drumchork 155 J13
Drumclog 119 F6
Drumderfit 151 F9
Drumeldrie 129 D6
Drumelzier 120 F4
Drumfearn 149 G11
Drumgask 138 E2
Drumgley 134 D4
Drumguish 138 E3
Drumin 152 E1
Drumlasie 140 D5
Drumlemble 143 G7
Drumligair 141 C8
Drumlithie 141 F6
Drummoddie 105 E7
Drummond 151 E9
Drummore 104 F5
Drummuir 152 D3
Drummuir Castle 152 D3
Drumnadrochit 137 B8
Drumnagorrach 152 C5
Drumoak 141 E6
Drumpark 107 A5
Drumphail 105 C6
Drumrash 106 B3
Drumrunie 156 J4
Drums 141 B8
Drumsallie 130 B3
Drumstinchall 107 D5
Drumsturdy 134 F4
Drumtochty Castle 135 B6
Drumtroddan 105 E7
Drumuie 149 D9
Drumuillie 138 B5
Drumvaich 127 D5
Drumwhindle 153 E9
Drunkendub 135 E6
Drury 73 C6
Drury Square 68 C2
Drybeck 100 C1
Drybridge
Moray 152 B4
N Ayrs 118 F3
Drybrook 36 C3
Dryburgh 121 F8
Dry Doddington 77 E8
Dry Drayton 54 C4
Dryhope 115 B5
Drylaw 120 B5
Drym 2 C5
Drymen 126 F3
Drymuir 153 D9
Drynoch 149 E9
Dryslwyn 33 B6
Dryton 61 D5
Dubford 153 B8
Dubton 135 D5
Duchally 156 H6
Duchlage 126 F2
Duck Corner 57 E7
Duckington 73 D8
Ducklington 38 D3
Duckmanton 76 B4
Duck's Cross 54 D2
Duddenhoe End 55 F5
Duddingston 121 B5
Duddington 65 D6
Duddleswell 17 B8
Duddo 122 E5
Duddon 74 C2
Duddon Bridge 98 F4
Dudleston 73 F7
Dudleston Heath 73 F7
Dudley
T&W 111 B5
W Mid 62 E3
Dudley Port 62 E3
Duffield 76 E3
Duffryn
Neath 34 E2
Newport 35 F6
Dufftown 152 E3
Duffus 152 B1
Dufton 100 B1
Duggleby 96 C4
Duirinish 149 E12
Duisdalemore 149 G12
Duisky 130 B4
Dukestown 35 C5
Dukinfield 87 E7
Dulas 82 C4
Dulcote 23 E7
Dulford 11 D5
Dull 133 E5
Dullatur 119 B7
Dullingham 55 D7
Dulnain Bridge 139 B5
Duloe
Bedford 54 C2
Corn 5 D7
Dulsie 151 G12
Dulverton 10 B4
Dulwich 28 B4
Dumbarton 118 B3
Dumbleton 50 F5
Dumcrieff 114 D4
Dumfries 107 B6
Dumgoyne 126 F4
Dummer 26 E3
Dumpford 16 B2
Dumpton 31 C7
Dun 135 D6
Dunain House 151 G9
Dunalastair 132 D4
Dunan 149 F10
Dunans 145 D9
Dunball 22 E5
Dunbar 122 B2
Dunbeath 158 H3
Dunbeg 124 B4
Dunblane 127 D6
Dunbog 128 C4
Duncanston 151 F8
Duncanstone 140 B4
Dun Charlabhaigh 154 C6
Dunchurch 52 B2
Duncote 52 D4
Duncow 114 F2
Duncraggan 126 D4
Duncrievie 128 D3
Duncton 16 C3
Dundas House 159 K5
Dundee 134 F4
Dundeugh 113 F5
Dundon 23 F6
Dundonald 118 F3
Dundonnell 150 C3
Dundonnell Hotel 150 C3
Dundonnell House 150 C4
Dundraw 108 E2
Dundreggan 137 C6
Dundreggan Lodge 137 C6
Dundrennan 106 E4
Dundry 23 C7
Dunecht 141 D6
Dunfermline 128 F2
Dunfield 37 E8
Dunford Bridge 88 D2
Dungworth 88 F3
Dunham 77 B8
Dunham-on-the-Hill 73 B8
Dunhampton 50 C3
Dunham Town 86 F5
Dunholme 78 B3
Dunino 129 C7
Dunipace 127 F7
Dunira 127 B6
Dunkeld 133 E7
Dunkerton 24 D2
Dunkeswell 11 D6
Dunkeswick 95 E6
Dunkirk
Kent 30 D4
Norf 81 E8
Dunk's Green 29 D7
Dunlappie 135 C5
Dunley
Hants 26 D2
Worcs 50 C2
Dunlichity Lodge 151 H9
Dunlop 118 E4
Dunmaglass Lodge 137 B8
Dunmore
Argyll 144 G6
Falk 127 F7
Dunnet 158 C4
Dunnichen 135 E5
Dunninald 135 D7
Dunning 128 C2
Dunnington
E Yorks 97 D7
Warks 51 D5
York 96 D2
Dunnockshaw 87 B6
Dunollie 124 B4
Dunoon 145 F10
Dunragit 105 D5
Dunrostan 144 E6
Duns 122 D3
Dunsby 65 B8
Dunscore 113 F8
Dunscroft 89 D7
Dunsdale 102 C4
Dunsden Green 26 B5
Dunsfold 27 F8
Dunsford 10 F3
Dunshalt 128 C4
Dunshillock 153 D9
Dunskey House 104 D4
Dunsley 103 C6
Dunsmore 40 D1
Dunsop Bridge 93 D6
Dunstable 40 B3
Dunstall 63 B5
Dunstall Common 50 E3
Dunstall Green 55 C8
Dunstan 117 C8
Dunstan Steads 117 B8
Dunster 21 E8
Duns Tew 38 B4
Dunston
Lincs 78 C3
Norf 68 D5
Staffs 62 C3
T&W 110 C5
Dunsville 89 D7
Dunswell 97 F6
Dunsyre 120 E3
Dunterton 5 B8
Duntisbourne Abbots 37 D6
Duntisbourne Leer 37 D6
Duntisbourne Rouse 37 D6
Duntish 12 D4
Duntocher 118 B4
Dunton
Bucks 39 B8
C Beds 54 E3
Norf 80 D4
Dunton Bassett 64 E2
Dunton Green 29 D6
Dunton Wayletts 42 E2
Duntulm 149 A9
Dunure 112 C2
Dunvant 33 E6
Dunvegan 148 D7
Dunwich 57 B8
Dunwood 75 D6
Dupplin Castle 128 C2
Durdar 108 D4
Durgates 18 B3
Durham 111 E5
Durisdeer 113 D8
Durisdeermill 113 D8
Durkar 88 C4
Durleigh 22 F4
Durley
Hants 15 C6
Wilts 25 C7
Durnamuck 150 B3
Durness 156 C7
Durno 141 B6
Duror 130 D3
Durran
Argyll 125 E5
Highld 158 D3
Durrington
Wilts 25 E6
W Sus 16 D5
Dursley 36 E4
Durston 11 B7
Durweston 13 D6
Dury 160 G6
Duston 52 C5
Duthil 138 B5
Dutlas 48 B4
Duton Hill 42 B2
Dutson 8 F5
Dutton 74 B2
Duxford
Cambs 55 E5
Oxon 38 E3
Dwygyfylchi 83 D7
Dwyran 82 E4
Dyce 141 C7
Dye House 110 D2
Dyffryn
Bridgend 34 E2
Carms 32 B4
Pembs 44 B4
Dyffryn Ardudwy 71 E6
Dyffryn Castell 58 F4
Dyffryn Ceidrych 33 B8
Dyffryn Cellwen 34 D2
Dyke
Lincs 65 B8
Moray 151 F12
Dykehead
Angus 134 C3
N Lanark 119 D8
Stirling 126 E4
Dykelands 135 C7
Dykends 134 D2
Dykeside 153 D7
Dykesmains 118 E2
Dylife 59 E5
Dymchurch 19 C7
Dymock 50 F2
Dyrham 24 B2
Dysart 128 E5
Dyserth 72 B4

E

Eadar Dha Fhadhail 154 D5
Eagland Hill 92 E4
Eagle 77 C8
Eagle Barnsdale 77 C8
Eagle Moor 77 C8
Eaglescliffe 102 C2
Eaglesfield
Cumb 98 B2
Dumfries 108 B2
Eaglesham 119 D5
Eaglethorpe 65 E7
Eairy 84 E2
Eakley Lanes 53 D6
Eakring 77 C6
Ealand 89 C8
Ealing 40 F4
Eals 109 D6
Eamont Bridge 99 B7
Earby 94 E2
Earcroft 86 B4
Eardington 61 E7
Eardisland 49 D6
Eardisley 48 E5
Eardiston
Shrops 60 B3
Worcs 49 C8
Earith 54 B4
Earle 117 B5
Earley 27 B5
Earlham 68 D5
Earlish 149 B8
Earls Barton 53 C6
Earls Colne 42 B4
Earl's Croome 50 E3
Earlsdon 51 B8
Earlsferry 129 E6
Earlsfield 78 F2
Earlsford 153 E8
Earl's Green 56 C4
Earlsheaton 88 B3
Earl Shilton 63 E8
Earlsmill 151 F12
Earl Soham 57 C6
Earl Sterndale 75 C7
Earlston
Borders 121 F8
E Ayrs 118 F4
Earl Stonham 56 D5
Earlswood
Mon 36 E1
Sur 28 E3
Warks 51 B6
Earnley 16 E2
Earsairidh 148 J2
Earsdon 111 B6
Earsham 69 F6
Earswick 96 D2
Eartham 16 D3
Easby
N Yorks 101 D6
N Yorks 102 D3
Easdale 124 D3
Easebourne 16 B2
Easenhall 52 B2
Eashing 27 E7
Easington
Bucks 39 C6
Durham 111 E7
E Yorks 91 C7
Northumb 123 F7
Oxon 39 E6
Oxon 52 F2
Redcar 103 C5
Easington Colliery 111 E7
Easington Lane 111 E6
Easingwold 95 C8
Easole Street 31 D6
Eassie 134 E3
East Aberthaw 22 C2
East Adderbury 52 F2
East Allington 7 E5
East Anstey 10 B3
East Appleton 101 E7
East Ardsley 88 B4
East Ashling 16 D2
East Auchronie 141 D7
East Ayton 103 F7
East Bank 35 D6
East Barkwith 91 F5
East Barming 29 D8
East Barnby 103 C6
East Barnet 41 E5
East Barns 122 B3
East Barsham 80 D5
East Beckham 81 D7
East Bedfont 27 B8
East Bergholt 56 F4
East Bilney 68 C2
East Blatchington 17 D8
East Boldre 14 D4
Eastbourne 18 F3
East Brent 22 D5
Eastbridge 57 C8
East Bridgford 77 E6
East Buckland 21 F5
East Budleigh 11 F5
Eastburn 94 E3
East Burrafirth 160 H5
East Burton 13 F6
Eastbury
London 40 E3
W Berks 25 B8
East Butsfield 110 E4
East Butterwick 90 D2
Eastby 94 D3
East Cairnbeg 135 B7
East Calder 120 C3
East Carleton 68 D4
East Carlton
N Nhants 64 F5
W Yorks 94 E5
East Chaldon 13 F5
East Challow 38 F3
East Chiltington 17 C7
East Chinnock 12 C2
East Chisenbury 25 D6
Eastchurch 30 B3
East Clandon 27 D8
East Claydon 39 B7
East Clyne 157 J12
East Coker 12 C3
Eastcombe 37 D5
East Combe 22 F3
East Common 96 F2
East Compton 23 E8
Eastcote
London 40 F4
W Mid 51 B6
W Nhants 52 D4
Eastcott
Corn 8 C4
Wilts 24 D5
East Cottingwith 96 E3
Eastcourt
Wilts 25 C7
Wilts 37 E6
East Cowes 15 E6
East Cowick 89 B7
East Cowton 101 D8
East Cramlington 111 B5
East Cranmore 23 E8
East Creech 13 F7
East Croachy 138 B2
East Croftmore 139 C5
East Curthwaite 108 E3
East Dean
E Sus 18 F2
Hants 14 B3
W Sus 16 C3
East Down 20 E5
East Drayton 77 B7
East Ella 90 B4
East End
Dorset 13 E7
E Yorks 91 B6
Hants 14 E4
Hants 15 B7
Hants 26 C2
Herts 41 B7
Kent 18 B5
N Som 23 B6
Oxon 38 C3
Easter Ardross 151 D9
Easter Balmoral 139 E8
Easter Boleskine 137 B8
Easter Compton 36 F2
Easter Cringate 127 F6
Easter Davoch 140 D3
Easter Earshaig 114 D3
Easter Fearn 151 C9
Easter Galcantray 151 G11
Eastergate 16 D3
Easterhouse 119 C6
Easter Howgate 120 C5
Easter Howlaws 122 E3
Easter Kinkell 151 F8
Easter Lednathie 134 C3
Easter Milton 151 F12
Easter Moniack 151 G8
Eastern Green 63 F6
Easter Ord 141 D7
Easter Quarff 160 K6
Easter Rhynd 128 C3
Easter Row 127 E6
Easter Silverford 153 B7
Easter Skeld 160 J5
Easterton 24 D5
Eastertown 22 D5
Eastertown of Auchleuchries 153 E10
Easter Whyntie 152 B6
East Farleigh 29 D8
East Farndon 64 F4
East Ferry 90 E2
Eastfield
N Lanark 119 C8
N Yorks 103 F8
Eastfield Hall 117 D8
East Fortune 121 B8
East Garston 25 B8
Eastgate
Durham 110 F2

Eastgate *continued*
Norf 81 E7
East Ginge 38 F4
East Goscote 64 C3
East Grafton 25 C7
East Grimstead 14 B3
East Grinstead 28 F4
East Guldeford 19 C6
East Haddon 52 C4
East Hagbourne 39 F5
East Halton 90 C5
Eastham 85 F4
East Ham 41 F7
Eastham Ferry 85 F4
Easthampstead 27 C6
East Hanney 38 E4
East Hanningfield 42 D3
East Hardwick 89 C5
East Harling 68 F2
East Harlsey 102 E2
East Harnham 14 B2
East Harptree 23 D7
East Hartford 111 B5
East Harting 15 C8
East Hatley 54 D3
East Hauxwell 101 E6
East Haven 135 F5
Eastheath 27 C6
East Heckington 78 E4
East Hedleyhope 110 E4
East Hendred 38 F4
East Herrington 111 D6
East Heslerton 96 B5
East Hoathly 18 D2
Easthope 61 E5
Easthorpe
Essex 43 B5
Leics 77 F8
Notts 77 D7
East Horrington 23 E7
East Horsley 27 D8
East Horton 123 F6
Easthouses 121 C6
East Huntspill 22 E5
East Hyde 40 C4
East Ilkerton 21 E6
East Ilsley 38 F4
Eastington
Devon 10 D2
Glos 36 D4
Glos 37 C8
East Keal 79 C6
East Kennett 25 C6
East Keswick 95 E6
East Kilbride 119 D6
East Kirkby 79 C6
East Knapton 96 B4
East Knighton 13 F6
East Knoyle 24 F3
East Kyloe 123 F6
East Lambrook 12 C2
East Lamington 151 D10
East Langdon 31 E7
East Langton 64 E4
East Langwell 157 J10
East Lavant 16 D2
East Lavington 16 C3
East Layton 101 D6
Eastleach Martin 38 D2
Eastleach Turville 38 D1
East Leake 64 B2
East Learmouth 122 F4
Eastleigh
Devon 9 B6
Hants 14 C5
East Leigh 9 D8
East Lexham 67 C8
East Lilburn 117 B6
Eastling 30 D3
East Linton 121 B8
East Liss 15 B8
East Looe 5 D7
East Lound 89 E8
East Lulworth 13 F6
East Lutton 96 C5
East Lydford 23 F7
East Mains 141 E5
East Malling 29 D8
East March 134 F4
East Marden 16 C2
East Markham 77 B7
East Marton 94 D2
East Meon 15 B7
East Mere 10 C4
East Mersea 43 C6
East Mey 158 C5
East Molesey 28 C2
Eastmoor
Derbys 76 B3
Norf 67 D7
East Morden 13 E7
East Morton 94 E3
East Ness 96 B2
East Newton 97 F8
Eastney 15 E7
Eastnor 50 F2
East Norton 64 D4
East Nynehead 11 B6
East Oakley 26 D3
Eastoft 90 C2
East Ogwell 7 B6
Eastoke 15 E8
Easton
Cambs 54 B2
Cumb 108 B4
Cumb 108 D2
Devon 10 F2
Dorset 12 G4
Hants 26 F3
Lincs 65 B6
Norf 68 C4
Som 23 E7
Suff 57 D6
Wilts 24 B3
Easton Grey 37 F5
Easton-in-Gordano 23 B7
Easton Maudit 53 D6
Easton on the Hill 65 D7
Easton Royal 25 C7
East Orchard 13 C6
East Ord 123 D5
East Panson 9 E5
Eastpark 107 C7
East Peckham 29 E7
East Pennard 23 F7
East Perry 54 C2
East Portlemouth 6 F5
East Prawle 7 F5
East Preston 16 D4
East Putford 9 C5
East Quantoxhead 22 E3
East Rainton 111 E6
East Ravendale 91 E6
East Raynham 80 E4
Eastrea 66 E2
East Rhidorroch Lodge 150 B5
Eastriggs 108 C2
East Rigton 95 E6
Eastrington 89 B8
East Rounton 102 D2
East Row 103 C6
East Rudham 80 E4
East Runton 81 C7
East Ruston 69 B6
Eastry 31 D7
East Saltoun 121 C7
East Sleekburn 117 F8
East Somerton 69 C7
East Stockwith 89 E8
East Stoke
Dorset 13 F6
Notts 77 E7
East Stour 13 B6
East Stourmouth 31 C6
East Stowford 9 B8
East Stratton 26 F3
East Studdal 31 E7
East Suisnish 149 E10
East Taphouse 5 C6
East-the-Water 9 B6
East Thirston 117 E7
East Tilbury 29 B7
East Tisted 26 F5
East Torrington 90 F5
East Tuddenham 68 C3
East Tytherley 14 B3
East Tytherton 24 B4
East Village 10 D3
Eastville
Bristol 23 B8
Lincs 79 D7
East Wall 60 E5
East Walton 67 C7
Eastwell 64 B4
East Wellow 14 B4
East Wemyss 128 E5
East Whitburn 120 C2
Eastwick
Herts 41 C7
Shetland 160 F5
East Williamston 32 D1
East Winch 67 C6
East Winterslow 25 F7
East Wittering 15 E8
East Witton 101 F6
Eastwood
Notts 76 E4
Southend 42 F4
W Yorks 87 B7
East Woodburn 116 F5
East Woodhay 26 C2
East Worldham 26 F5
East Worlington 10 C2
East Worthing 17 D5
Eathorpe 51 C8
Eaton
Ches E 75 C5
Ches W 74 C2
Leics 64 B4
Norf 68 D5
Notts 77 B7
Oxon 38 D4
Shrops 60 F3
Shrops 60 F5
Eaton Bishop 49 F6
Eaton Bray 40 B2
Eaton Constantine 61 D5
Eaton Green 40 B2
Eaton Hastings 38 E2
Eaton on Tern 61 B6
Eaton Socon 54 D2
Eavestone 94 C5
Ebberston 103 F6
Ebbesbourne Wake 13 B7
Ebbw Vale
= *Glyn Ebwy* 35 D5
Ebchester 110 D4
Ebford 10 F4
Ebley 37 D5
Ebnal 73 E8
Ebrington 51 E6
Ecchinswell 26 D2
Ecclaw 122 C3
Ecclefechan 107 B8
Eccles
Borders 122 E3
Gtr Man 87 E5
Kent 29 C8
Ecclesall 88 F4
Ecclesfield 88 E4
Ecclesgreig 135 C7
Eccleshall 62 B2
Eccleshill 94 F4
Ecclesmachan 120 B3
Eccles on Sea 69 B7
Eccles Road 68 E3
Eccleston
Ches W 73 C8
Lancs 86 C3
Mers 86 E2
Eccleston Park 86 E2
Eccup 95 E5
Echt 141 D6
Eckford 116 B3
Eckington
Derbys 76 B4
Worcs 50 E4
Ecton 53 C6
Edale 88 F2
Edburton 17 C6
Edderside 107 E7
Edderton 151 C10
Eddistone 8 B4
Eddleston 120 E5
Edenbridge 28 E5
Edenfield 87 C5
Edenhall 109 F5
Edenham 65 B7
Eden Park 28 C4
Edensor 76 C2
Edentaggart 126 E2
Edenthorpe 89 D7
Edentown 108 D3
Ederline 124 E4
Edern 70 D3
Edgarley 23 F7
Edgbaston 62 F4
Edgcott
Bucks 39 B6
Som 21 F7
Edge 60 D3
Edgebolton 61 B5
Edge End 36 C2
Edgefield 81 D6
Edgefield Street 81 D6
Edge Green 73 D8
Edge Hill 85 F4
Edgeside 87 B6
Edgeworth 37 D6
Edgmond 61 C7
Edgmond Marsh 61 B7
Edgton 60 F3
Edgware 40 E4
Edgworth 86 C5
Edinample 126 B4
Edinbane 149 C8
Edinburgh 121 B5
Edingale 63 C6
Edingight House 152 C5
Edingley 77 D6
Edingthorpe 69 A6
Edingthorpe Green 69 A6
Edington
Som 23 F5
Wilts 24 D4
Edintore 152 D4
Edithmead 22 E5
Edith Weston 65 D6
Edlesborough 40 C2
Edlingham 117 D7
Edlington 78 B5
Edmondsham 13 C8
Edmondsley 110 E5
Edmondthorpe 65 C5
Edmonstone 159 F6
Edmonton 41 E6
Edmundbyers 110 D3
Ednam 122 F3
Ednaston 76 E2
Edradynate 133 D5
Edrom 122 D4
Edstaston 74 F2
Edstone 51 C6
Edvin Loach 49 D8
Edwalton 77 F5
Edwardstone 56 E3
Edwinsford 46 F5
Edwinstowe 77 C6
Edworth 54 E3
Edwyn Ralph 49 D8
Edzell 135 C5
E Eachwick 110 B4
Efail Isaf 34 F4
Efailnewydd 70 D4
Efailwen 32 B2
Efenechtyd 72 D5
Effingham 28 D2
Effirth 160 H5
Efford 10 D3
Egdon 50 D4
Egerton
Gtr Man 86 C5
Kent 30 E3
Egerton Forstal 30 E2
Eggborough 89 B6
Eggbuckland 6 D3
Eggington 40 B2
Egginton 63 B6
Egglescliffe 102 C2
Eggleston 100 B4
Egham 27 B8
Egleton 65 D5
Eglingham 117 C7
Egloshayle 4 B5
Egloskerry 8 F4
Eglwysbach 83 D8
Eglwys-Brewis 22 C2
Eglwys Cross 73 E8
Eglwys Fach 58 E3
Eglwyswen 45 F3
Eglwyswrw 45 F3
Egmanton 77 C7
Egremont
Cumb 98 C2
Mers 85 E4
Egton 103 D6
Egton Bridge 103 D6
Eight Ash Green 43 B5
Eignaig 130 E1
Eil 138 C4
Eilanreach 149 G13
Eileanach Lodge 151 E8
Eilean Darach 150 C4
Einacleite 154 E6
Eisgean 155 F8
Eisingrug 71 D7
Elan Village 47 C8
Elberton 36 F3
Elburton 6 D3
Elcho 128 B3
Elcombe 37 F8
Eldernell 66 E3
Eldersfield 50 F3
Elderslie 118 C4
Eldon 101 B7
Eldrick 112 F2
Eldroth 93 C7
Eldwick 94 E4
Elfhowe 99 E6
Elford
Northumb 123 F7
Staffs 63 C5
Elgin 152 B2
Elgol 149 G10
Elham 31 E5
Elie 129 D6
Elim 82 C3
Eling 14 C4
Elishader 149 B10
Elishaw 116 E4
Elkesley 77 B6
Elkstone 37 C6
Ellan 138 B4
Elland 88 B2
Ellary 144 F6
Ellastone 75 E8
Ellemford 122 C3
Ellenbrook 84 E3
Ellenhall 62 B2
Ellen's Green 27 F8
Ellerbeck 102 E2
Ellerburn 103 F6
Ellerby 103 C5
Ellerdine Heath 61 B6
Ellerhayes 10 D4
Elleric 130 E4
Ellerker 90 B3
Ellerton
E Yorks 96 F3
Shrops 61 B7
Ellesborough 39 D8
Ellesmere 73 F8
Ellesmere Port 73 B8
Ellingham
Norf 69 E6
Northumb 117 B7
Ellingstring 101 F6
Ellington
Cambs 54 B2
Northumb 117 E8
Elliot 135 F6
Ellisfield 26 E4
Ellistown 63 C8
Ellon 153 E9
Ellonby 108 F4
Ellough 69 F7
Elloughton 90 B3
Ellwood 36 D2
Elm 66 D4
Elmbridge 50 C4
Elmdon
Essex 55 F5
W Mid 63 F5
Elmdon Heath 63 F5
Elmers End 28 C4
Elmesthorpe 63 E8
Elmfield 15 E7
Elm Hill 13 B6
Elmhurst 62 C5
Elmley Castle 50 E4
Elmley Lovett 50 C3
Elmore 36 C4
Elmore Back 36 C4
Elm Park 41 F8
Elmscott 8 B4
Elmsett 56 E4
Elmstead Market 43 B6
Elmsted 30 E5
Elmstone 31 C6
Elmstone Hardwicke 37 B6
Elmswell
E Yorks 97 D5
Suff 56 C3
Elmton 76 B5
Elphin 156 H5
Elphinstone 121 B6
Elrick 141 D7
Elrig 105 E7
Elsdon 117 E5
Elsecar 88 E4
Elsenham 41 B8
Elsfield 39 C5
Elsham 90 C4
Elsing 68 C3
Elslack 94 E2
Elson 73 F7
Elsrickle 120 E3
Elstead 27 E7
Elsted 16 C2
Elsthorpe 65 B7
Elstob 101 B8
Elston
Notts 77 E7
Wilts 25 E5
Elstone 9 C8
Elstow 53 E8
Elstree 40 E4
Elstronwick 97 F8
Elswick 92 F4
Elsworth 54 C4
Elterwater 99 D5
Eltham 28 B5
Eltisley 54 D3
Elton
Cambs 65 E7
Ches W 73 B8
Derbys 76 C2
Glos 36 C4
Hereford 49 B6
Notts 77 F7
Stockton 102 C2
Elton Green 73 B8
Elvanfoot 114 C2
Elvaston 76 F4
Elveden 56 B2
Elvingston 121 B7
Elvington
Kent 31 D6
York 96 E2
Elwick
Hrtlpl 111 F7
Northumb 123 F7
Elworth 74 C4
Elworthy 22 F2
Ely
Cambs 66 F5
Cardiff 22 B3
Emberton 53 E6
Embleton
Cumb 107 F8
Northumb 117 B8
Embo 151 B11
Emborough 23 D8
Embo Street 151 B11
Embsay 94 D3
Emersons Green 23 B8
Emery Down 14 D3
Emley 88 C3
Emmbrook 27 C5
Emmer Green 26 B5
Emmington 39 D7
Emneth 66 D4
Emneth Hungate 66 D5
Empingham 65 D6
Empshott 27 F5
Emstrey 60 C5
Emsworth 15 D8
Enborne 26 C2
Enchmarsh 60 E5
Enderby 64 E2
Endmoor 99 F7
Endon 75 D6
Endon Bank 75 D6
Enfield 41 E6
Enfield Wash 41 E6
Enford 25 D6
Engamoor 160 H4
Engine Common 36 F3
Englefield 26 B4
Englefield Green 27 B7
Englesea-brook 74 D4
English Bicknor 36 C2
Englishcombe 24 C2
English Frankton 60 B4
Enham Alamein 25 E8
Enmore 22 F4
Ennerdale Bridge 98 C2
Enoch 113 D8
Enochdhu 133 C7
Ensay 146 G6
Ensbury 13 E8
Ensdon 60 C4
Ensis 9 B7
Enstone 38 B3
Enterkinfoot 113 D8
Enterpen 102 D2
Enville 62 F2
Eolaigearraidh 148 H2
Eorabus 146 J6
Eòropaidh 155 A10
Epperstone 77 E6
Epping 41 D7
Epping Green
Essex 41 D7
Herts 41 D5
Epping Upland 41 D7
Eppleby 101 C6
Eppleworth 97 F6
Epsom 28 C3
Epwell 51 E8
Epworth 89 D8
Epworth Turbary 89 D8
Erbistock 73 E7
Erbusaig 149 F12
Erchless Castle 150 G7
Erdington 62 E5
Eredine 125 E5
Eriboll 156 D7
Ericstane 114 C3
Eridge Green 18 B2
Erines 145 F7
Eriswell 55 B8
Erith 29 B6
Erlestoke 24 D4
Ermine 78 B2
Ermington 6 D4
Erpingham 81 D7
Errogie 137 B8
Errol 128 B4
Erskine 118 B4
Erskine Bridge 118 B4
Ervie 104 C4
Erwarton 57 F6
Erwood 48 E2
Eryholme 101 D8
Eryrys 73 D6
Escomb 101 B6
Escrick 96 E2
Esgairdawe 46 E5
Esgairgeiliog 58 D4
Esh 110 E4
Esher 28 C2
Esholt 94 E4
Eshott 117 E8
Eshton 94 D2
Esh Winning 110 E4
Eskadale 150 H7
Eskbank 121 C6
Eskdale Green 98 D3
Eskdalemuir 115 E5
Eske 97 E6
Eskham 91 E7
Esk Valley 103 D6
Esprick 92 F4
Essendine 65 C7
Essendon 41 D5
Essich 151 H9
Essington 62 D3
Esslemont 141 B8
Eston 102 C3
Eswick 160 H6
Etal 122 F5
Etchilhampton 24 C5
Etchingham 18 C4
Etchinghill
Kent 19 B8
Staffs 62 C4
Ethie Castle 135 E6
Ethie Mains 135 E6
Etling Green 68 C3
Eton 27 B7
Eton Wick 27 B7
Etteridge 138 E2
Ettersgill 100 B3
Ettingshall 62 E3
Ettington 51 E7
Etton
E Yorks 97 E5
Pboro 65 D8
Ettrick 115 C5
Ettrickbridge 115 B6
Ettrickhill 115 C5
Etwall 76 F2
Euston 56 B2
Euximoor Drove 66 E4
Euxton 86 C3
Evanstown 34 F3
Evanton 151 E9
Evedon 78 E3
Evelix 151 B10
Evenjobb 48 C4
Evenley 52 F3
Evenlode 38 B2
Evenwood 101 B6
Evenwood Gate 101 B6
Everbay 159 F7
Evercreech 23 F8
Everdon 52 D3
Everingham 96 E4
Everleigh 25 D7
Everley 103 F7
Eversholt 53 F7
Evershot 12 D3
Eversley 27 C5
Eversley Cross 27 C5
Everthorpe 96 F5
Everton
C Beds 54 D3
Hants 14 E3
Mers 85 E4
Notts 89 E7
Evertown 108 B3
Evesbatch 49 E8
Evesham 50 E5
Evington 64 D3
Ewden Village 88 E3
Ewell 28 C3
Ewell Minnis 31 E6
Ewelme 39 E6
Ewen 37 E7
Ewenny 21 B8
Ewerby 78 E4
Ewerby Thorpe 78 E4
Ewes 115 E6
Ewesley 117 E6
Ewhurst 27 E8
Ewhurst Green
E Sus 18 C4
Sur 27 F8
Ewloe 73 C7
Ewloe Green 73 C6
Ewood 86 B4
Eworthy 9 E6
Ewshot 27 E6
Ewyas Harold 35 B7
Exbourne 9 D8
Exbury 14 E5
Exebridge 10 B4
Exelby 101 F7
Exeter 10 E4
Exford 21 F7
Exhall 51 D6
Exley Head 94 F3
Exminster 10 F4
Exmouth 10 F5
Exnaboe 160 M5
Exning 55 C7
Exton
Devon 10 F4
Hants 15 B7
Rutland 65 C6
Som 21 F8
Exwick 10 E4
Eyam 76 B2
Eydon 52 D3
Eye
Hereford 49 C6
Pboro 66 D2
Suff 56 B5
Eye Green 66 D2
Eyemouth 122 C5
Eyeworth 54 E3
Eyhorne Street 30 D2
Eyke 57 D7
Eynesbury 54 D2
Eynort 149 F8
Eynsford 29 C6
Eynsham 38 D4
Eype 12 E2
Eyre
Highld 149 C9
Highld 149 E10
Eythorne 31 E6
Eyton
Hereford 49 C6
Shrops 60 F3
Wrex 73 E7
Eyton upon the Weald Moors 61 C6

F

Faceby 102 D2
Facit 87 C6
Faddiley 74 D2
Fadmoor 102 F4
Faerdre 33 D7
Failand 23 B7
Failford 112 B4
Failsworth 87 D6
Fain 150 D4
Fairbourne 58 C3
Fairburn 89 B5
Fairfield
Derbys 75 B7
Stockton 102 C2
Worcs 50 B4
Worcs 50 E5
Fairford 38 D1
Fair Green 67 C6
Fairhaven 85 B4
Fair Hill 108 F5
Fairlie 118 D2
Fairlight 19 D5
Fairlight Cove 19 D5
Fairmile 11 E5
Fairmilehead 120 C5
Fairoak 74 F4
Fair Oak 15 C5
Fair Oak Green 26 C4
Fairseat 29 C7
Fairstead
Essex 42 C3
Norf 67 C6
Fairwarp 17 B8
Fairy Cottage 84 D4
Fairy Cross 9 B6
Fakenham 80 E5
Fakenham Magna 56 B3
Fala 121 C7
Fala Dam 121 C7
Falahill 121 D6
Falcon 49 F8
Faldingworth 90 F4
Falfield 36 E3
Falkenham 57 F6
Falkirk 119 B8
Falkland 128 D4
Falla 116 C3
Fallgate 76 C3
Fallin 127 E7
Fallowfield 87 E6
Fallsidehill 122 E2
Falmer 17 D7
Falmouth 3 C7
Falsgrave 103 F8
Falstone 116 F3
Fanagmore 156 E4
Fangdale Beck 102 E3
Fangfoss 96 D3
Fankerton 127 F6
Fanmore 146 G7
Fannich Lodge 150 E5
Fans 122 E2
Far Bank 89 C7
Far Bletchley 53 F6
Farcet 66 E2
Far Cotton 52 D5
Farden 49 B7
Fareham 15 D6
Farewell 62 C4
Far Forest 50 B2
Farforth 79 B6
Faringdon 38 E2
Farington 86 B3
Farlam 109 D5
Farlary 157 J10
Far Laund 76 E3
Farleigh
N Som 23 C6
Sur 28 C4
Farleigh Hungerford 24 D3
Farleigh Wallop 26 E4
Farlesthorpe 79 B7
Farleton
Lancs 93 C5
W&F 99 F7
Farley
Shrops 60 D3
Staffs 75 E7
Wilts 14 B3
Farley Green 27 E8
Farley Hill
Luton 40 B3
Wokingham 26 C5
Farleys End 36 C4
Farlington 96 C2
Farlow 61 F6
Farmborough 23 C8
Farmcote
Glos 37 B7
Shrops 61 E7
Farmington 37 C8
Farmoor 38 D4
Farmtown 152 C5
Farnborough
Hants 27 D6
London 28 C5
Warks 52 E2
W Berks 38 F4
Farnborough Green 27 D6
Farncombe 27 E7
Farndish 53 C7
Farndon
Ches W 73 D8
Notts 77 D7
Farnell 135 D6
Farnham
Dorset 13 C7
Essex 41 B7
N Yorks 95 C6
Suff 57 C7
Sur 27 E6
Farnham Common 40 F2
Farnham Green 41 B7
Farnham Royal 40 F2
Farnhill 94 E3
Farningham 29 C6
Farnley
N Yorks 94 E5
W Yorks 95 F5
Farnley Tyas 88 C2
Farnsfield 77 D6
Farnworth
Gtr Man 86 D5
Halton 86 F3
Farr
Highld 138 D4
Highld 151 H9
Highld 157 C10
Farr House 151 H9
Farringdon 10 E5
Farrington Gurney 23 D8
Far Sawrey 99 E5
Farsley 94 F5
Farthinghoe 52 F3
Farthingloe 31 E6
Farthingstone 52 D4
Fartown 88 C2
Farway 11 E6
Fasag 149 C13
Fascadale 147 D8
Faslane Port 145 E11
Fasnacloich 130 E4
Fasnakyle Ho 137 B6
Fassfern 130 B4
Fatfield 111 D6
Fattahead 153 C6
Faugh 108 D5
Fauldhouse 120 C2
Faulkbourne 42 C3
Faulkland 24 D2
Fauls 74 F2
Faversham 30 C4
Favillar 152 E2
Fawdington 95 B7
Fawfieldhead 75 C7
Fawkham Green 29 C6
Fawler 38 C3
Fawley
Bucks 39 F7
Hants 15 D5
W Berks 38 F3
Fawley Chapel 36 B2
Fawley Waterside 15 D5
Faxfleet 90 B2
Faygate 28 F3
Fazakerley 85 E4
Fazeley 63 D6
Fearby 101 F6
Fearn 151 D11
Fearnan 132 E4
Fearnbeg 149 C12
Fearnhead 86 E4
Fearn Lodge 151 C9
Fearnmore 149 B12
Fearn Station 151 D11
Featherstone
Staffs 62 D3
W Yorks 88 B5
Featherwood 116 D4
Feckenham 50 C5
Feering 42 B4
Feetham 100 E4
Feizor 93 C7
Felbridge 28 F4
Felbrigg 81 D8
Felcourt 28 E4
Felden 40 D3
Felin-Crai 34 B2
Felindre
Carms 33 B6
Carms 33 B8
Carms 46 F2
Carms 47 F5
Ceredig 46 D4
Powys 59 F8
Swansea 33 D7
Felindre Farchog 45 F3
Felinfach
Ceredig 46 D4
Powys 48 F2
Felinfoel 33 D6
Felingwmisaf 33 B6
Felingwmuchaf 33 B6
Felinwynt 45 D4
Felixkirk 102 F2
Felixstowe 57 F6
Felixstowe Ferry 57 F7
Felkington 122 E5
Felkirk 88 C4
Felling 111 C5
Fell Side 108 F3
Felmersham 53 D7
Felmingham 81 E8
Felpham 16 E3
Felsham 56 D3
Felsted 42 B2
Feltham 28 B2
Felthorpe 68 C4
Felton
Hereford 49 E7
Northumb 117 D7
N Som 23 C7
Felton Butler 60 C3
Feltwell 67 E7
Fenay Bridge 88 C2
Fence 93 F8
Fence Houses 111 D6
Fen Ditton 55 C5
Fen Drayton 54 C4
Fen End 51 B7
Fengate
Norf 81 E7
Pboro 66 E2
Fenham 123 E6
Fenhouses 79 E5
Feniscliffe 86 B4
Feniscowles 86 B4
Feniton 11 E6
Fenlake 53 E8
Fenny Bentley 75 D8
Fenny Bridges 11 E6
Fenny Compton 52 D2
Fenny Drayton 63 E7
Fenny Stratford 53 F6
Fenrother 117 E7
Fen Side 79 D6
Fenstanton 54 C4
Fenton
Cambs 54 B4
Lincs 77 B8
Lincs 77 D8
Stoke 75 E5
Fenton Barns 129 F7
Fenton Town 123 F5
Fenwick
E Ayrs 118 E4
Northumb 110 B3
Northumb 123 E6
S Yorks 89 C6
Feochaig 143 G8
Feock 3 C7
Feolin Ferry 144 G3
Ferindonald 149 H11
Ferinquarrie 148 C6
Ferlochan 130 E3
Fern 134 C4
Ferndale 34 E4
Ferndown 13 D8
Ferness 151 G12
Ferney Green 99 E6
Fernham 38 E2
Fernhill Heath 50 D3
Fernhurst 16 B2
Fernie 128 C5
Ferniegair 119 D7
Fernilea 149 E8
Fernilee 75 B7
Ferrensby 95 C6
Ferring 16 D4
Ferrybridge 89 B5
Ferryden 135 D7
Ferryhill
Aberdeen 141 D8
Durham 111 F5
Ferry Hill 66 F3
Ferryhill Station 111 F6
Ferry Point 151 C10
Ferryside 32 C4
Fersfield 68 F3
Fersit 131 B7
Ferwig 45 E3
Feshiebridge 138 D4
Fetcham 28 D2
Fetterangus 153 C9
Fettercairn 135 B6
Fettes 151 F8
Fewcott 39 B5
Fewston 94 D4
F Faccombe 25 D8
Ffairfach 33 B7
Ffair-Rhos 47 C6
Ffaldybrenin 46 E5
Ffarmers 47 E5
Ffawyddog 35 C6
Fforest 33 D6
Fforest-fâch 33 E7
Ffostrasol 46 E2
Ffos-y-ffi 46 C3
Ffridd-Uchaf 83 F5
Ffrith 73 D6
Ffrwd 82 F4
Ffynnon ddrain 33 B5
Ffynnongroyw 85 F2
Ffynnon-oer 46 D4
Fidden 146 J6
Fiddes 141 F7
Fiddington
Glos 50 F4
Som 22 E4
Fiddleford 13 C6
Fiddlers Hamlet 41 D7
Field 75 F7
Field Broughton 99 F5
Field Dalling 81 D6
Field Head 63 D8
Fifehead Magdalen 13 B5
Fifehead Neville 13 C5
Fifield
Oxon 38 C2
Wilts 25 D6
Windsor 27 B7
Fifield Bavant 13 B8
Figheldean 25 E6
Filands 37 F6
Filby 69 C7
Filey 97 A7
Filgrave 53 E6
Filkins 38 D2
Filleigh
Devon 9 B8
Devon 10 C2
Fillingham 90 F3
Fillongley 63 F6
Filton 23 B8
Fimber 96 C4
Finavon 134 D4
Finchairn 124 E5
Fincham 67 D6
Finchampstead 27 C5
Finchdean 15 C8
Finchingfield 55 F7
Finchley 41 E5
Findern 76 F3
Findhorn 151 E13
Findhorn Bridge 138 B4
Findochty 152 B4
Findo Gask 128 B2
Findon
Aberds 141 E8
W Sus 16 D5
Findon Mains 151 E9
Findrack House 140 D5
Finedon 53 B7
Fingal Street 57 C6
Fingask 141 B6
Fingerpost 50 B2
Fingest 39 E7
Finghall 101 F6
Fingland
Cumb 108 D2
Dumfries 113 C7
Finglesham 31 D7
Fingringhoe 43 B6
Finlarig 132 F2
Finmere 52 F4
Finnart 132 D2
Finningham 56 C4
Finningley 89 E7
Finnygaud 152 C5
Finsbury 41 F6
Finstall 50 C4
Finsthwaite 99 F5
Finstock 38 C3
Finstown 159 G4
Fintry
Aberds 153 C7
Dundee 134 F4
Stirling 126 F5
Finzean 140 E5
Fionnphort 146 J6
Fionnsbhagh 154 J5
Firbeck 89 F6
Firby
N Yorks 96 C3
N Yorks 101 F7
Firgrove 87 C7
Firsby 79 C7
Firsdown 25 F7
First Coast 150 B2
Fir Tree 110 F4
Fishbourne
IoW 15 E6
W Sus 16 D2
Fishburn 111 F6
Fishcross 127 E7
Fisherford 153 E6
Fisher Place 99 C5
Fisher's Pond 15 B5
Fisherstreet 27 F7
Fisherton
Highld 151 F10
S Ayrs 112 C2
Fishguard
= *Abergwaun* 44 B4
Fishlake 89 C7
Fishleigh Barton 9 B7
Fishponds 23 B8
Fishpool 36 B3
Fishtoft 79 E6
Fishtoft Drove 79 E6
Fishtown of Usan 135 D7
Fishwick 122 D5
Fiskavaig 149 E8
Fiskerton
Lincs 78 B3
Notts 77 D7
Fitling 97 F8
Fittleton 25 E6
Fittleworth 16 C4
Fitton End 66 C4
Fitz 60 C4
Fitzhead 11 B6
Fitzwilliam 88 C5
Fiunary 147 G9
Five Acres 36 C2
Five Ashes 18 C2
Fivecrosses 74 B2
Fivehead 11 B8
Five Oak Green 29 E7
Five Oaks
Jersey 17 I3
W Sus 16 B4
Five Roads 33 D5
Flack's Green 42 C3
Flackwell Heath 40 F1
Fladbury 50 E4
Fladdabister 160 K6
Flagg 75 C8
Flamborough 97 B8
Flamstead 40 C3
Flamstead End 41 D6
Flansham 16 D3
Flanshaw 88 B4
Flasby 94 D2
Flash 75 C7

Flashader....149 C8
Flask Inn....103 D7
Flaunden....40 D3
Flawborough....77 E7
Flawith....95 C7
Flax Bourton....23 C7
Flaxby....95 D6
Flaxholme....76 E3
Flaxley....36 C3
Flaxpool....22 F3
Flaxton....96 C2
Fleckney....64 E3
Flecknoe....52 C3
Fledborough....77 B8
Fleet
  Hants....15 D8
  Hants....27 D6
  Lincs....66 B3
Fleetham....117 B7
Fleet Hargate....66 B3
Fleetlands....15 D6
Fleetville....40 D4
Fleetwood....92 E3
Flemingston....22 B2
Flemington....119 D6
Flempton....56 C2
Fleoideabhagh....154 J5
Fletchertown....108 E2
Fletching....17 B8
Flexbury....8 D4
Flexford....27 E7
Flimby....107 F7
Flimwell....18 B4
Flint = Y Fflint....73 B6
Flintham....77 E7
Flint Mountain....73 B6
Flinton....97 F8
Flintsham....48 D5
Flitcham....80 E4
Flitton....53 F8
Flitwick....53 F8
Flixborough....90 C2
Flixborough
  Stather....90 C2
Flixton
  Gtr Man....86 E5
  N Yorks....97 B6
  Suff....69 F6
Flockton....88 C3
Flodaigh....148 C3
Flodden....122 F5
Flodigarry....149 A9
Flood's Ferry....66 E3
Flookburgh....92 B3
Florden....68 E4
Flore....52 C4
Flotterton....117 D5
Flowton....56 E4
Flush House....88 D2
Flushing
  Aberds....153 D10
  Corn....3 C7
Flyford Flavell....50 D4
Foals Green....57 B6
Fobbing....42 F3
Fochabers....152 C3
Fochriw....35 D5
Fockerby....90 C2
Fodderletter....139 B7
Fodderty....151 F8
Foel....59 C6
Foel-gastell....33 C6
Foffarty....134 E4
Foggathorpe....96 F3
Fogo....122 E3
Fogorig....122 E3
Foindle....156 E4
Folda....134 C1
Fole....75 F7
Foleshill....63 F7
Folke....12 C4
Folkestone....31 F6
Folkingham....78 F3
Folkington....18 E2
Folksworth....65 F8
Folkton....97 B6
Folla Rule....153 E7
Follifoot....95 D6
Folly Gate....9 E7
Fonthill Bishop....24 F4
Fonthill Gifford....24 F4
Fontmell Magna....13 C6
Fontwell....16 D3
Foolow....75 B8
Foots Cray....29 B5
Forbestown....140 C2
Force Mills....99 E5
Forcett....101 C6
Ford
  Argyll....124 E4
  Bucks....39 D7
  Devon....9 B6
  Glos....37 B7
  Northumb....122 F5
  Shrops....60 C4
  Staffs....75 D7
  Wilts....24 B3
  W Sus....16 D3
Fordcombe....29 E6
Fordell....128 F3
Forden....60 D2
Ford End....42 C2
Forder Green....7 C5
Fordham
  Cambs....55 B7
  Essex....43 B5
  Norf....67 E6
Fordhouses....62 D3
Fordingbridge....14 C2
Fordon....97 B6
Fordoun....135 B7
Ford's Green....56 C4
Fordstreet....43 B5
Ford Street....11 C6
Fordwells....38 C3
Fordwich....31 D5
Fordyce....152 B5
Forebridge....62 B3
Forest....109 F8
Forest Becks....93 D7
Forestburn Gate....117 E6
Foresterseat....152 C1
Forest Gate....41 F7
Forest Green....28 E2
Forest Hall....99 D7

Forest Head....109 D5
Forest Hill....39 D5
Forest Lane Head....95 D6
Forest Lodge
  Argyll....131 E6
  Highld....139 C6
  Perth....133 B6
Forest Mill....127 E8
Forest Row....28 F5
Forestside....15 C8
Forest Town....77 C5
Forfar....134 D4
Forgandenny....128 C2
Forge....58 E4
Forge Side....35 D6
Forgewood....119 D7
Forgie....152 C3
Forglen House....153 C6
Formby....85 D4
Forncett End....68 E4
Forncett St Mary....68 E4
Forncett St Peter....68 E4
Forneth....133 E7
Fornham All
  Saints....56 C2
Fornham
  St Martin....56 C2
Forres....151 F13
Forrestfield....119 C8
Forrest Lodge....113 F5
Forsbrook....75 E6
Forse....158 G4
Forse House....158 G4
Forsinain....157 E12
Forsinard....157 E11
Forsinard
  Station....157 E11
Forston....12 E4
Forteviot....128 C2
Fort George
  Guern....16 I2
  Highld....151 F10
Forth....120 D2
Forthampton....50 F3
Forth Road
  Bridge....120 B4
Fortingall....132 E4
Forton
  Hants....26 E2
  Lancs....92 D4
  Shrops....60 C4
  Som....11 D8
  Staffs....61 B7
Forton Heath....60 C4
Fortrie....153 D6
Fortrose....151 F10
Fortuneswell....12 G4
Fort William....131 B5
Forty Green....40 E2
Forty Hill....41 E6
Forward Green....56 D4
Fosbury....25 D8
Fosdyke....79 F6
Foss....132 D4
Foss Cross....37 D7
Fossebridge....37 C7
Fosterhouses....89 C7
Foster Street....41 D7
Foston
  Derbys....75 F8
  Lincs....77 E8
  N Yorks....96 C2
Foston on the
  Wolds....97 D7
Fotherby....91 E7
Fotheringhay....65 E7
Foubister....159 H6
Foulby....88 C4
Foulden
  Borders....122 D5
  Norf....67 E7
Foul Mile....18 D3
Foulridge....93 E8
Foulsham....81 E6
Fountainhall....121 E7
Four Ashes
  Staffs....62 F2
  Suff....56 B4
Four Crosses
  Powys....59 D7
  Powys....60 C2
  Wrex....73 D6
Four Elms....29 E5
Four Forks....22 F4
Four Gotes....66 C4
Fourlane Ends....76 D3
Four Lane Ends....74 C2
Four Lanes....3 C5
Fourlanes End....74 D5
Four Marks....26 F4
Four Mile Bridge....82 D2
Four Oaks
  E Sus....19 C5
  W Mid....62 E5
  W Mid....63 F6
Fourpenny....151 B11
Four Roads
  Carms....33 D5
  IoM....84 F2
Fourstones....109 C8
Four Throws....18 C4
Fovant....13 B8
Foveran....141 B8
Fowey....5 D6
Fowley Common....86 E4
Fowlis....134 F3
Fowlis Wester....127 B8
Fowlmere....54 E5
Fownhope....49 F7
Foxbar....118 C4
Foxcombe Hill....38 D4
Fox Corner....27 D7
Foxdale....84 E2
Foxearth....56 E2
Foxfield....98 F4
Foxham....24 B4
Foxhole
  Corn....4 D4
  Swansea....33 E7
Foxholes....97 B6
Foxhunt Green....18 D2
Fox Lane....27 D6
Foxley
  Norf....81 E6
  Wilts....37 F5
Fox Street....43 B6

Foxt....75 E7
Foxton
  Cambs....54 E5
  Durham....102 B1
  Leics....64 E4
Foxup....93 B8
Foxwist Green....74 C3
Foxwood....49 B8
Foy....36 B2
Foyers....137 B7
Fraddam....2 C4
Fraddon....4 D4
Fradley....63 C5
Fradswell....75 F6
Fraisthorpe....97 C7
Framfield....17 B8
Framingham Earl....69 D5
Framingham
  Pigot....69 D5
Framlingham....57 C6
Frampton
  Dorset....12 E4
  Lincs....79 F6
Frampton
  Cotterell....36 F3
Frampton
  Mansell....37 D6
Frampton on
  Severn....36 D4
Frampton West
  End....79 E5
Framsden....57 D5
Framwellgate
  Moor....111 E5
Franche....50 B3
Frankby....85 F3
Frankley....62 F3
Frank's Bridge....48 D3
Frankton....52 B2
Frant....18 B2
Fraserburgh....153 B9
Frating Green....43 B6
Fratton....15 E7
Freathy....5 D8
Freckenham....55 B7
Freckleton....86 B2
Freeby....64 B5
Freehay....75 E7
Freeland....38 C4
Freester....160 H6
Freethorpe....69 D7
Freiston....79 E6
Fremington
  Devon....20 F4
  N Yorks....101 E5
Frenchay....23 B8
Frenchbeer....9 F8
French....126 D3
Frensham....27 E6
Fresgoe....157 C12
Freshfield....85 D3
Freshford....24 C2
Freshwater....14 F4
Freshwater Bay....14 F4
Freshwater East....32 E1
Fressingfield....57 B6
Freston....57 F5
Freswick....158 D5
Fretherne....36 D4
Frettenham....68 C5
Freuchie....128 D4
Freuchies....134 C2
Freystrop....44 D4
Friar's Gate....29 F5
Friarton....128 B3
Friday Bridge....66 D4
Friday Street....18 E3
Fridaythorpe....96 D4
Friern Barnet....41 E5
Friesland....146 F4
Friesthorpe....90 F4
Frieston....78 E2
Frieth....39 E7
Frilford....38 E4
Frilsham....26 B3
Frimley....27 D6
Frimley Green....27 D6
Frindsbury....29 B8
Fring....80 D3
Fringford....39 B6
Frinsted....30 D2
Frinton-on-Sea....43 B8
Friockheim....135 E5
Friog....58 C3
Frisby on the
  Wreake....64 C3
Friskney....79 D7
Friskney Eaudike....79 D7
Friskney Tofts....79 D7
Friston
  E Sus....18 F2
  Suff....57 C8
Fritchley....76 D3
Fritham....14 C3
Frith Bank....79 E6
Frith Common....49 C8
Frithelstock....9 C6
Frithelstock Stone....9 C6
Frithville....79 D6
Frittenden....30 E2
Frittiscombe....7 E6
Fritton
  Norf....68 E5
  Norf....69 D7
Fritwell....39 B5
Frizinghall....94 F4
Frizington....98 C2
Frocester....36 D4
Frodesley....60 D5
Frodingham....90 C2
Frodsham....74 B2
Frogden....116 B3
Froggatt....76 B2
Froghall....75 E7
Frogmore
  Devon....7 E5
  Hants....27 D6
Frognall....65 C8
Frogshail....81 D8
Frolesworth....64 E2
Frome....24 E2
Frome St Quintin....12 D3
Fromes Hill....49 E8
Fron
  Denb....72 C4
  Gwyn....70 D4
  Gwyn....82 F5
  Powys....48 D2

Fron continued
  Powys....59 E8
  Powys....60 D2
Froncysyllte....73 E6
Frongoch....72 F3
Frostenden....69 F7
Frosterley....110 F3
Frotoft....159 F5
Froxfield....25 C7
Froxfield Green....15 B8
Froyle....27 E5
Fryerning....42 D2
Fryton....96 B2
Fulbeck....78 D2
Fulbourn....55 D6
Fulbrook....38 C2
Fulford
  Som....11 B7
  Staffs....75 F6
  York....96 E2
Fulham....28 B3
Fulking....17 C6
Fullarton
  Glasgow....119 C6
  N Ayrs....118 F3
Fuller's Moor....73 D8
Fuller Street....42 C3
Fullerton....25 F8
Fulletby....79 B5
Full Sutton....96 D3
Fullwood....118 D4
Fulmer....40 F2
Fulmodeston....81 D5
Fulnetby....78 B3
Fulstow....91 E7
Fulwell....111 D6
Fulwood
  Lancs....92 F5
  S Yorks....88 F4
Fundenhall....68 E4
Fundenhall
  Street....68 E4
Funtington....15 D8
Funtley....15 D6
Funtullich....127 B6
Funzie....160 D8
Furley....11 D7
Furnace
  Argyll....125 E6
  Carms....33 D6
Furnace End....63 E6
Furneaux Pelham....41 B7
Furness Vale....87 F8
Furzehill....21 E6
Furze Platt....40 F1
Fyfett....11 C7
Fyfield
  Essex....42 D1
  Glos....38 D2
  Hants....25 E7
  Oxon....38 E4
  Wilts....25 C6
Fylingthorpe....103 D7
Fyvie....153 E7

G

Gabhsann bho
  Dheas....155 B9
Gabhsann bho
  Thuath....155 B9
Gablon....151 B10
Gabroc Hill....118 D4
Gaddesby....64 C3
Gadebridge....40 D3
Gaer....35 B5
Gaerllwyd....35 E8
Gaerwen....82 D4
Gagingwell....38 B4
Gaick Lodge....138 F3
Gailey....62 C3
Gainford....101 C6
Gainsborough
  Lincs....90 E2
  Suff....57 E5
Gainsford End....55 F7
Gairloch....149 A13
Gairlochy....136 F4
Gairney Bank....128 E3
Gairnshiel
  Lodge....139 D8
Gaisgill....99 D8
Gaitsgill....108 E3
Galashiels....121 F7
Galgate....92 D4
Galhampton....12 B4
Gallaberry....114 F2
Gallachoille....144 E6
Gallanach
  Argyll....124 C4
  Argyll....146 E5
Gallantry Bank....74 D2
Gallatown....128 E4
Galley Common....63 E7
Galleyend....42 D3
Galley Hill....54 C4
Galleywood....42 D3
Gallin....132 E2
Gallowfauld....134 E4
Gallows Green....75 E7
Galltair....149 F13
Galmisdale....146 C7
Galmpton
  Devon....6 E4
  Torbay....7 D6
Galphay....95 B5
Galston....118 F5
Galtrigill....148 C6
Gamblesby....109 F6
Gamesley....87 E8
Gamlingay....54 D3
Gammersgill....101 F5
Gamston....77 B7
Ganarew....36 C2
Ganavan....124 B4
Gang....5 C8
Ganllwyd....71 E8
Gannochy
  Angus....135 B5
  Perth....128 B3
Gansclet....158 F5
Ganstead....97 F7
Ganthorpe....96 B2
Ganton....97 B5
Garbat....150 E7
Garbhallt....125 F6
Garboldisham....68 F3

Garden City....73 C7
Gardenstown....153 B7
Garden Village
  Wrex....73 D7
  W Yorks....95 F7
Garderhouse....160 J5
Gardham....97 E5
Gardin....160 G6
Gare Hill....24 E2
Garelochhead....145 D11
Garford....38 E4
Garforth....95 F7
Gargrave....94 D2
Gargunnock....127 E6
Garlic Street....68 F5
Garlieston....105 E8
Garlinge Green....30 D5
Garlogie....141 D6
Garmond....153 C8
Garmony....147 G9
Garmouth....152 B3
Garn-Dolbenmaen....71 C5
Garnedd....83 F7
Garnett Bridge....99 E7
Garnfadryn....70 D3
Garnkirk....119 C6
Garnlydan....35 C5
Garn-yr-erw....35 C6
Garrabost....155 D10
Garraron....124 E4
Garras....3 D6
Garreg....71 C7
Garrick....127 C7
Garrigill....109 E7
Garriston....101 E6
Garroch....113 F5
Garrogie Lodge....137 C8
Garros....149 B9
Garrow....133 E5
Garryhorn....113 E5
Garsdale....100 F2
Garsdale Head....100 E2
Garsdon....37 F6
Garshall Green....75 F6
Garsington....39 D5
Garstang....92 E4
Garston....86 F2
Garswood....86 E3
Gartcosh....119 C6
Garth
  Bridgend....34 E2
  Gwyn....83 D5
  Powys....47 E8
  Shetland....160 H4
  Wrex....73 E6
Garthamlock....119 C6
Garthbrengy....48 F2
Garthdee....141 D8
Gartheli....46 D4
Garthmyl....59 E8
Garthorpe
  Leics....64 B5
  N Lincs....90 C2
Garth Row....99 E7
Gartly....152 E5
Gartmore....126 E4
Gartnagrenach....144 H6
Gartness
  N Lanark....119 C7
  Stirling....126 F4
Gartocharn....126 F3
Garton....97 F8
Garton-on-the-
  Wolds....97 D5
Gartsherrie....119 C7
Gartymore....157 H13
Garvald....121 B8
Garvamore....137 E8
Garvard....144 D2
Garvault Hotel....157 F10
Garve....150 E6
Garvestone....68 D3
Garvock
  Aberds....135 B7
  Invclyd....118 B2
Garway....36 B1
Garway Hill....35 B8
Gaskan....130 B1
Gastard....24 C3
Gasthorpe....68 F2
Gatcombe....15 F5
Gateacre....86 F2
Gatebeck....99 F7
Gate Burton....90 F2
Gateford....89 F6
Gateforth....89 B6
Gatehead....118 F3
Gate Helmsley....96 D2
Gatehouse....116 F3
Gatehouse of
  Fleet....106 D3
Gatelawbridge....114 E2
Gateley....81 E5
Gatenby....101 F8
Gateshead....111 C5
Gatesheath....73 C8
Gateside
  Aberds....140 C5
  Angus....134 E4
  E Renf....118 D4
  Fife....128 D3
  N Ayrs....118 D3
Gathurst....86 D3
Gatley....87 F6
Gattonside....121 F8
Gaufron....47 C8
Gaulby....64 D3
Gauldry....129 B5
Gaunt's
  Common....13 D8
Gautby....78 B4
Gavinton....122 D3
Gawber....88 D4
Gawcott....52 F4
Gawsworth....75 C5
Gawthorpe....88 C3
Gawthrop....100 F1
Gawthwaite....98 F4
Gaydon....51 D8
Gayfield....159 C5
Gayhurst....53 E6
Gayle....100 F3
Gayles....101 D6

Gayton
  Mers....85 F3
  Norf....67 C7
  Staffs....62 B3
  W Nhants....52 D5
Gayton le Marsh....91 F8
Gayton le Wold....91 F6
Gayton Thorpe....67 C7
Gaywood....67 B6
Gazeley....55 C8
Geanies House....151 D11
Gearraidh
  Bhailteas....148 F2
Gearraidh
  Bhaird....155 E8
Gearraidh na h-
  Aibhne....154 D7
Gearraidh na
  Monadh....148 G2
Geary....148 B7
Geddes House....151 F11
Gedding....56 D3
Geddington....65 F5
Gedintailor....149 E10
Gedling....77 E6
Gedney....66 B4
Gedney
  Broadgate....66 B4
Gedney Drove
  End....66 B4
Gedney Dyke....66 B4
Gee Cross....87 E7
Geilston....118 B3
Geirinis....148 D2
Geisiadar....154 D6
Geise....158 D3
Geldeston....69 E6
Gell....83 E8
Gelli
  Pembs....32 C1
  Rhondda....34 E3
Gellideg....34 D4
Gellifor....72 C5
Gelligaer....35 E5
Gellilydan....71 D7
Gellinudd....33 D8
Gellyburn....133 F7
Gellywen....32 B3
Gelston
  Dumfries....106 D4
  Lincs....78 E2
Gembling....97 D7
Gentleshaw....62 C4
Geocrab....154 H6
George Green....40 F3
Georgeham....20 F3
George Nympton....10 B2
Georgetown....35 D5
Gerlan....83 E6
Germansweek....9 E6
Germoe....2 D4
Gerrans....3 C7
Gerrards Cross....40 F3
Gestingthorpe....56 F2
Geuffordd....60 C2
Gibbet Hill....64 F2
Gibbshill....106 B4
Gib Hill....74 B3
Gidea Park....41 F8
Gidleigh....9 F8
Giffnock....119 D5
Gifford....121 C8
Giffordland....118 E2
Giffordtown....128 C4
Giggleswick....93 C8
Gilberdyke....90 B2
Gilchriston....121 C7
Gilcrux....107 F8
Gildersome....88 B3
Gildingwells....89 F6
Gileston....22 C2
Gilfach....35 E5
Gilfach Goch....34 F3
Gilfachrheda....46 D3
Gillamoor....102 F4
Gillar's Green....86 E2
Gillen....148 C7
Gilling East....96 B2
Gillingham
  Dorset....13 B6
  Medway....29 C8
  Norf....69 E7
Gilling West....101 D6
Gillock....158 E4
Gillow Heath....75 D5
Gills....158 C5
Gill's Green....18 B4
Gilmanscleuch....115 B6
Gilmerton
  Edin....121 C5
  Perth....127 B7
Gilmonby....100 C4
Gilmorton....64 F2
Gilmourton....119 E6
Gilsland....109 C6
Gilsland Spa....109 C6
Gilston
  Borders....121 D7
  Herts....41 C7
Gilwern....35 C6
Gimingham....81 D8
Giosla....154 E6
Gipping....56 C4
Gipsey Bridge....79 E5
Girdle Toll....118 E3
Girlsta....160 H6
Girsby....102 D1
Girthon....106 D3
Girton
  Cambs....54 C5
  Notts....77 C8
Girvan....112 E1
Gisburn....93 E8
Gisleham....69 F8
Gislingham....56 B4
Gissing....68 F4
Gittisham....11 E6
Gladestry....48 D4
Gladsmuir....121 B7
Glais....33 D8
Glaisdale....103 D5
Glame....149 D10
Glamis....134 E3
Glan Adda....83 D5
Glanaman....33 C8

Glan Conwy
  Conwy....83 D8
  Conwy....83 F8
Glandford....81 C6
Glan-Duar....46 E4
Glandwr....32 B2
Glan-Dwyfach....71 C5
Glandy Cross....32 B2
Glandyfi....58 E3
Glan Gors....82 D4
Glangrwyney....35 C6
Glanmule....59 E8
Glanrafon....58 F3
Glanrhyd
  Gwyn....70 D3
  Pembs....45 E3
Glan-rhyd....82 F4
Glanton....117 C6
Glanton Pike....117 C6
Glan-traeth....82 D2
Glanvilles
  Wootton....12 D4
Glan-y-don....73 B5
Glan-y-nant....59 F6
Glan-yr-afon
  Anglesey....83 C6
  Gwyn....72 E3
  Gwyn....72 E4
Glan-y-wern....71 D7
Glapthorn....65 E7
Glapwell....76 C4
Glas-allt Shiel....139 F8
Glasbury....48 F3
Glaschoil....151 H13
Glascoed
  Denb....72 B3
  Mon....35 D7
  Powys....59 C8
Glascorrie....140 E2
Glascote....63 D6
Glascwm....48 D3
Glasdrum....130 E4
Glasfryn....72 D3
Glasgow....119 C5
Glashvin....149 B9
Glasinfryn....83 E5
Glasnacardoch....147 B9
Glasnakille....149 G10
Glasphein....148 D6
Glaspwll....58 E4
Glassburn....150 H6
Glasserton....105 F8
Glassford....119 E7
Glasshouse Hill....36 B4
Glasshouses....94 C4
Glasslie....128 D4
Glasson
  Cumb....108 C2
  Lancs....92 D4
Glassonby....109 F5
Glasterlaw....135 D5
Glaston....65 D5
Glastonbury....23 F7
Glatton....65 F8
Glazebrook....86 E4
Glazebury....86 E4
Glazeley....61 F7
Gleadless....88 F4
Gleadsmoss....74 C5
Gleann
  Tholàstaidh....155 C10
Gleaston....92 B2
Gleiniant....59 E6
Glemsford....56 E2
Glen
  Dumfries....106 B5
  Dumfries....106 D2
Glenamachrie....124 C5
Glen Auldyn....84 C4
Glenbarr....143 E7
Glenbeg
  Highld....139 B6
  Highld....147 E8
Glen Bernisdale....149 D9
Glenbervie....141 F6
Glenboig....119 C7
Glenborrodale....147 E9
Glenbranter....125 F7
Glenbreck....114 B3
Glenbrein
  Lodge....137 C7
Glenbrittle
  House....149 F9
Glenbuchat
  Lodge....140 C2
Glenbuck....113 B7
Glenburn....118 C4
Glencalvie
  Lodge....150 C7
Glencanisp
  Lodge....156 G4
Glencaple....107 C6
Glencarron
  Lodge....150 F3
Glencarse....128 B3
Glencassley
  Castle....156 J7
Glenceitlein....131 E5
Glencoe....130 D4
Glencraig....128 E3
Glencripesdale....147 F9
Glencrosh....113 F7
Glendavan
  House....140 D3
Glendevon....127 D8
Glendoebeg....137 D7
Glendoe Lodge....137 D7
Glendoick....128 B4
Glendoll Lodge....134 B2
Glendoune....112 E1
Glenduckie....128 C4
Glendye Lodge....140 F5
Gleneagles
  Hotel....127 C8
Gleneagles
  Station....127 C8
Glenegedale....142 C4
Glenelg....149 G13
Glenernie....151 G13
Glenfarg....128 C3
Glenfarquhar
  Lodge....141 F6
Glenferness
  House....151 G12
Glenfeshie
  Lodge....138 E4
Glenfield....64 D2
Glenfinnan....147 C11

Glenfoot....128 C3
Glenfyne Lodge....125 D8
Glengap....106 D3
Glengarnock....118 D3
Glengorm Castle....146 F7
Glengrasco....149 D9
Glenhead Farm....134 C2
Glen Ho....121 F5
Glenhoul....113 F6
Glenhurich....130 C2
Glenkerry....115 C5
Glenkiln....106 B5
Glenkindie....140 C3
Glenlatterach....152 C1
Glenlee....113 F6
Glenlichorn....127 C6
Glenlivet....139 B7
Glenlochsie....133 C7
Glenloig....143 E10
Glenluce....105 D6
Glenmallan....125 E8
Glenmarksie....150 F6
Glenmassan....145 E10
Glenmavis....119 C7
Glenmaye....84 E2
Glenmidge....113 F8
Glen Mona....84 D4
Glenmore
  Argyll....124 D4
  Highld....149 D9
Glenmore
  Lodge....139 D5
Glenmoy....134 C4
Glen Nevis
  House....131 B5
Glenogil....134 C4
Glen Parva....64 E2
Glenprosen
  Lodge....134 C3
Glenprosen
  Village....134 C3
Glenquiech....134 C4
Glenreasdell
  Mains....145 H7
Glenree....143 F10
Glenridding....99 C5
Glenrossal....156 J7
Glenrothes....128 D4
Glensanda....130 E2
Glensaugh....135 B6
Glenshero
  Lodge....137 E8
Glen Sluain....125 F6
Glenstockadale....104 C4
Glenstriven....145 F9
Glentaggart....113 B8
Glen Tanar
  House....140 E3
Glentham....90 E4
Glentirranmuir....127 E5
Glenton....140 B5
Glentress....121 F5
Glentromie
  Lodge....138 E3
Glen Trool
  Lodge....112 F4
Glentrool
  Village....105 B7
Glentruan....84 B4
Glentruim
  House....138 E2
Glentworth....90 F3
Glenuig....147 D9
Glenurquhart....151 E10
Glen Village....119 B8
Glen Vine....84 E3
Glespin....113 B8
Gletness....160 H6
Glewstone....36 B2
Glinton....65 D8
Glooston....64 E4
Glororum....123 F7
Glossop....87 E8
Gloster Hill....117 D8
Gloucester....37 C5
Gloup....160 C7
Glusburn....94 E3
Glutt Lodge....157 F12
Glutton Bridge....75 C7
Glympton....38 B4
Glynarthen....46 E2
Glynbrochan....59 F6
Glyn-Ceiriog....73 F6
Glyncoch....34 E4
Glyncorrwg....34 E2
Glynde....17 D8
Glyndebourne....17 C8
Glyndyfrdwy....72 E5
Glyn Ebwy
  = Ebbw Vale....35 D6
Glynedd
  = Glynneath....34 D2
Glyn-neath
  = Glynedd....34 D2
Glynogwr....34 F3
Glyntaff....34 F4
Glyntawe....34 C2
Gnosall....62 B2
Gnosall Heath....62 B2
Goadby....64 E4
Goadby Marwood....64 B4
Goatacre....24 B5
Goathill....12 C4
Goathland....103 D6
Goathurst....22 F4
Goat Lees....30 E4
Gobernuisgach
  Lodge....156 E7
Gobhaig....154 G5
Gobowen....73 F7
Godalming....27 E7
Godley....87 E7
Godmanchester....54 B3
Godmanstone....12 E4
Godmersham....30 D4
Godney....23 E6
Godolphin Cross....2 C5
Godre'r-graig....34 D1
Godshill
  Hants....14 C2
  IoW....15 F6
Godstone....28 D4
Godwinscroft....14 E2
Goetre....35 D7
Goferydd....82 C2
Goff's Oak....41 D6
Gogar....120 B4

Goginan....58 F3
Golan....71 C6
Golant....5 D6
Golberdon....5 B8
Golborne....86 E4
Golcar....88 C2
Goldcliff....35 F7
Golden Cross....18 D2
Golden Green....29 E7
Golden Grove....33 C6
Goldenhill....75 D5
Golden Hill....14 E3
Golden Pot....26 E5
Golden Valley....37 B6
Golders Green....41 F5
Goldhanger....43 D5
Gold Hill....66 E5
Golding....60 D5
Goldsborough
  N Yorks....95 D6
  N Yorks....103 C6
Goldsithney....2 C4
Goldsworthy....9 B6
Goldthorpe....89 D5
Gollanfield....151 F11
Golspie....157 J11
Golval....157 C11
Gomeldon....25 F6
Gomersal....88 B3
Gomshall....27 E8
Gonalston....77 E6
Gonfirth....160 G5
Good Easter....42 C2
Gooderstone....67 D7
Goodleigh....20 F5
Goodmanham....96 E4
Goodnestone
  Kent....30 C4
  Kent....31 D6
Goodrich....36 C2
Goodrington....7 D6
Goodshaw....87 B6
Goodwick = Wdig....44 B4
Goodworth
  Clatford....25 E8
Goole....89 B8
Goonbell....3 B6
Goonhavern....4 D2
Goose Eye....94 E3
Goose Green
  Gtr Man....86 D3
  Norf....68 F4
  W Sus....16 C5
Gooseham....8 C4
Goosey....38 E3
Goosnargh....93 F5
Goostrey....74 B4
Gorcott Hill....51 C5
Gord....160 L6
Gordon....122 E2
Gordonbush....157 J11
Gordonsburgh....152 B4
Gordonstoun....152 B1
Gordonstown
  Aberds....152 C5
  Aberds....153 E7
Gore....31 D7
Gorebridge....121 C6
Gore Cross....24 D5
Gorefield....66 C4
Gore Pit....42 C4
Gorey....17 I3
Gorgie....120 B5
Goring....39 F6
Goring-by-Sea....16 D5
Goring Heath....26 B4
Gorleston-on-
  Sea....69 D8
Gornalwood....62 E3
Gorrachie....153 C7
Gorran
  Churchtown....3 B8
Gorran Haven....3 B9
Gorrenberry....115 E7
Gors....46 B5
Gorsedd....73 B5
Gorse Hill....38 F1
Gorseinon....33 E6
Gorseness....159 G5
Gorsgoch....46 D3
Gorslas....33 C6
Gorsley....36 B3
Gorstan....150 E6
Gorstanvorran....130 B2
Gorsteyhill....74 D4
Gorsty Hill....62 B5
Gortantaoid....142 A4
Gorton....87 E6
Gosbeck....57 D5
Gosberton....78 F5
Gosberton
  Clough....65 B8
Gosfield....42 B3
Gosford....49 C7
Gosforth
  Cumb....98 D2
  T&W....110 C5
Gosmore....40 B4
Gosport....15 E7
Gossabrough....160 E7
Gossington....36 D4
Goswick....123 E6
Gotham....76 F5
Gotherington....37 B6
Gott....160 J6
Goudhurst....18 B4
Goulceby....79 B5
Gourdas....153 D7
Gourdon....135 B8
Gourock....118 B2
Govan....119 C5
Govanhill....119 C5
Goveton....7 E5
Govilon....35 C6
Gowanhill....153 B10
Gowdall....89 B7
Gowerton....33 E6
Gowkhall....128 F2
Gowthorpe....96 D3
Goxhill
  E Yorks....97 E7
  N Lincs....90 B5
Goxhill Haven....90 B5
Goytre....34 F1
Grabhair....155 F8
Graby....65 B7
Grade....3 E6

Graffham 16 C3
Grafham
Cambs. 54 C2
Sur 27 E8
Grafton
Hereford. 49 F6
N Yorks 95 C7
Oxon 38 D2
Shrops 60 C4
Worcs 49 C7
Grafton Flyford. .50 D4
Grafton Regis . . .53 E5
Grafton
Underwood 65 F6
Grafty Green 30 E2
Graianrhyd 73 D6
Graig
Conwy 83 D8
Denb 72 B4
Graig-fechan 72 D5
Grain 30 B2
Grainsby 91 E6
Grainthorpe 91 E7
Grampound 3 B8
Grampound Road. .4 D4
Gramsdal 148 C3
Granborough. 39 B7
Granby 77 F7
Grandborough . . .52 C2
Grandtully 133 D6
Grange
Cumb 98 C4
E Ayrs 118 F4
Medway 29 C6
Mers 85 F3
Perth. 128 B4
Grange
Crossroads. 152 C4
Grange Hall 151 E13
Grange Hill. 41 E7
Grangemill. 76 D2
Grange Moor 88 C3
Grangemouth . . .127 F8
Grange of
Lindores 128 C4
Grange-over-
Sands. 92 B4
Grangepans 128 F2
Grangetown
Cardiff. 22 B3
Redcar 102 B3
Grange Villa 110 D5
Granish 138 C5
Gransmoor 97 D7
Granston 44 B3
Grantchester 54 D5
Grantham 78 F2
Grantley 94 C5
Grantlodge 141 C6
Granton
Dumfries. 114 D3
Edin. 120 B5
Grantown-on-
Spey 139 B6
Grantshouse 122 C4
Grappenhall. 86 F4
Grasby 90 D4
Grasmere 99 D5
Grasscroft 87 D7
Grassendale 85 F4
Grassholme 100 B4
Grassington 94 C3
Grassmoor 76 C4
Grassthorpe 77 C7
Grateley 25 E7
Gratwich 75 F7
Graveley
Cambs. 54 C4
Herts. 41 B5
Gravelly Hill 62 E5
Gravels 60 D3
Graven 160 F6
Graveney 30 C4
Gravesend
Herts. 41 B7
Kent 29 B7
Grayingham. 90 E3
Grayrigg 99 E7
Grays 29 B7
Grayshott. 27 F6
Grayswood 27 F7
Graythorp. 102 B3
Grazeley 26 C4
Greasbrough. 88 E5
Greasby. 85 F3
Great Abington. . .55 E6
Great Addington. .53 B7
Great Alne 51 D6
Great Altcar. 85 D4
Great Amwell 41 C6
Great Asby 100 C1
Great Ashfield. . . .56 C3
Great Ayton 102 C3
Great Baddow 42 D3
Great Bardfield. . . .55 F7
Great Barford 54 D2
Great Barr 62 E4
Great Barrington. .38 C2
Great Barrow 73 C8
Great Barton 56 C2
Great Barugh. 96 B3
Great Bavington.117 F5
Great Bealings. . . .57 E6
Great Bedwyn 25 C7
Great Bentley 43 B7
Great Billing 53 C6
Great Bircham 80 D3
Great Blakenham 56 D5
Great Blencow . . .108 F4
Great Bolas 61 B6
Great Bookham . . .28 D2
Great Bourton. . . .52 E2
Great Bowden 64 F4
Great Bradley 55 D7
Great Braxted 42 C4
Great Bricett 56 D4
Great Brickhill 53 F7
Great Bridge 62 E3
Great Bridgeford .62 B2
Great Brington . . .52 C4
Great Bromley 43 B6
Great Broughton
Cumb 107 F7
N Yorks 102 D3
Great Budworth . .74 B3
Great Burdon. . . .101 C8
Great Burgh 28 D3
Great Burstead . .42 E2

Great Busby 102 D3
Great Canfield. . . .42 C1
Great Carlton 91 F8
Great Casterton . .65 D7
Great Chart 30 E3
Great Chatwell . . .61 C7
Great
Chesterton 55 E6
Great Cheverell . .24 D4
Great Chishill 54 F5
Great Clacton 43 C7
Great Cliff 88 C4
Great Clifton 98 B2
Great Coates 91 D6
Great Comberton .50 E4
Great Corby 108 D4
Great Cornard 56 E2
Great Cowden 97 E8
Great Coxwell 38 E2
Great Crakehall .101 E7
Great Cransley . . .53 B6
Great
Cressingham . . .67 D8
Great Crosby 85 E4
Great Cubley 75 F8
Great Dalby 64 C4
Great Denham 53 E8
Great
Doddington 53 C6
Great Dunham . . .67 C8
Great Dunmow . . .42 B2
Great Durnford . . .25 F6
Great Easton
Essex 42 B2
Leics 64 E5
Great Eccleston . .92 E4
Great Edstone. . . .103 F5
Great Ellingham . .68 E3
Great Elm 24 E2
Great Eversden . .54 D4
Great Fencote . . .101 E7
Great
Finborough 56 D4
Greatford 65 C7
Great Fransham . .67 C8
Greatgate. 75 E7
Great Gidding 65 F8
Great Givendale . .96 D4
Great Glemham . .57 C7
Great Glen 64 E3
Great Gonerby . . .77 F8
Great Gransden . .54 D3
Great Green
Norf 69 F5
Suff. 56 D3
Great Habton 96 B3
Great Hale 78 E4
Great Hallingbury 41 C8
Greatham
Hants 27 F5
Hrtlpl 102 B2
W Sus 16 C4
Great Hampden . .39 D8
Great Harrowden .53 B6
Great Harwood . . .93 F7
Great Haseley 39 D6
Great Hatfield. . . .97 E7
Great Haywood . .62 B4
Great Heath 63 F7
Great Heck. 89 B6
Great Henny 56 F2
Great Hinton 24 D4
Great Hockham . . .68 E2
Great Holland 43 C8
Great Horkesley . .56 F3
Great Hormead. . . .54 F6
Great Horton 94 F4
Great Horwood . . .53 F5
Great Houghton
S Yorks 88 D5
W Nhants 53 D5
Great Hucklow 75 B8
Great Kelk 97 D7
Great Kimble 39 D8
Great Kingshill . . .40 E1
Great Langton . . .101 E7
Great Leighs 42 C3
Great Lever 86 D5
Great Limber 90 D5
Great Linford 53 E6
Great Livermere . .56 B2
Great Longstone .76 B2
Great Lumley 111 E5
Great Lyth 60 D4
Great Malvern 50 E2
Great Maplestead 56 F2
Great Marton 92 F3
Great
Massingham . . .80 E3
Great Melton 68 D4
Great Milton 39 D6
Great Missenden 40 D1
Great Mitton 93 F7
Great Mongeham.31 D7
Great Moulton. . . .68 E4
Great Munden 41 B6
Great Musgrave .100 C2
Great Ness 60 C3
Great Notley 42 B3
Great Oakley
Essex 43 B7
N Nhants 65 F5
Great Offley 40 B4
Great Ormside . . .100 C2
Great Orton 108 D3
Great Ouseburn . .95 C7
Great Oxendon . . .64 F4
Great Oxney
Green 42 D2
Great Palgrave . . .67 C7
Great Parndon. . . .41 D7
Great Paxton 54 C3
Great Plumpton . .92 F3
Great Plumstead 69 C6
Great Ponton 78 F8
Great Preston 88 B5
Great
Raveley 66 F2
Great Rissington 38 C1
Great Rollright . . .38 B3
Great Ryburgh . . .81 E5
Great Ryle 117 C6
Great Ryton 60 D4
Great Saling 42 B3
Great Salkeld . . .109 F5
Great Sampford . .55 F7
Great Sankey 86 F3

Great Saxham 55 C8
Great Shefford . . .25 B8
Great Shelford . . .55 D5
Great Smeaton . .101 D8
Great Snoring 80 D5
Great Somerford .37 F6
Great Stainton . .101 B8
Great Stambridge 42 E4
Great Staughton. .54 C2
Great Steeping . . .79 C7
Great Stonar 31 D7
Great Strickland. .99 B7
Great Stukeley . . .54 B3
Great Sturton 78 B5
Great Sutton
Ches W 73 B7
Shrops 60 F5
Great
Swinburne 110 B2
Great Tew 38 B3
Great Tey 42 B4
Great Thurkleby . .95 B7
Great Thurlow 55 D7
Great Torrington .117 D6
Great Tosson 117 D6
Great Totham 42 C4
Great Tows 91 E6
Great Urswick 92 B2
Great Wakering . . .43 F5
Great
Waldingfield . . .56 E3
Great
Walsingham . . .80 D5
Great Waltham . . .42 C2
Great Warley 42 E1
Great
Washbourne . . .50 F4
Great Weldon 65 F6
Great Welnetham 56 D2
Great Wenham . . .56 F4
Great
Whittington . . .110 B3
Great
Wigborough . . .43 C5
Great Wilbraham 55 D6
Great Wishford . . .25 F5
Great Witcombe. .37 C6
Great Witley. 50 C2
Great Wolford 51 F7
Greatworth 52 E3
Great Wratting . . .55 E7
Great Wymondley 41 B5
Great Wyrley 62 D3
Great Wytheford .61 C5
Great Yarmouth . .69 D8
Great Yeldham . . .55 F8
Greave. 87 B6
Greeba 84 D3
Green 72 C4
Green
Hammerton 95 D7
Greenbank 160 C7
Greenburn 120 C2
Greendikes 117 B6
Green End 54 D2
Greenfield
C Beds. 53 F8
Flint 73 B5
Gtr Man. 87 D7
Highld 136 D5
Oxon 39 E7
Greenford 40 F4
Greengairs 119 B7
Greenham 26 C2
Green
Hammerton 95 D7
Greenhaugh. 116 F3
Greenhead 109 C6
Greenhill
Falk. 119 B8
Kent 31 C5
Leics 63 C8
London 40 F4
Greenhills 118 D3
Greenhithe. 29 B6
Greenholm. 118 F5
Greenholme 99 D7
Greenhouse 115 B8
Greenhow Hill 94 C4
Greenigoe 159 H5
Greenland 158 D4
Greenlands 39 F7
Greenlaw 122 D3
Greenlea 107 B7
Greenloaning 127 D7
Greenmount 87 C5
Greenmow 160 L6
Greenock 118 B2
Greenock West . .118 B2
Greenodd 99 F5
Green Ore. 23 D7
Greenrow 107 D8
Greenside
Oxon 38 E4
T&W 110 C4
Greensidehill 117 C5
Greens Norton . . .52 E4
Greenstead
Green 42 B4
Greensted 41 D8
Green Street 40 E4
Greenwich 28 B4
Greet 50 F5
Greete 49 B7
Greetham
Lincs 79 B6
Rutland 65 C6
Greetland 87 B8
Gregg Hall 99 E6
Gregson Lane 86 B3
Greinetobht. 148 A3
Greinton. 23 F6
Gremista 160 J6
Grenaby 84 E2
Grendon
N Nhants 53 C6
Warks 63 D6
Grendon
Common 63 E6
Grendon Green . . .49 D7
Grendon
Underwood 39 B6
Grenofen 6 B2
Grenoside. 88 E4
Greosabhagh. . . .154 H6
Gresford 73 D7

Gresham 81 D7
Greshornish 149 C8
Gressenhall 68 C2
Gressingham. 93 C5
Gresty Green 74 D4
Greta Bridge 101 C5
Gretna 108 C3
Gretna Green. . . .108 C3
Gretton
Glos 50 F5
N Nhants 65 E5
Shrops 60 E5
Grewelthorpe 94 B5
Greygarth. 94 B4
Grey Green. 89 D8
Greynor. 33 D6
Greysouthen 98 B2
Greystoke 108 F4
Greystone
Angus 135 E5
Dumfries. 107 B6
Greywell 26 D5
Griais 155 C9
Grianan 155 D9
Gribthorpe. 96 F3
Gridley Corner 9 E5
Griff 63 F7
Griffithstown. 35 E6
Grimbister 159 G4
Grimblethorpe . . .91 F6
Grimeford
Village 86 C4
Grimethorpe 88 D5
Griminis 148 C2
Grimister 160 D6
Grimley 50 C3
Grimoldby. 91 F7
Grimpo 60 B3
Grimsargh 93 F5
Grimsbury 52 E2
Grimsby 91 C6
Grimscote 52 D4
Grimscott. 8 D4
Grimsthorpe 65 B7
Grimston
E Yorks 97 F8
Leics 64 B3
Norf 80 E3
York 96 D2
Grimstone 12 E4
Grinacombe Moor .9 E6
Grindale 97 B7
Grindigar 159 H6
Grindiscol. 160 K6
Grindle 61 D7
Grindleford 76 B2
Grindleton 93 E7
Grindley 62 B4
Grindley Brook . . .74 E2
Grindlow 75 B8
Grindon
Northumb 122 E5
Staffs 75 D7
Grindonmoor
Gate 75 D7
Gringley on the
Hill 89 E8
Grinsdale 108 D3
Grinshill 60 B5
Grinton 101 E5
Griomsidar. 155 E8
Grishipoll 146 F4
Grisling Common .17 B8
Gristhorpe 103 F8
Griston 68 E2
Gritley 159 H6
Grittenham 37 F7
Grittleton 37 F5
Grizebeck 98 F4
Grizedale 99 E5
Grobister 159 F7
Groby 64 D2
Groes
Conwy 72 C4
Neath 34 F1
Groes-faen 34 F4
Groesffordd Marli72 B4
Groeslon
Gwyn. 82 E5
Gwyn. 82 F4
Groes-lwyd 60 C2
Grogport. 143 D9
Gromford 57 D7
Gronant 72 A4
Groombridge. 18 B2
Grosmont
Mon. 35 B8
N Yorks 103 D6
Groton 56 E3
Groudfoot 120 B3
Grouville. 17 I3
Grove
Dorset. 12 G5
Kent 31 C6
Notts. 77 B7
Oxon 38 E4
Grove Park 28 B5
Grovesend 33 D6
Grove Vale 62 E4
Grudie 150 E6
Gruids 157 J8
Gruinard House .150 B2
Grula 149 F8
Grunasound. 160 K5
Grundisburgh 57 D6
Grunsagill. 93 D7
Grutness 160 N6
Gualachulain 131 E5
Gualin House. . . .156 D6
Guardbridge 129 C6
Guarlford 50 E3
Guay 133 E7
Guestling Green . .19 D5
Guestling Thorn . .18 D5
Guestwick 81 E6
Guestwick Green .81 E6
Guide 86 B5
Guide Post 117 F8
Guilden Morden . .54 E3
Guilden Sutton . . .73 C8
Guildford 27 E7
Guildtown 133 F8
Guilsborough 52 B4
Guilsfield 60 C2
Guilton 31 D6

Guineaford 20 F4
Guisborough 102 C4
Guiseley 94 E4
Guist 81 E5
Guith 159 E6
Guiting Power. . . .37 B7
Gulberwick 160 K6
Gullane 129 F6
Gulval 2 C3
Gulworthy 6 B2
Gumfreston 32 D2
Gumley 64 E3
Gummow's
Shop. 4 D3
Gunby
E Yorks 96 F3
Lincs 65 B6
Gundleton 26 F4
Gun Hill 18 D2
Gunn 20 F5
Gunnerside 100 E4
Gunnerton 110 B2
Gunness 90 C2
Gunnislake 6 B2
Gunnista. 160 J7
Gunthorpe
Norf 81 D6
Notts. 77 E6
Pboro 65 D8
Gunville 15 F5
Gunwalloe 3 D5
Gurnard 15 E5
Gurnett 75 B6
Gurney Slade 23 E8
Gurnos 34 D1
Gussage All
Saints. 13 C8
Gussage
St Michael 13 C7
Guston. 31 E7
Gutcher 160 D7
Guthrie 135 D5
Guyhirn 66 D3
Guyhirn Gull. 66 D3
Guy's Head. 66 B4
Guy's Marsh 13 B6
Guyzance 117 D8
Gwaenysgor. 72 A4
Gwalchmai 82 D3
Gwaun-Cae-
Gurwen 33 C8
Gwaun-Leision. . .33 C8
Gwbert 45 E3
Gweek 3 D6
Gwehelog 35 D7
Gwenddwr 48 E2
Gwennap 3 C6
Gwenter 3 E6
Gwernaffield 73 C6
Gwernesney. 35 D8
Gwernogle. 46 F4
Gwernymynydd. . .73 C6
Gwersyllt 73 D7
Gwespyr 85 F2
Gwithian 2 B4
Gwredog 82 C4
Gwyddelwern 72 E4
Gwyddgrug 46 F3
Gwydyr Uchaf . . .83 E7
Gwynfryn 73 D6
Gwystre. 48 C2
Gwytherin 83 E8
Gyfelia 73 E7
Gyffin 83 D7
Gyre 159 H4
Gyrn-goch 70 C5

H
Habberley. 60 D3
Habergham 93 F8
Habrough 90 C5
Haceby 78 F3
Hacheston 57 D7
Hackbridge 28 C3
Hackenthorpe. . . .88 F5
Hackford 68 D3
Hackforth 101 E7
Hackland 159 F4
Hackleton 53 D6
Hackness
N Yorks 103 E7
Orkney 159 J4
Hackney. 41 F6
Hackthorn 90 F3
Hackthorpe. 99 B7
Haconby 65 B8
Hacton 41 F8
Hadden 122 F3
Haddenham
Bucks 39 D7
Cambs. 55 B5
Haddington
E Loth 121 B8
Lincs 78 C2
Haddiscoe 69 E7
Haddon
Cambs. 65 E8
Ches E. 75 C6
Hade Edge 88 D2
Hademore 63 D5
Hadfield 87 E8
Hadham Cross. . . .41 C7
Hadham Ford 41 B7
Hadleigh
Essex 42 F4
Suff. 56 E4
Hadley
Telford 61 C6
Hadley End. 62 B5
Hadlow 29 E7
Hadlow Down 18 C2
Hadnall 60 C5
Hadstock 55 E6
Hady 76 B3
Hadzor 50 C4
Haffenden
Quarter 30 E2
Hafod-Dinbych. . .83 F8
Hafod-Iom 83 D8
Haggate 93 F8
Haggbeck 108 B4
Haggerston 123 E6
Haggrister 160 F5
Hagley
Hereford 49 E7
Worcs 62 F3
Hagworthingham 79 C6

Haigh
Gtr Man. 86 D4
S Yorks 88 C3
Haigh Moor 88 B3
Haighton Green . .93 F5
Haile 98 D2
Hailes 50 F5
Hailey
Herts. 41 C6
Oxon 38 C3
Hailsham 18 E2
Haimer 158 D3
Hainault 41 E7
Hainford 68 C5
Hainton 91 F5
Hairmyres 119 D6
Haisthorpe 97 C7
Hakin 44 E3
Halam 77 D6
Halbeath 128 F3
Halberton 10 C5
Halcro 158 D4
Hale
Gtr Man. 87 F5
Halton 86 F2
Hants 14 C2
Medway 30 B2
Hale Bank 86 F2
Halebarns. 87 F5
Hales
Norf 69 E6
Staffs 74 F4
Halesfield. 61 D7
Halesgate. 66 B3
Halesowen. 62 F3
Hales Place 30 D5
Hale Street. 29 E7
Halesworth 57 B7
Halewood. 86 F2
Halford
Shrops 60 F4
Warks 51 E7
Halfpenny Furze. .32 C3
Halfpenny Green .62 E2
Halfway
Carms. 46 F5
Carms. 47 F7
W Berks 26 C2
Halfway Bridge. . .16 B3
Halfway House . . .60 C3
Halfway Houses . .30 B3
Halifax. 87 B8
Halket 118 D4
Halkirk 158 E3
Halkyn 73 B6
Hall 118 D4
Hallaton 64 E4
Hallatrow 23 D8
Hallbankgate. . . .109 D5
Hall Dunnerdale . .98 E4
Hallen 36 F2
Hall Green
W Mid 62 F5
W Yorks 88 C4
Hall Grove. 41 C5
Halliburton 122 E2
Hallin 148 C7
Halling 29 C8
Hallington
Lincs 91 F7
Northumb 110 B2
Halliwell 86 C5
Hall of
Tankerness. . . .159 H6
Hall of the Forest .60 F2
Halloughton 77 D6
Hallow 50 D3
Hallrule 115 C8
Halls 122 B2
Hall's Green. 41 B5
Hallthwaites 98 F3
Hallworthy 8 F3
Hallyburton
House. 134 F2
Hallyne 120 E4
Halmer End 74 E4
Halmore 36 D3
Halmyre Mains . .120 E4
Halnaker. 16 D3
Halsall 85 C4
Halse
Som. 11 B6
W Nhants 52 E3
Halsetown 2 C4
Halsham 91 B6
Halsinger 20 F4
Halstead
Essex 56 F2
Kent 29 C5
Leics 64 D4
Halstock 12 D3
Haltham 78 C5
Halton End 79 E6
Halton
Bucks 40 C1
Halton 86 F3
Lancs 92 C5
Northumb 110 C2
Wrex 73 F7
W Yorks 95 F6
Halton East 94 D3
Halton Gill 93 B8
Halton Holegate . .79 C7
Halton Lea Gate 109 D6
Halton West 93 D8
Haltwhistle 109 C7
Halvergate. 69 D7
Halwell 7 D5
Halwill 9 E6
Halwill Junction. . .9 D6
Ham
Devon 11 D7
Glos 36 E3
Highld 158 C4
Kent 31 D7
London 28 B2
Shetland 160 K1
Wilts 25 C8
Hambleden 39 F7
Hambledon
Hants 15 C7
Sur 27 E7
Hamble-le-Rice . .15 D5
Hambleton
Lancs 92 E3
N Yorks 95 F8
Hambridge 11 B8

Hambrook
S Glos 23 B8
W Sus 15 D8
Ham Common . . .13 B6
Hameringham. . . .79 C6
Hamerton 54 B2
Hametoun 160 K1
Ham Green
Hereford 50 E2
Kent 30 C2
N Som 23 B7
Worcs 50 C5
Hamilton 119 D7
Hammer 27 F6
Hammerpot 16 D4
Hammersmith. . . .28 B3
Hammerwich 62 D4
Hammerwood 28 F5
Hammond Street 41 D6
Hammoon 13 C6
Hamnavoe
Shetland 160 E6
Shetland 160 E6
Shetland 160 F6
Shetland 160 K5
Hampden Park . . .18 E3
Hamperden End . .55 F6
Hampnett 37 C7
Hampole 89 C6
Hampreston. 13 E8
Hampstead 41 F5
Hampstead
Norreys 26 B3
Hampsthwaite . . .95 D5
Hampton
London 28 C2
Shrops 61 F7
Worcs 50 E5
Hampton Bishop .49 F7
Hampton Heath . .73 E8
Hampton in
Arden. 63 F6
Hampton Loade . .61 F7
Hampton Lovett . .50 C3
Hampton Lucy . . .51 D7
Hampton on the
Hill 51 C7
Hampton Poyle . .39 C5
Hamrow 80 E5
Hamsey 17 C8
Hamsey Green. . .28 D4
Hamstall Ridware 62 C5
Hamstead
IoW. 14 E5
W Mid 62 E4
Hamstead
Marshall 26 C2
Hamsterley
Durham 110 D4
Durham 110 D4
Hamstreet 19 B7
Ham Street. 23 F7
Hamworthy 13 E7
Hanbury
Staffs 62 B5
Worcs 50 C4
Hanbury
Woodend 63 B5
Hanby 78 F3
Hanchurch 74 E5
Handbridge 73 C8
Handcross 17 B6
Handforth. 87 F6
Handley. 73 D8
Handsacre 62 C4
Handsworth
S Yorks 88 F5
W Mid 62 E4
Handy Cross. 9 B6
Hanford 75 E5
Hanging
Langford 24 F5
Hangleton 16 D4
Hanham 23 B8
Hankelow 74 E3
Hankerton 37 E6
Hankham 18 E3
Hanley 75 E5
Hanley Castle . . .50 E3
Hanley Child 49 C8
Hanley Swan 50 E3
Hanley William . .49 C8
Hanlith 94 C2
Hanmer 73 F8
Hannah. 79 B8
Hannington
Hants 26 D3
Swindon 38 E1
W Nhants 53 B6
Hannington Wick 38 E1
Hansel Village. . . .118 F3
Hanslope 53 E6
Hanthorpe 65 B7
Hanwell
London 40 F4
Oxon 52 E2
Hanwood 60 D4
Hanworth
London 28 B2
Norf 81 D7
Happendon 119 F8
Happisburgh 69 A6
Happisburgh
Common 69 B6
Hapsford. 73 B8
Hapton
Lancs 93 F7
Norf 68 E4
Harberton 7 D5
Harbertonford 7 D5
Harbledown 30 D5
Harborne 62 F4
Harborough
Magna 52 B2
Harbottle 117 D5
Harbury 51 D7
Harby
Leics 77 F7
Notts. 77 B8
Harcombe 11 E6
Harden
W Mid 62 D4
W Yorks 94 F3
Hardenhuish 24 B4
Hardgate
Aberds 141 D6
N Yorks 95 C5
Hardham 16 C4

Hardingham 68 D3
Hardingstone 53 D5
Hardington 24 D2
Hardington
Mandeville 12 C3
Hardington
Marsh. 12 D3
Hardley 14 D5
Hardley Street . . .69 D6
Hardmead 53 E7
Hardrow 100 E3
Hardstoft 76 C4
Hardway
Hants 15 D7
Som. 24 F2
Hardwick
Bucks 39 C8
Cambs. 54 D4
N Nhants 53 C6
Norf 67 C6
Norf 68 F5
Notts. 77 B6
Oxon 38 D3
Oxon 39 B5
W Mid 62 E4
Hardwicke
Glos 36 C4
Glos 37 B6
Hereford 48 E4
Hardy's Green. . . .43 B5
Hareby 79 C6
Harefield 40 E3
Hare Green 43 B6
Hare Hatch 27 B6
Harehills 95 F6
Harehope 117 B6
Haresceugh. 109 E6
Harescombe 37 C5
Haresfield 37 C5
Hareshaw 119 C8
Hareshaw Head . .116 F4
Hare Street 41 B6
Harewood 95 E6
Harewood End . . .36 B2
Harford
Carms. 46 E5
Devon 6 D4
Hargate 68 E4
Hargatewall. 75 B8
Hargrave
Ches W 73 C8
N Nhants 53 B8
Suff. 55 C8
Harker 108 C3
Harkland 160 E6
Harkstead 57 F5
Harlaston 63 C6
Harlaw House . . .141 B6
Harlaxton 77 F8
Harlech 71 D6
Harlequin 77 F6
Harlescott 60 C5
Harlesden 41 F5
Harleston
Devon 7 E5
Norf 68 F5
Suff. 56 D4
Harlestone 52 C5
Harle Syke 93 F8
Harley
Shrops 61 D5
S Yorks 88 E4
Harleyholm 120 F2
Harlington
C Beds. 53 F8
London 27 B8
S Yorks 89 D5
Harlosh 149 D7
Harlow. 41 C7
Harlow Hill
Northumb 110 C3
N Yorks 95 D5
Harlthorpe 96 F3
Harlton 54 D4
Harman's Cross . .13 F7
Harmby 101 F6
Harmer Green 41 C5
Harmer Hill 60 B4
Harmondsworth. .27 B8
Harmston 78 C2
Harnham 110 B3
Harnhill 37 D7
Harold Hill 41 E8
Haroldston West .44 D3
Haroldswick 160 B8
Harold Wood 41 E8
Harome 102 F4
Harpenden 40 C4
Harpford 11 E5
Harpham 97 C6
Harpley
Norf 80 E3
Worcs 49 C8
Harpole 52 C4
Harpsdale 158 E3
Harpswell 90 F3
Harpurhey 87 D6
Harpur Hill 75 B7
Harraby 108 D4
Harrapool 149 F11
Harrier 160 J1
Harrietfield 127 B8
Harrietsham 30 D2
Harrington
Cumb 98 B1
Lincs 79 B6
N Nhants 64 F4
Harringworth. 65 E6
Harris 146 E5
Harrogate 95 D6
Harrold 53 D7
Harrow 40 F4
Harrowbarrow 5 C8
Harrowden 53 E8
Harrowgate Hill 101 C7
Harrow on the
Hill 40 F4
Harrow Street. . . .56 F3
Harrow Weald. . . .40 E4
Harston
Cambs. 54 D5
Leics 77 F8
Harswell 96 E4
Hart 111 F7
Hartburn
Northumb 117 F6

Hartburn continued
Stockton 102 C2
Hart Common 86 D4
Hartest 56 D2
Hartfield. 29 F5
Hartford
Cambs. 54 B3
Ches W 74 B3
Hartfordbridge. . .27 D5
Hartford End 42 C2
Hartforth 101 D6
Harthill
Ches W 74 D2
N Lanark 120 C2
S Yorks 89 F5
Hart Hill 40 B4
Hartington 75 C8
Hartland 8 B4
Hartlebury 50 B3
Hartlepool 111 F7
Hartley
Kent 18 B4
Kent 29 C7
Northumb 111 B6
W&F 100 D2
Hartley Westpall 26 D4
Hartley Wintney .27 D5
Hartlip 30 C2
Hartoft End 103 E5
Harton
N Yorks 96 C3
Shrops 60 F4
T&W 111 C6
Hartpury. 36 B4
Hartshead 88 B2
Hartshill 63 E7
Hartshorne 63 B7
Hartsop. 99 C6
Hart Station 111 F7
Hartwell 53 D5
Hartwood 119 D8
Harvieston 126 F4
Harvington. 51 E5
Harvington Cross .51 E5
Harwell 38 F4
Harwich 57 F6
Harwood
Durham 109 F8
Gtr Man. 86 C5
Harwood Dale . . .103 E7
Harworth 89 F7
Hasbury 62 F3
Hascombe 27 E7
Haselbech 52 B5
Haselbury
Plucknett 12 C2
Haseley 51 C7
Haselor 51 D6
Hasfield 37 B5
Hasguard 44 E3
Haskayne 85 D4
Hasketon 57 D6
Hasland 76 C3
Haslemere 27 F7
Haslingden 87 B5
Haslingfield 54 D5
Haslington 74 D4
Hassall 74 D4
Hassall Green . . .74 D4
Hassell Street . . .30 E4
Hassendean 115 B8
Hassingham 69 D6
Hassocks 17 C6
Hassop 76 B2
Hastigrow 158 D4
Hastingleigh 30 E4
Hastings 18 E5
Hastingwood 41 D7
Hastoe 40 D2
Haswell 111 E6
Haswell Plough. .111 E6
Hatch
C Beds. 54 E2
Hants 26 D4
Wilts 13 B7
Hatch
Beauchamp 11 B8
Hatch End 40 E4
Hatch Gate 26 C5
Hatch Green 11 C8
Hatching Green . .40 C4
Hatchmere 74 B2
Hatcliffe 91 D6
Hatfield
Hereford 49 D7
Herts. 41 D5
S Yorks 89 D7
Worcs 50 D3
Hatfield Broad
Oak. 41 C8
Hatfield Garden
Village 41 D5
Hatfield Heath . . .41 C8
Hatfield Hyde 41 C5
Hatfield Peverel. .42 C3
Hatfield
Woodhouse 89 D7
Hatford 38 E3
Hatherden 25 D8
Hatherleigh 9 D7
Hathern 63 B8
Hatherop 38 D1
Hathersage 88 F3
Hathershaw 87 D7
Hatherton
Ches E 74 D3
Staffs 62 D3
Hatley St George 54 D3
Hatt 5 C8
Hattingley 26 F4
Hatton
Aberds 153 E10
Derbys 63 B6
Lincs 78 B4
Shrops 60 E4
Warks 51 C7
Warr 86 F3
Hatton Castle . . .153 D7
Hattoncrook 141 B7
Hatton Heath 73 C8
Hatton of
Fintray 141 C7
Haugh
E Ayrs 112 B4
Gtr Man. 87 C7

Haugh *continued*
Lincs. 79 B7
Haugham. 91 F7
Haugh Head. . . 117 B6
Haughley. 56 C4
Haughley Green. . 56 C4
Haugh of Glass . . 152 E4
Haugh of Urr . . 106 C5
Haughs of
Clinterty . . . 141 C7
Haughton
Notts. 77 B6
Shrops. 60 B3
Shrops. 61 C5
Shrops. 61 D7
Shrops. 61 E6
Staffs. 62 B2
Haughton Castle 110 B2
Haughton Green . 87 E7
Haughton Moss . 74 D2
Haultwick. . . 41 B6
Haunn
Argyll. 146 G6
W Isles. 148 G2
Haunton. 63 C6
Hauxley. 117 D8
Hauxton. 54 D5
Havant. 15 D8
Haven. 49 D6
Haven Bank . . 78 D5
Haven Side . . . 91 B5
Havenstreet. . . 15 E6
Havercroft . . . 88 C4
Haverfordwest
= *Hwlffordd* . . 44 D4
Haverhill. 55 E7
Haverigg. 92 B1
Havering-atte-
Bower. 41 E8
Haveringland . . 81 E7
Haversham . . . 53 E6
Haverthwaite . . 99 F5
Haverton Hill . . 102 B2
Hawarden
= *Penarlâg* . . 73 C7
Hawcoat. 92 B2
Hawen. 46 E2
Hawes. 100 F3
Hawes' Green . . 68 E5
Hawes Side . . 92 F3
Hawford. 50 C3
Hawick. 115 C8
Hawkchurch . . 11 D8
Hawkedon. . . 55 D8
Hawkenbury
Kent. 18 B2
Kent. 30 E2
Hawkeridge . . 24 D3
Hawkerland . . 11 F5
Hawkesbury
S Glos. 36 F4
Warks. 63 F7
Hawkesbury
Upton. 36 F4
Hawkes End . . 63 F7
Hawk Green . . 87 F7
Hawkhill. 117 C8
Hawkhurst . . 18 B4
Hawkinge. . . 31 F6
Hawkley. 15 B8
Hawkridge . . 21 F7
Hawkshead . . 99 E5
Hawkshead Hill . . 99 E5
Hawksland . . 119 F8
Hawkswick . . 94 B2
Hawksworth
Notts. 77 E7
W Yorks. 94 E4
W Yorks. 95 F5
Hawkwell . . 42 E4
Hawley
Hants. 27 D6
Kent. 29 B6
Hawling. 37 B7
Hawnby. 102 F3
Haworth. 94 F3
Hawstead . . 56 D2
Hawthorn
Durham. 111 E7
Rhondda . . 35 F5
Wilts. 24 C3
Hawthorn Hill
Brack. 27 B6
Lincs. 78 D5
Hawthorpe . . 65 B7
Hawton. 77 D7
Haxby. 96 D2
Haxey. 89 D8
Haydock . . 86 E3
Haydon. 12 C4
Haydon Bridge 109 C8
Haydon Wick . . 37 F8
Haye. 5 C8
Hayes
London. 28 C5
London. 40 F4
Hayfield
Derbys. 87 F8
Fife. 128 E4
Hay Green . . 66 C5
Hayhill. 112 C4
Hayhillock . . 135 E5
Hayle. 2 C4
Haynes. 53 E8
Haynes Church
End. 53 E8
Hay-on-Wye
= *Y Gelli Gandryll* . . 48 E4
Hayscastle . . 44 C4
Hayscastle Cross 44 C4
Hayshead . . 135 E6
Hay Street . . 41 B6
Hayton
Aberdeen . . 141 D8
Cumb. 107 D8
Cumb. 108 D5
E Yorks. 96 E4
Notts. 89 F8
Hayton's Bent . . 60 F5
Haytor Vale . . 7 F5
Haywards Heath . . 17 B7
Haywood . . 89 C6
Haywood Oaks . . 77 D6
Hazelbank . . 119 E8
Hazelbury Bryan . 12 D5

Hazeley. 26 D5
Hazel Grove . . 87 F7
Hazelhurst . . 87 D7
Hazelslade . . 62 C4
Hazel Street . . 18 B3
Hazelton. 37 C7
Hazelton Walls . 128 B5
Hazelwood . . 76 E3
Hazlemere . . 40 E1
Hazlerigg . . 110 B5
Hazlewood . . 94 D3
Hazon. 117 D7
Heacham . . 80 D2
Headbourne
Worthy. 26 F2
Headbrook . . 48 D5
Headcorn . . 30 E2
Headingley . . 95 F5
Headington . . 39 D5
Headlam . . 101 C6
Headless Cross . . 50 C5
Headley
Hants. 26 C3
Hants. 27 F6
Sur. 28 D3
Head of Muir . . 127 F7
Headon. 77 B7
Heads. 119 E7
Heads Nook . . 108 D4
Heage. 76 D3
Healaugh
N Yorks. 95 E7
N Yorks. 101 E5
Heald Green . . 87 F6
Heale
Devon. 20 E5
Som. 23 E8
Healey
Gtr Man. 87 C6
Northumb . . 110 D3
N Yorks. 101 F6
Healing. 91 C6
Heamoor . . 2 C3
Heanish . . 146 G3
Heanor. 76 E4
Heanton
Punchardon . . 20 F4
Heapham . . 90 F2
Hearthstane . . 114 B4
Heasley Mill . . 21 F6
Heast. 149 G11
Heath
Cardiff. 22 B3
Derbys. 76 C4
Heath and Reach . 40 B2
Heathcote . . 75 C8
Heath End
Hants. 26 C3
Sur. 27 E6
Warks. 51 C7
Heather. 63 C7
Heatherfield . . 149 D9
Heathfield
Devon. 7 B6
E Sus. 18 C2
Som. 11 B6
Heathhall . . 107 B6
Heath Hayes . . 62 C4
Heath Hill . . 61 C7
Heath House . . 23 E6
Heathrow Airport 27 B8
Heathstock . . 11 D7
Heathton . . 62 E2
Heath Town . . 62 E3
Heatley. 86 F5
Heaton
Lancs. 92 C4
Staffs. 75 C6
T&W. 111 C5
W Yorks. 94 F4
Heaton Moor . . 87 E6
Heaverham . . 29 D6
Heaviley . . 87 F7
Heavitree . . 10 E4
Hebburn . . 111 C6
Hebden . . 94 C3
Hebden Bridge . . 87 B7
Hebron
Anglesey . . 82 C4
Carms. 32 B2
Northumb . . 117 F7
Heck. 114 F3
Heckfield . . 26 C5
Heckfield Green . . 57 B5
Heckfordbridge . . 43 B5
Heckington . . 78 E4
Heckmondwike . . 88 B3
Heddington . . 24 C4
Heddle. 159 G4
Heddon-on-the-
Wall. 110 C4
Hedenham . . 69 E6
Hedge End . . 15 C5
Hedgerley . . 40 F2
Hedging. 11 B8
Hedley on the
Hill. 110 D3
Hednesford . . 62 C4
Hedon. 91 B5
Hedsor. 40 F2
Hedworth . . 111 C6
Hegdon Hill . . 49 D7
Heggerscales . . 100 D2
Heglibister . . 160 H5
Heighington
Darl. 101 B7
Lincs. 78 C3
Heights of Brae . . 151 E8
Heights of
Kinlochewe . . 150 E3
Heilam. 156 C7
Heiton. 122 F3
Hele
Devon. 10 D4
Devon. 20 E4
Helensburgh . . 145 E11
Helford. 3 D6
Helford Passage . . 3 D6
Helions
Bumpstead . . 55 E7
Hellaby. 89 E6
Helland
Corn. 5 B5
Som. 11 B7
Hellandbridge . . 5 B5
Hellesdon . . 68 C5
Hellidon. 52 D3
Hellifield . . 93 D8
Hellingly . . 18 D2
Hellington . . 69 D6

Hellister . . 160 J5
Helm. 117 E7
Helmdon . . 52 E3
Helmingham . . 57 D5
Helmington Row 110 F4
Helmsdale . . 157 H13
Helmshore . . 87 B5
Helmsley . . 102 F4
Helperby . . 95 C7
Helperthorpe . . 97 B5
Helpringham . . 78 E4
Helpston . . 65 D8
Helsby. 73 B8
Helsey. 79 B8
Helston. 3 D5
Helstone . . 8 F2
Helton. 99 B7
Helwith Bridge . . 93 C8
Hemblington . . 69 C6
Hemel
Hempstead . . 40 D3
Hemingbrough . . 96 F2
Hemingby . . 78 B5
Hemingford
Abbots. 54 B3
Hemingford Grey 54 B3
Hemingstone . . 57 D5
Hemington
Leics. 63 B8
N Nhants. 65 F7
Som. 24 D2
Hemley. 57 E6
Hemlington . . 102 C3
Hemp Green . . 57 C7
Hempholme . . 97 D6
Hempnall . . 68 E5
Hempnall Green . . 68 E5
Hempriggs
House. 158 F5
Hempstead
Essex. 55 F7
Medway . . 29 C8
Norf. 69 B7
Norf. 81 D7
Hempsted . . 37 C5
Hempton
Norf. 80 E5
Oxon. 52 F2
Hemsby . . 69 C7
Hemswell . . 90 E3
Hemswell Cliff . . 90 F3
Hemsworth . . 88 C5
Hemyock . . 11 C6
Henbury
Bristol. 23 B7
Ches E. 75 B5
Hendon
London. 41 F5
T&W. 111 D7
Hendre. 73 C5
Hendre-ddu . . 83 E8
Hendreforgan . . 34 F3
Hendy. 33 D6
Heneglwys . . 82 D4
Hen-feddau fawr . . 45 F4
Henfield
Essex. 17 C6
S Sus. 17 C6
Henford. 9 E5
Henghurst . . 19 B6
Hengoed
Caerph. 35 E5
Powys. 48 D4
Shrops. 73 F6
Hengrave . . 56 C2
Henham . . 41 B8
Heniarth . . 59 D8
Henlade. 11 B7
Henley
Shrops. 49 B7
Som. 23 F6
Suff. 57 D5
W Sus. 16 B2
Henley-in-Arden . . 51 C6
Henley-on-
Thames. 39 F7
Henley's Down . . 18 D4
Henllan
Ceredig. 46 E2
Denb. 72 C4
Henllan Amgoed . . 32 B2
Henllys. 35 E6
Henlow. 54 F2
Hennock . . 10 F3
Henny Street . . 56 F2
Henryd. 83 D7
Henry's Moat . . 32 B1
Hensall. 89 B6
Henshaw . . 109 C7
Hensingham . . 98 C1
Henstead . . 69 F7
Henstridge . . 12 C5
Henstridge Ash . . 12 B5
Henstridge Marsh 12 B5
Henton
Oxon. 39 D7
Som. 23 E6
Henwood . . 5 B7
Heogan . . 160 J6
Heol-las. 33 E7
Heol Senni . . 34 B3
Heol-y-Cyw . . 34 F3
Hepburn . . 117 B6
Hepple. 117 D5
Hepscott . . 117 F8
Heptonstall . . 87 B7
Hepworth
Suff. 56 B3
W Yorks. 88 D2
Herbrandston . . 44 E3
Hereford. 49 E7
Heriot. 121 D6
Hermiston . . 120 B4
Hermitage
Borders. 115 E8
Dorset. 12 D4
W Berks. 26 B3
W Sus. 15 D8
Hermon
Anglesey . . 82 E3
Carms. 32 B2
Carms. 46 F2
Pembs. 45 F4
Herne. 31 C6
Herne Bay . . 31 C6
Herner. 9 B7
Hernhill. 30 C4
Herodsfoot . . 5 C7
Herongate . . 42 E2
Heronsford . . 104 A5

Herriard. 26 E4
Herringfleet . . 69 E7
Herringswell . . 55 B8
Hersden. 31 C6
Hersham
Corn. 8 D4
Sur. 28 C2
Herstmonceux . . 18 D3
Herston. 159 J5
Hertford. 41 C6
Hertford Heath . . 41 C6
Hertingfordbury . . 41 C6
Hesketh Bank . . 86 B2
Hesketh Lane . . 93 E6
Hesket
Newmarket . . 108 F3
Heskin Green . . 86 C3
Hesleden . . 111 F7
Hesleyside . . 116 F4
Heslington . . 96 D2
Hessay. 95 D8
Hessenford . . 5 D8
Hessett. 56 C3
Hessle. 90 B4
Hest Bank . . 92 C4
Heston. 28 B2
Hestwall . . 159 G3
Heswall. 85 F3
Hethe. 39 B5
Hethersett . . 68 D4
Hethersgill . . 108 C4
Hethpool . . 116 B4
Hett. 111 F5
Hetton. 94 D2
Hetton-le-Hole 111 F6
Hetton Steads . . 123 F6
Heugh. 110 B3
Heugh-head . . 140 C2
Heveningham . . 57 B7
Hever. 29 E5
Heversham . . 99 F6
Hevingham . . 81 E7
Hewas Water . . 3 B8
Hewelsfield . . 36 D2
Hewish
N Som. 23 C6
Som. 12 D2
Heworth . . 96 D2
Hexham . . 110 C2
Hextable . . 29 B6
Hexton. 54 F2
Hexworthy . . 6 B4
Hey. 93 E8
Heybridge
Essex. 42 D4
Essex. 42 D4
Heybridge Basin . . 42 D4
Heybrook Bay . . 6 E3
Heydon
Cambs. 54 E5
Norf. 81 E7
Heydour. 78 F3
Heyford Park *Oxon* 39 B5
Heylipol . . 146 G2
Heylor. 160 E4
Heysham . . 92 C4
Heyshott . . 16 C2
Heyside. 87 D7
Heytesbury . . 24 E4
Heythrop . . 38 B3
Heywood
Gtr Man. 87 C6
Wilts. 24 D3
Hibaldstow . . 90 D3
Hickleton . . 89 D5
Hickling
Norf. 69 B7
Notts. 64 B3
Hickling Green . . 69 B7
Hickling Heath . . 69 B7
Hickstead . . 17 B6
Hidcote Boyce . . 51 E6
High Ackworth . . 88 C5
Higham
Derbys. 76 D3
Kent. 29 B8
Lancs. 93 F8
Suff. 55 C8
Suff. 56 F4
Higham Dykes . . 110 B4
Higham Ferrers . . 53 C7
Higham Gobion . . 54 F2
Higham on the
Hill. 63 E7
Highampton . . 9 D6
Higham Wood . . 29 E6
High Angerton . . 117 F6
High Bankhill . . 109 E5
High Barnes . . 111 D6
High Beach . . 41 E7
High Bentham . . 93 C6
High Bickington . . 9 B8
High Birkwith . . 93 B7
High Blantyre . . 119 D6
High
Bonnybridge . . 119 B8
High Bradfield . . 88 E3
High Bray . . 21 F5
Highbridge
Highld. 136 F4
Som. 22 E5
Highbrook . . 28 F4
High Brooms . . 29 E6
High Bullen . . 9 B7
Highburton . . 88 C2
Highbury . . 23 E8
High Buston . . 117 D8
High Callerton . . 110 B4
High Catton . . 96 D3
Highclere . . 26 C2
Highcliffe . . 14 E3
High Cogges . . 38 D3
High Coniscliffe 101 C7
High Cross
Hants. 15 B8
Herts. 41 C6
High Easter . . 42 C2
High Eggborough 89 B6
High Ellington . . 101 F6
Higher Ansty . . 13 D5
Higher Ashton . . 10 F3
Higher Ballam . . 92 F3
Higher Bartle . . 92 F4
Higher Boscaswell . . 2 C2
Higher
Burwardsley . . 74 D2
Higher Clovelly . . 8 B5

Higher End . . 86 D3
Higher Kinnerton 73 C7
Higher
Penwortham . . 86 B3
Higher Town . . 2 E1
Higher Walreddon . . 6 B2
Higher Walton
Lancs. 86 B3
Warr. 86 F3
Higher Wheelton 86 B4
Higher Whitley . . 86 F4
Higher Wincham . . 74 B3
Higher Wych . . 73 E8
High Etherley . . 101 B6
Highfield
E Yorks. 96 F3
Gtr Man. 86 D5
N Yorks. 118 E3
S Yorks. 88 F4
T&W. 110 D4
Highfields
Cambs. 54 D4
Northumb . . 123 D5
Highgate
Glasgow. 118 C5
Norf. 80 E3
High Garrett . . 42 B3
Highgate. 41 F5
High Grange . . 110 F4
High Green
Norf. 68 D4
S Yorks. 88 E4
Worcs. 50 E3
High Halden . . 19 B5
High Halstow . . 29 B8
High Ham . . 23 F6
High Harrington . . 98 B2
High Hatton . . 61 B6
High Hawsker . . 103 D7
High Hesket . . 108 E4
High Hesleden . . 111 F7
High Hoyland . . 88 C3
High Hunsley . . 97 F5
High Hurstwood . . 17 B8
High Hutton . . 96 C3
High Ireby . . 108 F2
High Kelling . . 81 C7
High Kilburn . . 95 B8
High Lands . . 101 B6
High Lane
Ches E. 75 C5
Derbys. 88 F5
High Lane
Gtr Man. 87 F7
Worcs. 49 C8
High Laver . . 41 D8
Highlane
Derbys. 88 F4
Ches E. 75 C5
Highlaws . . 107 E8
Highleadon . . 36 B4
High Legh . . 86 F5
Highleigh . . 16 E2
High Leven . . 102 C2
Highley. 61 F7
High Littleton . . 23 D8
High Lorton . . 98 B3
High Marishes . . 96 B4
High Marnham . . 77 B8
High Melton . . 89 D6
High Mickley . . 110 C3
High Mindork . . 105 D7
Highmoor Cross . . 39 F7
Highmoor Hill . . 36 F1
Highnam . . 36 C4
Highnam Green . . 36 B4
High Newton . . 99 F6
High Newton-by-the-
Sea. 117 B8
High Nibthwaite . . 98 F4
High Offley . . 61 B7
High Ongar . . 42 D1
High Onn . . 62 C2
High Roding . . 42 C2
High Row . . 108 F3
High Salvington . . 16 D5
High Sellafield . . 98 D2
High Shaw . . 100 E3
High Spen . . 110 D4
Highsted. 30 C3
High Stoop . . 110 E4
High Street
Corn. 4 D4
Kent. 18 B4
Suff. 56 E2
Suff. 57 B8
Suff. 57 D8
Highstreet Green . . 55 F8
High Street
Green. 56 D4
Hightae. 107 B7
High Throston . . 111 F7
Hightown
Ches E. 75 C5
Mers. 85 D3
Hightown Green . . 56 D3
High Toynton . . 79 C6
High Trewitt . . 117 D6
High Valleyfield 128 F2
Highway. 24 B5
Highweek . . 7 B6
High Westwood 110 D4
Highworth . . 38 E2
High Wray . . 99 E5
High Wych . . 41 C7
High Wycombe . . 40 E1
Hilborough . . 67 D8
Hilcote. 76 D4
Hilcott. 25 D6
Hildenborough . . 29 E6
Hilden Park . . 29 E6
Hildersham . . 55 E6
Hilderstone . . 75 F6
Hilderthorpe . . 97 C7
Hilfield. 12 D4
Hilgay. 67 E6

Hill End
Durham. 110 F3
Fife. 128 E2
N Yorks. 94 D3
Hillerton . . 10 E2
Hillesden . . 39 B6
Hillesley . . 36 F4
Hillfarance . . 11 B6
Hillhead
Aberds. 152 E5
Devon. 7 D7
S Ayrs. 112 C4
Hill Head
Hants. 15 D6
Northumb . . 110 C2
Hillhead of
Auchentumb . . 153 C9
Hillhead of
Cocklaw . . 153 D10
Hillhouse . . 121 D8
Hilliclay . . 158 D3
Hillingdon . . 40 F3
Hillington
Glasgow. 118 C5
Norf. 80 E3
Hill Mountain . . 44 E4
Hillockhead
Aberds. 140 C3
Aberds. 140 D2
Hill of Beath . . 128 E3
Hill of Fearn . . 151 D11
Hill of
Mountblairy . . 153 C6
Hill Ridware . . 62 C4
Hillside
Aberds. 141 E8
Angus. 135 C7
Mers. 85 C4
Orkney. 159 J5
Shetland . . 160 G6
Hillswick . . 160 F4
Hill Top
Durham. 100 B4
Hants. 14 D5
N Yorks. 62 E3
W Yorks. 88 C4
Hill View . . 13 E7
Hillway. 15 F7
Hillwell . . 160 M5
Hilmarton . . 24 B5
Hilperton . . 24 D3
Hilsea. 15 D7
Hilston. 97 F8
Hilton
Aberds. 153 E9
Cambs. 54 C3
Derbys. 76 F2
Dorset. 13 D5
Durham. 101 B6
Highld. 151 C10
Shrops. 61 E7
Stockton . . 102 C2
W&F. 100 B2
Hilton of
Cadboll . . 151 D11
Himbleton . . 50 D4
Himley. 62 E2
Hincaster . . 99 F7
Hinckley . . 63 E8
Hinderclay . . 56 B4
Hinderton . . 73 B7
Hinderwell . . 103 C5
Hindford . . 73 F7
Hindhead . . 27 F6
Hindley. 86 D4
Hindley Green . . 86 D4
Hindlip. 50 D3
Hindolveston . . 81 E6
Hindon. 24 F4
Hindringham . . 81 D5
Hingham . . 68 D3
Hinstock . . 61 B6
Hintlesham . . 56 E4
Hinton
Hants. 14 E3
Hereford. 48 F5
S Glos. 24 B2
Shrops. 60 D4
W Nhants. 52 D3
Hinton Ampner . . 15 B6
Hinton Blewett . . 23 D7
Hinton
Charterhouse . . 24 D2
Hinton-in-the-
Hedges. 52 F3
Hinton Martell . . 13 D8
Hinton on the
Green. 50 E5
Hinton Parva . . 38 F2
Hinton St George . . 12 C2
Hinton St Mary . . 13 C5
Hinton Waldrist . . 38 E3
Hints
Shrops. 49 B8
Staffs. 63 D5
Hinwick . . 53 C7
Hinxhill. 30 E4
Hinxton. 55 E5
Hinxworth . . 54 E3
Hipperholme . . 88 B2
Hipswell . . 101 E6
Hirael. 83 D5
Hiraeth. 32 B2
Hirn. 141 D6
Hirnant. 59 B7
Hirst
N Lanark. 119 C8
Northumb . . 117 F8
First Courtenay . . 89 B7
Hirwaen. 72 C5
Hirwaun . . 34 D3
Hiscott. 9 B7
Histon. 54 C5
Hitcham . . 56 D3
Hitchin. 40 B4
Hither Green . . 28 B4
Hittisleigh . . 10 E2
Hive. 96 F3
Hixon. 62 B4
Hoaden. 31 D6
Hoaldalbert . . 35 B7
Hoar Cross . . 62 B5
Hoarwithy . . 36 B2
Hoath. 31 C6
Hobarris . . 48 B5
Hobbister . . 159 H4
Hobkirk . . 115 C8

Hobson. 110 D4
Hoby. 64 C3
Hockering . . 68 C3
Hockerton . . 77 D7
Hockley. 42 E4
Hockley Heath . . 51 B6
Hockliffe . . 40 B2
Hockwold cum
Wilton. 67 F7
Hockworthy . . 10 C5
Hoddesdon . . 41 D6
Hoddlesden . . 86 B5
Hoddomcross . . 107 B8
Hoddom Mains . . 107 B8
Hodgeston . . 32 E1
Hodley. 59 E8
Hodnet. 61 B6
Hodthorpe . . 76 B5
Hoe
Hants. 15 C6
Norf. 68 C2
Hoe Gate . . 15 C7
Hoff. 100 C1
Hoggard's Green 56 D2
Hoggeston . . 39 B8
Hogha
Gearraidh . . 148 A2
Hoghton . . 86 B4
Hognaston . . 76 D2
Hog Patch . . 27 E6
Hogsthorpe . . 79 B8
Holbeach . . 66 B3
Holbeach Bank . . 66 B3
Holbeach Clough 66 B3
Holbeach Drove . . 66 C3
Holbeach Hurn . . 66 B3
Holbeach
St Johns . . 66 C3
Holbeach
St Marks . . 79 F7
Holbeach
St Matthew . . 79 F7
Holbeck
Notts. 76 B5
W Yorks. 95 F5
Holbeck
Woodhouse . . 76 B5
Holberrow Green 50 D5
Holbeton . . 6 D4
Holborn . . 41 F6
Holbrook
Derbys. 76 B3
Suff. 57 F5
S Yorks. 88 F5
Holburn . . 123 F6
Holbury . . 14 D5
Holcombe
Devon. 7 B7
Som. 23 E8
Holcombe Rogus . 11 C5
Holcot. 53 C5
Holden. 93 E7
Holdenby . . 52 C4
Holdenhurst . . 14 E2
Holdgate . . 61 F5
Holdingham . . 78 E3
Holditch . . 11 D8
Holefield . . 122 F4
Holehouses . . 74 B4
Hole-in-the-Wall . . 36 B3
Holemoor . . 9 D6
Holestane . . 113 E8
Holford. 22 E3
Holgate. 95 D8
Holker. 92 B3
Holkham . . 80 C4
Hollacombe . . 9 D5
Holland
Orkney. 159 C5
Orkney. 159 F7
Holland Fen . . 78 E5
Holland-on-Sea . . 43 C8
Hollandstoun . . 159 C8
Hollee. 108 C2
Hollesley . . 57 E7
Hollicombe . . 7 C6
Hollingbourne . . 30 D2
Hollington
Derbys. 76 F2
E Sus. 18 D4
Staffs. 75 F7
Hollington Grove 76 F2
Hollingworth . . 87 E8
Hollins. 87 D6
Hollinsclough . . 75 C7
Hollins Green . . 86 E4
Hollins Lane . . 92 D4
Hollinwood
Gtr Man. 87 D7
Shrops. 74 F2
Hollocombe . . 9 C8
Holloway . . 76 D3
Hollowell . . 52 B4
Hollow Meadows . . 88 F3
Holly Bush
Caerph. 35 D5
E Ayrs. 112 C3
Worcs. 50 F2
Holly End . . 66 D4
Holly Green . . 50 E3
Hollym. 91 B7
Hollywood . . 51 B5
Holmbridge . . 88 D2
Holmbury
St Mary . . 28 E2
Holmbush . . 4 D5
Holmcroft . . 62 B3
Holme
Cambs. 65 F8
Cumb. 99 F7
Notts. 77 D8
N Yorks. 102 F1
W&F. 92 B5
W Yorks. 88 D2
Holme Chapel . . 87 B6
Holme Green . . 95 E8
Holme Hale . . 67 D8
Holme Lacy . . 49 F7
Holme Marsh . . 48 D5
Holme next the
Sea. 80 C3
Holme-on-Spalding-
Moor. 96 F4
Holme on the
Wolds. 97 E5
Holme
Pierrepont . . 77 F6
Holmer. 49 E7
Holmer Green . . 40 E2

Holme
St Cuthbert . . 107 E8
Holmes Chapel . . 74 C4
Holmesfield . . 76 B3
Holmeswood . . 86 C2
Holmewood . . 76 C4
Holme Wood . . 94 F4
Holmfirth . . 88 D2
Holmhead
Dumfries . . 113 F7
E Ayrs. 113 B5
Holmisdale . . 148 D6
Holmpton . . 91 B7
Holmrook . . 98 E2
Holmsgarth . . 160 J6
Holmwrangle . . 108 E5
Holne. 6 C5
Holnest . . 12 D4
Holsworthy . . 8 D5
Holsworthy
Beacon. 9 D5
Holt
Dorset. 13 D8
Norf. 81 D6
Wilts. 24 C3
Wrex. 73 D8
Worcs. 50 C3
Holt End
Hants. 26 F4
Worcs. 51 C5
Holt Fleet . . 50 C3
Holt Heath . . 50 C3
Holton
Oxon. 39 D6
Som. 12 B4
Suff. 57 B7
Holton cum
Beckering . . 90 F5
Holton Heath . . 13 E7
Holton le Clay . . 91 D6
Holton le Moor . . 90 E4
Holton St Mary . . 56 F4
Holt Park . . 95 F5
Holwell
Dorset. 12 C5
Herts. 54 F2
Leics. 64 B4
Oxon. 38 D2
Holwick . . 100 B4
Holworth . . 13 F5
Holybourne . . 26 E5
Holy Cross . . 50 B4
Holyhead
= *Caergybi* . . 82 C2
Holy Island . . 123 E7
Holymoorside . . 76 C3
Holyport . . 27 B6
Holystone . . 117 D5
Holytown . . 119 C7
Holywell
Cambs. 54 B4
Corn. 4 D2
Dorset. 12 D3
E Sus. 18 F2
Northumb . . 111 B6
Holywell
= *Treffynnon* . . 73 B5
Holywell Green . . 87 C8
Holywell Lake . . 11 B6
Holywell Row . . 55 B8
Holywood . . 114 F2
Homer. 61 D6
Homersfield . . 69 F5
Hom Green . . 36 B2
Homington . . 14 B2
Honeyborough . . 44 E4
Honeybourne . . 51 E6
Honeychurch . . 9 D8
Honey Hill . . 30 C5
Honey Street . . 25 C6
Honey Tye . . 56 F3
Honiley. 51 B7
Honing. 69 B6
Honingham . . 68 C4
Honington
Lincs. 78 E2
Suff. 56 B3
Warks. 51 E7
Honiton . . 11 D6
Honley. 88 C2
Hood Green . . 88 D4
Hooe
E Sus. 18 E3
Plym. 6 D3
Hooe Common . . 15 B8
Hoo Green . . 86 F5
Hook
E Yorks. 89 B8
Hants. 15 D6
Hants. 26 D5
London. 28 C2
Pembs. 44 D4
Wilts. 37 F7
Hooke. 12 E3
Hookgate . . 74 F4
Hook Green
Kent. 18 B3
Kent. 29 C7
Hook Norton . . 51 F8
Hookway . . 10 E3
Hookwood . . 28 E3
Hoole. 73 C8
Hooley. 28 D3
Hoop. 36 D2
Hoo St Werburgh . . 29 B8
Hooton. 73 B7
Hooton Levitt . . 89 E6
Hooton Pagnell . . 89 D5
Hooton Roberts . . 89 E5
Hope
Derbys. 88 F2
Devon. 6 F4
Highld. 156 B7
Powys. 60 D2
Shrops. 60 D3
Staffs. 75 D8
Hope = *Yr Hôb* . . 73 D7
Hope Bagot . . 49 B7
Hope Bowdler . . 60 E4
Hope End Green . . 42 B2
Hope Green . . 87 F7
Hopeman . . 152 B1
Hope Mansell . . 36 C3
Hopesay . . 60 F3
Hope's Green . . 42 F3
Hope under
Dinmore . . 49 D7
Hopley's Green . . 48 D5

Hopperton . . 95 D7
Hop Pole . . 65 C8
Hopstone . . 61 E7
Hopton
Shrops. 60 B3
Shrops. 61 B5
Staffs. 62 B3
Suff. 56 B3
Hopton
Cangeford . . 60 F5
Hopton Castle . . 49 B5
Hoptonheath . . 49 B5
Hopton on Sea . . 69 D8
Hopton Wafers . . 49 B8
Hopwas . . 63 D5
Hopwood
Gtr Man. 87 D6
Worcs. 50 B5
Horam. 18 D2
Horbling . . 78 F4
Horbury . . 88 C3
Horcott . . 38 D1
Horden . . 111 E7
Horderley . . 60 F4
Hordle. 14 E3
Hordley . . 73 F7
Horeb
Carms. 33 B6
Carms. 33 D5
Ceredig. 46 E2
Horfield . . 23 B8
Horham . . 57 B6
Horkesley Heath . . 43 B5
Horkstow . . 90 C3
Horley
Oxon. 52 E2
Sur. 28 E3
Hornblotton
Green. 23 F7
Hornby
Lancs. 93 C5
N Yorks. 101 E7
N Yorks. 102 D1
Horncastle . . 79 C5
Hornchurch . . 41 F8
Horncliffe . . 122 E5
Horndean
Borders. 122 E4
Hants. 15 C8
Horndon . . 6 B3
Horndon on the
Hill. 42 F2
Horne. 28 E4
Horniehaugh . . 134 C4
Horning . . 69 C6
Horninghold . . 64 E5
Horninglow . . 63 B6
Horningsea . . 55 C5
Horningsham . . 24 E3
Horningtoft . . 80 E5
Hornsby . . 108 D5
Horns Corner . . 18 C4
Horns Cross
Devon. 9 B5
E Sus. 18 C5
Hornsea . . 97 E8
Hornsea Bridge . . 97 E8
Hornsey . . 41 F6
Hornton . . 51 E8
Horrabridge . . 6 C3
Horringer . . 56 C2
Horringford . . 15 F6
Horse Bridge . . 75 D6
Horsebridge
Devon. 6 B2
Hants. 25 F8
Horsebrook . . 62 C2
Horsehay . . 61 D6
Horseheath . . 55 E7
Horsehouse . . 101 F5
Horsell. 27 D7
Horseman's
Green. 73 E8
Horseway . . 66 F4
Horsey. 69 B7
Horsford . . 68 C4
Horsforth . . 94 F5
Horsham
Worcs. 50 D2
W Sus. 28 F2
Horsham St Faith 68 C5
Horsington
Lincs. 78 C5
Som. 12 B5
Horsley
Derbys. 76 E3
Glos. 37 E5
Northumb . . 110 C3
Northumb . . 116 F4
Horsley Cross . . 43 B7
Horsleycross
Street. 43 B7
Horsleyhill . . 115 C8
Horsleyhope . . 110 E3
Horsley
Woodhouse . . 76 E3
Horsmonden . . 29 E7
Horspath . . 39 D5
Horstead . . 69 C5
Horsted Keynes . . 17 B7
Horton
Bucks. 40 C2
Dorset. 13 D8
Lancs. 93 D6
S Glos. 36 F4
Shrops. 60 B4
Som. 11 C8
Staffs. 75 D6
Swansea . . 33 F5
Wilts. 25 C5
Windsor . . 27 B8
Horton-cum-
Studley . . 39 C5
Horton Green . . 73 E8
Horton Heath . . 15 C5
Horton in
Ribblesdale . . 93 B8
Horton Kirby . . 29 C6
Hortonlane . . 60 C4
Horwich . . 86 C4
Horwich End . . 87 F8
Horwood . . 9 B7
Hose. 64 B4
Hoselaw . . 122 F4
Hoses. 98 E4
Hosh. 127 B7
Hosta. 148 A2

Hoswick 160 L6
Hotham 96 F4
Hothfield 30 E3
Hoton 64 B2
Houbie 160 D8
Houdston 112 E1
Hough
  Ches E 74 D4
  Ches E 75 B5
Hougham 77 E8
Hough Green 86 F2
Hough-on-the-
  Hill 78 E2
Houghton
  Cambs 54 B3
  Cumb 108 D4
  Hants 25 F8
  Pembs 44 E4
  W Sus 16 C4
Houghton
  Conquest 53 E8
Houghton Green
  E Sus 19 C6
  Warr 86 E4
Houghton-le-
  Side 101 B7
Houghton-le-
  Spring 111 E6
Houghton on the
  Hill 64 D3
Houghton Regis .40 B3
Houghton
  St Giles 80 D5
Houlland
  Shetland 160 F7
  Shetland 160 H5
Houlsyke 103 D5
Houlton Warks . . .52 B3
Hound 15 D5
Hound Green 26 D5
Houndslow 122 E2
Houndwood 122 C4
Hounslow 28 B2
Hounslow Green .42 C2
Housay 160 F8
House of
  Daviot 151 G10
House of
  Glenmuick 140 E2
Housetter 160 E5
Houss 160 K5
Houston 118 C4
Houstry 158 G3
Houton 159 H4
Hove 17 D6
Hoveringham 77 E6
Hoveton 69 C6
Hovingham 96 B2
How 108 D5
Howbrook 88 E4
How Caple 49 F8
Howden
  Borders 116 B2
  E Yorks 89 B8
Howden-le-
  Wear 110 F4
Howe
  Highld 158 D5
  Norf 69 D5
  N Yorks 101 F8
Howe Bridge 86 D4
Howe Green 42 D3
Howell 78 E4
How End 53 E8
Howe of
  Teuchar 153 D7
Howe Street
  Essex 42 C2
  Essex 55 F7
Howey 48 D2
Howgate 120 D5
How Green 29 E5
Howick 117 C8
Howle
  Durham 101 B5
  Telford 61 B6
Howlett End 55 F6
Howley 11 D7
Hownam 116 C3
Hownam Mains . .116 B3
Howpasley 115 D6
Howsham
  N Lincs 90 D4
  N Yorks 96 C3
Howslack 114 D3
Howtel 122 F4
Howton 35 B8
Howtown 99 C6
Howwood 118 C3
Hoxne 57 B5
Hoy 159 H3
Hoylake 85 F3
Hoyland 88 D4
Hoylandswaine . .88 D3
Hubberholme 94 B2
Hubbert's Bridge .79 E5
Huby
  N Yorks 95 C8
  N Yorks 95 E5
Hucclecote 37 C5
Hucking 30 D2
Hucknall 76 E5
Huddersfield 88 C2
Huddington 50 D4
Hudswell 101 D6
Huggate 96 D4
Hugglescote 63 C8
Hughenden
  Valley 40 E1
Hughley 61 E5
Hugh Town 2 E4
Huish
  Devon 9 C7
  Wilts 25 C6
Huish
  Champflower . . .11 B5
Huish Episcopi . .12 B2
Huisinis 154 F4
Hulcott 40 C1
Hulland 76 E2
Hulland Ward 76 E2
Hullavington 37 F5
Hullbridge 42 E4
Hulme 87 E6
Hulme End 75 D8
Hulme Walfield . . .74 C5
Hulverstone 14 F4
Hulver Street 69 F7

Humber 49 D7
Humber Bridge . . .90 B4
Humberston 91 D7
Humbie 121 C7
Humbleton
  E Yorks 97 F8
  Northumb 117 B5
Humby 78 F3
Hume 122 E3
Humshaugh 110 B2
Huna 158 C5
Huncoat 93 F7
Huncote 64 E2
Hundalee 116 C2
Hunderthwaite . . .100 B4
Hundleby 79 C6
Hundle Houses . . .79 D5
Hundleton 44 E4
Hundon 55 E8
Hundred Acres . . .15 C6
Hundred End 86 B2
Hundred House . . .48 D3
Hungarton 64 D3
Hungerford
  Hants 14 C2
  W Berks 25 C8
Hungerford
  Newtown 25 B8
Hungladder 149 A8
Hunmanby 97 B6
Hunmanby
  Moor 97 B7
Hunningham 51 C8
Hunny Hill 15 F5
Hunsdon 41 C7
Hunsingore 95 D7
Hunslet 95 F6
Hunsonby 109 F5
Hunspow 158 C4
Hunstanton 80 C2
Hunstanworth 110 E2
Hunsterson 74 E3
Hunston
  Suff 56 C3
  W Sus 16 D2
Hunstrete 23 C8
Hunt End 50 C5
Hunter's Quay . . .145 F10
Hunthill Lodge . . .134 B4
Huntingdon 54 B3
Huntingfield 57 B7
Huntingtower 24 F3
Huntington
  E Loth 121 B7
  Hereford 48 D4
  Staffs 62 C3
  York 96 D2
Huntingtower 128 B2
Huntley 36 C4
Huntly 152 E5
Huntlywood 122 E2
Hunton
  Kent 29 E8
  N Yorks 101 E6
Hunt's Corner 68 F3
Hunt's Cross 86 F2
Huntsham 10 B5
Huntspill 22 E5
Huntworth 22 F5
Hunwick 110 F4
Hunworth 81 D6
Hurdsfield 75 B6
Hurley
  Warks 63 E6
  Windsor 39 F8
Hurlford 118 F4
Hurliness 159 K3
Hurn 14 E2
Hurn's End 79 E7
Hursley 14 B5
Hurst
  N Yorks 101 D5
  Som 12 C2
  Wokingham 27 B5
Hurstbourne
  Priors 26 E2
Hurstbourne
  Tarrant 25 D8
Hurst Green
  E Sus 18 C4
  Lancs 93 F6
Hurstpierpoint . . .17 C6
Hurst Wickham . .17 C6
Hurstwood 93 F8
Hurtmore 27 E7
Hurworth
  Place 101 D7
Hury 100 C4
Husabost 148 C7
Husbands
  Bosworth 64 F3
Husborne
  Crawley 53 F7
Huthwaite 95 B8
Hutchwns 21 B7
Huthwaite 76 D4
Huttoft 79 B8
Hutton
  Borders 122 D5
  Essex 42 E2
  E Yorks 97 D6
  Lancs 86 B2
  N Som 22 D5
  W&F 99 B6
Hutton Buscel . . .103 F7
Hutton Conyers . .95 B6
Hutton
  Cranswick 97 D6
Hutton End 108 F4
Hutton Gate 102 C3
Hutton Henry 111 F7
Hutton-le-Hole . . .103 E5
Hutton Magna . . .101 C6
Hutton Roof
  Lincs 90 F3
  Norf 69 B6
  Suff 56 B2
Ingham Corner . . .69 B6
Ingleborough 66 C4
Ingleby
  Derbys 63 B7
  Lincs 77 B8
Ingleby
  Arncliffe 102 D2
Ingleby Barwick .102 C2
Ingleby
  Greenhow 102 D3
Inglemire 97 F6

Hwlffordd
  = Haverfordwest . 44 D4
Hycemoor 98 F2
Hyde
  Glos 37 D5
  Gtr Man 87 E7
  Hants 14 C2
Hyde Heath 40 D2
Hydestile 27 E7
Hylton Castle 111 D6
Hyndford
  Bridge 120 E2
Hynish 146 H2
Hyssington 60 E3
Hythe
  Hants 14 D5
  Kent 19 B8
Hythe End 27 B8
Hythie 153 C10

I

Ibberton 13 D5
Ible 76 D2
Ibsley 14 D2
Ibstock 63 C8
Ibstone 39 E7
Ibthorpe 25 D8
Ibworth 26 D3
Ichrachan 125 B6
Ickburgh 67 E8
Ickenham 40 F3
Ickford 39 D6
Ickham 31 D6
Ickleford 54 F2
Icklesham 19 D5
Ickleton 55 E5
Icklingham 55 B8
Ickwell Green 54 E2
Icomb 38 B2
Idbury 38 C2
Ide 10 E3
Ideford 7 B6
Ide Hill 29 D5
Iden 19 C6
Iden Green
  Kent 18 B4
  Kent 18 B5
Idle 94 F4
Idlicote 51 E7
Idmiston 25 F6
Idole 33 C5
Idridgehay 76 E2
Idrigill 149 B8
Idstone 38 F2
Idvies 135 E5
Iffley 39 D5
Ifield 28 F3
Ifold 27 F8
Iford 17 D8
Ifton Heath 73 F7
Ightfield 74 F2
Ightham 29 D6
Iken 57 D8
Ilam 75 D8
Ilchester 12 B3
Ilderton 117 B6
Ilford 41 F7
Ilfracombe 20 E4
Ilkeston 76 E4
Ilketshall
  St Andrew 69 F6
Ilketshall
  St Lawrence 69 F6
Ilketshall
  St Margaret 69 F6
Ilkley 94 E4
Illey 62 F3
Illingworth 87 B8
Illogan 3 B5
Illston on the Hill .64 E4
Ilmer 39 D7
Ilmington 51 E7
Ilminster 11 C8
Ilsington 7 B5
Ilston 33 E6
Ilton
  N Yorks 94 B4
  Som 11 C8
Imachar 143 D9
Imeraval 142 D4
Immingham 91 C5
Impington 54 C5
Ince 73 B8
Ince Blundell 85 D4
Ince in
  Makerfield 86 D3
Inchbare 135 C6
Inchberry 152 C3
Inchbraoch 135 D7
Incheril 150 E3
Inchgrundle 134 B4
Inchina 150 B2
Inchinnan 118 C4
Inchkinloch 157 E8
Inchlaggan 136 D4
Inchlumpie 151 D8
Inchmore 150 G6
Inchnacardoch
  Hotel 137 C6
Inchnadamph 156 G5
Inch of Arnhall . . .135 B6
Inchree 130 C4
Inchture 128 B4
Inchyra 128 B3
Indian Queens . . .4 D4
Inerval 142 E2
Ingatestone 42 E2
Ingbirchworth 88 D3
Ingestre 62 B3
Ingham
  Lincs 90 F3

Inglesbatch 24 C2
Inglesham 38 E2
Ingleton
  Durham 101 B6
  N Yorks 93 B6
Inglewhite 92 E5
Ingliston 120 B4
Ingoe 110 B3
Ingol 92 F5
Ingoldisthorpe . . .80 D2
Ingoldmells 79 C8
Ingoldsby 78 F3
Ingon 51 D7
Ingram 117 C6
Ingrow 94 F3
Ings 99 E6
Ingst 36 F2
Ingworth 81 E7
Inham's End 66 E2
Inkberrow 50 D5
Inkpen 25 C8
Inkstack 158 C4
Inn 99 D6
Innellan 145 F10
Innerleithen 121 F6
Innerleven 128 D5
Innermessan 104 C4
Innerwick
  E Loth 122 B3
  Perth 132 E2
Innis Chonain . . .125 C7
Insch 140 B5
Inshore 156 C6
Inskip 92 F4
Intake 89 D6
Inver
  Aberds 139 E8
  Highld 151 C11
  Perth 133 E7
Inverailort 147 C10
Inveraldie 134 F4
Inverallign 149 C13
Inverallochy 153 B10
Inveran 151 B8
Inveraray 125 E6
Inverarish 149 E10
Inverarity 134 E4
Inverarnan 126 C2
Inverasdale 155 J13
Inverbeg 126 E2
Inverbervie 135 B8
Inverboyndie 153 B6
Inverbroom 150 C4
Invercassley 156 J7
Invercauld
  House 139 E7
Inverchaolain . . .145 F9
Invercharnan 131 E5
Inverchoran 150 F5
Invercreran 130 E4
Inverdruie 138 C5
Inverebrie 153 E9
Invereck 145 E10
Inverernan
  House 140 C2
Invereshie
  House 138 D4
Inveresk 121 B6
Inverey 139 F6
Inverfarigaig 137 B8
Invergarry 137 D6
Invergelder 139 E8
Invergeldie 127 B6
Invergordon 151 E10
Invergowrie 134 F3
Inverguseran 149 H12
Inverhadden 132 D3
Inverharroch 152 E3
Inverherive 126 B2
Inverie 147 B10
Inverinan 125 D5
Inverinate 136 B2
Inverkeilor 135 E6
Inverkeithing 128 F3
Inverkeithny 153 D6
Inverkip 118 B2
Inverkirkaig 156 H3
Inverlael 150 C4
Inverlochlarig 126 C3
Inverlochy
  Argyll 125 C7
  Highld 131 B5
Inverlussa 144 E5
Inver Mallie 136 F4
Invermark
  Lodge 140 F3
Invermoidart 147 D9
Invermoriston 137 C7
Invernaver 157 C10
Inverneill 145 E7
Inverness 151 G9
Invernettie 153 D11
Invernoaden 125 F7
Inveroran Hotel .131 E6
Inverpolly
  Lodge 156 H3
Inverquharity 134 D4
Inverquhomery .153 D10
Inverroy 137 F5
Inversanda 130 D3
Invershiel 136 C2
Invershin 151 B8
Inversnaid Hotel .126 D2
Inveruglas 126 D2
Inveruglass 138 D4
Inverurie 141 B6
Invervar 132 E3
Inverythan 153 D7
Inwardleigh 9 E7
Inworth 42 C4
Iochdar 148 D2
Iping 16 B2
Ipplepen 7 C6
Ipsden 39 F6
Ipsley 51 C5
Ipstones 75 D7
Ipswich 57 E5
Irby 85 F3
Irby in the Marsh .79 C7
Irby upon
  Humber 91 D5
Irchester 53 C7
Ireby
  Cumb 108 F2

Ireby continued
  Lancs 93 B6
Ireland
  Orkney 159 H4
  Shetland 160 L5
Ireland's Cross . . .74 E4
Ireleth 92 B2
Ireshopeburn 109 F8
Irlam 86 E5
Irnham 65 B7
Iron Acton 36 F3
Ironbridge 61 D6
Iron Cross 51 D5
Irongray 107 B6
Ironmacannie 106 B3
Ironside 153 C8
Ironville 76 D4
Irstead 69 B6
Irthington 108 C4
Irthlingborough . .53 B7
Irton 103 F8
Irvine 118 F3
Isauld 157 C12
Isbister
  Orkney 159 F3
  Orkney 159 G4
  Shetland 160 D5
  Shetland 160 G7
Isfield 17 C8
Isham 53 B6
Isle Abbotts 11 B8
Isle Brewers 11 B8
Isleham 55 B7
Isle of Whithorn .105 F8
Isleornsay 149 G12
Islesburgh 160 G5
Islesteps 107 B6
Isleworth 28 B2
Isley Walton 63 B8
Islibhig 154 E4
Islington 41 F6
Islip
  N Nhants 53 B7
  Oxon 39 C5
Istead Rise 29 C7
Isycoed 73 D8
Itchen 14 C5
Itchen Abbas 26 F3
Itchen Stoke 26 F3
Itchingfield 16 B5
Itchington 36 F3
Itteringham 81 D7
Itton 9 E8
Itton Common 36 E1
Ivegill 108 E4
Iver 40 F3
Iver Heath 40 F3
Iveston 110 D4
Ivinghoe 40 C2
Ivinghoe Aston . . .40 C2
Ivington 49 D6
Ivington Green . . .49 D6
Ivybridge 6 D4
Ivy Chimneys 41 D7
Ivychurch 19 C7
Ivy Cross 13 B6
Ivy Hatch 29 D6
Iwade 30 C3
Iwerne Courtney or
  Shroton 13 C6
Iwerne Minster . .13 C6
Ixworth 56 B3
Ixworth Thorpe . .56 B3

J

Jack Hill 94 D5
Jack in the Green .10 E5
Jacksdale 76 D4
Jackstown 153 E7
Jacobstow 8 E3
Jacobstowe 9 D7
Jameston 32 E1
Jamestown
  Dumfries 115 E6
  Highld 150 F7
  W Dunb 126 F2
Jarrow 111 C6
Jarvis Brook 18 C2
Jasper's Green . . .42 B3
Java 124 B3
Jawcraig 119 B8
Jaywick 43 C7
Jealott's Hill 27 B6
Jedburgh 116 B2
Jeffreyston 32 D1
Jellyhill 119 B6
Jemimaville 151 E10
Jersey Farm 40 D4
Jesmond 111 C5
Jevington 18 E2
Jockey End 40 C3
Johnby 108 F4
John o'Groats . . .158 C5
John's Cross 18 C4
Johnshaven 135 C7
Johnston
  E Renfs 118 C4
  Pembs 44 D4
Johnstonebridge
  . . . . .114 E3
Johnstown
  Carms 33 C5
  Wrex 73 E7
Joppa
  Edin 121 B6
  S Ayrs 112 C4
Jordans 40 E2
Jordanthorpe 88 F4
Jump 88 D4
Jumpers Green . .14 E2
Juniper Green . . .120 C4
Jurby East 84 C3
Jurby West 84 C3

K

Kaber 100 C2
Kaimend 120 E2
Kaimes 121 C5
Kalemouth 116 B3
Kames
  Argyll 124 D4
  Argyll 145 F8
  E Ayrs 113 B6
Kea 3 B7

Keadby 90 C2
Keal Cotes 79 C6
Kearsley 87 D5
Kearstwick 99 F8
Kearton 100 E4
Kearvaig 156 B5
Keckwick 86 F3
Keddington 91 F7
Kedington 55 E8
Kedleston 76 E3
Keelby 91 C5
Keele 74 E5
Keeley Green 53 E8
Keeston 44 D4
Keevil 24 D4
Kegworth 63 B8
Kehelland 2 B5
Keig 140 C5
Keighley 94 E3
Keil 130 D3
Keilarsbrae 127 E7
Keilhill 153 C7
Keillmore 144 E5
Keillor 134 E2
Keillour 127 B8
Keills 142 B5
Keils 144 G4
Keinton
  Mandeville 23 F7
Keir Mill 113 E8
Keisby 65 B7
Keiss 158 D5
Keith 152 C4
Keith Inch 153 D11
Keithock 135 C6
Kelbrook 94 E2
Kelby 78 E3
Keld
  N Yorks 100 D3
  W&F 99 C7
Keldholme 103 F5
Kelfield
  N Lincs 90 D2
  N Yorks 95 F8
Kelham 77 D7
Kellan 147 G8
Kellas
  Angus 134 F4
  Moray 152 C1
Kellaton 7 F6
Kelleth 100 D1
Kelleythorpe 97 D5
Kelling 81 C6
Kellingley 89 B6
Kellington 89 B6
Kelloholm 113 C7
Kelly 9 F5
Kelly Bray 5 B8
Kelmarsh 52 B5
Kelmscot 38 E2
Kelsale 57 C7
Kelsall 74 C2
Kelsall Hill 74 C2
Kelshall 54 F4
Kelsick 107 D8
Kelso 122 F3
Kelstedge 76 C3
Kelstern 91 E6
Kelston 24 C2
Keltneyburn 132 E4
Kelton 107 B6
Kelty 128 E3
Kelvedon 42 C4
Kelvedon
  Hatch 42 E1
Kelvin 119 D6
Kelvinside 119 C5
Kelynack 2 C2
Kemback 129 C6
Kemberton 61 D7
Kemble 37 E6
Kemerton 50 F4
Kemeys
  Commander 35 D7
Kemnay 141 C6
Kempley 36 B3
Kempsey 50 E3
Kempsford 38 E1
Kemps Green 51 B6
Kempshott 26 D4
Kempston 53 E8
Kempston
  Hardwick 53 E8
Kempton 60 F3
Kemp Town 17 D7
Kemsing 29 D6
Kemsley 30 C3
Kenardington 19 B6
Kenchester 49 E6
Kencot 38 D2
Kendal 99 E7
Kendoon 113 F6
Kendray 88 D4
Kenfig 34 F2
Kenfig Hill 34 F2
Kenilworth 51 B7
Kenknock 132 F1
Kenley
  London 28 D4
  Shrops 61 D5
Kenmore
  Highld 149 C12
  Perth 132 E4
Kenn
  Devon 10 F4
  N Som 23 C6
Kennacley 154 H6
Kennacraig 145 G7
Kennerleigh 10 D3
Kennet 127 E8
Kennethmont 140 B4
Kennett 55 C7
Kennford 10 F4
Kenninghall 68 F3
Kenninghall
  Heath 68 F3
Kennington
  Kent 30 E4
  Oxon 39 D5
Kennoway 129 D5
Kenny Hill 55 B7
Kennythorpe 96 C3
Kenovay 146 G2
Kensaleyre 149 C9
Kensington 28 B3
Kensworth 40 C3

Kensworth
  Common 40 C3
Kentallen 130 D4
Kentchurch 35 B8
Kentford 55 C8
Kentisbeare 11 D5
Kentisbury 20 E5
Kentisbury Ford . .20 E5
Kentmere 99 D6
Kenton
  Devon 10 F4
  Suff 57 C5
  T&W 110 C5
Kenton
  Bankfoot 110 C5
Kentra 147 E9
Kenwick 73 F8
Kenwyn 3 B7
Keoldale 156 C6
Keppanach 130 C4
Keppoch 136 B2
Keprigan 143 G7
Kepwick 102 E2
Kerchesters 122 F3
Keresley 63 F7
Kernborough 7 E5
Kerne Bridge 36 C2
Kerris 2 D3
Kerry 59 F8
Kerrycroy 145 G10
Kerrysdale 149 A13
Kerry's Gate 49 F5
Kersall 77 C7
Kersey 56 E4
Kershopefoot . . .115 F7
Kersoe 50 F4
Kerswell 11 D5
Kerswell Green . . .50 E3
Kesgrave 57 E6
Kessingland 69 F8
Kessingland
  Beach 69 F8
Kessington 119 B5
Kestle 3 B8
Kestle Mill 4 D3
Keston 28 C5
Keswick
  Cumb 98 B4
  Norf 68 D5
  Norf 81 D9
Ketley 61 C6
Ketley Bank 61 C6
Ketsby 79 B6
Kettering 53 B6
Ketteringham 68 D4
Kettins 134 F2
Kettlebaston 56 D3
Kettlebridge 128 D5
Kettleburgh 57 C6
Kettlehill 128 D5
Kettleholm 107 B8
Kettleness 103 C6
Kettlesing 95 D5
Kettlesing
  Bottom 94 D5
Kettlesing Head . .94 D5
Kettlestone 81 D5
Kettlethorpe 77 B8
Kettletoft 159 E7
Kettlewell 94 B2
Ketton 65 D6
Kew 28 B2
Kew Bridge 28 B2
Kewstoke 22 C5
Kexbrough 88 D4
Kexby
  Lincs 90 F2
  York 96 D3
Key Green 75 C5
Keyham 64 D3
Keyhaven 14 E4
Keyingham 91 B6
Keymer 17 C7
Keynsham 23 C8
Keysoe 53 C8
Keysoe Row 53 C8
Keyston 53 B8
Keyworth 77 F6
Kibblesworth 110 D5
Kibworth
  Beauchamp 64 E3
Kibworth
  Harcourt 64 E3
Kidbrooke 28 B5
Kiddemore Green .62 D2
Kidderminster . . .50 B3
Kiddington 38 B4
Kidlington 38 C4
Kidmore End 26 B4
Kidsgrove 74 D5
Kidstones 100 F4
Kidwelly
  = Cydweli 33 D5
Kiel Crofts 124 B5
Kielder 116 E2
Kierfiold Ho 159 G3
Kilbagie 127 F8
Kilbarchan 118 C4
Kilbeg 149 H11
Kilberry 144 G6
Kilbirnie 118 D3
Kilbride
  Argyll 124 C4
  Argyll 124 C4
  Highld 149 F10
Kilburn
  Angus 134 C3
  Derbys 76 E3
  London 41 F5
  N Yorks 95 B8
Kilby 64 E3
Kilchamaig 145 G7
Kilchattan 144 D2
Kilchattan Bay . .145 H10
Kilchenzie 143 F7
Kilcheran 124 B4
Kilchiaran 142 B3
Kilchoan
  Argyll 124 D3
  Highld 146 E7
Kilchoman 142 B3

Kilchrenan 125 C6
Kilconquhar 129 D6
Kilcot 36 B3
Kilcoy 151 F8
Kilcreggan 145 E11
Kildale 102 D4
Kildalloig 143 G8
Kildary 151 D10
Kildermorie
  Lodge 151 D8
Kildonan
  Highld 151 C9
Kildonan
  Bridge 127 F8
Kildonan
  Lodge 157 G12
Kildonnan 146 C7
Kildrummy 140 C3
Kildwick 94 E3
Kilfinan 145 E8
Kilfinnan 137 E5
Kilgetty 32 D2
Kilgwrrwg
  Common 36 E1
Kilham
  E Yorks 97 C6
  Northumb 122 F4
Kilkenneth 146 G2
Kilkerran 143 G8
Kilkhampton 8 C5
Killamarsh 89 F5
Killay 33 E7
Killbeg 147 G9
Killean 143 D7
Killearn 126 F4
Killen 151 F9
Killerby 101 C6
Killichonan 132 D2
Killiechonate 136 F5
Killiechronan 147 G8
Killiecrankie 133 C6
Killiemor 146 H7
Killiemore
  House 146 J7
Kililan 150 H2
Killimster 158 E5
Killin 132 F2
Killinallan 142 A4
Killinghall 95 D5
Killington 99 F8
Killingworth 111 B5
Killin Lodge 137 D8
Killmahumaig . . .144 D6
Killochyett 121 E7
Killocraw 143 E7
Killundine 147 G8
Kilmacolm 118 C3
Kilmaha 124 E5
Kilmahog 126 D5
Kilmalieu 130 D2
Kilmaluag 149 A9
Kilmany 129 B5
Kilmarie 149 G10
Kilmarnock 118 F4
Kilmaron Castle .129 C5
Kilmartin 124 F4
Kilmaurs 118 E4
Kilmelford 124 D4
Kilmeny 142 B4
Kilmersdon 23 D8
Kilmeston 15 B6
Kilmichael 143 F7
Kilmichael
  Glassary 145 D7
Kilmichael of
  Inverlussa 144 E6
Kilmington
  Devon 11 E7
  Wilts 24 F2
Kilmonivaig 136 F4
Kilmorack 150 G7
Kilmore
  Argyll 124 C4
  Highld 149 H11
Kilmory
  Argyll 144 F6
  Highld 147 D8
  Highld 149 H8
  N Ayrs 143 F10
Kilmuir
  Highld 148 D3
  Highld 149 A8
  Highld 151 D10
  Highld 151 G9
Kilmun
  Argyll 124 D5
  Argyll 145 E10
Kilncadzow 119 E8
Kilndown 18 B4
Kilnhurst 89 E5
Kilninian 146 G6
Kilninver 124 C4
Kiln Pit Hill 110 D3
Kilnsea 91 C8
Kilnsey 94 C2
Kilnwick 97 E5
Kilnwick Percy . . .96 D4
Kiloran 144 D2
Kilpatrick 143 F10
Kilpeck 49 F6
Kilphedir 157 H12
Kilpin 89 B8
Kilpin Pike 89 B8
Kilrenny 129 D7
Kilsby 52 B3
Kilspindie 128 B4
Kilsyth 119 B7
Kiltarlity 151 G8
Kilton
  Notts 77 B5
  Som 22 E3
Kilton Thorpe 102 C4
Kilvaxter 149 B8
Kilve 22 E3
Kilvington 77 E7
Kilwinning 118 E3
Kimberley
  Norf 68 D3
  Notts 76 E5
Kimberworth 88 E5
Kimblesworth . . .111 E5
Kimble Wick 39 D8
Kimbolton
  Cambs 53 C8
  Hereford 49 C7
Kimcote 64 F2
Kimmeridge 13 G7
Kimmerston 123 F5
Kimpton
  Hants 25 E7
  Herts 40 C4

Kinbrace 157 F11
Kinbuck 127 D6
Kincaple 129 C6
Kincardine
  Fife 127 F8
  Highld 151 C9
Kincardine
  Bridge 127 F8
Kincardine
  O'Neil 140 E4
Kinclaven 134 F1
Kincorth 141 D8
Kincorth House 151 E13
Kincraig 138 D4
Kincraigie 133 E6
Kindallachan 133 E6
Kineton
  Glos 37 B7
  Warks 51 D8
Kinfauns 128 B3
Kingairloch 130 D2
Kingarth 145 H9
Kingcoed 35 D8
King Edward 153 C7
Kingerby 90 E4
Kingham 38 B2
Kingholm Quay . .107 B6
Kinghorn 128 F4
Kingie 136 D4
Kinglassie 128 E4
Kingoodie 128 B5
King's Acre 49 E6
Kingsand 6 D2
Kingsbarns 129 C7
Kingsbridge
  Devon 6 E5
  Som 21 F8
King's Bromley . .62 C5
Kingsburgh 149 C8
Kingsbury
  London 41 F5
  Warks 63 E6
Kingsbury
  Episcopi 12 B2
King's Caple 36 B2
Kingsclere 26 D3
King's Cliffe 65 E7
Kingscote 37 E5
Kingscott 9 C7
King's Coughton . .51 D5
Kingscross 143 F11
Kingsdon 12 B3
Kingsdown 31 E7
Kingseat 128 E3
Kingsey 39 D7
Kingsfold 28 F2
Kingsford
  E Ayrs 118 E4
  Worcs 62 F2
Kingsforth 90 C4
Kingsgate 31 B7
Kingsheanton 20 F4
King's Heath 62 F4
Kings Hedges . . .55 C5
King's Hill 29 D7
Kingshouse
  Hotel 131 D6
Kingside Hill 107 D8
Kingskerswell 7 C6
Kingskettle 128 D5
Kingsland
  Anglesey 82 C2
  Hereford 49 C6
Kings Langley . . .40 D3
Kingsley
  Ches W 74 B2
  Hants 27 F5
  Staffs 75 E7
Kingsley Green . .27 F6
Kingsley Holt 75 E7
Kingsley Park 53 C5
King's Lynn 67 B6
King's Meaburn . .99 B8
King's Mills 73 E7
Kingsmuir
  Angus 134 E4
  Fife 129 D7
Kings Muir 121 F5
King's Newnham .52 B2
King's Newton . . .63 B7
Kingsnorth 19 B7
King's Norton
  Leics 64 D3
  W Mid 51 B5
King's Nympton . .9 C8
King's Pyon 49 D6
King's Ripton 54 B3
King's
  Somborne 25 F8
King's Stag 12 C5
King's Stanley . . .37 D5
King's Sutton 52 F2
Kingstanding 62 E4
King Sterndale . . .75 B7
King's Thorn 49 F7
Kingsthorpe 53 C5
Kingston
  Cambs 54 D4
  Devon 6 E4
  Dorset 13 D5
  Dorset 13 G7
  E Loth 129 F7
  Hants 14 D2
  IoW 15 F5
  Kent 31 D5
  Moray 152 B3
Kingston
  Bagpuize 38 E4
Kingston Blount . .39 E7
Kingston by Sea .17 D6
Kingston Deverill .24 F3
Kingstone
  Hereford 49 F6
  Som 11 C8
  Staffs 62 B4
Kingston Gorse . .16 D4
Kingston Lisle . . .38 F3
Kingston
  Maurward 12 E5
Kingston near
  Lewes 17 D7
Kingston on Soar .64 B2
Kingston Russell .12 E3
Kingston St Mary .11 B7

Kingston
Seymour 23 C6
Kingston upon Hull 90 B4
Kingston upon Thames 28 C2
Kingston Vale 28 B3
Kingstown 108 D3
King's Walden 40 B4
Kingswear 7 D6
Kingswells 141 D7
Kingswinford 62 F2
Kingswood
Bucks 39 C6
Glos 36 E4
Hereford 48 D4
Kent 30 D2
Powys 60 D2
S Glos 23 B8
Sur 28 D3
Warks 51 B6
Kings Worthy 26 F2
Kingthorpe 78 B4
Kington
Hereford 48 D4
Worcs 50 D4
Kington Langley 24 A4
Kington Magna 13 B5
Kington St Michael 24 B4
Kingussie 138 D3
Kingweston 23 F7
Kininvie House 152 D3
Kinkell Bridge 127 C8
Kinknockie 153 D10
Kinlet 61 F7
Kinloch
Fife 128 C4
Highld 146 B6
Highld 149 G11
Highld 156 F6
Perth 133 E8
Perth 134 E2
Kinlochan 130 C2
Kinlochard 126 D3
Kinlochbeoraid 147 C11
Kinlochbervie 156 D5
Kinlocheil 130 B3
Kinlochewe 150 E3
Kinloch Hourn 136 D2
Kinloch Laggan 137 F8
Kinlochleven 131 C5
Kinloch Lodge 157 D8
Kinlochmoidart 147 D10
Kinlochmorar 147 B11
Kinlochmore 131 C5
Kinloch Rannoch 132 D3
Kinlochspelve 124 C2
Kinloid 147 C9
Kinloss 151 E13
Kinmel Bay 72 A3
Kinmuck 141 C7
Kinmundy 141 C7
Kinnadie 153 D9
Kinnaird 128 B4
Kinnaird Castle 135 D6
Kinneff 135 B8
Kinnelhead 114 D3
Kinnell 135 D6
Kinnerley 60 B3
Kinnersley
Hereford 48 E5
Worcs 50 E3
Kinnerton 48 C4
Kinnesswood 128 D3
Kinninvie 101 B5
Kinnordy 134 D3
Kinoulton 77 F6
Kinross 128 D3
Kinrossie 134 F1
Kinsbourne Green 40 C4
Kinsey Heath 74 E3
Kinsham
Hereford 49 C5
Worcs 50 F4
Kinsley 88 C5
Kinson 13 E8
Kintbury 25 C8
Kintessack 151 E12
Kintillo 128 C3
Kintocher 140 C4
Kinton
Hereford 49 B6
Shrops 60 C3
Kintore 141 C6
Kintour 142 C5
Kintra
Argyll 142 D4
Argyll 146 J6
Kintraw 124 E4
Kinuachdrachd 124 F3
Kinveachy 138 C5
Kinver 62 F2
Kippax 95 F7
Kippen 127 E5
Kippford or Scaur 106 D5
Kirbister
Orkney 159 F7
Orkney 159 H4
Kirbuster 159 F3
Kirby Bedon 69 D5
Kirby Bellars 64 C4
Kirby Cane 69 E6
Kirby Cross 43 B8
Kirby Grindalythe 96 C5
Kirby Hill
N Yorks 95 C6
N Yorks 101 D6
Kirby Knowle 102 F2
Kirby-le-Soken 43 B8
Kirby Misperton 96 B3
Kirby Muxloe 64 D2
Kirby Row 69 E6
Kirby Sigston 102 E2
Kirby Underdale 96 D4
Kirby Wiske 102 F1
Kirdford 16 B4
Kirk 158 E4
Kirkabister 160 K6
Kirkandrews 106 E3

Kirkandrews upon Eden 108 D3
Kirkbampton 108 D3
Kirkbean 107 D6
Kirk Bramwith 89 C7
Kirkbride 108 D2
Kirkbuddo 135 E5
Kirkburn
Borders 121 F5
E Yorks 97 D5
Kirkburton 88 C2
Kirkby
Lincs 90 E4
Mers 86 E2
N Yorks 102 D3
Kirkby Fleetham 101 E7
Kirkby Green 78 D3
Kirkby-in-Ashfield 76 D5
Kirkby-in-Furness 98 F4
Kirkby la Thorpe 78 E3
Kirkby Lonsdale 93 B6
Kirkby Malham 93 C8
Kirkby Mallory 63 D8
Kirkby Malzeard 94 B5
Kirkby Mills 103 F5
Kirkbymoorside 102 F4
Kirkby on Bain 78 C5
Kirkby Overflow 95 E6
Kirkby Stephen 100 D2
Kirkby Thore 99 B8
Kirkby Underwood 65 B7
Kirkby Wharfe 95 E8
Kirkcaldy 128 E4
Kirkcambeck 108 C5
Kirkcarswell 106 E4
Kirkcolm 104 C4
Kirkconnel 113 C7
Kirkconnell 107 C6
Kirkcowan 105 C7
Kirkcudbright 106 D3
Kirkdale 85 E4
Kirk Deighton 95 D6
Kirk Ella 90 B4
Kirkfieldbank 119 E8
Kirkgunzeon 107 C5
Kirk Hallam 76 E4
Kirkham
Lancs 92 F4
N Yorks 96 C3
Kirkhamgate 88 B3
Kirk Hammerton 95 D7
Kirkharle 117 F6
Kirkheaton
Northumb 110 B3
W Yorks 88 C2
Kirkhill
Angus 135 C6
Highld 151 G8
Midloth 120 C5
Moray 152 E2
Kirkhope 115 B6
Kirkhouse 121 F6
Kirkiboll 157 D8
Kirkibost 149 G10
Kirkinch 134 E3
Kirkinner 105 D8
Kirkintilloch 119 B6
Kirk Ireton 76 D2
Kirkland
Cumb 98 C2
Dumfries 113 C7
Dumfries 113 E8
W&F 109 F6
Kirk Langley 76 F2
Kirkleatham 102 B3
Kirklevington 102 D2
Kirkley 69 E8
Kirklington
Notts 77 D6
N Yorks 101 F8
Kirklinton 108 C4
Kirkliston 120 B4
Kirkmaiden 104 F5
Kirk Merrington 111 F5
Kirkmichael
Perth 133 D7
S Ayrs 112 D3
Kirk Michael 84 C3
Kirkmuirhill 119 E7
Kirknewton
Northumb 122 F5
W Loth 120 C4
Kirkney 152 E5
Kirk of Shotts 119 C8
Kirkoswald
Cumb 108 B5
S Ayrs 112 D2
Kirkpatrick
Durham 106 B4
Kirkpatrick-Fleming 108 B2
Kirk Sandall 89 D7
Kirksanton 98 F3
Kirk Smeaton 89 C6
Kirkstall 95 F5
Kirkstead 78 C4
Kirkstile 152 E5
Kirkstyle 158 C5
Kirkton
Aberds 140 B5
Aberds 153 D6
Angus 134 E4
Angus 134 F4
Borders 115 C8
Dumfries 114 F2
Fife 129 B5
Highld 149 F13
Highld 150 G2
Highld 151 B10
Highld 151 F10
Perth 127 C8
S Lanark 114 B2
Stirling 126 D4
Kirktonhill 121 D7
Kirkton Manor 120 F5
Kirkton of Airlie 134 D3
Kirkton of Auchterhouse 134 F3
Kirkton of Auchterless 153 D7
Kirkton of Barevan 151 G11
Kirkton of Bourtie 141 B7

Kirkton of Collace 134 F1
Kirkton of Craig 135 D7
Kirkton of Culsalmond 153 E6
Kirkton of Durris 141 E6
Kirkton of Glenbuchat 140 C2
Kirkton of Glenisla 134 C2
Kirkton of Kingoldrum 134 D3
Kirkton of Largo 129 D6
Kirkton of Lethendy 133 E8
Kirkton of Logie Buchan 141 B8
Kirkton of Maryculter 141 E7
Kirkton of Menmuir 135 C5
Kirkton of Monikie 135 F5
Kirkton of Oyne 141 B5
Kirkton of Rayne 153 F6
Kirkton of Skene 141 D7
Kirkton of Tough 140 C5
Kirktown 153 C10
Kirktown of Alvah 153 B6
Kirktown of Deskford 152 B5
Kirktown of Fetteresso 141 F7
Kirktown of Mortlach 152 E3
Kirktown of Slains 141 B9
Kirkurd 120 E4
Kirkwall 159 G5
Kirkwhelpington 117 F5
Kirk Yetholm 116 B4
Kirmington 90 C5
Kirmond le Mire 91 E5
Kirn 145 F10
Kirriemuir 134 D3
Kirstead Green 69 E5
Kirtlebridge 108 B2
Kirtleton 115 F5
Kirtling 55 D7
Kirtling Green 55 D7
Kirtlington 38 C4
Kirtomy 157 C10
Kirton
Lincs 79 F6
Notts 77 D6
Suff 57 F6
Kirton End 79 E5
Kirton Holme 79 E5
Kirton in Lindsey 90 E3
Kislingbury 52 D4
Kites Hardwick 52 C2
Kittisford 11 B5
Kittle 33 F6
Kitt's Green 63 F5
Kitt's Moss 87 F6
Kittybrewster 141 D8
Kitwood 26 F4
Kivernoll 49 F6
Kiveton Park 89 F5
Knaith 90 F2
Knaith Park 90 F2
Knap Corner 13 B6
Knaphill 27 D7
Knapp
Perth 134 F2
Som 11 B8
Knapthorpe 77 D7
Knapton
Norf 81 D9
York 95 D8
Knapton Green 49 D6
Knapwell 54 C4
Knaresborough 95 D6
Knarsdale 109 D6
Knauchland 152 C5
Knaven 153 D8
Knayton 102 F2
Knebworth 41 B5
Knedlington 89 B8
Kneesall 77 C7
Kneesworth 54 E4
Kneeton 77 E7
Knelston 33 F5
Knenhall 75 F6
Knettishall 68 F2
Knightacott 21 F5
Knightcote 51 D8
Knightley Dale 62 B2
Knighton
Devon 6 E3
Leicester 64 D2
Staffs 61 B7
Staffs 74 E4
Knighton =Tref-y-Clawdd 48 B4
Knightswood 118 C5
Knightwick 50 D2
Knill 48 C4
Knipton 77 F8
Knitsley 110 E4
Kniveton 76 D2
Knock
Argyll 147 H8
Moray 152 C5
W&F 100 B1
Knockally 158 H3
Knockan 156 H5
Knockandhu 152 E1
Knockando House 152 D2
Knockbain 151 F9
Knockbreck 148 B7
Knockbrex 106 E2
Knockdee 158 D3
Knockdolian 104 A5
Knockenkelly 143 F11
Knockentiber 118 F3
Knockespock House 140 B4
Knockfarrel 151 F8
Knockglass 104 D4
Knockholt 29 D5
Knockholt Pound 29 D5

Knockie Lodge 137 C7
Knockin 60 B3
Knockinlaw 118 F4
Knocklearn 106 B4
Knocknaha 143 G7
Knocknain 104 C3
Knockrome 144 F4
Knocksharry 84 D2
Knodishall 57 C8
Knolls Green 74 B5
Knolton 73 F7
Knolton Bryn 73 F7
Knook 24 E4
Knossington 64 D5
Knott End-on-Sea 92 E3
Knotting 53 C8
Knotting Green 53 C8
Knottingley 89 B6
Knotts
Lancs 93 D7
W&F 99 B6
Knotty Ash 86 E2
Knotty Green 40 E2
Knowbury 49 B7
Knowe 105 B7
Knowehead 113 E6
Knowesgate 117 F5
Knowes of Elrick 152 C6
Knoweton 119 D7
Knowhead 153 C9
Knowle
Bristol 23 B8
Devon 10 D2
Devon 11 F5
Devon 20 F3
Shrops 49 B7
W Mid 51 B6
Knowle Green 93 F6
Knowle Park 94 E3
Knowl Hill 27 B6
Knowlton
Dorset 13 C8
Kent 31 D6
Knowsley 86 E2
Knowstone 10 B3
Knox Bridge 29 E8
Knucklas 48 B4
Knuston 53 C7
Knutsford 74 B4
Knutton 74 E5
Knypersley 75 D5
Kuggar 3 E6
Kyleakin 149 F12
Kyle of Lochalsh 149 F12
Kylerhea 149 F12
Kylesknoydart 147 B11
Kylesku 156 F5
Kylesmorar 147 B11
Kylestrome 156 F5
Kyllachy House 138 B3
Kynaston 60 B3
Kynnersley 61 C6
Kyre Magna 49 C8

L

Labost 155 C7
Lacasaidh 155 E8
Lacasdal 155 D9
Laceby 91 D6
Lacey Green 39 E8
Lach Dennis 74 B4
Lackford 55 B8
Lacock 24 C4
Ladbroke 52 D2
Laddingford 29 E7
Lade Bank 79 D6
Ladock 4 D3
Lady 159 D7
Ladybank 128 C5
Ladykirk 122 E4
Ladysford 153 B9
La Fontenelle 16 I2
Laga 147 E9
Lagalochan 124 D4
Lagavulin 142 D5
Lagg
Argyll 144 F4
N Ayrs 143 F10
Laggan
Argyll 142 C3
Highld 137 E5
Highld 138 E2
Highld 147 D10
S Ayrs 112 F2
Lagganulva 146 G7
Laide 155 H13
Laigh Fenwick 118 E4
Laigh Glengall 112 C3
Laighmuir 118 E4
Laindon 42 F2
Lair 150 G3
Lairg 157 J8
Lairg Lodge 157 J8
Lairgmore 151 H8
Lairg Muir 157 J8
Laisterdyke 94 F4
Laithes 108 F4
Lake
IoW 15 F6
Wilts 25 F6
Lakenham 68 D5
Lakenheath 67 F7
Lakesend 66 E5
Lakeside 99 F5
Laleham 27 C8
Laleston 21 B7
Lamarsh 56 F2
Lamas 81 E8
Lambden 122 E3
Lamberhurst 18 B3
Lamberhurst Quarter 18 B3
Lamberton 123 D5
Lambeth 28 B4
Lambhill 119 C5
Lambley
Northumb 109 D6
Notts 77 E6
Lamborough Hill 38 D4
Lambourn 25 B8
Lambourne End 41 E7
Lambs Green 28 F3
Lambston 44 D4

Lambton 111 D5
Lamerton 6 B2
Lamesley 111 D5
Laminess 159 E7
Lamington
Highld 151 D10
S Lanark 120 F2
Lamlash 143 E11
Lamloch 112 E5
Lamonby 108 F4
Lamorna 2 D3
Lamorran 3 B7
Lampardbrook 57 C6
Lampeter =Llanbedr Pont Steffan 46 E4
Lampeter Velfrey 32 C2
Lamphey 32 D1
Lamplugh 98 B2
Lamport 53 B5
Lamyatt 23 F8
Lana
Devon 8 E5
Devon 8 D5
Lanark 119 E8
Lancaster 92 C4
Lanchester 110 E4
Lancing 17 D5
Landbeach 55 C5
Landcross 9 B6
Landerberry 141 D6
Landford 14 C3
Landford Manor 14 B3
Landimore 33 E5
Landkey 20 F4
Landore 33 E7
Landrake 5 C8
Landscove 7 C5
Landshipping 32 C1
Landshipping Quay 32 C1
Landulph 6 C2
Landwade 55 C7
Lane 4 C3
Laneast 8 F4
Lane End
Bucks 39 E8
Cumb 98 E3
Dorset 13 E6
Hants 15 B7
IoW 15 F7
Lancs 93 E8
Lane Ends
Lancs 93 D7
Lancs 93 F7
N Yorks 94 E2
Northumb 117 F8
Lanehead
Durham 109 E8
Northumb 116 F3
Lane Head
Derbys 75 B8
Durham 101 C6
Gtr Man 86 E4
W Yorks 88 D2
Lanercost 109 C5
Laneshaw Bridge 94 E2
Lane Side 87 B5
Lanfach 35 E6
Langar 77 F7
Langbank 118 B3
Langbar 94 D3
Langburnshiels 115 D9
Langcliffe 93 C8
Langdale End 103 E7
Langdon 8 D5
Langdon Beck 109 F8
Langdon Hills 42 F2
Langdyke 128 D5
Langenhoe 43 C6
Langford
C Beds 54 E2
Devon 10 D5
Essex 42 D4
Notts 77 D8
Oxon 38 D2
Langford Budville 11 B6
Langham
Essex 56 F4
Norf 81 C6
Rutland 64 C5
Suff 56 C3
Langhaugh 120 F5
Langho 93 F7
Langholm 115 F6
Langleeford 117 B5
Langley
Ches E 75 B6
Hants 14 D5
Herts 41 B5
Kent 30 D2
Northumb 109 C8
Slough 27 B8
Warks 51 C6
W Sus 16 B2
Langley Burrell 24 B4
Langley Common 76 F2
Langley Heath 30 D2
Langley Lower Green 54 F5
Langley Marsh 11 B5
Langley Park 110 E5
Langley Street 69 D6
Langley Upper Green 54 F5
Langney 18 E3
Langold 89 F6
Langore 8 F5
Langport 12 B2
Langrick 79 E5
Langridge 24 C2
Langridge Ford 9 B7
Langrigg 107 E8
Langsett 88 D3
Langshaw 121 F8
Langside 127 C6
Langskaill 159 D5
Langstone
Hants 15 D8
Newport 35 E7
Langthorne 101 E7
Langthorpe 95 C6
Langthwaite 101 D5
Langtoft
E Yorks 97 C6
Lincs 65 C8
Langton
Durham 101 C6
Lincs 78 C5
Lincs 79 C6

Langton continued
Lincs 79 B6
N Yorks 96 C3
Langton by Wragby 78 B4
Langton Green
Kent 18 B2
Suff 56 B5
Langton Herring 12 F4
Langton Matravers 13 G8
Langtree 9 C6
Langwathby 109 F5
Langwell House 158 H3
Langwell Lodge 156 J4
Langwith 76 C5
Langwith Junction 76 C5
Langworth 78 B3
Lanivet 4 C5
Lanivery 5 D5
Lanner 3 C6
Lanreath 5 D6
Lansallos 5 D6
Lansdown 37 B6
Lanteglos Highway 5 D6
Lanton
Borders 116 B2
Northumb 122 F5
Lapford 10 D2
Laphroaig 142 D4
La Planque 16 I2
Lapley 62 C2
Lapworth 51 B6
Larachbeg 147 G9
Larbert 127 F7
Larden Green 74 D2
Largie 152 E6
Largiemore 145 E8
Largoward 129 D6
Largs 118 D2
Largybeg 143 F11
Largymore 143 F11
Larkfield 118 B2
Larkhall 119 D7
Larkhill 25 E6
Larling 68 F2
Larriston 115 E8
Lartington 101 C5
Lary 140 D2
Lasham 26 E4
Lashenden 30 E2
Lassington 36 B4
Lassodie 128 E3
Lastingham 103 E5
Latcham 23 E6
Latchford
Herts 41 B6
Warr 86 F4
Latchingdon 42 D4
Latchley 6 B2
Lately Common 86 E4
Lathbury 53 E6
Latheron 158 G3
Latheronwheel 158 G3
Latheronwheel House 158 G3
Lathones 129 D6
Latimer 40 E3
Latteridge 36 F3
Lattiford 12 B4
Latton 37 E7
Latton Bush 41 D7
Lauchintilly 141 C6
Lauder 121 E8
Laugharne 32 C4
Laughterton 77 B8
Laughton
E Sus 18 D2
Leics 64 F3
Lincs 78 F3
Lincs 90 E2
Laughton Common 89 F6
Laughton en le Morthen 89 F6
Launcells 8 D4
Launceston 8 F5
Launton 39 B6
Laurencekirk 135 B7
Laurieston
Dumfries 106 C3
Falk 120 B2
Lavendon 53 D7
Lavenham 56 E3
Laverhay 114 E4
Laversdale 108 C4
Laverstock 25 F6
Laverstoke 26 E2
Laverton
Glos 51 F5
N Yorks 94 B5
Som 24 D2
Lavister 73 D7
Law 119 D8
Lawers
Perth 127 B6
Perth 132 F3
Lawford 56 F4
Lawhitton 9 F5
Lawkland 93 C7
Lawley 61 D6
Lawnhead 62 B2
Lawrenny 32 D1
Lawshall 56 D2
Lawton 49 D6
Laxey 84 D4
Laxfield 57 B6
Laxfirth
Shetland 160 H6
Shetland 160 J6
Laxo 160 G6
Laxobigging 160 F6
Laxton
E Yorks 89 B8
Nhants 65 E6
Notts 77 C7
Laycock 94 E3
Layer Breton 43 C5
Layer de la Haye 43 C5
Layer Marney 43 C5
Laytham 96 F3
Layton 92 F3
Lazenby 102 B3
Lazonby 108 F5

Lea
Derbys 76 D3
Hereford 36 B3
Lincs 90 F2
Shrops 60 D4
Wilts 37 F6
Leabrooks 76 D4
Leac a Li 154 H6
Leachkin 151 G9
Leadburn 120 D5
Leadenham 78 D2
Leaden Roding 42 C1
Leadgate
Durham 110 D4
T&W 110 D4
W&F 109 E7
Leadhills 113 C8
Leafield 38 C3
Leagrave 40 B3
Leake 102 E2
Leake Commonside 79 D6
Lealholm 103 D5
Lealt
Argyll 144 D5
Highld 149 B10
Leamington Hastings 52 C2
Leamonsley 62 D5
Leanach 151 H8
Leanaig 151 F8
Leargybreck 144 F4
Leasgill 99 F6
Leasingham 78 E3
Leasingthorne 101 B7
Leasowe 85 E3
Leatherhead Common 28 D2
Leatherhead 28 D2
Leathley 94 E5
Leaton 60 C4
Lea Town 92 F4
Leaveland 30 D4
Leavening 96 C3
Leaves Green 28 C5
Leazes 110 D4
Lebberston 103 F8
Lechlade-on-Thames 38 E2
Leck 93 B6
Leckford 25 F8
Leckfurin 157 D10
Leckgruinart 142 B3
Leckhampstead
Bucks 52 F5
W Berks 26 B2
Leckhampstead Thicket 26 B2
Leckhampton 37 C6
Leckie 150 E3
Leckmelm 150 B4
Leckwith 22 B3
Leconfield 97 E6
Ledaig 124 B5
Ledburn 40 B2
Ledbury 50 F2
Ledcharrie 126 B4
Ledgemoor 49 D6
Ledicot 49 C6
Ledmore 156 H5
Lednagullin 157 C10
Ledsham
Ches W 73 B7
W Yorks 89 B5
Ledston 88 B5
Ledston Luck 95 F7
Ledwell 38 B4
Lee
Argyll 146 J7
Devon 20 E3
Hants 14 C4
Lancs 93 D5
Shrops 73 F8
Lee Brockhurst 60 B5
Leebotwood 60 E4
Lee Clump 40 D2
Leeds
Kent 30 D2
W Yorks 95 F5
Leedstown 2 C5
Leek 75 D6
Leek Wootton 51 C7
Lee Mill 6 D4
Leeming 101 F7
Leeming Bar 101 E7
Lee Moor 6 C3
Lee-on-the-Solent 15 D6
Lees
Derbys 76 F2
Gtr Man 87 D7
W Yorks 94 F3
Leeswood 73 C6
Legbourne 91 F7
Legerwood 121 E8
Legsby 90 F5
Leicester 64 D2
Leicester Forest East 64 D2
Leigh
Dorset 12 D4
Glos 37 B5
Gtr Man 86 E4
Kent 29 E6
Shrops 60 D3
Sur 28 E3
Wilts 37 E7
Worcs 50 D2
Leigh Beck 42 F4
Leigh Common 12 B5
Leigh Delamere 24 B3
Leigh Green 19 B6
Leigh on Sea 42 F4
Leigh Park 15 D8
Leigh Sinton 50 D2
Leighswood 62 D4
Leighterton 37 E5
Leighton
N Yorks 94 B4
Powys 60 D2
Shrops 61 D6

Leighton continued
Som 24 E2
Leighton Bromswold 54 B2
Leighton Buzzard 40 B2
Leigh upon Mendip 23 E8
Leigh Woods 23 B7
Leinthall Earls 49 C6
Leinthall Starkes 49 C6
Leintwardine 49 B6
Leire 64 E2
Leirinmore 156 C7
Leiston 57 C8
Leitfie 134 E2
Leith 121 B5
Leitholm 122 E3
Lelant 2 C4
Lelley 97 F8
Lem Hill 50 B2
Lemmington Hall 117 C7
Lempitlaw 122 F3
Lenchwick 50 E5
Lendalfoot 112 F1
Lendrick Lodge 126 D3
Lenham 30 D2
Lenham Heath 30 E3
Lennel 122 E4
Lennoxtown 119 B6
Lenton
Lincs 78 F3
Nottingham 77 F5
Lentran 151 G8
Lenwade 68 C3
Leny House 126 D5
Lenzie 119 B6
Leoch 134 F3
Leochel-Cushnie 140 C4
Leominster 49 D6
Leonard Stanley 37 D5
Leorin 142 D4
Lepe 15 E5
Lephin 148 D6
Lephinchapel 145 D8
Lephinmore 145 D8
Le Planel 16 I2
Leppington 96 C3
Lepton 88 C3
Lerryn 5 D6
Lerwick 160 J6
Lesbury 117 C8
Le Skerne Haughton 101 C8
Leslie
Aberds 140 B4
Fife 128 D4
Lesmahagow 119 F8
Lesnewth 8 E3
Lessendrum 152 D5
Lessingham 69 B6
Lessonhall 108 D2
Leswalt 104 C4
Letchmore Heath 40 E4
Letchworth Garden City 54 F3
Letcombe Bassett 38 F3
Letcombe Regis 38 F3
Letham
Angus 135 E5
Falk 127 F7
Fife 128 C5
Perth 128 B2
Letham Grange 135 E6
Lethenty 153 D8
Letheringham 57 D6
Letheringsett 81 D6
Lettaford 10 F2
Letter 159 D8
Letterewe 150 D3
Letterfearn 149 F13
Letterfinlay 137 E5
Lettermorar 147 C10
Lettermore 146 G7
Letters 150 C4
Letterston 44 C4
Lettoch
Highld 139 B6
Highld 151 H13
Letton
Hereford 48 E5
Hereford 49 B5
Letton Green 68 D2
Letty Green 41 C5
Letwell 89 F6
Leuchars 129 B6
Leuchars House 152 B2
Leumrabhagh 155 F8
Levan 118 B2
Levaneap 160 G6
Levedale 62 C2
Leven
E Yorks 97 E7
Fife 129 D5
Levencorroch 143 F11
Levens 99 F6
Levens Green 41 B6
Levenshulme 87 E6
Levenwick 160 L6
Leverburgh =An t-Ob 154 J5
Leverington 66 C4
Leverton 79 E7
Leverton Highgate 79 E7
Leverton Outgate 79 E7
Le Villocq 16 I2
Levington 57 F6
Levisham 103 E6
Levishie 137 C7
Lew 38 D3
Lewannick 8 F4
Lewdown 9 F6
Lewes 17 C8
Leweston 44 C4
Lewisham 28 B4
Lewiston 137 B8
Lewistown 34 F3
Lewknor 39 E7
Leworthy
Devon 8 D5
Devon 21 F5
Lewtrenchard 9 F6
Lexden 43 B5

Ley
Aberds 140 C4
Corn 5 C6
Leybourne 29 D7
Leyburn 101 E6
Leyfields 63 D6
Leyhill 40 D2
Leyland 86 B3
Leylodge 141 C6
Leymoor 88 C2
Leys
Aberds 153 C10
Perth 134 F2
Leys Castle 151 G9
Leysdown-on-Sea 30 B4
Leysmill 135 E6
Leys of Cossans 134 E3
Leysters Pole 49 C7
Leyton 41 F6
Leytonstone 41 F6
Lezant 5 B8
Leziate 67 C6
Lhanbryde 152 B2
Liatrie 150 H5
Libanus 34 B3
Libberton 120 E2
Liberton 121 C5
Liceasto 154 H6
Lichfield 62 D5
Lickey 50 B4
Lickey End 50 B4
Lickfold 16 B3
Liddel 159 K5
Liddesdale 130 D1
Liddington 38 F2
Lidgate 55 D8
Lidget 89 D7
Lidget Green 94 F4
Lidgett 77 C6
Lidlington 53 F7
Lidstone 38 B3
Lieurary 158 D2
Liff 134 F3
Lifton 9 F5
Liftondown 9 F5
Lighthorne 51 D8
Lightwater 27 C7
Lightwood 75 E6
Lightwood Green
Ches E 74 E3
Wrex 73 E7
Lilbourne 52 B3
Lilburn Tower 117 B6
Lilleshall 61 C7
Lilley
Herts 40 B4
W Berks 26 B2
Lilliesleaf 115 B8
Lillingstone Dayrell 52 F5
Lillingstone Lovell 52 E5
Lillington
Dorset 12 C4
Warks 51 C8
Lilliput 13 E8
Lilstock 22 E3
Lilyhurst 61 C7
Limbury 40 B3
Limebrook 49 C5
Limefield 87 C6
Limekilnburn 119 D7
Limekilns 128 F2
Limerigg 119 B8
Limerstone 14 F5
Limington 12 B3
Limpenhoe 69 D6
Limpley Stoke 24 C2
Limpsfield 28 D5
Limpsfield Chart 28 D5
Linby 76 D5
Linchmere 27 F6
Lincluden 107 B6
Lincoln 78 B2
Lincomb 50 C3
Lindale 99 F6
Lindal in Furness 92 B2
Lindean 121 F7
Lindfield 17 B7
Lindford 27 F6
Lindifferon 128 C5
Lindley 88 C2
Lindley Green 94 E5
Lindores 128 C4
Lindridge 49 C8
Lindsell 42 B2
Lindsey 56 E3
Linford
Hants 14 D2
Thurrock 29 B7
Lingague 84 E2
Lingards Wood 87 C8
Lingbob 94 F3
Lingdale 102 C4
Lingen 49 C5
Lingfield 28 E4
Lingreabhagh 154 J5
Lingwood 69 D6
Linicro 149 B8
Linkenholt 25 D8
Linkhill 18 C5
Linkinhorne 5 B8
Linklater 159 K5
Linksness 159 H3
Linktown 128 E4
Linley 60 E3
Linley Green 49 D8
Linlithgow Bridge 120 B2
Linshiels 116 D4
Linsiadar 154 D7
Linsidemore 151 B8
Linslade 40 B2
Linstead Parva 57 B7
Linstock 108 D4
Linthwaite 88 C2
Lintlaw 122 D4
Lintmill 152 B5
Linton
Borders 116 B3
Cambs 55 E6
Derbys 63 C6
Hereford 36 B3
Kent 29 E8
Northumb 117 E8

Linton *continued*
N Yorks ... 94 C2
W Yorks ... 95 E6
Linton-on-Ouse ..95 C7
Linwood
Hants ... 14 D2
Lincs ... 90 F5
Renfs ... 118 C4
Lionacleit ... 148 D2
Lional ... 155 A10
Liphook ... 27 F6
Liscard ... 85 E4
Liscombe ... 21 F7
Liskeard ... 5 C7
L'Islet ... 16 I2
Liss ... 15 B8
Lissett ... 97 C7
Liss Forest ... 15 B8
Lissington ... 90 F5
Lisvane ... 35 F5
Liswerry ... 35 F7
Litcham ... 67 C8
Litchborough ... 52 D4
Litchfield ... 26 D2
Litherland ... 85 E4
Litlington
Cambs ... 54 E4
E Sus ... 18 E2
Little Abington ..55 E6
Little Addington ..53 B7
Little Alne ... 51 C6
Little Altcar ... 85 D4
Little Asby ... 100 D1
Little Assynt ... 156 G4
Little Aston ... 62 D4
Little Atherfield ..15 F5
Little Ayre ... 159 J4
Little-ayre ... 160 G5
Little Ayton ... 102 C3
Little Baddow ... 42 D3
Little Badminton .37 F5
Little Ballinluig ..133 D6
Little Bampton ..108 D2
Little Bardfield ..55 F7
Little Barford ... 54 D2
Little Barningham ...81 D7
Little Barrington 38 C2
Little Barrow ... 73 B8
Little Barugh ... 96 B3
Little Bavington 110 B2
Little Bealings ... 57 E6
Littlebeck ... 103 D6
Little Bedwyn ... 25 C7
Little Bentley ... 43 B7
Little Berkhamsted ...41 D5
Little Billing ... 53 C6
Little Birch ... 49 F7
Little Blakenham .56 E5
Little Blencow ... 108 F4
Little Bollington ..86 F5
Little Bookham ...28 D2
Littleborough
Gtr Man ... 87 C7
Notts ... 90 F2
Littlebourne ... 31 D6
Little Bowden ... 64 F4
Little Bradley ... 55 D7
Little Brampton ..60 F3
Little Brechin ... 135 C5
Littlebredy ... 12 F3
Little Brickhill ... 53 F7
Little Brington ... 52 C4
Little Bromley ... 43 B6
Little Broughton 107 F7
Little Budworth ..74 C2
Little Burstead ... 42 E2
Littlebury ... 55 F6
Littlebury Green .55 F5
Little Bytham ... 65 C7
Little Carlton
Lincs ... 91 F7
Notts ... 77 D7
Little Casterton ..65 D7
Little Cawthorpe .91 F7
Little Chalfont ... 40 E2
Little Chart ... 30 E3
Little Chesterford 55 E6
Little Cheverell ... 24 D4
Little Chishill ... 54 F5
Little Clacton ... 43 C7
Little Clifton ... 98 B2
Little Colp ... 153 D7
Little Comberton .50 E4
Little Common ... 18 E4
Little Compton ... 51 F7
Little Cornard ... 56 F2
Little Cowarne ... 49 D8
Little Coxwell ... 38 E2
Little Crakehall ..101 E7
Little Cressingham ... 67 D8
Little Crosby ... 85 D4
Little Dalby ... 64 C4
Little Dawley ... 61 D6
Littledean ... 36 C3
Little Dens ... 153 D10
Little Dewchurch 49 F7
Little Downham ..66 F5
Little Driffield ... 97 D6
Little Dunham ... 67 C8
Little Dunkeld ... 133 E7
Little Dunmow ... 42 B2
Little Easton ... 42 B2
Little Eaton ... 76 E3
Little Eccleston ..92 E4
Little Ellingham ..68 E3
Little End ... 41 D8
Little Eversden ..54 D4
Little Faringdon ..38 D2
Little Fencote ... 101 E7
Little Fenton ... 95 F8
Littleferry ... 151 B11
Little Finborough 56 D4
Little Fransham .68 C2
Little Gaddesden 40 C2
Little Gidding ... 65 F8
Little Glemham ...57 D7
Little Glenshee ..133 F6
Little Gransden ..54 D3
Little Green ... 24 E2
Little Grimsby ... 91 E7
Little Gruinard ..150 C2
Little Habton ... 96 B3
Little Hadham ... 41 B7
Little Hale ... 78 E4
Little Hallingbury .41 C7

Littleham
Devon ... 9 B6
Devon ... 10 F5
Little Hampden ..40 D1
Littlehampton ... 16 D4
Little Harrowden ..53 B6
Little Haseley ... 39 D6
Little Hatfield ... 97 E7
Little Hautbois ..81 E8
Little Haven ... 44 D3
Little Hay ... 62 D5
Little Hayfield ... 87 F8
Little Haywood ..62 B4
Little Heath ... 63 F7
Littlehempston ... 7 C6
Little Hereford ...49 C7
Little Horkesley ..56 F3
Little Horsted ... 17 C8
Little Horton ... 94 F4
Little Horwood ..53 F5
Littlehoughton ..117 C8
Little Houghton
S Yorks ... 88 D5
W Nhants ... 53 D6
Little Hucklow ... 75 B8
Little Hulton ... 86 D5
Little Humber ... 91 B5
Little Hungerford ... 26 B3
Little Irchester ...53 C7
Little Kimble ... 39 D8
Little Kineton ... 51 D8
Little Kingshill ...40 E1
Little Langdale ...99 D5
Little Langford ...25 F5
Little Laver ... 41 D8
Little Leigh ... 74 B3
Little Leighs ... 42 C3
Little Lever ... 87 D5
Little London
Bucks ... 39 C6
E Sus ... 18 D2
Hants ... 25 E8
Hants ... 26 D4
Lincs ... 66 B2
Lincs ... 66 B4
Norf ... 81 E7
Powys ... 59 F7
Little Longstone ..75 B8
Little Lynturk ... 140 C4
Little Malvern ... 50 E2
Little Maplestead .56 F3
Little Marcle ... 49 F8
Little Marlow ... 40 F1
Little Marsden ... 93 F8
Little Massingham ... 80 E3
Little Melton ... 68 D4
Littlemill
Aberds ... 140 E2
E Ayrs ... 112 C4
Highld ... 151 F12
Northumb ... 117 C8
Little Mill ... 35 D7
Little Milton ... 39 D6
Little Missenden .40 E2
Littlemoor ... 12 F4
Littlemore ... 39 D5
Little Musgrave 100 C2
Little Ness ... 60 C4
Little Neston ... 73 B6
Little Newcastle ..44 C4
Little Newsham 101 C6
Little Oakley
Essex ... 43 B8
N Nhants ... 65 F5
Little Orton ... 108 D3
Little Ouseburn ..95 C7
Littleover ... 76 F3
Little Paxton ... 54 C2
Little Petherick ... 4 B4
Little Pitlurg ... 152 D4
Little Plumpton ..92 F3
Little Plumstead 69 C6
Little Ponton ... 78 F2
Littleport ... 67 F5
Little Raveley ... 54 B3
Little Reedness ..90 B2
Little Ribston ... 95 D6
Little Rissington ..38 C1
Little Ryburgh ...81 E5
Little Ryle ... 117 C6
Little Salkeld ... 109 F5
Little Sampford ..55 F7
Little Sandhurst ..27 C6
Little Saxham ... 55 C8
Little Scatwell ... 150 F6
Little Sessay ... 95 B7
Little Shelford ... 54 D5
Little Singleton ..92 F3
Little Skillymarno ... 153 C9
Little Smeaton ... 89 C6
Little Snoring ... 81 D5
Little Sodbury ... 36 F4
Little Somborne ..25 F8
Little Somerford .37 F6
Little Stainforth ..93 C8
Little Stainton ... 101 B8
Little Stanney ... 73 B8
Little Staughton ..54 C2
Little Steeping ... 79 C7
Little Stoke ... 75 F6
Littlestone on Sea ... 19 C7
Little Stonham ... 56 C5
Little Stretton
Leics ... 64 D3
Shrops ... 60 E4
Little Strickland ..99 C7
Little Stukeley ... 54 B3
Little Sutton ... 73 B7
Little Tew ... 38 B3
Little Thetford ... 55 B6
Little Thirkleby ...95 B7
Little Thornton ... 92 E3
Little Thorpe ... 58 C2
Littlethorpe
Leics ... 64 E2
N Yorks ... 95 C6
Little Thurlow ... 55 D7
Little Thurrock ... 29 B7
Littleton
Ches W ... 73 C8
Hants ... 26 F2
Perth ... 134 F2
Som ... 23 F6
Sur ... 27 C8
Sur ... 27 E7
Littleton Drew ... 37 F5

Littleton-on-Severn ... 36 F2
Littleton Pannell 24 D5
Little Torboll ... 151 B10
Little Torrington ...9 C6
Little Totham ... 42 C4
Little Toux ... 152 C5
Littletown ... 111 E6
Little Town
Cumb ... 98 C4
Lancs ... 93 F6
Little Urswick ... 92 B2
Little Wakering ..43 F5
Little Walden ... 55 E6
Little Waldingfield ... 56 E3
Little Walsingham ... 80 D5
Little Waltham ... 42 C3
Little Warley ... 42 E2
Little Weighton ..97 F5
Little Weldon ... 65 F6
Little Welnetham ...56 C3
Little Wenlock ... 61 D6
Little Whittingham Green ... 57 B6
Littlewick Green .27 B6
Little Wilbraham 55 D6
Little Wishford ..25 F5
Little Witley ... 50 C2
Little Wittenham .39 E5
Little Wolford ... 51 F7
Littleworth
Bedford ... 53 E8
Glos ... 37 D5
Oxon ... 38 E3
Staffs ... 62 C4
Worcs ... 50 D4
Little Wratting ... 55 E7
Little Wymington 53 C7
Little Wymondley 41 B5
Little Wyrley ... 62 D4
Little Yeldham ... 55 F8
Litton
Derbys ... 75 B8
N Yorks ... 94 B2
Som ... 23 D7
Litton Cheney ... 12 E3
Liurbost ... 155 E8
Liverpool ... 85 E4
Liverpool Airport .86 F2
Liversedge ... 88 B3
Liverton
Devon ... 7 B6
Redcar ... 103 C5
Livingston ... 120 C3
Livingston Village ... 120 C3
Lixwm ... 73 B5
Lizard ... 3 E6
Llaingoch ... 82 C2
Llaithddu ... 59 F7
Llan ... 59 D5
Llanaber ... 58 C3
Llanaelhaearn ... 70 C4
Llanafan ... 47 B5
Llanafan-fawr ...47 D8
Llanallgo ... 82 C4
Llanandras
=*Presteigne* ... 48 C5
Llanarmon ... 70 D5
Llanarmon Dyffryn Ceiriog ...73 F5
Llanarmon-yn-Ial ... 73 D5
Llanarth
Ceredig ... 46 D3
Mon ... 35 C7
Llanarthne ... 33 B6
Llanasa ... 85 F2
Llanbabo ... 82 C3
Llanbadarn Fawr .58 F3
Llanbadarn Fynydd ... 48 B3
Llanbadarn-y-Garreg ... 48 E3
Llanbadoc ... 35 E7
Llanbadrig ... 82 B3
Llanbeder ... 35 E7
Llanbedr
Gwyn ... 71 E6
Powys ... 35 B6
Powys ... 48 E3
Llanbedr-Dyffryn-Clwyd ... 72 D5
Llanbedrgoch ... 82 C5
Llanbedrog ... 70 D4
Llanbedr Pont Steffan
=*Lampeter* ... 46 E4
Llanbedr-y-cennin ... 83 E7
Llanberis ... 83 E5
Llanbethêry ... 22 C2
Llanbister ... 48 B3
Llanblethian ... 21 B8
Llanboidy ... 32 B3
Llanbradach ... 35 E5
Llanbrynmair ... 59 D5
Llancarfan ... 22 B2
Llancayo ... 35 D7
Llancloudy ... 36 B1
Llancynfelyn ... 58 E3
Llandaff ... 22 B3
Llandanwg ... 71 E6
Llandarcy ... 33 E8
Llandawke ... 32 C3
Llanddaniel Fab .82 D4
Llanddarog ... 33 C6
Llanddeiniol ... 46 B4
Llanddeiniolen ..82 E5
Llandderfel ... 72 F3
Llanddeusant
Anglesey ... 82 C3
Carms ... 34 B1
Llanddew ... 48 F2
Llanddewi ... 33 F5
Llanddewi-Brefi ..47 D5
Llanddewi'r Cwm .48 E2
Llanddewi Rhydderch ... 35 C7
Llanddewi Velfrey ... 32 C2
Llanddoged ... 83 E8
Llanddona ... 83 D5
Llanddowror ... 32 C3
Llanddulas ... 72 B3
Llanddwywe ... 71 E6
Llanddyfnan ... 82 D5

Llandefaelog Fach ... 48 F2
Llandefaelog-tre'rgraig ... 35 B5
Llandefalle ... 48 F3
Llandegai ... 83 D5
Llandegfan ... 83 D5
Llandegla ... 73 D5
Llandegley ... 48 C3
Llandegveth ... 35 E7
Llandegwning ... 70 D3
Llandeilo ... 33 B7
Llandeilo Graban ... 48 E2
Llandeilo'r Fan ...47 F7
Llandeloy ... 44 C3
Llandenny ... 35 D8
Llandevenny ... 35 F8
Llandewednock ...3 E6
Llandewi Ystradenny ... 48 C3
Llandinabo ... 36 B2
Llandinam ... 59 F7
Llandissilio ... 32 B2
Llandogo ... 36 D2
Llandough
V Glam ... 21 B8
V Glam ... 22 B3
Llandovery
=*Llanymddyfri* ...47 F6
Llandow ... 21 B8
Llandre
Carms ... 47 E5
Ceredig ... 58 F3
Llandrillo ... 72 F4
Llandrillo-yn-Rhos ... 83 C8
Llandrindod
=*Llandrindod Wells* ... 48 C2
Llandrindod Wells
=*Llandrindod* ... 48 C2
Llandrinio ... 60 C2
Llandudno ... 83 C7
Llandudno Junction
=*Cyffordd Llandudno* ... 83 D7
Llandwrog ... 82 F4
Llandybie ... 33 C7
Llandyfaelog ... 33 C5
Llandyfan ... 33 C7
Llandyfriog ... 46 E2
Llandyfrydog ... 82 C4
Llandygwydd ... 45 E4
Llandynan ... 73 E5
Llandyrnog ... 72 C5
Llandysilio ... 60 C2
Llandyssil ... 59 E8
Llandysul ... 46 E3
Llanedeyrn ... 35 F6
Llanedi ... 33 D6
Llaneglwys ... 48 F2
Llanegryn ... 58 D2
Llanegwad ... 33 B6
Llaneilian ... 82 B4
Llanelian-yn-Rhos ... 83 D8
Llanelidan ... 72 D5
Llanelieu ... 48 F3
Llanellen ... 35 C7
Llanelli ... 33 E6
Llanelltyd ... 58 C4
Llanelly ... 35 C6
Llanelly Hill ... 35 C6
Llanelwedd ... 48 D2
Llanelwy
=*St Asaph* ... 72 B4
Llanenddwyn ... 71 E6
Llanengan ... 70 E3
Llanerchymedd .82 C4
Llanerfyl ... 59 D7
Llanfachraeth ... 82 C3
Llanfachreth ... 71 E8
Llanfaelog ... 82 D3
Llanfaelrhys ... 70 E3
Llanfaenor ... 35 C8
Llanfaes
Anglesey ... 83 D6
Powys ... 34 B4
Llanfaethlu ... 82 C3
Llanfaglan ... 82 E4
Llanfair ... 71 E6
Llanfair-ar-y-bryn ...47 F7
Llanfair Caereinion ... 59 D8
Llanfair Clydogau 46 D5
Llanfair-Dyffryn-Clwyd ... 72 D5
Llanfairfechan ... 83 D6
Llanfair Kilgheddin ... 35 D7
Llanfair-Nant-Gwyn ... 45 F3
Llanfairpwllgwyngyll ... 82 D5
Llanfair Talhaiarn 72 B3
Llanfair Waterdine ... 48 B4
Llanfair-ym-Muallt
=*Builth Wells.* ... 48 E2
Llanfairyneubwll 82 D3
Llanfairynghornwy ...82 B3
Llanfallteg ... 32 C2
Llanfaredd ... 48 D2
Llanfarian ... 46 B4
Llanfechain ... 59 B8
Llanfechan ... 47 D8
Llanfechell ... 82 B3
Llanfendigaid ... 58 D2
Llanferres ... 73 C5
Llan Ffestiniog ..71 C8
Llanfflewyn ... 82 C3
Llanfihangel-ararth ... 46 F3
Llanfihangel-Crucorney ... 35 B7
Llanfihangel Glyn Myfyr ...72 E3
Llanfihangel Nant Bran ... 47 F8
Llanfihangel-nant-Melan ... 48 D3
Llanfihangel Rhydithon ... 48 C3
Llanfihangel Rogiet ... 35 F8

Llanfihangel Tal-y-llyn ... 35 B5
Llanfihangel-uwch-Gwili ... 33 B5
Llanfihangel-y-Creuddyn ...47 B5
Llanfihangel-yn-Ngwynfa ... 59 C7
Llanfihangel yn Nhowyn ... 82 D3
Llanfihangel-y-pennant
Gwyn ... 58 D3
Gwyn ... 71 C6
Llanfihangel-y-traethau ... 71 D6
Llanfilo ... 48 F3
Llanfoist ... 35 C6
Llanfor ... 72 F3
Llanfrechfa ... 35 E7
Llanfrothen ... 71 C7
Llanfrynach ... 34 B4
Llanfwrog
Anglesey ... 82 C3
Denb ... 72 D5
Llanfyllin ... 59 C8
Llanfynydd
Carms ... 33 B6
Flint ... 73 D6
Llanfyrnach ... 45 F4
Llangadfan ... 59 C7
Llangadog ... 33 B8
Llangadwaladr
Anglesey ... 82 E3
Powys ... 73 F5
Llangaffo ... 82 E4
Llangain ... 32 C4
Llangammarch Wells ... 47 E8
Llangan ... 21 B8
Llangarron ... 36 B2
Llangasty Talyllyn 35 B5
Llangathen ... 33 B6
Llangattock ... 35 C6
Llangattock Lingoed ... 35 B7
Llangattock nigh Usk ...35 D7
Llangattock-Vibon-Avel. ... 36 C1
Llangedwyn ... 59 B8
Llangefni ... 82 D4
Llangeinor ... 34 F3
Llangeitho ... 46 D5
Llangeler ... 46 F2
Llangelynin ... 58 D2
Llangendeirne ... 33 C5
Llangennech ... 33 D6
Llangennith ... 33 E5
Llangenny ... 35 C6
Llangernyw ... 83 E8
Llangian ... 70 E3
Llanglydwen ... 32 B2
Llangoed ... 83 D6
Llangoedmor ... 45 E3
Llangollen ... 73 E6
Llangolman ... 32 B2
Llangors ... 35 B5
Llangovan ... 36 D1
Llangower ... 72 F3
Llangranog ... 46 D2
Llangristiolus ... 82 D4
Llangrove ... 36 C2
Llangua ... 35 B7
Llangunllo ... 48 B4
Llangunnor ... 33 C5
Llangurig ... 47 B8
Llangwm
Conwy ... 72 E3
Mon ... 35 D8
Pembs ... 44 E4
Llangwnnadl ... 70 D3
Llangwyfan ... 72 C5
Llangwyfan-isaf .82 E3
Llangwyllog ... 82 D4
Llangwyryfon ... 46 B4
Llangybi
Ceredig ... 46 D5
Gwyn ... 70 C5
Mon ... 35 E7
Llangyfelach ... 33 E7
Llangynhafal ... 72 C5
Llangynidr ... 35 C5
Llangynin ... 32 C3
Llangynog
Carms ... 32 C4
Powys ... 59 B7
Llangynwyd ... 34 F2
Llanhamlach ... 34 B4
Llanharan ... 34 F4
Llanharry ... 34 F4
Llanhennock ... 35 E7
Llanhiledd
=*Llanhilleth.* ... 35 D6
Llanhilleth
=*Llanhiledd.* ... 35 D6
Llanidloes ... 59 F6
Llaniestyn ... 70 D3
Llanifyny ... 59 F5
Llanigon ... 48 F4
Llanilar ... 46 B5
Llanilid ... 34 F3
Llanilltud Fawr
=*Llantwit Major.* 21 C8
Llanishen
Cardiff. ... 35 F5
Mon. ... 36 D1
Llanllawddog ... 33 B6
Llanllechid ... 83 E6
Llanllowell ... 35 E7
Llanllugan ... 59 D7
Llanllwch ... 32 C4
Llanllwchaiarn ..59 E8
Llanllwni ... 46 F3
Llanllyfni ... 82 F4
Llanmadoc ... 33 E5
Llanmaes ... 21 C8
Llanmartin ... 35 F7
Llanmihangel ... 21 B8
Llanmorlais ... 33 E6
Llannefydd ... 72 B3
Llannon ... 33 D6
Llannor ... 70 D4
Llanover ... 35 D7
Llanpumsaint ... 33 B5
Llanreithan ... 44 C3
Llanrhaeadr ... 72 C4

Llanrhaeadr-ym-Mochnant ... 59 B8
Llanrhian ... 44 B3
Llanrhidian ... 33 E5
Llanrhos ... 83 C7
Llanrhyddlad ... 82 C3
Llanrhystud ... 46 C4
Llanrosser ... 48 F4
Llanrothal ... 36 C1
Llanrug ... 82 E5
Llanrumney ... 35 F6
Llanrwst ... 83 E8
Llansadurnen ... 32 C3
Llansadwrn
Anglesey ... 83 D5
Carms ... 47 F5
Llansaint ... 32 D4
Llansamlet ... 33 E7
Llansanffraid-ym-Mechain ... 60 B2
Llansannan ... 72 C3
Llansannor ... 21 B8
Llansantffraed
Ceredig ... 46 C4
Powys ... 35 B5
Llansantffraed Cwmdeuddwr ... 47 C8
Llansantffraed-in-Elvel ... 48 D2
Llansawel ... 46 F5
Llansilin ... 60 B2
Llansoy ... 35 D8
Llanspyddid ... 34 B4
Llanstadwell ... 44 E4
Llansteffan ... 32 C4
Llanstephan ... 48 E3
Llantarnam ... 35 E7
Llanteg ... 32 C2
Llanthony ... 35 B6
Llantilio Crossenny ... 35 C7
Llantilio Pertholey ... 35 C7
Llantood ... 45 E3
Llantrisant
Anglesey ... 82 C3
Mon ... 35 E7
Rhondda ... 34 F4
Llantrithyd ... 22 B2
Llantwit Fardre ...34 F4
Llantwit Major
=*Llanilltud Fawr.* 21 C8
Llanuwchllyn ... 72 F2
Llanvaches ... 35 E8
Llanvair Discoed .35 E8
Llanvapley ... 35 C7
Llanvetherine ... 35 C7
Llanveynoe ... 48 F5
Llanvihangel Gobion ... 35 D7
Llanvihangel-Ystern-Llewern 35 C8
Llanwarne ... 36 B2
Llanwddyn ... 59 C7
Llanwenog ... 46 E3
Llanwern ... 35 F7
Llanwinio ... 32 B3
Llanwnda
Gwyn ... 82 F4
Pembs ... 44 A4
Llanwnnen ... 46 E4
Llanwnog ... 59 E7
Llanwrda ... 47 F6
Llanwrin ... 58 D4
Llanwrthwl ... 47 C8
Llanwrtud
=*Llanwrtyd Wells* .47 E7
Llanwrtyd ... 47 E7
Llanwrtyd Wells
=*Llanwrtud* ... 47 E7
Llanwyddelan ... 59 D7
Llanyblodwel ... 60 B2
Llanybri ... 32 C4
Llanybydder ... 46 E4
Llanycefn ... 32 B1
Llanychaer ... 44 B4
Llanycil ... 72 F3
Llanycrwys ... 46 E5
Llanymawddwy ..59 C6
Llanymddyfri
=*Llandovery* ...47 F6
Llanymynech ... 60 B2
Llanynghenedl ..82 C3
Llanynys ... 72 C5
Llan-y-pwll ... 73 D7
Llanyre ... 48 C2
Llanystumdwy ... 71 D5
Llanywern ... 35 B5
Llawhaden ... 32 C1
Llawndy ... 85 F2
Llawnt ... 73 F6
Llawr Dref ... 70 E3
Llawryglyn ... 59 E6
Llay ... 73 D7
Llechcynfarwy ...82 C3
Llecheiddior ... 71 C5
Llechfaen ... 34 B4
Llechryd
Caerph ... 35 D5
Ceredig ... 45 E4
Llechrydau ... 73 F6
Lledrod ... 46 B5
Llenmerewig ... 59 E8
Llethrid ... 33 E6
Llidiad Nenog ...46 F4
Llidiardau ... 72 F2
Llidiart-y-parc ...72 E5
Llithfaen ... 70 C4
Llong ... 73 C6
Llowes ... 48 E3
Llundain-fach ... 46 D4
Llwydcoed ... 34 D3
Llwyn ... 60 F2
Llwyncelyn ... 46 D3
Llwyndafydd ... 46 D2
Llwynderw ... 60 D2
Llwyn-du ... 35 C6
Llwyngwril ... 58 D2
Llwynhendy ... 33 E6
Llwynmawr ... 73 F6
Llwyn-têg ... 33 D6
Llwyn-y-brain ... 32 C2
Llwyn-y-groes ...46 D4
Llwynypia ... 34 E4
Llynclys ... 60 B2
Llynfaes ... 82 D4
Llysfaen ... 83 D8

Llyswen ... 48 F3
Llysworney ... 21 B8
Llys-y-frân ... 32 B1
Llywel ... 47 F7
Loan ... 120 B2
Loanend ... 122 D5
Loanhead ... 121 C5
Loans ... 118 F3
Loans of Tullich ... 151 D11
Lobb ... 20 D7
Loch a' Charnain 148 D2
Loch a' Ghainmhich ... 155 F7
Lochailort ... 147 C10
Lochaline ... 147 G9
Lochanhully ... 138 B5
Lochans ... 104 D4
Locharbriggs ... 114 F2
Lochassynt Lodge ... 156 G4
Lochavich House ... 124 D5
Lochawe ... 125 C7
Loch Baghasdail
=*Lochboisdale* 148 G2
Lochboisdale
=*Loch Baghasdail* ... 148 G2
Lochbuie ... 124 C2
Lochcarron ... 149 E13
Loch Choire Lodge ... 157 F9
Lochdhu ... 157 E13
Lochdochart House ... 126 B3
Lochdon ... 124 B3
Lochdrum ... 150 D5
Lochead ... 144 F6
Lochearnhead ... 126 B4
Lochee ... 134 F3
Lochend
Highld ... 151 H8
Highld ... 158 D4
Locherben ... 114 E2
Loch Euphoirt ...148 B3
Lochfoot ... 107 B5
Lochgair ... 145 D8
Lochgarthside ...137 C8
Lochgelly ... 128 E3
Lochgilphead ... 145 E7
Lochgoilhead ... 125 E8
Loch Head ... 105 E7
Lochhill ... 152 B2
Lochindorb Lodge ... 151 H12
Lochinver ... 156 G3
Lochlane ... 127 B7
Loch Loyal Lodge ... 157 E9
Lochluichart ... 150 E6
Lochmaben ... 114 F3
Lochmaddy
=*Loch nam Madadh* ... 148 B4
Lochmore Cottage ... 158 F2
Lochmore Lodge ... 156 F5
Loch nam Madadh
=*Lochmaddy* ... 148 B4
Lochore ... 128 E3
Lochportain ... 148 A4
Lochranza ... 143 C10
Lochs Crofts ... 152 B3
Loch Sgioport ...148 E2
Lochside
Aberds ... 135 C7
Highld ... 151 F11
Highld ... 156 D7
Highld ... 157 F11
Lochslin ... 151 C11
Lochstack Lodge ... 156 E5
Lochton ... 141 E6
Lochty
Angus ... 135 C5
Fife ... 129 D7
Perth ... 128 B2
Lochuisge ... 130 D1
Lochurr ... 113 F7
Lochwinnoch ... 118 D3
Lochwood ... 114 E3
Lochyside ... 131 B5
Lockengate ... 4 C5
Lockerbie ... 114 F4
Lockeridge ... 25 C6
Lockerley ... 14 B3
Locking ... 23 D5
Lockinge ... 38 F4
Lockington
E Yorks ... 97 E5
Leics ... 63 B8
Locklywood ... 61 B6
Locks Heath ... 15 D6
Lockton ... 103 E6
Lockwood ... 88 C2
Loddington
Leics ... 64 D4
N Nhants ... 53 B6
Loddiswell ... 6 E5
Loddon ... 69 E6
Lode ... 55 C6
Loders ... 12 E2
Lodsworth ... 16 B3
Lofthouse
N Yorks ... 94 B4
W Yorks ... 88 B4
Loftus ... 103 C5
Logan ... 113 B5
Loganlea ... 120 C2
Logan Mains ... 104 E4
Loggerheads ... 74 F4
Logie
Angus ... 135 C6
Fife ... 129 B6
Moray ... 151 F13
Logiealmond Lodge ... 133 F6
Logie Coldstone 140 D3
Logie Hill ... 151 D10
Logie Pert ... 135 C6
Logierait ... 133 D6
Login ... 32 B2
Lolworth ... 54 C4
Lonbain ... 149 C11
Londesborough ..96 E4
London Colney ...40 D4

Londonderry ... 101 F8
Londonthorpe ... 78 F2
Londubh ... 155 J13
Lonemore ... 151 C10
Long Ashton ... 23 B7
Longbar ... 118 D3
Long Bennington 77 E8
Longbenton ... 111 C5
Longborough ... 38 B1
Long Bredy ... 12 E3
Longbridge
Warks ... 51 C7
W Mid ... 50 B5
Longbridge Deverill ... 24 E3
Long Buckby ... 52 C4
Longburton ... 12 C4
Long Clawson ... 64 B4
Longcliffe ... 76 D2
Long Common ...15 C6
Long Compton
Staffs ... 62 B2
Warks ... 51 F7
Longcot ... 38 E2
Long Crendon ... 39 D6
Long Crichel ... 13 C7
Longcroft ... 119 B7
Longden ... 60 D4
Long Ditton ... 28 C2
Longdon
Staffs ... 62 C4
Worcs ... 50 F3
Longdon Green ..62 C4
Longdon on Tern .61 C6
Longdown ... 10 E3
Longdowns ... 3 C6
Long Drax ... 89 B7
Long Duckmanton ..76 B4
Long Eaton ... 76 F4
Longfield
Kent ... 29 C7
Shetland ... 160 M5
Longford
Derbys ... 76 F2
Glos ... 37 B5
London ... 27 B8
Shrops ... 74 F3
Telford ... 61 C7
W Mid ... 63 F7
Longfordlane ... 76 F2
Longforgan ... 128 B5
Longformacus ... 122 D2
Longframlington ... 117 D7
Long Green ... 50 F3
Longham
Dorset ... 13 E8
Norf ... 68 C2
Long Hanborough ... 38 C4
Longhaven ... 153 E11
Longhill ... 153 C9
Longhirst ... 117 F8
Longhope
Glos ... 36 C3
Orkney ... 159 J4
Longhorsley ... 117 E7
Longhoughton ..117 C8
Long Itchington .52 C2
Longlane
Derbys ... 76 F2
W Berks ... 26 B2
Long Lawford ... 52 B2
Longlevens ... 37 B5
Longley ... 88 D2
Longley Green ... 50 D2
Long Load ... 12 B2
Longmanhill ... 153 B7
Long Marston
Herts ... 40 C1
N Yorks ... 95 D8
Warks ... 51 E6
Long Marton ... 100 B1
Long Melford ... 56 E2
Longmoor Camp ..27 F5
Longmorn ... 152 C2
Long Newnton ... 37 E6
Longnewton
Borders ... 115 B8
Stockton ... 102 C1
Long Newton ... 121 C8
Longney ... 36 C4
Longniddry ... 121 B7
Longnor
Shrops ... 60 D4
Staffs ... 75 C7
Longparish ... 26 E2
Longport ... 75 E5
Long Preston ... 93 D8
Longridge
Lancs ... 93 F6
Staffs ... 62 C3
W Loth ... 120 C2
Longriggend ... 119 B8
Long Riston ... 97 E7
Longsdon ... 75 D6
Longshaw ... 86 D3
Longside ... 153 D10
Long Sight ... 87 D7
Longstanton ... 54 C4
Longstock ... 25 F8
Longstone ... 32 D2
Longstowe ... 54 D4
Long Stratton ... 68 E4
Long Street ... 53 E5
Long Sutton
Hants ... 26 E5
Lincs ... 66 B4
Som ... 12 B2
Longthorpe ... 65 E8
Long Thurlow ... 56 C4
Longthwaite ... 99 B6
Longton
Lancs ... 86 B2
Stoke ... 75 E6
Longtown
Cumb ... 108 C3
Hereford ... 35 B7
Longview ... 86 E2
Longville in the Dale ... 60 E5
Long Whatton ...63 B8
Longwick ... 39 D7
Long Wittenham ... 39 E5
Longwitton ... 117 F6
Longwood ... 61 D6
Longworth ... 38 E3

Longyester ... 121 C8
Lonmay ... 153 C10
Lonmore ... 148 D7
Looe ... 5 D7
Loose ... 29 D8
Loosley Row ... 39 D8
Lopcombe Corner 25 F7
Lopen ... 12 C2
Loppington ... 60 B4
Lopwell ... 6 C2
Lorbottle ... 117 D6
Lorbottle Hall ... 117 D6
Lornty ... 134 E1
Loscoe ... 76 E4
Losgaintir ... 154 H5
Lossiemouth ... 152 A2
Lossit ... 142 C2
Lostford ... 74 F3
Lostock Gralam ..74 B3
Lostock Green ...74 B3
Lostock Hall ... 86 B3
Lostock Junction 86 D4
Lostwithiel ... 5 D6
Loth ... 159 E7
Lothbeg ... 157 H12
Lothersdale ... 94 E2
Lothmore ... 157 H12
Loudwater ... 40 E2
Loughborough ...64 C2
Loughor ... 33 E6
Loughton
Essex ... 41 E7
M Keynes ... 53 F6
Shrops ... 61 F6
Lound
Lincs ... 65 C7
Notts ... 89 F7
Suff ... 69 E8
Lount ... 63 C7
Louth ... 91 F7
Love Clough ... 87 B6
Lovedean ... 15 C7
Lover ... 14 B3
Loversall ... 89 E6
Loves Green ... 42 D2
Lovesome Hill ...102 E1
Loveston ... 32 D1
Lovington ... 23 F7
Low Ackworth ...89 C5
Low Barlings ... 78 B3
Low Bentham ...93 C6
Low Bradfield ...88 E3
Low Bradley ... 94 E3
Low Braithwaite 108 E4
Lowbridge House 99 D7
Low Brunton ... 110 B2
Low Burnham ... 89 D8
Low Burton ... 101 F7
Low Buston ... 117 D8
Lowca ... 98 B1
Low Catton ... 96 D3
Low Clanyard ...104 F5
Low Coniscliffe ..101 C7
Low Crosby ... 108 D4
Low Dalby ... 103 F6
Lowdham ... 77 E6
Low Dinsdale ...101 C8
Lowe ... 74 F2
Lowe Hill ... 75 D6
Low Ellington ...101 F7
Lower Aisholt ... 22 F4
Lower Arncott ...39 C6
Lower Ashton ... 10 F3
Lower Assendon .39 F7
Lower Badcall ...156 E4
Lower Bartle ... 92 F4
Lower Basildon ..26 B4
Lower Beeding ..17 B6
Lower Benefield .65 F6
Lower Boddington ... 52 D2
Lower Brailes ...51 F8
Lower Breakish 149 F11
Lower Broadheath ... 50 D3
Lower Bullingham ... 49 F7
Lower Cam ... 36 D4
Lower Chapel ... 48 F2
Lower Chute ... 25 D8
Lower Cragabus 142 D4
Lower Crossings .87 F8
Lower Cumberworth ... 88 D3
Lower Darwen ... 86 B4
Lower Dean ... 53 C8
Lower Diabaig 149 B12
Lower Dicker ... 18 D2
Lower Dinchope ..60 F4
Lower Down ... 60 F3
Lower Drift ... 2 D3
Lower Dunsforth .95 C7
Lower Egleton ... 49 E8
Lower Elkstone ..75 D7
Lower End ... 40 B2
Lower Everleigh ..25 D6
Lower Farringdon 26 F5
Lower Foxdale ...84 E2
Lower Frankton ..73 F7
Lower Froyle ... 27 E5
Lower Gledfield 151 B8
Lower Green ... 81 D5
Lower Hacheston .57 D7
Lower Halistra ...148 C7
Lower Halstow ...30 C2
Lower Hardres ...31 D5
Lower Hawthwaite ... 98 F4
Lower Heath ... 75 C5
Lower Hempriggs ... 151 E14
Lower Hergest ...48 D4
Lower Heyford ...38 B4
Lower Higham ...29 B8
Lower Holbrook .57 F5
Lower Hordley ...60 B3
Lower Horsebridge ... 18 D2
Lower Killeyan 142 D3
Lower Kingswood ... 28 D3
Lower Kinnerton 73 C7
Lower Langford ..23 C6
Lower Largo ... 129 D6
Lower Leigh ... 75 F7

Lower Lemington .51 F7
Lower Lenie 137 B8
Lower Lydbrook . 36 C2
Lower Lye 49 C6
Lower Machen . . .35 F6
Lower Maes-
 coed 48 F5
Lower Mayland . 43 D5
Lower Midway . . .50 B4
Lower Milovaig . 148 G6
Lower Moor 50 E4
Lower Nazeing . 41 D6
Lower
 Netchwood . . .61 E6
Lower Ollach . 149 E10
Lower Penarth . . .22 B3
Lower Penn 62 E2
Lower
 Pennington 14 E4
Lower Peover . . .74 B4
Lower Pexhill . . .75 B5
Lower Place 87 C7
Lower Quinton . .51 E6
Lower Rochford . 49 C8
Lower Seagry . . .37 F6
Lower Shelton . . .53 E7
Lower Shiplake . .27 B5
Lower
 Shuckburgh . . .52 C2
Lower Slaughter. 38 B1
Lower Stanton
 St Quintin 37 F6
Lower Stoke 30 B2
Lower Stondon . .54 F2
Lower Stow
 Bedon 68 E2
Lower Street
 Norf 69 C6
 Norf 81 D8
Lower Strensham. 50 E4
Lower Stretton . .86 F4
Lower Sundon . . .40 B3
Lower Swanwick 15 D5
Lower Swell 38 B1
Lower Tean 75 F7
Lower Thurlton . .69 E7
Lower Tote . . . 149 B10
Lower Town 44 B4
Lower Tysoe 51 E8
Lower Upham . . .15 C6
Lower Vexford . . .22 F3
Lower Weare 23 D6
Lower Welson . . .48 D4
Lower Whitley . . .74 B3
Lower Wield 26 E4
Lower
 Winchendon . . 39 C7
Lower
 Withington 74 C5
Lower Woodend . 27 F7
Lower Woodford .25 F6
Lower Wyche 50 E2
Lowesby 64 D4
Lowestoft 69 E8
Loweswater 98 B3
Low Etherley . . 101 B6
Low Fell 111 D5
Lowford 15 C5
Low Fulney 66 B2
Low Garth 103 D5
Low Gate 110 C2
Lowgill
 Lancs 93 C6
 W&F 99 E8
Low Grantley . . .94 B5
Low Habberley . .50 B3
Low Ham 12 B2
Low Hesket 108 E4
Low Hesleyhurst 111 E4
Low Hutton 96 C3
Lowick
 N Nhants 65 F6
 Northumb 123 F6
Lowick Bridge . .98 A4
Lowick Green . . .98 A4
Low Laithe 94 C4
Lowlands 35 E6
Low Leighton . . .87 F8
Low Lorton 98 B3
Low Marishes . . .96 B4
Low Marnham . . .77 C8
Low Mill 102 E4
Low Moor
 Lancs 93 E7
 W Yorks 88 B2
Lowmoor Row . . .99 B8
Low Moresley . . . 111 E6
Low Newton 99 F6
Low Newton-by-the-
 Sea 117 B8
Lownie Moor . . . 134 E4
Low Row
 Cumb 108 F3
 Cumb 109 C5
 N Yorks 100 E4
Low Salchrie . . . 104 C4
Low Smerby . . . 143 F8
Lowsonford 51 C6
Lowther 99 B7
Lowthorpe 97 C6
Lowton 86 E4
Lowton Common .86 E4
Low Torry 128 F2
Low Worsall . . . 102 D1
Low Wray 99 D5
Loxbeare 10 C4
Loxhill 27 F8
Loxhore 20 F5
Loxley 51 D7
Loxton 23 D5
Loxwood 27 F8
Lubcroy 156 J6
Lubenham 64 F4
Luccombe 21 E8
Luccombe
 Village 15 G6
Lucker 123 F7
Luckett 5 B8
Luckington 37 F5
Lucklawhill . . . 129 B6
Luckwell Bridge . .21 F8
Lucton 49 C6
Ludag 148 G2
Ludborough 91 E6
Ludchurch 32 C2

Luddenden 87 B8
Luddenden Foot . .87 B8
Luddesdown 29 C7
Luddington
 N Lincs 90 C2
 Warks 51 D6
Luddington in the
 Brook 65 F8
Lude House . . . 133 C5
Ludford
 Lincs 91 F6
 Shrops 49 B7
Ludgershall
 Bucks 39 C6
 Wilts 25 D7
Ludgvan 2 C4
Ludham 69 C6
Ludlow 49 B7
Ludwell 13 B7
Ludworth 111 E6
Luffincott 8 E5
Lugar 113 B5
Luggate Burn . . 122 B2
Lugg Green 49 C6
Luggiebank 119 B7
Lugton 118 D4
Lugwardine 49 E7
Luib 149 F10
Lulham 49 E6
Lullenden 28 E5
Lullington
 Derbys 63 C6
 Som 24 D2
Lulsgate Bottom. 23 C7
Lulsley 50 D2
Lumb 87 B8
Lumby 95 F7
Lumloch 119 C6
Lumphanan . . . 140 D4
Lumphinnans . . 128 E3
Lumsdaine 122 C4
Lumsden 140 B3
Lunan 135 D6
Lunanhead 134 D4
Luncarty 128 B2
Lund
 E Yorks 97 E5
 N Yorks 96 F3
 Shetland 160 C2
Lunderton 153 D11
Lundie
 Angus 134 F2
 Highld 136 C4
Lundin Links . . 129 D6
Lunga 124 E3
Lunna 160 G6
Lunning 160 G6
Lunnon 33 F6
Lunsford's Cross 18 D4
Lunt 85 D4
Luntley 49 D5
Luppitt 11 D6
Lupset 88 C4
Lupton 99 F7
Lurgashall 16 B3
Lusby 79 C6
Luson 6 E4
Lussagiven 144 E5
Lusta 149 C7
Lustleigh 10 F2
Luston 49 C6
Luthermuir 135 C6
Luthrie 128 C5
Luton
 Devon 7 B7
 Luton 40 B3
 Medway 29 C8
Lutterworth 64 F2
Lutton
 Devon 6 D3
 Lincs 66 B4
 N Nhants 65 F8
Lutworthy 10 C2
Luxborough 21 F8
Luxulyan 5 D5
Lybster 158 G4
Lydbury North . .60 F3
Lydcott 21 F5
Lydd 19 C7
Lydden
 Kent 31 E6
 Kent 31 D8
Lyddington 65 E5
Lydd on Sea 19 C7
Lydeard
 St Lawrence . . .22 F3
Lyde Green 26 D5
Lydford 9 F7
Lydford-on-
 Fosse 23 F7
Lydgate 87 B7
Lydham 60 E3
Lydiard Green . . .37 F7
Lydiard Millicent .37 F7
Lydiate 85 D4
Lydlinch 12 C5
Lydney 36 D3
Lydstep 32 E1
Lye 62 F3
Lye Green
 Bucks 40 D2
 E Sus 18 B2
Lyford 38 E3
Lymbridge Green .30 E5
Lyme Regis 11 E8
Lyminge 31 E5
Lymington 14 E4
Lyminster 16 D4
Lymm 86 F4
Lymore 14 E3
Lympne 19 B8
Lympsham 22 D5
Lympstone 10 F4
Lynchat 138 D3
Lyndale House . 149 C8
Lyndhurst 14 D4
Lyndon 65 D6
Lyne 27 C8
Lyneal 73 F8
Lyne Down 49 F8
Lyneham
 Oxon 38 B2
 Wilts 24 B5
Lynemore 139 B6
Lynemouth 117 E8
Lyne of
 Gorthleck 137 B8
Lyne of Skene . . 141 C6
Lyness 159 J4

Lyng
 Norf 68 C3
 Som 11 B8
Lynmouth 21 E6
Lynsted 30 C3
Lynton 21 E6
Lyon's Gate 12 D4
Lyonshall 48 D5
Lytchett
 Matravers 13 E7
Lytchett Minster .13 E7
Lyth 158 D4
Lytham 85 B4
Lytham St Anne's .85 B4
Lythe 103 C6
Lythes 159 K5

M

Mabe Burnthouse . 3 C6
Mabie 107 B6
Mablethorpe 91 F9
Macclesfield 75 B6
Macclesfield
 Forest 75 B6
Macduff 153 B7
Mace Green 56 E5
Macharioch . . . 143 H8
Machen 35 F6
Machrihanish . . 143 F7
Machynlleth 58 D4
Machynys 33 E6
Mackerel's
 Common 16 B4
Mackworth 76 F3
Macmerry 121 B7
Madderty 127 B8
Maddiston 120 B2
Madehurst 16 C3
Madeley
 Staffs 74 E4
 Telford 61 D6
Madeley Heath . .74 E4
Madeley Park . . .74 E4
Madingley 54 C4
Madley 49 F6
Madresfield 50 E3
Madron 2 C3
Maenaddwyn . . .82 C4
Maenclochog . . .32 B1
Maendy 22 B2
Maentwrog 71 C7
Maen-y-groes . . 46 D2
Maer 74 F4
Maerdy
 Conwy 72 E4
 Rhondda 34 E3
Maesbrook 60 B2
Maesbury 60 B3
Maesbury Marsh .60 B3
Maesgwyn-Isaf . .59 C8
Maesgwynne . . .32 B3
Maeshafn 73 C6
Maesllyn 46 E2
Maesmynis 48 E2
Maesteg 34 E2
Maestir 46 E4
Maes-Treylow . . .48 C4
Maesybont 33 C6
Maesycrugiau . . .46 E3
Maesy cwmmer . .35 E5
Maesymeillion . .46 E3
Magdalen Laver . 41 D8
Maggieknockater
 . . . . 152 D3
Magham Down . 18 D3
Maghull 85 D4
Magor 35 F8
Magpie Green . . .56 B4
Maiden Bradley . .24 F3
Maidencombe 7 C7
Maidenhall 57 E5
Maidenhead 40 F1
Maiden Law 110 E4
Maiden Newton .12 E3
Maidens 112 D2
Maidensgrave . . .57 E6
Maiden's Green . .27 B6
Maidenwell
 Corn 5 B6
 Lincs 79 B6
Maiden Wells . . .44 F4
Maidford 52 D4
Maids Moreton . .52 F5
Maidwell 52 B5
Mail 160 L6
Main 59 C8
Maindee 35 F7
Mainsforth 111 F6
Mains of Airies . 104 C3
Mains of
 Allardice 135 B8
Mains of
 Annochie 153 D9
Mains of
 Ardestie 135 F5
Mains of Balhall 135 C5
Mains of
 Ballindarg . . . 134 D4
Mains of
 Balnakettle . . 135 B6
Mains of
 Birness 153 E9
Mains of
 Burgie 151 F13
Mains of
 Clunas 151 G11
Mains of Crichie 153 D9
Mains of
 Dalvey 151 H14
Mains of
 Dellavaird . . . 141 F6
Mains of Drum . 141 E7
Mains of
 Edingight . . . 152 C5
Mains of
 Fedderate . . . 153 D8
Mains of
 Inkhorn 153 E9
Mains of Mayen 152 D5
Mains of
 Melgund 135 D5
Mains of
 Thornton 135 B6
Mains of Watten 158 E4
Mainsriddle . . . 107 D6

Mainstone 60 F2
Maisemore 37 B5
Malacleit 148 A2
Malborough 6 F5
Malcoff 87 F8
Maldon 42 D4
Malham 94 C2
Maligar 149 B9
Mallaig 147 B9
Malleny Mills . . 120 C4
Malling 126 D4
Malltraeth 82 E4
Mallwyd 59 C5
Malmesbury 37 F6
Malmsmead 21 E6
Malpas
 Ches W 73 E8
 Corn 3 B7
 Newport 35 E7
Malswick 36 B4
Maltby
 Stockton 102 C2
 S Yorks 89 E6
Maltby le Marsh .91 F8
Malting Green . . .43 B5
Maltman's Hill . . .30 E3
Malton 96 B3
Malvern Link . . .50 E2
Malvern Wells . . .50 E2
Mamble 49 B8
Mamhilad 35 D7
Manaccan 3 D6
Manafon 59 D8
Manais 154 J6
Manar House . . . 141 B6
Manaton 10 F2
Manby 91 F7
Mancetter 63 E7
Manchester 87 E6
Manchester
 Airport 87 F6
Mancot 73 C7
Mandally 137 D5
Manea 66 F4
Manfield 101 C7
Mangaster 160 F5
Mangotsfield . . .23 B8
Mangurstadh . . 154 D5
Mankinholes . . .87 B7
Manley 74 B2
Manmoel 35 D5
Mannal 146 G2
Mannerston . . . 120 B3
Manningford
 Bohune 25 D6
Manningford
 Bruce 25 D6
Manningham . . .94 F4
Mannings Heath .17 B6
Mannington 13 D8
Manningtree 56 F4
Mannofield 141 D8
Manor 41 F7
Manorbier 32 E1
Manordeilo 33 B7
Manor Estate . . .88 F4
Manorhill 122 F2
Manorowen 44 B4
Manselfield 33 F6
Mansel Lacy 49 E6
Mansell Gamage .49 E5
Mansergh 99 F8
Mansfield
 E Ayrs 113 C6
 Notts 76 C5
Mansfield
 Woodhouse . .76 C5
Mansriggs 98 F4
Manston
 Dorset 13 C6
 Kent 31 C7
 W Yorks 95 F6
Manswood 13 D7
Manthorpe
 Lincs 65 C7
 Lincs 78 F2
Manton
 N Lincs 90 D3
 Notts 77 B5
 Rutland 65 D5
 Wilts 25 C6
Manuden 41 B7
Maperton 12 B4
Maplebeck 77 C7
Maple Cross 40 E3
Mapledurham . . .26 B4
Mapledurwell . . .26 D4
Maplehurst 17 B5
Maplescombe . . .29 C6
Mapleton 75 E8
Mapperley 76 E4
Mapperley Park . .77 E5
Mapperton 12 E3
Mappleborough
 Green 51 C5
Mappleton 97 E8
Mappowder 12 D5
Maraig 154 G6
Marazanvose 4 D3
Marazion 2 C4
Marbhig 155 F9
Marbury 74 E2
March
 Cambs 66 E4
 S Lanark 114 C3
Marcham 38 E4
Marchamley 61 B5
Marchington 75 F7
Marchington
 Woodlands . . .62 B5
Marchroes 70 E4
Marchwiel 73 E7
Marchwood 14 C4
Marcross 21 C8
Marden
 Hereford 49 E7
 Kent 29 E8
 T&W 111 B6
 Wilts 25 D5
Marden Beech . . .29 E8
Marden Thorn . . .29 E8
Mardy 35 C7
Marefield 64 D4
Mareham le Fen . 79 C5
Mareham on the
 Hill 79 C5
Marehay 76 E3
Marehill 16 C4
Maresfield 17 B8

Marfleet 90 B5
Marford 73 D7
Margam 34 E1
Margaret Marsh . 13 C6
Margaret Roding .42 C1
Margaretting 42 D2
Margate 31 B7
Margnaheglish 143 E11
Margrove Park . . 102 C4
Marham 67 C7
Marhamchurch . . .8 D4
Marholm 65 D8
Mariandyrys 83 C6
Marianglas 82 C5
Mariansleigh 10 B2
Marionburgh . . . 141 D6
Marishader 149 B9
Marjoriebanks . . 114 F3
Mark
 Dumfries 104 D5
 S Ayrs 104 B4
 Som 23 E5
Markbeech 29 E5
Markby 79 B7
Mark Causeway . .23 E5
Mark Cross 18 B2
Market
 Harborough . . .64 F4
Markethill 134 F2
Market Lavington 24 D5
Market Overton . .65 C5
Market Rasen . . .90 F5
Market Stainton . 78 B5
Market Warsop . .77 C5
Market Weighton .96 E4
Market Weston . .56 B3
Markfield 63 C8
Markham 35 D5
Markham Moor . .77 B7
Markinch 128 D4
Markington 95 C5
Marksbury 23 C8
Marks Tey 43 B5
Markyate 40 C3
Marland 87 C6
Marlborough 25 C6
Marlbrook
 Hereford 49 D7
 Worcs 50 B4
Marlcliff 51 D5
Marldon 7 C6
Marlesford 57 D7
Marley Green . . .74 E2
Marley Hill 110 D5
Marley Mount . . .14 E3
Marlingford 68 D4
Mar Lodge 139 E6
Marlow
 Bucks 39 F8
 Hereford 49 B6
Marlow Bottom . .40 F1
Marlpit Hill 28 E5
Marlpool 76 E4
Marnhull 13 C5
Marnoch 152 C5
Marnock 119 C7
Marple 87 F7
Marple Bridge . . .87 F7
Marr 89 D6
Marrel 157 H13
Marrick 101 E5
Marrister 160 G7
Marros 32 D3
Marsden
 T&W 111 C6
 W Yorks 87 C8
Marsett 100 F4
Marsh
 Devon 11 C7
 W Yorks 94 F3
Marshall's Heath 40 C4
Marshalsea 11 D8
Marshalswick . . .40 D4
Marsham 81 E7
Marshaw 93 D5
Marshborough . . .31 D7
Marshbrook 60 F4
Marshchapel 91 E7
Marshfield
 Newport 35 F6
 S Glos 24 B2
Marshgate 8 E3
Marsh Green
 Devon 10 E5
 Kent 28 E5
 Staffs 75 D5
Marshland
 St James 66 D5
Marsh Lane 76 B4
Marsh Street 21 E8
Marshwood 11 E8
Marske 101 E6
Marske-by-the-
 Sea 102 B4
Marston
 Ches W 74 B3
 Hereford 49 D5
 Lincs 77 E8
 Oxon 39 D5
 Staffs 62 B3
 Staffs 62 C3
 Warks 63 E6
 Wilts 24 D4
Marston Doles . . .52 D2
Marston Green . . .63 F5
Marston Magna . . 12 B3
Marston Meysey . .37 E8
Marston
 Montgomery . .75 F8
Marston
 Moretaine 53 E7
Marston on Dove .63 B6
Marston
 St Lawrence . . .52 E3
Marston Stannett .49 D7
Marston Trussell .64 F3
Marstow 36 C2
Marsworth 40 C2
Marten 25 D7

Marthall 74 B5
Martham 69 C7
Martin
 Hants 13 C8
 Kent 31 E7
 Lincs 78 C5
 Lincs 78 D4
Martin Dales 78 C4
Martin Drove End .13 B8
Martinhoe 21 E5
Martinhoe Cross .21 E5
Martin
 Hussingtree . . .50 C3
Martin Mill 31 E7
Martinscroft 86 F4
Martinstown 12 F4
Martlesham 57 E6
Martlesham
 Heath 57 E6
Martletwy 32 C1
Martley 50 D2
Martock 12 C2
Marton
 Ches E 75 C5
 E Yorks 97 F7
 Lincs 90 F2
 Mbro 102 C3
 N Yorks 95 C7
 N Yorks 103 F5
 Shrops 60 B4
 Shrops 60 D2
 Warks 52 C2
Marton-le-Moor .95 B6
Martyr's Green . . 27 D8
Martyr Worthy . .26 F3
Marwick 159 F3
Marwood 20 F4
Marybank 150 F7
Maryburgh 151 F8
Maryhill 119 C5
Marykirk 135 C6
Marylebone 86 D3
Marypark 152 E1
Maryport
 Cumb 107 F7
 Dumfries 104 F5
Mary Tavy 6 B3
Maryton 135 D6
Marywell
 Aberds 140 E4
 Aberds 141 E8
 Angus 135 E6
Masham 101 F7
Mashbury 42 C2
Masongill 93 B6
Masonhill 112 B3
Mastin Moor 76 B4
Mastrick 141 D7
Matching 41 C8
Matching Green . .41 C8
Matching Tye . . .41 C8
Matfen 110 B3
Matfield 29 E7
Mathern 36 E2
Mathon 50 E2
Mathry 44 B3
Matlaske 81 D7
Matlock 76 C2
Matlock Bath . . .76 D2
Matson 37 C5
Matterdale End . .99 B5
Mattersey 89 F7
Mattersey Thorpe 89 F7
Mattingley 26 D5
Mattishall 68 C3
Mattishall Burgh 68 C3
Mauchline 112 B4
Maud 153 D9
Maugersbury . . .38 B2
Maughold 84 C4
Mauld 150 H7
Maulden 53 E8
Maulds Meaburn 99 C8
Maunby 102 F1
Maund Bryan . . .49 D7
Maundown 11 B5
Mautby 69 C7
Mavis Enderby . .79 C6
Mawbray 107 E7
Mawdesley 86 C2
Mawdlam 34 F2
Mawgan 3 D6
Mawgan Porth . . .4 C3
Maw Green 74 D4
Mawla 3 B6
Mawnan 3 D6
Mawnan Smith . . .3 D6
Mawsley 53 B6
Maxey 65 D8
Maxstoke 63 F6
Maxton
 Borders 122 F2
 Kent 31 E7
Maxwellheugh . . 122 F3
Maxwelltown . . . 107 B6
Maxworthy 8 E4
Mayals 33 E7
May Bank 75 E5
Maybole 112 D3
Mayfield
 E Sus 18 C2
 Midloth 121 C6
 Staffs 75 E8
 W Loth 120 C2
Mayford 27 D7
Mayland 43 D5
Maynard's Green 18 D2
Maypole
 Mon 36 C1
 Scilly 2 E4
Maypole Green
 Essex 43 B5
 Norf 69 E7
 Suff 57 C6
Maywick 160 L5
Meadle 39 D8
Meadowtown . . .60 D3
Meaford 75 F5
Mealabost
 Bhuirgh 155 B9
Mealabost 155 D9
Meal Bank 99 E7
Mealsgate 108 E2
Meanwood 95 F5
Mearbeck 93 C8
Meare 23 E6
Meare Green 11 B8
Mears Ashby 53 C6

Measham 63 C7
Meath Green 28 E3
Meathop 99 F6
Meaux 97 F6
Meavy 6 C3
Medbourne 64 E4
Medburn 110 B4
Meddon 8 C4
Meden Vale 77 C5
Medlam 79 D6
Medmenham 39 F8
Medomsley 110 D4
Medstead 26 F4
Meerbrook 75 C6
Meer End 51 B7
Meers Bridge . . .91 F8
Meesden 54 F5
Meeth 9 D7
Meggethead . . . 114 B4
Meidrim 32 B3
Meifod
 Denb 72 D4
 Powys 59 C8
Meigle
 N Ayrs 118 C1
 Perth 134 E2
Meikle Earnock . 119 D7
Meikle Ferry . . . 151 C10
Meikle Forter . . 134 C1
Meikle Gluich . . 151 C9
Meikleour 134 F1
Meikle
 Pinkerton . . . 122 B3
Meikle Strath . . 135 B6
Meikle Tarty . . . 141 B8
Meikle Wartle . . 153 E7
Meinciau 33 C5
Meir 75 E6
Meir Heath 75 E6
Melbourn 54 E4
Melbourne
 Derbys 63 B7
 E Yorks 96 E3
 S Lanark 120 E3
Melbury Abbas . .13 B6
Melbury Bubb . . .12 D3
Melbury Osmond 12 D3
Melbury
 Sampford 12 D3
Melby 160 H3
Melchbourne 53 C8
Melcombe
 Bingham 13 D5
Melcombe Regis. 12 F4
Meldon
 Devon 9 E7
 Northumb 117 F7
Meldreth 54 E4
Meldrum House . 141 B7
Melfort 124 D4
Melgarve 137 E7
Meliden 72 A4
Melinbyrhedyn . .58 E5
Melincourt 34 D2
Melin-y-coed . . .83 E8
Melin-y-ddôl 59 D7
Melin-y-grug 59 D7
Melin-y-Wig 72 E4
Melkinthorpe . . .99 B7
Melkridge 109 C7
Melksham 24 C4
Melldalloch 145 E8
Melling
 Lancs 93 B5
 Mers 85 D4
Melling Mount . . 86 D2
Mellis 56 B5
Mellon Charles 155 H13
Mellon Udrigle . 155 H13
Mellor
 Gtr Man. 87 F7
 Lancs 93 F6
Mellor Brook . . .93 F6
Mells 24 E2
Melmerby
 N Yorks 95 B6
 N Yorks 101 F5
 W&F 109 F5
Melplash 12 E2
Melrose 121 F8
Melsetter 159 K3
Melsonby 101 D6
Meltham 88 C2
Melton 57 D6
Meltonby 96 D3
Melton Constable 81 D6
Melton Mowbray 64 C4
Melton Ross 90 C4
Melvaig 155 J12
Melverley 60 C3
Melverley Green . 60 C3
Melvich 157 C11
Membury 11 D7
Memsie 153 B9
Memus 134 D4
Menabilly 5 D5
Menai Bridge
 = Porthaethwy . 83 D5
Mendham 69 F5
Mendlesham 56 C5
Mendlesham
 Green 56 C4
Menheniot 5 C7
Mennock 113 D8
Menston 94 E4
Menstrie 127 E7
Menthorpe 96 F2
Mentmore 40 C2
Meoble 147 C10
Meole Brace 60 C4
Meols 85 E3
Meonstoke 15 C7
Meopham 29 C7
Meopham Green 29 C7
Meopham Station 29 C7
Mepal 66 F4
Meppershall 54 F2
Merbach 48 E5
Mere
 Ches E 86 F5
 Wilts 24 F3
Mere Brow 86 C2
Mereclough 93 F8
Mere Green 62 E5
Mereside 92 F3
Merewich 29 D7
Mergie 141 F6
Meriden 63 F6
Merkadale 149 E8

Merkland
 Dumfries 106 B4
 S Ayrs 112 E2
Merkland Lodge 156 G7
Merley 13 E8
Merlin's Bridge . .44 D4
Merrington 60 B4
Merrion 44 F4
Merriott 12 C2
Merrivale 6 B3
Merrow 27 D8
Merrymeet 5 C7
Mersham 19 B7
Merstham 28 D3
Merston 16 D2
Merstone 15 F6
Merther 3 B7
Merthyr 32 B4
Merthyr Cynog . .47 F8
Merthyr-Dyfan . . 22 C3
Merthyr Mawr . . .21 B7
Merthyr Tudful
 = Merthyr Tydfil . 34 D4
Merthyr Tydfil
 = Merthyr Tudful . 34 D4
Merthyr Vale 34 E4
Merton
 Devon 9 C7
 London 28 B3
 Norf 68 E2
 Oxon 39 C5
Mervinslaw 116 C2
Meshaw 10 C2
Messing 42 C4
Messingham 90 D2
Metfield 69 F5
Metheringham . . .78 C3
Methil 129 E5
Methlem 70 D2
Methley 88 B4
Methlick 153 E8
Methven 128 B2
Methwold 67 E7
Methwold Hythe . 67 E7
Mettingham 69 F6
Mevagissey 3 B9
Mewith Head 93 C7
Mexborough 89 D5
Mey 158 C4
Meysey Hampton .37 E8
Miabhag
 W Isles 154 G5
 W Isles 154 H6
Miabhig 154 D5
Michaelchurch . .36 B2
Michaelchurch
 Escley 48 F5
Michaelchurch on
 Arrow 48 D4
Michaelston-le-
 Pit 22 B3
Michaelston-y-
 Fedw 35 F6
Michaelstow 5 B5
Michaelston-super-
 Ely 22 B3
Micheldever 26 F3
Michelmersh 14 B4
Mickfield 56 C5
Micklebring 89 E6
Mickleby 103 C6
Mickleham 28 D2
Mickleover 76 F3
Micklethwaite . . .94 E4
Mickleton
 Durham 100 B4
 Glos 51 E6
Mickletown 88 B4
Mickley 95 B5
Mickley Square . 110 C3
Mid Ardlaw 153 B9
Mid Auchinlech 118 B3
Midbea 159 D5
Mid Beltie 140 D5
Mid Calder 120 C3
Mid Cloch
 Forbie 153 C7
Mid Clyth 158 G4
Middle
 Assendon 39 F7
Middle Aston . . .38 B4
Middle Barton . . .38 B4
Middlebie 108 B2
Middle
 Cairncake . . . 153 D8
Middle Claydon . .39 B7
Middle Drums . . 135 D5
Middleforth
 Green 86 B3
Middleham 101 F5
Middle Handley . .76 B4
Middlehope 60 F4
Middle Littleton . .51 E5
Middle Maes-
 coed 48 F5
Middle Mill 44 C3
Middlemuir 141 B8
Middle Rasen . . .90 F4
Middle Rigg . . . 128 D2
Middlesbrough . 102 B3
Middleshaw
 Dumfries 107 B8
 W&F 99 F7
Middlesmoor 94 B3
Middlestone 111 F5
Middlestone
 Moor 110 F5
Middlestown 88 C3
Middlethird 122 E2
Middleton
 Aberds 141 C7
 Argyll 146 G2
 Derbys 75 C8
 Derbys 76 D2
 Essex 56 F2
 Gtr Man. 87 D6
 Hants 26 E2
 Hereford 49 C7
 Lancs 92 D4
 Midloth 121 D6
 N Nhants 64 F5
 Norf 67 C6
 Northumb 117 F6
 Northumb 123 F7
 N Yorks 94 E4
 N Yorks 103 F5

Middleton continued
 Perth 128 D3
 Perth 133 E8
 Shrops 49 B7
 Shrops 60 B3
 Shrops 60 D2
 Suff 57 C8
 Swansea 33 F5
 Warks 63 E5
 W&F 99 F8
 W Yorks 88 B3
Middleton
 Cheney 52 E2
Middleton Green .75 F6
Middleton Hall . 117 B5
Middleton-in-
 Teesdale 100 B4
Middleton Moor . 57 C8
Middleton One
 Row 102 C1
Middleton-on-
 Leven 102 D2
Middleton-on-
 Sea 16 D3
Middleton on the
 Hill 49 C7
Middleton-on-the-
 Wolds 96 E5
Middleton Priors .61 E6
Middleton
 Quernham 95 B6
Middleton
 St George 101 C8
Middleton
 Scriven 61 F6
Middleton Stoney 39 B5
Middleton Tyas . 101 D7
Middletown
 Cumb 98 D1
 Powys 60 C3
Middle Tysoe 51 E8
Middle Wallop . . .25 F7
Middlewich 74 C3
Middle
 Winterslow . . .25 F7
Middle Woodford. 25 F6
Middlewood
 Green 56 C4
Middlezoy 23 F5
Midfield 157 C8
Midge Hall 86 B3
Midgeholme . . . 109 D6
Midgham 26 C3
Midgley
 W Yorks 87 B8
 W Yorks 88 C3
Midhopestones . .88 E3
Midhurst 16 B2
Mid Lavant 16 D2
Midlem 115 B8
Mid Main 150 H7
Midsomer Norton 23 D8
Midton 118 B2
Midtown
 Highld 155 J13
 Highld 157 C8
Midtown of
 Buchromb . . . 152 D3
Mid Urchany . . 151 G11
Midville 79 D6
Mid Walls 160 H4
Midway 87 F7
Mid Yell 160 D7
Migdale 151 B9
Migvie 140 D3
Milarrochy 126 E3
Milber 7 B6
Milborne Port . . .12 C4
Milborne
 St Andrew 13 E6
Milborne Wick . .12 B4
Milbourne 110 B4
Milburn 100 B1
Milbury Heath . . .36 E3
Milcombe 52 F2
Milden 56 E3
Mildenhall
 Suff 55 B8
 Wilts 25 C7
Milebrook 48 B5
Milebush 29 E8
Mile Cross 68 C5
Mile Elm 24 C4
Mile End
 Essex 43 B5
 Glos 36 C2
Mileham 68 C2
Mile Oak 17 D6
Milesmark 128 F2
Milfield 122 F5
Milford
 Derbys 76 E3
 Devon 8 B4
 Powys 59 E7
 Staffs 62 B3
 Sur 27 E7
 Wilts 14 B2
Milford Haven
 = Aberdaugleddau
 . . . . 44 E4
Milford on Sea . .14 E3
Milkwall 36 D2
Milkwell 13 B7
Milland 16 B2
Millarston 118 C4
Millbank
 Aberds 153 D11
 Highld 158 D3
Mill Bank 87 B8
Millbeck 98 B4
Millbounds 159 E6
Millbreck 153 D10
Millbridge 27 E6
Millbrook
 C Beds 53 F8
 Corn 6 D2
 Soton 14 C4
Millburn 112 B4
Millcombe 7 E6
Mill Common . . .69 F7
Millcorner 18 C5
Milldale 75 D8
Millden Lodge . . 135 B5
Milldens 135 D5
Mill End
 Bucks 39 F7
 Herts 54 F4